THE PHILOSOPHY OF
KARL POPPER

BOOK II

THE LIBRARY OF LIVING PHILOSOPHERS

Paul Arthur Schilpp, Editor

Already Published:

THE PHILOSOPHY OF JOHN DEWEY (1939)
THE PHILOSOPHY OF GEORGE SANTAYANA (1940)
THE PHILOSOPHY OF ALFRED NORTH WHITEHEAD (1941)
THE PHILOSOPHY OF G. E. MOORE (1942)
THE PHILOSOPHY OF BERTRAND RUSSELL (1944)
THE PHILOSOPHY OF ERNST CASSIRER (1949)
ALBERT EINSTEIN: PHILOSOPHER-SCIENTIST (1949)
THE PHILOSOPHY OF SARVEPALLI RADHAKRISHNAN (1952)
THE PHILOSOPHY OF KARL JASPERS (1957)
THE PHILOSOPHY OF C. D. BROAD (1959)
THE PHILOSOPHY OF RUDOLF CARNAP (1963)
THE PHILOSOPHY OF MARTIN BUBER (1967)
THE PHILOSOPHY OF C. I. LEWIS (1968)
THE PHILOSOPHY OF KARL POPPER (1974)

In Preparation:

THE PHILOSOPHY OF GABRIEL MARCEL
THE PHILOSOPHY OF BRAND BLANSHARD
THE PHILOSOPHY OF GEORG HENRIK von WRIGHT
THE PHILOSOPHY OF W. V. QUINE
THE PHILOSOPHY OF JEAN-PAUL SARTRE

Other volumes to be announced

Karl Popper

THE LIBRARY OF LIVING PHILOSOPHERS
VOLUME XIV BOOK II

THE PHILOSOPHY OF
KARL POPPER

EDITED BY

PAUL ARTHUR SCHILPP

NORTHWESTERN UNIVERSITY &
SOUTHERN ILLINOIS UNIVERSITY

LA SALLE, ILLINOIS • OPEN COURT • ESTABLISHED 1887

THE PHILOSOPHY OF KARL POPPER

FIRST EDITION

Library of Congress Catalog Card Number: 76-186983
ISBN Number: 0-87548-141-8 Vol. I cloth
0-87548-142-6 Vol. II cloth

"Hypothesis and Imagination" by Peter Medawar was first published in *The Art of the Soluble* (London: Methuen & Co., 1971).

ADVISORY BOARD

ACKNOWLEDGMENTS

by the editor

The editor hereby gratefully acknowledges his obligation and sincere gratitude to all the publishers of Professor Popper's books and publications for their kind and uniform courtesy in permitting us to quote—sometimes at some length—from Professor Popper's writings.

PAUL A. SCHILPP

ACKNOWLEDGMENTS

by Professor Popper

I am deeply grateful to Ernst Gombrich, Bryan Magee, Arne Petersen, Jeremy Shearmur, and most of all to David Miller and to my wife, for their patience in reading and improving my manuscript.

After the manuscript was completed, there arose many problems in connection with the proofs. The work done in this connection by Professor Eugene Freeman, Mrs. Ann Freeman and by their editorial staff was immense, and done under very trying circumstances since most of the corrections suggested by them and by myself had to be discussed by letters between California and England. I cannot thank them enough for their criticism, their meticulous care, and their infinite patience.

KARL POPPER

TABLE OF CONTENTS

PART THREE: THE PHILOSOPHER REPLIES
Karl Popper: "Replies to My Critics"

I. Introduction

II. The Problem of Demarcation

THE PHILOSOPHY OF
KARL POPPER

BOOK II

G. Schlesinger

POPPER ON SELF-REFERENCE

I

Popper objects to the received view on the nature of self-referential sentences and holds they are not in all cases devoid of meaning. He advances his views in a Socratic dialogue entitled 'Self-Reference and Meaning in Ordinary Language'.[1] His essay makes delightful reading; however, from a logical point of view, it is surprising to see on what loose arguments he proposes to establish his case. A defender of the orthodox view would find very little difficulty in rebutting each point made by Popper. This seems a pity, for I believe the general sentiments underlying the paper are commendable: the received view ought to be challenged.

Popper's line of attack is to cite counterexamples to the rule that self-referring sentences are always meaningless and finally to proceed to demonstrate that the solution to the Liar's Paradox based on this rule anyhow fails.

Let us first look at the alleged demonstration of the inadequacy of the traditional solution to the Liar's Paradox. What Popper has to say amounts to the following: suppose someone utters 'S_1: The proposition now being asserted is false'. This raises the ancient paradox that, if S_1 conveys a true proposition, then it must be conveying a false proposition, and vice versa. It is commonly claimed that we can avoid the paradox by simply declaring S_1 as devoid of all meaning. But, says Popper, this merely shifts the difficulty. Meaningless utterances convey neither true nor false propositions. It is therefore a false claim which attributes falsehood to something devoid of meaning. Philosophers have declared S_1 meaningless; hence to claim that S_1 expresses a falsehood is to make a false claim. But it is this very claim that S_1 is being employed to express with. We are forced to conclude therefore that S_1 is being used to express a falsehood. Thus, after having declared S_1 meaningless, we find that it expresses a falsehood. This result is bad enough in itself. This situation is worse than this, however; for, as we very well know, if S_1 conveys a false proposition it must be conveying a true proposition; thus, we have the old paradox back with us again.

It is not difficult to point out where Popper has gone seriously wrong. Once we agree that S_1, in spite of whatever it may appear to mean, is devoid of all meaning, the old paradox cannot be resuscitated. For, if S_1 is meaningless, then it asserts nothing, conveys no proposition, carries no claim. To claim that S_1 conveys a false proposition is indeed to make a false claim, but S_1 has not been used to make such a claim; S_1 cannot be used to make such a claim, since it is meaningless.

Popper seems to fare even worse when it comes to the counterexamples he produces to show the inadequacy of the orthodox view. One of these is put forward in the following manner:

Socrates   Could you produce an example of a self-referring asser-
              tion which is empirically true?

Theatetus   .   .   .   .   .

S.   I could not hear what you were saying Theatetus. Please
              repeat it a little louder. My hearing is no longer what it
              used to be.

Th.   I said: 'I am now speaking so softly that dear old
              Socrates cannot make out what I am saying.'

S.   I like this example; and I cannot deny that when you were
              speaking so softly, you were speaking truthfully. Nor can
              I deny the empirical character of this truth; for had my
              ears been younger it would have turned out an untruth.
              [P. 306]

The immediate reaction of some readers might be to conclude that the present argument collapses for exactly the same reason as the previous one. It is simply not the case—it might be said—that when Theatetus spoke softly he spoke the truth. Admittedly a proposition has to be regarded true if it corresponds to facts, and it is a fact that Socrates could not hear what Theatetus was saying. But no facts can correspond to the proposition asserted by Theatetus' softly spoken utterance, nor, indeed, can any counter it, since no proposition was asserted by Theatetus. All self-referring utterances are meaningless, and Theatetus' utterance was self-referring.

This, however, would not destroy Popper's case. He could argue, not entirely without justification, that such a conclusion would be based on arbitrary presuppositions. Naturally, if we dogmatically decree that all self-referring utterances are meaningless, then it follows that Theatetus has said nothing, and, *ipso facto*, the truth or falsity of what he said does not arise. But after all, the very decision to rule all self-referring utterances meaningless is now under review. Is it a reasonable decision? Popper seems to have shown that it is not. He has produced an example where no room for uncertainty would seem to exist for anyone, regarding the question: 'What are the relevant facts which determine the truth value of what has been said?' If it is a fact that Socrates could not hear Theatetus speaking, then everyone, unless he feels compelled to protect a special dogma about self-reference, will agree that the facts correspond to what Theatetus said, and hence that he spoke truly. On the other hand, if Theatetus' utterance was audible to Socrates, then that utterance conveyed a falsehood. Popper's attack here differs from his other one concerning S_1. There his move was to allow us to declare the utterance meaningless, and then to claim to have demonstrated that this at once leads to the attaching of falsity to the proposition conveyed by S_1. In that demonstration, he failed. Here, however, he questions the reasonableness of declaring the self-referring utterance as devoid of meaning in the first place. He seems to have raised a very valid question.

Indeed, Theatetus' utterance is meaningful; but it proves nothing. Surely Popper cannot fail to acknowledge the distinction between that which is being asserted and that by which an assertion is being made. The former is normally called a proposition; the latter a sentence. What we hear or fail to hear, just as what we are able or unable to read, is not a proposition to which truth value attaches. It is rather the physical vehicle, such as a combination of sounds or a collection of marks on a paper through which a proposition is purported to be conveyed, i.e. a sentence. Those who ruled self-referring sentences as not succeeding in carrying propositions were concerned with the kind of sentence which is employed to convey a proposition purported to refer to that very proposition itself. The sentence voiced by Theatetus clearly does not belong to this category. The proposition he has asserted does not refer to itself but to the sentence conveying it. Everybody agrees that there is nothing wrong with this kind of self-reference. There are innumerably many examples showing this, e.g. 'This sentence is . . . .

(i) ... in English
(ii) ... written in longhand   ... on a piece of paper
(iii) ... uttered on a Monday... in a room'.

Another example of Popper concerns sentences referring to themselves not directly but via each other; that is, the first sentence refers to the second, where the second refers to the first. Such sentences are also commonly regarded as not succeeding in conveying a proposition. A well-known example is 'S_2: The next sentence conveys a true proposition', 'S_3: The previous sentence expressed a false proposition'. S_2 and S_3 seem to create a paradox; however, the paradox disappears—it is claimed—as soon as we realize that S_2 and S_3 are meaningless because self-referring. For we cannot decide the truth value of P_2 (the proposition purported to be expressed by S_2) until we decide the truth value of P$_3$ which in turn depends on the truth value of P$_2$. Popper attempts to show that such sentences may nevertheless succeed in expressing propositions:

Theatetus	The very next question which I am going to ask you is an extraordinary one, although expressed in perfectly ordinary language.
Socrates	There is no need to warn me. I am all ears.
Th.	What did I say between your last two interruptions, Socrates? [P. 304]

In the present case Theatetus' first sentence referred to the last and his last sentence to the first; yet it would be again most unreasonable to rule them out as meaningless. But this example is just as bad as the previous one, for it is perfectly clear that Theatetus has committed no self-reference of the sort which has ever been ruled out as illegitimate. His second sentence, which expresses a question, has an established meaning entirely independent of the meaning of the first sentence. Whatever has been conveyed or has not been conveyed by the first sentence, Theatetus is now asking to repeat it. Nor is there any problem with the first sentence. By employing the term 'extraordinary', Theatetus presumably intended to convey the proposition that his next sentence is going to be self-referring. This, however, turns out not to be the case, as we have just seen; therefore we conclude that his first sentence conveyed a false proposition.

Finally, Popper's general conclusion that self-referring sentences are not as a rule meaningless, but in case they lead to paradoxes, we must avoid them, will not satisfy many. The less tolerant reader may well be tempted to ask whether this advice is meant as a general short cut to the solution of all sorts of philosophical problems: all talk which is liable to give rise to perplexities should be avoided. But the more sympathetic reader will assume that what Popper actually had in mind was that even though there are many self-referring sentences which are free of all blemish, those which give rise to paradoxes are to be regarded as constituting nonpermissible constructions. They must be avoided then, not because we are otherwise faced with a perplexing situation, but because they are not legitimate sentences of the language.

But this does not get us much further. We need something better than *ad hoc* ruling that certain self-referring sentences, namely, those which otherwise would give rise to intolerable paradoxes, are to be treated as ill formed sentences. We need a general theory of sentence construction which will entail among many other things that these troublesome expressions are not well formed.

One might conceivably wish to attempt, on Popper's behalf, to claim that his ruling was not an *ad hoc* one. It is generally the case, it might be pointed out, that under no circumstances are we prepared to assent to the tautologously false assertion. Now $P_1 \leftrightarrow {\sim} P_1$ is a tautologously false assertion. But if 'S_1 = The proposition now being asserted is false' be allowed as a legitimate construction, $P_1 \rightarrow {\sim} P_1$ is imposed upon us as an analytic truth, since it follows from the meaning of S_1. Under these peculiar circumstances, there is no other way, then, to avoid assenting to the tautologically false assertion but by disqualifying S_1 from being a well formed sentence.

I do not believe that the situation is improved by these arguments. While the motive behind declaring S_1 ill formed is certainly a legitimate one, this does not lessen the arbitrariness of the act of declaring it so. We shall remain dissatisfied until we find some general reason why S_1 is anyhow ill formed or meaningless, and will no longer need specifically to disqualify it because of its paradoxicality.

There is also another even more important objection to the way Popper intended to leave things. No provisions have been made for disqualifying '$S_1{}^*$ = The proposition now being asserted is true'. It is quite obvious that a theory of ordinary discourse which allows $S_1{}^*$ to feature as a well formed significant sentence, is unsatisfactory. For what sort of significance might $S_1{}^*$ have? It makes absolutely no difference whether it has been uttered or not; nothing can be derived from it, it introduces no information, and there is no way to appraise whether it has conveyed a truth or a falsehood, nor could it of course be construed as conveying a value judgment, command or apology.

Some may perhaps be tempted to claim that provision for the disqualification of $S_1{}^*$ has been made as soon as S_1 has been disqualified, since the negation of an ill formed sentence is itself ill formed. This obviously would be a mistake. The proposition expressed by $S_1{}^*$—if there was such—is not the contradictory of what is purported to be denied by S_1, since it 'affirms' a different proposition—namely $P_1{}^*$ and not P_1.

Yet, in spite of these serious deficiencies and fallacies, the spirit which informs Popper's essay is, I believe, a sound one. Because he has not succeeded in presenting any valid counterexamples to the accepted view on self-reference, nor has he formulated an alternative theory, logicians will tend to dismiss him altogether. But Popper's conviction of the inadequacy of the accepted view motivating his paper does not stand or fall with the arguments put forward in it. The core of his attitude derives probably from the fact that he is primarily a philosopher of science. Popper believes that the question of the meaning which attaches or fails to attach to a given sentence cannot be settled by a mere examination of the internal structure of that sentence without any reference made to the setting in which it has been uttered and to the various uses it may have in different contexts. It is highly implausible that a complex, rich and ever-changing system like everyday language should permit the existence of such a powerful and simple rule like 'All self-referring sentences are meaningless', whereby, irrespective of any other facts or utterances which may have bearing on it, a sentence is automatically excluded from significant discourse.

In what follows I shall try to establish, first, more decisively the untenability of the orthodox view through what I hope will be genuine counterexamples, and then attempt to replace it by a view which does not treat self-referring expressions on any special basis. Those which are meaningless are so for perfectly general reasons that apply equally to sentences of any form.

II

Suppose I assert the following:

Q: An event e is going to happen at time t.

R: If an event e is to happen *at any other time* than t then the proposition correctly stating e's occurrence is not strictly implied by anything I have said (including what I am saying now).

R is obviously self-referential and the self-reference here at last is made not to the physical casing but to the proposition encased, since the entity which is capable of entering into the logical relationship of strict implication is a proposition and not the sentence expressing that proposition. At the same time, R will universally be judged true by all persons without prior commitment to the view that all self-referring utterances must be deemed meaningless.

Those who subscribe to the received view might, however, not regard R as constituting a decisive counterexample doing damage to their position. Genuinely self-referring expressions—they might maintain—never succeed in conveying any meaning: R, however, is not ineradicably self-referring. This can easily be seen once we consider the two strict equivalences to which the definitions of Q and R give rise:

$$Q \leftrightarrow te.(\theta)\sim(\theta e.\theta \neq t) \ldots \text{(i)}$$

('te' stands for 'e at t' and θ

$$R \leftrightarrow (\theta)((\theta e.\theta \neq t) \supset \sim(Q.R \rightarrow \theta e)) \ldots \text{(ii)}$$

ranges over time predicates. The second conjunct is obvious, since a given event can occur at one time only.)

Conjoin (i) and (ii):

$$Q.R \leftrightarrow te.(\theta)(\sim(\theta e.\theta \neq t).((\theta e.\theta \neq t) \supset \sim(QR \rightarrow \theta e)))$$

$\therefore$ $Q.R \leftrightarrow te.(\theta)\sim(\theta e.\theta \neq t)$ (Since in general $\sim A.(A \supset B)$ may be

$\therefore$ $Q.R \leftrightarrow Q$ replaced by its equivalent $\sim A$)

Substituting on the basis of this for Q.R into the R.H.S. of (ii):
R $\leftrightarrow$ (θ)(($\theta e . \theta \neq t$)$\supset \sim$(Q $\rightarrow$ θe)) the R.H.S, of which no longer contains R. Thus (ii) is not 'really' self-referring.

Suppose now I assert Q, in conjunction not with R, but with T:

T: If event *e* is to occur at *any time at all* then the proposition correctly stating the time of *e*'s occurrence is not strictly implied by what I have said (including what I am saying now).

Q, of course, is true only in case *e* occurs at *t*, in which case T is false.

Thus Q and T are inconsistent. Consequently the conjunction of Q and T strictly implies anything. In other words (θ)(Q.T $\rightarrow$ θe). But T asserts that

$$(\theta)(\theta e \supset \sim(Q.T \rightarrow \theta e)) \ldots . \text{(iii)}$$

Thus, no matter when *e* occurs, T is false. Does T, therefore, not constitute a proper counterexample to the traditional view? T is after all self-referring in the proper sense and false, hence meaningful? The answer again will be that the self-reference in case of T may be eliminated. Since T is true, if and only if *e* does not materialize at all, it is strictly equivalent to $\sim(\exists\theta)(\theta e)$ which does not contain T.

The same can be obtained formally by combining Q and T as represented by (iii):

Q.T $\leftrightarrow$ *te*.(θ)($\theta e \supset \sim$(Q.T $\rightarrow$ θe))

∴   Q.T $\leftrightarrow$ *te*.(*te* $\supset \sim$(Q.T $\rightarrow$ *te*)) (Universal Instantiation)

Q.T $\rightarrow \sim$(Q.T $\rightarrow$ *te*)   (Modus Ponens)

but $\sim$(Q.T $\rightarrow$ *te*) is logically false hence $\Box \sim$Q.T, since Q.T is seen to strictly imply a logical falsehood. Substituting 2 + 2 = 5 into (iii) which is strictly equivalent to Q.T:

T $\leftrightarrow$ (θ)($\theta e \supset \sim$(2+2=5 $\rightarrow$ θe))

∴   T $\leftrightarrow$ (θ) $\sim \theta e$ as before.

On reflection, however, the introduction of the notion of the eliminability of self-reference is seen to be of no help whatever in defending the orthodox view. There is nothing surprising in that whenever one can give an exhaustive account of all the circumstances C_T, under which a given self-referring expression is true and of C_F, under which it is false, one can replace that expression with a non-self-referring one. In general, 'C_T obtains and C_F does not obtain' is a sentence which can always replace such a self-referring expression. Naturally when one is prevented from naming C_T and C_F because of the paradox generated by the self-referring expression, one cannot possibly find an appropriate expression to which the self-referring one is strictly equivalent. But one has still not made a single step toward explaining why some self-referring expressions create paradoxes and have to be treated as meaningless while others can be treated as true or false in which case, of course, they are strictly equivalent to some non self-referring expression.

Another line of defence for someone upholding the received view might be to attempt to claim that R and T, even though meaningful, constitute no proper counterexamples for a different reason. He might wish to maintain that self-reference is not vicious as long as reference is made to the form and not to the content of a proposition. 'Strict-implication' is a matter of form, as distinct 'truth' or 'falsity', which is a matter of content; hence a proposition may refer meaningfully to its own form as well as to the sentence expressing it.

To defeat this last move let us consider the case in which I assert U in conjunction with Q:

> U: If *e* occurs *at any time at all* then the proposition correctly stating the time of *e*'s occurrence is not uniquely strictly implied by what I have said (including what I am saying now).[2]

Is U true in case *e* occurs at *t*? Suppose it is; then there exists a situation in which Q and U are concurrently true. Thus the two are consistent and while Q.U $\rightarrow$ *te*, it is not the case that also Q.U $\rightarrow \sim te$. In other words, Q.U uniquely strictly implies *te*. U however *denies* this and therefore must be false in this case. Thus Q and U can never together be true and are therefore logically inconsistent and their conjunction strictly implies anything. Hence not only Q.U $\rightarrow$ *te* but also Q.U $\rightarrow \sim te$. Thus Q.U does not uniquely strictly imply *te*. But this is what is *affirmed* by U; hence U is true in this case. Consequently Q and U *are* consistent etc.

The paradox generated by U bears the familiar hallmark of paradoxes which arise through self-reference and have in the past been thought to disappear by declaring all self-referring sentences meaningless. This move, however, is clearly no longer available to us since it has been agreed, as a result of the problems raised by R and T, that the kind of self-reference committed in our case, where reference is not made to the truth value of the proposition concerned but to purely formal features of it, is not a vicious kind of self-reference. We are forced then to the conclusion that this kind of paradoxes demand a different treatment from the one hitherto accorded to them.

III

It seems to me, that the solution to the various difficulties raised before lies, to put it briefly, in not singling out self-referring sentences for any special treatment. The meaninglessness of the sentences which are associated with paradoxes need not specially be stipulated; it follows at once from the universally accepted and most basic criterion of cognitive significance.

According to the natural standard of cognitive meaningfulness, a sentence conveys no proposition unless the proposition purported to be conveyed by it is amenable to confirmation or disconfirmation. If I specified the characteristics a process requires in order to qualify as a confirmation, then of course I could not guarantee that my description would meet universal approval. My present account, however, is rendered wholly inoffensive by my not restricting the meaning to be attached to 'confirmation' beyond its minimal sense: anything that may be construed as lending support to a claim; anything that will make us inclined to subscribe to it, rather than to its rival will, for the purposes of the current discussion, be regarded as a confirmation of that claim. This general meaning-criterion, therefore, is in no way prejudicial as to the status of metaphysical assertions (and Popper, as is well known, is among those who refuse to equate metaphysics with nonsense). Metaphysicians, obviously, do not hold that nothing whatever provides the remotest basis for their beliefs and that there are no facts in the universe which are relevant to the maintaining of some and to the rejection of other metaphysical propositions. There are certain forms of arguments, metaphysicians claim, which are typically employed to support metaphysical statements. These arguments constitute, for whatever they are worth, the confirmation of metaphysical statements.

Let me hasten to make understood that I do not wish in any way to provide support for the verification principle. What the verificationist programme consists of is the provision of a complete definition of the term 'confirmation' at least insofar as it is employed in the context of empirical science. If the numerous attempts to achieve this have failed, this was because every suggestion was deficient either because, if accepted, on its basis well established scientific hypotheses had to be regarded as unconfirmable in principle, or conversely, obvious nonsense had to be acknowledged as scientifically confirmed. Consequently, those who have objected to the verificationist programme have done so because they believed that future attempts are not going to fare better. But everybody without exception agrees that we do not subscribe to a scientific hypothesis unless we believe it to have received some confirmation and that statements which are in principle not amenable to any sort of confirmation have no place in scientific discourse. What antiverificationists deny is the possibility of giving a full description of the process of confirmation. Some of them have taken this attitude not merely because of the past failures of verificationists to provide a satisfactory description, but because they believed there were profound reasons why in principle such a uniform description is nonexistent. This, of course, by no means amounts to the questioning of the existence and importance of the process of confirmation. Indeed, if called upon, in any individual instance, everyone can quite easily say what constitutes the confirmatory basis of a given scientific hypothesis.

On the other hand, we must not now be carried in the opposite direction and believe that because of its extreme liberality the criterion I put forward is useless. It is still possible to rule out on its basis utterances which constitute an extreme group about which all will agree that no facts or arguments could be found relevant to their retaining or rejection. A case in point is 'S_1* = The proposition now being asserted is true', which must by our criterion be deemed as devoid of cognitive meaning, since no one would suggest that anything might tend to confirm or disconfirm it to the slightest degree.

Matters will become clearer if we probe somewhat deeper into the question of what constitutes confirmation. Suppose that just before uttering S_1* one utters 'S_4 = The proposition now being asserted implies the next'. Let us for a moment be prepared tentatively to entertain that both S_1* and S_4 convey propositions. By virtue of the meaning of S_4 we have now the following compound proposition (α):

$$P_4 \leftrightarrow (P_4 \supset P_1\text{*}). \ldots\ldots\ldots(\alpha)$$

P_1* is either true or false. Suppose it is false. Then if P_4 is true the R.H.S. of (α) is false and so must therefore the L.H.S. be, e.g. P_4. In other words, if P_4 is true then it is false. On the other hand, if P_4 is false, then the R.H.S. of (α) is true and so must therefore the L.H.S. be. That is, if P_4 is false then it is true—all of which show that the supposition that P_1* is false leads to a contradiction. If, however, P_1* is assumed to be true, then (α) entails that P_4 is true too, and there is no contradiction.

Thus, in case prior to S_1*, S_4 has been uttered, it is no longer correct to say that there is absolutely no reason why S_1* should be deemed a true rather than a false proposition. The fact that the compound proposition (α) can be treated as coherent only on the assumption that P_1* is true should be given some weight, tipping the balance in favour of regarding it true. Therefore, should not the uttering of S_4, together with its giving rise to (α), be regarded as providing grounds for the confirmation of S_1*? Similarly, if instead of S_4, the sentence uttered just prior to S_1* was 'The proposition now being asserted implies the falsity of the next', we should regard it as having been disconfirmed and hence false. And even if nothing has been said closely before uttering S_1*, as long as someone somewhere sometime in the past or future ever utters the words 'The proposition now being asserted implies the truth (or falsity) of the proposition asserted by X at time t', it should provide confirmation (or disconfirmation) for S_1* which has been uttered by X at time t. Yet one feels that a theory of meaning which attributed meaning to S_1* because of the foregoing arguments must be unsatisfactory.

This feeling can, I believe, adequately be accounted for. It was suggested that, when S_4 is uttered, giving rise to (α), then the fact that (α) is coherent only if P_1^* is true, provides a reason why we should regard P_1^* true rather than false. But, if this be conceded, then there is no sentence which is not amenable to confirmation since the argument remains unchanged no matter what you substitute instead of S_1^* into (α). We accept, however, the general principle that a fact which can be construed as confirming to an equal extent everything, constitutes no confirmation of anything. We are thus led to deny that the fact that (α) cannot be prevented from yielding a self-contradiction but by assigning truth to P_1^*, tends to confirm P_1^* to any extent.

Turning now our attention to one of the sentences which has been the prime source of trouble, S_1, we at once see even stronger reasons than in the case of S_1^*, why it must be regarded as being in principle unconfirmable. Whatever might present itself as a candidate for supporting S_1, it immediately turns into an evidence that S_1 is false, simply because if S_1 is true it must be false. Thus, even if there could be any relevant fact adducible in favour or against S_1, the evidence would be self-cancelling. This applies equally to U and indeed to any sentence which presents us with the compound proposition of the form $p \leftrightarrow \sim p$.

IV

To sum up: my suggestion consists of a negative and a positive part. The negative part is an amplification of a view which may be found in Popper's quoted article, that no proposition is to be judged solely on the basis of its internal structure or the structure of the sentence conveying it. I was trying to strengthen this negative proposal by what I believe to be firmer than Popper's counterexample to the orthodox view. The core of the positive thesis is that our approach to all sentences should be a uniform one. They ought to be regarded as cognitively meaningful if and only if they are amenable to some kind of confirmation, that is, if one can adduce some reasons why they, rather than their denial, ought to be given a certain truth value.

Just one more example which may help to shed further light on the position adopted here. It concerns expressions which are self-referring via each other like S_2 and S_3.

Suppose the following three sentences are uttered:

'S_5:   The next two propositions are both true'

'S_6:   The previous proposition was true but the next proposition is false'

'S_7:   The previous propositions were both false'.

If we assign falsity to the first two propositions and truth to the last proposition everything comes out correct. For P_5 is false by virtue of its claim that P_6 is true which is not the case. P_6 is false since it makes two false assertions. P_7 is true for, indeed, the first two propositions are false. Try, however, assigning any one of the other seven combinations of truth values and you run into contradiction.

But of course one need not arrive at this by trial and error, as this result is imposed on us by the method of deduction. We have the following three premises:

(i) $P_5 \leftrightarrow P_6 . P_7$

(ii) $P_6 \leftrightarrow P_5 . \sim P_7$

(iii) $P_7 \leftrightarrow \sim P_5 . \sim P_6$
        hence

(iv) $P_5 \leftrightarrow P_6 . \sim P_5 . \sim P_6$ Substituting into (i) for P_7
        the R.H.S. of (iii).

(v) $\sim P_5$ The R.H.S. of (iv) being
        _____ logically false.

(vi) $\sim P_5 \text{ v } P_7$ From (v) by the Law of Addition.

(vii) $\sim (P_5 . \sim P_7)$ From (vi) by De Morgan's Law.

(viii) $\sim P_6$ Combining (vii) and (ii).
        _____

(ix) P_7 Combining (v) (viii) and (iii).
        _____

Having shown why P_5 and P_6 must be false while P_7 must be true on the basis of no other information about these but what has been conveyed through S_5, S_6 and S_7 and through grasping the meaning of these and the logical relationships which are created through S_5, S_6 and S_7, would it not be unreasonable dogmatically to maintain that S_5, S_6 and S_7 are meaningless and they do not succeed to convey any propositions at all? Do we then not have here another set of counterexamples to the view that all self-referring expressions are meaningless?

Not quite perhaps. It could, after all, be objected that it has not categorically been shown that S_5 and S_6 convey false propositions while S_7 conveys a true proposition. All we have succeeded is to show that *if* S_5, S_6 and S_7 carry propositions then they can have no other than these truth values. It is therefore not unreasonable to maintain that, since such propositions would be self-referential, these three sentences are not to be regarded as expressing any propositions at all.

But is this defence of the traditional position a sound one? It must, after all, be admitted that the conditional assertion that if S_5, S_6 and S_7 carry propositions, etc. is a significant one, and it was arrived at with the aid of nothing else but the rules of logic and S_5, S_6 and S_7. Is it not absurd to claim that such a meaningful assertion may be derived from meaningless empty sentences?

I believe that the reasonable thing is to concede that, with the sole aid of the present example, we would not succeed in converting anyone strongly committed to the view that all self-referential expressions are meaningless. He could insist that S_5, S_6 and S_7 are barren sentences. The counterfactual asserting that, if propositions were conveyed through them, then such and such truth values would have to be assigned to them, is derived not from the nonexistent P_5, P_6 and P_7. We are conducting here—so it would be claimed—a thought experiment. We treat S_5, S_6 and S_7 as candidates for sentences which convey propositions and 'observe' what happens. The report that if P_5 and P_6 are assigned falsity and P_7 truth then, and only then, would we have a coherent set of propositions, is a report of our observing the results of our experiment and derives from this observation. Just as in the case 'S_1: The proposition now being asserted is false', where all agree that no proposition attaches to the sentence S_1, we derive that if S_1 conveyed a true proposition it would convey a false proposition, etc. by observing what would be, but is not, the case if S_1 conveyed a true proposition, etc.

However, now we have adopted a pragmatic line and permit a sentence to carry a proposition as long as there is a slight asymmetry in the total situation, inclining one to assign this, rather than that, truth value to the proposition in question. We may therefore in good conscience say that P_5, P_6 and P_7 do attach to the sentences and that the first two are false, while the last one is true. For there are some grounds upon which one is to favour this, rather than any one of the other seven possible distributions of truth values. Furthermore these grounds are unique to P_5, P_6 and P_7: you cannot arbitrarily replace anyone of them without thereby removing these grounds.

G. SCHLESINGER

DEPARTMENT OF PHILOSOPHY
UNIVERSITY OF NORTH CAROLINA
SEPTEMBER, 1965

NOTES

[1] First published in *Mind*, 1954; subsequently reprinted in Popper's *Conjectures and Refutations*. Page references are to the latter.

[2] Note: *p uniquely* strictly implies q if and only if $(p \rightarrow q)$. $\sim (p \rightarrow \sim q)$.

A. J. Ayer

TRUTH, VERIFICATION AND VERISIMILITUDE

In the original version of his *Logik der Forschung*, Professor Popper found himself able to dispense with the concepts of empirical truth and falsehood. He did not think that they were defective concepts or that their use led to any serious difficulties; on the contrary, he argued that the very fact that they could be eliminated showed them to be innocent. It was just that he did not think he needed them. He could obtain all he wanted by referring to the logical relations in which different types of empirical statement stood to one another. An empirical statement which did not belong to the class of basic statements was to be accounted false if it was contradicted by a set of accepted basic statements; so long as our attempts to test it did not result in such a contradiction we might provisionally hold it to be true. Basic statements themselves were characterized by their form. They were singular existential statements to the effect that an event of such and such a kind occurred at such and such a particular place and time; the only restriction placed upon the range of these events was that their presence or absence should be publicly observable. For reasons which I shall later examine, Popper did not think that any justification could be given for ascribing truth or falsehood to a basic statement. To count a basic statement as true came down to accepting it; to count a basic statement as false came down to rejecting it; but this acceptance or rejection was a matter for decision. Such decisions are not entirely arbitrary, since they are motivated by our experiences, but they are not substantiated by them. They can be right or wrong only in the sense that we may or may not decide to adhere to them.[1]

As Popper recognized, this treatment of truth and falsehood brought him very close to pragmatism. He claimed to differ from the pragmatists in that he resisted their tendency to identify truth with verification. His reason was that truth, if one was going to speak of it at all, could not be regarded as admitting of degrees or as capable of change. A statement can be strongly or weakly corroborated, but it cannot be strongly or weakly true. It can be accepted at one time and not at another; but it is true or false without any temporal qualification. Here I think that he was clearly in the right.

Nevertheless he agreed with the pragmatists in choosing to work with the concepts of corroboration and acceptance rather than with the concept of truth.

In his notes to *The Logic of Scientific Discovery*, the English translation of *Logik der Forschung*, and in the essays which he collected and published under the title of *Conjectures and Refutations*, Popper took the view that his previous reluctance to employ the concepts of truth and falsehood was unjustified. He explained that he had been convinced by Tarski that the use of these concepts need not lead to antinomies, and he argued, in my view correctly, that Tarski's schema "S is true in L if and only if p", as exemplified in such propositions as that the English sentence "Snow is white" is true if and only if snow is white, achieves what was aimed at in the classical idea of truth as correspondence with fact. This explanation would have been more to the point if Popper's original reason for dispensing with the concept of truth had been that he thought it unclear or defective, rather than that he simply had no need of it. He is, however, now prepared to say that he relies on the notion of truth at least as a "regulative principle".[2] For instance the view, which Popper shares with Peirce, that all our beliefs are fallible, would seem to imply that there is a standard of truth of which they may fall short. It might be taken also to be a presupposition of scientific enquiry that truth is attainable.

But how do we know when we have attained it? Are we ever in a position to be sure that we have reached a true conclusion about any matter of fact? Popper's answer to this question seems to be that we are not. In his essay "On the Sources of Knowledge and of Ignorance" he argues both against the rationalist view that some truths are self-evident and against the empiricist view that it is a sufficient condition of the truth of some beliefs that they arise immediately out of sense-experiences.[3] His own position, as stated in the essay on "Truth, Rationality and the Growth of Knowledge," is that "though there are no general criteria by which we can recognize truth—except perhaps tautological truth—there are something like criteria of progress towards the truth. . . ."[4] We shall see later on what he takes these criteria of progress to be.

First, however, I want to examine his claim that, at any rate so far as empirical propositions are concerned, there are no general criteria by which we can recognize truth. In the essay from which this quotation is taken, it becomes clear that Popper is thinking almost exclusively of scientific theories, and with respect to such theories his thesis is not very controversial. The difference in this connection between him and the inductivists, whom he so sharply opposes, is that whereas they hold that the accumulation of positive instances confirms a universal hypothesis, he prefers to say that the failure of the instances to be negative corroborates it. I confess that I have never been able to see that this difference amounted to very much. Admittedly, to speak of a hypothesis as having been confirmed carries the suggestion that it has acquired some credit in the process, that the more favourable instances we find, with none unfavourable, the better reason we have to rely upon it; and it may be objected that this is an unwarranted assumption, since no one has yet been able to answer the arguments which Hume brought against it. But, if there is a difficulty here, it is by no means obvious that Popper's own approach avoids it. He lays great emphasis upon the need for testing hypotheses as rigorously as we can, which means that we are to make every effort to discover counterexamples to them. It is, however, not clear why we should make this effort if the hypotheses gain no credit from passing the test. Popper himself remarks, in the course of making some telling criticisms of Carnap's version of inductive logic that ". . . the better a statement can be tested, the better it can be confirmed, i.e. attested by its tests".[5] I do not know what the word "attested" means in this context if it carries no suggestion that we have acquired any reason at all to expect the statement to maintain itself in the future. Of course, to the extent that a hypothesis is open to further tests, there can be no question of our having any guarantee of its truth; but it is now generally admitted that no such guarantee could be forthcoming.

To say that there are no general criteria for recognizing truth is, therefore, correct in its application to theories, if it is taken to mean that there is no infallible means of telling in advance what the result of testing a theoretical statement will be. There is, however, a sense in which we do have a general criterion for deciding whether or not a theoretical statement is true. It is true if and only if there is no counterexample to it. Admittedly, in the case of universal statements, this works as a criterion of falsity rather than as a criterion of truth. Finding a counterexample proves the statement false, but failing to find one does not prove it true, since we can never be sure that we have run through all the instances. Nevertheless it remains the case that the absence of any counterexample, whether or not we are able to establish it, is both a necessary and sufficient condition of truth; and from this an important consequence follows. Since the only way in which any empirical statement can meet with a counterexample is by its coming into conflict with a basic statement, it can be concluded that the truth or falsity of any empirical statement, whatever its form or content, is entirely determined by the truth or falsity of some set of basic statements. Accordingly, if we can lay down a general criterion for recognizing the truth of basic statements, there is a sense in which we shall after all have a general criterion for recognizing empirical truth.

Now, as we have seen, Popper does have a very simple way of assessing the truth or falsity of basic statements. True basic statements are those that we decide to accept; false basic statements are those that we decide to reject.

It may be objected that this way of putting it is unfair to him, since even in this case he does not equate truth with acceptance or falsity with rejection. He leaves open the formal possibility of our accepting a false basic statement or rejecting a true one. But this possibility is entirely abstract, since there is nothing that would actually count as our discovering that we had been mistaken, one way or the other. All that is open to us is to decide not to abide by a previous decision. We cannot even claim to be justified in taking this course, any more than we can claim to be justified in accepting or rejecting any basic statement in the first place. If we were to be justified, it could only be in virtue of our experiences; but Popper explicitly denies that this is possible. "Experiences", he says, "can *motivate a decision*, and hence an acceptance or rejection of a statement, but a basic statement cannot be justified by them—no more than by thumping the table".[6]

If this conclusion is to be taken literally, there no longer appears to be any good reason why basic statements should be required to refer to observable events. The principle which underlay this requirement was that empirical statements had to be testable by observation. But if observation can only motivate but never justify the acceptance of any statement, this principle becomes entirely arbitrary. One might have equally strong motives for accepting statements which did not refer to anything observable. Indeed, if our experiences supply us with no better ground for accepting any statements than a blow on the table, it is not clear what sense can be attached to speaking of observation as a test. For Popper it is enough that other empirical statements should stand in certain logical relations to basic statements. But what is this to the purpose if basic statements themselves are not empirically justifiable?

This refusal to allow that any statement can find its justification in experience is the outcome of Popper's hostility to what he calls psychologism. He remarks, correctly, that if one takes the view that statements can be justified only by other statements, one seems to be committed to an infinite regress; any statement which is put forward as justifying another will have to be justified in its turn and so ad infinitum. In order to put a stop to this regress, empirical philosophers have commonly invoked a class of statements which they took to be self-evident: these were the subject's own reports of the experiences which he was having. It was held that he could not be mistaken about the character of the sense-data with which he was currently presented. Statements of this kind were, therefore, thought to supply us with the sure foundation on which all our claims to empirical knowledge could be made to rest.

Popper's main objection to this view is that there can be no such thing as a pure report of experience. There is a "transcendence inherent in any description".

> Every description uses *universal* names (or symbols, or ideas); every statement has the character of a theory, of a hypothesis. The statement, 'Here is a glass of water' cannot be verified by any observational experience. The reason is that the *universals* which appear in it cannot be correlated with any specific sense-experience. (An 'immediate experience' is *only once* 'immediately given'; it is unique.) By the word 'glass', for example, we denote physical bodies which exhibit a certain *law-like behaviour,* and the same holds for the word 'water'. Universals cannot be reduced to classes of experiences; they cannot be 'constituted'.[7]

From this Popper infers that the attempt to found empirical statements upon reports of immediate experiences fails. All empirical statements, including those that are taken to be basic, remain on indefinite probation. The only way in which we can put a stop to the regress is by simply deciding to accept certain basic statements without further tests.

The weakness in this argument is the assumption that if what purports to be the record of an observation "transcends" the experience on which it is based, we are left with no reason for accepting it. But why should this be so? Let it be granted that even the most cautious description of an experience is liable to error; at the very least one may classify the experience incorrectly. It still does not follow that the description has no warrant at all. If I were asked how I knew that there was a glass of water in front of me, to say that I could see it would be a perfectly good answer. It is conceivable that I should be misusing the words 'glass' or 'water', or that, without making any verbal mistake, I should have misindentified one or the other, or that I should be the victim of a hallucination. None of this prevents it from being true that my having this "observational experience" supplies me not only with a motive but also with a ground for accepting the interpretation which I put upon it.

But what makes the experience a ground for one interpretation rather than another? If I had mistaken an inkpot for the glass of water, should I still have been justified? The answer is that my command of the language which I am using fundamentally consists in my having acquired the habit of accepting certain statements as the result of having the appropriate experiences. To the extent that these statements transcend the experiences on which they are based, they set up expectations which may be disappointed. It is, however, a condition of my being able to apply my language to the world that they are commonly not disappointed. My experiences license the interpretations which I have learned to put upon them, because the world has been found to answer to them; and this general rule is not invalidated by the fact that the interpretations now and then miscarry. There is, indeed, a circle here, inasmuch as the proof that I commonly do interpret my observations successfully itself depends upon a suitable interpretation of my memory experiences and other observations; but I am afraid that some such circle is unavoidable in any account of inductive reasoning. So much the worse, it may be said, for inductive reasoning. But if I am never justified in coming to any conclusion on inductive grounds, then I have no reason to think that my language does have any application to the world: and equally no reason to think that any hypothesis ever passes any test.

It is to be noted that in arguing that basic statements can find a justification in experience, I have not found it necessary to cast them in the form of statements which refer exclusively to present sense-data. This is not because I have any objection to such statements in principle: I am not even convinced that it is wrong to treat them as "incorrigible", in the sense that they do not leave room for anything other than merely verbal mistakes. It is rather that I do not think that they are strictly needed for the role which has here been assigned to them. They were intended to stop the infinite regress of justifying one statement by another, as being statements which needed no further justification. But the only ground for holding that these statements need no further justification is that they are sufficiently justified by the actual occurrence of the experiences which they describe. That is to say, one's right to be sure of the truth of such a statement is founded, not on one's having the right to be sure of the truth of some other statement, but directly on the fact that one is having the experience in question. But if this is so, we have to reject the view that statements can be justified only by one another; and once this view has been rejected, there seems to be no good reason why we should not regard our experiences as directly justifying, not only sense-data statements, but the sort of statements which Popper treats as basic. We cannot hold that they verify them conclusively; but this is not a bar to our holding that they give us an adequate ground for accepting them.

This runs directly counter to Popper's thesis that the sources of our claims to knowledge have no authoritative, and in general no very strong, bearing on their validity.[8] But beyond making the point that such claims are fallible, this thesis is surely mistaken. The argument which Popper advances for it is that "in general we do not test the validity of an assertion or information by tracing its sources or its origin, but we test them, much more directly, by a critical examination of what has been asserted—of the asserted facts themselves".[9] This is correct in that finding out what caused a speaker to make his assertion is commonly not the only and very often not the best way of determining whether what he asserts is true; and it is also the case that we are commonly more interested in assessing the value of the information which we are given than in assessing the qualifications of the speaker to impart it. Even so, the argument does not vindicate Popper's thesis. The reason why it does not is that it requires the false assumption that the knowledge which we gain from examining the facts is not validated by its source. For what must be meant here by examining the facts is making observations which lead one to accept or reject certain basic statements. If these observations give us no authority for accepting any basic statement, they do not constitute a test of anything, so that there is nothing to be gained by examining the facts: if they do give us this authority, our claims to know basic statements are validated by their sources. There are, indeed, facts, such as historical facts, which we are not in a position to examine, but here too our claims to knowledge must ultimately rest upon observation. Popper does his best to play down the extent to which our acceptance of historical assertions depends upon our belief that they are causally connected with the reports made by eyewitnesses of the events to which they refer. He reminds us that eyewitnesses are notoriously fallible, forgetting that in the last analysis the only ground that we can have for mistrusting one eyewitness is that his report conflicts with that of other eyewitnesses whom we trust. No doubt our assessment of firsthand evidence is partly conditioned by our previous acceptance of certain theories: but this makes no essential difference to the argument. Unless the theories had been attested by observation, we should have no reason for accepting them.

It would seem absurd, then, not to take as our criterion of progress towards truth the persistent accord of our hypotheses with our observations. At no stage would the further survival of any hypothesis be guaranteed: they are engaged, as it were, in a steeplechase without a winning post; if any sense at all is to be given to the idea of their progressing towards victory, it must surely be taken to consist in their putting an ever longer stretch of the course behind them. But this amounts to adopting "a theory of the attainment of truth through verification,"[10] which Popper dismisses as subjectivist. The question is what he can find to put in its place.

So far as I can see, nothing whatsoever. What he does is to introduce a new technical concept to which he gives the name of "verisimilitude". The verisimilitude of a statement is defined as the difference between its truth-content and its falsity-content; its truth-content being the conjunction of all the true statements which it entails, and its falsity-content the conjunction of all the false statements which it entails. In the case of any true statement, the falsity-content is nil, but the converse does not hold, since false statements can have true consequences. Indeed, since every statement entails the disjunction of itself with every other statement, any false statement, in an infinite universe of discourse, may have an infinite number of true consequences. This does not mean, of course, that it will have a positive verisimilitude, since it will also in these circumstances have an infinite number of false consequences. If trivial entailments of this kind are left out of consideration, we cannot assess the verisimilitude of a statement unless we already know its truth-value, and even this would not always be sufficient. The verisimilitude of a statement which is known to be true can be equated with its logical content, but that of a statement which is known to be false cannot be determined unless we also know what false statements it entails.

It is, however, possible to make certain comparisons. For instance if a theory T_2 supersedes another theory T_1 in the sense that it accounts for all the facts for which T_1 accounts but also for some facts for which T_1 fails to account, then if it can be assumed that any new information which was fatal to T_2 would also be fatal to T_1, we can safely conclude that T_2 has the greater verisimilitude. This gives us no guarantee that T_2 will not be refuted in its turn, but at least we shall be able to say in retrospect that T_2 was a better theory than T_1.

Considerations of this kind lead Popper to assume that his concept of comparative verisimilitude will apply to all the cases in which we should be inclined to say of two theories not known to be true, or even known not to be true, that one corresponded better than the other to the facts. It is, however, doubtful if this conclusion is correct. For example, among the cases of this kind which Popper lists are those in which T_2 makes more precise assertions than T_1, and those in which it explains the facts in more detail. Now it is quite true, as he claims, that in these circumstances T_2 will have a greater verisimilitude than T_1, provided that its falsity-content is not greater, but this proviso is not at all likely to be satisfied. The reason why it is not is just that the less precise theory runs less risk of falsification. It is like making a safe, as opposed to a speculative, investment. The yield is smaller; yet, since the danger of the company's going out of business is also smaller, one may end by making more money out of it. This is not to say that one ought to prefer the less precise theory. It is rather that the pursuit of verisimilitude may conflict with the principle, which Popper most of all favours, that in the choice of hypotheses preference should be given to those that run the greater risk of being falsified.

In what way, then, does the concept of verisimilitude afford us a criterion for assessing our progress towards truth? So far from aiding us in our search for true hypotheses, it only becomes effective when it is applied to hypotheses which have already been refuted. It then makes it possible for us to award them consolation prizes. But the hypotheses in which we are interested are those which have not yet been refuted; and their comparative verisimilitude cannot be known. As Popper says, one can only guess. One can only guess at which stage, if any, each of the competing hypotheses will break down; one can only guess which, if any of them, will maintain its position in the face of any test. What is surprising is that he does not leave it there. He goes on to say that "I can examine my guess critically, and if it withstands severe criticism, then this fact may be taken as a good critical reason in favour of it".[11] But how can a hypothesis better withstand criticism than by passing the hardest test to which we can subject it? And how does this in the end differ from the idea of progress through verification which Popper believes that he rejects?

SIR ALFRED AYER, F.B.A.

NEW COLLEGE
OXFORD, ENGLAND
MARCH, 1967

NOTES

[1] *Vide* K. R. Popper, *Logik der Forschung* (Vienna: Julius Springer-Verlag, 1934), Sec. 84.

[2] *Vide* K. R. Popper, "Truth, Rationality and the Growth of Knowledge," *Conjectures and Refutations: The Growth of Scientific Knowledge* (London: Routledge & Kegan Paul, 1963; New York: Basic Books, 1963), p. 226. Hereinafter cited as *C.&R.*

[3] *C.&R.*, pp. 3-30 *passim.*

[4] *C.&R.*, p. 226.

[5] *C.&R.*, p. 287.

[6] *The Logic of Scientific Discovery* (London: Hutchinson, 1959; New York: Basic Books, 1959), Sec. 28, p. 105. Hereinafter cited as *L.Sc.D.*

[7] *L.Sc.D.*, pp. 94-95.

[8] "On the Sources of Knowledge and of Ignorance," in *C.&R.*, pp. 3-30.

[9] *C.&R.*, pp. 24-25.

[10] *C.&R.*, p. 227.

[11] "Truth, Rationality and the Growth of Knowledge," in *C.&R.*, p. 239.

Joseph Agassi

MODIFIED CONVENTIONALISM IS MORE COMPREHENSIVE THAN MODIFIED ESSENTIALISM*

Let me begin by boasting that my moderate reputation is that of a purist Popperian, aiming at a position more Popperian than Popper's. I am quite happy to attempt here (though not in general) to live up to my reputation. The title of this essay alludes, of course, to Popper's "Three Views Concerning Human Knowledge," where the two traditional views, of science as knowledge and of science as utility, are labelled "essentialism" and "instrumentalism" respectively, and where Popper endorses a third view, of the approximation to the truth in stages, a view which has since been labelled as modified essentialism. It makes no good sense to speak of modified instrumentalism, since the bold idea that science is merely instrumental for technology with the slightest modification becomes rather trite. My desire to view the third view as a modified conventionalism has to do with Popper's third view in his *Open Society* within social philosophy and the methodology of the social sciences. The contrast between nature and convention in that field is unsatisfactory, as naturalism is either psychologistic or organicist, whereas conventionalism is somewhat cynical; Popper proposes there a modified conventionalism as a basis for reformist social philosophy. And he associates with it an institutionalistic individualism as a new methodology. All we have to do to link the two modified views—of science and of society—is to refer to Popper's view of science as a social institution (rather than a state of mind). But, in addition I wish to contrast essentialism with conventionalism so as to be able to declare Popper's third view as a synthesis, i.e., as a modification of both. But there is a little snag here. In his *Logic of Scientific Discovery* Popper contrasts conventionalism with inductivism and in his

---

* Paper read to the philosophy seminar in the London School of Economics on Tuesday, February 25, 1969. I am grateful to all its members for their comments—particularly to Sir Karl Popper. Though my intention was to publish this paper with many lengthy footnotes, I have decided, after a discussion with Sir Karl, to omit them.

"Three Views" he contrasts essentialism with instrumentalism; the correlation is fairly intuitive, but for my purpose I wish to make it explicit and rectify it somewhat. I apologize for my pedantry in advance. I put matters in a table of 3 x 3. The columns present the contemplative view of science, the active view, and the new gradualist view. The rows present the aim of science, the method of science, dealing with the problem of induction, and the status of science, dealing with the problem of the demarcation of science. Popper's identification of the two last problems, then, are here taken with some reservation. Let me name the three rows as rationality, methodology, and epistemology, in accord with tradition.

THREE VIEWS ON SCIENCE

	CONTEMPLATIVE	ACTIVE	GRADUALIST
Rationality of Science	True and ultimate explanation ESSENTIALISM	Pragmatic truth or utility INSTRUMENTALISM	As in ESSENTIALISM
Methodology of Science	PASSIVISM Intuition of essences, essentialism; divided into inductivism and apriorism	Trial and error ACTIVISM	ACTIVISM
Epistemology (the status of Science)	Essential definitions, final truths, ultimate explanations ESSENTIALISM	Nominal definitions further divided into fictionalism or tautologism CONVENTIONALISM	Tentative explanations, refuted and succeeding better tentative ones GRADUALISM

A few comments. Kant does not fit here, nor does Whewell, nor the inductive school of probability. This holds for Popper's "Three Views" as much as the present schema. The inductive school of probability may be viewed as an alternative modified essentialism—indeed, unlike Popper's modified essentialism, inductive probability cannot be consistently viewed as modified conventionalism (pace Carnap)

The contemplative methodology of intuiting essences (methodological essentialism) is, either inductivist or apriorist. The contemplative epistemology of viewing science as certainty (epistemological essentialism) may contrast with the active epistemology either by contrasting the alleged true nature of scientific theories with the alleged fictitious nature of scientific theories, or with their alleged empty tautologous nature. Croce, Marcel, and others, are contemplative and active in metaphysics and in science respectively; so is Duhem, who allows one to view scientific theory as either fiction or empty definition—preferring the latter. The empty definitions view is less traditional than the claim for the fictitious nature of scientific theory, but it still is to be found in older writings; and even the implicit definition idea may be found in Torricelli's conventionalist twist of Galileo's theory of the inclined plane. But it was Poincaré who gave it the necessary precision. Eddington saw the fiction as inescapable but private and the empty implicit definition as the convention.

The third view, endorsing the contemplative view on rationality and the active view of method, raises severe difficulties—hence its rarity; they can be solved by the gradualist theory of science approaching the truth by approximations and by the view of scientific theories as improbable though refutable conjectures. The status of science, however, is not clear in Popper's theory. What status has a refuted theory? An untested refutable theory? A tested unrefuted theory? All these are open since the major questions of traditional philosophy are answered by Popper without going into the question of status. The question of status may refer back to the question of rationality (as Bartley claims), in which case degrees of approximation to the truth—of verisimilitude—may be defined to answer it. This may perhaps be done after the incorporation of additional desiderata—which means changing our view of the rationality of science. Beforehand, I feel, we may do better to explore only the desideratum of degrees of explanatory power—a modification of Leibniz's view to include refutations—and see if it cannot suffice. I suppose it will not, but cannot say. If it will not, then, obviously, our view of either rationality or methodology will have to be altered.

The additional possible desiderata may define more stringent kinds of rationality plus status; these may be credibility, if one likes (I do not), usefulness, challenge, or depth (this I like very much). I wish, however, to say that it is difficult for me to place the role of corroboration—failed refutation—here, seeing that a scientific theory may be corroborated scientifically—through a genuine test—or not, just as an unscientific theory, say

		THEORY	
		SCIENTIFIC	UNSCIENTIFIC
TEST	SCIENTIFIC	Michelson Eddington	Renaissance refutations of mediaeval superstitions especially medical, astrological, etc.
	UNSCIENTIFIC	Ad hoc technology. Classroom demonstrations. Much of popular science so-called	Almost all confirmations of mediaeval superstitions.

not explanatory yet of technological import, may be corroborated scientifically or not.(we have scientific technology, pre, pseudo, etc.).

For the sake and in the name of social responsibility a theory must be corroborated before it is allowed to be institutionally implemented. Viewing
scientific theory as a contemplative institution (the textbook of science) or as
technology of sorts—educational or otherwise—may resolve some of the difficulty.

JOSEPH AGASSI

DEPARTMENT OF PHILOSOPHY
BOSTON UNIVERSITY AND TEL AVIV UNIVERSITY
SEPTEMBER 26, 1969

Tom Settle

INDUCTION AND PROBABILITY UNFUSED*

In recent philosophy of science, there has been a widespread confusion of induction with probability. This confusion is engendered by other confusions: the identification of induction with scientific method and the identification of probability with the key criterion of rational betting or of decision making under uncertainty. Both these identifications have deep roots in modern philosophy. The more recent confusion of induction with probability has come about as a result of the recent recognition that scientific method does not yield demonstrative truths but only refutable hypotheses. The overthrow of Newtonianism shattered what was left of a considerably shaken faith in the reliability of scientific knowledge. In place of the earlier view that the acceptance of a theory into the body of scientific knowledge depended upon its being proved (inductively) to be true—beyond any reasonable doubt!—there came the view that a theory was more or less acceptable as it was rendered more or less probable by the available evidence. This view, the equating of degrees of acceptability with degrees of confirmation and degrees of confirmation with degrees of probability, was very seductive. Alone among philosophers of the first half-century, Sir Karl Popper heard the song of the sirens but did not find it sweet: he has persistently refused to confuse scientific method with induction or probability with rational justification or induction with probability or scientific method with rational justification.

It is not the purpose of this essay to expose the confusions I have indicated, even though they underlie much contemporary philosophizing about science: exposés have already been given by Sir Karl himself as well as by students of his. Rather it is the purpose of this essay to explore somewhat the two concepts of induction and probability, given Popper's unfusing of them, and in the spirit of Popper's critical philosophy. I choose to explore the problem of induction not only because of its importance but principally because of the neglect many aspects of the problem have suffered in Popper's

* I am indebted to Sir Karl Popper, Professor Mario Bunge, Professor Joseph Agassi, Professor R. B. Braithwaite, Professor Alex Michalos, and Professor Cliff Hooker for their very helpful criticisms of early drafts of this article.

published works. On the other hand, I choose to explore the problem of the interpretation of probability somewhat, because of the neglect Popper's published works on the subject have received in recent literature.

In Part One, I pay attention to the popular demand for a guide of life based on science. This demand was, I guess, partly responsible for the various confusions to which I have referred: if we want to make rational decisions in conditions of uncertainty, what better procedure to imitate than that of science, that paradigm of the rational pursuit of truth? The demand is, it seems to me, doomed to disappointment if what is sought is a criterion which would uniquely, unequivocally, and indisputably pick out the right, correct, proper, or rational decision. But, instead of neglecting the doomed demand, as Popper understandably has, I wish to try to meet it in some way: I wish to try to characterize (even if only crudely) the rationality implicit in science so as to aid the construction of a guide of life based on science.

In Part Two, I turn my attention to the other fork in the road, and explore that avenue a little. Popper has several times explained carefully what he had in mind when he introduced his propensity interpretation of probability, but it has been more or less neglected where it has not been confused with other interpretations. One confusion in particular seemed to me to be worth a closer scrutiny: when Popper first publicly introduced his propensity interpretation, Professor Braithwaite suggested that this interpretation was already to be found in the works of Charles Peirce and moreover is not different from the frequency interpretation which Popper appeared to think he was improving upon. This confusion seemed to be worth looking at because it offered an opportunity to bring out either the novelty or the antiquity of Popper's interpretation. As it transpired, the scrutiny led also to a critical assessment of various axiomatizations of the probability calculus, a further area in which Popper has made interesting contributions.

Thus whereas the first part of the essay aims to draw Sir Karl's attention to aspects of the problem of induction which he had hitherto neglected, the second part aims to draw the attention of other philosophers to Sir Karl's contributions to probability theory. Even so, the second part is not without criticism: I invite Sir Karl to say whether he agrees with some views which arise from a fairly natural reading of his publications or with views which I hold after some criticism of this natural reading.

PART ONE:
THE PROBLEM OF A GUIDE OF LIFE BASED ON SCIENCE

1. Science is Golden

The old quest for the philosopher's stone, with which we might have turned base metals into gold and thereby made a fortune for ourselves and produced unspeakable benefits for mankind—or so at least, some who longed for the coming of Midas would have us believe—was frustrated. Perhaps it was as well. It might have been more beneficial to have turned stones into bread, as Jesus of Nazareth declined to do—or so at least some who longed for the coming of the Messiah would have us believe—when it was suggested to him by God's travelling examiner, Satan.

Looking for the philosopher's stone is not like looking for a needle in a haystack. It is much harder. We know where the haystack is, and thus roughly where to look; we know what a needle is, and thus what to look for; we know the needle is there, and thus that it is worthwhile to search. But we do not know where to look for the philosopher's stone; we do not know what it looks like; and we do not know whether there is one. Nonetheless, men have searched for it just as they have looked for a device to turn stones to bread, or a talisman to turn bad luck to good, or a way to take the future by the forelock and choose what may befall.

The new quest for the philosopher's stone exhibits many features of the old and has much in common with the common quest for certainty about the unknowable. This time we want a rational or scientific guide of life: we want to solve the problem of induction. Hume said it cannot be done: there is no 'new philosopher's stone'; but the search for it persists. If only we knew what it looked like. There is no need here to demonstrate men's motivation. Nowadays it is commonplace: by the popular standards of success, science is successful; by the popular standards of certainty, science is certain; by the popular standards of a safe bet, science is a safe bet; by the popular standards of trust, science is to be trusted. All this is no accident. Science has won the position that it occupies not by meeting old standards of success, certainty, safety, and trust, but by challenging the old standards and shaping new ones. Science and technology between them set the standards today as theology did in the infancy of science. Science is virtuous. Science is golden. What more could one hope for of life than that it be scientific. The lovers of reason see science as rational; lovers of adventure, laud its challenges; lovers of art, its creativity and beauty.

But hold! Do we already know so much about science that we can judge its qualities so surely? And knowing so much about science, do we not already possess the philosopher's stone? Anyone now with a good grasp of scientific method may chisel out his own stone. The popular view is that induction is the method of science and that the solution to the problems of induction will provide the prize in the quest for a guide of life based on science. The popular view of induction is that it is a method by which we achieve as much rational certainty as possible, go as near as we can to proving ourselves correct, rely only upon the most reliable information and build our maximally reliable house or maximally reliable foundations. But the prize still eludes us.[1]

Sir Karl Popper, for years more or less alone in dissenting from the popular view, has not allowed himself to be sidetracked from his task of assaying the gold—the task of solving the problem of the nature of science—by the question whether base life could be rendered scientific. He examined the problem of induction, declared inductive logic to be nonexistent[2]—and so the popular search for the philosopher's stone to be futile. But the failure of one stone to work the alchemic trick is no proof of the nonexistence of a stone that works. Sir Karl's answer to the question, 'How do we gain theoretical knowledge from experience?' is now very widely accepted.[3] Attention could perhaps now be given to whether the theory that knowledge grows by conjecture and refutation may not inspire conjectures to solve other aspects of the problem of induction.

According to Lakatos this has already been done. He claims two problems emerged with the demise of what Carnap called "the grand old problem of induction":[4] (1) "the problem of the growth of knowledge" and (2) "the problem of the appraisal of conjectural knowledge" (*PIL*, p. 322), and that while many philosophers have tried to solve the problem of appraisal and ignored the problem of growth, Popper started by solving the problem of growth and then showed that his 'solution' to that one solved "the most interesting aspects of the (other problem). . .too" (*PIL*, p. 322).

I disagree. I think Popper's proposed solution to the problem of induction is much more austere. Because ordinary people regard valid induction as virtuous, and laud science just because it seems to them to guarantee induction, the vulgar demand is for a guide of life to rely upon, a recipe for valid induction. Popper says there is none. In 1789, outside the Palace of Versailles, the vulgar demand was for bread. There was none. That time, there was no cake either, despite Marie Antoinette's alleged saying, "Qu'ils mangent de la brioche". Perhaps in our case, however, to the surprise of the crowd, we may be able to serve cake even though there is no bread.

The austerity of Popper's proffered solution to the problem of induction would be exposed, I think, if an analysis of the problem whose complexity is hinted at by Lakatos's two main problems, should reveal a number of interesting subproblems to which Popper's solution does not immediately apply. I do not propose to conduct here an exhaustive analysis, but to offer the following sketch to expose the complex within which lies the main problem to which Part One is addressed: the problem of a guide of life based on science.

A. Growth

On the face of it, there would seem to be more to the growth of knowledge in science than, simply, shifts in theoretical knowledge. Without going to the extreme of suggesting that any new fact recorded is an example, however small or mean, of growth in scientific knowledge, and without suggesting that anyone could know which facts were worth trying to record without at least the embryo of a law in mind, it is possible to see that what may deserve the name of 'progress' may be made in science without any theory being proposed, challenged, tested, or refuted. Examples of such prima facie non-Popperian progress might be: the improvement of the foundations of a theory through partial axiomatization[5] (Foundations Research); the improvement of the grip of a theory on experience by improved precision in the measurement of the value of some constant[6] or the exposure of the scope of a theory by a series of experiments over areas to which the theory is expected to apply[7] (Consolidation); the exploitation of the power of a theory by making use of its suggestiveness in new directions[8] (Exploitation).

Of course, it could be claimed that a necessary condition for progress in science was the positing or testing of a theory. Such a claim would exclude from being properly called science much of what is normally called science, including all of what Kuhn calls normal science.[9] One does not want to squabble over words, but it seems more appropriate to me to let the term 'science' be wide enough to refer to the professional activities of professional scientists. On this view, it would be possible to distinguish several different types of research. Perhaps there is a spectrum shading off into mathematics at the violet end and technology at the red end:

TABLE 1

Spectrum of Types of Scientific Research,
Showing Contiguous Nonscientific Types of Research

"Ultra-Violet"					"Red"	"Infrared"
	1	2	3	4	5	
Mathematics	Foundations Research	Theory Conjecturing	Testing	Consolidation	Exploitation	Technology

We may very well want to talk about the progress or growth of science with reference to the results of research of types 1, 4, and 5 without it being implied that there was progress of types 2 or 3. We could then say that

Popper has characterized what might be called the core of science: conjecturing and refuting theories.[10]

A number of interesting problems of the induction complex, other than
those to which Popper has addressed himself, are hinted at by this spectrum:
Corresponding to Lakatos's (1) above is:

(1a) How do we gain theoretical knowledge from experience?

And then there are:

(1b) How do we lay the foundations of a theory?

(1c) What are the techniques of consolidation of a theory?

(1d) What steps do we take to exploit a theory?

B. Appraisal

The problem of appraisal appears to require not only some criteria of
appraisal—but also some specification of purpose. A judgment as to the truth
value of an hypothesis may turn on different cirteria than a judgment as to
the worthwhileness of setting up a test for an hypothesis; and the criteria may
be different again, if we had in mind a judgment of the rationality of acting
upon an hypothesis. Indeed, we choose rationally not to test an hypothesis
that is "worth testing" if the test may be beyond our capabilities or our
means, or the hypothesis may not interest us. Or we may decide rationally not
to act on an hypothesis that is truthworthy, if a different hypothesis is better
suited as an assumption in pursuit of our goal. Even the question of
judgments of truth is not clear-cut despite the logical asymmetry between
theories and basic statements (a strictly universal statement may be refuted
but is not implied by relevant basic statements); Duhem showed, a long time
ago, that the results of a so-called crucial experiment do not have a unique interpretation, and drew certain instrumentalist conclusions from the impossibility of unequivocal interpretation. Popper realized that the decision to
accept a basic statement as falsifying a specific universal hypothesis was not
justifiable though, of course, he eschewed instrumentalism.[11] Some
philosophers, who hold a justificationist theory of rationality, have taken this
to mean the collapse of Popper's programme: no refutations can take place,
they supposed, if no justifiable decisions could be taken.[12] Popper, of course,
is not disturbed by a lack of justification: on his theory of rationality,
justification not only is not possible, it is not even called for. What is called
for is criticism. A decision is required, to count an hypothesis as refuted; and
the decision is criticizable and corrigible. Nevertheless, even when we accept
Popper's position on 'refutation', we get no good guidance from Popper as to
how to choose which hypothesis or theory, from the complex used to set up
and interpret an experiment, to take as refuted.

Thus at least three problems may be usefully distinguished:

(2a) How do we make judgments as to the truth value of hypotheses?

(2b) How do we choose hypotheses to test?

(2c) How do we choose the right hypotheses to act upon?

Popper has, of course, already made these distinctions—distinctions between the truth, the testworthiness, and the trustworthiness of hypotheses. Moreover, he has dealt very satisfactorily with (2a) and has contributed to the solution of (2b).[13] Nevertheless he has largely ignored (2c), the problem to which Part One calls attention. I do not think he shares with inductivists the common confusion of science with technology: I think he simply ignores technology and is thus at cross purposes with those who take it into account and then confuse its demands and problems with science's. Problem (2c), the choice of hypotheses to act upon, is not a problem in philosophy of (strictly) science—although unless scientists had some relevant decision procedure they would never implement any tests: science needs technology in order to get started, as it were: which is, however, no excuse for confusing the two: a race is distinct from a starter's pistol. Problem (2c) is a problem in technology and in life. We should not confuse the greatness of science with the success of technology,[14] the growth of scientific knowledge with the conquest of nature—even Francis Bacon avoided that confusion—or the problem of appraising general hypotheses in science with the problem of appraising an hypothesis to act upon.[15]

Inductivists usually present the problem of induction as the problem of choice between rival hypotheses as bases for action and subsume the appraisal of the truth value of an hypothesis as a special case of that choice; they know that positive evidence is relevant to rational decisions how to act—every judge, every banker, every insurance agent, knows as much—and they conclude that it must be relevant to judgments of truth of general hypotheses. Thus do they threaten to turn science into lead rather than life to gold: the weight of the accumulating cargo of favourable evidence would be enough to stop the train of ideas in science.[16] It needs careful consideration what it is the vulgar ask for when they want life to be like science; but we are not bound to give them what they fancy themselves as wanting. We may sympathize with their admiration for science without concurring with their explanation of their trust.

The vulgar demand is no doubt for a guide of life that can be trusted as science is trusted. Inductivists commonly confuse the trustworthiness of science with the trustworthiness of hypotheses in science, and trustworthiness with nearness to truth. Of course, if statements that were nearly true were trustworthy and if hypotheses in science were nearly true then science would be trustworthy for those reasons; however, since statements that are nearly true may easily let us down, and since we in any case lack a measure of the nearness of hypotheses to truth, we need another explanation of the vulgar trust in science[17] especially if we share the trust. The assigning of an important role to the confirmation of an hypothesis by the data it explains is not a surprise in the light of the confusions which may have engendered it. Conventionalists—like Duhem—do not explain the importance of an hypothesis by its trustworthiness: they know that the less precise an hypothesis is, the more trustworthy it becomes—a trick every fortuneteller knows: so the scientists' demand for precision runs counter to any hope for trustworthy hypotheses: every general hypothesis can be rendered false by raising the demanded level of precision.[18] Nevertheless, inductivists explain the popular demand for a guide of life based on science as a demand for a decision procedure that will enable us to approximate certainty of being right every time, much as the theoretician in science approximates truth by stages. For example, Ayer understands knowing as "having the right to be sure" and the right to be sure is guaranteed by induction—though we are not told what induction is: Ayer sets aside the nub of Hume's problem, the question: What guarantees induction?[19] I do not think the problem of the justification of induction can be so easily dismissed: but I shall leave it for another paper. For now, it suffices to remark that many philosophers of science see the vulgar demand for a guide of life as a demand for a vindication of rational decisions. To this cry for bread, Popper has turned a deaf ear. To my teacher's deaf ear, I turn a blind eye—and join in the new quest for the philosopher's stone: I want a solution to problem (2c) (How do we choose hypotheses to act upon?) which is consistent with—and even suggested by—Sir Karl's solutions to problems (1a) (How do we gain theoretical knowledge from experience?) and (2a) (How do we make judgments of the truth value of hypotheses?).

2. Bread Is Lead

There is a basic conflict of intent between the *critical attitude*, which is the kernel of rationality for Popper, and a desire for *justification*. The difference between Popper's philosophy of science and that of his opponents or critics is sharp on this issue: should the hypotheses we choose be criticized, in the hope of improving them, or justified in the hope that we can show ourselves to have been as near correct as we could be? Being right is very attractive. Being obviously right, even more attractive. And being demonstratively right, most attractive of all. But the widely held hope to be able to demonstrate how right we are is at odds with the aim of improving our knowledge. So that skepticism ('enquiry'; *'skeptomai'* = 'I examine'), despite its creative power, has never been widely acclaimed. Few people like to have their mistakes pointed out, and fewer admit to them gladly.

I explain the desire for justification as the last link, in contemporary philosophy of science, with the confident philosophies of science of the seventeenth century—Baconian inductivism and Cartesian intellectualism—both of which assumed that scientific knowledge could be secure, certain and stable. The prevailing views in metaphysics and theology at that time most likely contributed to this confidence. The chief problem for both philosophies was to find the *method* by which such secure scientific knowledge could be achieved. Although both Bacon and Descartes criticized Aristotle, they did not abandon his aim to provide incontestable knowledge of the world of our experience—indeed, this aim has not yet been completely abandoned. David Hume raised serious doubts as to the possibility of such secure knowledge; Kant failed to supply an incontestable rationale for synthetic a priori statements; and the nineteenth century saw a split between positivism—according to which *only observation reports* were certain (Comte, Mach)—and inductivism—with Mill making a last ditch stand for Bacon's hopes. (As early as the nineteenth century there were adumbrations of Popper's startling break with the science-is-stable-and-near-certain school, but only adumbrations.) Nowadays, nevertheless, *confidence* in science is still widespread and high. This is particularly so in the teaching of science. Were Socrates alive today, he would not be allowed to publish in the *American Journal of Physics*, I imagine. This journal, which is devoted to the "Instructional and Cultural Aspects of the Physical Sciences" recently contained the following statement of editorial policy:

> Papers presenting original research that clarifies past misunderstandings or allow a more encompassing view of a subject are certainly acceptable. Controversial results yet to be judged in the research literature are not acceptable. Included in the latter category are papers purporting to discredit bodies of physical theory (such as spatial relativity, quantum mechanics, and thermodynamics) which are part of the generally accepted physics curricula.[20]

The most charitable construction which I can put upon this prohibition of critical debate is that it is regarded as inappropriate that difficult or abstruse discussion should be published in the journal. But, no charitable construction is possible if the prohibition applies (as I suspect it does) to criticisms which teachers of physics (as distinct from specialist research workers) could follow. Students of physics most emphatically should *not* be protected from the truths that physics is in flux, that a number of theories in physics are in an underdeveloped state, that sometimes in experimental design (notoriously in quantum physics) one has to work with *incompatible* theories—for example, classical physics, used in the design of apparatus, is incompatible with quantum physics—and that knowledge grows in physics partly by a critical examination (rigorous testing is only one facet of the examination) of the "established" theories in a field.

Can the intent of someone seeking a guide of life and its justification be anything other than anticritical? Is there any way in which the search may be conducted that would attract a Popperian to join it? I think so, as I explain more fully later. But I am aware of the anticritical intent of many seekers after a guide of life and its justification, for example, A. J. Ayer with his theory of "knowing as having the right to be sure" and Wesley Salmon, with his insistence that inductive acceptance rules are needed.[21] Popper certainly distanced himself from members of the Vienna Circle in its early days. Carnap reports, "I believed that the task of philosophy consists in reducing all knowledge to a basis of certainty".[22] However, I imagine that many members of that Circle have since modified their views.[23]

What sort of modification has taken place? What has replaced the quest for certainty, for contemporary inductivists? And is the quest for whatever has replaced certainty still an anticritical quest?

There are two fairly obvious certainty-substitutes, differing on whether 'certainty' is to be construed psychologically or epistemologically. The psychological substitute is 'belief'; the epistemological substitute is 'probability'. The distinction between these two is sometimes confused, because some students of 'belief' want measures of belief to obey what is called the calculus of 'probability'. Perhaps a neater way of making the distinction would be between subjectivist and objectivist interpretations of the probability calculus. But this way of making the distinction would add a further confusion: Popper's propensity interpretation of 'probability' is objectivist, but is not designed to help 'probability' substitute for 'certainty'. I prefer to say that there is a school of thought which maintains that there is some way of treating *actual beliefs* that will deal satisfactorily with what used to be problems of knowledge or problems of certainty[24] and that there is a different school of thought which maintains that there is some *objective* way of assigning *probabilities* to hypotheses as a surrogate for knowledge or certainty.[25]

A quick glance at each of these will serve to show why a Popperian cannot allow either of them as a solution to the problem of a guide of life based on science. Such a quick glance will not permit us to see, except in a very cursory way, what role either has to play in philosophy or in life, and, as a result, what I have to say may appear to be unjust to both. I hope not, but I take the risk.

First, then, a study of the way actual beliefs function—that is, an attempt to answer questions like 'What sort of criteria do people use in choosing to believe this or that?', and 'Under what sorts of conditions do people give up beliefs?', and 'How do people's beliefs shift when elements in their set of beliefs do not chime?', and 'What counts as *strong* or *weak* belief?' and 'What relations do beliefs have to actions or to evidence or to betting quotients?'—is a very useful study for some purposes, but does not immediately obviously serve to aid solutions to the problems 'What counts as a rational decision for action?', or 'What criteria exist for a rational choice between hypotheses?' or 'Is there any sense to the concept of 'acceptability' such that the acceptance of an hypothesis is a rational act?' These problems appear to me to be associated with the question 'What is rationality?', a question which can easily get left behind by enquirers after 'What is belief?', unless an equation is made of the type: 'rationality' = 'the way people's minds work' = 'the way they choose beliefs'. I cannot see good reasons for making an equation of that sort; but I can see good reasons for not doing: my (close) acquaintance with religions has supplied me with so much evidence that beliefs lead to a cessation of enquiry after truth, and even lead to the persecution of proponents of alternative beliefs, that I am very reluctant, to opt for 'belief' as a substitute for 'certainty' or 'knowledge' without, first, a serious scrutiny of any alternatives. Belief notoriously conceals and protects errors (as every believer knows, at least with respect to his opponents' beliefs).

I think Popper's philosophy offers a serious alternative characterization of rationality. Indeed, I think that Popper's attempt to draw the attention of philosophers to the ancient method of Socratic debate is about his most important contribution to philosophy (and to history). Popper was led to this attempt by his discovery of the *critical* character of scientific method—a discovery which is now fast becoming "old hat".[26] What is not yet taken sufficiently seriously is the possibility that the theory that scientific method is a form of critical debate (or Socratic dialogue), which goes a long way towards solving the question 'How do we gain theoretical knowledge from experience?', may be able to solve other problems within the induction-complex as well. It seems that many contemporary students are ready to admit Popper's contributions to the solution of the one problem, but prefer to try to solve the *other* problems using a theory of rationality that is radically different from that which Popper's philosophy of science presupposes. Because of the existence of this alternative theory of rationality which has been successful in one area, I think there is a good reason for not falling back upon the concept of 'belief' as a surrogate for 'certainty' or 'knowledge'. The incentive for the "falling back" appears to me to be a reluctance to accept what the story of the growth of knowledge in science appears to teach us, namely, that knowledge is conjectural, corrigible and unreliable. It is poor advice to men faced with the ogre of uncertainty to invite them to pretend that it does not exist. Popper's theory of rationality might be able to yield a theory of how to make friends with the ogre; and this article is intended to contribute to the formulation of such a theory.

Secondly, I think the objectivist school of thought, which is oriented to solve the problem of assigning measures of probability ("degree of confirmation", "degree of rational belief", etc.) to hypotheses, is much less anticritical, on the face of it, than the subjectivist school. There is a large number of important ordinary life situations, as well as a number of situations which merit scientific study (particularly in psychology and sociology), which have *sufficient resemblance* to the balls-from-the-urn model to give some warrant to the search for a guide of life based on the assignment of probabilities to predictions. "Sufficient resemblance" refers, for example, to the following structural properties: (a) the membership of a particular population is restricted: the population can contain only certain sorts of individuals and not just any sort; and frequently it can be supposed to contain only a finite number of members. (b) Some features of the members of the population are supposed to be distributed randomly among the population, or the sampling technique is supposed to pick out members of the population in a random fashion. If a particular situation is such that an abstraction of the type to which the balls-from-the-urn model (or any other statistical model) belongs is not too farfetched—how one is to judge farfetchedness is another question, to which I shall eventually come—then it appears to me to be legitimate to use statistical theory for handling the situation. And, if a particular situation is such that it is permissible—I shall eventually come, also, to the question of how one is to judge permissibleness—to assume that the variables under consideration are the only important variables, then I think it is legitimate to use decision theory or operations research theory to handle the situation. Statistics, decision theory, game theory, operations research, etc., are appropriate theories to yield predictions (and even explanations) within certain model frameworks. Among the questions that are left over, however, when one has indicated the sorts of models to which these theories apply are the following:

(a) How is one to judge when the abstraction to the appropriate model is not farfetched?
(b) How is one to judge when all the important variables are under consideration?
(c) How is one to explicate the concept 'legitimate' in usages similar to those immediately above?

In other words, granting all the claims which are made for various theories which apply to situations of uncertainty, how are we to assess the claim that the *uncertainties* are of a known kind and have an estimable effect—and are not, rather, of an unknown kind? Lakatos has this delightful distinction between 'controlled' uncertainty and 'uncontrolled' uncertainty:

> According to Carnap, for instance, even if you rationally predict that you will pull out a blue ball from an urn, you must be prepared (to a well-defined degree) to pull out a white or a red one. . . .But, for Popper, the possible variety of the universe is unlimited: you may equally well pull out a rabbit, or your hand may be caught in the urn, or the urn may explode, or, rather, you may pull out something dramatically unexpected that you cannot possibly understand or even describe.[27]

Just so!

That some of the uncertainties in a situation may be of a kind that have not been foreseen—or even of a kind that are not foreseeable—amounts to an objection to the use of any (objectively) probabilistic decision procedure as a guide of life and, in particular, as a guide of scientific research, unless the decision procedure has a built-in *search* instruction, and a built-in *standard of responsibility*. Let me put the objection this way: the usual probabilistic decision procedures instruct us how to assign probabilities to hypotheses given certain evidence, or how to decide on a possible course of action given the utility measures of certain possible outcomes; but they do not prescribe whether more evidence should be sought, or whether some evidence already given may be ignored, or whether it is rational to look for other possible outcomes than those given or whether one should reconsider the given utility measures of the given possibilities. A man betting on the outcome of a horse race will consider it rational to make certain enquiries about the horses if he has a small stake, and much more searching enquiries if he has a large stake; a man supplied with data by his advisors may ask for a check of crucial data if much is at stake, but trust the advisors, if not; manufacturers of cheap egg-slicers will not be thought irresponsible if 5 percent of the slicers fail to work and are returned by the customers; but an automobile manufacturer is expected not to sell a single automobile that does not work; the up-to-date character and the accuracy of road maps is less important if one is going a short way or has time to spare than if one is going a long distance on a tight schedule. In all these examples, there are pairs of cases such that, whereas, for one of the pair, a decision arrived at by using some decision procedure on given evidence looks rational, for the other of the pair, rationality demands further enquiry or further precautions before use is made of the appropriate decision procedure. And in all these examples, it is the character of the particular *case*, or the *context*, that is crucial.

The character of particular cases, however, cannot be taken into account in the use of formal decision procedures: there will be more peculiarities to each case than there are variables in any practicable procedure, so the crucial question before any standard procedure is applied is as to whether that procedure is appropriate. Teachers of, even, elementary arithmetic, know well that, over and above instructing their pupils in the mechanical procedures of adding, subtracting and so on, they have to try to instruct their pupils in recognizing when it is appropriate to add and when not. Rational decision making consists not only in using standard procedures but, crucially, in picking out which procedure is appropriate. The central problem in the search for a guide of life is to find an overarching procedure which teaches us, among other things, how to pick out formal procedures as appropriate to particular cases. Is there such a procedure? Or is the search for a procedure for choosing procedures an infinite regress? Without such a procedure all other procedures are useless or even mischievous.

The episcopal procedure we seek needs, then, not only to teach us what to look for—take precautions, collect relevant evidence, check relevant evidence, check given evidence, and so on—and not only, in addition, to teach us when to stop looking—when, that is, we have taken as many precautions, and so on, as may reasonably be expected—but also to teach us which formal procedures we ought to use in processing the data, evaluating the results of tests, exploiting our having satisfied safety precautions. Happily, there is such a procedure and it is already in use. Unhappily, few philosophers admit the role it plays. My explanation for their neglect is that this procedure to oversee procedures does not have the characteristics that many philosophers expect a rational guide of life to have.

The episcopal procedure we seek is already in wide use: it is standard practice for scientists to engage in critical debate provoked by the inadequacies of objectivist guides of life—critical debate, that is, centred round questions like: 'Shall we use a game-theoretical model here or models drawn from traditional economics theories?'; 'What constitutes "reasonable doubt" in a court of law?'; 'Is it more reasonable to back a well-confirmed hypothesis that does not promise so much chance of gain than to back a less well-confirmed hypothesis with a high possible pay-off?'; 'Shall we abolish the death penalty for illegal possession of arms?'; 'Can some better model than the "wave-and/or-particle" model in quantum physics (Bohr's Complementary Principle) be found?'; 'Have we taken sufficient precautions against undesirable side effects that may result from the use of this drug, before we market it?'.

Critical debate is rarely given the credit it deserves because of the widespread hope that a scientific or rational guide of life will furnish us with a reliable guide or will enable us to justify our actions. There are very few philosophers today, and there have been very few in the history of philosophy in the West, favouring skepticism. Traditionally skepticism has been viewed as a prolegomenon to philosophy and, especially in modern times, has been confused with doubt or negative approach to knowledge. Descartes's first meditation is taken to be the paradigm of skepticism. The skeptical paradigm science provides is not universal doubt but, rather, one enquiry. In science, skepticism is not a prolegomenon: it is the whole method. So, at least, Sir Karl teaches us.

Nevertheless, if formal criteria for the justification of decisions on given evidence are used within a critical context, the question needs to be asked whether the use of such criteria *presupposes* a "justificationist" (and therefore anti-Popperian) theory of rationality. I think not—although it is very attractive to focus upon the core of decision making and blur the context. Philosophers who pay attention to the core are apt to think of reliability as a key concept in explicating rationality. Thus, it is widely held that it is rational to act upon the most reliable hypothesis. Such an explication of 'rational' requires that we already know what is meant by 'reliable'; but a closer examination reveals that 'reliability' is not only not a clear concept, it can be more of a hindrance than a help in explicating the idea of rational action.

To start with, no philosopher of science nowadays (as far as I know) seriously maintains that we may have full reliability. To have a fully reliable hypothesis we should require some absolute (or final or demonstrable or indisputable) justification for the hypothesis and this cannot be given.

The "comprehensive rationalism" (Bartley's phrase)[28] of the intellectualist and empiricist traditions—the equivalent of the double injunction: 'accept any position demonstrable by reason; accept only positions demonstrable by reason'—has been abandoned by most philosophers of science in favour of what might be construed as a weakened form: 'Because full justification of an hypothesis cannot be given, it is rational to justify hypotheses *as far as one can*'. Out of this (weakened) theory of rationality comes a weakened form of reliability: partial reliability. A partially reliable hypothesis is one which has been justified as far as we can justify it.

The problem about a partially reliable hypothesis is that one does not know when, or how disastrously, it is going to let him down. Having a partially reliable timetable for a rail service may be only slightly more helpful than having no timetable at all; it could be more mischievous than no timetable at all, should one rely on it—which is what its being partially reliable invites one to do. We should be in a very bad case if partial reliability were all we had to go on in making rational choices in life: a theory of rationality has to explain why it is rational sometimes to doubt the most reliable available hypothesis and to seek a different one—as when a gambler looks for further evidence which alters the probability of particular horses winning a particular race, or a scientist challenges a well-established theory. This is a problem for a "justificationist" rationalism. The corresponding problem for a comprehensively critical rationalism is to explain why it is rational sometimes to stop doubting and questioning some hypotheses—say, that the earth is an oblate spheroid, or that water boils at more or less the same temperature under normal pressure conditions, or that chickenpox is contagious, or that aspirin eases pain.

It seems to me that a basic requirement of rationality is that no position, procedure, theory, person, institution or document be regarded as sacrosanct—that is, immune from criticism. Further, it is a fact of life that no argument could be convincing unless the premisses of the argument were accepted, or agreed upon, as true, and the logical structure of the argument, as valid. For rational discussion we need agreements which are themselves held to be corrigible. If 'partial justification' means arguing from agreed premises by an agreed procedure, and if 'partial reliability' were defined as a characteristic of the conclusions of such arguments, then I can see nothing intrinsically anticritical in partial justification and partial reliability—on the contrary, I think they are indispensable as components in a rational guide of life. The reason why I think partial reliability needs replacing as the key concept in a theory of rationality is that rationality may become anticritical unless partial reliability is embedded in an overtly critical framework or context.

The partial reliability of an hypothesis or a decision procedure is dependent upon the correctness of a corrigible agreement. This is a trivial observation in the case of patently uncontroversial hypotheses such as the theory of terrestrial gravitation, or 'the average specific gravity of the human body with inflated lungs is slightly less than one'. Anybody who has dived or jumped into a swimming pool would testify to those hypotheses and nobody knows of any counterinstances. But, it is a less trivial observation in the case of macroeconomic theory, when politicians are surprised to discover the failure of certain classical fiscal measures to curb domestic consumption, or in the case of the disasters to the Comet aircraft, when established scientific theories and well-tested techniques and equipment failed to guarantee the safety of the aircraft in flight. It is well known that the *Titanic* sank partly because she was thought to be unsinkable. The key concept in the theory of rationality I am recommending is criticism and the key concept in my candidate for a rational guide of life is responsibility which requires being as critical as one can reasonably be expected to be.

Whereas consideration of responsibility may lead to the use of formal decision procedures, which may emerge under criticism as the best available devices for calculating rational choices on the given evidence, consideration of partial reliability without a critical context could lead to quite irrational decisions—that is to say, decisions which we would not have made had we taken time out to criticize our procedures. Just such a separation of partial reliability from a critical context is what mars the only other serious attempt I know of to develop a guide of life from Popper's philosophy. Lakatos offers the following practical rule:

"Act upon the unrefuted theories which are 'contained' in the existent body of science, rather than on theories which are not".[29] Concerning this rule, Lakatos warns us that it

> offers us limited guidance only concerning the choice of the most 'reliable' theory. But what about particular predictions? There we opt for the relevant prediction of the chosen theory.
> The 'reliability' of particular propositions may then be characterized in two

distinct steps: *first* we decide, if we can, which is the most 'reliable' theory among the relevant ones and *secondly* we decide, on the basis of this chosen theory, which is the most 'reliable' prediction for the given practical problem. Thus, while theories may be said to be supported by evidence, 'predictions' are supported by theories.[30]

This practical rule had already been assumed by Feigl in his characterization of inductive inference[31]—though not, of course, with the intention of capturing Popper's view of the matter: indeed it is doubtful whether this rule is really in the *spirit* of Popper's philosophy: It appears rather to be a rule permitting the uncritical acceptance of "established" scientific theories—as the editors of the *American Journal of Physics* would prefer. I do not think Lakatos can have intended it this way, but it does appear to be equivalent to the claim: 'the only criticism of scientific theories that can reasonably be required is that which scientists indulge in in the attempts to refute theories; no further criticism of any sort is called for'. Happily, the (subsequently celebrated) clerk in the Patents Office at Berne was not aware of this practical rule; he (Einstein) offered theoretical criticism of accepted scientific theories. Happily also, the designers of things my life depends upon from time to time (automobiles, aeroplanes, elevators, etc.) did not follow the practical rule; they put what they designed to further tests and were not satisfied only to have their "predictions" supported by theories. A guide of life in the spirit of Popper's philosophy would be expected to *prescribe* criticism not to *proscribe* it (even by implication). Perhaps Lakatos was overattracted by the song of that siren, Reliability.

Charles II of England was supposed to have said of himself that he had been an unconscionable time dying but he hoped it would be excused. 'Reliability' was dealt a mortal blow by Hume, but is not yet dead—though admittedly it is now much weaker ('partial reliability') than it was. Perhaps it may be excused for living so long: it was such an attractive fellow. It is not my intention to hasten the death of partial reliability, but rather to have the concept replaced because it is now seen to be unable to do, unaided, the task reliability was earlier supposed to do: guide our lives. I shall try to show that the requirement to be *responsible* according to certain agreed upon but corrigible standards follows rather naturally from the application of *the critical attitude* to specific practical goals.

3. The Stone is Cake

In our sophisticated civilization the distinction can readily be drawn between 'being wrong' and 'being to blame for being wrong'. It might be interesting—but not altogether relevant—to trace the chequered history in legal and religious practice of this very important distinction; in particular, it might be interesting to see what criteria were used for distinguishing right from wrong, and to see what counted as a good excuse for being wrong. Now that it is proposed to replace 'partial reliability' by 'responsibility', it might be relevant (as well as interesting) to see what sort of excuse would count nowadays in mitigation of being wrong. 'Ignorance' is the most obvious candidate as an excuse; but it will not do: we readily distinguish between 'ignorance' and 'culpable ignorance'—between 'he did not know any better' and 'he could not reasonably have been expected to have known better'. We do not blame the man whose actions led to disaster if it is the case that the situation was beyond his control in some crucial respect, that is, if there was some unforeseen (and possibly unforeseeable) factor which partially caused the disaster, provided that he took all the precautions he could reasonably have been expected to have taken.

Our increased awareness nowadays of the unreliability of predictions has perhaps made us more sensitive to the blamelessness of the man who has taken all the precautions he could reasonably be expected to take in the circumstances, but whose actions still lead to disaster. When the slag heap moved and buried the schoolhouse at Aberfan (Wales) the enquiry into the disaster sought to discover *what precautions could have been taken* that might have averted the disaster, and *who* should have taken them. And everybody wanted to be sure that those precautions would be taken consistently in the future.

Taking precautions against foreseeable disasters is entirely in the spirit of critical debate. It might look, at first sight, that the caution involved in precautions does not chime with the boldness and imaginativeness of theoretical conjectures. But let me put it this way: If one's aim is growth of knowledge, then imagination is called for in conjecturing, and toughness is called for in testing; but if one's aim is designing an aeroplane for civil aviation or discovering a drug that will relieve arthritic pains, quite apart from the ingenuity called for in research and design, a great deal of imagination and persistence will be needed to think up and try out all possible ways in which the plane could fail to function or the drug have undesired side effects. The desire not to endanger the lives of future passengers or future patients is a sufficient reason for taking precautions; and the general desire of the public not to have their lives endangered is a sufficient reason for the public *requirement* that precautions be taken. What is more important, for our purposes in this paper, is that the requirement of persistent critical enquiry together with the aim of designing a marketable product, appears to provide a sufficient reason for taking the same sorts of precautions as the public requirement would lead to.

But now here is a problem: How is it that there are limits to the precautions that one may reasonably be expected to take in certain circumstances? More specifically, is the existence of standards of responsibility consistent with the theory of rationality as critical debate? At first sight, it might appear not. If the standards of responsibility are equivalent to permission to cease from critical debate, then there may be an imcompatibility between the use to which the standards are put and the critical attitude. On the other hand, standards of responsibility may themselves be subject to critical debate. We may, for example, debate whether the standard of safety precautions taken by automobile manufacturers is a high enough standard. If the attitude to the standards is *critical*, it is not anticritical to have standards. Standards are called for in a social context: people with practical goals to fulfill in a social context—for instance, building a bridge, marketing a food product, breeding cattle or raising a family—are obliged to make decisions and take actions. What is demanded by the aim to be rational with respect to action or decision making in pursuit of a specific goal? It would be absurd for us to say that being rational demanded that no action or decision be taken until all possible critical debate was at an end: nothing would ever be done. If rationality is critical debate then being rational requires that choices of goal be criticized; that standards of responsibility be criticized; that guesses as to whether certain actions would produce certain results be criticized. In short, the critical debate to be engaged in if one is to be rational embraces every criterion and every choice—including the criterion of critical debate and the choice of being rational.[32]

Standards of responsibility come to aid decisions about culpability. They are conventions that would not be required if reliable knowledge were obtainable. They presuppose the theory that responsible enquiry is critical enquiry oriented to some specific goal. The basic meaning of 'responsible' is 'expected or obliged to account (*for* something, *to* someone)'. I am using 'responsible' in the (derived) sense of '*able* to fulfill or *having done what is needed to fulfill* the expectations or obligations to give account. . .'. Popper's theory of rationality throws light on 'responsibility' by first throwing light on what is expected of a responsible person. Because 'partial reliability' is not capable of providing a guide of life on its own, what is expected of a person, in place of the expectation that he be right, is that he takes steps to avoid being *more wrong* than he need be—not, merely, wrong *more often* than he need be. Some errors in theories can be discovered by analysis, some by empirical tests; some defects in machines can be discovered by inspection, others by doing a test run; some mistakes of ethical judgment can be discovered by examination of the conceivable outcomes of actions, others by acting, and watching for the (unforeseeable) consequences. Whether the search is for truth (true explanations of experience) or for success in performance or for rightness of action, the search is aided by critical examination, of the hypothesis, the machines, or the contemplated actions, which will uncover errors that can be eliminated by fresh conjectures or repair or acting differently. The elimination of error as far as possible contributes to the pursuit of truth, operational success, and goodness. A responsible person is one who eliminates errors as·far as he can reasonably be expected to. Thus 'responsibility' comes to mean 'being critical in pursuit of certain goals, as far as prevailing standards require'.

Arising from this discussion of the outcome of applying the theory of critical debate in the service of specific goals, a cake can be baked with the following ingredients:

(1) A theory of what consititutes critical debate.

(2) A set of goals towards which critical debate may be oriented—some of the goals may be value-impregnated, like the maximizing of certain utilities (goods).

(3) A set of standards of responsibility, standards of how far the critical debate has to be pushed—some elements of the set may be public standards agreed by social institutions (universities, governments, courts of law).

(4) A set of alternative actions from which rational actions are to be selected.

(5) A body of (scientific) knowledge comprised of data reporting matters of fact, and hypotheses and theories aimed at explaining the data in a more or less systematic fashion. These are needed for predicting the outcome of various actions.

(6) A set of techniques for achieving the various goals, including techniques for getting started.

The rationality of a choice of actions depends upon there being an ongoing critical discussion of goals, of standards of responsibility, of scientific knowledge, and of the matching of actions to desired outcomes. In that context, any particular action is rationally (responsibly) chosen if and only if it matches the outcome of critical debate,[33] *oriented towards an appropriate goal, and pursued as well as may be expected according to appropriate standards.*

It is entirely in the spirit of Popper's theory of rationality that the decision to regard an action as rational should not be a cut and dried affair, but should itself be criticizable (disputable), as would be the case with decisions made in accordance with this definition.

The answers to the questions I postponed earlier (concerning judging the farfetchedness of an abstraction or the exhaustiveness of one's bundle of variables, or deciding when the use of decision theory or game theory is legitimate) follow quite naturally if science be characterized as responsibly conducted, goal-oriented, critical debate. The issues in those questions are not decided finally: they are discussed: abstractions, etc., are criticized. It is all part of the critical debate: at any particular period of time, there is a more or less widely accepted convention, which alters under criticism, for what counts as 'farfetched', or 'exhaustive' or 'legitimate'. Responsibly used standards of responsibility take care of those questions.

The New Philosopher's Stone, the guide of life based on science, here proposed may be set out as a game for one or more players up to a maximum permitted by the practical requirement of reaching agreement. Here is a crude sketch of how the rules might look:

Aim of Game: To pursue a chosen aim rationally
Rules:

A   1. Specify your aim carefully.
      2. Criticize your aim, for instance by asking whether it is worth pursuing.
      3. When the aim is agreed upon by the players, proceed to B.
      4. If there is no agreement upon aim, find fresh players and start again.

B   1. Conjecture methods of realizing the agreed aim, including ways of getting started and ways of stopping when the aim is realized.
      2. Criticize conjectured methods in order to pick out the best.
      3. If you are ignorant of some relevant laws of nature proceed to C.
      4. If no method of realizing agreed aim can be thought of or if all methods thought of cost too much or if no agreement on method can be reached, go back to A1.
      5. When the method is agreed upon proceed to D.

C   1. Conjecture explanations of relevant phenomena.
      2. Criticize conjectured explanations to eliminate error as far as possible.
      3. When the appropriate explanatory hypotheses are agreed upon go back to B1.
      4. If there is no agreement upon an hypothesis to assume in designing methods to reach aim go back to A1 and be more specific.

D   1. Proceed towards agreed aim by agreed method assuming agreed background knowledge.
      2. If unforeseen challenge to background knowledge arises go back to C1.
      3. If agreed method does not realize agreed aim or if unforeseen obstacles arise go back to B1.
      4. If there is an unforeseen shift in value of aim go back to A1.

4. Ale with the Cake

Popper's theory of rationality has suffered something of a modification in the process of trying to discover a guide of life that follows from it. According to Popper, rationality is critical debate. According to the above discussion, rationality includes responsible, goal-oriented critical debate. Is *all* rationality of this type, or, is there some critical debate which merits the accolade 'rational' but which is pursued without termination and without goal. I think there are examples of goal-less (pointless) critical debate—but I would not want to call them 'rational'. And I think there are people who sometimes prefer to continue a critical debate instead of deciding upon a course of action (and by default, as it were "decide" upon inactivity), but I would not want to call what they were doing 'rational', without qualification. If Popper intends that 'rationality' shall refer to *any* critical debate then I think his theory is in need of modification. Popper himself discusses the orientation of critical debate towards the solution of problems. For example, Popper thinks that for philosophy to be interesting and for its discussions to be fruitful, the dialogue in philosophy has to be oriented towards the solution of problems.[34] Further, Popper sometimes characterizes science by its aim: "to find satisfactory explanations of whatever strikes us as being in need of an explanation".[35] But, as far as I know, Popper does not characterize rationality as goal-oriented critical debate, but rather only as critical debate. Growth of knowledge is then characterized as critical debate oriented towards specific problems in an effort to answer them (P_1) with tentative theories (TT) and eliminate errors (EE) from the theories by criticism. In this way, on Popper's schema,[36] we achieve a deeper problem (P_2):

$$P_1 \rightarrow TT \rightarrow EE \rightarrow P_2$$

The modification here called for in the attempt to find a rational guide of life is identical to the modification proposed by Agassi[37] in the course of his discussion of the problem of stability in science. From the point of view of inductivists (and other justificationists) the stability of science needs little explanation—their main problem is explaining change; but from a Popperian point of view, stability is an anomaly—which Popper does not adequately explain. Agassi proposes this modification: ". . .rationality is not any critical debate, but only that which is oriented towards a specific goal as well as might be reasonably expected".[38] (Agassi also mentions 'responsibility': he explains the role of positive evidence—or "corroborations"—in technology as "proving decisions to be responsible".)[39]

The fruitfulness of the Agassi-modification to Popper's theory of rationality is not restricted to the explanation of stability in science—which can be explained "as the stability of the social institutions which administer and apply science, rather than the stability of science itself"[40]—or to the solution of the problem 'What is a rational procedure for choosing hypotheses to act upon?' (the problem of a rational guide of life). If it were, it might appear as an *ad hoc* modification invented to deal with problems peripheral to Popper's main interest. Let us see how the modified theory of rationality deals with one of Popper's main problems: the problem of demarcation. Popper's solution to this problem is well known, very interesting, but unsatisfactory. His criterion is: science is distinguished by the falsifiability of scientific theories, plus the critical policy of trying to refute theories, that is, the policy of trying to eliminate error as far as possible from the system of theoretical explanation of experience. Note that there are *two* parts to it: some philosophers have mistakenly supposed there to be only one. This criterion is unsatisfactory because, first, the aim of eliminating error as far as possible is not unique to science, but can be carried over into other disciplines and, secondly, theories other than scientific theories are falsifiable: I have worked in *theology* with the aim of eliminating error as far as possible; and I find one can offer *empirical disproofs* of theological theories.[41] For instance, in the classical problem of evil, the empirical assertion of the existence of evil in the world falsifies the conjunction of two theological theories: 'God is all-powerful' and 'God is all-good'.[42] It is perhaps startling to find that, on Popper's criterion, Amos and Isaiah were among the world's early scientists: they were aware that the impending destruction of Samaria—threatened by the rise to power of Tiglath-Pileser III of Assyria (745 B.C.)—was a refutation of the covenant of unconditional favouritism "cut" by Jacob and persisting for about 1000 years. They rewrote the convenant and added obedience, righteousness, and justice as necessary conditions for the LORD'S favouritism.[43]

As a criterion of demarcation between science and nonscience, Popper's 'falsifiability'-plus-a-critical-policy does not work.

If we follow Popper's advice, before trying to improve upon a solution to a problem, we should take a closer look at the problem. What, then, was the problem which Popper's criterion was supposed to solve? Happily, we have Popper's own story to go by.[44] He originally (1919) wanted to distinguish *science as typified by Einstein's theory of gravitation from nonscience as typified by the theories of Marx, Freud and Adler*. His solution was prepared in 1920. He could distinguish between the theories of Einstein and the theories of Freud by the falsifiability of the former and the unfalsifiability (at least as Freud handled them) of the latter. Later this criterion was generalized into a criterion of demarcation of *all* science (not just that part that was typified by Einstein's theory) from *all* nonscience (not just that part that was typified by the theories of Marx, Freud and Adler). In 1934, Popper saw his task as "to formulate a suitable characterization of empirical science, or to define the concepts 'empirical science' and 'metaphysics' in such a way that we shall be able to say of a given system of statements whether or not its closer study is the concern of empirical science" (*L.Sc.D.*, p. 37). Incidentally, Popper's regarding modern theoretical physics as the most complete realization to date of what he called 'empirical science' (*L.Sc.D.*, p. 38) may explain in part why what distinguished Einstein's work from, say, Freud's work, should be regarded as effecting the more general distinction also.

The exciting revolutionary facet of the character of science is captured for us by this criterion, and by the theory of growth of knowledge which grew out of the criterion as an attempted solution to the problem of induction. However, there is much to what one wants to call 'empirical science' which is not typified by the work of Einstein. A scrutiny of the history of science and of the contemporaneous professional activities of professional scientists would reveal much in science markedly different from what Popper understood Einstein to be doing. On the other side of the fence there is much in nonscience not typified by the work of Marx, Freud or Adler.[45] In short, Popper's criterion performed the function he invented it for in 1920; but it has not been able to perform the function he gave it in 1934. Science is *not* distinguished from nonscience by the falsifiability of its theories or by the critical character of its method or by both together. Of the two, Popper's criterion was much nearer the truth than the positivists' verifiability criterion—but I shall not sidetrack into a criticism of that.

Perhaps now we can state the problem of demarcation in a slightly more complex fashion than Popper usually does:

(1) 'How shall we distinguish between a discipline typified by the work of Einstein and a discipline typified by the work of Freud?' (Popper's 1919 version)

(2) 'How shall we distinguish between science as a whole and nonscience as a whole?' (Popper's 1934 version)

(3) 'How shall we distinguish between two disciplines that are nonscientific—under distinction (2)—but differ from each other as markedly as the two disciplines distinguished under distinction (1) (for instance, how shall we distinguish Barth's dogmatic theology from Mackie's philosophical theology)?'

The first and third distinctions are effected by the distinction between rational and irrational disciplines. This is perhaps the most important demarcation to be drawn. It enables us to distinguish rational metaphysics from dogmatic theology, and from pseudosciences, for example, dianetics.[46] The demarcation of science as a whole from nonscience as a whole is largely uninteresting by comparison: nonscience is so heterogenous a mixture that it is rather uninstructive to treat it as a whole. Indeed, it is almost mischievous to treat it as a whole, because there are many theories in the nonscience ragbag which are highly desirable from the point of view of science.[47] I think it is more important to distinguish rational disciplines from irrational disciplines than to distinguish science from nonscience. I am assuming, of course, that being scientific is a proper special case of being rational. There remains then a modified version of the second element of the demarcation problem:

(2') How shall we distinguish science from other rational disciplines?

This may be done by remarking upon the goal of science and upon the standards of responsibility that guide critical enquiry in the discipline. In a general way, science could, I suppose, be characterized by the long term goal of systematically explaining experience and by a standard of responsibility which requires the empirical testing of scientific theories. Technology, which sometimes appears to be rendered almost nonscientific (and hence not really respectable) on Popper's characterization of science, is here given status as a rational discipline, which has standards of responsibility as empirical and as tough as those of "pure" research, but is distinguished from "pure" research, by its prime goal. Francis Bacon already made this distinction in his *Novum Organum*: to understand nature and to conquer her.

Incidentally, should it turn out on close investigation—and I strongly suspect that it will—that science is not a homogeneous enterprise, the modified theory of rationality here proposed will function as a delicate instrument of demarcation, taking into account the various goals and standards of responsibility which are appropriate to the subdivisions of science. Thus we may distinguish, if we wish, between more or less dissimilar enterprises within the discipline of science: theoretical criticism of theories;[48] empirical criticism of theories;[49] search for things to fit the gaps in a taxonomy;[50] solving problems in topography;[51] answering queries arising within a given theoretical framework.[52] These types of enterprises and perhaps many other types could be distinguished *within* science by paying attention to the *goal*, the particular short-term aim of the enquiry. Perhaps a taxonomy of scientific aims would be a useful exercise (a proto-science of science?)—not to help us to understand and control Nature, but, rather, to help us understand and control our own efforts at understanding and controlling Nature.

PART TWO:
PEIRCE *VERSUS* POPPER ON PROBABILITY AS PROPENSITY

1. The Case Before Us

Is it interesting to discuss the anticipation of new ideas? Let us suppose it is and ask, why should this be so? Is it because the discovery that an idea has been anticipated is interesting? Hardly, since, as we already know, all novelties are anticipated to some extent—which explains the plausibility of the continuity theory of the growth of ideas: the theory that all thinkers are greatly indebted to their predecessors, and all progress is in small steps. Incidentally, I think the continuity theory is inadequate despite its plausibility, because it leaves so little room for controversy, for the clash of ideas, and thus clashes with the idea that critical debate explains the growth of scientific knowledge.[53] This idea, due to Sir Karl Popper, that critical debate explains growth of knowledge in science, is itself novel. Not that it is new to say that we learn by trial and error, nor to say that the conjecturing of hypotheses and their subsequent testing is part of the method of science—all this has been known since the seventeenth century; what is novel is Popper's use of the old idea of learning by trial and error as a solution to the old problem of induction.[54] Popper's theory of science has, unfortunately, been widely misrepresented by writers who failed to comprehend the startling novelty that science has no secure foundations of any sort, not even in experience.[55] In contrast to Carnap's aim, in the Vienna Circle days, of reducing knowledge to a basis of certainty,[56] Popper abandoned certainty and gave a novel explanation of the growth of ideas in which all scientific knowledge was taken to be conjectural, tentative, and corrigible. It seems to me that Popper's novel suggestion of a propensity interpretation of probability has suffered a similar fate, having been misrepresented (though not so widely). Popper's view has been mistaken for a frequency interpretation, perhaps because, after avoiding the mistake that there should be only one interpretation of probability, it was thought there should be only one *objective* interpretation of probability, or perhaps because it was thought that 'propensity' could not mean anything but 'disposition to a certain frequency in the long run'. In contrast to the history of the calculation of probabilities,[57] the history of interpretations of probability is quite short. Perhaps it begins with Robert Leslie Ellis,[58] who raised the problem of interpretation by insisting upon a relative frequency theory and protesting against the Principle of Indifference as a ground for inference; protesting, that is, against the view that judgments of probability are properly based upon equally balanced degrees of ignorance. In the debates that ensued, it was generally assumed that there was only one correct interpretation of probability. Popper, in 1935, was the first to maintain that there might properly be several different interpretations.[59] Even so, more recent discussions have assumed only one,[60] or, at most, two.[61] Until very recently, Popper was the only philosopher to insist upon the propriety of there being several interpretations.[62] Moreover, Popper has presented a fresh one, addressed to a particular problem: his propensity interpretation[63] is intended to elucidate probabilities in theories in physics. Whatever other interpretations there may properly be, this paper is an exercise in examining anticipations and novelty with respect to the propensity interpretation: specifically, I ask in what respects Peirce anticipated Popper, and in what respects Popper has introduced novelty, concerning this interpretation of probability. But let us return to our opening line of enquiry!

Is the discussion of anticipation interesting because of the identification of the personalities involved? Trivially so, perhaps. There may be some historical interest in intellectual genealogies, but hardly any philosophical interest. Are anticipations interesting because some accolade is due to a man who has a novel idea? Is the debunking of false claims interesting or is it simply a form of rough justice? Or do we perhaps find the discussion of anticipations interesting precisely because we are interested in doing justice? Let us suppose this is so, and ask how justice may best be done. Is it not unjust to rob a man of his property—in this case a new idea—and ascribe it to some other person? A stress on the similarity of a new idea to its anticipation might thus be an injustice, and the claim that an idea has been anticipated might be unjust unless accompanied by some account of differences, in order to avoid bestowing upon an anticipator title to more than he owns, thus robbing the innovator. However, I do not think the search for justice suffices to explain our interest, despite its requiring that we examine both the earlier and the later ideas with care, with the consequence that we understand better both the new idea and its (partial) anticipation. I think it is this latter result, the increased understanding, which explains the chief interest we have in the discussion of anticipations: perhaps striving for justice causes it; but satisfaction that justice has been done is a bonus.

To take the analogy slightly further, perhaps we have a case to hear: Peirce versus Popper. I shall try to act as advocate for both parties. Readers are invited to be judge, with the reservation that I be allowed to sit on the bench with them for a while and express my own judgments. Perhaps readers would sooner consider themselves a higher court of appeal, to assess pleas of misconduct of the enquiry or miscarriage of justice.

Here is the case in brief: when Sir Karl Popper first explained how he had discovered the propensity interpretation of probability[64] any possible claim to priority—not, however, made by Popper, who himself claimed only independence—was immediately challenged by Professor Braithwaite,[65] who pointed to an anticipation in the writings of C. S. Peirce.[66] Neither Braithwaite nor Popper—nor has, as far as I know, anyone else—discussed the anticipation: it was simply noted. More recently, moreover, Professor Hacking[67] has suggested that the propensity interpretation may be found in the writings of Venn and von Mises. Again, there was no discussion of the differences between the new idea and its anticipation: pointing to the similarities was perhaps thought to suffice, whereas, as I have suggested above, pointing to the similarities is not very interesting and may even be unjust.

Contrariwise, part of my aim in this paper is to distinguish views which it has been the achievement—if not the purpose—of others to confuse. Specifically, by examining the views of Peirce and Popper, the accounts given of these views by Braithwaite and Hacking, and, for good measure, Bunge's criticisms of these views, I hope to expose six different propensity interpretations of probability. There is, here, no attempt to be exhaustive. I set out the differing views in a table of 3 x 2 (see Table 2) distinguishing rows by whether the philosopher named regards absolute (A) or relative (B) probability as fundamental; and distinguishing between columns as follows: Column (2) names Popper, who specifically introduced his propensity interpretation to elucidate probabilities in experimental situations in physics, and Peirce, who elucidated probabilities in practical situations in games of chance. Neither has generalized their interpretation beyond empirical situations (hence Bunge's criticism of what he calls "empiricist" traits in Popper's theory of probability);[68] but, both have divorced the interpretation from actual sets of observations, thus distinguishing the propensity theory from the frequency theory. Column (3) picks out the generalizations of Column (2); Column (1) indicates views not yet severed from the frequentist roots from which propensity theory grew. These distinctions are discussed more fully in Section 5

TABLE 2

	(1)	(2)	(3)
A	Hacking	Peirce	Bunge
B	Braithwaite	Popper?	Settle

The query after Popper's name indicates that I regard it as questionable whether his actual views, as opposed to his published views, warrant his being in position B(2) and not rather in position B(3).[69] I hope Sir Karl will clear up this matter in his Reply.

Our enquiry into anticipation and novelty over an interpretation of probability leads us into questions about axiomatizations of the probability calculus, including a second question of priority: Popper versus Kolmogorov, as the first to give an uninterpreted axiomatization. There arises also a third question of novelty and anticipation: in what sense do Peircean and Popperian propensities differ from Aristotelian occult qualities?

2. Alleged Anticipations of Popper's View

Let us begin by examining how Braithwaite and Hacking present the propensity interpretation of probability in the passages in which they draw attention to anticipations. First, Braithwaite.

Braithwaite says Popper's language resembles Peirce's. He paraphrases Peirce thus:

. . .to state that a die has a certain probability of falling, for instance, with six up-
permost is to state that it has a certain 'would-be' which is analogous to a habit,
and this 'would-be', like other habits, though testable by experiment, cannot be
reduced to results of experiment.[70]

Before the Colston Conference, at which Popper introduced the propensity
interpretation, Braithwaite had already mentioned Peirce's views in his
Scientific Explanation,[71] where his account of those views corresponds very
well with that given above. It is clear from the book that Braithwaite understood Peirce to hold much the same interpretation of probability as he
himself holds, namely the frequency interpretation, and to have found a
rather picturesque way of expressing it. It is clear from the passage which I
quote next that Braithwaite further thought that Popper shared that view,
despite the point of Popper's paper having been the introduction of the
propensity interpretation as an improvement, for certain purposes in physics,
over the frequency interpretation. The next sentence follows immediately
upon the above quotation from Braithwaite:

"Popper expresses the frequency theory in the same admirable way by
using the term 'propensity' to emphasize the similarity of a probability to a
habit".[72]

The only difference which Braithwaite notes between Popper's view,
which Braithwaite thought he both understood and shared, and Peirce's, was
that, for Peirce, the propensity was a property of the die instead of being, as
for Popper, a property of the die with respect to a die-throwing situation.
Braithwaite's stress upon the similarity of a probability to a habit, however,
distorts Peirce's view. The performance of a certain type of action through
an endless succession of occasions without exception, would, as Peirce remarked, constitute a habit but would not constitute a "would-be": Peirce distinguished between any *actual* series of die-throws and an endless *virtual*
series, suggesting that a "would-be" is more analogous to a virtual habit than
to, simply, a habit. If I read Peirce aright, a "would-be" is a propensity, bent,
tendency or disposition—rather than a habit—which may or may not find expression: a particular die may never be cast; nonetheless, a propensity is a
property of the object in question by virtue of its composition and structure:

. . .the 'would-be' of the die is presumably as much simpler and more definite
than a man's habit as the die's homogeneous composition and cubical shape is
simpler than the nature of the man's nervous system and soul.[73]

I may be reading too much into this quotation from Peirce (and thus robbing
his successors of some title to novelty) but, nevertheless, it seems that he had
it in mind that there was some connection between a "would-be" on the one
hand and the structure and composition of the die on the other, at least in this
respect, that the "would-be" of an object shared degrees of simplicity and

definiteness with the object's composition and shape.

There seems to be no resemblance here to the frequency interpretation of probability as it was presented by von Mises,[74] Reichenbach[75] or Popper.[76] Thus it may seem on the face of it that Braithwaite is wrong in suggesting that Peirce and Popper both express the frequency interpretation when, according to my reading, they are expressing a propensity interpretation. However, it is clear from *Scientific Explanation* (p. 191) that Braithwaite's account of the frequency interpretation, in which the probability in question—a theoretical entity—is a property of whatever causes the events whose frequency is being measured, is different from that given by von Mises, in which the probability in question is a property of a class of events of a certain kind within a universe of events of a number of kinds. Furthermore, on investigation we find that Reichenbach's account of the frequency interpretation is different from that of von Mises, and that Popper's old view is different again from both of those. Thus, despite repeated references, in discussions of interpretations of probability, to *the* frequency interpretation, it turns out that there is no such thing, except perhaps as a genus with many species. And, moreover, Braithwaite's view more closely resembles a propensity interpretation than it does the other frequency views: Braithwaite's insistence upon the possibility of testing probabilities by comparing them with actual frequency ratios is not sufficient to show that his view is a frequency interpretation, since everybody, whatever his view as to what a probability is, agrees that an appropriate *test* of a probability statement would be a set of appropriate observations, say, a long sequence of actual runs of the device in question, should that be possible. Thus, it now appears, Braithwaite may be right in claiming that Peirce and Popper hold views similar to his own, but mistaken in confusing the propensity interpretation, which they may share, with various frequency interpretations, which they do not share. Nevertheless, there are important differences between Braithwaite's view and those of Peirce and Popper. One important difference, which has been hinted at by my emphasis on the relation of propensity to composition and structure, will be discussed later. Perhaps I may mention in passing one further difference: Braithwaite alone of the three thinks that the reason why he needs the possibility of testing the propensities by a number of actual observations is in order to give meaning to statements of this or that probability: the criterion for the meaning of probability statements is to be found (bizarrely) in the human propensity to reject or to fail to reject them on the basis of tests. This is bizarre because it is a ruinous double deformation of Popper's falsifiability criterion of demarcation between science and metaphysics: deformation (1): take falsifiability to be a criterion of meaningfulness rather than of demarcation; deformation (2): take the existence of a set of semantic rules for the rejection under certain circumstances of what can not be formally falsified, instead of its possible falsification, as a guarantee of its falsifiability. On this basis, all metaphysical statements could be rendered meaningful simply by there being a set of rules for rejecting some of them on the basis of some tests—a result few positivists would relish. But let us leave aside such positivistic black magic and return to the case before our court. Let us now turn to a consideration of Hacking's claims.

Hacking asks of what kind of thing is chance a property—by 'chance', he means 'frequency in the long run'—and suggests that a rather naive answer stands out, namely that chance is a property of a chance setup. This, Hacking tells us, runs counter to suggestions of von Mises (chance is a property of a sequence), Neyman (chance is a property of fundamental probability sets) and Fisher (chance is a property of an hypothetical infinite population). Nevertheless, according to Hacking, this naive view has proponents:

> Venn's descriptions make it plain that he has a chance set-up in mind, and that it is this which leads him to the idea of an unending series of trials. Von Mises' probability. . .is intended as a model of a property of. . .an experimental set-up. . . .Popper has urged that the dispositional property of frequency in the long run is a property of an experimental 'arrangement'.[77]

Hacking's puzzling claims hardly merit much attention for a variety of reasons: first, he gives no reference for the alleged views of Venn and von Mises, therefore making it impossible to debate exegetically with him whether he has correctly interpreted their writings; secondly, he definitely misrepresents Popper's propensity interpretation, which can easily be checked,[78] thus raising the suspicion that he may have done the same with the views of Venn and von Mises; and thirdly, he appears unable to distinguish a propensity interpretation from a frequency interpretation. However, Hacking's claims do raise some interesting questions which are worth attention: could Popper have had many precursors? If not, and supposing Peirce to have anticipated Popper publicly by a quarter of a century, why was Peirce's idea not taken up?

Before turning to those questions let us quickly set aside Hacking's claim that Venn and von Mises anticipated Popper. Von Mises definitely embraced a frequency interpretation of probability and defined probability as a property of an ensemble of events of a certain kind: no ensemble, no probability.[79] In addition, he was careful to point out that even stochastic events were caused by the interaction of the random system (or device) with its environment.[80] This is about as near to a propensity view as I have found in von Mises's work. Interestingly enough, the view that probabilistic events are caused is shared by Venn[81] who promotes the frequency concept of probability, though not in a way which would line him up distinctly for or against a propensity view. Peirce wrote his 1910 note with all the air of one who has formed a new view, and this after having been a student of logic for fifty years. I am inclined to think that Venn did not anticipate Peirce and that von Mises neither followed Peirce's lead nor introduced a propensity view independently. This judgment is supported by a consideration of the philosophical climate in the modern period, to which we now turn.

Our attention is drawn to the influence of the climate on interpretations of probability by Keynes:

> . . .a careful examination of all the cases in which various writers claim to detect the presence of 'objective chance' confirms the view that 'subjective chance', which is concerned with knowledge and ignorance, is fundamental, and that so-called 'objective chance', is really a special kind of 'subjective chance'. . . .For none of the adherents of 'objective chance' wish to question the determinist character of natural order.[82]

The determinist character of natural order receives its classic statement by Laplace, who was responsible for so improving Newton's equations for planetary motion as to be able to dispense with the hypothesis of divine interference to explain the stability of the solar system. With Laplace, Newtonianism joined Cartesianism in secular determinism, and the mechanization of the world picture was more or less complete. As Keynes remarked, determinism of this sort leaves no room for objective chance. (This is not to say that other versions of determinism do not leave room for objective chance. This is discussed at length in my essay, "Human Freedom and 1,568 Versions of Determinism and Indeterminism",[83] where I also remark the astonishing paucity, in the philosophical literature, of an analysis of large numbers of different possible versions of determinism, including many interesting versions of partial indeterminism.) Thus the climate of opinion with which Peirce had to reckon and which has continued popular to this day is a confusion: the view that the physical world was thoroughgoingly deterministic, but that this did not stop human beings from being free. James called this "soft" determinism.[84] Of course, our freedom depends upon our ignorance: if we shared the omniscience of Laplace's demon not only should we know what all our future actions would be, but also we should neither be free nor even feel free. Similarly with probability: in a thoroughgoingly deterministic world, those who knew enough about the past and who knew the laws of nature would not need the concept of probability. As Joseph Butler remarked, "nothing which is the possible object of knowledge. . .can be probable to an infinite Intelligence; since it cannot but be discerned absolutely as it is in itself—certainly true, or certainly false".[85] And Keynes thought "judgements of probability do seem to be based on equally balanced degrees of ignorance".[86] No ignorance, no probability. Perhaps it is natural to agree that no man could have such knowledge and then to leave it to the philosophical theologians to debate the problems of God's omniscience. Thus what we might call epistemic *indeterminism* comes to be coupled with ontic *determinism*.

Peirce himself, knowing that the climate of opinion was against him, argued forcefully and at length in favour of objective chance[87] and against ontic determinism. It appears to be a necessary condition for the emergence of a propensity interpretation of probability that strict ontic determinism be denied: this partially explains, what I think is the case, that there was no propensity interpretation of probability in modern times before Peirce. However, the abandonment of determinism is not sufficient to entail a propensity view: if ontic indeterminism be coupled with empiricism, no propensity view will emerge. 'Empiricism', here, names that general philosophical outlook which places more weight upon reports of human experience than upon human speculation.

Perhaps some empiricists would prefer to say that empiricism is the view that there is something special about *experience* as opposed to mere "talk"; but this is not a distinctive view: any nonempiricist could agree to that: Parmenides, for example, thought experience specially deceptive. What empiricists frequently do is to suppose, mistakenly, that experience may provide a reliable basis for talk about experience and thus for science.[88] Empiricism may be contrasted with intellectualism (or rationalism in the narrow sense) and has its modern roots in the works of Bacon, Boyle, and Newton. Hume gave considerable force to empiricism by his incisive criticisms of attempts to ground speculation in experience. In the nineteenth century, a narrow version of empiricism, namely positivism, was invented in view of Kant's failure to meet Hume's criticisms. The revolutions in physical theory in that century and the present one, particularly the introduction of statistical assumptions in the gas laws and in thermodynamics, in the study of Brownian motion, and, most importantly, in quantum mechanics undermined ontic determinism. By the 1930s Einstein was one of the few physicists of note who was a determinist; moreover, he had returned to a belief in determinism after a quarter of a century of believing in objective chance. Philosophers, who could afford to ignore the rumpus in physics, continued to be ontic determinists, "soft" determinism, "a quagmire of evasion" (as James called it), being almost universal. Philosophers of physics, eschewing the reintroduction of speculative notions (occult qualities) into physics sought to give a thoroughly empiricist account of theoretical physics, so that the meaningfulness of theoretical terms was made to depend upon their reducibility to empirical terms. It was even tried to give operational definitions to theoretical concepts. In such a climate as this, nothing so occult as propensities could be supported as an explication of probability in physics. Instead, when stochastic properties of physical systems were interpreted objectively, they were interpreted as comparative frequencies of certain kinds of events (outcomes of trials), and, when subjectively, as the best guesses the state of human ignorance would permit. Subjective interpretations were of two kinds: logical (Keynes) or psychological (de Finetti). Positivism, as it then was, left little or no room for a propensity interpretation. Some philosophers, however, such as Poincaré, were quite confused in their interpretation.[89]

This completes my explanation of why views similar to Peirce's did not emerge independently and why Peirce's ideas were not taken up after their publication in 1932. It is worth noting that Popper's early view was a frequency view and that he did not come to the propensity view until he had criticized the empiricist traits of his early philosophy of science. Indeed, Professor Bunge claims to detect traces of empiricism still in Popper's propensity interpretation. We shall return to that point below.

I wish to digress for a moment to remark upon the influence of the usual macroscopic models of chance setups upon interpretations of probability. Whatever may be our views as to the indeterminism in quantum physics, most people would agree that the outcome of coin-tossing or die-throwing experiments are governed by laws which are deterministic on macroscopic scales, any indeterminism having been introduced by a randomness in the initial conditions. It is easy, then, to suppose that it is a matter of our ignorance that we cannot predict precisely the outcome of a particular throw. Thus the traditional probabilistic paradigms permit or even foster, on the one hand, a subjective interpretation of probability, which appears out of place when we turn to physics. Quantum theory does not make reference to measuring instruments or to observers, but rather refers to microscopic systems and their environments. Of course, predictions of the outcome of experiments will be possible only after consideration of the apparatus used; but such a consideration would be an addition to, rather than a part of, quantum theory. Nevertheless some empiricists (physicists and philosophers) have imported apparatus and observers into their accounts of quantum physics in an effort to render "meaningful" a theory which otherwise would be about occult entities: Heisenberg's principles of indeterminacy (which are "theorems" in quantum theory)[90] are given a subjective interpretation as measures of our invincible ignorance. Against the intrusion of subjective interpretations of probability into physics one must protest.[91] On the other hand, a frequency interpretation is the most obvious nonpsychologistic view permitted by macroscopic betting setups, because, whereas we know nothing about the specific initial conditions of each trial, we do know the outcomes. Furthermore, it is the outcomes which interest the gambler. The use of a frequency interpretation in physics, however, is quite inappropriate because it focusses attention upon the outcomes of experiments, rather than upon the objects to which the theories of physics refer. When Popper introduced his propensity view, he did so deliberately as a preferable interpretation from the point of view of physics: the propensities were, in his view, properties of the microsystem-environment complex rather than of long runs of outcomes; which made it possible to attach a meaning to the probability of individual events. This brings us back to Bunge's criticism of Popper's view.

Over against claims that the view had been anticipated, Bunge claimed[92] that Popper's propensity interpretation is a newcomer. However, Bunge's presentation of the propensity interpretation differs radically from Popper's in that Bunge interprets $P(A)$ as "the natural disposition of event(s) A to happen"[93] whereas Popper's view applies only to a system within an environment: $p(a,b)$ is the propensity of an experimental setup b to yield result(s) a. Bunge offers what he calls a generalization of Popper's interpretation[94] and makes use of it in his discussion of the foundations of quantum theory.[95] Bunge criticizes Popper for not having freed his propensity interpretation from consideration of experiments, and thus for not having removed all empiricist traits; and offers an experiment-free propensity interpretation, by using absolute probability as fundamental. It may be questioned, however, whether the reference to experimental arrangements is not merely accidental to Popper's view, and also whether the use of absolute probability as fundamental is relevant and if so whether it is entirely satisfactory. These questions will be taken up in Section 4.

The difference here indicated between Popper's and Bunge's views resembles the difference already noted between Peirce's and Popper's. Bunge agrees with Peirce in assigning probability to the physical system independently of its environment, whereas Popper (along with Braithwaite) assigns probability to the system-environment complex. This difference is focussed for us by Bunge's choice of absolute probability as fundamental, following Kolmogorov[96] against Popper's choice of relative probability as fundamental.[97] If our interpretation of probability is to be natural rather than forced—or, to put it another way round, if our axiomatization of probability is to capture what we have in mind as probability—we want our interpretation to match our axiomatization in the following way: whatever we consider as the more fundamental (propensities of things or propensities of things-in-an-environment) should be the fundamental concept in the axioms. Bunge therefore chooses Kolmogorov's axioms with $p(a)$ as primitive whereas Popper chooses $p(a,b)$ as primitive. It is not, however, entirely satisfactory to make the decision which axiomatization to prefer primarily upon grounds such as these. We shall therefore immediately entertain other considerations. Although attendance upon the question of which axiomatization to prefer might appear as a digression from our main purpose, it is not entirely a digression, since the discussion furnishes us with considerations leading to a more detailed comparison of the views of Peirce and Popper.

The discussion of axiomatizations will be in two stages. First (Section 3), we shall look at the claim Popper made to be the first to give an uninterpreted set of axioms for the probability calculus. This scrutiny introduces us to a number of considerations indispensable to a mature decision on which axiomatization to prefer. The second stage (Section 4) will consist in displaying a few arguments in support of Popper's preference for a relative probability as fundamental over against the Peirce-Bunge preference for absolute probability.

3. Priority in Axiomatizing the Probability Calculus

Popper's claim to be the first to give a completely uninterpreted axiomatization of the calculus of probability has never, so far as I know, been challenged explicitly. Rather, it has been more or less completely ignored. And not only his claim but also his axiomatization has been ignored. I have found no reference to Popper's axiomatization in standard textbooks on probability theory, all of which use some version of Kolmogorov's axioms. For example Fisz[98] lists works devoted to an axiomatization of the probability calculus without referring to Popper,[99] and the compilers of the supplementary bibliography to the second English edition (1956) of Kolmogorov's work omit reference to Popper, claiming that "the axiomatic theory advanced by Kolmogorov is considered by workers in probability and statistics to be the correct one" (p. 77). This latter view (that Kolmogorov's 1933 axiomatization is correct) is, however, false: there are a number of well-known (see below) inadequacies in that axiomatization, although fortunately these are not irreparable. Somehow, the compilers of the bibliography could not quite bring themselves to say both that Kolmogorov was great and that he was wrong—exhibiting the widespread inductivist historiographic dilemma of being unable to explain the greatness of men whose views turn out to be false.[100] Furthermore, Russell, when looking for an axiomatization in which probability is a function of two arguments rather than, as for Kolmogorov, a function of one argument, chose that given by Broad[101] instead of that given by Popper in the same journal a few years earlier, and this despite Russell's having to reinterpret the axioms Broad gave in order to fit in his finite frequency interpretation.[102] Whereas Popper's system was completely uninterpreted, the one given by Broad, which (Russell failed to mention) was due to von Wright[103] and was being reported by Broad, was, like that of Keynes, a theory of logical probability, and not a very good one at that: von Wright bemoaned its many shortcomings in the Preface to the second edition, and completely rewrote the system without, however, succeeding in meeting all the objections advanced by Kemeny.[104] Bunge, who views Popper's system as "more refined",[105] nevertheless used Kolmogorov's in elucidating the physical theory of probability.[106]

To assess Popper's claim to priority we need to discover whether the axiomatic work which preceded his 1938 paper gave uninterpreted axiom systems. This would be an exhausting task to perform exhaustively; I have, therefore, contented myself with examining axiomatizations referred to by Kolmogorov,[107] Popper,[108] and Fisz[109] with the exception of Bernstein,[110] concerning whose work I shall take Kolmogorov's word that it is not an uninterpreted system. Thus, I think we may set aside any possible claim by von Mises[111] for whom probability is a defined rather than a primitive concept, by Steinhaus[112] whose axiomatization is restricted to the special case of *rouge et noir*, and by Reichenbach,[113] whose confusion of conditional probability with the probability of conditionals restricts interpretations. Keynes[114] is an interesting case: despite the highly interpretative context of the presentation of his axiomatization, it is largely uninterpreted. That is to say, his three main axioms are susceptible of any interpretation, even though his three preliminary axioms, in which the arguments of the probability function are taken to be propositions or conjunctions of propositions are not. With a little adjustment even that deficiency could perhaps be removed, since conjunction need not mean propositional conjunction.

This leaves us with Kolmogorov's axiomatization. Obviously, it was prior to Popper's: it is not so obvious that it was as adequate. Three inadequacies stand out: (1) the arguments of the probability functions are defined as sets, which thus restricts the application of the calculus to those arguments which may properly be viewed as sets. From this point of view, Popper's axiomatization, which has no such restriction is preferable. (2) The definition of relative probability—'p(*a,b*)'—is such that calculations of relative probability must always be conditional upon p(*b*) $\neq$ 0. This rather severe restriction, discussed at length by Popper, is not always mentioned in works on probability theory.[115] Popper's system suffers from no such handicap. (3) Kolmogorov's system is intentionally elementary, in the sense that it is designed on finite sets. Additional postulates extend its application to infinite sets, but not until Renyi's work was the system generalized to unbounded measures. Renyi drew attention to a report that Kolmogorov had himself had the idea of generalizing his axiomatization but had not published his ideas on the question. It is interesting that to generalize the theory so as to take account of unbounded measures, according to Renyi, *"conditional probability must be taken as a fundamental concept"*.[116] Although Renyi made this shift from absolute probability to relative probability, he retained Kolmogorov's measure-theoretic treatment, and thus did not remove the restriction (1) above. Thus it appears that Popper's was the first uninterpreted axiomatization of the probability calculus. Whether or not it is of importance to have an *uninterpreted* axiomatization, I leave to the end of the next section; here, however, it may be remarked that Popper's system was the first adequate axiomatization from a number of other points of view. Let us turn now to the question whether to follow Kolmogorov and Bunge in preferring a single argument function or Renyi and Popper in preferring a double argument function, as fundamental.

4. *Absolute* versus *Relative Probability*

It is interesting to notice, in passing—though it is not at all decisive on the point at issue—that most philosophers writing on probability make use of two arguments, that is, use relative probability as fundamental. Thus Keynes[117] discusses the logical relation between the proposition a and the hypothesis h; von Mises[118] discusses the relative frequency of events of one kind occurring within a collective of events of (perhaps) more than one kind; von Wright[119] follows Keynes; Kneale[120] compares the range of α-ness to the range of β-ness; Russell[121] discusses the chance that a member of a finite class B may be a member of some other class A; and Braithwaite[122] discusses the probability of an A thing's being B. It is the mathematicians who use absolute probability as fundamental: but they, unlike the philosophers mentioned, do not treat us to a discussion of the meaning that their fundamental concept (absolute probability) could have.

Bunge, however, does discuss philosophically the preference he shares with the mathematicians for absolute probability.[123] His argument is roughly this: if we are to apply probability theory *objectively* to quantum theory eschewing all talk of the probability of the outcomes of experiments, since experiments do not figure in quantum theory, then we require absolute probabilities, since the stochastic character of quantum mechanics does not inhere in the wave function, ψ, as is popularly supposed, although the wave function is interpreted as a probability density, but in the relation between ψ and the *eigen*values of the dynamical variables, so that a fully physical interpretation of quantum theory requires us to take the spread of value of a dynamical variable as an objective scatter rather than as a subjective uncertainty or as an expression of the purely empirical elusiveness of ultimate precision or even as the distribution of the weights of possible outcomes of experiments and thus as perhaps referring to an isolated microsystem.

I am entirely in sympathy with Bunge's motive in removing what he takes to be a trace of "empiricism" from Popper's interpretation, which was, after all, introduced explicitly to deal with the interpretation of certain experiments in physics. A physical theory should not be restricted to explaining the results of experiments we actually have performed or may perhaps perform. Thus, the generalization which Bunge intends, such that probabilities may refer to microsystems which are isolated (free), at least to a first approximation, is quite proper. I question, however, whether that generalization calls for the regarding of absolute probability as fundamental. Certainly by regarding absolute probability as fundamental we rule out the view that experimental results, rather than experiment-free states of the universe are the prior concern of physics. But perhaps we rule out too much. What concerns us in quantum theory is not, simply, isolated microsystems or, simply, microsystems upon which we perform an experiment, or even, simply, a conjunction of these two. Our concern includes microsystems which are neither free nor under experiment. Although we need to generalize our propensity interpretation to cover isolated microsystems, which were not part of the problem to which Popper addressed himself we could do so without regarding absolute probability as fundamental by considering the application of propensity interpretation to isolated microsystems as a proper special case of its general application to microsystem-environment pairs. An analogy for this is already at hand in Bunge's axiomatization of elementary quantum mechanics[124] in which he considers as fundamental the ordered pair $\{\sigma,\bar\sigma\}$ where σ is a member of the set Σ of microsystems and $\bar\sigma$ is a member of the set $\bar\Sigma$ of environments of microsystems. In this axiomatization, there exists a Hilbert space for every ordered pair $\{\sigma,\bar\sigma\}$ $\epsilon\Sigma x\bar\Sigma$; and the wave functions ψ, which are points in the Hilbert space, are complex-valued functions on the Cartesian product of $\Sigma,\bar\Sigma$, Euclidean 3-space, and time. A special case here is the free quanton, when $\bar\sigma$ is nonexistent (the null individual of the kind $\bar\Sigma$).[125] Unfortunately, Popper has never carried through his application of the two-argument propensity interpretation into an axiomatization of quantum theory, and I do not have the expertise to do it for him. Plea: would some kind theoretical physicist come to our aid?

At this point, the views of two further critics of Popper's propensity proposal call for consideration: Feyerabend and Mellor.[126] Both these philosophers follow Bunge in supposing that Popper's emphasis upon experimental arrangements exposes empiricist traits. Perhaps this is a fairly natural reading of Popper's recent publications on probability. Nevertheless it may be a misreading.

Feyerabend assimilates Popper's views on probability to those of Niels Bohr in claiming "that complementarity and the propensity interpretation *coincide*—as far as probabilities are concerned".[127] This is a surprising claim, in view of Popper's rejection of complementarity. However, this claim receives little support from Popper's writings. Feyerabend's claim is consistent with Popper's application of propensity interpretation to experimental situations in quantum physics; but it entails that Popper denies the possibility (and, perhaps, the meaningfulness) of ascriptions of propensities to individual physical systems. So far as I know Popper has never done this, and I am inclined to think that he would agree with Bunge rather than with Bohr in this matter.[128]

Mellor claims that Popper confounds "propensity with the chance distribution which is the display of it", and this, because of Popper's insistence

that propensity is ascribable to experimental arrangements rather than simply to isolated systems. According to Mellor, in the case of coin-tossing,

> the propensity is *not* to be ascribed to the whole assembly of coin, tossing device,
> and their environs that is only present when the coin is actually tossed. To do that
> is to remove completely the point of ascribing a *disposition*, as something present
> whether or not it is being displayed. [P. 29]

Mellor is quite correct, I think, to draw our attention to the distinction
between propensity and chance, showing propensities to be occult qualities
which are displayed, if at all, in chance distributions of outcomes.[129]
However, Mellor is far from convincing with his claim that propensity is *not*
ascribable to experimental arrangements but rather to individual systems. He
offers no argument which could counter Popper's example of a loaded die in
varying gravitational fields:[130] if the probability of throwing six with the next
throw of a loaded die near the surface of the earth is 1/4, the propensity 1/4 is
not a property of the loaded die but only of the loaded die relative to certain
gravitational conditions. In a stronger field, the load would have a stronger
effect and may give a propensity of 1/3 or even 1/2; in a weaker field, conversely, the propensity might drop to 1/5 or even very nearly 1/6. This argument is used by Popper not to support the view (which Mellor rightly rejects)
that propensities are always and only the properties of actual total experimental arrangements, but rather that they are properties of individual
physical systems only relative to specific (but not necessarily actual) environmental conditions. A special case (which Popper nowhere mentions) is
the isolated system. Dice, considered, *per impossibile*, as isolated systems,
would not have any propensity for falling this way or that at all. Their
gravitating properties are specified (in physics) by means of gravitational
theory, which assumes gravity as a relative effect. Some isolated systems
have absolute propensities, according to contemporary physical theories, but
ordinary dice are not among them. For example, the spontaneous decay rate
of samples of radioactive elements represents an environment-independent
propensity of individual physical systems. In general, however, it is not possible to state a propensity of a physical systems without specifying the (virtual)
conditions related to the propensity. The conventional ellipsis of ordinary
language masks a relativity of propensities which physical theories in general
make explicit.

Perhaps Mellor's preference for ascribing propensities to individual
systems conceals a confusion between, on the one hand, the composition or
inner structure of the systems, which in many cases one might want to say
was independent of environment and which one might want to say was a
cause or the seat of the various propensities a system might have, and, on the
other hand, the propensities the system has, relative to various (virtual) environments. Many physical theories[131] relate the structure of systems to their

propensities relative to various environments. The elastic propensities of a coiled metal spring are importantly different from those of the same metal uncoiled, as are its electromagnetic propensities. It would be impossible to state either sets of propensities without reference to related external conditions.

It seems to me, thus, that when we interpret probability as a propensity, we are better off taking the relative concept, rather than the absolute, as fundamental. There are, however, other arguments we may consider in favour of this, arguments which Popper has already advanced.[132] I want to point only to the one I find especially attractive: the argument regarding strength. This argument exposes, also, why I think Popper's uninterpreted axioms are preferable to Renyi's, even though Renyi's generalization of Kolmogorov's system overcomes its most important inadequacies: the set-theoretical interpretation which is built into the system for Renyi restricts the models of the probability calculus to set-theoretical models. I take it that a system of axioms which may have various models (in the sense of mathematical models) is stronger and preferable *ceteris paribus* to an alternative system which has fewer models, especially if all the models of the latter are also models of the former. In the standard axiom system used by statisticians, Kolmogorov's system, set theory has to be added to the axioms if a set-theoretical model of the probability calculus is needed: indeed set theory has to be assumed if any conditional probabilities at all are to be used, since the relation of conjunction is not defined in Kolmogorov's axioms nor derivable from them. Kolmogorov's system is then creative (in the sense discussed by Popper)[133] in the presence of set theory, but barren in its absence; and even more creative under Renyi's generalization. Similarly, one cannot proceed with Keynes's axioms without assuming the propositional calculus. From Popper's axioms, however, Boolean algebra may be derived.[134] Since set theory and the calculus of sentences may be viewed as models of Boolean algebra, Popper's system may be considered to be rather strong. In particular, in its logical interpretation, it may be considered as a generalized logic of derivation. In view of all this it is difficult to explain the neglect Popper's system has suffered.

Let us now return to the comparison of Peirce's view with Popper's.

5. A Spectrum of Propensity Interpretations

In this section, I propose to display a spectrum of propensity interpretations and compare the views of Peirce and Popper by suggesting where each should be located on the spectrum. If we begin by supposing that the fairly natural reading of Popper's works referred to above, the reading shared by Bunge, Feyerabend and Mellor, is correct, then we may distinguish the views of Peirce, Popper, Bunge and myself by a simple table of 2 x 2 (see Table 3).[135] I am assuming, here, also, that it is proper to ascribe similar empiricist traits to Peirce, whose discussion of "would-be"s is confined to experimental (gambling) situations. In the matrix below, let the rows distinguish *absolute probability as fundamental* (Row A) from *relative probability as fundamental* (Row B); and let the columns distinguish views with *alleged "empiricist" traits* (Column 2) from views which are more *"metaphysical"* (propensities as occult properties of things in themselves) (Column 3). I reserve the numeral (1) for a column of a more avowedly empiricist kind, to be added later.

TABLE 3

	(2)	(3)
A	Peirce	Bunge
B	Popper	Settle

We may perhaps, now, extend our considerations to include Braithwaite and Hacking. To do this, I introduce the consideration of how firmly tied the propensity is to the structure of the object and how firmly to the frequencies of results of trials. Both Braithwaite and Hacking espouse a species of frequency interpretation in which the set of observations is a fundamental concept. For Braithwaite, it is fundamental in order to give meaning to propensity; for Hacking it is fundamental since, for him, 'chance' is synonymous with 'frequency in the long run'. Neither of these philosophers has quite succeeded in shaking off the historical context in which the problems of probability arose: betting situations. Even, however, leaving aside the question of frequency interpretations, the claims that probability is propensity, even if the propensity never is actualized, and that it makes sense to talk of the probability of *unique* events taking place, separate both Braithwaite and Hacking from the rest of us. Popper claimed, for his own view, that the probability of the result of a single experiment with respect to its conditions rather than the frequency of results in a sequence of experiments, is to be taken as fundamental.[136] I guess that Bunge would go further and claim (and I would agree with him) that the local structure of a system (e.g., the scatter of quasi-position and quasi-momentum in the case of a microsystem) is to be taken as fundamental.

Furthermore, we may distinguish between the views of Braithwaite and Hacking: Hacking, but not Braithwaite, follows Kolmogorov in using absolute probability as fundamental, although his presentation of absolute probability is somewhat confusing: he writes of '$P(E)$' as an *abbreviation*.

"Strictly speaking, we are concerned with an ordered triad: the set-up, the kind of trial, the outcome. . . .Nevertheless when the context makes evident which kind of triad is in question, it suffices to write $P(E)$".[137] Although it is evident that the economy of writing $P(E)$ for $P(E,K)$ (where K names the setup and the kind of trial in question) is innocuous in practical work in statistics, nevertheless, absolute probability is *not* primary wherever $P(E)$ is an abbreviation; and if it is an abbreviation, it is not the same concept as the '$P(A)$' in Kolmogorov's axioms: that measure is independent of setups and kinds of trials. The "abbreviation" '$P(E)$' could be equivalent to $P_K(E)$ (in Kolmogorov's notation): that is, the conditional probability $P(EK)/P(K)$. Be that as it may, Hacking's espousing of absolute probability separates him from Braithwaite.

We thus have a table of six, as introduced in Section 1 of Part Two (Table 2 Column (1) distinguishing a frequentist view from the other views:

TABLE 4

	(1)	(2)	(3)
A	Hacking	Peirce	Bunge
B	Braithwaite	Popper	Settle

The distinction drawn between the frequentists and the others is of considerable theoretical significance. Bunge has drawn attention to the concept of theoretical depth with his contrast between phenomenological (black-box) and representational (translucid box) theories and has attacked black-boxism, the view that conversion of black boxes into translucid boxes is neither necessary nor desirable.[138] Analogously, we may say that a frequency interpretation of probability is phenomenological, that is, deals only with the output of black-box devices, whereas propensity interpretation attempts to be representational by focussing attention upon the innards or local structure of the systems in question. This is, of course, a question of emphasis; but it is significant since the representational view, but not the phenomenological views, invites the question, What is it about the local structure of the system and of the system-environment complex which accounts for the propensities it has? Trivially, the flatness and roundness of a penny and the flatness of a table help account for there being only two outcomes (heads or tails) from the toss of a penny. Of course, the assumption of some theories would be needed for a full account to be given: gravitational theory, the kinematics of spin, elasticity theory (to account for damping of the bounces) and so on. The representational approach even suggests to us that we may, if we know enough, be able to predict the propensities of some systems in novel environments, and so dispense with the requirement to perform long runs of trials.

To prefer a representational view of propensity to a phenomenological view, is not, of course, to say that the frequency interpretation is dispensable. It is not. We make good use of a version of the frequency view for handling long (and short) runs of a trial setup as well as for the treatment of, say, population statistics in preparing actuarial tables for life insurance companies.

Table 4, nonetheless, is not entirely satisfactory in the way it locates people's views. First, it may very well be that Popper's actual views do not warrant his being in B(2), which is where a natural reading of his publications may locate him. Perhaps, we should rather put Bohr's name in B(2) and move Popper's name over to B(3) to join mine. Secondly, I may have misrepresented Peirce's views somewhat. Mellor, whose views appear to warrant his being located in B(2), agrees with Braithwaite that Peirce's views are frequentist. If Mellor is right, Peirce's name should be in A(1), and the table would then look like this:

TABLE 5

	(1)	(2)	(3)
A	Peirce Hacking	Mellor	Bunge
B	Braithwaite	Bohr	Popper Settle

Ironically, if Table 5 properly represents the views of the persons named, Braithwaite's remarks which provoked this enquiry turn out to have been widely mistaken: Popper's views could not differ more widely from Peirce's under this analysis.

6. Propensity as an Occult Quality

The tradition, following the early pioneers of modern science, is to eschew occult qualities. Thus Newton criticized Aristotle's explanations: "To tell us that every species of Things is endow'd with an occult specifick Quality by which it acts and produces manifest Effects, is to tell us nothing. . ."[139] In contrast to this tradition Popper closed the paper in which he introduced his propensity interpretation in this way:

Aristotle put the propensities as potentialities *into* the things. Newton's was the first *relational* theory of physical dispositions and his gravitational theory led, almost inevitably, to a theory of fields of forces. I believe that the propensity interpretation of probability may take this development one step further. [*OIPP*, p. 70]

It may sound to many people, particularly to those brought up in the contemporary positivist atmosphere, as though the introduction of propensities does no more for us than Aristotle's occult specific qualities did, so that the step is retrograde. I think, by contrast, that a propensity view is a considerable improvement upon the metaphysically sterile positivist approach which tells us to pay attention only to experimental results and does not satisfy at all our curiosity as to how those results came about. The representationalist approach does more to satisfy this curiosity. It does this by the positing of occult qualities, the positing of an internal structure to things. The qualities posited may, or they may not, exist; or perhaps whatever exists may resemble the posited qualities in some respects. In any case, the positing of hidden structural elements may be fruitful in scientific enquiry, by being vindicated or by being condemned (indirectly) by tests. Either vindication or condemnation will do just as well because it is *ad hoc* occult qualities rather than occult qualities as such which are not fruitful.

Thus perhaps we should regard Newton's scientific indignation as aimed at only *ad hoc* occult qualities (did Newton mean by 'specifick' what we mean by *'ad hoc'*?). However, it is a problem to decide which qualities are *ad hoc* and which not. There seems to be no agreed a priori test for picking out in all cases the *ad hoc* from the potentially fruitful, although there is, of course, the a posteriori check that whatever turns out to be fruitful was not *ad hoc*, and there are some *ad hoc* explanatory devices which are deliberately and almost patently *ad hoc*—but even these may be indirectly fruitful, such as Lorentz's treatment of the null result of the Michelson and Morley experiment. Could propensities serve as non-*ad hoc* explanations of the outcomes of trials or must all propensities be *ad hoc* qualities? I think that it would be very easy to give *ad hoc* propensity explanations of outcomes, but possible to avoid the *ad hoc* character and reap benefits not available to the frequentist. For example, suppose we know the results of many trials upon a particular pin table; and suppose we find one day that the pin table is behaving quite differently from before. A nonpropensity frequentist would have no suggestion to make to us: quite long runs of "strange" results would be acceptable on his view. On the propensity view, however, one would suspect that a shift of behaviour indicated a shift in propensity caused by a change in the local structure: one would be inclined to examine the table for changes. Or, to take another example, one that particularly puzzled Professor Ayer,[140] we may explain the poor showing of a well-fancied horse by a change in its propensity to win, suspect a change in its inner qualities and, in some cases, look for signs of its having been doped. The best example, perhaps, for the fruitfulness of propensities for scientific enquiry is quantum theory, a thoroughgoing physical interpretation of which requires us to regard the scatters in values of dynamic variables as properties of the systems involved, and thus, to regard propensities as fundamental in that theory.

On the propensity interpretation, a statement of probability is an empirical hypothesis which may, In principle, be testable, though its tests will be statistical and only conventionally decidable. The conventional decidability, however, is not unique to statistical tests: the result of any test may be questioned without contradiction, the decision to stop testing being a convention.[141] This exposes the social character of scientific enquiry,[142] and invites a modified conventionalist approach to theory of knowledge. But that is another story altogether, and belongs to Part One of this article.[143]

It thus appears that Peirce, like Aristotle, puts propensities into things, although Aristotle, of course, did not discuss propensities in relation to probabilities. In this, Peirce is followed by Bunge, who removes, however, all empiricist traces from his treatment. On the other hand, Popper regards propensities primarily as relational, as properties of a system-environment complex. If we are to give a thoroughly physical interpretation of probability, I prefer the relational view yielding the Peirce-Bunge position as a special case, the case of the isolated system. I look forward to Sir Karl's clarification of his own position, in the light of distinctions which I have here displayed.

TOM SETTLE

DEPARTMENT OF PHILOSOPHY
UNIVERSITY OF GUELPH, CANADA
APRIL, 1970

NOTES

[1] It has not yet been found possible to give a satisfactory account of induction, let alone to give a satisfactory justification of it—and this, despite the efforts not only of Boyle, Bacon, Kant, Mill, Keynes and Russell but of Reichenbach, Carnap, Feigl and many others. In the light of the failure yet adequately to characterize induction, the claim of Ayer and Strawson that induction justifies itself is, to say the least, strangely premature.

[2] Popper has made this point many times, most recently in his contributions to *The Problem of Inductive Logic*, ed. by Imre Lakatos (Amsterdam: North-Holland Publishing Co., 1968). Hereinafter cited as *PIL*.

[3] Joseph Agassi has drawn attention to a new game: that of tracking down writers who found Popper's theory first. Whewell and Peirce are the best known philosophers who anticipate Popper to some extent. Less well-known examples are given by Agassi. See J. Agassi, "The Novelty of Popper's Philosophy of Science," *International Philosophical Quarterly*, 8, No. 3 (1968), 442-63. To these examples may be added Jevons and Stewart (see P. B. Medawar, *The Art of the Soluble* [London: Methuen, 1967], pp. 147-51) and Lukasciewicz (see J. Giedymin,

"Empiricism, Refutability, Rationality," in *Problems in the Philosophy of Science*, ed. by Imre Lakatos and Alan Musgrave [Amsterdam: North-Holland Publishing Co., 1968], p. 67). No doubt historians of the philosophy of science will discover more and more examples. I mention this game, not to detract from Popper's originality, which is not, as far as I am concerned, in dispute, but to show the general acceptance of his views; there is perhaps less interest in discovering historical precedents for people's mistaken views than there is for discovering precedents for ideas which appear to be substantially correct. [See also the essays by Freeman and by Skolimowski and Popper's *Replies* to them in this volume.—Editor]

[4] Rudolf Carnap, "Inductive Logic and Inductive Intuition," in *PIL*, p. 258. Lakatos's claim is made and discussed in I. Lakatos, "Changes in the Problem of Inductive Logic," in *PIL*, pp. 315-417.

I do not agree with Carnap that there is only one problem of induction, although I agree that considerable attention may have been focussed from time to time on only one of the problems suggested by Hume's enquiry into the foundations of scientific knowledge. I think philosophers have neglected until recently another problem which is an alternative way to construe the relevant passages in Hume's work: what if the course of nature is not stable? What if the laws according to which the universe operates change with time? What if the laws of nature were radically different at some future time, t, from how they are now, the alteration taking place suddenly? The puzzle is, of course, older than Hume. Leibnitz debated the matter with Clarke in their celebrated correspondence: may God alter or suspend laws of nature or are they unalterable? The problem has been revived recently—though without acknowledgement to earlier discussions—in the so-called new riddle of induction posed by Goodman (Nelson Goodman, *Fact, Fiction and Forecast* [New York: Bobbs-Merrill, 1965]), and the problem of nocturnal doubling of the size of everything. Goodman's riddle is a linguistic, and thus comparatively uninteresting, variant of the problem of the variability of natural laws. Grünbaum's revival of the puzzle whether we would notice the difference if the world doubled in size overnight raises the question whether any laws would need to change for the world to double in size, and whether any of the changes would be empirically testable.

Incidentally, my wife Margaret, accustomed as she is to the idea of the sun never setting on the Christian Church, and remembering when we lived so far away from our families that there was no time normally when no member of our families was awake, asked what sense there was in considering the doubling as having taken place at night: it was never nighttime for everybody: somebody would be awake to notice! It is a quaint hangover from flat-earth days or from the days before what we call civilization spread around the world, that the doubling should be thought of as happening after dark. Why not try the problem of the world doubling in size while we are having lunch?

[5] For example, Mario Bunge, *Foundations of Physics* (New York: Springer-Verlag, 1967).

[6] For example, the Millikan oil drop experiment, which is cited by Achinstein as a counterexample to Popper's theory that knowledge grows by conjecture and refutation. (Achinstein's review of *Conjectures and Refutations* is in the *British Journal for the Philosophy of Science*, **19** [1968], 160 ff.) Popper, as far as I read him, does not confuse progress with growth of knowledge, and is only interested in progress which is also growth of knowledge. Thus Achinstein's counterexamples of progress which is not growth do not touch Popper's theory of growth, though they do suggest (as I argue in this paper, although Achinstein did not make the point clear because, I suspect, he made the confusion which Popper avoids) that there may be important progress which is not growth in theoretical knowledge. Another, perhaps more interesting example, is the search for the value of the mechanical equivalent of heat in a series of experiments in widely differing domains.

[7] For example, the discovery of Neptune (1846) to whose existence Leverrier's calculations from the theory of planetary motions (plus accumulated observations) pointed. Another example is the search for gallium, scandium and germanium after their existence and properties had been predicted by Mendeléev.

[8] Examples are the exploitation for developments in nuclear physics of the equivalence of mass and energy suggested by Relativity Theory; Einstein's use of Planck's idea of a quantum of

energy in offering an explanation of the photoelectric effect; and de Broglie's inversion of the principle in his programme in search of matter waves.

[9] T. S. Kuhn, *The Structure of Scientific Revolutions* (Chicago: Chicago University Press, 1962).

[10] For a discussion of the merits of foundations research see Mario Bunge, "Physical Axiomatics," *Reviews of Modern Physics*, **39** (1967), 463 ff.

[11] The relation between Popper's philosophy of science on the one hand, and conventionalism and instrumentalism on the other hand, is discussed very neatly by Agassi in his contribution to this volume.

[12] This criticism was invented by Ayer, who also invented the pseudo-Popperian theory against which the criticism is devastating. (A. J. Ayer, *Language, Truth and Logic*, rev. ed. [London: Victor Gollancz, 1946], p. 38.) Most recently, the misinterpretation and the criticism have been set out by Max Deutscher, though without acknowledgement to Ayer, in his, "Popper's Problem of an Empirical Basis," *Australasian Journal of Philosophy*, **46** (1968), 277-88. Compare T. W. Settle, "Deutscher's Problem is not Popper's Problem," *Australasian Journal of Philosophy*, **47** (August, 1969), 216-19.

[13] There have, however, been misinterpretations of the idea of test-worthiness. For example, Salmon has twice claimed that corroboration is crypto-induction. (W. C. Salmon, *The Foundations of Scientific Inference* [Pittsburgh: University of Pittsburgh Press, 1966], p. 26; and "Justification of Inductive Rules of Inference," in *PIL*, p. 28.) Compare T. W. Settle, "Is Corroboration a Nondemonstrative Form of Inference?", *Ratio*, **12**, No. 2 (December, 1970), 151-53.

[14] The confusion of pure science with applied science and with technology is discussed in J. Agassi, "The Confusion Between Science and Technology in Standard Philosophies of Science," *Technology and Culture*, **7** (1966), 348-66 and in my unpublished Ph.D. dissertation in Hong Kong University, "The Impact of Science on Contemporary Protestant Theology" (1965), especially Section 5.v., pp. 189-94.

[15] T. W. Settle, "The Point of Positive Evidence—Reply to Professor Feyerabend," *British Journal for the Philosophy of Science*, **20**, No. 4 (1969), 352-55.

[16] Compare P. K. Feyerabend, "How to be a Good Empiricist: A Plea for Tolerance in Matters Epistemological," in *Philosophy of Science*, ed. by B. Baumrin (New York: John Wiley & Sons, 1963), Vol. II.

[17] In my doctoral dissertation (see note 14 above) I discuss and try to explain the shift in vulgar trust from religion to science. Unfortunately there is a temptation for scientists to emulate priests as the custodians of the true faith, forgetting that it is a crucial difference between science and religion rather than any similarities they may have which earns the shift in trust. See also T. W. Settle, "Scientists: Priests of Pseudo-Certainty or Prophets of Enquiry?", *Science Forum*, **2**, No. 3 (1969), 21-24.

[18] Pierre Duhem, *The Aim and Structure of Physical Theory* (Princeton: Princeton University Press, 1954).

[19] A. J. Ayer, *The Problem of Knowledge* (London: Penguin, 1956). Compare Goodman, *Fact, Fiction and Forecast*, p. 65: ". . .the problem of justifying induction is not something over and above the problem of describing or defining valid induction."

[20] *American Journal of Physics*, **36** (1968), 2. Dr. Mario Bunge drew my attention to this editorial.

[21] W. C. Salmon, "Who Needs Inductive Acceptance Rules?" in *PIL*, pp. 142-43.

[22] R. Carnap, "Intellectual Autobiography," in *The Philosophy of Rudolf Carnap* (The Library of Living Philosophers, Vol. i1), ed. by Paul A. Schilpp (La Salle, Illinois: Open Court Publishing Co., 1963), p. 50.

[23] For instance, Victor Kraft, "Induction, Confirmation and Method," in *Mind, Matter and*

Method, ed. by P. K. Feyerabend and G. Maxwell (Minneapolis: University of Minnesota Press, 1966), p. 317.

[24] See R. C. Jeffrey, "Probable Knowledge," in *PIL*, pp. 166-80, esp. p. 166.

[25] Carnap's programme of inductive logic is an important example. See, for instance, Rudolf Carnap, "The Aim of Inductive Logic," in *Logic, Methodology and Philosophy of Science*, ed. by Nagel, Tarski and Suppes (Stanford: Stanford University Press, 1962), pp. 303-18.

[26] As Agassi observes in "Novelty of Popper's Philosophy of Science," p. 443.

[27] I. Lakatos, "Changes in the Problem of Inductive Logic," in *PIL*, pp. 400 f.

[28] W. W. Bartley III, "Rationality versus Theories of Rationality," in *The Critical Approach to Science and Philosophy*, ed. by Mario Bunge (New York: Free Press, 1964).

[29] Lakatos, "Changes in Inductive Logic," in *PIL*, p. 405.

[30] *Ibid.*, p. 406.

[31] Herbert Feigl, "De principiis non disputandum. . ." in *Philosophical Analysis*, ed. by M. Black (Englewood Cliffs, N. J.: Prentice-Hall, 1950), p. 116.

[32] W. W. Bartley III has an interesting discussion of what he calls "comprehensively critical rationalism" in *Retreat to Commitment* (New York: A. A. Knopf, 1962).

[33] Ordinarily, many 'rational' actions are more or less habitual; rationality does not require that each action be preceded by deliberation.

[34] K. R. Popper, "Philosophical Problems and their Roots in Science," in *Conjectures and Refutations: The Growth of Scientific Knowledge* (London: Routledge & Kegan Paul, 1963; New York: Basic Books, 1963), pp. 66-96. Hereinafter cited as *C.&R.*

[35] K. R. Popper, "The Aim of Science," *Ratio,* 1 (1957), 24.

[36] K. R. Popper, "On the Theory of the Objective Mind," in *Akten des XIV Internationalen Kongresses für Philosophie* (Vienna, 1968), Vol. I, p. 32.

[37] J. Agassi, "Science in Flux: Footnotes to Popper," in *Boston Studies in the Philosophy of Science, 1964-1966*, ed. by R. S. Cohen and M. W. Wartofsky (Dordrecht-Holland: D. Reidel, 1967), pp. 293-323.

[38] *Ibid.*, p. 318.

[39] *Ibid.*, p. 321.

[40] *Ibid.*, p. 294.

[41] T. W. Settle, "A Prolegomenon to Intellectually Honest Theology," *Philosophical Forum,* 1 (1968), 136-70.

[42] *Ibid.*, pp. 145-52.

[43] Amos, Chap. 2, vv. 4-16; Chap. 5, vv. 18-24; and Isaiah, Chap. 1, vv. 16-20.

[44] K. R. Popper, "Science: Conjectures and Refutations," in *C.&R.*, pp. 33-65.

[45] See for example the arguments in J. Agassi, "The Nature of Scientific Problems and Their Roots in Metaphysics," in *The Critical Approach to Science and Philosophy*, ed. by Mario Bunge (New York: Free Press, 1964), pp. 189-211; Feyerabend, "How to Be a Good Empiricist," pp. 3-39; and M. Bunge, *Scientific Research* (New York: Springer-Verlag New York, 1967), pp. 346-57.

[46] Martin Gardner, *Fads and Fallacies in the Name of Science* (New York: Dover Publications, 1957), pp. 263-80.

[47] This point was made by Bartley in his article criticizing Popper's criterion of demarcation: W. W. Bartley III, "Theories of Demarcation Between Science and Metaphysics," in *Problems in the Philosophy of Science*, ed. by Imre Lakatos and Alan Musgrave (Amsterdam: North-Holland Publishing Co., 1968), p. 51. For other references see p. 51 n.

[48] For example, Copernicus's criticism of Ptolemy's system of the world, and Einstein's criticism of Newton's.

[49] For example, the criticism offered to phlogiston theory by the experiments of Lavoisier and that offered to the corpuscular theory of light by the experiments of Fresnel and Foucault.

[50] For example, Louis B. Leakey's search in East Africa for the fossil remains of early man—that is, remains of precursors to homo sapiens. Leakey rejected the popular palaeanthropological view of the 1920s, a view still purveyed for the layman in D. Morris, *The Naked Ape* (New York: McGraw-Hill, 1967), that homo sapiens is a development of a vegetarian tree-dwelling primate comparable to apes. His arguments for the rejection of the vulgar view and in favour of a search for 20,000,000-year-old remains in East Africa show his case to be a classic of theory consolidation, particularly the removal of anomalies in a taxonomy. For instance: if homo sapiens were a recent (2,000,000 to 5,000,000 years) development from an early primate, the speed of evolution of man would be disproportionately fast over against other mammalian rates and would have begun disproportionately late, all other mammalian speciation having been accomplished by 20,000,000 years ago. Leakey took up a suggestion from Darwin to look in Africa for the origins of man and has recently had some very interesting finds.

[51] For example, William Harvey's search for the flow pattern of blood in mammals, and the race between Linus Pauling in California and Watson and Crick in Cambridge for a structure for DNA.

[52] For example, the quantitative analysis of organic compounds which was undertaken by Dalton, Gay-Lussac and others who assumed the results of Lavoisier's qualitative analysis.

[53] Compare Pierre Duhem, *La Théorie Physique: Son Objet, Sa Structure* (Paris, 1907), with Joseph Agassi, *Towards an Historiography of Science* (Middletown, Conn.: Wesleyan University Press, 1963).

[54] For a discussion of this point, see Joseph Agassi's contribution to this volume.

[55] I have discussed this in T. W. Settle, "Deutscher's Problem is not Popper's Problem," *Australasian Journal of Philosophy*, **47**, No. 2 (1969), 216-19.

[56] Carnap, "Intellectual Autobiography."

[57] Isaac Todhunter, *A History of the Mathematical Theory of Probability from the Time of Pascal to that of Laplace* (London: Macmillan, 1865).

[58] W. Walton, ed., *The Mathematical and Other Writings of Robert Leslie Ellis* (Cambridge: Deighton Bell and Co., 1863).

[59] K. R. Popper, *Logik der Forschung* (Vienna: Julius Springer-Verlag, 1935). Hereinafter cited as *L.d.F.* Compare K. R. Popper, "Probability Magic or Knowledge Out of Ignorance," *Dialectica*, **11** (1957), 354-74.

[60] For example, Bertrand Russell, *Human Knowledge: Its Scope and Limits* (London: Allen and Unwin, 1948); William Kneale, *Probability and Induction* (Oxford: Oxford University Press, 1949); R. B. Braithwaite, *Scientific Explanation* (Cambridge: Cambridge University Press, 1953); Ian Hacking, *Logic of Statistical Inference* (Cambridge: Cambridge University Press, 1965).

[61] R. Carnap, "The Two Concepts of Probability," *Philosophy and Phenomenological Research*, **5** (1945), reprinted in *Readings in Philosophical Analysis*, ed. by H. Feigl and W. Sellars (New York: Appleton-Century-Crofts, 1949), pp. 330-48; G. H. von Wright, "The Logical Problem of Induction," *Acta Philosophica Fennica*, **3** (1941), and *The Logical Problem of Induction*, rev. ed. (Oxford: Basil Blackwell, 1965).

[62] See now, however, Mario Bunge, *Foundations of Physics* (New York: Springer-Verlag New York, 1967)—hereinafter cited as *FP*; *Scientific Research I* (New York: Springer-Verlag New York, 1967)—hereinafter cited as *SR*.

[63] K. R. Popper, "The Propensity Interpretation of the Calculus of Probability and the Quantum Theory," in *Observation and Interpretation in the Philosophy of Physics*, ed. by S. Körner (New York: Dover, 1957), pp. 65-70—hereinafter cited as *OIPP*; "The Propensity Interpretation of Probability," *British Journal for the Philosophy of Science*, **10** (1959), 25-42; "Quantum Mechanics without the Observer," in *Quantum Theory and Reality*, ed. by Mario Bunge (New

York: Springer-Verlag New York, 1967)—hereinafter cited as *QTR*.

[64] Popper, *OIPP*, p. 67.

[65] In the discussion following Popper's paper, *OIPP*, p. 78.

[66] C. S. Peirce, "Notes on the Doctrine of Chances" (1910), *Collected Papers of Charles Sanders Peirce*, ed. by Charles Hartshorne and Paul Weiss, Vol. II (Cambridge, Mass.: Harvard University Press, 1931), pp. 405-14.

[67] Hacking, *Logic of Statistical Inference*.

[68] M. Bunge, "Philosophy and Physics," in *Contemporary Philosophy, A Survey*, ed. by Raymond Klibansky (Florence: La Nuova Italia Editrice, 1968).

[69] Compare M. Bunge, "What Are Physical Theories About?," in *American Philosophical Quarterly*, Monograph No. 3 (1969), p. 83, n. 15.

[70] *OIPP*, p. 78.

[71] Braithwaite, *Scientific Explanation*.

[72] *OIPP*, p. 78.

[73] Peirce, "Notes on the Doctrine of Chances," p. 409.

[74] Richard von Mises, "Fundamentalsätze der Wahrscheinlichkeitsrechnung," *Mathematische Zeitschrift*, **4** (1919), 1 ff.; "Grundlagen der Wahrscheinlichkeitsrechnung," *Mathematische Zeitschrift*, **5** (1919), 52-99; *Probability, Statistics and Truth* (London: Allen and Unwin, 1957). (The last mentioned is a translation of the 3d German edition [1951] of a work originally published in 1928.)

[75] Hans Reichenbach, "Axiomatik der Wahrscheinlichkeitsrechnung," *Mathematische Zeitschrift*, **34** (1932).

[76] *L.d.F.*

[77] *Logic of Statistical Inference*, pp. 13-14.

[78] *OIPP*, pp. 65-70.

[79] "Grundlagen."

[80] *Probability, Statistics and Truth*, pp. 71-75.

[81] John Venn, *Logic of Chance* (New York: Chelsea Publishing Co., 1962), pp. 244-50, 276-77. This is a reprint of the 3d edition (1888).

[82] J. M. Keynes, *A Treatise on Probability* (London: Macmillan, 1921), pp. 286-87. Hereinafter cited as *TP*.

[83] To appear in *Philosophy of Science Symposium*, ed. by Mario Bunge. Theory and Decision Supp. Series (Dordrecht-Holland: D. Reidel, forthcoming).

[84] William James, "The Dilemma of Determinism," in *Essays on Faith and Morals*, ed. by R. B. Perry (New York: Meridian, 1942). James delivered this essay as an address in 1884.

[85] Joseph Butler, *The Analogy of Religion* (New York: Frederick Ungar, n. d. [first published in 1736]), Introduction.

[86] *TP*.

[87] "The Doctrine of Necessity Examined" (1892), *Collected Papers*, Vol. VI, pp. 28-45.

[88] For fuller discussion see K. R. Popper, *The Logic of Scientific Discovery* (London: Hutchinson, 1959; New York: Basic Books, 1959), Chap. 5—hereinafter cited as *L.Sc.D.*; and Joseph Agassi, "Sensationalism," *Mind,* **75** (1966), 1-24; and compare M. Deutscher, "Popper's Problem of an Empirical Basis," *Australasian Journal of Philosophy,* **46** (1968), 277-88 with T. W. Settle, "Deutscher's Problem is not Popper's Problem," *Australasian Journal of Philosophy,* **47** (1969), 216-19.

[89] Henri Poincaré, *La Science et l'hypothèse* (Paris, 1903); *Science et Méthode* (Paris, 1908).

[90] See, for example, Bunge, *FP*.

[91] See, for example, Popper, *L.Sc.D.*, *OIPP*, *QTR*, and Bunge, *QTR*.

[92] Mario Bunge, "Quanta and Philosophy," in *Actes du 7ème Congrès Inter Américain de Philosophie* (Quebec, 1967), p. 178.

[93] *FP*, p. 90; compare *SR*, p. 428.

[94] *SR*.

[95] *QTR* and "Philosophy and Physics."

[96] A. N. Kolmogorov, *Foundations of Probability* (New York: Chelsea Publishing Co., 1950; English translation of original German monograph, 1933).

[97] *L.Sc.D.*, Appendices *ii and *iv.

[98] Marek Fisz, *Probability Theory and Mathematical Statistics* (New York: John Wiley & Sons, 1963; English translation of Polish original, 1954).

[99] K. R. Popper, "A Set of Independent Axioms for Probability," *Mind*, **47** (1938), 275.

[100] Compare Agassi, *Historiography*.

[101] C. D. Broad, "Mr. von Wright on the Logic of Induction (II)," *Mind*, **53** (January, 1944), 97-119.

[102] Russell, *Human Knowledge*, Part V, esp. pp. 363-79.

[103] *The Logical Problem of Induction.*

[104] John Kemeny, review of *The Logical Problem of Induction* in *Philosophical Review*, **62** (1953), 93.

[105] *FP*, p. 89.

[106] *FP* and *SR*.

[107] *Foundations of Probability.*

[108] *L.Sc.D.*

[109] *Probability Theory.*

[110] S. N. Bernstein, "An Axiomatic Foundation of the Theory of Probability," published in Russia in 1917 and cited by Kolmogorov.

[111] "Fundamentalsätze" and "Grundlagen."

[112] M. Steinhaus, "Les probabilitiés dénombrables et leur rapport à la théorie de la mesure," *Fundamenta Mathematica*, **4** (1923), 286.

[113] "Axiomatik."

[114] *TP*.

[115] *L.Sc.D.*, Appendix *iv.

[116] Alfred Renyi, "On a New Axiomatic Theory of Probability," *Acta Mathematica*, **6** (1955), 285. (Renyi's italics.)

[117] *TP*.

[118] "Grundlagen."

[119] *The Logical Problem of Induction.*

[120] *Probability and Induction.*

[121] *Human Knowledge.*

[122] *Scientific Explanation.*

[123] "Philosophy and Physics" and "What are Physical Theories About?"

[124] "A Ghost-Free Axiomatization of Quantum Mechanics," in *QTR* and *FP*.

[125] Bunge, *QTR*, pp. 109-11.

[126] P. K. Feyerabend, "On a Recent Critique of Complementarity," *Philosophy of Science*, **35**

(1968), 309-29 and **36** (1969), 80-105; D. H. Mellor, "Chance," *Proceedings of the Aristotelian Society*, Supp. Vol. **43** (1969).

[127] "On a Recent Critique," **35**, p. 314.

[128] Compare Bunge, "What are Physical Theories About?" p. 83, n. 15.

[129] This distinction is present in Popper's writings, but is perhaps most clear in his 1967 essay to which Mellor makes no reference.

[130] *OIPP*. Sir Karl has drawn my attention, in private correspondence, to the effect upon a loaded die of varying elasticity of the surface on to which the die is thrown, the effect of the load in such a die being very marked if, say, a surface of soft butter is used and minimized if, say, a taut drum skin is used as the surface.

[131] For a very interesting discussion of varieties of theories see Mario Bunge, "Phenomenological Theories," in *The Critical Approach to Science and Philosophy*, ed. by Mario Bunge (New York: Free Press, 1964).

[132] Especially in *L.Sc.D.*, Appendix *iv.

[133] K. R. Popper, "Creative and Non-Creative Definitions in the Calculus of Probability," *Synthese*, **15**, No. 2 (June, 1963), 167-86.

[134] *L.Sc.D.*, Appendix *iv.

[135] When I wrote the first draft of this paper, I shared this view that Popper's treatment of propensity exposed empiricist traits, and I criticized these traits aiming to improve upon Popper's view if possible. I found, however, that my "improvement" was consistent with what Popper wrote. This posed the question, which I ask Sir Karl to answer, whether my "improved" view is not what he intended after all, appearances to the contrary being the result of the specific context of his published discussions of propensity theory.

[136] *OIPP*, p. 68.

[137] *Logic of Statistical Inference*, p. 18.

[138] "Phenomenological Theories" and "The Maturation of Science," in *Problems in the Philosophy of Science*.

[139] Isaac Newton, *Opticks*, Query 31.

[140] A. J. Ayer comments on Popper's paper in *OIPP*, p. 79.

[141] This is Popper's view in *L.Sc.D.* (see also my defence against Deutscher, "Deutscher's Problem is not Popper's Problem").

[142] For a further discussion of this see Joseph Agassi, "Positive Evidence as a Social Institution," *Philosophia* **1** (1971), 143-57; and "The Confusion Between Science and Technology in the Standard Philosophies of Science," *Technology and Culture*, **7** (1966), 348-66; and Settle, "Reply to Professor Feyerabend," pp. 352-55, and "Scientists: Priests or Prophets," pp. 22-24. Similar views, but set against different background assumptions may be found in John Ziman, *Public Knowledge* (Cambridge: Cambridge University Press, 1968).

[143] See also Agassi's contribution to this volume.

[144] See note 143 above.

Henry Margenau

ON POPPER'S PHILOSOPHY OF SCIENCE

This contribution, wholly inadequate to its purpose, is meant to be a respectful tribute to Karl Popper, whose philosophy and whose gracious person I came to know and appreciate, unfortunately, late in life, when my own views were already formed. Since then I have felt a modest sort of kinship with him in the world of ideas, a sort of distant admiration that prevented me from stating publicly where I would differ from his detailed conclusions, and certainly from defending him needlessly against a late host of vociferous critics who have attacked his position vis-à-vis the modern theories of physics. The verdict there, I felt, was that Sir Karl, in contradistinction to many of his opponents, had taken the trouble to learn the subjects he was philosophizing about.

For these and many other reasons this note will say little about the major things in which his views and mine concur: his indictment of all extreme kinds of positivism, logical and otherwise; the search for substance, not mere form, in philosophy; the places where that substance is to be found, namely the sciences and mathematics; his acknowledgement of a moderate measure of conventionalism in the definition of what is scientifically true or valid; his acknowledgement of the inevitable flux of accepted truth; his indictment of the logical basis for a principle of induction; his deep concern with probability, a concept which dominates imperiously larger and larger areas of modern science and will doubtless not go away or resolve itself into the older rigid certainties. This leaves me with the humble task of stating where, and in what manner, I would alter or augment Popper's approach and where special results I have previously published throw added light upon his conclusions.

One reason why his writings have a genuine and natural appeal to working scientists is his frank avowal of the insuffiency of linguistic analysis and of the limitations of logic as places from which the start into philosophy of science is to be made. My own liquidation of these launching pads is even more severe than his. They are, it seems, along with mathematics, important analytic tools which no philosopher may ignore, but neither words, nor sentences, nor propositions, nor logical rules can replace *experiences* as the unique foundations of all science, and of all philosophy of science. Every creative person, scientist, artist, historical or literary scholar knows instinctively that experience is prior to verbalization, indeed to any sort of symbolization or communication; and prior certainly to the perception of logical relations, which by and large do not even bear reference to the inchoate elements of immediate experience. This is being said here, however, with an important proviso. I do not mean by experience the bare "empirical" sort of stuff in terms of which theories are ultimately tested: empirical, *en peira*, is a satisfactory designation for that. Experience is here taken in its original Latin sense, which includes sensing, thinking, feeling, remembering, indeed every form of awareness within the flow of our consciousness. A theory, for instance, when known is part of experience. Here is perhaps a place where linguistics is able to enlighten the scene. The English language has no simple word to render this original, extended meaning of experience; in German it is preserved as "*Erlebnis*".

In Popper's writings the word statement is still commonplace; as the accomplished logician he still occasionally describes, confusingly I think, his own philosophy of science as an analysis of statements or a theory as a set of sentences; to be sure, sentences that can be tested. He evidently knows that such phrases are at odds with the language of science itself, for the context frequently indicates this; he is equally aware, I am sure, that every scientific theory engenders, and is equivalent to, an infinite set of sentences all differing minutely in shades of meaning. What in fact a theory is will be briefly set forth below in a language that may offend the pure logician, but is, I trust, satisfactory enough to escape Popper's disapproval. Here, then, is a rapid summary of my epistemology within the context of Popper's philosophy.

Human experience ("*Erlebnisse*") can be divided roughly into two classes: those which lead to knowledge, understanding or, more specifically, are susceptible to explanation in a scientific or everyday sense of that word, are called cognitive; the others noncognitive. There are experiences, like the view of a sunset, which are cognitive for the physicist but remain noncognitive for the artist or the person who merely enjoys them. The distinction between these classes is surely not logically sharp; yet I refuse to regard this as an indictment; the demand for precise constitutive definitions that go beyond denotation or illustration by examples is absurd when applied to some of the ingredients of experience. Only constructs (cf. next paragraph below) engendered deliberately by the intellect are susceptible of sharp, exclusive definition.

Science, probably tautologically, deals with cognitive experience, indeed it is designed to render some experiences cognitive. To outline its function it is necessary to make another distinction within the domain of cognitive experience; roughly that between percepts and concepts. However psychology

and analytic philosophy have made the traditional meanings of these terms
not only insecure but factually false, and I chose to replace them by protocol
experiences[1] and constructs. Their meaning is elaborated in footnotes 1 a, b, c
and 2.[2] The term protocol is used in the sense of Neurath, Carnap and
Popper, but applied to experiences, not statements. Popper's "basic
statement" is, I believe, the symbolization of a protocol experience.
Constructs, on the other hand, are the kernels within theoretical contexts,
commonly called concepts, ideas or, among liguistic philosophers, theoretical
terms. They are not abstracted from protocols, but conceived in a creative
sense, and thus indeed constructed.[3] P-facts are unsuited for rational
manipulation, because they are intrinsically subjective, unstable, rhapsodic,
contingent and qualitative. This last defect is perhaps the most significant, for
it prevents the assignment of a *measure*, either numerical or topological or
even set-theoretical, to protocols, and this makes exact science in terms of
them impossible. The scientist must organize the raw P-data (better habita!)
in a way whose description and analysis is the business of philosophy of
science.

Roughly, this involves the following. First, certain passages from P to C,
called *rules of correspondence*. Such a rule links, for example, the
temperature felt in my fingertip (P-aspect of temperature) to the number
measured by means of a thermometer, or the force felt in my muscles to the
number of pounds or dynes indicated by a spring balance or a dynamometer.
The vehicles for these passages are Bridgman's operational definitions, which
form an important set of rules of correspondence. There are others. Their
role I deem extremely important, their neglect by most philosophers of
science disastrous. Without them, every analysis of science lacks recognition
of one of the most vital phases of modern exact science, the creative matching
of ideas to observations, of constructs to protocol experiences, an act performed with increasing finesse and elaboration which is *not* controlled by the
data nor by the meaning of the constructs. The ideal structure related to a P-
fact by a rule of correspondence is a construct.[4] Thus there is a P-experience
called temperature, force etc., and a construct bearing the same name; but
these are not identical either logically or epistemologically. The latter usually
carry numbers. In contrast to the former, they are connected by logical or
mathematical relations, and a well-connected complex of them is called a
theory. Certain relations in the C-field are termed laws, others principles,
postulates or theorems.

Now it is of paramount significance to recognize (and this, I feel, is the
reason for Popper's felicitous concession to conventionalism) that rules of
correspondence are subject to the scientist's choice. That choice is controlled
by what I have called metaphysical principles, using the odious adjective in its
time-honored (e.g., Kantian) sense. To name but one example: we choose

among all possible operational definitions of the construct "time" the one that produces the *simplest* law of motion, namely Newton's first law, and this singles out a time definition based on the astronomical, not a pendulum or a solar clock. Of these, each of the latter would provide a different rule of correspondence, which is ruled out by what might loosely be called a principle of simplicity.

Scientific theories can change in several ways, usually by modifications within the texture of constructs or by the discovery of new constructs vis-à-vis new P-experiences. But it also happens that within an accepted complex of constructs only a rule of correspondence changes. For instance, in the theory of special relativity, it is possible to retain Newton's second law of motion, provided one alters the operational definition of mass (by incorporating its change with velocity).

To have a valid and complete scientific theory means to have a C-field, equipped with rules of correspondence relating certain C's to P, and a P-plane of sufficient extent. But what is meant by a valid theory?

Here we encounter the problem of validation, of testing, of falsification to which Popper pays so much careful attention. It has two parts, one metaphysical (or, if you detest that term, methodological) and one empirical. To be a valid part of a scientific theory, i.e., to become a *verifact*, a given construct (like mass, electron, gene, Ψ-function, G.N.P.) must satisfy a set of metaphysical requirements (see footnotes 1 and 2) and form a necessary ingredient within a sufficient (but finite!) number of "circuits of empirical confirmation". (Cf. footnote 1.) A complex obeying both of these criteria is promoted from a hypothesis to a theory, and that theory is said to be *true* (meaning correct) in view of available evidence; it is not said to be probable by many scientists. For theories are thought of as true or false. If one were to name them probable, because they are not ultimately or eternally true, one would be wasting an otherwise meaningful adjective and furthermore incur the infelicity of having to assign to every known, empirical theory the probability zero.

Within this epistemological framework Popper's philosophy of science can be readily accommodated, the solutions to some of his problems can be obtained in alternative and occasionally simpler ways, and minor differences can be exposed.

The Logic of Scientific Discovery[5] advances good reasons for rejecting a discipline often called inductive logic. Within our schema, inductive logic is the passage from P to C, whereas deductive logic allows a transition within C (from left to right in the diagrams of footnote 1 b) from regions remote to the P-plane to the border of it, where rules of correspondence complete the transit to P. The deductive passage is certain, not fraught with probabilities; it obeys the rules of logic. The inductive one, viewed as logic, is impossible for two reasons. First, it cannot perform a passage from P even to the adjacent regions of C, because it lacks rules of correspondence, and second, a movement to the left in the C-field, which involves inferences from particulars to universals, is known to be logically insecure (except for the modus tollens which, as Popper points out, allows falsification but not confirmation). This rules out inductive *logic*, but not all inductive inferences such as those practiced in many descriptive sciences which make no or very little use of elaborate constructs. What is done there may be described as follows.

One *assumes*, without a priori justification, that a set of data forms a collective, a probability aggregate to which the rules of that calculus can be applied. It is then possible, as shown in footnote 1 b, to establish correlations, in fact to calculate correlation coefficients that allow predictions within a penumbra of probabilities. And if the predictions are correct, one regards the initial assumption as justified. This is the practical gist of all inductive procedures.

But the story does not quite end at this point. For, when the correlation coefficient between two sets of data approaches the value 1, the scientist surmises that there must be a C-field context upon which these experiences can be mapped. This surmise easily becomes a conviction imparting a confidence which inspires a search for rules of correspondence and suitable constructs, often a successful search. It is the frequency, indeed the likelihood of such success which instills among scientists the (false) belief in the existence of a discipline called inductive logic.

One further point. Popper uses the fictitious character of inductive logic as an argument for rejecting sense perceptions, *and thus our experiences* (*L.Sc.D.*, p. 13) as bases of the empirical sciences. I believe he does not use "experiences" in this passage in my extended sense. Given his sense, the statement is true, and this for an even more cogent reason: again, sense perceptions, which are P-data, do not automatically suggest the rules of correspondence which link them to constructs, the living cells of science. When thus seen, Popper's argument does not indict experience in my version as the foundation and the medium of all science; it does not reduce science to a bundle of sentences.

Several more specific problems also deserve comment here. I turn first to that of demarkation, the task of "finding a criterion which would enable us to distinguish between the empirical sciences on the one hand, and mathematics and logic as well as 'metaphysical' systems on the other". From my point of view this criterion is simple: it is the presence or the lack of rules of correspondence. A set of constructs satisfying the metaphysical requirements (footnote 1), e.g., Hilbert space before the advent of quantum mechanics, belongs to the latter class. It has now become an empirical science, because we know how to connect its ingredients with observational data.

A little more needs to be said about Popper's view on falsifiability. As a guiding methodological principle falsifiability is included among the "metaphysical" requirements mentioned earlier. In my listing it would appear as part of the criterion of logical fertility; but it surely deserves a better name and merits the attention Popper accords it. But he also seems to hold to the belief in an asymmetry between falsifiability and verifiability, regarding the latter as impossible.

At this point the traditional conceptions, or shall I say professional prejudices I have acquired as a physicist, begin to trouble me, as they seem to trouble many of my friends and students. For, it seems to be generally recognized that a scientific theory of the empirical (nonmetaphysical) sort *can* be shown to be correct or incorrect, valid or false, in the face of the observational material available. Perhaps this matter is obscured so long as a theory remains identified with a lot of propositions. To the physical scientist, however, and increasingly to the social and biological scientist, it is a conceptual structure implying quantitative aspects which can be observed in measurements. The measurements are invariably subject to statistical dispersion, usually (though not always!) occasioned by uncontrollable factors introduced by the measuring device. In terms of this dispersion one defines a probable error, and this is taken *by convention* as an index of tolerance in the adjudication of the correctness of a theory. If the value it predicts lies within the range of the probable error it is said to be confirmed, verified; if it lies outside, it is disconfirmed or falsified. Hence there is a practical symmetry between the process of verification and falsification.

It is true, of course, that neither of these tests is absolute or final. The nature of the dispersive deviations from a "true" value, being regulated by probability considerations, is such that a later measurement can convert a valid theory into a false one, but also a reputedly false theory into a valid one. Hence again, there is symmetry.

Scientists often speak of crucial experiments, seemingly suggesting that a single test can, on occasion, validate or invalidate a theory. In a practical understanding this is perfectly true, but only in the sense here suggested. The criterion is whether or not the measured value falls within a range of tolerance, i.e., probable error, that contains the predicted one, and the probable error is computable from previous experience with the measuring apparatus. The possibility that the inference as to the theory's validity may be false is always entertained, but never in a way that allows the assignment of probabilities to the remaining doubt.

But the point of issue here is subtle, and perhaps it is merely verbal. What Popper's argument in terms of his modus tollens proves is not that a theory is incapable of being verified; it shows that there is no absolute, ultimate or final truth in science (cf. my footnote 1 c), that the basis even of science is not secure *knowledge*, but *faith* in a sense articulated elsewhere (*ibid*.). Truth in science is the asymptotic limit, if such a limit exists, upon which our progressive penetration of the C-field converges. However, in using this mathematical figure of speech I beg the reader's indulgence; perhaps such precise language is inappropriate in discussing epistemology. Popper's view is set forth in a beguiling simile. He says:

> Science does not rest upon rock bottom. The bold structure of its theories rises, as it were, above a swamp. It is like a building erected on piles. The piles are driven from above into the swamp, but not down to any natural or 'given' base; and when we cease our attempts to drive our piles into a deeper layer, it is not because we have reached firm ground. We simply stop when we are satisfied that they are firm enough to carry the structure, at least for the time being. [*L.Sc.D.*, p. 277]

I like this picture very much, except for a few features. I am not sure whether up and down should not be reversed, whether we do not build from a swamp of protocol experiences into a lofty sky of theoretical constructs—(for my own part I have been noncommittal, placing facts and theories on the same vertical level). But that is not very important. Retaining Popper's spatial orientation, one might suggest these alterations. Forget the swamp—for the ocean is bottomless and we float on its surface. The bold structure is first built down from the top. There are no piles that hold it at the bottom. But the deeper you go the calmer is the ocean, and this provides relative stability to the infrastructure against the movements on the surface. If there is, or were, a bottom, it might be conceived as motionless, satisfying some ontological principle of permanence or the qualities of Kant's elusive *Ding-an-sich*. Sometimes an entire structure is abandoned and a better one is built, in which perhaps parts of the old may be incorporated. Very often a structure is repaired. And the greater the surface area from which man operates, the deeper he seems to be compelled to go.

There is one aspect, however, which this account (and Popper's) ignores, an aspect of growing importance in contemporary physics. It is this. We sometimes sink a floating submarine platform down to a certain depth and build up from there. Some of the most spectacular modern theories arise from postulates deep below the surface. The structures built upon them (by rules of logic and mathematics) finally reach the surface at points dotted with known or previously unrecognized objects or peculiarities, hence "explaining" them. To name but one, the mathematical principle of invariance (of nature's laws) is such a submarine platform of extreme, almost miraculous efficacy.

This contribution would be incomplete if it failed to mention Popper's philosophical approach to probability, which matches Carnap's in excellence and seizes upon the crucial logical difficulties inherent in this concept at a time when they were hardly recognized by philosophers. His attempts to resolve the difficulties of von Mises, especially his treatment of randomness, are ingenious, and his use of the concept of accumulation points to establish a meaning of randomness parallels the classic work of Kolmogorov, which is now generally accepted.

If there is anything of philosophic interest to be added it is this. Popper distinguishes 3 kinds of probability interpretations: Laplace's (or a priori), a logical subjective, and an objective (a posteriori) interpretation. Of these, I would omit the second, which speaks of a degree of entailment between statements, because logicians have other names for such a relation and the concept has, so far as I know, never been used in an empirical science. Of the other two, Popper prefers the last, the frequency interpretation and gives it an elaborate treatment.

It seems imperative to me that one should go beyond this position, which marks von Mises's stand, and recognize the "a priori" and the frequency definition not as opposed or unrelated but as complementary in the following sense. As shown in footnote 1 b, every observable, to be scientifically useful, must be definable in two independent ways. It must be susceptible of at least one constitutive definition and one operational definition. In the case of probability, Laplace's is one of many possible constitutive definitions; the frequency definition is an operational one. The availability of both proves, as it does with all other scientific quantitics, that probability is an acceptable, legitimate and possibly irreducible scientific observable.

This has an important bearing upon the quantum theory, to which I now turn. And I confront this last topic of my discourse with special pleasure, for the area of agreement between Popper's interpretation of quantum mechanics and my own is very large. He was among the first philosophers to interpret Heisenberg's uncertainty principle as a statistical scatter relation[6] which does not permit any conclusion with respect to single measurements.[7] And he foresaw that this principle does not forbid the simultaneous measurement, with arbitrary precision, of observables whose operators do not commute. This is a point to which some of my recent researches have been devoted,[8] and I take the liberty here of extending Popper's comments in only one important respect. For his view, as well as mine, is contradicted by a famous theorem of von Neumann's, which is universally acclaimed as *proving* that two noncommuting observables can not be measured simultaneously at all, and the proof is based on the accepted postulates of quantum mechanics. That proof is not in error. The escape from this dilemma is by way of the following consideration. The premises of von Neumann's proof include the assumption of an isomorphism between all possible physical operations, all measurements, on the one hand, and the set of all hermitean operators in Hilbert space. As shown in footnote 8, this assumption is unreasonable: There are known to be formally satisfactory operators in Hilbert space for which a physical operation does not exist; hence we postulate that the reverse is also true, that there are operations which can not be matched by hermitean operators. Simultaneous measurement of p and q is one of them. In other words, the isomorphism breaks down. In footnote 8 and other papers cited here a search is undertaken for the mathematical formulation of a concept which is now free from contradictions, namely the joint probability of measuring noncommuting observables simultaneously. The results are in many respects reassuring—such joint distributions do exist—but some of their features are not yet understood.

There are other developments that lie in the extended line of Popper's early proposals and conjectures. He refuted von Neumann's projection postulate (in the special form of the reduction of a wave packet). The current literature is full of arguments and strange misunderstandings over this philosophically vital issue; textbooks still propagate a myth which Popper already rejected. (The present writer suggested the incorrectness of the projection postulate in connection with the Einstein, Podolski, Rosen paradox.)[9]

I do not know, and my present whereabouts do not allow me to discover, whether Popper still assigns a meaningful path to electrons. If so, I disagree with him, and this for a reason which I think he accepts, namely that an atomic entity, being too small to be the carrier of visual attributes, must not be endowed with them in our physical description of it. For this reason I have proposed the thesis of latent observables (footnotes 1 b, 8) which assigns to the denizens of the microcosm something like Heisenberg's "potentia". Unfortunately I am not clear on Popper's meaning of "propensity" (his *Postscript* continues to be unavailable to me here), but I should not be surprised if it were close to my conception of latency.

Finally, I wish to applaud Popper's insistence on objectivity in quantum mechanical description. The reasons he has given against the view that the state function represents human knowledge are utterly convincing, and I dare say they are accepted by the great majority of physicists today. He saw, much earlier than many physicists, that quantum mechanics did not effect a degeneration of physics to a shallow and wholly incompetent kind of psychology but the reverse, it accomplished the restoration of a powerful objectivity of description by reliance upon "statistical scatter" theories, to which he himself devoted so much attention.

HENRY MARGENAU

DEPARTMENT OF PHILOSOPHY
UNIVERSITY OF HEIDELBERG
FEBRUARY, 1971

NOTES

[1] Extensive accounts are found in the following publications (aside from special articles in periodicals):

    a. Henry Margenau, "Methodology of Modern Physics", *Philosophy of Science*, 2, No. 48 (1935), 164.

    b. Henry Margenau, *The Nature of Physical Reality* (New York: McGraw-Hill, 1950).

    c. Henry Margenau, *Open Vistas: Philosophical Perspectives of Modern Science* (New Haven: Yale University Press, 1961).

[2] See my chapter in *The Structure of Economic Science,* ed. by S. R. Krupp (New York: Prentice-Hall, 1960).

[3] In my early writings I chose the letter P for primary, perceptual, and called their domain the P-plane. I would now rather have P stand for protocol. The domain of constructs was called the C-field. Reasons for the use of "plane" and "field" are given in 1 b and 2. Several recent texts have adopted and sometimes generalized the terms C-field and P-plane or P-field. See, for instance,

    H. G. Cassidy, *The Sciences and the Arts* (New York: Harper & Row, 1962).

    _____, *Knowledge, Experience and Action* (New York: Teachers College Press, 1967).

    _____, *Science Restated* (San Francisco: Freeman, Cooper & Co., 1970).

    H. K. Schilling, *Science and Religion* (New York: Charles Scribner's Sons, 1962).

    T. T. Segerstedt, *The Nature of Social Reality* (Totowa, New Jersey: Bedminster, 1966).

    J. T. Robinson, *The Nature of Science and Science Teaching* (Belmont, Calif.: Wadsworth Publishing Co., 1968).

    V. L. Parsegian, *The Physical Sciences* (New York: Academic Press, 1968).

[4] This term, I should like here to acknowledge, was recommended to me as especially suitable in this context by Professor Ernst Cassirer when he taught at Yale.

[5] K. R. Popper, *The Logic of Scientific Discovery* (London: Hutchinson, 1959; New York: Basic Books, 1959). Hereinafter cited as *L.Sc.D.*

[6] In spite of Popper's mild polemic against Heisenberg in this connection, his interpretation can not have been "news" to Heisenberg, who soon after its discovery derived the uncertainty principle in a way which clearly identifies Δp and Δq as standard deviations in an ensemble of measurements. This ensemble, I would add to Popper's remarks, need not be a space ensemble, it can also be a time ensemble (see footnote 8 below), i.e., a collective composed of similar measurements on a single system reprepared in time. As to the important distinction between the act called measurement and that called preparation, see footnotes 1 b and 8, along with numerous special publications.

[7] In this context, see also Robert B. Lindsay and H. Margenau, *Foundations of Physics* (New York: John Wiley & Sons, 1936).

[8] The most recent and extensive reference is J. L. Park and H. Margenau, "Simultaneous Measurability in Quantum Theory", *International Journal of Theoretical Physics,* 1 (1968), 211.

[9] H. Margenau, "Quantum Mechanical Description", *Physical Review,* 47 (1935), 777.

Patrick Suppes

POPPER'S ANALYSIS OF PROBABILITY
IN QUANTUM MECHANICS

Since the early 1930s, Popper has been publishing articles about the foundations of quantum mechanics, and he has had many useful things to say in a number of books and articles. With some hesitation, I have narrowed the scope of what I shall discuss to two topics: the propensity interpretation of probability and quantum mechanics as a statistical theory. Throughout his writings, but especially in *The Logic of Scientific Discovery,* Popper has a great deal to say also about measurement in the quantum mechanics. I shall not discuss these matters except as they bear upon his conception of the role of probability in quantum mechanics.

1. Propensity Interpretation of Probability

Popper has spent considerable effort in elaborating and defending his propensity interpretation of probability, and the term itself has become a widely used one for a certain conception about probability. More than anyone else, he has been responsible for making this view of the foundations of probability well known, and he says in several places that he was led to the propensity interpretation as part of his reflections on the role of probability in quantum mechanics.

I shall concentrate on comparing the propensity interpretation with the other major views of the foundations of probability: the classical Laplacean definition, the relative-frequency interpretation, and the subjective interpretation. Only after a fairly detailed scrutiny of the propensity interpretation as an alternative to one of these three positions will I have anything to say about the particular case of quantum mechanics. I shall not discuss confirmation or corroboration as an additional way of looking at the foundations of probability. I think a case can be made for considering confirmation theory as a fourth alternative; but Popper has rather different views of this matter, and some rather special views of his own about corroboration. I believe the issues surrounding the propensity interpretation can be discussed by restricting the frame of reference to the three major views mentioned.

To begin with, I think Popper has brought to the surface some intuitions that many of us share about the foundations of probability. He has had the insight to recognize that there is something misleading about each of the main classical views of the foundations of probability in at least some applications. The propensity viewpoint or what we might also call the dispositional viewpoint toward probability is very appealing, not only when we deal with the physics of atomic and subatomic particles, but also with many straightforward applications in medicine, psychology, sociology, etc. Moreover, Popper has properly emphasized that we cannot simply think of the propensity or disposition as inhering in the object independent of the circumstances surrounding the object. In other words, propensity, as Popper remarks, like the concept of force "is a relational concept."[1]

Although I am sympathetic with these intuitions and with the insight that Popper has verbalized for all of us, a central issue about the propensity interpretation dominates all other issues for me, and I would like to concentrate on it in this discussion. In broad terms, the issue is that of characterizing the explicit meaning of the propensity interpretation. To ask for the meaning of the interpretation without making any more definite statement of the methodology to be used or the approach to be taken is to ask in philosophers' jargon the ordinary question, What is the propensity interpretation? However, in the case of probability, a strong intellectual tradition of analysis can be used.

The matter can be formulated this way. With an important exception in quantum mechanics to be discussed below but not an exception that affects the conceptual point being made at this stage, the scientific applications of probability all rest on the acceptance of Kolmogorov's axiomatization, and the formal properties of probability that flow from that axiomatization. On occasion, Popper has indicated some reservations about that axiomatization (*PI,* p. 40), but those reservations are minor and not a serious issue here. The mathematical applications of probability in sciences as diverse as sociology and statistical mechanics all use the standard properties of probability, and the theorems asserted or claimed about probabilistic phenomena depend upon the formal properties that flow from the Kolmogorov axiomatization, plus possibly other special assumptions needed in particular applications. For example, the theory of stochastic processes is of increasingly great importance.

Because of the significance I shall attach to the relation of any interpretation of probability to the Kolmogorov axiomatization, it will probably be worthwhile to formulate the Kolmogorov approach. The axioms are based on three primitive concepts: a nonempty set X of possible outcomes, a family $\mathscr{F}$ of subsets of X representing possible events, and a real-valued function P on $\mathscr{F}$; for event A in $\mathscr{F}$; $P(A)$ is interpreted as the probability of A. It is important to note in this connection that events are always formally represented as subsets of the basic sample space X. (It is assumed throughout that X is nonempty.) The notion of an algebra of events is caught in the following definition.

Definition 1. $\mathcal{F}$ is an algebra of events on X if and only if $\mathcal{F}$ is a nonempty family of subsets of X and for every A and B in $\mathcal{F}$:

$$1.\ \sim A \in \mathcal{F};$$
$$2.\ A \cup B \in \mathcal{F}.$$

Moreover, if $\mathcal{F}$ is closed under countable unions, that is, if for $A_1, A_2,$ $\ldots, A_n \ldots \in \mathcal{F}, \bigcup_{i=1}^{\infty} A_i \in \mathcal{F}$, then $\mathcal{F}$ is a σ-algebra on X.

Assuming the set-theoretical structure of X, $\mathcal{F}$, and P already described, we may now turn to the definition of probability spaces.

Definition 2. A structure $\mathcal{X} = \langle X, \mathcal{F}, P \rangle$ is a finitely additive probability space if and only if for every A and B in $\mathcal{F}$:

P1. *$\mathcal{F}$ is an algebra of events on X;*
P2. *$P(A) \geq 0$;*
P3. *$P(X) = 1$;*
P4. *If $A \cap B = 0$, then $P(A \cup B) = P(A) + P(B)$.*

Moreover, $\mathcal{X}$ is a probability space (without restriction to finite additivity) if the following two axioms are also satisfied:

P5. *$\mathcal{F}$ is a σ-algebra of events on X;*
P6. *If $A_1, A_2, \ldots$, is a sequence of pairwise incompatible events in $\mathcal{F}$, i.e., $A_i \cap A_j = 0$ for $i \neq j$, then*

$$P\left(\bigcup_{i=1}^{\infty} A_i\right) = \sum_{i=1}^{\infty} P(A_i).$$

Some more special probabilistic notions will be needed in later parts of this paper, but I shall defer until then their formal definition. Also, although I have included the countable cases for the sake of completeness in Definitions 1 and 2, I shall mainly ignore them in the sequel. These concepts are of central importance in advanced applications, but explicit consideration of them here does not add much of conceptual interest, and the notation and theorems will remain simpler if they are ignored. We can, if we desire, think of the sequel as being restricted to finite probability spaces, that is, to spaces in which the basic set X is finite. But, I would emphasize that the conceptual remarks are not at all bound by this imposition of finiteness.

On the assumption that any interpretation of probability must come to terms with the Kolmogorov set-theoretical approach as embodied in Definitions 1 and 2, we can ask ourselves how is that "coming to terms" to be expressed. There is a classical mathematical way of formulating the matter. We must be able to prove that the set-theoretical entities defined under the particular interpretation of probability are themselves either objects that satisfy Definition 2 or lead in a completely explicit way to the construction of objects that satisfy Definition 2. This rather abstract formulation of the representation problem is made more concrete by consideration of the classical interpretations of probability.

The place to begin is with Laplacean or classical probability. Laplace begins this way. "The first of these principles is the definition itself of probability, which, as has been seen, is the ratio of the number of favorable cases to that of all the cases possible." There are severe difficulties with the application of this definition; but it is clear how it leads to a representation in terms of probability spaces. We may incorporate the idea of Laplace's first principle in the following formal definition. (In the statement of this definition I use $K(A)$ for the cardinality of the set A.)

Definition 3. A structure $\mathscr{X} = \langle X, \mathscr{F}, P \rangle$ is a finite Laplacean probability space if and only if:

P1. *X is a finite set;*
P2. *$\mathscr{F}$ is an algebra of events on X;*
P3. *For A in $\mathscr{F}$,*

$$P(A) = \frac{K(A)}{K(X)}.$$

It is apparent that the following theorem is a trivial consequence of this definition, but the theorem does express the way in which the Laplacean definition provides a strict interpretation of the set-theoretical formalization of probability.

Theorem 1. Any finite Laplacean probability space $\mathscr{X} = \langle X, \mathscr{F}, P \rangle$ is a finitely additive probability space in the sense of Definition 2.

Almost everybody recognizes criticisms that can be leveled at the classical Laplacean definition. It is only when very strong principles of symmetry are satisfied that the definition in a strict sense can be applied. Most of Laplace's own work in probability did not use the principle. I mean by this that the detailed applications in astronomy and other complicated phenomena did not proceed from a strict application of the classical definition.

However, I find myself unable to agree with some of Popper's criticisms of the classical definition. These criticisms are expressed in *PI* (p. 36).

> . . . mere possibilities could never give rise to any prediction. It is possible, for example, that an earthquake will destroy tomorrow *all* the houses between the 13th parallels north and south (and *no* other houses). Nobody can calculate this possibility, but most people would estimate it as exceedingly small; and while the sheer possibility as such does not give rise to any prediction, the estimate that it is exceedingly small may be made the basis of the prediction that the event described will not take place ("in all probability").

Thus the estimate of the *measure* of a possibility — that is, the estimate of the probability attached to it — has always a predictive function, while we should hardly predict an event upon being told no more than that this event is possible. In other words, we do not assume that a possibility as such has any tendency to realise itself; but we do interpret probability measures, or "weights" attributed to the possibility, as measuring its disposition, or tendency, or propensity to realise itself; . . .

It seems to me that in this discussion there is an abuse of the Laplacean notion of possibility. It is precisely the point that it is simply the enumeration of possibilities that are used in the definition of probability. I think Popper can rightly object, as he does, that in many instances this is not what we do, or we do not know how to enumerate the possibilities. On the other hand, in the examples given by Laplace as paradigm cases of his definition, namely, games of chance, we do agree on the enumeration of possibilities, and we can claim that it is the enumeration of possibilities that provides the basis for the definition of probability. It is not a case, as Popper puts it, of assuming "that a possibility as such has any tendency to realise itself." It is just that the computation of probabilities is based upon the enumeration of possibilities. As we look deeper into the matter, we are willing to accept these enumerations in cases where certain implicit principles of symmetry are satisfied and not in other cases. My quarrel with Popper here is not a large one. I do think that the notion of possible outcomes or possible cases is a fundamental aspect of thinking about probability. It is also a fundamental aspect to tend to impose a uniform distribution on the set of possible outcomes. We do not do this because of any ideas about propensity itself or probability weights, but because we see no reason to treat one possible outcome in a manner different from another. I want to be perfectly clear on this point. I am not trying to defend the classical definition as a workable interpretation of probability. I am taking exception to Popper's remarks about the way in which possibility does enter in the classical definition. The important point for our discussion here is that a well-defined formal relation between the classical interpretation of probability and the set-theoretical approach is embodied in Definition 2. This formal relation is caught by Theorem 1.

Let us now take a quick look at the relative-frequency interpretation of probability. I shall first state several formal notions and a theorem, but then indicate how the models brought under the framework of probability spaces by the theorem are not fully satisfactory. However, I shall not enter into the formal details of how the definitions are to be more restricted. These are standard matters in the discussion of relative-frequency theory. The point is to show how one is led from the relative-frequency interpretation in a formal way to models of Definition 2.

An *(infinite) sequence* is a function whose domain of definition is the set of positive integers. If s is a sequence then $s(n)$ (or in a common notation: s_n) is the nth *term* of the sequence s. A sequence of *positive integers* is a sequence all of whose terms are positive integers.

Let s be a sequence of real numbers. Then the $\lim_{n \to \infty} s_n = k$ if and only if for every $\in > 0$, there is an integer N such that for all integers n if $n > N$ then

$$|s_n - k| < \in.$$

Definition 4. Let s be a sequence and let $\mathscr{F}$ be the family of all sub-sets of $R(s)$, the range of s. Let t be the function defined on $\mathscr{F} \times \omega$ where ω is the set of all positive integers, such that for all A in $\mathscr{F}$,

$$t(A, n) = K\{i : i \leq n \ \& \ s_i \in A\}.$$

We call the number $t(A, n)/n$ the *relative frequency* of A in the first n terms of s. If the limit of the function $t(A, n)/n$ exists, then this limit is the *limiting relative frequency* of A in s.

Theorem 2. Let s be a sequence and $\mathscr{F}$ an algebra of events on $R(s)$ such that if $A \in \mathscr{F}$ then the limiting relative frequency of A in s exists. Let P be the function defined on $\mathscr{F}$ such that for every A in $\mathscr{F}$

$$P(A) = \lim_{n \to \infty} \frac{t(A, n)}{n}.$$

Then $\langle R(s), \mathscr{F}, P \rangle$ is a finitely additive probability space.

The proof of Theorem 2 requires more argument than the proof of Theorem 1, but it is straightforward in terms of standard facts about the limits of sequences and will be omitted here.

I emphasize that to have a realistic relative-frequency theory, the conditions of Theorem 2 need to be strengthened. Many sequences satisfy the hypothesis of Theorem 2 and thus generate a finitely additive probability space, but we would not at all be willing to accept them as falling within the framework of what we intuitively consider to be probabilistic phenomena. For example, the deterministic sequence consisting of alternating 1's and 0's would satisfy Theorem 2 and the event of a 1 occurring would be 1/2, and the event of a 0 occurring, 1/2; but, clearly, no reasonable notion of probability in an intuitive sense would admit such a sequence. The point of the present discussion, however, is not disturbed by this aspect of things. I am interested only in how we formulate a formal relation between a relative-frequency theory and the notion of probability space embodied in Definition 2.

I turn now to a brief exposition of the subjective theory of probability and the way in which it formally provides an interpretation of Definition 2. I shall restrict my analysis of the subjective theory to a simple example to avoid technical complexities. The spirit of the axioms embodied in the definition given below places restraints on qualitative judgments of probability, which on the one hand seem intuitively sensible and on the other hand seem sufficient to guarantee the existence of a numerical probability measure in the sense of Definition 2. The subjective aspect enters directly in the sense that the qualitative relation is meant to reflect the qualitative judgments of subjective probability: $A \geq B$ if and only if A is judged subjectively at least as probable as B.

Definition 5. A structure $\mathscr{X} = \langle X, \mathscr{F}, \geq \rangle$ is a finite qualitative probability structure with equivalent atoms if and only if X is a finite set, $\mathscr{F}$ is an algebra of events on X, $\geq$ is a binary relation on $\mathscr{F}$, and the following axioms are satisfied for every A, B, and C in $\mathscr{F}$:

1. *The relation $\geq$ is a weak ordering of $\mathscr{F}$;*
2. *If $A \cap C = \phi$ and $B \cap C = \phi$, then $A \geq B$ if and only if $A \cup C \geq B \cup C$;*
3. *$A \geq \phi$;*
4. *Not $\phi \geq X$;*
5. *If $A \geq B$ then there is a C in $\mathscr{F}$ such that $A \geq B \cup C$ and $B \cup C \geq A$.*

The first four axioms are standard axioms that originate with de Finetti (the symbol ϕ stands for the empty set); the fifth axiom is the structural axiom that implies the equivalence of the atoms; the exact theorem that can be proved is the following:

Theorem 3. Let $\mathscr{X} = \langle X, \mathscr{F}, \geq \rangle$ be a finite qualitative subjective probability structure with equivalent atoms. Then there exists a probability measure P in the sense of Definition 2 such that for every A and B in $\mathscr{F}$

$$P(A) \geq P(B) \text{ if and only if } A \geq B.$$

Moreover, there are at most two equivalence classes of atomic events in $\mathscr{F}$; and if there are two rather than one, one of these contains the empty event.

The proof of this theorem I shall omit.[2]

It is not my purpose in this paper to defend any one of the three views of probability I have sketched above. Rather, in the present context I want to distinguish the three classical views sketched above from the propensity interpretation advocated by Popper on the grounds that I do not see what the corresponding theorem for the propensity interpretation is. I have gone to some length to make this point, because I think it is an important one about the propensity interpretation. I very much agree with Popper that there is much that is attractive in the idea of probability as propensity. What I find difficult to envisage, and what I find missing in his own discussions of the propensity interpretation, is the more explicit formal characterization of the propensity interpretation that permits us to prove a theorem like Theorem 1, 2 or 3. Until an interpretation of probability is given sufficient systematic definiteness to permit the proof of such a theorem, it seems fair to say that it is still at a presystematic level, and no clear concept has as yet been explicated.

Popper tells us in *PI* that he was especially led to the propensity concept by the problem of interpreting the use of probability in quantum theory. He felt that the Bohr-Heisenberg interpretation was inextricably bound up with the subjectivistic interpretation of probability. On the other hand, the difficulty of the relative-frequency theory lay in providing an appropriate straightforward interpretation of the probability of singular events. A number of his remarks in this connection seem to me sensible, as for example, his insistence that the so-called "problem of the reduction of the wave packet" is a problem inherent in every probabilistic theory, and not special to any particular interpretation.

There are a number of tantalizing remarks about the propensity view in *PI*. In several places Popper compares propensities to forces in Newtonian physics. As he puts it, "there is an analogy between the idea of propensities and that of forces." However, I would again raise the same question I have been raising. Already in the case of Newtonian forces there are explicit formal laws that these forces are required to obey: the laws of addition of forces and also the more special laws for internal forces in a system of particle mechanics; namely, the law that the force exerted by one particle on another be equal and opposite, and also the law that the direction of these two internal forces be along the line connecting the position of the two particles. I find no systematic laws whatsoever that the propensity interpretation is to satisfy, except the formal laws of probability already embodied in Definition 2.

In other passages, Popper indicates the close relation between the propensity interpretation and the relative-frequency interpretation, but again I would want to press the point and ask if there is indeed a formal difference between the two and, if so, what it is.

Of the three views I have sketched above, the relative-frequency and subjective views each provide a sharply defined formal theory that does lead to an interpretation in the formal sense of the axioms of Definition 2. The classical theory also provides such an interpretation, but it is weaker and less interesting.

Toward the close of *PI*, Popper says the following:

> . . . what I propose is *a new physical hypothesis* (or perhaps a metaphysical hypothesis) analogous to the hypothesis of Newtonian forces. It is the hypothesis that every experimental arrangement (and therefore every state of a system) generates physical propensities which can be tested by frequencies. This hypothesis is testable, and it is corroborated by certain quantum experiments. The two-slit experiment, for example, may be said to be something like a crucial experiment between the purely statistical and the propensity interpretation of probability, and to decide the issue against the purely statistical interpretation.

What troubles me about this passage is the vagueness of his new physical hypothesis in contrast to the sharpness of formulation of the hypothesis of Newtonian forces. From what he says it is also not clear how the two-slit experiment provides a crucial experiment between the relative-frequency and propensity interpretations. Indeed, I have found it difficult to try to infer what formal properties the propensity interpretation is supposed to have from consideration of the two-slit experiment.

Let me sum up the situation as I see it in three points.

1. Much of what Popper says about the use of probability in quantum mechanics and the way he has used the idea of propensity to say these things seem eminently sensible to me.

2. I find the systematic case for the propensity interpretation badly worked out and not at all in a state comparable to that of the classical, relative-frequency or subjective interpretations.

3. I recognize at the same time that the subjective theory, especially in its simply providing a qualitative ordering relation, has not provided an interpretation at a very deep level. I do not wish to defend the adequacy of the subjective interpretation in any fundamental way. It does stand in sharp contrast, however, to the propensity interpretation because there does exist a systematic body of analysis and resulting theorems that can be proved about the subjective view. Until such an analysis and resulting theorems are produced for the propensity interpretation, I find it impossible to embark upon a more thoroughgoing critique.

2. Quantum Mechanics as a Statistical Theory

Popper has written extensively on the conceptual nature of quantum mechanics. I shall not cite here the many references, for these are available in the general bibliography. I agree with much of what he has had to say about quantum mechanics as a statistical theory. He has had many sane and sensible things to say in his analyses and criticisms of the doctrines advanced by physicists. Our points of agreement are too many to enumerate, although I cannot help mentioning my pleasure in his recent article on Birkhoff and von Neumann's interpretation of quantum mechanics.[3] He points out the conceptual inadequacy of the argument given in Birkhoff and von Neumann's famous article in a way that is perhaps the clearest of anything I have seen in print. I shall not review the details of the argument here, but note that he shows how unsatisfactory is their claim that quantum mechanics uses a nondistributive lattice. It is not the result that is so unsatisfactory, but the total lack of serious argument for their position.

I could list other points of agreement, but the more constructive and useful thing is to focus on the major issues where I find myself in disagreement with Popper, or where I do not think he has pushed hard enough or dealt as yet sufficiently explicitly with matters of central importance.

The central theme of what I want to say can be posed as a question. Is indeed quantum mechanics a genuinely statistical theory? By this, I do not question whether there are many statistical aspects of quantum mechanics, but rather, can quantum mechanics as a theory be regarded as a statistical theory in the way that classical statistical mechanics, population genetics or theories of mental testing are statistical theories? It seems to me that much in Popper's writings indicates that he would want to make this claim. I shall not try to document the many places where he discusses these matters, but I would refer the reader especially to his recent article, "Quantum Mechanics Without 'The Observer'."[4] In this article Popper sets forth 13 theses about quantum mechanics. It is not possible to examine each of these theses and to comment on them, especially as to how each thesis relates to the view of quantum mechanics as a statistical theory. I shall begin by concentrating on the interpretation of the Heisenberg uncertainty relations, and then go on from there to problems about probability that are not explicitly treated by Popper.

To begin with, if one starts from the idea that quantum mechanics is a statistical theory, as Popper evidently does, a first point of peculiarity about the Heisenberg principle needs to be mentioned. The principle asserts that the product of the standard deviations of two noncommuting variables is always greater than some positive constant. In the particular example of position and momentum it is asserted that the products of the standard deviations of the position and momentum of a particle at a given time are always greater than a certain fixed constant, which is positive. A statement of this kind can be derived in many classical theories. In fact, it will be true in any classical theory in which we are dealing with a nondegenerate joint distribution of at least two random variables. Nearly the first thing we would want to do is ask about a closer relation between the two variables. We would want information about the covariation of the two random variables and their possible causal relation—that causal relation either being between the variables or due to a common cause. The standard statistical way in which these matters are studied would be in terms of looking at the covariance or the correlation of the two variables. (Because the notion of correlation is familiar in a wide range of scientific disciplines, let us deal with the correlation and recall that the correlation of two random variables is defined as the covariance divided by the product of the standard deviations.) Given that the product of the standard deviations is greater than some fixed constant, we can still produce examples in which the correlation has the entire range from -1 to 1; in particular, examples for which the correlation between the values of the random variables is 1, and also cases for which the correlation of the random variables is 0. From a general statistical viewpoint, it is often more important and almost always at least as important to know whether the random variables are independent or highly correlated as it is to know that the product of their standard deviations is greater than some constant. When Popper talks about quantum mechanics as a statistical theory, he is talking, it seems to me, with that surprise evinced by those who look at quantum mechanics from the standpoint of classical physics — surprise that the theory brings within its purview certain statistical relations and denies at the theoretical level the determinism so characteristic of classical physics. Looked at from the standpoint of standard statistical theories, the surprise about quantum mechanics is rather different. The first glance would be something like the one I have sketched. The surprise is that natural questions are not asked or discussed. Popper's own neglect of these standard questions of covariation or correlation is a reflection that he has not really taken seriously as yet the rethinking of quantum mechanics as a statistical theory. What Heisenberg, for example, has had to say about these matters would make the hair of any right-thinking statistician stand on end.

I emphasize the importance of these questions of correlation. If, for example, the Heisenberg uncertainty relation is satisfied by position and momentum in a given direction at a given time, we would be enormously surprised if the correlation between position and momentum were one. This would indicate a deterministic relation between the two that would be most disturbing to most physicists. I stress, however, that such a model is mathematically consistent with the Heisenberg relations. This is an obvious and elementary fact of statistics. It is of course not my claim that such an interpretation is consistent with the actual empirical data of quantum mechanics or with the theory taken in a larger framework than that of the simple statement of the Heisenberg principle.

That physicists and Popper as well do not really take seriously their claim that quantum mechanics is a statistical theory is evident from the complete absence of discussion of the problems of correlation just raised. In Popper's case, I suspect that he has simply been caught up in the discussions of physicists and has tried to respond in a direct way to the many kinds of things they have had to say; he has not looked at the problems from the standpoint of a genuine statistical theory.

Let me now turn to the second part of my remarks in this connection. There are good reasons why the questions I have raised are not raised. There are many ways of explaining what the reason for failure is. The essential idea, however, is that quantum mechanics is not a standard statistical theory — it is a peculiar, mystifying, and as yet, poorly understood radical departure from the standard methodology of probability and statistics. There is as yet no uniform agreement on how the probabilistic aspects or statistical aspects of quantum mechanics should be formulated. But it is widely agreed that there are unusual problems that must be dealt with and that do not arise in standard statistical theories of the sort I mentioned earlier. In fact, the kind of problems I now want to raise do not, so far as I know, exist in any other scientific theories of any scientific discipline.

The difficulty is that when the standard formalism of quantum mechanics is used the joint distribution of noncommuting random variables turns out not to be a proper joint distribution in the classical sense of probability. These ideas have been discussed now by a good many people, and I shall not quote chapter and verse here. I am sure that Popper is familiar with several of these discussions, although I have been a little surprised not to find more explicit comment on these matters in his own writings. I do think the difficulties raised by the nonexistence of joint distributions within the framework of the standard formalism are the most direct challenge to a straightforward interpretation of quantum mechanics as a standard statistical theory.

To have a concrete instance in front of us, I give an example that I computed some years ago,[5] but I emphasize that these matters have been discussed by many people and general proofs of the impossibility of having proper joint distributions within the classical framework have been given by several people.

Consider the momentum and position random variables P and Q. The characteristic function $\varphi(t, u)$ is defined by:

$$(1) \qquad \varphi(u, v) = E(e^{iup + ivq}).$$

Using the Hilbert space formulation, let (ψ, ψ) be the inner product of a state with itself. Following the usual formalism, the expectation $E(R)$ of an operator R when the quantum mechanical system is in state ψ is simply $(\psi, R\psi)$. In view of (1) the characteristic function $\varphi(u, v)$ for the joint distribution of P and Q is given by:

$$(2) \qquad \varphi(u, v) = (\psi, e^{i(up + vq)}\psi).$$

We then have from (1) and (2) by Fourier inversion:

$$(3) \qquad f(p, q) = \frac{1}{4\pi^2} \int_{-\infty}^{\infty} \int_{-\infty}^{\infty} e^{-i(up + vq)}(\psi, e^{i(up + vq)}\psi) \, du \, dv.$$

For canonically conjugate operators P and Q, i.e., $PQ - QP = \hbar/i$, it may be shown that (2) simplifies to[6]

$$\varphi(u, v) = \int \psi^* \left(q - \frac{1}{2}\hbar u \right) e^{ivq} \psi \left(q + \frac{1}{2}\hbar u \right) dq$$

and so by Fourier inversion

(4) $$f(p, q) - \frac{1}{2\pi} \int \psi^* \left(q - \frac{1}{2}\hbar u \right) e^{-iup} \psi \left(q + \frac{1}{2}\hbar u \right) du.$$

As is well known in probability theory not every characteristic function determines a proper probability distribution, and this is the difficulty with (4). (The expression given by (4) for the joint density was first proposed by Wigner [1932] and the derivation just sketched follows Moyal [1949].[7])

Let us now look at a simple example, the harmonic oscillator in the ground state and also in the first excited state.

Ground State. The potential energy is given by

$$V(x) = \frac{1}{2}Kx^2,$$

and the time-independent wave equation is

$$-\frac{\hbar^2}{2m} \frac{d^2\psi(x)}{dx^2} + \frac{1}{2}Kx^2\psi(x) = E\psi(x).$$

The solution of this equation in terms of Hermite polynomials is familiar from the literature. In the lowest energy state H_0

(5) $$\psi(x) = \left(\frac{\alpha}{\pi^{1/2}} \right)^{1/2} \exp\left(-\frac{1}{2}\alpha^2 x^2 \right),$$

where

$$\alpha^2 = \sqrt{\frac{Km}{\hbar^2}}.$$

Thus

(6) $$|\psi(x)|^2 = \frac{\alpha}{\pi^{1/2}} e^{-\alpha^2 x^2}$$

which is a normal density with mean zero and variance $\sigma^2 = 1/2\alpha^2 = \hbar/2 \sqrt{Km}$.

We now apply (4) and (5) to obtain the joint distribution of momentum and position. For convenience of calculation, we replace p by the propagation vector $k = p/\hbar$. We have at once:

$$f(k, x) = \frac{1}{2\pi} \int \psi^* \left(x - \frac{u}{2}\right) e^{-iku} \psi\left(x + \frac{u}{2}\right) du$$

$$= \frac{1}{2\pi} \left(\frac{\alpha}{\pi^{1/2}}\right) \int \exp\left[a^2\left(x^2 + \left(\frac{u}{2}\right)^2\right)\right] e^{-iku} du$$

$$= \frac{1}{2\pi} \left(\frac{\alpha}{\pi^{1/2}}\right) e^{-\alpha^2 x^2} \frac{\pi^{1/2}}{\alpha/2} \exp\left[-\frac{k^2}{4(\alpha/2)^2}\right]$$

$$= \frac{1}{\pi} \exp\left(-\alpha^2 x^2 - \frac{k^2}{\alpha^2}\right).$$

First Excited State. We have from the literature

$$\psi(x) = \left(\frac{4\alpha^3}{\pi^{1/2}}\right)^{1/2} x \exp\left(-\frac{1}{2}\alpha^2 x^2\right),$$

whence

$$|\psi(x)|^2 = \frac{4\alpha^3}{\sqrt{\pi}} x^2 e^{-\alpha^2 x^2}.$$

Applying now (4) and (5), and again replacing p by the propagation vector $k = p/\hbar$, we have:

(7) $f(k, x) = \left(\frac{1}{2\pi}\right)\left(\frac{4\alpha^3}{\sqrt{\pi}}\right) \int \left(x^2 - \left(\frac{u}{2}\right)^2\right) \exp\left[-\alpha^2\left(x^2 + \left(\frac{u}{2}\right)^2\right)\right] e^{-iku} du.$

Integrating (7) we obtain

$$f(k, x) = \frac{4}{\pi}\left[\exp\left(-\alpha^2 x^2 - \frac{k^2}{\alpha^2}\right)\right]\left(\alpha^2 x^2 + \frac{k^2}{\alpha^2} - \frac{1}{2}\right),$$

and the function $f(k, x)$ is negative for those values of k and x such that

$$\alpha^2 x^2 + \frac{k^2}{\alpha^2} < \frac{1}{2},$$

which means that $f(k, x)$ is not a proper joint density.

To my mind the problems posed by this elementary example and others like it, as well as general results about the impossibility of having a joint distribution, constitute the really central question of how to treat quantum mechanics as a statistical theory. This is not the proper place to examine possible viewpoints or to review some of the few proposals that have been made; for example, that by Margenau and his collaborators to adopt the special joint distribution that makes noncommuting random variables independent. What I consider important in the present context is to bring to the surface the deep-running nature of the difficulties of interpreting quantum mechanics as a standard statistical theory.

The thirteenth and last thesis of *QM* is "the peculiarity of quantum mechanics is the principle of the superposition of wave amplitudes—a kind of probabilistic dependence . . . that apparently has no parallel in classical probability theory." It is also part of this last thesis to say that both classical physics and quantum physics are indeterministic. What I would urge upon Popper is not the view of the peculiarity of quantum mechanics in terms of the principle of the superposition of wave amplitudes, but rather, the peculiarity of quantum mechanics as a nonstandard statistical theory. Given the wide applicability in all ordinary domains of science of the standard statistical theory and methodology, it is surprising and intellectually unsettling to encounter the fundamental difficulties that seem to be present in quantum mechanics. These difficulties disturb a much deeper level of scientific methodology than do any mere issues of determinism.

In my judgment, these formal difficulties of interpreting quantum mechanics as a standard statistical theory will turn out to be the most revolutionary aspect of the theory. My own historical sense is that these difficulties will come to play the same fundamental role in the foundations of physics and probability that the three classical problems of the Greeks have played in the foundations of mathematics. We now all accept that we cannot trisect an angle or find a square whose area is equivalent to that of a given circle by elementary means. I do not think we have as yet digested in any deep and serious way the profound ramifications of the nonstandard statistical character of quantum mechanics.

PATRICK SUPPES

DEPARTMENT OF PHILOSOPHY
STANFORD UNIVERSITY
MAY, 1970

NOTES

[1] K. R. Popper, "The Propensity Interpretation of Probability," *The British Journal for the Philosophy of Science,* **10**, No. 37 (1959), 25-42. Hereinafter cited as *PI.*

[2] The elementary proof is to be found in Patrick Suppes, *Studies in the Methodology and Foundations of Science* (Amsterdam: D. Reidel Publishing Co., 1969), pp. 7-8.

[3] K. R. Popper, "Birkhoff and von Neumann's Interpretation of Quantum Mechanics," *Nature,* **219** (1968), 682-85.

[4] K. R. Popper, "Quantum Mechanics Without 'The Observer'," in *Quantum Theory and Reality,* ed. by Mario Bunge (Berlin: Springer-Verlag, 1967), pp. 7-44. Hereinafter cited as *QM.*

[5] P. Suppes, "Probability Concepts in Quantum Mechanics," *Philosophy of Science,* **28**, No. 4 (1961), 378-89.

[6] Henceforth the range of integration is understood to be $(-\infty, \infty)$ and notation for it is omitted.

[7] Eugene Wigner, "On the Quantum Correction for Thermodynamic Equilibrium," *Physical Review,* **40** (1932), 749-59.

J. E. Moyal, "Quantum Mechanics as a Statistical Theory," *Proceedings of the Cambridge Philosophical Society,* **45** (1949), 99-124.

Adolf Grünbaum

POPPER'S VIEWS ON THE ARROW OF TIME

1. Introduction

In my contribution to the Popper *Festschrift* of 1964,[1] I discussed the provocative ideas on the "arrow of time" which Professor Popper had expounded in *Nature* during the years 1956-58.[2] Since then, he has published three additional notes on the subject in the same journal.[3] The first of the latter three publications constitutes an important extension of his ideas.[4] Hence it prompts me to present here a more comprehensive critical appreciation of the extended range of his views on the arrow of time.

2. What is Meant by "The Arrow of Time"?

Just as we can coordinatize one of the dimensions of space by means of real numbers *without* being committed to the anisotropy of that spatial dimension, so also we can coordinatize a topologically open time continuum without being committed to the existence of irreversible kinds of processes which would render that continuum anisotropic. For so long as the states of the world (as defined by some one simultaneity criterion) are ordered by a relation of temporal *betweenness* having the same formal properties as the spatial betweenness on a Euclidean straight line, there will be two time senses which are opposite to each other. And we can then assign increasing real-number coordinates in one of these senses and decreasing ones in the other by convention *without* assuming that these two senses are *further distinguished* by the structural property that some kinds of sequences of states encountered along one of them are never (or hardly ever) encountered along the other. Thus, we can use the locutions 'initial state', 'final state', 'before', and 'after' on the basis of such a time-coordinatization, entirely without prejudice as to whether the two ordinally opposite time senses turn out to be further distinguished structurally by the existence of irreversible kinds of processes. By an "irreversible process" (*à la* Planck) we understand a process such that no counterprocess is capable of restoring the original *kind* of state of the system at another time. Note that the temporal vocabulary used in this definition of what is *meant* by an irreversible kind of process does *not* assume tacitly that there *are* irreversible processes: as used here, the terms 'original state', 'restore' and 'counterprocess' presuppose only the coordinatization based on the assumed betweenness.

There is both a weak sense and a strong sense in which a process might be claimed to be 'irreversible' within the framework of a physical theory that allows a sharp distinction between laws and boundary conditions. The weak sense is that the *temporal inverse* of the process in fact never (or hardly ever) occurs with increasing time for the following reason: Certain boundary or initial conditions obtaining in the universe independently of any law (or laws) combine with a relevant law (or laws) to render the temporal inverse *de facto* nonexistent or unreversed, although no law or combination of laws itself disallows that inverse process. The strong or nomological sense of 'irreversible' is that the temporal inverse is impossible in virtue of being ruled out by a law alone or by a combination of laws. Since the weaker kind of irreversibility arises from boundary conditions which are *contingent* with respect to the laws of nature, I shall refer to the weaker kind of irreversibility as 'nomologically-contingent' or as 'contingent'.

If there are irreversible kinds of processes in either of these two senses, then the two ordinally opposite time senses are indeed *further* distinguished structurally as follows: There are certain kinds of sequences of states of systems specified in the order of increasing time coordinates such that these same kinds of sequences do *not* likewise exist in the order of decreasing time coordinates. Or, equivalently, the existence of irreversible processes *structurally* distinguishes the two opposite time senses as follows: there are certain kinds of sequences of states of systems specified in the order of *decreasing* time coordinates such that these same kinds of sequences do *not* likewise obtain in the order of increasing time coordinates. Accordingly, if there are irreversible kinds of processes, then time is *anisotropic*. By the same token, if the temporal inverses of all kinds of processes belonging to a certain very wide class actually materialized, then time would be isotropic with respect to that important class of process-types. When physicists say with Eddington that time has an "arrow," it is this anisotropy to which they are referring metaphorically. Specifically, the spatial opposition between the head and the tail of the arrow represents the structural anisotropy of time.

It is clear that the anisotropy of time resulting from the existence of irreversible processes consists in the mere structural differences between the two opposite senses of time, but provides no basis at all for singling out *one* of the two opposite senses as '*the* direction' of time. Hence the assertion that irreversible processes render time anisotropic is *not at all* equivalent to such statments as 'time flows one way'. And the metaphor of time's 'arrow', which Eddington intended to refer to the anisotropy of time, can be misleading:

attention to the head of the arrow to the exclusion of the tail may suggest that there is a 'flow' in *one* of the two anisotropically related senses. But since the instants of anisotropic time are ordered by the relation 'earlier than' no less than by the converse relation 'later than', the anisotropy of time provides no warrant at all for singling out the 'later than' sense as '*the*' direction of time. Instead, the inspiration for speaking about 'the' direction of time derives from the supposition that there is a transient 'now' or 'present' which can be claimed to shift so as to single out the future direction of time as the sense of its 'advance'. But the claim that there is such an 'advance' is a tautology. For the terms 'shift' or 'flow' are used in their literal kinematic senses in such a way that the *spatial* direction of a shift or flow is specified by where the shifting object is at *later* times. Hence when we speak metaphorically of the now as 'shifting' temporally in a particular *temporal* direction, it is then simply a matter of definition that the now shifts or advances in the direction of the future. For this declaration tells us no more than that the nows corresponding to later times are later than those corresponding to earlier ones, which is just as uninformative as the truism that the earlier nows precede the later ones.[5]

3. Statement of Popper's Two Theses

Professor Popper puts forward two theses as follows: (1) He asserts the existence of a physical basis for the anisotropy of time which is both nomologically-contingent and *non*thermodynamic, thereby denying that the statistical behavior of the entropy of physical systems is the *sole* basis for time's arrow, and (2) he claims further that the statistics of thermodynamic phenomena do not contribute *at all* to the existence of that arrow. Thus, he maintains the "untenability of the widespread, though surely not universal, belief that the 'arrow of time' is closely connected with, or dependent upon, the law that disorder (entropy) tends to increase" (Irreversibility II).

I shall examine each of these two major theses and some of their important ramifications in turn.

4. The Nonthermodynamic Basis of Time's Arrow

Independently of O. Costa de Beauregard, who had used the same illustration before him,[6] Popper (Irreversibility I) considers a large surface of water initially at rest into which a stone is dropped, thereby producing an outgoing wave of decreasing amplitude spreading concentrically about the point of the stone's impact. And Popper argues that this process is irreversible in the sense that the "spontaneous" (Irreversibility IV) concatenation on all points of a circle of the initial conditions requisite to the occurrence of a corresponding *contracting* wave is physically impossible, a '*spontaneous*' concatenation being understood to be one which is *not* brought about by coor-

dinated influences emanating from a common center. Since the laws of
nature governing elementary processes do indeed allow the temporal inverse
of the outgoing wave process, the latter process is only *de facto* or contingently irreversible. Noting that "Although the arrow of time is not implied by the
fundamental equations [laws governing elementary processes], it nevertheless
characterizes most solutions" (Irreversibility I), Popper therefore rejects the
claim that "every non-statistical or 'classical' mechanical process is reversible" (Irreversibility IV). Being predicated on the spontaneity of the requisite
initial conditions, this nomologically-contingent irreversibility (*de facto*
unreversedness) is of a *conditional* kind, i.e., it does not hold for those cases
in which the initial conditions issuing in the temporal inverse are in fact in-
stituted from a common center.

Now, one might object that the attribution of the irreversibility of the
outgoing water wave motion to *nonthermodynamic* causal factors is unsound.
The grounds would be that the statistical entropy law is *not irrelevant* to this
irreversibility, because the diminution in the amplitude of the outgoing wave
is due to the superposition of two independent effects, as follows: (1) the requirements of the law of conservation of energy (first law of thermodynamics), and (2) an entropy increase in an essentially closed system
through dissipative viscosity. To be sure, the entropy increase through dissipative viscosity is a sufficient condition (in the *statistical* sense of my Section 5, below) for the irreversibility of the outgoing wave motion, i.e., for the
absence of a corresponding (spontaneously initiated) contracting wave motion. But this fact cannot detract from the soundness of Popper's claim that
the nonexistence of a spontaneously contracting water wave does not depend
on the fact that actual outgoing waves involve an entropy increase through
dissipative viscosity. For, let us consider an idealized outgoing water wave
whose propagation involves no entropy increase because there is no
amplitude-diminution due to dissipative viscosity. It is then clear that the initial conditions requisite for the corresponding contracting water wave do not
occur spontaneously. Hence the spontaneous *non*occurrence of the latter initial conditions is itself sufficient to assure that outgoing water waves are *de
facto* irreversible in Popper's conditional sense. And we see that he rightly ad-
duces the need for the *coherence* of these initial conditions as his basis for
denying the possibility of their spontaneous concatenation, i.e., their concatenation without first having been coordinated by an influence emanating
from a central source. Says he (Irreversibility III):

> Only such conditions can be causally realized as can be organized from one cen-
> tre . . . causes which are not centrally correlated are causally unrelated, and can
> co-operate [i.e., produce coherence in the form of isotropic contraction of waves
> to a precise point] only by accident. . . . The probability of such an accident will
> be zero.

Note, however, that in a spatially *finite* system it is indeed possible to produce *non*spontaneously the initial conditions for contracting waves and for implosions of gas particles which converge to a point. Thus, assuming negligible viscosity, there are expanding water waves in finite systems of which the temporal inverses could be produced nonspontaneously by dropping a very large circular object onto the water surface so that all parts of the circular object strike the water surface simultaneously. And hence there are conditions under which contracting waves do actually exist in finite systems. But Popper's spontaneity proviso is not necessary to assert the *de facto* irreversibility of the eternal expansion of a spherical light wave from a center through infinite space. If space is infinite, the existence of the latter process of expansion is assured by the facts of observation in conjunction with electromagnetic theory; but despite the fact that the laws for a homogeneous and isotropic medium allow the inverse process no less than the actual one,[7] we never encounter the inverse process of spherical waves closing in isotropically to a sharp point of extinction.

In response to the first two of his notes, E. L. Hill and I endorsed Popper's contention of the existence of a nonentropic species of *de facto* irreversibility.[8] But we were able to dispense with Popper's restrictive proviso of spontaneity by asserting the following: if the universe is spatially infinite, then there are outgoing centrosymmetric processes which do not involve any (Boltzmannian) entropy increase but are unconditionally *de facto* irreversible and extend over infinite space and time. Thus, the processes in infinite space considered by Hill and myself are *de facto* irreversible categorically. By contrast, Popper's processes are merely *conditionally de facto* irreversible by lacking only *spontaneously*-produced temporal inverses. Without presuming to speak for Professor Hill, I can say, for my part, that in making that existential claim I was guided by the following considerations:

(i) Popper (Irreversibility II) briefly remarks correctly that the eternal expansion of a very thin gas from a center·into a spatially infinite universe does not involve an entropy increase, and the *de facto* irreversibility of this process is therefore nonentropic. For by its definition as a measure of frequency of occurrence in time, the statistical Maxwell-Boltzmann entropy is assigned on the assumption that all coarse-grained microstates are equiprobable, and, as a result, is not even defined for a spatially infinite universe: the quasi-ergodic hypothesis, which provides the essential basis for the stated equiprobability ingredient in the Maxwell-Boltzmann entropy concept, is presumably false for an infinite phase-space, since walls are required to produce the collisions which are essential to its validity. In the absence of some kind of wall, whose very existence would assure the finitude of the system, the rapidly moving particles will soon overtake those moving slowly, leaving them ever further behind for all future eternity instead of mixing with them in a space-filling manner. Thus, in a spatially infinite universe, the equiprobability assumption for all microstates is at best unfounded or simply false. Moreover, if the number of particles in the infinite universe is only finite, the state of maximum entropy then does *not* correspond to a *uniform* distribution of the particles among the cells of the phase space, since a finite number of particles cannot be uniformly distributed in a phase space of infinitely many cells. On the other hand, if the number n of particles is denumerably infinite, the number W of microscopic complexions in $S = k \log W$ becomes infinite, and no entropy increase or decrease is defined, since $W = n!/\Pi n_i!$, where the symbol "Π" means product, so that the denominator of the expression for W is the product of the factorials of the numbers n_i ($i = 1, 2, 3 \ldots$) of particles in the various cells.

Despite these strictures on the applicability of the probability-metric of the Maxwell-Boltzmann entropy concept to a spatially infinite universe, the physicist Robert B. Griffiths has called my attention to the following: A generalized coarse-grained entropy function $S = k \log W$ is definable for a spatially infinite universe so as to have some physically interesting uses in just the kind of case considered by Popper, viz., the expansion of a thin ideal gas with a finite number n of noninteracting particles from a central point in a spatially infinite universe. Thus, for a suitable choice of the cell size of the coarse-grained 6-dimensional position-velocity phase space, all of the n particles of the thin gas might start out in one cell even though their precise velocities are all different while still falling within the ranges of the increments in the velocity components corresponding to the chosen cell size. For this initial state, the numerical value of W will be 1, being given by $n!/n!$, since all of the other terms in the denominator of the expression for W are 0! and hence have the value 1. Since the particles are presumed to be essentially noninteracting, their respective velocities will not change. And hence Griffiths points out that if one waits long enough, they will each be in a *different* cell of the chosen partitioning of the phase space, so that W will then be $n!$. Not only will W thus have *increased* from 1 to $n!$, but W never needs to decrease again, since the recurrence time will be infinite. A corresponding increase will, of course, take place in the values of S. More generally, Griffiths notes that for a suitable partitioning of the position-velocity phase space, there are many cases where W and hence S will increase quasi-monotonically with time, i.e., with only occasional downward fluctuations. And this conclusion is *not* made to depend on any assumption of a probability metric for the coarse-grained microstates.

In the light of Griffiths's proposed generalization of S to the case of a spatially infinite universe, it is to be understood hereafter that when I refer to Popper's *de facto* unreversed processes as "nonentropic", I mean that they are nonentropic in the specified full-blown Maxwell-Boltzmann sense, but I allow that, in the spatially infinite case, they *may* be entropic in the weaker generalized sense of R. B. Griffiths.

(ii) Though allowed by the laws of mechanics, there seem to exist no 'implosions' at all which would qualify as the temporal inverses of eternally progressing 'explosions' of very thin gases from a center into infinite space. In the light of this fact, one can assert the *de facto* irreversibility of an eternal 'explosion' *unconditionally*, i.e., without Popper's restrictive proviso of spontaneity with regard to the production of the coherent initial conditions requisite for its inverse. For in an infinite space, there is no possibility at all of even a *non*spontaneous production of the coherent 'initial' conditions for an implosion having the following properties: the gas particles converge to a point, after having been moving through infinite space for all past eternity, in a manner constituting the temporal inverse of the expansion of a very thin gas from a point for all future eternity. There can be no question of a nonspontaneous realization of the 'initial' conditions required for the latter kind of implosion, since that would involve a self-contradictory condition akin to that in Kant's fallacious First Antinomy: the requirement that a process which has been going on for all infinite past time must have had a finite beginning (production by past initial conditions) after all.

In view of the decisive role of the infinitude or 'openness' of a physical system (the universe)—as opposed to the finitude of closed systems—in rendering Popper's spontaneity proviso dispensable, Hill and I[9] made the following existential claim concerning processes whose irreversibility is non-entropic and *de facto* in 'open' (infinite) systems:

> In classical mechanics the closed systems have quasi-periodic orbits, whereas the open systems have at least some aperiodic orbits which extend to infinity . . . there exists a fundamental distinction between the two kinds of system in the following sense. In open systems there always exists a class of allowed elementary processes the inverses of which are unacceptable on physical grounds by requiring a *deus ex machina* for their production. For example, in an open universe, matter or radiation can travel away indefinitely from the 'finite' region of space, and so be permanently lost. The inverse process would require matter or radiant energy coming from 'infinity', and so would involve a process which is not realizable by physical sources. Einstein's example of an outgoing light wave and Popper's analogous case of a water wave are special finite illustrations of this principle.

Note also that in their subsequent paper of 1962 on "The Direction of Time,"[10] Penrose and Percival independently introduced the core idea underlying the revision of Popper's claim set forth by Hill and myself. Specifically, they derive their fundamental principle of temporal asymmetry or "law of conditional independence" from the assumption that "the causal influences coming from infinity in different directions are independent" and hence not coherent.

I was therefore quite puzzled to find that the communication by Hill and myself prompted the following dissent by Popper (Irreversibility III):

> In this connection, I must express some doubt as to whether the principle proposed by Profs. Hill and Grünbaum is adequate. In formulating their principle, they operate with two ideas: that of the 'openness' of a system, and that of a *deus ex machina*. Both seem to me insufficient. For a system consisting of a sun, and a comet coming from infinity and describing a hyperbolic path around the sun, seems to me to satisfy all the criteria stated by them. The system is open; and the reversion of the comet on its track would require *a deus ex machina for* its realization: it would 'require matter . . . coming from "infinity".' Nevertheless, this is an example of just that kind of process which, I take it, we all wish to describe as completely reversible.

Popper's proposed counterexample of the comet coming from "infinity" into the solar system seems to me to fail for the following reasons: (1) neither the actual motion of the comet nor its inverse involve any *coherence*, a feature which I, for my part, had conceived to be essential to the obtaining of nonentropic *de facto* irreversibility in open systems. In my own view, the fact that particles or photons came from "infinity" in the course of an infinite past does not per se require a *deus ex machina*, any more than does their going to "infinity" in the course of an infinite future: in this context, I regard as innocuous the asymmetry involved in the fact that a particle which has come from infinity can be said to have traversed an infinite space by *now*, whereas a particle embarking on an infinite journey will only have traversed a *finite* distance at *any one time* in the future. It is a *coherent* 'implosion' from infinity that I believe to require a *deus ex machina*, i.e., to be *de facto* nonexistent, while coherent 'explosions' actually do exist. (2) Even ignoring the fact that the motion of Popper's comet does not involve coherence, the issue is *not*, as he seems to think, whether it would require a *deus ex machina* to produce the reversal of any given actual comet in its track; rather, the issue is whether, if no *deus ex machina* would be needed to realize the actual comet motion, a *deus ex machina* would be needed to have another comet execute *instead* a motion inverse to the first one. The answer to this question is an emphatic *no*. Unlike the case of outgoing and contracting waves (explosions and implosions), the two comet motions, which are temporal inverses of each other, are *on a par* with respect to the role of a *deus ex machina* in their realization. And even the reversal of the motion of an actual comet at a suitable point in its orbit might in fact be effected by an elastic collision with an oppositely moving other comet of equal mass, and hence would *not* involve, as Popper would have it (Irreversibility III), "a *deus ex machina* who is something like a gigantic tennis player."

It seems to me, therefore, that far from being vulnerable to Popper's proposed counterexample, the existential claim by Hill and myself is fully as viable as Popper's, while having the merit of achieving generality through freedom from Popper's spontaneity proviso. I therefore cannot see any justification at all for the following two assertions which H. Mehlberg made in a very informative paper: (1) He states incorrectly that Hill and I have claimed *de facto* irreversibility for "the class of all conceivable physical processes provided that the latter meet the mild requirement of happening in an 'open' physical system," and (2) he asserts that "Popper has shown the untenability of the Hill-Grünbaum criterion by constructing an effective counterexample which illustrates the impossibility of their sweeping generalization of his original criterion."[11]

Mehlberg's critical estimate of Popper's own affirmation of nonentropic *de facto* irreversibility likewise seems to me to be unconvincing in important respects. After asking whether the irreversibility asserted by Popper is "lawlike or factlike"—a question to which the answer is: 'avowedly factlike'—Mehlberg[12] concludes that Popper's temporal asymmetry "seems to be rather interpretable as a local, factlike particularity of the terrestrial surface than as a universal, lawlike feature . . . which may be expected to materialize always and everywhere." There are two points in Mehlberg's conclusion which invite comment: (1) the significance he attaches to the circumstance that the irreversibility of certain classes of processes is *de facto* or factlike rather than nomological or lawlike, when he assesses the bearing of that irreversibility on the issue of anisotropy versus isotropy of time, and (2) the contrast between the epistemological parsimony of Mehlberg's characterization of Popper's irreversibility as a "local . . . particularity of the terrestrial surface" and the inductive boldness of his willingness to affirm a cosmically pervasive nomological isotropy of time on the basis of attributing cosmic relevance, both spatially and temporally, to the fundamental time-symmetric laws which have been confirmed in modern man's limited sample of the universe.

As to the first of these two points in Mehlberg's denial of the anisotropy of time, I note preliminarily that human hopes for an eternal biological life are no less surely frustrated if all men are indeed *de facto* mortal, i.e., mortal on the strength of 'boundary conditions' which do obtain permanently, than if man's mortality were assured by some law. By the same token, I see no escape from the conclusion that if *de facto* irreversibility does actually obtain everywhere and forever, such irreversibility confers anisotropy on time. And this anisotropy prevails not one iota less than it would if its existence were guaranteed by temporally *asymmetrical* fundamental *laws* of cosmic scope. It is of considerable interest, of course, if such irreversibility as obtains in nature is *de facto* rather than nomological. But, in my view, when evaluating the evidence for the anisotropy of time, Mehlberg engages in misplaced emphasis: he wrongly discounts *de facto* irreversibility vis-à-vis nomological irreversibility by failing to show that our warrant for a cosmic extrapolation

of time-symmetric *laws* is actually greater than for a corresponding extrapolation of the factlike conditions making for observed *de facto* irreversibility. For on what grounds can it be maintained that the ubiquitous and
permanent existence of the *de facto* probabilities of "boundary conditions"
on which Popper rests his affirmation of temporal anisotropy is less well confirmed than that of those laws on whose time-symmetry Mehlberg is willing
to base his *denial* of the anisotropy of time?

In particular, one wonders how Mehlberg could inductively justify his
contention that we are only confirming a "particularity of the terrestrial surface" when we find with Popper (Irreversibility III) that:

> Only such conditions can be causally realized as can be organized from one cen-
> tre . . . causes which are not centrally correlated are causally unrelated, and can
> co-operate [i.e., produce coherence in the form of *isotropic* contraction of waves
> to a precise point] only by accident. . . . The probability of such an accident will
> be zero.

If this finding cannot be presumed to hold on all planetlike bodies in the universe, for example, then why are we entitled to assume with Mehlberg that
time-symmetric laws of mechanics, for example, are exemplified by the
motions of binary stars throughout the universe? Since I see no valid grounds
for Mehlberg's double standard of inductive credibility of pervasiveness as
between laws and factlike regularities, I consider his negative estimate of
Popper's nonentropic *de facto* anisotropy of time as unfounded.

Mehlberg presents an account of the reversibility status of the process
constituted by the concentric spread of light from a point source. He does *not*
offer this account as a basis for objecting to Popper's conception, but rather
as further support for his own disparagement of the significance of any
irreversibility which is *de facto* rather than lawlike. But if Mehlberg's account
were indeed correct, then it would have the following two important consequences: (1) the photon character of light would make for a telling optical
counterexample to Popper's conditional assertion of *de facto* irreversibility,
and (2) in the context of present-day assumptions concerning the symmetries
in the spatial distribution of stars and galaxies, the centrosymmetric emission
and propagation of light from a point P would be *de facto* irreversible *only
because* of the expansion of the universe, i.e., only because the stellar light
sources lying on spheres about P are *receding* from P, so that the energy
$E = h\nu$ of light received at P is very low due to the drastic reduction of its frequency by a Doppler shift. It therefore behooves us to examine Mehlberg's
account. He writes:[13]

> A less speculative example of cosmological irreversibility is provided by the
> propagation of light *in vacuo*, which several authors have discussed from this
> point of view. . . . In accordance with Maxwell's theory of light conceived as an
> electromagnetic phenomenon, they point out that light emitted by a pointlike

source, or converging towards a point, can spread on concentric spherical surfaces which either expand or contract monotonically. Yet, independently of Maxwell's theory, the incidence of expanding optical spheres is known to exceed by far the incidence of shrinking optical spheres. The reason for this statistical superiority of expanding optical spheres is simply the fact that pointlike light-emitting atoms are much more numerous than perfectly spherical, opaque surfaces capable of generating shrinking optical spheres, mainly by the process of reflection. If true, this ratio of the incidences of both types of light waves would provide a cosmological clue to a pervasive irreversibility of a particular class of optical processes.

The bearing of this optical irreversibility upon time's arrow was often discussed. A long time before the asymmetry of expanding and contracting light waves was promoted to the rank of time's arrow, Einstein[14] pointed out that the asymmetry of these two types of optical propagation holds only on the undulatory theory of light. Once light is identified instead with a swarm of photons, the asymmetry vanishes. This conclusion holds at least for a spatially finite universe or for optical phenomena confined to a finite spatial region.

Once more, however, the decisive point seems to be that the asymmetry between the two types of light waves depends on factual, initial conditions which prevail in a given momentary cross section of cosmic history or at the 'boundaries' of a finite or infinite universe rather than on nomological considerations concerning this history: any other ratio of the incidences of expanding and shrinking light waves would also be in keeping with the relevant laws of nature contained in Maxwell's theory of electromagnetic phenomena. Of course, the aforementioned non-nomological conditions, responsible for the factual ratio of these incidences, are not 'local' either, since the *whole* world is involved—they belong to cosmology. These conditions are nevertheless factlike rather than lawlike, as a comparison with the pertinent laws which can be derived from Maxwell's theory clearly shows.[15]

To assess the adequacy of Mehlberg's account, let us first quote the pertinent statement from the 1909 paper by Einstein cited by him.[16] Being concerned to note that the wave theory of light fails to account for a phenomenon like the photoelectric effect, in which a large amount of energy suddenly appears at a single point even if the light intensity is very low, Einstein writes there:[17]

> The basic feature of the wave theory, which entails these difficulties, seems to me to be rooted in the following: Whereas in the kinetic molecular theory there exists an inverse process for every process involving only a small number of elementary particles, for example for every collision of molecules, this is not the case for elementary processes of radiation according to the wave theory. According to that familiar theory, an oscillating ion produces an expanding spherical wave. The reverse process does not exist as an *elementary process*. To be sure, a contracting spherical wave is possible mathematically; but its approximate realization requires an enormous number of emitting elementary structures. Thus the elementary process of light emission as such does not have the attribute of reversibility. I believe that, in this respect, our wave theory is in error. It would appear that in respect to this point Newton's corpuscular theory of light contains more truth than the wave theory, since according to the former the energy imparted to a light particle upon emission is not scattered over infinite space but

remains available for an elementary process of absorption. Think of the laws of the production of secondary cathode rays by x-rays . . . the elementary process of radiation appears to proceed such that it does not distribute and scatter the energy of the primary electron via a spherical wave which propagates itself in all directions, as demanded by the wave theory. Instead, it appears that at least a large part of this energy is available at some one place or other. . . . *The elementary process of radiation emission appears to be [spatially] directional.*[18]

It would seem that the proper conclusions relevant to the reversibility status of concentric light propagation which are to be drawn from Einstein's statement here are the following:[19]

Let a large but finite number of observers or other absorption-instruments be uniformly distributed on a spatial sphere about the point P as center. If now a single light quantum is emitted at P, then these observers could *not* each register light coming from P. Hence if light does spread centrosymmetrically about P such that each of our large number of absorbers on the sphere register its arrival simultaneously, then the required light emission at P *cannot* be an *elementary* process in the context of the photon theory. Indeed in the case of such light emission, the point P would qualify as a source of *coherent* light from the point of view of the wave theory in the following sense: if two neighboring observers Q and R on the sphere were each to pipe through a slit the light received through repeated emissions at P, then the slits at Q and R would be *coherent* sources of light in virtue of giving rise to stable interference patterns on a suitably placed screen in the manner of Young's double-slit experiment. But a light emission from P which is coherent in the sense of having this capability is one for which the *number* of photons emanating from P is *not* defined (determinate) in quantum electrodynamics, since the respective operators corresponding to coherence and to the number of photons do not commute in its theoretical formalism. What follows then from the fact that the *elementary* process of single photon emission is reversible as explained by Einstein?

This reversibility does not seem to sustain Mehlberg's contention that "the asymmetry of expanding and contracting light . . . propagation holds only on the undulatory theory of light. Once light is identified instead with a swarm of photons, the asymmetry vanishes." Specifically, suppose that a group of stars or other light sources which are uniformly distributed on a sphere about P each simultaneously though *independently* emit photons of a certain frequency toward P, thereby producing a centrosymmetrically *contracting* swarm of photons. Then it does *not* follow from the reversibility of the elementary process of photon emission that this contracting light configuration qualifies as the temporal inverse of our optically *coherent*, centrosymmetrically *expanding* light disturbance. Indeed, there is every reason to think that our *spontaneously* produced contracting light configuration does not so qualify, and hence that the electromagnetic *de facto* irreversibility of centrosymmetric light propagation at issue holds for this *non*elementary process in the photon theory of light no less than in the wave theory. Let this be granted. Then our *de facto* optical irreversibility does *not* depend on the recession of the stellar light sources from the point P(expansion of the universe), although that expansion makes for the darkness of the sky at night. For even in the absence of the recession of the stellar light sources, a spherically distributed set of these would not spontaneously produce an optically coherent contracting configuration of photons.

Accordingly, Popper's conditional assertion of *de facto* irreversibility is not invalidated by the reversibility of the elementary process of photon emission. Nor is the significance of Popper's assertion lessened by the consequences of the expansion of the universe. Furthermore, for the reasons given above, the *de facto* rather than nomological character of the irreversibility of centrosymmetric light propagation does not disqualify this optical process as a physical basis for the anisotropy of time.

5. *Is There Also a Thermodynamic Basis for the Arrow of Time?*

Popper has expressed his denial of the relevance of the statistical entropy law to the anisotropy of time as follows:

> The suggestion has been made (first by Boltzmann himself) that the arrow of time is, either by its very nature, or by definition, connected with the increase in entropy; so that entropy cannot decrease in time because a decrease would mean a reversal of its arrow, and therefore an increase relative to the reversed arrow. Much as I admire the boldness of this idea, I think that it is absurd, especially in view of the undeniable fact that thermodynamic fluctuations do exist. One would have to assert that, within the spatial region of the fluctuation, all clocks run backwards if seen from outside that region. But this assertion would destroy that very system of dynamics on which the statistical theory is founded. (Moreover, most clocks are non-entropic systems, in the sense that their heat production, far from being essential to their function, is inimical to it.)
>
> I do not believe that Boltzmann would have made his suggestion after 1905, when fluctuations, previously considered no more than mathematically calculable near-impossibilities, suddenly became the strongest evidence in favour of. the physical reality of molecules. (I am alluding to Einstein's theory of Brownian motion.) As it is, a statistical theory of the arrow of time seems to me unacceptable. The purpose of my first communication was to propose an example of a non-statistical process such that no physicist who finds a film strip of this particular process would need to doubt where the film begins and where it ends: he could determine its arrow of time.[20]

More recently, Popper has presented the following further arguments in an endeavor to show that the statistics of thermodynamic phenomena cannot be validly regarded as a physical foundation for the anisotropy of time:

... we can split the change of entropy dS_X in any system X into two parts: dS_{X_e}, or the flow of entropy due to interaction with the exterior of X, and dS_{X_i}, the contribution to the change of entropy due to changes inside the system X. We have of course:

$$dS_X = dS_{X_e} + dS_{X_i} \qquad (1)$$

and we can express the second law by:

$$dS_{X_i} \geq 0 \qquad (2)$$

For an energetically closed (or 'isolated') system X, for which by definition $dS_{X_e} = 0$, expression (2) formulates the classical statement that entropy never decreases. But if X is open towards a cooler exterior:

$$dS_{X_e} < 0 \qquad (3)$$

holds, and the question whether its total entropy increases or decreases depends, of course, on both its entropy production dS_{X_i} and its entropy loss dS_{X_e}.

... With very few and short-lived exceptions, the entropy in almost all known regions (of sufficient size) of our universe either remains constant or decreases, although energy is dissipated (by escaping from the system in question). ...

... in almost all sufficiently large systems known to us, entropy production seems to be equalled, or even exceeded, by entropy loss through heat radiation. ...

So there do not seem to be theoretical or empirical reasons to attribute to expression (2) any cosmic significance or to connect 'time's arrow' with that expression; especially since the equality sign in expression (2) may hold for almost all cosmical regions (and especially for regions empty of matter). Moreover, we have good reason to interpret expression (2) as a statistical law; while the 'arrow' of time, or the 'flow' of time, does not seem to be of a stochastic character: nothing suggests that it is subject to statistical fluctuation, or connected with a law of large numbers.[21]

I shall now endeavor to show in detail that *when coupled with specified assumptions as to the boundary conditions*, (1) the statistical behavior of the entropy of physical systems does qualify as a basis for a statistical anisotropy of time, and (2) the modified version of Boltzmann's basic conception to be set forth is *not* beset by any of the absurdities adduced by Popper. And I shall then give my reasons for being unconvinced by the further arguments against a thermodynamic basis for the anisotropy of time which Popper put forward in 1965 (in Irreversibility V).

We saw that the *non*entropic irreversibilities countenanced by Popper as a criterion of temporal anisotropy depend on the role played by boundary conditions (in conjunction with the relevant laws). And we shall see that in the context of entropic phenomena, a statistical anisotropy of time is also *not* assured by the laws alone but rather by their conjunction with certain boundary conditions to be specified. Indeed, the complete time symmetry of the basic laws like those of dynamics is entirely compatible with the existence of contingent irreversibility (unreversedness). In the concise and apt words of Penrose and Percival, the reason for this compatibility is that "dynamics relates the states of a system at two different times, but it puts no restriction whatever on the state at any one time, nor on the probability distribution at any one time." (See p. 606 of the reference given in n. 10.)

We shall now find that finite thermodynamic systems which are closed for only relatively *short* time periods exhibit an entropy behavior which is contingently statistically irreversible. H. Reichenbach has given a detailed discussion of the kind of thermodynamic irreversibility which we are about to consider.[22] But since I believe that Reichenbach's treatment requires significant modification in order to be satisfactory, I shall now set forth what I believe to be a corrected elaboration of his main conception.

Reichenbach points out that there are subsystems which branch off from the wider solar system, galactic system, or from other portions of the universe, remain quasi-closed for a *limited* period of time, and then merge again with the wider system from which they had been separated. And he uses the term "branch-system" to designate this kind of subsystem.[23] Branch-systems are formed not only in the natural course of things, but also through human intervention, such as when an ice cube is placed into a glass of warm gingerale by a waiter and then covered for hygienic purposes until it merges with the wider universe by being consumed by a person. Most but not all branch-systems branch off in initial states of relatively low entropy which are the products of their earlier coupling or interaction with outside agencies of one kind or another. This rather constant and ubiquitous formation of a branch-system in a relatively low entropy state resulting from interaction often proceeds at the expense of an entropy increase in some wider quasi-closed system from which it originated. And the *de facto* occurrence of these branch-systems, which is contingent with respect to the laws of nature, has the following *fundamental consequence*, at least for our region of the universe and during the current epoch: among the quasi-closed systems whose entropy is relatively low and which behave as if they might remain isolated, the vast majority have not been and will not remain permanently-closed systems, being branch-systems instead.

Hence, upon encountering a quasi-closed system in a state of fairly low entropy, we know the following to be overwhelmingly probable: the system has *not* been isolated for millions and millions of years and does *not* just *happen* to be in one of the infrequent but ever-recurring low entropy states exhibited by a permanently-isolated system. Instead, our system was formed not too long ago by branching off after an interaction with an outside agency. For example, suppose that an American geologist is wandering in an isolated portion of the Sahara desert in search of an oasis and encounters a portion of the sand in the shape of 'Coca-Cola'. He would then infer that, with overwhelming probability, a kindred person had interacted with the sand in the recent past by tracing 'Coca-Cola' in it. The geologist would not suppose that he was in the presence of one of those relatively low entropy configurations which are assumed by the sand particles spontaneously but very rarely, if beaten about by winds for millions upon millions of years in a state of effective isolation from the remainder of the world.

Branch systems have a property which has the character of a *boundary condition* in the context of (coarse-grained) classical statistical mechanics and which enters into the temporally asymmetrical statistical regularities which we shall find to be exhibited in the entropic behavior of these systems. This property consists in the following *randomness* obtaining *as a matter of contingent fact* in the occurrence of the microstates belonging to the initial macrostates of a *space* ensemble of branch-systems, each of which has the same initial entropy $S_1 = k \log W_1$: for each class of *like* branch-systems having the *same* initial entropy value S_1, the microstates constituting the identical initial macrostates of entropy S_1 are *random samples* of the set of all microstates yielding a macrostate of entropy S_1.[24] This attribute of randomness of microstates on the part of the initial states of the members of the space ensemble will be recognized as the counterpart of the following attribute of the microstates of one single, permanently closed system: there is equiprobability of occurrence among the microstates belonging to the *time* ensemble of states of equal entropy $S_1 = k \log W_1$ exhibited by one single, permanently-closed system.

We can now state the statistical regularities which obtain as a consequence of the *de facto* contingent properties of branch-systems just set forth, when coupled with the principles of statistical mechanics. These regularities, which will be seen to yield a temporally asymmetric statistical behavior of the entropy of branch-systems, fall into two main groups as follows.

Group 1. In most space ensembles of quasi-closed branch-systems each of which is initially in a state of nonequilibrium of relatively *low* entropy, the majority of branch-systems in the ensemble will have *higher* entropies *after* a given time t.[25] But these branch-systems simply did not exist as quasi-closed, distinct systems at a time t *prior* to the occurrence of their initial, branching-off states. Hence, not existing then as such, the branch-systems did in fact *not* also exhibit the same higher entropy states at the *earlier* times t, which they would indeed have done then had they existed as closed systems all along.

The increase after a time t in the entropy of the overwhelming majority of branch-systems of initially low entropy—as confirmed abundantly by observation—can be made fully intelligible. To do so, we note the following property of the *time* ensemble of entropy values belonging to a single, permanently-closed system and then affirm that property of the space ensembles of branch-systems: since *large* entropic downgrades or decreases are *far less* probable (frequent) than moderate ones, the *vast majority* of *non*-equilibrium entropy states of a permanently-closed system are located either at or in the immediate temporal vicinity of the *bottom* of a *dip* of the one-system entropy curve. In short, the vast majority of the *sub*maximum entropy states are on or temporally very near the *upgrades* of the one-system curve. The application of this result to the space ensemble of branch-systems whose initial states exhibit the aforementioned *de facto* property of randomness then yields the following: among the initial low entropy states of these systems, the vast majority lie at or in the immediate temporal vicinity of the bottoms of the one-system entropy curve at which an upgrade begins.

Group 2. A decisive *temporal asymmetry* in the statistics of the temporal evolution of branch-systems arises from the further result that in most space ensembles of branch-systems each of whose members is initially in a state of *equilibrium* or very *high* entropy (for example, a covered glass of lukewarm water just drawn from a reservoir of water at the same uniform temperature), the vast majority of these systems in the ensemble will *not* have *lower* entropies *after* a finite time *t*, but will still be in equilibrium.[26] For the aforementioned randomness property assures that the vast majority of those branch-systems whose initial states are equilibrium states have maximum entropy values lying somewhere *well within* the plateau of the one-system entropy curve, rather than at the extremity of the plateau at which an entropy *decrease* is initiated.[27]

We see therefore that, in the vast majority of branch-systems, either one end of their finite entropy curves is a point of low entropy and the other a point of high entropy, or they are in equilibrium states at both ends as well as during the intervening interval. And it is likewise apparent that the statistical distribution of these entropy values on the time axis is such that the vast majority of branch-systems have the *same direction of entropy increase* and hence also the same opposite direction of entropy decrease. Thus, the statistics of entropy increase among branch-systems assures that in most space ensembles the vast majority of branch-systems will increase their entropy in *one* of the two opposite time directions and decrease it in the other. In this way, *the entropic behavior of branch-systems confers the same statistical anisotropy on the vast majority of all those epochs of time during which the universe exhibits the requisite disequilibrium and contains branch-systems satisfying initial conditions of 'randomness'.*

Let us now call the direction of entropy increase of a typical representative of these epochs the direction of 'later', as indeed we have done from the outset by the mere assignment of higher time numbers in that direction, but without prejudice to our findings concerning the issue of the anisotropy of time. Then our results pertaining to the entropic behavior of branch-systems show that the directions of 'earlier than' and 'later than' are not merely opposite directions bearing decreasing and increasing time coordinates respectively, but are statistically *anisotropic* in an objective physical sense. This statistical anisotropy is an objective *macroscopic* fact even though the behavior of the entropy function as a mathematical entity depends on human choices as to the size of the cells in phase space.[28]

As we just saw, the entropic statistical anisotropy of time can be described without having to characterize the direction of entropy increase as the direction of increasing time coordinates. Thus, this anisotropy surely does not depend on our assigning the lower of two time coordinates t_1 and t_2 to the lower of two entropy states of a branch-system. Nor is that anisotropy implicit in designating the lower of these two states as the 'initial' state rather than as the 'final' state, a designation which results from the customary coordinatization of the time continuum. Using either the usual time coordinatization or one obtained from it via the transformation $t \rightarrow -t$, we are able to assert that for each branch-system there is a finite time interval $t_1 \leq t \leq t_2$ to which its existence is confined. And if the boundary conditions governing the branch-systems are specified for *either one* of the extremities of their finite careers, then the one-system entropy curve yields both the states of these systems at their other extremities and their behavior during the intervening time. Let us now utilize the latter fact to clarify our results further by showing the following: the same entropic statistical anisotropy of time results *both* from the boundary conditions governing the initial states at time t_1 *and* also from those pertaining to the final states at time t_2.

If we use the language of the usual time coordinatization, we can assert that during a cosmic epoch of disequilibrium, the following is a *de facto* property of a typical space ensemble of branch-systems which form at a given time t_1: a good many of its members are in relatively low entropy states at the given time t_1 ('subclass A'), while others are in essentially equilibrium states at that time ('subclass B'). Now let us be mindful of the aforementioned randomness of the initial states at t_1 and of the fact that branch-systems do not as such endure for a period comparable to that of a typical entropy plateau of the one-system curve. Then we see that at the time t_2 ($t_2 > t_1$), the existing A-systems and B-systems are in entropy states as follows: higher states of the A-systems at time t_2 lie temporally near or at the near *extremity of a plateau* of the one-system curve, whereas the equilibrium states of the B-systems prevailing at time t_2 lie *well within a plateau* of the one-system curve. Again using the language of the usual time coordinatization, the boundary conditions can be given *alternatively* for the time t_2 by the following compound specification: (1) At time t_2, there exist branch systems (of type 'A') which are in relatively high entropy states lying temporally very near or at the extremity of a plateau of the one-system curve; hence the microstates underlying these high entropy states of the A-systems are *not* random (typical) samples of the totality of microstates, each one of which constitutes a macrostate of the same high entropy, and (2) at time t_2, there also exist branch systems (of type

'B') which are in equilibrium states lying well within a plateau of the one-system curve; hence the microstates underlying the equilibrium states of these B-systems are indeed random (typical) samples of the totality of microstates, each one of which constitutes an equilibrium state of the same entropy.

But if we are thus given that at the time t_2 branch systems of types A and B exist in high entropy states *as specified*, then the one-system entropy curve tells us that the A-systems *decrease* their entropies in the direction of time t_1 while the B-systems maintain equilibrium states in that direction. For this curve shows us that the 'nonrandom' high states of the A-systems at time t_2 evolved from lower ones at time t_1, whereas the 'random' equilibrium states of the B-systems at time t_2 came from like equilibrium states prevailing throughout their careers. It is now clear that, if the boundary conditions are correctly specified for *either one* of the two ends of the careers of the branch systems, the otherwise time-symmetric one-system entropy curve yields a statistical anisotropy of time. And it is further evident that the same conclusion would have been reached, if the *de facto* obtaining boundary conditions had been correspondingly codified in a time language based on replacing the usual time coordinatization according to the transformation $t \rightarrow -t$.

It should be noted that I have characterized the positive direction of time as the direction of entropy increase for a *typical representative* of all those epochs of time during which the universe exhibits the requisite disequilibrium and contains branch systems satisfying initial conditions of 'randomness'. Accordingly, it is entirely possible and consistent to speak of the *atypically* behaving branch systems, whose entropy increases are *counterdirected* with respect to those of the majority, as *decreasing* their entropies in the positive direction of time. Since we are able to give the usual temporal description of fluctuation phenomena in this way, I must therefore reject the cited argument by Karl Popper, which he offered in an endeavor to show that a thermodynamic basis for the relation 'later than' yields an absurd temporal description of fluctuation phenomena.

This brings me to my doubts concerning Popper's further arguments of 1965, which relate to equations (1), (2), and (3) in my citation from his Irreversibility V. My reasons for being unconvinced by them are the following:

1. Most of the systems which we encounter in our physical environment and whose (thermodynamic) behavior we observe are *not* Popper's "sufficiently large systems" (for example, our solar system, known stars) for which dS_x is zero or even negative; instead, they are systems for which $dS_x = dS_{x_i}$ to a fairly good approximation and which qualify as branch-systems in Reichenbach's sense (for example, mixing processes such as hot and cold water forming a lukewarm mixture, wood burning in a fireplace, floating ice melting in a lake). Hence the failure of dS_x to be positive in the minority case

of "sufficiently large systems" cannot detract from the fact that for the majority of the relevant systems, the total entropy change dS_x is indeed adequately rendered by equation (2). Thus, while there is an interesting sense in which the existence of Popper's sufficiently large systems erodes the "cosmic significance" of equation (2), he is apparently not entitled to his conclusion that there is no reason to connect time's arrow with that equation.

2. When Popper declares that "the 'arrow' of time . . . does not seem to be of a stochastic character," one must ask what context of experience or presumed fact he is invoking in support of this statement. Surely the daily experiences of life as conceptualized in common sense are not competent to yield a verdict on the stochasticity of those physical features of the world which are presumed to constitute the foundations for the observed 'arrow'.

I have contended against Popper that the entropic behavior of branch systems confers the *same* statistical anisotropy on the vast majority of all those cosmic epochs of time during which the universe exhibits the requisite disequilibrium and contains branch-systems satisfying the specified initial conditions of 'randomness'. My conclusion that the *same* statistical anisotropy pervasively characterizes the overwhelming majority of the cosmic epochs of disequilibrium is supported by the findings of Penrose and Percival, who reject Boltzmann's contrary view on the basis of their Law of Conditional Independence.[29] But my claim of statistical anisotropy departs significantly from Reichenbach's "hypothesis of the branch structure"[30] in two ways. (1) Since the universe may be spatially infinite, I do *not* assume with Reichenbach that the entropy is defined for the entire universe such that the universe as a whole can be presumed to exhibit the entropic evolution of the statistical entropy curve for a permanently closed, *finite* system. Therefore (2) I do *not* conclude, as Reichenbach does, that there is a parallelism of the direction of entropy increase of the universe and of the branch-systems at any time, such that cosmically the statistical anisotropy of time is only local by 'fluctuating' in the sense that the supposed alternations of epochs of entropy increase and decrease of the universe go hand in hand with the alleged alternations of the direction of entropy increase in the ensembles of branch-systems associated with those respective epochs, successive disequilibrium epochs allegedly being entropically *counterdirected* with respect to each other.

In view of the reservations which Reichenbach himself expressed[31] concerning the reliability of assumptions regarding the universe as a whole in the present state of cosmology, one wonders why he invoked the *entropy* of the universe at all instead of confining himself, as I have done, to the much weaker assumption of the existence of states of disequilibrium in the universe. More fundamentally, it is unclear how Reichenbach thought he could reconcile the assumption that the branch-systems satisfy initial conditions of randomness during whatever cosmic epoch they may form—an assumption which, as we saw, makes for the *same* statistical anisotropy on the part of *most* disequilibrium epochs of the universe—with his claim of alternation: "When we come to the downgrade [of the entropy curve of the entire universe], always proceeding in the same direction [along the time axis], the branches begin at states of high entropy . . . and they end at points of low entropy."[32] Contrary to Reichenbach, we saw in our statement of the consequences of the postulate of randomness under Group 2 above that, in the vast majority of cases, branch-systems beginning in a state of equilibrium (high entropy) will *remain* in equilibrium for the duration of their finite careers instead of decreasing their entropies!

If the universe were finite and such that an entropy is defined for it as a whole which conforms to the one-system entropy curve of statistical mechanics, then my contention of a *cosmically pervasive statistical anisotropy* of time could no longer be upheld. For I am assuming that the vast majority of branch-systems in most epochs increase their entropy in the same direction and that space ensembles of branch-systems do form during most periods of disequilibrium. And if one may further assume that the entropy of a finite, spatially closed universe depends *additively* on the entropies of its component subsystems, then the assumed temporal asymmetry of the entropy behavior of the branch-systems would appear to contradict the complete *time symmetry* of the one-system entropy behavior of the finite universe. This conclusion, if correct, therefore poses the question—which I merely wish to ask here—whether in a closed universe the postulate of the randomness of the initial conditions would not hold. For in that case, the cosmically *pervasive* statistical anisotropy of time which is assured by the randomness postulate would not obtain; instead, one could then assume initial conditions in branch-systems that issue in Reichenbach's cosmically local kind of anisotropy of time, successive overall disequilibrium epochs having *opposite* directions of entropy increase both in the universe and in the branch-systems associated with these epochs.

I have expressed doubts regarding Popper's denial of the relevance of statistico-thermodynamic phenomena to the anisotropy of time. But I was primarily concerned to show that we are in his debt for advancing our understanding of time's arrow by calling attention to the role of nonentropic *de facto* irreversibility.

ADOLF GRÜNBAUM

DEPARTMENT OF PHILOSOPHY
CENTER FOR PHILOSOPHY OF SCIENCE
UNIVERSITY OF PITTSBURGH
AUGUST 25, 1965

NOTES

[1] Adolf Grünbaum, "Popper on Irreversibility," in *The Critical Approach to Science and Philosophy*, ed. by Mario Bunge (New York: Free Press, 1964), pp. 316-31. [Added in proofs: See Adolf Grünbaum, *Falsifiability and Rationality* (Pittsburgh: University of Pittsburgh Press, forthcoming in 1974), for a statement of my views on other major tenets of Popper's philosophy of science not covered in either my 1964 Festschrift essay or in the present essay.—E DITOR]

[2] K. R. Popper, *Nature*, **177** (1956), 538; **178** (1956), 382; **179** (1957), 1297; **181** (1958), 402. These four publications will be cited hereinafter as 'Irreversibility I', 'Irreversibility II', 'Irreversibility III', and 'Irreversibility IV', respectively.

[3] K. R. Popper, *Nature*, **207** (1965), 233-34; **213** (1967), 320; **214** (1967), 322.

[4] The 1965 paper in question will be cited hereinafter as 'Irreversibility V'.

[5] For a detailed discussion of the *non*tautological sense in which there is a transient now, see the account of temporal becoming in Chap. I of my *Modern Science and Zeno's Paradoxes* (Middletown, Conn.: Wesleyan University Press); 2d ed. rev. (London: Allen & Unwin, 1968). [The most recent statement of Professor Grünbaum's views on becoming is found in his essay "The Meaning of Time," in *Basic Issues in the Philosophy of Time*, ed. by Eugene Freeman and Wilfrid Sellars (La Salle, Ill.: Open Court Publishing Co., 1971).—EDITOR]

[6] O. Costa de Beauregard, "L'Irréversibilité Quantique, Phénomène Macroscopique," in *Louis de Broglie*, ed. by A. George (Paris: Albin Michel, 1953), p. 402.

[7] See G. J. Whitrow, *The Natural Philosophy of Time* (London: Thomas Nelson & Sons, 1961), pp. 8-10 and 269; also E. Zilsel, "Über die Asymmetrie der Kausalität und die Einsinnigkeit der Zeit," *Naturwissenschaften*, **15** (1927), 283.

[8] E. L. Hill and Adolf Grünbaum, "Irreversible Processes in Physical Theory," *Nature*, **179** (1957), 1296.

[9] *Ibid.*

[10] O. Penrose and I. C. Percival, "The Direction of Time," *Proceedings of the Physical Society*, **79** (1962), 611.

[11] H. Mehlberg, "Physical Laws and Time's Arrow," in *Current Issues in the Philosophy of Science*, ed. by H. Feigl and G. Maxwell (New York: Holt, Rinehart and Winston, 1961), p. 128.

[12] *Ibid.*, p. 126.

[13] *Ibid.*, pp. 123-24.

[14] A. Einstein, "Über die Entwicklung unserer Anschauungen über die Konstitution und das Wesen der Strahlung," *Physikalische Zeitschrift*, **10** (1909), 817-28.

[15] H. Mehlberg, "Physical Laws and Time's Arrow," pp. 123-24.

[16] Through an oversight, Mehlberg lists 1910 rather than 1909 as the date of the pertinent paper by Einstein.

[17] Einstein, "Konstitution und Wesen der Strahlung," 821. The translation into English is mine.

[18] For a helpful historical account of the context of Einstein's thought here, cf. M. J. Klein, "Thermodynamics in Einstein's Thought," *Science*, **157** (1967), 509-16.

[19] I am indebted to my colleague Allen Janis for clarifying comments concerning the interpretation and import of Einstein's statement.

[20] Irreversibility IV.

[21] Irreversibility V.

[22] H. Reichenbach, *The Direction of Time* (Berkeley: University of California Press, 1956).

[23] *Ibid.*, p. 118.

[24] Cf. R. C. Tolman, *The Principles of Statistical Mechanics* (Oxford: Oxford University Press, 1938), p. 149.

[25] Cf. R. Fürth, "Prinzipien der Statistik," *Handbuch der Physik,* 4 (1929), 192-93, 270.

[26] *Ibid.,* p. 270.

[27] Although the decisive asymmetry just noted was admitted by H. Mehlberg ("Physical Laws and Time's Arrow," in *Current Issues in the Philosophy of Science*, ed. by H. Feigl and G. Maxwell [New York: Holt, Rinehart and Winston, 1961], p. 129), he dismisses it as expressing "merely the factual difference between the two relevant values of probability." But an asymmetry is no less an asymmetry for depending on *de facto* contingent boundary conditions rather than being assured by a *law* alone. Since our verification of laws generally has the same partial and indirect character as that of our confirmation of the existence of complicated *de facto* boundary conditions, the assertion of an asymmetry depending on *de facto* conditions is generally no less reliable than one wholly grounded on a law. Hence, when Mehlberg (*ibid.*, p. 117, n. 30) urges against Schrödinger's claim of entropic asymmetry that, for every pair of branch-systems which change their entropy in one direction, "there is nothing to prevent" another pair of closed subsystems from changing their entropy in the opposite direction, the reply is: Mehlberg's criticism can be upheld only by gratuitously neglecting the statistical asymmetry admitted but then dismissed by him as "merely" factual. For it is the existence of the specified boundary conditions which statistically prevents the existence of entropic time symmetry in this context. The reader is referred to my book, *Philosophical Problems of Space and Time* (New York: Alfred A. Knopf, 1964), p. 219, n. 8 for a critique of Mehlberg's further contention that Caratheodory's axiomatic account of the second law of thermodynamics "has also stripped the second phenomenological principle of thermodynamics of its irreversible and anisotropic implications."

[28] For the details of my justification of this claim as well as for my rebuttal of the charge that the entropy statistics *merely* measure the extent of human ignorance as to the microstates, see A. Grünbaum, "Is the Coarse-Grained Entropy of Classical Statistical Mechanics an Anthropormorphism?" in *Festschrift for Henry Margenau*, ed. by E. Laszlo and E. B. Sellon (forthcoming). This essay is also published as Chapter 19 of the second, enlarged edition of A. Grünbaum, *Philosophical Problems of Space and Time* (Boston and Dordrecht: D. Reidel, 1973).

[29] Cf. Penrose and Percival, "The Direction of Time," Sec. 9, p. 614.

[30] Reichenbach, *The Direction of Time*, p. 136.

[31] *Ibid.*, pp. 132-33.

[32] *Ibid.*, p. 126.

Thomas S. Kuhn
LOGIC OF DISCOVERY OR PSYCHOLOGY OF RESEARCH?

My object in these pages is to juxtapose the view of scientific development outlined in my book, *The Structure of Scientific Revolutions*, with the better known views to which the whole of this volume is appropriately devoted.[1] Ordinarily I should decline such an undertaking, for I am not so sanguine as Sir Karl about the utility of confrontations. Besides, I have admired his work for too long to turn critic easily at this date. Nevertheless, I am persuaded that, for this occasion, the attempt must be made. Even before my book was first published in 1962, I had begun to discover special and often puzzling characteristics of the relation between Sir Karl's views and my own. That relation and the divergent reactions I have encountered to it suggest that a disciplined comparison of the two may produce peculiar enlightenment. Let me say why I think this could occur.

On almost all the occasions when we turn explicitly to the same problems, Sir Karl's view of science and my own are very nearly identical.[2] We are both concerned with the dynamic process by which scientific knowledge is acquired rather than with the logical structure of the products of scientific research. Given that concern, both of us emphasize, as legitimate data, the facts and also the spirit of actual scientific life, and both of us turn often to history to find them. From this pool of shared data, we draw many of the same conclusions. Both of us reject the view that science progresses by accretion; both emphasize instead the revolutionary process by which an older theory is rejected and replaced by an incompatible new one;[3] and both deeply underscore the role played in this process by the older theory's occasional failure to meet challenges posed by logic, experiment, or observation. Finally, Sir Karl and I are united in opposition to a number of classical positivism's most characteristic theses. We both emphasize, for example, the intimate and inevitable entanglement of scientific observation with scientific theory; we are correspondingly sceptical of efforts to produce any neutral observation language; and we both insist that scientists may properly aim to invent theories that *explain* observed phenomena and that do so in terms of *real* objects, whatever the latter phrase may mean.

That list, though it by no means exhausts the issues about which Sir Karl and I agree,[4] is already extensive enough to place us in the same minority among contemporary philosophers of science. Presumably that is why Sir Karl's followers have with some regularity provided my most sympathetic philosophical audience, one for which I continue to be grateful. But my gratitude is not unmixed. The same agreement that evokes the sympathy of this group too often misdirects its interest. Apparently Sir Karl's followers can often read much of my book as chapters from a late (and, for some, a drastic) revision of his classic, *The Logic of Scientific Discovery*. One of them asks whether the view of science outlined in my *Scientific Revolutions* has not long been common knowledge. A second, more charitably, isolates my originality as the demonstration that discoveries-of-fact have a life cycle very like that displayed by innovations-of-theory. Still others express general pleasure in the book, but will discuss only the two comparatively secondary issues about which my disagreement with Sir Karl is most nearly explicit: my emphasis on the importance of deep commitment to tradition and my discontent with the implications of the term "falsification." All these men, in short, read my book through a quite special pair of spectacles; but there is another way to read it. The view through those spectacles is not wrong—my agreement with Sir Karl is real and substantial. Yet readers outside of the Popperian circle almost invariably fail even to notice that the agreement exists, and it is these readers who most often recognize (not necessarily with sympathy) what seem to me the central issues. I conclude that a Gestalt switch divides readers of my book into two or more groups. What one of these sees as striking parallelism is virtually invisible to the others. The desire to understand how this can be so motivates the present comparison of my view with Sir Karl's.

The comparison must not, however, be a mere point by point juxtaposition. What demands attention is not so much the peripheral area in which our occasional secondary disagreements are to be isolated but the central region in which we appear to agree. Sir Karl and I do appeal to the same data; to an uncommon extent we are seeing the same lines on the same paper; asked about those lines and those data, we often give virtually identical responses, or at least responses that inevitably seem identical in the isolation enforced by the question-and-answer mode. Nevertheless, experiences like those mentioned above convince me that our intentions are often quite different when we say the same things. Though the lines are the same, the figures which emerge from them are not. That is why I call what separates us a Gestalt switch rather than a disagreement and also why I am at once perplexed and intrigued about how best to explore the separation. How am I to persuade Sir Karl, who knows everything I know about scientific development and who has somewhere or other said it, that what he calls a duck can be seen as a rabbit? How am I to show him what it would be like to wear my spectacles when he has already learned to look at everything I can point to through his own?

In this situation a change in strategy is called for, and the following suggests itself. Reading over once more a number of Sir Karl's principal books and essays, I encounter again a series of recurrent phrases which, though I understand them and do not quite disagree, are locutions that I could never have used in the same places. Undoubtedly they are most often intended as metaphors applied rhetorically to situations for which Sir Karl has elsewhere provided unexceptionable descriptions. Nevertheless, for present purposes these metaphors, which strike me as patently inappropriate, may prove more useful than straightforward descriptions. They may, that is, be symptomatic of contextual differences that a careful literal expression hides. If that is so, then these locutions may function not as the lines-on-paper but as the rabbit-ear, the shawl, or the ribbon-at-the-throat which one isolates when teaching a friend to transform his way of seeing a Gestalt diagram. That, at least, is my hope for them. I have four such differences of locutions in mind and shall treat them seriatim.

I

Among the most fundamental issues on which Sir Karl and I agree is our insistence that an analysis of the development of scientific knowledge must take account of the way science has actually been practiced. That being so, a few of his recurrent generalizations startle me. One of these provides the opening sentences of the first chapter of *The Logic of Scientific Discovery*: "A scientist," writes Sir Karl, "whether theorist or experimenter, puts forward statements, or systems of statements, and tests them step by step. In the field of the empirical sciences, more particularly, he constructs hypotheses, or systems of theories, and tests them against experience by observation and experiment."[5] The statement is virtually a cliché; yet in application it presents three problems. It is ambiguous in its failure to specify which of two sorts of "statements" or "theories" are being tested. That ambiguity can, it is true, be eliminated by reference to other passages in Sir Karl's writings; but the generalization that results is historically mistaken. Furthermore, the mistake proves important, for the unambiguous form of the description misses just that characteristic of scientific practice which most nearly distinguishes the sciences from other creative pursuits.

There is one sort of "statement" or "hypothesis" that scientists do repeatedly subject to systematic test. I have in mind statements of an individual's best guesses about the proper way to connect his own research problem with the corpus of accepted scientific knowledge. He may, for example, conjecture that a given chemical unknown contains the salt of a rare earth, that the obesity of his experimental rats is due to a specified component in their diet, or that a newly discovered spectral pattern is to be understood as an effect of nuclear spin. In each case, the next steps in his research are intended to try out or test the conjecture or hypothesis. If it passes enough or stringent enough tests, the scientist has made a discovery or has at least resolved the puzzle he had been set. If not, he must either abandon the puzzle entirely or attempt to solve it with the aid of some other hypothesis. Many research problems, though by no means all, take this form. Tests of this sort are a standard component of what I have elsewhere labelled "normal science" or "normal research," an enterprise which accounts for the overwhelming majority of the work done in basic science. In no usual sense, however, are such tests directed to current theory. On the contrary, when engaged with a normal research problem, the scientist must *premise* current theory as the rules of his game. His object is to solve a puzzle, preferably one at which others have failed, and current theory is required to define that puzzle and to guarantee that, given sufficient brilliance, it can be solved.[6] Of course, the practitioner of such an enterprise must often test the conjectural puzzle solution that his ingenuity suggests. But only his personal conjecture is tested. If it fails the test, only his own ability not the corpus of current science is impugned.

This is not, however, the sort of test Sir Karl has in mind. He is above all concerned with the procedures through which science grows, and he is convinced that "growth" occurs not primarily by accretion but by the revolutionary overthrow of an accepted theory and its replacement by a better one.[7] (The subsumption under "growth" of "repeated overthrow" is itself a linguistic oddity whose *raison d'être* may become more visible as we proceed.) Taking this view, the tests which Sir Karl emphasizes are those which were performed to explore the limitations of accepted theory or to subject a current theory to maximum strain. Among his favorite examples, all of them startling and destructive in their outcome, are Lavoisier's experiments on calcination, the eclipse expedition of 1919, and the recent experiments on parity conservation.[8] All, of course, are classic tests; but, in using them to characterize scientific activity, Sir Karl misses something terribly important about them. Episodes like these are very rare in the development of science. When they occur, they are generally called forth either by a prior crisis in the relevant field (Lavoisier's experiments or Lee and Yang's)[9] or by the existence of a theory which competes with the existing canons of research (Einstein's general relativity). These are, however, aspects of or occasions for what I have elsewhere called "extraordinary research," an enterprise in which scientists do display very many of the characteristics Sir Karl emphasizes, but one which, at least in the past, has arisen only intermittently and under quite special circumstances in any scientific speciality.[10]

I suggest then that Sir Karl has characterized the entire scientific enterprise in terms that apply only to its occasional revolutionary parts. His emphasis is natural and common: the exploits of a Copernicus or Einstein make better reading than those of a Brahe or Lorentz; Sir Karl would not be the first, if he mistook what I call normal science for an intrinsically uninteresting enterprise. Nevertheless, neither science nor the development of knowledge is likely to be understood if research is viewed exclusively through the revolutions it occasionally produces. For example, though testing of basic commitments occurs only in extraordinary science, it is normal science that discloses both the points to test and the manner of testing. Or again, it is for the normal, not the extraordinary, practice of science that professionals are trained; if they are nevertheless eminently successful in displacing and replacing the theories on which normal practice depends, that is an oddity which must be explained. Finally, and this is for now my main point, a careful look at the scientific enterprise suggests that it is normal science, in which Sir Karl's sort of testing does not occur, rather than extraordinary science which most nearly distinguishes science from other enterprises. If a demarcation criterion exists (we must not, I think, seek a sharp or decisive one), it may lie just in that part of science which Sir Karl ignores.

In one of his most evocative essays, Sir Karl traces the origin of "the tradition of critical discussion [which] represents the only practicable way of expanding our knowledge" to the Greek philosophers between Thales and Plato, the men who, as he sees it, encouraged critical discussion both between schools and within individual schools.[11] The accompanying description of Presocratic discourse is most apt; but what is described does not at all resemble science. Rather, it is the tradition of claims, counterclaims, and debates over fundamentals which, except perhaps during the Middle Ages, have characterized philosophy and much of social science ever since. Already by the Hellenistic period, mathematics, astronomy, statics, and the geometric parts of optics had abandoned this mode of discourse in favor of puzzle solving. Other sciences, in increasing numbers, have undergone the same transition since. In a sense, to turn Sir Karl's view on its head, it is precisely the abandonment of critical discourse that marks the transition to a science. Once a field has made that transition, critical discourse recurs only at moments of crisis when the bases of the field are again in jeopardy.[12] Only when they must choose between competing theories do scientists behave like philosophers. That, I think, is why Sir Karl's brilliant description of the reasons for the choice between metaphysical systems so closely resembles my description of the reasons for choosing between scientific theories.[13] In neither choice, as I shall shortly try to show, can testing play a quite decisive role.

There is, however, good reason why testing has seemed to do so, and, in exploring it, Sir Karl's duck may at last become my rabbit. No puzzle-solving enterprise can exist unless its practitioners share criteria which, for that group and for that time, determine when a particular puzzle has been solved. The same criteria necessarily determine failure to achieve a solution, and anyone who chooses may view that failure as the failure of a theory to pass a test. Normally, as I have already insisted, it is not viewed that way. Only the practitioner is blamed, not his tools. But, under the special circumstances which induce a crisis in the profession (e.g., gross failure, or repeated failure by the most brilliant professionals), the group's opinion may change. A failure that had previously been personal may then come to seem the failure of a theory under test. And thereafter, because the test arose from a puzzle and thus carried settled criteria of solution, it proves both more severe and harder to evade than the tests available within a tradition whose normal mode is critical discourse rather than puzzle solving.

In a sense, therefore, severity of test criteria is simply one side of a coin whose other face is a puzzle-solving tradition. That is why the *outcome* of applying Sir Karl's line of demarcation and my own so frequently coincide. The *process* of applying them is, however, very different; it isolates distinct aspects of the activity about which the decision—science or nonscience—is to be made. Examining the vexing cases, e.g., psychoanalysis or Marxist historiography, for which Sir Karl tells us his criterion was initially designed,[14] I concur that they cannot now properly be labelled "science." But I reach that conclusion by a route far surer and more direct than his. One brief example may suggest that, of the two criteria, testing and puzzle solving, the latter is at once the less equivocal and the more fundamental.

To avoid irrelevant contemporary controversies, I consider astrology rather than, say, psychoanalysis. Astrology is Sir Karl's most frequently cited example of a "pseudo-science."[15] About it he says: "By making their interpretations and prophecies sufficiently vague they [astrologers] were able to explain away anything that might have been a refutation of the theory, had the theory and the prophecies been more precise. In order to escape falsification they destroyed the testability of the theory."[16] Those generalizations catch something of the spirit of the astrological enterprise. But taken at all literally, as they must be if they are to provide a demarcation criterion, they are impossible to support. The history of astrology during the centuries when it was intellectually reputable records many predictions that categorically failed.[17] Not even astrology's most convinced and vehement exponents doubted the recurrence of such failures. Astrology cannot be barred from the sciences because of the form in which its predictions were cast.

Nor can it be barred because of the way its practitioners explained failure. Astrologers pointed out, for example, that, unlike general predictions about, say, an individual's propensities or a natural calamity, the forecast of an individual's future was an immensely complex task, demanding the utmost skill, and extremely sensitive to minor errors in relevant data. The configuration of the stars and eight planets was constantly changing; the astronomical tables used to compute the configuration at an individual's birth were notoriously imperfect; few men knew the instant of their birth with the requisite precision.[18] No wonder, then, that forecasts often failed. Only after astrology itself became implausible did these arguments come to seem question-begging.[19] Similar arguments are regularly used today when explaining, for example, failures in medicine or meteorology. In times of trouble they are also deployed in the exact sciences, fields like physics, chemistry, and astronomy.[20] There was nothing unscientific about the astrologer's explanation of failure.

Nevertheless, astrology was not a science. Instead, it was a craft, one of the practical arts, with close resemblances to engineering, meteorology, and medicine, as these fields were practiced until little more than a century ago. The parallels to an older medicine and to contemporary psychoanalysis are, I think, particularly close. In each of these fields shared theory was adequate only to establish the plausibility of the discipline and to provide a rationale for the various craft rules which governed practice. These rules had proved their use in the past; but no practitioner supposed they were sufficient to prevent recurrent failure. A more articulated theory and more powerful rules were desired; but it would have been absurd to abandon a plausible and badly needed discipline with a tradition of limited success simply because these desiderata were not yet at hand. In their absence, however, neither the astrologer nor the doctor could do research. Though they had rules to apply, they had no puzzles to solve and therefore no science to practice.[21]

Compare the situations of the astronomer and the astrologer. If an astronomer's prediction failed and his calculations checked, he could hope to set the situation right. Perhaps the data were at fault: old observations could be reexamined and new measurements made, tasks which posed a host of calculational and instrumental puzzles. Or, perhaps, theory needed adjustment, either by the manipulation of epicycles, eccentrics, equants, etc., or by more fundamental reforms of astronomical technique. For more than a millennium these were the theoretical and mathematical puzzles around which, together with their instrumental counterparts, the astronomical research tradition was constituted. The astrologer, by contrast, had no such puzzles. The occurrence of failures could be explained, but particular failures did not give rise to research puzzles; for no man, however skilled, could make use of them in a constructive attempt to revise the astrological tradition. There were too many possible sources of difficulty, most of them beyond the astrologer's knowledge, control, or responsibility. Individual failures were correspondingly uninformative, and they did not reflect on the competence of the prognosticator in the eyes of his professional compeers.[22] Though astronomy and astrology were regularly practiced by the same people, including Ptolemy, Kepler, and Tycho Brahe, there was never an astrological equivalent of the puzzle-solving astronomical tradition. And without puzzles, able first to challenge and then to attest the ingenuity of the individual practitioner, astrology could not have become a science even if the stars had, in fact, controlled human destiny.

In short, though astrologers made testable predictions and recognized that these predictions sometimes failed, they did not and could not engage in the sorts of activities that normally characterize all recognized sciences. Sir Karl is right to exclude astrology from the sciences; but his overconcentration on science's occasional revolutions prevents his seeing the surest reason for doing so.

That fact, in turn, may explain another oddity of Sir Karl's historiography. Though he repeatedly underlines the role of tests in the replacement of scientific theories, he is also constrained to recognize that many theories, for example the Ptolemaic, were replaced before they had in fact been tested.[23] On some occasions, at least, tests are not requisite to the revolutions through which science advances. But that is not true of puzzles. Though they had not deliberately been put to the test before their displacement, none of the theories Sir Karl cites were set aside before some of the men who used it professionally came to feel that it no longer adequately supported a puzzle-solving tradition. The state of astronomy was a scandal in the early sixteenth century. Most astronomers nevertheless felt that normal adjustments of a basically Ptolemaic model would set the situation right. In this sense the theory had not failed a test. But a few astronomers, Copernicus among them, felt that the difficulties must lie in the Ptolemaic approach itself rather than in the particular versions of Ptolemaic theory so far developed, and the results of that conviction are already recorded. The situation is typical.[24] With or without tests, a puzzle-solving tradition can prepare the way for its own displacement. To rely on testing as the mark of a science is to miss what scientists mostly do and, with it, the most characteristic feature of their enterprise.

II

With the background supplied by the preceding remarks we can quickly discover the occasion and consequences of another of Sir Karl's favorite locutions. The preface to *Conjectures and Refutations* opens with the sentence: "The essays and lectures of which this book is composed are variations upon one very simple theme—the thesis that *we can learn from our mistakes*." The emphasis is Sir Karl's; the thesis recurs in his writing from an early date;[25] taken in isolation, it inevitably commands assent. Everyone can and does learn from his mistakes; isolating and correcting them is an essential technique in teaching children; Sir Karl's rhetoric has roots in everyday experience. Nevertheless, in the contexts for which he invoked this familiar imperative, its application seems decisively askew. I am not sure a mistake has been made, at least not a mistake to learn from.

One need not confront the deeper philosophical problems presented by mistakes to see what is presently at issue. It is a mistake to add three plus three and get five, or to conclude from "All men are mortal" to "All mortals are men." For different reasons, it is a mistake to say, "He is my sister," or to report the presence of a strong electric field when test charges fail to indicate it. Presumably there are still other sorts of mistakes; but all the normal ones are likely to share the following characteristics. A mistake is made, or is committed, at a specifiable time and place by a particular individual. That individual has failed to obey some established rule of logic or of language or of the relations between one of these and experience. Or, he may instead have failed to recognize the consequences of a particular choice among the alternatives which the rules allow him. Only because the group whose practice embodies these rules can isolate the individual's failure in applying them can the individual learn from his mistake. In short, the sorts of mistakes to which Sir Karl's imperative most obviously applies are an individual's failures of understanding or of recognition within an activity governed by preestablished rules. In the sciences such mistakes occur most frequently and perhaps exclusively within the practice of normal puzzle-solving research.

That is not, however, where Sir Karl seeks them; for his concept of science obscures even the existence of normal research. Instead, he looks to the extraordinary or revolutionary episodes in scientific development. The mistakes to which he points are not usually acts at all, but rather out-of-date scientific theories: Ptolemaic astronomy, the phlogiston theory, or Newtonian dynamics; and, "learning from our mistakes" is, correspondingly, what occurs when a scientific community rejects one of these theories and replaces it with another.[26] If this does not immediately seem an odd usage, that is mainly because it appeals to the residual inductivist in us all. Believing that valid theories are the product of correct inductions from facts, the inductivist must also hold that a false theory is the result of a mistake in induction. In principle, at least, he is prepared to answer the questions: what mistake was made, what rule broken, when and by whom, in arriving at, say, the Ptolemaic system? To the man for whom those are sensible questions and to him alone Sir Karl's locution presents no problems.

But neither Sir Karl nor I is an inductivist. We do not believe that there are rules for inducing correct theories from facts, or even that theories, correct or incorrect, are induced at all. Instead, we view them as imaginative posits, invented in one piece for application to nature. And, though we point out that such posits can and usually do at last encounter puzzles they cannot solve, we also recognize that those troublesome confrontations rarely occur for some time after a theory has been both invented and accepted. In our view, then, no mistake was made in arriving at the Ptolemaic system; and it is therefore difficult for me to understand what Sir Karl has in mind when he calls that system, or any other out-of-date theory, a mistake. At most one may wish to say that a theory which was not previously a mistake has become one or that a scientist has made the mistake of clinging to a theory for too long. And even these locutions, of which at least the first is extremely awkward, do not return us to the sense of mistake with which we are most familiar. Those mistakes are the normal ones which a Ptolemaic (or a Copernican) astronomer makes within his system, perhaps in observation, calculation, or the analysis of data. They are, that is, the sort of mistake which can be isolated and then at once corrected, leaving the original system intact. In Sir Karl's sense, on the other hand, a mistake infects an entire system and can be corrected only by replacing the system as a whole. No locutions and no similarities can disguise these fundamental differences, nor can it hide the fact that, before infection set in, the system had the full integrity of what we today call sound knowledge.

Quite possibly Sir Karl's sense of "mistake" can be salvaged; but a successful salvage operation must deprive it of certain still current implications. Like the term "testing," "mistake" has been borrowed from normal science, where its use is reasonably clear, and applied to revolutionary episodes, where its application is at best problematic. That transfer creates, or at least reinforces, the prevalent impression that whole theories can be judged by criteria of the same sort one employs when judging a theory's individual research applications. The discovery of applicable criteria then becomes a primary desideratum for many people. That Sir Karl should be among them is strange, for the search runs counter to the most original and fruitful thrust in his philosophy of science. But I can understand his methodological writings since the *Logik der Forschung* in no other way. Despite explicit disclaimers, he has, I shall now suggest, consistently sought evaluation procedures which can be applied to theories with the apodictic assurance characteristic of the techniques by which one identifies mistakes in arithmetic, logic, or measurement. I fear that he is pursuing a will-o'-the-wisp born from the same conjunction of normal and extraordinary science which made tests seem so fundamental a feature of the sciences.

III

In his *Logik der Forschung*, Sir Karl underlined the asymmetry of a generalization and its negation in their relation to empirical evidence. A scientific theory cannot be shown to apply successfully to all its possible instances, but it can be shown to be unsuccessful in particular applications. Emphasis upon that logical truism and its implications seems to me a forward step from which there must be no retreat. The same asymmetry plays a fundamental role in my *Structure of Scientific Revolutions*, where a theory's failure to provide rules that identify solvable puzzles is viewed as the source of professional crises which often result in the theory's being replaced. My point is very close to Sir Karl's, and I may well have taken it from what I had heard of his work.

But Sir Karl describes as "falsification" or "refutation" what happens when a theory fails in an attempted application, and these are the first of a series of related locutions that again strike me as extremely odd. Both "falsification" and "refutation" are antonyms of "proof." They are drawn principally from logic and from formal mathematics; the chains of argument to which they apply end with a "Q.E.D."; invoking these terms implies the ability to compel assent from any member of the relevant professional community. No reader of this volume, however, still needs to be told that, where a whole theory or often even a scientific law is at stake, arguments are seldom so apodictic. All experiments can be challenged, either as to their relevance or their accuracy. All theories can be modified by a variety of *ad hoc* adjustments without ceasing to be, in their main lines, the same theories. It is important, furthermore, that this should be so; for it is often by challenging observations or adjusting theories that scientific knowledge grows. Challenges and adjustments are a standard part of normal research in empirical science, and adjustments, at least, play a dominant role in informal mathematics as well. Dr. Lakatos's brilliant analysis of the permissible rejoinders to mathematical refutations provides the most telling arguments I know against a naive falsificationist position.[27]

Sir Karl is not, of course, a naive falsificationist. He knows all that has just been said and has emphasized it from the beginning of his career. Very early in his *Logic of Scientific Discovery*, for example, he writes:

> In point of fact, no conclusive disproof of a theory can ever be produced; for it is always possible to say that the experimental results are not reliable or that the discrepancies which are asserted to exist between the experimental results and the theory are only apparent and that they will disappear with the advance of our understanding.[28]

Statements like these display one more parallel between Sir Karl's view of science and my own; but what we make of them could scarcely be more different. For my view they are fundamental, both as evidence and as source. For Sir Karl's, in contrast, they are an essential qualification which threatens the integrity of his basic position. Having barred conclusive disproof, he has provided no substitute for it, and the relation he does employ remains that of logical falsification. Though he is not a naive falsificationist, Sir Karl may, I suggest, legitimately be treated as one.

If his concern were exclusively with demarcation, the problems posed by the unavailability of conclusive disproofs would be less severe and perhaps eliminable. Demarcation might, that is, be achieved by an exclusively syntactic criterion.[29] Sir Karl's view would then be, and perhaps is: a theory is scientific if and only if *observation statements*—particularly the negations of singular existential statements—can be logically deduced from it, perhaps in conjunction with stated background knowledge. The difficulties (to which I shall shortly turn) in deciding whether the outcome of a particular laboratory operation justifies asserting a particular observation statement would then be irrelevant. Perhaps, though the basis for doing so is less apparent, the equally grave difficulties in deciding whether an observation statement deduced from an approximate (e.g., mathematically manageable) version of the theory should be considered consequences of the theory itself could be eliminated in the same way. Problems like these would belong not to the syntactics but to the pragmatics or semantics of the language in which the theory was cast, and they would therefore have no role in determining its status as a science. To be scientific a theory need be falsifiable only by an observation statement not by actual observation. The relation between statements, unlike that between a statement and an observation, could be the conclusive disproof familiar from logic and mathematics.

For reasons suggested above (note 26) and elaborated immediately below, I doubt that scientific theories can, without decisive change, be cast in a form which permits the purely syntactic judgments which this version of Sir Karl's criterion would require. But, even if they could, these reconstructed theories would provide a basis only for his demarcation criterion, not for the logic of knowledge so closely associated with it. The latter has, however, been Sir Karl's most persistent concern, and his notion of it is quite precise. "The logic of knowledge . . . ," he writes, "consists solely in investigating the methods employed in those systematic tests to which every new idea must be subjected if it is to be seriously entertained."[30] From this investigation, he continues, result methodological rules or conventions like the following: "Once a hypothesis has been proposed and tested, and has proved its mettle, it may not be allowed to drop out without 'good reason'. A 'good reason' may be, for instance . . . the falsification of one of the consequences of the hypothesis."[31]

Rules like these, and with them the entire logical enterprise described above, are no longer simply syntactic in their import. They require that both the epistemological investigator and the research scientist be able to relate sentences derived from a theory not to other sentences but to actual observations and experiments. This is the context in which Sir Karl's term "falsification" must function, and Sir Karl is entirely silent about how it can do so. What is falsification if it is not conclusive disproof? Under what circumstances does the *logic* of knowledge require a scientist to abandon a previously accepted theory when confronted not with statements about experiments but with experiments themselves? Pending clarification of these questions, I am not clear that what Sir Karl has given us is a logic of knowledge at all. In my conclusion I shall suggest that, though equally valuable, it is something else entirely. Rather than a logic, Sir Karl has provided an ideology; rather than methodological rules, he has supplied procedural maxims.

That conclusion must, however, be postponed until after a last deeper look at the source of the difficulties with Sir Karl's notion of falsification. It presupposes, as I have already suggested, that a theory is cast, or can without distortion be recast, in a form which permits scientists to classify each conceivable event as either a confirming instance, a falsifying instance, or irrelevant to the theory. That is obviously required if a general law is to be falsifiable: to test the generalization $(x)\phi(x)$ by applying it to the constant a, we must be able to tell whether or not a lies within the range of the variable x and whether or not $\phi(a)$. The same presupposition is even more apparent in Sir Karl's recently elaborated measure of verisimilitude. It requires that we first produce the class of all logical consequences of the theory and then choose from among these, with the aid of background knowledge, the classes of all true and of all false consequences;[32] at least, we must do this if the criterion of verisimilitude is to result in a *method* of theory choice. None of these tasks can, however, be accomplished unless the theory is fully articulated logically and unless the terms through which it attaches to nature are sufficiently defined to determine their applicability in each possible case. In practice, however, no scientific theory satisfies these rigorous demands; and many people have argued that a theory would cease to be useful in research if it did so.[33] I have myself elsewhere introduced the term "paradigm" to underscore the dependence of scientific research upon concrete examples that bridge what would otherwise be gaps in the specification of the content and application of scientific theories. The relevant arguments cannot be repeated here. But a brief example, though it will temporarily alter my mode of discourse, may be even more useful.

My example takes the form of a constructed epitome of some elementary scientific knowledge. That knowledge concerns swans, and to isolate its presently relevant characteristic I shall ask three questions about it: How much can one know about swans without introducing explicit generalizations like "All swans are white"? Under what circumstances and with what consequences are such generalizations worth adding to what was known without them? And, finally, under what circumstances are such generalizations rejected once they have been made? In raising these questions my object is to suggest that, though logic is a powerful and ultimately an essential tool of scientific enquiry, one can have sound knowledge in forms to which logic can scarcely be applied. Simultaneously, I shall suggest that logical articulation for its own sake is not a value, but is to be undertaken only when and to the extent that circumstances demand it.

Imagine that you have been shown and can remember ten birds which have authoritatively been identified as swans; that you have a similar acquaintance with ducks, geese, pigeons, doves, gulls, etc.; and that you are informed that each of these types constitutes a natural family. A natural family you already know as an observed cluster of like objects, sufficiently important and sufficiently discrete to command a generic name. More precisely, though here I introduce more simplification than the concept requires, a natural family is a class whose members resemble each other more closely than they resemble the members of other natural families.[34] The experience of generations has to date confirmed that all observed objects fall into one or another natural family. It has, that is, shown that the entire population of the world can always be divided (though not once and for all) into perceptually discontinuous categories. In the perceptual spaces between these categories there are believed to be no objects at all.

What you have learned about swans from exposure to paradigms is very much like what children first learn about dogs and cats, tables and chairs, mothers and fathers. Its precise scope and content are, of course, impossible to specify, but it is sound knowledge nonetheless. Derived from observation, it can be infirmed by further observation, and it meanwhile provides a basis for rational action. Seeing a bird much like the swans you already know, you may reasonably presume that it will require the same food as the others and will breed with them. Provided swans are a natural family, no bird which closely resembles them on sight should display radically different characteristics on closer acquaintance. Of course, you may have been misinformed about the natural integrity of the swan family. But that can be discovered from experience, for example by the discovery of a number of animals (note that more than one is required) whose characteristics bridge the gap between swans and, say, geese by barely perceptible intervals.[35] Until that does occur, however, you will know a great deal about swans, though you will not be altogether sure what you know or what a swan is.

Suppose now that all the swans you have actually observed are white. Should you embrace the generalization, "All swans are white"? Doing so will

change what you know very little; that change will be of use only in the unlikely event that you meet a non-white bird which otherwise resembles a
swan; by making the change you increase the risk that the swan family will
prove not to be a natural family after all. Under those circumstances you are
likely to refrain from generalizing unless there are special reasons for doing
so. Perhaps, for example, you must describe swans to men who cannot be
directly exposed to paradigms; without superhuman caution both on your
part and on that of your readers, your description will acquire the force of a
generalization; this is often the problem of the taxonomist. Or perhaps you
have discovered some grey birds that look otherwise like swans but eat
different foods and have an unfortunate disposition; you may then generalize
to avoid a behavioral mistake. Or you may have a more theoretical reason for
thinking the generalization worthwhile. For example, you may have observed
that the members of other natural families share coloration. Specifying this
fact in a form which permits the application of powerful logical techniques to
what you know may enable you to learn more about animal color in general
or about animal breeding.

And now, having made the generalization, what will you do if you encounter a black bird that looks otherwise like a swan? Almost the same
things, I suggest, as if you had not previously committed yourself to the
generalization at all. You will examine the bird with care, externally and
perhaps internally as well, to find other characteristics that distinguish this
specimen from your paradigms. That examination will be particularly long
and thorough if you have theoretical reasons for believing that color
characterizes natural families or if you are deeply ego-involved with the
generalization. Very likely the examination will disclose other differentiae,
and you will announce the discovery of a new natural family. Or you may fail
to find such differentiae and may then announce that a black swan has been
found. Observation cannot, however, force you to that falsifying conclusion,
and you would occasionally be the loser if it could do so. Theoretical considerations may suggest that color alone is sufficient to demarcate a natural
family: the bird is not a swan because it is black. Or you may claim that a
characteristic others consider an individual idiosyncracy is really the index of
a distinct family. Or you may simply postpone the issue pending the discovery
and examination of other specimens. Only if you have previously committed
yourself to a full definition of "swan," one which will specify its applicability
to every conceivable object, can you be logically *forced* to rescind your
generalization.[36] And why should you have offered such a definition? It could
serve no cognitive function and would expose you to tremendous risks.[37]
Risks, of course, are often worth taking, but to say more than one knows
solely for the sake of risk is foolhardy.

I suggest that, though logically more articulate and far more complex, scientific knowledge is of this sort. The books and teachers from whom it is acquired present concrete examples together with a multitude of theoretical generalizations. Both are essential carriers of knowledge, and it is therefore Pickwickian to seek a methodological criterion that supposes the scientist can specify in advance whether each imaginable instance fits or would falsify his theory. The criteria at his disposal, explicit and implicit, are sufficient to answer that question only for the cases that clearly do fit or that are clearly irrelevant. These are the cases he expects, the ones for which his knowledge was designed. Confronted with the unexpected, he must always do more research in order further to articulate his theory in the area that has just become problematic. He may then reject it in favor of another and for good reason. But no exclusively logical criteria can entirely dictate the conclusion he must draw.

IV

Almost everything said so far rings changes on a single theme. The criteria with which scientists determine the validity of an articulation or an application of existing theory are not by themselves sufficient to determine the choice between competing theories. Sir Karl has erred by transferring selected characteristics of everyday research to the occasional revolutionary episodes in which scientific advance is most obvious and by thereafter ignoring the everyday enterprise entirely. In particular, he has sought to solve the problem of theory choice during revolutions by logical criteria that are applicable in full only when a theory can already be presupposed. That is the largest part of my thesis in this paper, and it could be the entire thesis if I were content to leave altogether open the questions that have been raised. How do scientists make the choice between competing theories? How are we to understand the way in which science does progress?

Let me at once be clear that, having opened that Pandora's box, I shall close it quickly. There is too much about these questions that I do not understand and must not pretend to. But I believe I see the directions in which answers to them must be sought, and I shall conclude with an attempt briefly to mark the trail. Near its end we shall once more encounter a set of Sir Karl's characteristic locutions.

I must first ask what it is that still requires explanation. Not that scientists discover the truth about nature, nor that they approach ever closer to the truth. Unless, as one of my critics suggests,[38] we simply define the approach to truth as the result of what scientists do, we cannot recognize progress towards that goal. Rather we must explain why science—our surest example of sound knowledge—progresses as it does, and we must first find out how, in fact, it does progress.

Surprisingly little is yet known about the answer to that descriptive question: a vast amount of thoughtful empirical investigation is still required. With the passage of time, scientific theories taken as a group are obviously more and more articulated. In the process, they are matched to nature at an increasing number of points and with increasing precision. Or, again, the number of subject matters to which the puzzle-solving approach can be applied clearly grows with time. Partly by an extension of the boundaries of science and partly by the subdivision of existing fields, there is a continuing proliferation of scientific specialties.

Those generalizations are, however, only a beginning. We know for example, almost nothing about what a group of scientists will sacrifice in order to achieve the gains that a new theory invariably offers. My own impression, though it is no more than that, is that a scientific community will seldom or never embrace a new theory unless it solves all or almost all the quantitative, numerical puzzles that have been treated by its predecessor.[39] They will, on the other hand, occasionally sacrifice explanatory power, however reluctantly, sometimes leaving previously resolved questions open and sometimes declaring them altogether unscientific.[40] Turning to another area, we know little about historical changes in the unity of the sciences. Despite occasional spectacular successes, communication across the boundaries between scientific specialties becomes worse and worse. Does the number of incompatible viewpoints employed by the increasing number of communities of specialists grow with time? Unity of the sciences is clearly a value for scientists, but for what will they give it up? Or again, though the bulk of scientific knowledge clearly increases with time, what are we to say about ignorance? The problems solved during the last thirty years did not exist as open questions a century ago. In any age, the scientific knowledge already at hand virtually exhausts what there is to know, leaving visible puzzles only at the horizon of existing knowledge. Is it not possible, or perhaps even likely, that contemporary scientists know less of what there is to know about their world than the scientists of the eighteenth century knew of theirs? Scientific theories, it must be remembered, attach to nature only here and there. Are the interstices between those points of attachment perhaps now greater than ever before?

Until we can answer more questions like these, we shall not know quite what scientific progress is and cannot therefore quite hope to explain it. On the other hand, answers to those questions will very nearly provide the explanation sought. The two come almost together. Already it should be clear that the explanation must, in the final analysis, be psychological or sociological. It must, that is, be a description of a value system—an ideology—together with an analysis of the institutions through which that system is transmitted and enforced. Knowing what scientists value, we may hope to understand what problems they will undertake and what choices they will make in particular circumstances of conflict. I doubt that there is another sort of answer to be found.

What form that answer will take, is, of course, another matter. At this point, too, my sense that I control my subject matter ends. But again, some sample generalizations will illustrate the sorts of answers which must be sought. For a scientist, the solution of a difficult conceptual or instrumental puzzle is a principal goal. His success in that endeavor is rewarded through recognition by other members of his professional group and by them alone. The practical merit of his solution is at best a secondary value, and the approval of men outside the specialists' group is a negative value or none at all. These values, which do much to dictate the form of normal science, are also significant at times when a choice must be made between theories. A man trained as a puzzle solver will wish to preserve as many as possible of the prior puzzle solutions obtained by his group, and he will also wish to maximize the number of puzzles that can be solved. But even these values frequently conflict, and there are others which make the problem of choice still more difficult. It is just in this connection that a study of what scientists will give up would be most significant. Simplicity, precision, and congruence with the theories used in other specialties are all significant values for the scientist; but they do not all dictate the same choice nor will they all be applied in the same way. That being the case, it is also important that group unanimity be a paramount value, causing the group to minimize the occasions for conflict and to reunite quickly about a single set of rules for puzzle solving even at the price of subdividing the specialty or excluding a formerly productive member.[41]

I do not suggest that these are the right answers to the problem of scientific progress, but only that they are the types of answers that must be sought. Can I hope that Sir Karl will join me in this view of the task still to be done? For some time I have assumed he would not: a set of phrases that recurs in his work seems to bar the position to him. Again and again he has rejected "the psychology of knowledge" or the "subjective" and insisted that his concern was instead with the "objective" or "the logic of knowledge."[42] The title of his most fundamental contribution to our field is *The Logic of Scientific Discovery*, and it is there that he most positively asserts that his concern is with the logical spurs to knowledge rather than with the psychological drives of individuals. Until very recently I have supposed that this view of the problem must bar the sort of solution I have advocated.

But now I am less certain; for there is another aspect of Sir Karl's work, not quite compatible with what precedes. When he rejects "the psychology of knowledge," Sir Karl's explicit concern is only to deny the methodological relevance of an *individual's* source of inspiration or of an individual's sense of certainty. With that much I cannot disagree. It is, however, a long step from the rejection of the psychological idiosyncrasies of an individual to the rejection of the common elements induced by nurture and training in the psychological makeup of the licensed membership of a *scientific group*. One need not be dismissed with the other. And this, too, Sir Karl seems sometimes to recognize. Though he insists he is writing about the logic of knowledge, an essential role in his methodology is played by passages which I can only read as attempts to inculcate moral imperatives in the membership of the scientific group.

> Assume [Sir Karl writes] that we have deliberately made it our task to live in this unknown world of ours; to adjust ourselves to it as well as we can;. . . and to explain it, *if* possible (we need not assume that it is) and as far as possible, with help of laws and explanatory theories. *If we have made this our task, then there is no more rational procedure than the method of . . . conjecture and refutation:* of boldly proposing theories; of trying our best to show that these are erroneous; and of accepting them tentatively if our critical efforts are unsuccessful.[43]

We shall not, I suggest, understand the success of science without understanding the full force of rhetorically induced and professionally shared imperatives like these. Institutionalized and articulated further (and also somewhat differently) such maxims and values may explain the outcome of choices that could not have been dictated by logic and experiment alone. The fact that passages like these occupy a prominent place in Sir Karl's writing is therefore further evidence of the resemblance of our views. That he does not, I think, ever see them for the social-psychological imperatives they are is further evidence of the Gestalt switch that still divides us deeply.

THOMAS S. KUHN

PROGRAM IN HISTORY AND PHILOSOPHY OF SCIENCE
PRINCETON UNIVERSITY
NOVEMBER, 1965

NOTES

[1] For purposes of the following discussion I have reviewed Sir Karl Popper's *The Logic of Scientific Discovery* (London: Hutchinson; New York: Basic Books, 1959), his *Conjectures and Refutations: The Growth of Scientific Knowledge* (London: Routledge & Kegan Paul; New York: Basic Books, 1963), and his *The Poverty of Historicism* (London: Routledge & Kegan Paul; Boston: Beacon Press, 1957). The first two of these volumes will hereinafter be cited as *L.Sc.D.* and *C.&R.*, respectively. I have also occasionally referred to the original *Logik der Forschung* (Vienna: Julius Springer, 1935) and to *The Open Society and Its Enemies*, rev. ed. (Princeton, N. J.: Princeton University Press, 1950). My own book, *The Structure of Scientific Revolutions* (Chicago: University of Chicago Press, 1962; Phoenix paperback edition, 1964), provides a more extended account of many of the issues discussed below. It will be hereinafter cited as *SSR*.

[2] More than coincidence is presumably responsible for this extensive overlap. Though I had

read none of Sir Karl's work before the appearance of *L.Sc.D.* in 1959 (by which time my book was in draft), I had repeatedly heard a number of his main ideas discussed. In particular, I had heard him discuss some of them as William James Lecturer at Harvard in the spring of 1950. These circumstances do not permit me to specify an intellectual debt to Sir Karl, but there must be one.

3. Elsewhere I use the term "paradigm" rather than "theory" to denote what is rejected and replaced during scientific revolutions. Some reasons for the change of term will emerge below.

4 Underlining one additional area of agreement about which there has been much misunderstanding may further highlight what I take to be the real differences between Sir Karl's views and mine. We both insist that adherence to a tradition has an essential role in scientific development. He has written, for example, "Quantitatively and qualitatively by far the most important source of our knowledge—apart from inborn knowledge—is tradition" (*C.&R.,* p. 27). Even more to the point, as early as 1948 Sir Karl wrote, "I do not think that we could ever free ourselves entirely from the bonds of tradition. The so-called freeing is really only a change from one tradition to another" (*C.&R.,* p. 122).

5 *L.Sc.D.,* p. 27.

6 For an extended discussion of normal science, the activity which practitioners are trained to carry on, see *SSR*, pp. 23-42, and 135-42. It is important to notice that when I describe the scientist as a puzzle solver and Sir Karl describes him as a problem solver (e.g., in *C.&R.,* pp. 67, 222), the similarity of our terms disguises a fundamental divergence. Sir Karl writes, "Admittedly, our expectations, and thus our theories, may precede, historically, even our problems. *Yet science starts only with problems.* Problems crop up especially when we are disappointed in our expectations, or when our theories involve us in difficulties, in contradictions" (Sir Karl's italics). I use the term "puzzle" in order to emphasize that the difficulties which *ordinarily* confront even the very best scientists are, like crossword puzzles or chess puzzles, challenges only to his ingenuity. *He* is in difficulty, not current theory. My point is almost the converse of Sir Karl's.

7 Cf. *C.&R.,* pp. 129, 215, 221, for particularly forceful statements of this position.

8 For example, *C.&R.,* p. 220.

9 For the work on calcination see Henry Guerlac, *Lavoisier—The Crucial Year* (Ithaca, N. Y.: Cornell University Press, 1961). For the background of the parity experiments see E. M. Hafner and Susan Presswood, "Strong Inference and Weak Interactions," *Science,* 149 (1965), 503-10.

10 The point is argued at length in Kuhn, *SSR*, pp. 52-97.

11 *C.&R.,* Chap. 5, esp. pp. 148-52.

12 Though I was not then seeking a demarcation criterion, just these points are argued at length in *SSR*, pp. 10-22, 87-90.

13 Compare *C.&R.,* pp. 192-200, with *SSR*, pp. 143-58.

14 *C.&R.,* p. 34.

15 The index to *C.&R.* has eight entries under the heading "astrology as a typical pseudoscience."

16 *C.&R.,* p. 37.

17 For examples see Lynn Thorndike, *A History of Magic and Experimental Science*, 8 vols. (New York: Columbia University Press, 1923-58), Vol. V, pp. 225 ff.; Vol. VI, pp. 71, 101, 114.

18. For reiterated explanations of failure see *ibid.,* Vol. I, pp. 11, 514 f.; Vol. IV, p. 368; Vol. V, p. 279.

19 A perceptive account of some reasons for astrology's loss of plausibility is included in William D. Stahlman, "Astrology in Colonial America: an Extended Query," *William and Mary Quarterly,* 13 (1956), 551-63. For an explanation of astrology's previous appeal see Lynn Thorndike, "The True Place of Astrology in the History of Science," *Isis,* 46 (1955), 273-78.

20 Kuhn, *SSR*, pp. 66-76.

[21] This formulation suggests that Sir Karl's criterion of demarcation might be saved by a minor restatement entirely in keeping with his apparent intent. For a field to be a science its conclusions must be *logically derivable* from *shared premises*. On this view astrology is to be barred, not because its forecasts were not testable, but because only the most general and least testable ones could be derived from accepted theory. Since any field that did satisfy this condition *might* support a puzzle-solving tradition, the suggestion is clearly helpful. It comes close to supplying a sufficient condition for a field's being a science. But in this form, at least, it is not even quite a sufficient condition, and it is surely not a necessary one. It would, for example, admit surveying and navigation as sciences, and it would bar taxonomy, historical geology, and the theory of evolution. The conclusions of a science may be both precise and binding without being fully derivable by logic from accepted premises. Compare *SSR*, pp. 35-51, and also the discussion in Sec. III below.

[22] This is not to suggest that astrologers did not criticize each other. On the contrary, like practitioners of philosophy and some social sciences, they belonged to a variety of different schools, and the interschool strife was sometimes bitter. But these debates ordinarily revolved about the *implausibility* of the particular theory employed by one or another school. Failures of individual predictions played very little role. Compare Thorndike, *Magic and Experimental Science*, Vol. V, p. 233.

[23] *C.&R.*, p. 246.

[24] Kuhn, *SSR*, pp. 77-87.

[25] The quotation is from *C.&R.*, p. vii, in the Preface dated 1962. Earlier Sir Karl had equated "learning from our mistakes" with "learning by trial and error" (*C.&R.*, p. 216), and the trial-and-error formulation dates from at least 1937 (*C.&R.*, p. 312) and is in spirit older than that. Much of what is said below about Sir Karl's notion of "mistake" applies equally to his concept of "error."

[26] *C.&R.*, pp. 215, 220. In these pages Sir Karl outlines and illustrates his thesis that science grows through revolutions. He does not, in the process, ever juxtapose the term "mistake" with the name of an out-of-date scientific theory, presumably because his sound historic instinct inhibits so gross an anachronism. Yet the anachronism is fundamental to Sir Karl's rhetoric, which does repeatedly provide clues to more substantial differences between us. Unless out-of-date theories are mistakes, there is no way to reconcile, say, the opening paragraph of Sir Karl's Preface (*C.&R.*, p. vii: "learn from our mistakes"; "our often mistaken attempts to solve our problems"; "tests which may help us in the discovery of our mistakes") with the view (*C.&R.*, p. 215) that "the growth of scientific knowledge. . .[consists in] the repeated overthrow of scientific theories and their replacement by better or more satisfactory ones."

[27] Imre Lakatos, "Proofs and Refutations," *British Journal for the Philosophy of Science,* **14** (1963-64).

[28] *L.Sc.D.*, p. 50.

[29] Though my point is somewhat different, I owe my recognition of the need to confront this issue to C. G. Hempel's strictures on those who misinterpret Sir Karl by attributing to him a belief in absolute rather than relative falsification. See his *Aspects of Scientific Explanation* (New York: Free Press, 1965), p. 45. I am also indebted to Professor Hempel for a close and perceptive critique of this paper in draft.

[30] *L.Sc.D.*, p. 31.

[31] *L.Sc.D.*, pp. 53 f.

[32] *C.&R.*, pp. 233-35. Notice also, at the foot of the last of these pages, that Sir Karl's comparison of the relative verisimilitude of two theories depends upon there being "no revolutionary changes in our background knowledge," an assumption which he nowhere argues and which is hard to reconcile with his conception of scientific change by revolutions.

[33] R. B. Braithwaite, *Scientific Explanation* (Cambridge, England: Cambridge University Press, 1953), pp. 50-87, esp. p. 76, and Kuhn, *SSR*, pp. 97-101.

[34] Note that the resemblance between members of a natural family is here a learned relationship and one which can be unlearned. Contemplate the old saw, "To an Occidental, all Chinamen look alike." That example also highlights the most drastic of the simplifications introduced at this point. A fuller discussion would have to allow for hierarchies of natural families with resemblance relations between families at the higher levels.

[35] This experience would not necessitate the abandonment of either the category "swans" or the category "geese," but it would necessitate the introduction of an *arbitrary* boundary between them. The families "swans" and "geese" would no longer be natural families, and you could conclude nothing about the character of a new swan-like bird that was not also true of geese. Empty perceptual space is essential, if family membership is to have cognitive content.

[36] Further evidence for the unnaturalness of any such definition is provided by the following question. Should "whiteness" be included as a defining characteristic of swans? If so, the generalization "All swans are white" is immune to experience. But if "whiteness" is excluded from the definition, then some other characteristic must be included for which "whiteness" might have substituted. Decisions about which characteristics are to be parts of a definition and which are to be available for the statement of general laws are often arbitrary and, in practice, are seldom made. Knowledge is not usually articulated in that way.

[37] This incompleteness of definitions is often called "open texture" or "vagueness of meaning," but those phrases seem decisively askew. Perhaps the definitions are incomplete, but nothing is wrong with the meanings. That is the way that meanings behave!

[38] David Hawkins, review of *Structure of Scientific Revolutions, American Journal of Physics,* **31** (1963).

[39] Compare T. S. Kuhn, "The Role of Measurement in the Development of Physical Science," *Isis,* **49** (1958), 161-93.

[40] Kuhn, *SSR*, pp. 102-8.

[41] Compare Kuhn, *SSR*, pp. 161-69.

[42] *L.Sc.D.*, pp. 22, 31 f., 46; *C.&R.*, p. 52.

[43] *C.&R.*, p. 51 (italics in original).

J. O. Wisdom

THE NATURE OF 'NORMAL' SCIENCE[1]

INTRODUCING THE PROBLEMS

The topic I wish to discuss concerns the processes of development of science. It has arisen of recent times because there is a renewed interest in the history of science and one or two new theories about the nature of the history of science have come on the market. It might seem strange that this should be so—at first sight it is fairly obvious in general terms what history is about, and therefore fairly obvious what the history of science is about. But this is not so, as we can see if we consider Kuhn's *The Structure of Scientific Revolutions* (1962), or Agassi's *Towards an Historiography of Science* (1963), which are the two most novel and important contributions to the subject.

First of all, I must try to indicate briefly what kind of problem it is that I wish to discuss. It is a metascientific problem, not a historical one. Though the canvas is the history of science, my discussion has to do with the role of metascience, or the philosophy of science operating in the medium of the history of science.

Thus the emphasis falls on metascience, although the medium is history; so one has to consider the nature of metascience. The application to the history of science will be one thing, if we take an inductive view of science, quite another if we follow Popper. I want to bring out some of the implications for history that ensue on Popper's theory of refutability as given in his *The Logic of Scientific Discovery* (1959), and to consider these in relation to Kuhn. Though at first sight it seems that Kuhn is doing something quite different from Popper, there is, despite some disparity of views, an extraordinary likeness. I want to try to bring out the relationship between these two. I want to open out what would be Popper's view of the metascience of the history of science, if this were worked out, and the relationship between it and Kuhn's, which is worked out to a high degree (though I think not completely) in his extraordinarily able and interesting book. This problem will become fully explicit only gradually in the first three main sections. For it has three

main facets: (1) refutability and puzzle-solving; (2) crisis; (3) logical corroboration and sociological acceptance. Then I want to go on to another connected topic, to do with the relation between the empirical content of a scientific theory and its philosophical framework. These two problems are in-
terwoven, as I hope will become clear.

Butterfield's Contribution

I should like to preface my remarks on Kuhn by a few remarks on an
earlier writer, because, before this recent reconsideration of the history of
science, there was a highly interesting work, quite a number of years ago now,
written in 1947 by Butterfield[2] on the origins of modern science. It is a work
that well repays reading today, is extraordinarily freshly written, and has the
merit of being written by a nonscientist who has genuinely come to grips with
science. In this last respect it is quite the opposite of Kuhn's, the great merit
of which is that it is written by a scientist who looks through the eyes of a
scientist, knows what scientific work feels like, both in its dramatic discoveries and its day-to-day work—a point, by the way, that is sometimes
overlooked by metascientific critics.

Butterfield's work suffers from one slight disavantage: It is a bit too
cursory. It is a work that would have been finer had it been more fully
developed. Indeed, it is so gently written that one can read it without noticing how good a book it is. This is a pity, because it contains, I think, an interesting thesis, and it is quite difficult to distil from it what exactly the thesis
is. There are a few negative points that come out clearly enough. Thus the
history of science—and in the context it is evident that Butterfield has in mind
the history of scientific revolutions—is not just a history of one great name
followed by another great name, that is to say, a kind of chart joining up
points from 1686, say, to the next great date; narration, or what I would call
chronography. Nor is it just a history of success stories. Nor is it a cumulative
doctrine that science is the accumulation of discoveries or the accumulation
of knowledge of facts. All these things Butterfield decries. More recently
many of them have been subject to heavy fire from Agassi, who has incisively
demolished them.[3] Butterfield makes no heavy weather over it. He makes it
plain that these are not reasonable approaches to history. Butterfield's
positive thesis can, I think, be put into two words. First, so far from
'revolutions' being traceable to external factors, the position is that scientists
are at some stage floundering with problems, in struggling with which they
undergo a change in the workings of their minds, they see old things in a new
way, and manage to get a key idea (this is a phrase he is very fond of); then,
with the key the lock is turned, so to speak. Second, when unlocked, the sluice
gates are opened. By which he means that discoveries then flow along very

easily, once you have got the key and unlocked the gates.

Kuhn would, I think, accept all of Butterfield's two major ideas, the metaphor of keys and the sluice gates. I do not think they do full justice to the nature of scientific discovery, but they are factors (though Kuhn has gone a long way beyond Butterfield);[4] in fact, it will become plain that Butterfield's key is Kuhn's paradigm, and the sluice gates are Kuhn's 'normal' science consisting of puzzle solving.

I. KUHN ON 'NORMAL' SCIENCE

Now Kuhn has a thesis that embraces a number of very different propositions, one of which is that there is a period in normal science, then a period of crisis. Although Kuhn's title concerns scientific revolution, he gives close attention to what he calls 'normal' science, which is nonrevolutionary. And this, I think, is where one metascientific problem arises.

The period of normal science is one which he spreads himself over and of which he gives a very fine description. This is the sort of thing that you do not readily find in books on the history of science or in books of metascience. I will try to give a bird's-eye view of what he has to say about this. In some periods the scientist is concerned with elaborating knowledge he already has, i.e., making and getting more accurate estimates of existing knowledge. For example, he may want to estimate the mass of the moon more accurately than it was done before. He may want to estimate melting points or densities and things of that sort more accurately, and a lot of highly careful experimental work may be involved. Such work is both factual and theoretical. It has to do with establishing facts which might be called general facts. One may need some of these facts for certain practical purposes like nautical almanacs; or it may be interesting to predict eclipses with more accuracy than you have previously predicted them. One needs these things for practical purposes and for developments in technology. But one also needs them because they have to do with relations of facts to theories, in particular with the possibility of further testing existing theories. For instance, getting the mass of the moon right is highly important for testing one of the applications/consequences of Newton's theory, namely the motion of the tides: as an application, this provides information about the tides needed for practical purposes; as a consequence, it provides a test (corroboration) of Newton's theory.

That would be one area which could be roughly described as investigating certain kinds of facts with greater discrimination than was done before. My main reason for highlighting this point is that it gives a picture of normal science that is usually overlooked by us philosophers of science. Another area of normal science concerns crucial predictions or calculations of such things as the acceleration due to gravity at different parts of the earth. This is of considerable interest because it can be used both to test a theory and to work out practical values for g at the same time. It brings out such interesting things as the role of experimental apparatus (the Atwood machine would not have been invented, if it had not been for the existence of the theory of gravitation). At the same time, it can be used for testing as well as for estimating.

In addition, there are other sorts of activities, such as 'articulating' a theory more precisely. This is different from making certain values of certain factual readings more exact. For example, if you take the Newtonian theory of gravitation, a good deal of work has gone on from time to time working out the value of the gravitational constant. This articulates the theory in a certain quite different sense, which is easily understandable. You have the theory stating that the force of gravitation is proportional to certain factors, but the factor of proportionality was not known at first. A further piece of work of an experimental kind was required to determine it. This articulates the law in making it more precise and definite. Such articulating of a law is different from getting a numerical value, say, for densities.

Then, quantitative laws, like the law of falling bodies or laws of constants which vary from material to material, come under the same heading, and study of the constant articulates a theory more exactly. According to Kuhn, you can also have a phenomenon like elaboration of the theory leading to Coulomb's law, or investigations to find the law of cooling. In this connection, mention should also be made of applications. This, I think is a vital heading, because again it is one that tends to be overlooked by metascientists. It is easy enough to find examples from Newtonian dynamics. You can first of all elaborate the theory in the simple terms in which it was originally given, and then you may decide that it would be interesting to exploit it in certain other fields, such as in other media like water or air or different fluids, and in this way you develop the science of hydrodynamics; or you can work out the theory of mechanics for resisting media and consider what would happen to projectiles if they were shot out in a resisting medium. This gives a vast amount of work of a normal kind which takes a great degree of originality to do, and is highly characteristic of ordinary science as it goes along from day to day. Kuhn's claim about it is that a new theory is not at stake here. The application of the original theory consists simply in the use of the theory in a specific field where you may have to introduce subsidiary hypotheses. But no revolution in theory is involved.

This is a rather cursory description of the kinds of activities that Kuhn refers to as going on in the day-to-day work of the scientist. I have skated over it rather fast because it is all set out in Kuhn, who puts it very much better than I have done in my summary account. (It is a pity, however, that

Kuhn should have used the term 'normal' science for this, for it implies that revolutions are not part of normal science. Certainly I would regard the revolutions by which one great theory is replaced by another as 'normal' to science. But this is not, as we shall see, the objection to Kuhn raised by some interpreters of Popper.)

'Normal' Science as Puzzle-Solving and as Daily Rebellion

When Kuhn comes to summarize this phase, he describes it as puzzle-solving. He means that, in exploiting a theory in some new direction, you have a succession of knotty tasks calling for great ingenuity, even genius; and what you set yourself to do is to unravel the puzzle. Let us expand this. In dealing with a puzzle, until it has yielded there is some difficulty. Now a difficulty is something to be got over, either a task or a problem. When the puzzle does not yield to repeated expert attention, the difficulty is regarded not as a task to be accomplished but as a problem requiring some new solution. However, when a difficulty arises, you do not at once go about it by regarding it as a problem and scrapping the fundamental theory; you first try all the devices of puzzle-solving you can think of, to accomplish the initial task.

This is the first big metascientific point that emerges from Kuhn and where he thinks he is differing from Popperian metascience, and where the followers of Popper also seem to think that Kuhn is differing from them. My first main point is that fundamentally there is no clash here at all, only an appearance of one which arises from the fairly simple oversight. To get at this we must go back over one or two metascientific matters.

Popper's fundamental metascientific thesis is that you are always concerned to refute hypotheses, to test hypotheses by seeing if they can be refuted. Naturally, you do not want to end up by having hypotheses or theories refuted; but they must be capable of being refuted if they are to be acceptable at all as scientific. (This, of course, is a very large-scale metascience which I am putting in a sentence, but later I shall expand it a little.) Popper's metascience has then been applied to the history of science, but the application has been oversimplified or hasty; it is to the effect that all history of science (apart from the formation of theories) must consist of attempts to test theories (and therefore consist of attempts to refute theories)—that this is so at all points all the time, even when the various kinds of activities described above as 'normal' science are engaged upon, even when checking a density point or applying a theory. In fact, it has been attributed to Popper that he has described the history of science as 'revolution in permanence'. This phrase has been used recently to describe the natural application to the history of science of Popper's metascience. I want to show that it is not a proper deduction from the Popperian metascience, and therefore that there is no clash with Kuhn (in this area). The difference between the two can be put roughly like this. On the view accorded to Popper, every theory is all the time in all circumstances being tested, no matter what applications are going on. Thus the daily work of science, if not revolutionary, aims at small-scale rebellion (which might blossom into a revolution at any moment). According to Kuhn, the situation is quite different: you are not attempting to test a theory at all; in certain circumstances you are concerned simply to exploit it, use it, extend it, apply it. The Popperian might, to this account, reply, "Of course, you may be extending the theory; but, if the extension goes wrong, this is taken as a test of the theory." It is this contention that requires investigation.

The Role of a Counterexample for Popper

The way we may lead into the issue is by considering one of the very few slips that I think Kuhn makes. He remarks, and quite rightly, that if something goes wrong with a test or some counterexample turns up, this is not regarded by a scientist as a counterexample to a fundamental theory—not at once.[5] But Kuhn supposes that, according to Popper, the counterexample is a counterexample to the theory and refutes it. Kuhn disagrees with the supposedly Popperian contention,[6] and says, rightly, that the scientist would, of course, be right. For the scientist a whole crop of questions would arise. In the case of an experimental test involving mathematics, the scientist would doubtless first check the mathematics, then enquire whether some accidental disturbance had spoilt the experiment, then check whether his instruments had been working properly, and then look into the possibility of bungling the experimental work; he might even begin to wonder whether there was some subsidiary hypothesis about the use of the instruments that was wrong, and he might go the length of considering whether the fundamental theory was correctly articulated for the purpose in hand. Many steps would have to be taken, which metascientists scarcely ever mention, before coming to those that interest them. So, Kuhn is right that a counterexample is not a refutation of a theory. But Popper knows this too. Kuhn, somehow, perhaps understandably, thought that Popper would deny it.

Let us now dwell on a relevant point in Popper's theory of refutability, which is quite clearly stated in his opening work of 1934, and which has not been modified since on the point at issue. The theory of refutability[7] in its intuitive outline is very simple. It is that a theory to be accredited as scientific has to be refutable, and you have to be able to specify what would constitute a refutation. This means that, if a consequence of a theory turns out to be wrong, then the theory is falsified. This is the rough intuitive way you can put it to begin with. Now this is misleading, for it might suggest that the falsification was absolute; but Popper[8] holds it is not; and he amplifies his theory in the body of his work. You have the theory as a major premiss. But you have other premisses as well—perhaps several of them—and you must have at least one other, which will state initial conditions; for it is impossible to derive an empirical consequence (or make a prediction) from a theory without bringing in initial conditions, or some form of observation-statement. Thus you have several premisses, at least two, when you make a test. When you get a prediction that is wrong, this tells you that, if the inference is valid, there is falsity to be unearthed and pin-pointed somewhere among the premisses. But it does not tell you where. Popper knows this perfectly well. He has emphasized it many times, it is in his first book, and he never overlooked the point. You do not know that the theory is falsified. You do know only that one of the premisses is false. The premiss *might* be the theory, but it might be the initial conditions. And this is as far as you get with the falsification.

Refutability-Theory Compatible with 'Normal Science'

We may now enquire how far this development of Popper squares with Kuhn's theory of 'normal' science and then with his theory of crisis.

The question arises for the working scientist, however, though not for the metascientist, whether the error is to be pin-pointed on one of the other features mentioned above. Do you suppose there was a mistake in the logical deduction?[9] Or a chance effect that altered the initial conditions? Or some failure of instruments, bearing on one of the minor premisses? Or some bungling which would do the same? Or some inaccurate articulation of the theory? Or what? The position may be put more sharply by classifying the premisses or other features of a scientific inference as follows: (i) the general premisses constituting the fundamental theory; (ii) the particular observational premisses constituting the initial conditions; (iii) subsidiary premisses/assumptions to do with miscellaneous conditions concerning chance effects, failure of instruments, theory of instruments, bungling, articulation of theory, validity of deductions. It seems to me good horse sense, which anyone doing any kind of practical or theoretical work would always do, on the grounds of economy of time, economy of labor, and perhaps for other reasons, that the scientist—though not the metascientist—will first concern himself with the possibilities of loopholes in the subsidiary premisses/assumptions, in case something will turn up that will save the prediction, save the theory. In other words, he will try to do puzzle-solving.

The only reason the metascientist is not at one with this is not disagreement but lack of interest: he assumes that such steps have been tried (assuming he knows about them), i.e., that the subsidiary premisses/assumptions have been checked and he becomes interested only when these steps have failed to work out the puzzle. What happens then? Supposing you cannot find anything wrong with the test, do you throw out the fundamental theory? The answer is still "No," both for the scientist and the metascientist: the fault may be in the initial conditions. In this situation, I think that, rationally speaking, the only thing to do is to suspend judgment. It is too early to know whether the fundamental theory is wrong, or whether something undetected about the initial conditions is involved. (The latter turned out to be the answer over the perturbations of Uranus, which were explained when the initial conditions were altered by Adams and Leverrier to include Neptune.)

Thus, even at this stage, a false consequence of a theory is not a counterexample to the theory. Even when the subisdiary premises/assumptions have been gone over, it is a counterexample only to the remaining set of premises/assumptions yielding it.[10] How does the scientist settle the question at this point of whether the fault, or falsity, lies in the theory or in the initial conditions? Again there is no specific metascientific prescription for this. Falling back once again on the notion of economy of time and effort when a business man considers how to handle a difficulty, the sensible thing to do is to work on the initial conditions first, simply because this is much easier than the immensely difficult task of altering the theory.

I propose to call this phase one of "paradigm-exploitation" (to anticipate a concept of Kuhn's) to cover elaboration, puzzle-solving, theoretical application, etc. I have presented it as compatible with Popper's refutability-theory of metascience, without interpreting the phrase as one of testing underlying theory. Thus Popper's metascience is entirely consonant with Kuhn's phase of 'normal' science.

II. FROM ANOMALY TO CRISIS

After serious attempts at puzzle-solving have failed, we have what Kuhn calls an "anomaly": the scientist does not yet know whether his theory is false or whether there is something about the initial conditions that has eluded him. Let us now make use of the foregoing elaboration of the falsifiability-theory for the second time.

Suppose this phenomenon, an anomaly, occurs a handful of times. Then you have a situation that Kuhn describes as a "crisis."[11] That is to say, a number of anomalies turn up, puzzles, which cannot be explained away or explained within the terms of the theory. When puzzles become anomalies, there is 'crisis' and then scientists may not know where to turn next.

It seems to me that this position is exactly what is required on Popper's metascientific theory and of Kuhn's theory of history. At this point one can get aid from ordinary simple considerations about what is most likely. If you have a number of situations in which predictions have gone wrong, say a handful, then it becomes highly unlikely that in every single one of those there is some mistake about the initial conditions (or even that there is some un-located mistake in the subsidiary premisses/assumptions); this becomes more and more unlikely with each particular anomaly that occurs. So, when you have a handful of these, the probability that they can *all* be explained in this way is extremely small. It is at that point that it becomes reasonable for scientists to consider that perhaps, after all, the fault lies not with the initial conditions but with the fundamental theory. It is at this point that the false consequences or counterexamples are regarded as a refutation specifically to the theory (though the refutation is not absolute).

The position is the same on Popper's metascience; for, on his view, falsification is not absolute, though often taken to be so. It has sometimes seemed to philosophers that, when Popper stressed the impossibility of ob-taining verification of a hypothesis no matter how many confirmations were found, whereas one disconfirmation would falsify it, this implied the ab-soluteness of falsification. But this is so, for Popper, only if the initial con-ditions are taken for granted and are not in question. This is a logical point. His theory puts falsification in a totally different position from verification: verification is impossible, even if the initial conditions are granted; falsifica-tion is possible (and would be absolute) if the statement of initial conditions is true. Thus the concept of falsifiability has applicability, even though it cannot be applied with absolute certainty. In the real situation, the initial conditions may be questioned and then the falsification of a hypothesis is not absolute.[12] On Popper's theory, then, one can accept Kuhn's thesis that there is a period of science consisting of elaborations, exploitations, applications, and things of that sort in which the fundamental aim is not the testing of a theory. When there are sufficient failures, i.e., there are enough anomalies to create a crisis, then the anomalies become tests of the theory and of the fundamental premiss of the theory rather than of the other premisses.

I think I have at one and the same time managed to outline Kuhn's theory and Popper's, because the apparent difference between their views evaporates in the way I have put the position. This result hinges on the fact, which Popper himself made explicit even in his first work, that falsification is not absolute, or that a false consequence is a counterexample only to a set of premisses and not necessarily to the premiss expressing the theory.[13]

III. KUHN'S SOCIOLOGY OF ACCEPTANCE OF NEW THEORIES

I should first try to bring out such differences in their views as Kuhn and Popper might suppose were there. For Kuhn there is an extralogical factor in the situation: the scientist simply does not wish to give up the theory when an anomaly first arises. But, when there are several anomalies, there is a crisis, and maybe a new theory is produced. The new theory cannot be adopted on any kind of logical grounds, for it creates too many new problems and there is no knowing whether they will be too difficult for it, and it is adopted at least partly because it gets over the immediate crisis.[14] Popper's theory, by contrast, looks as if it depended solely on logical considerations. Thus Kuhn takes a view of science that appears to be slightly less rationalistic than Popper's, in the sense (he does not speak of 'rationality') that he holds there is no specific logical procedure, nothing resembling a demonstration, that compels rejection or acceptance of a theory. Before discussing this, let us consider a cognate point.

Kuhn gives the impression first of all that scientists who develop a new theory cannot be on speaking terms with scientists of the first theory[15]—to be specific, that Einsteinian scientists could not really understand Newtonian physics, and the other way around. (This impression does, I think, more or less reflect Kuhn's view, but it should be borne in mind that he allows some role to logical considerations.) It certainly is true in practice that there is often great difficulty in communication between scientists who follow a new theory and those who follow an old; but certainly there are times when they can sift the matter out and understand one another. Nonetheless Kuhn does give a certain amount of powder and shot to those who criticize him for giving an irrationalistic account of scientific development. I think it is possible that, in his skillful depiction of the entire change, not only of theory, but of constituent concepts (e.g., mass) from Newtonian mechanics to relativity,[16] he may have gone beyond what was needed for this purpose and suggested the impossibility of communication in principle.

Kuhn[17] adds to the somewhat irrational flavor by suggesting that when a new theory is produced there is what I would call a bandwagon effect (though this expression somewhat exaggerates his sociological tendency). Somehow or other, the new theory becomes accepted, and the old one becomes rejected, as a result of a not fully rational change of attitude. Now there are, of course, all sorts of social reasons why this is so. A new generation of scientists grows up, and the old ones die off or retire, and we all know that in middle age we get hardening of the arteries and find it more difficult to understand new ideas. We reach middle years ourselves and this may happen to us without our always realizing it. This is a commonplace. Such facts give a sociological basis for the idea that scientific theories do not get refuted; like old soldiers, they only fade away. This is the sort of impression Kuhn conveys.[18] However, the question is whether such sociological pressures are a fundamental or merely an auxiliary effect that takes place on the surface. The question is whether there is also a rational factor involved, and whether it is decisive. I think, myself, that there is a different process at work, which I now wish to describe. And I shall at the same time try to show how Kuhn tries to include—I think unsuccessfully—logical considerations within his sociological theory of rejection and acceptance of paradigms.

Alternative Balancing of Logical and Sociological Determinants

When a new theory is propounded, there is, no doubt, a great shock to the middle-aged, who are perhaps emotionally tied to previous theory; and there may be a great deal of difficulty in understanding the new theory (some people may be able to remember the enormous difficulty people had in understanding Einstein in the first quarter of the century). Nonetheless, in the end the small number of top-grade scientists in a certain line will recognize that the evidence favors the new theory and will accept it, and thereby accept it on rational grounds.

Kuhn knows this just as well as I do, and he is overt about it. Why, therefore, does he give a sociological account, when he recognizes that there are rational factors to do with evidence? What he says is that evidence plays a part. The question is, what part; for it must play a decisive part, or the role it plays is not significant at all so far as a specific logical procedure for rejection or acceptance of a theory is concerned. Kuhn's answer is a rather curious one. Let us have some key passages.

> . . . to say . . . that paradigm change cannot be justified by proof, is not to say that no arguments are relevant . . . [151]
> All the arguments for a new paradigm discussed so far have been based upon the competitors' comparative ability to solve problems. To scientists these arguments are primarily the most significant and persuasive . . . But, for reasons to which we shall shortly revert, they are neither individually nor collectively compelling. [153]
> . . . if a new candidate for paradigm had to be judged from the start by hard-headed people who examined only relative problem-solving ability, the sciences would experience very few major revolutions. [156]
> Even today Einstein's general theory attracts men principally on aesthetical grounds . . . [157]
> If authority alone, and particularly if non-professional authority, were the arbiter of debates, the outcome of those debates might still be revolution, but it would not be *scientific* revolution. The very existence of science depends upon vesting the power to choose between paradigms in the members of a special kind of community. [166]
> . . . scientists will be reluctant to embrace a new candidate for paradigm unless convinced that two all-important conditions are being met. First, the new candidate must seem to resolve some outstanding and generally recognized problem that can be met in no other way. Second, the new paradigm must promise to preserve a relatively large part of the concrete problem-solving ability that was accrued to science through its predecessors. [168]

These passages display a shift of emphasis from the influence of argument to its lack of adequacy, back to a basis in what is scientific, thence to a community-judgment, and back to scientific efficacy. This last seems to be a wholly rational justification, i.e., it seems to place the whole emphasis on evidence: if a new paradigm solves problems an old one does not, the old one is refuted. But the role of sociological factors does not allow this to be decisive. How then are we to resolve the apparent ambiguity of Kuhn's position? There is one more passage, which supplies the key.

> Because scientists are reasonable men, one or another argument will ultimately persuade many of them. *But there is no single argument that can or should persuade them all.* [157] [Italics mine]

This is susceptible of the interpretation either that the pieces of evidence that appeal to one scientist are not necessarily the same as those that appeal to another, or that the same pieces of evidence are weighed differently. Now, if you will just dwell on this for a moment, it is much more curious than it looks. Supposing *you* are possessed of, say, three pieces of evidence that convince *you*. And suppose *I* am convinced by three different factors, or at any rate suppose not all of these are the same. Then there is agreement among the various scientists on the grounds of evidence, but there is nothing that you could call intersubjective testing. And the same holds if very different weights are attached to factors they agree upon. So, although they may be rational men and thinking in terms of evidence for the theory, since there is lack of agreement about the evidence, specific logical factors, though present, play no decisive role. You have a situation that I would describe as being like a syndrome of a disease, where the set of symptoms varies from patient to patient, or, if the same, varies as regards intensity, and is the same in several patients only in rare cases. The doctor makes a diagnosis on the basis of a syndrome which is not the same as the one the text book describes as typical, or differs from it markedly in intensity. This is a commonplace even in an epidemic of influenza. Of course, you hope that there is one characteristic feature which will reveal the disorder quite decisively; but this is very often not the case. Thus there is a question of skill in getting below a syndrome which does not follow, copybook-wise, what the text book describes. The doctor nonetheless does have an independent test, if he makes a diagnosis on the basis of a varying syndrome. He can test it by sending certain specimens to a laboratory for further examination.

But, in our situation, consisting of a varying syndrome of evidence, there is no independent test, no constant intersubjective observation or evidence.

So, despite Kuhn's holding that evidence or some specific logical factor is at work, or plays a role, it plays no *decisive* role. Therefore, it seems to me that fundamentally Kuhn comes down on one side of a knife edge, in favor of sociological explanations of scientific change.[19] Popper's metascience would come down on the other side of the knife edge; though there would, of course, be no reason to deny that sociological factors entered in as auxiliary influences. On Popper's metascience, it would have to be the same factors in comparable degree—the same evidence—that appeals to all scientists who are really competent to judge. And when they have let it be known that they accept the theory, then I think it is at that point that the bandwagon effect may take place. It convinces people on the fringe that they need worry about the controversy no longer. Supposing, for instance, that you are working in low temperature physics, but are not a specialist, say, in a theory of motion, you may not be too interested in going into the question of whether the tests in relativity are genuine, convincing, and decisive. But, if the recognized authorities on it are satisfied, then you tend to be, too. This is reasonably respectable and, in calling it a bandwagon effect, I do not want to cast too much of an aspersion on it (though there can of course be less noble bandwagon effects as well). Thus, so long as you have a specific logical procedure as a basis, e.g., uniform evidence accepted by the top-grade people in the line, it does not affect the rationality or the status of the theory if a lot of rank and file people, or top-grade people in another line, accept the theory mainly on sociological grounds.

With these three sections I conclude my comparison of Kuhn and Popper with respect to exploitation of paradigm, crisis, and corroboration versus sociological acceptance. On the first two I have tried to show that they are fundamentally at one. On the first, to do with 'normal science' or paradigm-exploitation, I have reconstructed Popper in a way that aligns him with Kuhn. On the second, to do with crisis and revolution, I have given a reconstruction that both Popper and Kuhn can fit. On the third there is a knife-edge difference which creates a deep and fundamental cleavage;[20] I have given a reconstruction which Popper can fit, but which, though it absorbs an element from Kuhn, is incompatible with his sociological theory of scientific knowledge.

IV. KUHN'S CONCEPT OF PARADIGM

Now I want to pass next to a point that does not come out clearly in Kuhn. It has to do with the concept of a paradigm. This is a nice idea; but it is not easy to say just what it means. He would give examples of paradigms, such as Newton's theory of gravitation or Einstein's general theory of relativity, meaning that they are *dominant* theories in terms of which you view all the problems that arise within a certain field. Confronted with any problem, say, if you hold out a piece of heavy string so that it sags like a telegraph wire and you want to find out what sort of equation would describe it, you would instinctively approach this matter through Newtonian statics which would be the paradigm for solving this problem.

Empirical Content, Embedded Ontology, and Weltanschauung

Kuhn often[21] speaks of a paradigm as if it stood for the *empirical content* of a dominant scientific theory. For example, the paradigm of Newton's celestial mechanics is the inverse square law of gravitation, i.e., that the force of gravitation between two masses is equal to the product of the masses divided by the square of the distance. And the paradigm for motion would be the law that force is proportional to acceleration. These examples at least suggest an emphasis on empirical content. However, there are places where Kuhn seems to extend the concept more widely, e.g., where he says that the paradigm tells you what sort of things a scientific theory leads you to expect the world to be constituted of.[22] The paradigm will tell you whether the world, for some particular branch of science, is composed of little atoms or waves or composed of monads or something else. Thus there is something more metaphysical that can come into the notion of a paradigm, if you take it in this wider sense. And there are several passages in Kuhn's discussions of paradigms where it is uncertain whether he is referring to the descriptive or the metaphysical components of a theory.[23]

To go further with this matter, I want to draw certain distinctions. First, I want to consider a distinction between the empirical concept of a theory and a mesh of ontology that goes with it.

Consider, first, empirical content. As an example, take the Newtonian theory of gravitation and let us suppose for simplicity that its empirical content consists of the inverse square law (if there should be more in it than the empirical content, this will not affect the main point). The obvious hallmark of empirical content is that it should be empirically testable, i.e., refutable by observation (in the sense already explained, of being falsifiable given the truth of the premises involving initial conditions and of the subsidiary premisses/assumptions).

With empirical content goes a conception that is apparently not empirical; at least, in highly developed areas like Newtonian mechanics there are conceptions for which there is no clearly developed empirical test. Let us take as an example that space is absolute, time is absolute, motion (or rest) is absolute, or that masses are composed of little corpuscles. If you are making a prediction, making a calculation of any sort, deriving the path of a planet, deriving any empirical consequence from the inverse square law, premises such as these typically never appear overtly in the deductions (possible exceptional cases will be taken up anon). No doubt Newtonian theory is so permeated by these conceptions that they are present implicitly in all deductions, if, as seems likely, it is impossible to state the pure empirical content without involving them. Thus, if you speak of measuring an object at rest and again as it moves away, you assume the Newtonian absolute about rigidity—an independence of reference frame, in fact the absoluteness of space. But these conceptions do not typically appear expressly. Further, if we articulated them, they would not be testable by observation, because there would be no way of testing them separately from the empirical content; put another way, if the empirical content is taken as true, this rules out the possibility of there being any observation left that could test them.

Such conceptions, which go with empirical content, even to the extent of permeating it, I propose to call the 'embedded ontology' of the theory.

Now there is the possibility of a flaw in the examples used, which is instructive. It is a classical argument for the absoluteness of rest, originating with Newton,[24] that the absoluteness of rotation can be shown by experiment. You take a bucket at rest, with water in it at rest, then the water has a plane surface; if you now rotate the bucket at uniform speed the water climbs up the side and develops a hollow, a paraboloid of revolution. That is the experiment. Here is the argument. If motion is relative, the parabolic water, with the hollow in it, could be regarded as at rest, with the Earth spinning round under it. But then there would be no centrifugal force to form the hollow, and the water would have a plane surface. But this is not the case. Therefore motion is not relative.

On this several comments are called for. (i) The argument is atypical, and might be said to be outside the paradigm, because it does not use the inverse square law or Newton's second law of motion (only the experience of centripetal force is needed to explain the existence of a hollow, though more, i.e., the second law, would be needed to explain its specific parabolic form). (ii) The experiment is used as a direct test of relative versus absolute rotation, as the hypothesis of absolute motion, *in this context,* is not a piece of embedded ontology but a piece of empirical content. (iii) It is sound to make every effort to test or find empirical consequences of a theory or hypothesis, even if it consists apparently only of ontological factors and lacks empirical content; for we can never tell a priori that a theory or hypothesis will be forever in the unempirical ontological list and not become empirically contentful. It would be wrong if metascience were a rigid legislative authority that restricted scientific activity. (iv) These considerations do not prevent absolute motion from being embedded ontology in another context, e.g., in that of gravitational theory. Moreover, (v) The inference is invalid. For, even on an absolutist view of space a bucket at 'rest' on the Earth is undergoing several relative rotations. These relative rotations are, of course, small in comparison with the rotation of the water round its own axis, and do not noticeably affect the shape of the hollow. Hence the hollow is mainly due to the rotation of the water round its own axis, but is compatible with being subject to other relative rotations having practically no effect. Hence Newton's conclusion must be, not that there is absolute rotation at an absolute place, but that there is an absolute rotation subject to movement in space, and for all we know to movement in relative space. And this does not yield the conclusion of absolute space. All that Newton can conclude is that there are, so to speak 'relative absolute rotations', and this is not what he wanted.

In short, if the inference is invalid, then absolute motion remains embedded ontology and is not part of the empirical content of Newtonian mechanics, and, if valid, all that ensues is that what is embedded ontology in one context is empirical content in another.

If it appears strange that a hypothesis might pass from being embedded ontology to being empirical content, we may reflect upon actual examples. The Greek atomic theory is perhaps one. Another would be the germ theory of disease as put forward before Koch and Pasteur. Even these may suffice to show that the status of a theory depends upon context.

The distinction in question has been implied by various writers, but I think unwittingly; the only distinction that was articulated was between a scientific theory and a metaphysical underlay. But this seems to me to have been a different conception, referring to presuppositions, but not part of the warp and weft of the theory. What I wish to stress about embedded ontology is its immanence.

Next I wish to effect a further distinction between embedded ontology and the outlook that goes with the empirical content and particularly with the embedded ontology. That is to say, when you have a large-scale theory and embedded ontology, you will have a special way of looking upon the world. I would call this the 'Weltanschauung' of the theory.

The embedded ontology and the Weltanschauung are conceptually quite distinct in the sense that the embedded ontology is a structure attributed to the world, whereas the Weltanschauung is a way of seeing the world in view of this structure. Further, such an account does not preclude the possibility of a Weltanschauung arising in some other way; and there might be a period in which there would be no empirical theory with embedded ontology corresponding to that Weltanschauung. In the case of Newtonian theory, for example, the Weltanschauung would consist of seeing the physical world as composed of purely material particles subject to rigid law governing their motion through a honeycombed space with their structure uninfluenced by the situation of their neighbours.

Returning to Kuhn, he does not seem to me to have fully articulated the embedded ontology of a paradigm. When he is discussing the change involved in a scientific revolution, he seems on the whole to mean by paradigm the change-over from the empirical content of one theory to the empirical content of another, although there are overtones in his work to suggest the contrary. I would submit that one cannot give an adequate account of what happens in the period of scientific revolution in terms of paradigms unless one gives it at least in terms both of the empirical content of a theory and also the embedded ontology.

Is Empirical Content or Embedded Ontology the Paradigm and Influence?

Having drawn the distinctions, I wish to investigate whether it is the empirical content of a predominant theory, or the embedded ontology, or the Weltanschauung that is paradigmatic and influential for the course of ingenious elaboration in science and for the nature of scientific revolution.

The phase of elaboration may seem to consist in exploiting the empirical content of a paradigm. And so, I think, it does, given the puzzle. But the selection of the puzzle depends upon its being amenable to treatment by the empirical content; and its being amenable to treatment would seem to consist in its conformity to the embedded ontology or to the Weltanschauung of the paradigm.

As regards scientific revolution, many scientists, and, indeed, metascientists, would hold that in the end what tells is the empirical content of a theory. What you test is always, apparently, the empirical content and not this other vague fringe of philosophical ideas. Although I believe that the empirical content is usually what tells in the end, I do not think it is what governs controversy about a change-over. Supposing you take the change-over from Newtonian to Einsteinian physics. One consequence of relativity physics was not only that the celestial mechanics of Newton was falsified, but also that space is not absolute. The interesting point is that observation—the observation, let us say, of Mercury or the observation to do with stars at times of total eclipse—will refute the Newtonian hypothesis, i.e., the empirical content of it. They will not refute the absoluteness of space.[25] To get a refutation of the idea that space is absolute, you have to have a new theory. It is a consequence of the Einstein theory, and not of the observations, that the absoluteness of space is refuted. I can perhaps make the point a little clearer by putting it another way. It is a consequence of Einstein's theory that space is relative and cannot be thought of as box-like. Therefore, it is a consequence that the Newtonian theory of absolute space is false. Thus the refutation of this embedded ontology comes from a new embedded ontology, that is, a consequence of a new empirical theory, i.e., the refutation is not obtained by an observation.

This is interesting for a number of reasons. It gives you a method by which embedded ontological ideas can, in the end, if you are lucky, be shown to be false. But further, it brings to our notice a point which I think is vital when we try to understand scientists who are judging between theories. Which was it, let us say, that appealed to a scientist of 1905, who was a good old Newtonian and believed in Euclidean geometry? Was it the empirical content of Newton's theory that appealed to him, or was it the ontology embedded in it? Was it the belief that space somehow must be absolute—anything else being 'unthinkable'—that made him tick? And when a change-over takes place, is the difficulty of persuading people of the validity of the new theory due to the fact that they are attached to the old empirical theory or to the old embedded ontology or Weltanschauung? I submit that it is the embedded ontology or Weltanschauung that catches scientists' emotions. I very much doubt if a scientist would really be so much attached to the empirical content of $F = M_1 M_2/r^2$ that he would be unwilling to give it up in the light of evidence for Einstein's theory, as so many people at the time were. If so, we can see why disputes about rival theories in a scientific revolution do not appear to be so rational as one would expect in a scientific setting. For, if they should be concerned fundamentally with the embedded ontology, or Weltanschauung of a theory rather than the empirical content, this would be much harder to discuss rationally, simply because the evidence is lacking in the sense that embedded ontology and Weltanschauung cannot be tested by observation. It is easy enough to point to the evidence that refutes the empirical content of a theory; it is much more difficult to handle the embedded ontology or the Weltanschauung. If this is right, there is much less reason to be hard on the supposed irrationality of scientists who would not give way when one paradigm was replacing another one.

There are, however, situations in which the reverse appears to hold. Thus, in the development of the modern atomic theory of chemistry, the attitude became current that the significant issue concerned the validity of actual chemical formulae and not the question whether atoms really exist. This was an area where an 'as if' philosophy flourished: there was no way of telling whether atoms exist or not, the chemical formulae could be used equally well with or without the assumption; atoms could be taken to be real or could be treated as if they were real without really being so. Thus what made chemists tick was the contents, the formulae, and they were prepared not to make a fuss about atoms in themselves. Now, in such cases it seems clear that the empirical content dominated the embedded ontology only when the situation encourages an attitude of logical positivism—concentrate on the empirical and distrust, dub as meaningless, treat as an 'as if ', or otherwise sweep under the carpet the ontology. Is this an exception to my thesis or an alternative attitude? To answer this, reflect that logical positivism was a Weltanschauung (in which the ontological was meaningless; but, though a nonentity, was constantly under the skin of logical positivists), for, according to it, the world was seen as what is outer: reality consists of appearances; the real is appearance and appearance is the real. In such cases, therefore, the empirical content of a theory is the sole object of reference of the Weltanschauung. It is thus at least a possibility that what excited chemists was not the chemical formulae but a Weltanschauung of chemical formulae.

It seems to me, then, that controversy rages over the Weltanschauung, centered on questions of embedded ontology; but that, if a controversy is resolved (and it need not be), tested empirical content is the decisive factor.

SUMMARY

Kuhn describes 'normal' science as consisting of elaborating existing knowledge, both as fact and in relation to theories, crucial predictions or calculations, the further articulation of theories, and applications of theories. He holds that all this has the nature of puzzle-solving. In other words, 'normal' science is puzzle-solving in the course of exploiting existing theories.

At the breakdown of puzzle-solving, a problem arises. According to Kuhn, you do not at once question the fundamental theory. He supposes that this is what you must do on Popper's metascience; and Popperians have ascribed to Popper the view that science is 'revolution in permanence', or in daily rebellion. Otherwise put, for Kuhn 'normal' science is not concerned with testing a theory, whereas for Popper it is said to be. But this interpretation of Popper must be questioned.

When a counterexample turns up, Kuhn claims it is not a counterexample to the fundamental theory and claims that scientists never treat it as such. I claim Popper's metascience likewise opposes this. Before taking such a step, a whole crop of loopholes have to be investigated: checking mathematics, accidental disturbances, instruments in working order, bungling, unsuspected misconceptions about the nature of the instruments, adequate articulation of the fundamental theory. We have to see that this is in line with Popper's theory. He stresses the role of initial conditions; so, for him, a counterexample is a counterexample to an inference containing not only the fundamental theory but also the initial conditions. There are also the other conditions listed, which may be called subsidiary premises/assumptions. Metascientists are not interested in these, they are interested in the situation only when these subsidiary premises/assumptions have been investigated. Even then the counterexample may point to an error, not in the fundamental theory but in the initial conditions. Only when the initial conditions have been investigated is it correct on Popper's metascience to consider pin-pointing the error on the fundamental theory. But even then this cannot be done with complete certainty, for some other factor may have been overlooked. So long as the fundamental theory is protected, puzzle-solving and paradigm-exploitation continue.

It follows that Kuhn is right that 'normal' science is exploitation of fundamental theory and not a test of it.

This was the first question I wished to sort out.

The second question concerns crisis.

When all the minor premisses that can be thought of, including the initial conditions have been investigated, the counterexample looks like being a refutation of the fundamental theory, but in view of doubt it is not yet taken to be so. It has the status of being an 'anomaly'.

However, when you get a handful of anomalies, it becomes highly improbable that something has been overlooked. At this point the handful of anomalies constitute a 'crisis' and the fundamental theory is taken to be refuted (though not with complete certainty).

It is, I claim, the same with Popper; for, falsification in his metascience is not absolute.

Thus Kuhn's theory and (when correctly interpreted) Popper's (when developed) are identical.[26]

The third question concerns replacement by a new theory, which involves revolution. Here Kuhn adopts what in the end comes down to being a sociological view; though logical factors, i.e., evidence, play a part in determining the acceptance of a new theory, they are not logically decisive. His reason would seem to be that the evidence is not the same, whether in kind or degree, for all competent judges. His view is extremely near to being a logical one, and only just comes down on the side of being a sociological one.

Against this I put forward an alternative account, according to which the logical evidence is the same for the most competent judges, and then nonspecialists jump on the bandwagon for a variety of sociological reasons.

The third question concerns Kuhn's concept of a paradigm. He appears to apply this to the empirical content of a dominant theory. But we have to distinguish from the empirical content the embedded ontology, and even the Weltanschauung, of the theory, which is the way of seeing the world in view of the ontology embedded in the theory.

It would seem that the empirical content of a paradigm is what counts in the phase of ingenious exploitation of a theory, but that the nature of the puzzles selected is determined by their satisfying the embedded ontology or the Weltanschauung of the paradigm. Scientific revolution, however, seems to concern primarily the embedded ontology or the Weltanschauung. For one of the factors keep keeping controversy alive is that questions of ontology and Weltanschauung cannot be settled by observational testing. When there appear to be exceptions to this situation, the appearance is probably due to a logical positivist Weltanschauung, which denies the meaningfulness of the embedded ontology and can make an issue only over empirical content.

In short, empirical content determines puzzle-solving; the puzzles themselves are selected in accordance with embedded ontology or Weltanschauung. Controversy, or a battle of paradigms, is due to the Weltanschauung centering on the embedded ontologies at issue, and it cannot be settled by observational test; but, in the end, it is specific empirical content evidence, intersubjectively available, that constitutes the rational grounds upon which leading scientists relinquish one paradigm and adopt another; and the new Weltanschauung leads to a bandwagon effect.

J. O. WISDOM

DEPARTMENT OF PHILOSOPHY AND DIVISION OF SOCIAL SCIENCE
YORK UNIVERSITY, TORONTO, CANADA
DECEMBER, 1968

NOTES

[1] Based upon a lecture given at Claremont Graduate School, California, February 22, 1966; written at the University of Southern California, 1966-67.

[2] Butterfield (1947).

[3] In addition, Agassi (1963) has attacked the idea of history as a continuous development in which any step forward can be found to contain transitional moves, and the idea of history as quasi-automatic unfolding of new truth from preceding phases. Further, Agassi has contributed two additional strong metascientific criticisms on the writing of history: he shows that most of it is based either on the inductivist approach or conventionalism, and he delivers a sustained attack on these as inadequate to the interpretation of history.

[4] Agassi (1966) has also pointed out the kinship of Butterfield and Kuhn.

[5] Kuhn (1962), esp. pp. 77, 81.

[6] Popper (1959), p. 145.

[7] Popper (1959), pp. 40 f.

[8] Popper (1959), Chap. 5, pp. 42, 47.

[9] Cf. Kuhn (1962), p. 81.

[10] For simplicity one may write of disposing of the possibility of mistakes in the subsidiary premisses/assumptions and then concentrating on the theory and initial conditions; but in fact we can never dispose of all the possible subsidiary premisses/assumptions.

[11] Kuhn (1962), p. 82.

[12] Popper (1959), Chap. 5, pp. 42, 47. It must be emphasized that there are two distinct problems, that of demarcation, in relation to which verification cannot be completed while falsification is absolute, and that of the nonabsoluteness of a refutation because of the possibility of questioning the initial conditions; this distinction was clear in Popper's original 1934 work; but he has recently explicitly contrasted them somewhat as I have done (Popper, 1963).

[13] Lakatos (1967).

Lakatos has discussed Popper and Kuhn from the point of view of what Popper apparently calls metaphysical research programmes (I have not seen Popper's unpublished work on this). This means that, if a theory is falsified, it is well known in advance what step (and succession of steps) will be taken to make an adjustment; thus, if the theory is that motion is circular, the next variant will be that it is elliptical, the next that the centre of force will be moved, and so on; all this within one programme. Such a procedure is highly important as a distinct part of 'normal' science; its characteristics are that refutation of the programme is not absolute (though after a time it may be found impossible to carry the programme a step further and it is dropped). I would classify this phase of science as the childhood of a paradigm. It belongs more to a period just before 'normal' science or just after revolution rather than to revolution itself. Kuhn discussed preparadigm science, though not this aspect of it; but he would surely be very ready to make room for it. I do not think it calls for separate discussion in the present context, because my aims concern different issues. I do think, however, that Lakatos has drawn attention to a highly important phase in the growth of science. In developing this idea Lakatos is certainly presupposing an expansion of Popper's methodology such as I have developed.

[14] Kuhn (1962), pp. 155-57.

[15] *Ibid.*, pp. 146-50.

[16] Kuhn (1962), pp. 100-01, pp. 148 f.

[17] *Ibid.*, Chap. 12.

[18] Hattiangadi (1965) has provided a well-argued criticism of Kuhn's sociological theory of scientific knowledge.

[19] Kuhn writes (in a personal communication): "I mean only to be insisting that, where choice of theories is at issue, there is no fully logical argument from agreed empirical evidence that will compel a choice or convict a man of irrationality. . .Adherents of an old theory can defend it until their deaths by fully rational arguments." I am grateful to Professor Kuhn for allowing me to quote this passage (and for other helpful comments and elucidations).

[20] Since they work out closer to one another than meets the eye, it is also worth remarking on the numerous features of Popper's metascience that Kuhn adopts: the need for refutability, the significance of unanticipated novelty, necessity for a new theory to reject an older one, the need to risk being wrong, the role of observation and experiment, the dominance of theory.

[21] Kuhn (1962), pp. 58, 61, 65.

[22] *Ibid.*, pp. 41, 108, 120, 129.

[23] Kuhn (1962), Chap. 10.

[24] Newton (1962).

[25] Wisdom, J. O. (1963).

[26] Lakatos (1967) has (independently) come to exactly the same conclusion. (Added in December, 1971: This footnote, written over four years ago, refers to views Lakatos put forward in 1967; obviously this paper could not take account of the numerous later writings on this subject by Kuhn and by Lakatos.)

REFERENCES

Agassi, Joseph (1963). *Towards an Historiography of Science*, published by *History and Theory*, as Beiheft 2. The Hague: Mouton & Co.

———————— (1966). "Revolutions in Science, Occasional or Permanent." *Organon*, **3**, pp. 47-61.

Butterfield, Herbert (1947). *Origins of Modern Science*. Cambridge: Cambridge University Press.

Hattiangadi, J. N. (1965). "Truth, Acceptance, and Agreement: A Discussion of Professor Kuhn's Theory of Science." Master's thesis, University of London, Chap. V.

Kuhn, T. S. (1962). *The Structure of Scientific Revolutions*. Chicago: University of Chicago Press.

Lakatos, Imre (1967). "Demarcation Criteria of Scientific Research Programmes." Paper given at the University of Southern California. Unpublished.

Newton, Isaac (1962). *Principia: Mathematical Principles of Natural Philosophy & His System of the World*. Translated by Andrew Motte. 2 vols. Berkeley and Los Angeles: University of California Press. Scholium to Definitions, 10-11.

Popper, K. R. (1959). *The Logic of Scientific Discovery*. London: Hutchinson; New York: Basic Books.

——————— (1963). *Conjectures and Refutations: The Growth of Scientific Knowledge*. London: Routledge & Kegan Paul; New York: Basic Books, Chap. 1, p. 41.

Wisdom, J. O. (1963). "The Refutability of Irrefutable Laws." *British Journal for the Philosophy of Science,* **13**, pp. 303-6.

Edward Boyle

KARL POPPER'S *OPEN SOCIETY* :
A PERSONAL APPRECIATION

I accepted the invitation to contribute to this volume with considerable diffidence, for two reasons. First, any attentive reader of Karl Popper's writings will be aware that he regards 'politicians', 'rulers'—even 'statesmen'—with a distinctly wary eye. For example, "I myself would rate many saints higher than most, or very nearly all, statesmen I know of, for I am generally not impressed by political success"[1] (*O.S.*, II, 257). Secondly, and more important, it is always risky for an amateur with no formal training in philosophy to venture, however modestly, into attempting a critical appreciation of one of the greatest minds of our age.

However, I will do my best. And I should like to start with a brief explanation of why Popper's *Open Society* impressed me so much when I first read it as an undergraduate, a quarter of a century ago. From (literally) its opening page, it is a book dedicated to the values of 'humaneness' and 'reasonableness', and these are the values which, above all others, seem to me at the heart of what we mean when we speak of 'a civilised society'. It is a book written from the viewpoint of one who does not fear, but rather seeks to set free, "the critical powers of man." It is a major contribution to the theory of how we can apply "the critical and rational methods of science" to the problems of society, and how we can establish sound principles of democratic social advance.

It was from the first the 'humanist' strain in Popper that I admired most of all. Nothing, for him, must be allowed to rank higher than humanitarianism—neither power, nor "the admiration of brilliance" (*O.S.*, II, 275), nor "the greatness and uniqueness of mediaeval craftsmanship" (*O.S.*, II, 302). Like John Stuart Mill, Popper's personal philosophy draws a clear distinction between the *impressive* and the *admirable*; in fact, there are pages in Popper which read like an eloquent expansion of Mill's great saying, "A man for whom awe automatically excites admiration may be aesthetically developed, but he is morally uncultivated."

Another aspect of Popper's humanism which has always appealed to me is his insistence that "We need hope. . . . But we do *not* need more, and we must not be given more. We do not need certainty" (*O.S.*, II, 279). *"Outside of pure logic and pure mathematics nothing can be proved"* (*O.S.*, II, 294)—in other words it is up to *us;* it is remarks like these which remind us that Popper indeed belongs to a 'great tradition' that includes not only Mill but also Bertrand Russell.

Popper is a hard-hitting, but never an unfair controversialist and he shows not only his humanism, but also his fundamental generosity, in his personal tribute to Karl Marx, whom he none the less regards as a "false prophet": "Fundamentally Marx was an individualist; his main interest was to help suffering human individuals" (*O.S.*, II, 319). It surprises me when people accuse Popper of being too unyielding in the face of criticism; on the occasions when I myself venture to feel critical of Popper, it is often because I feel he has yielded too much to his critics rather than too little.

Lastly, in accounting for my enthusiasm for Popper's writings, I should like briefly to recall the political climate of the late 1940s. On the one side there were those who still believed that one could run a peacetime economy like a wartime economy, who seemed to hold almost determinist beliefs in 'the onward march of socialism', and who appeared (or at least affected) to find value in legislation that contained vacuous clauses about 'using the resources of the nation for the good of the community as a whole'. Against this background, Popper's emphasis on criticism, on 'piecemeal' reform, and on evaluation of what was actually *done*, seemed to me just the corrective that was needed. On the other hand, I found myself equally divided in thought from those who still believed in 'normal' times, who advocated (then and subsequently) a more authoritarian approach to questions of individual and social morality, and who failed to realise the implications of the great change that had come over our society, once for all, during the Second World War, when public policy had come to accept a far 'stronger' definition of *the good of all*. Here again I welcomed Popper's anti-authoritarianism, his acceptance of the necessity for institutions coupled with his rejection of unthinking deference towards them, his belief in a concept of 'justice' which included *all* citizens equally, and his commitment to "a systematic fight against suffering and injustice and war" (*O.S.*, I, 158).

Rereading Popper recently, I have been impressed once again with the scale of his contribution to Western scientific and political thought:

(1) There has been, first of all, his central thesis that "the criterion of the scientific status of a theory is its falsifiability, or refutability, or testability. Every genuine test of a theory is an attempt to falisfy it, or to refute it. . . . As scientists we do not seek highly probable theories but explanations; that is to say, powerful and improbable theories"[2] (*C.&R.*, 37, 36, 58).

(2) Secondly Popper has time and again set out to refute the philosophical point of view which he calls "historicism"—"the view that the story of mankind has a plot, and that if we can succeed in unravelling this plot we shall hold the key to the future" (*C.&R.*, 338). In Popper's view, the task of the theoretical social sciences is not to prophesy, but "to trace the unintended repercussions of international social actions" (*C.&R.*, 342).

(3) Thirdly, Popper has shown himself a moral philosopher in the great tradition of Hume in his insistence that there is no logical argument from "is" to "ought": "It is impossible to derive a sentence stating a norm or a decision or, say, a proposal for a policy, from a sentence stating a fact" (*O.S.*, I, 64).

(4) This insistence on "the autonomy of ethics" has been the driving force behind Popper's passionate belief in the right of individuals to criticize their rulers and the institutional framework of their societies; and it has also been the reason for his notorious and most eloquent opposition to Plato's doctrine that "justice" is "a synonym for 'that which is in the interest of the best state' " (*O.S.*, I, 89).

(5) Finally, it is Popper's opposition to Plato's programme which has led him to elaborate that important distinction between "Utopian" and "piecemeal" social engineering—no doubt the best known and the most widely discussed aspect of Popper's work.

1. With Popper's notable contribution to scientific thought, I am not directly concerned. However, there is a connection, as Popper himself shows, between his emphasis on "refutability" as the criterion of the scientific status of a theory, and his belief in a society which aims at humaneness and reasonableness. One unifying principle, which runs through the whole of Popper's work, is the crucial importance of *learning from our own mistakes*, whether we are involved in science, in social science, or in government. Also, although Popper is entirely candid about this element of personal commentary in *The Open Society* (and it is of course this which gives the book a great deal of its fascination and power), he is insistent that science itself cannot be regarded as merely "a body of facts" (*O.S.*, II, 259); the scientific theory or hypothesis we wish to test—and on whose testability, indeed, its scientific status depends—will be determined by *our interests* as well as by *the facts themselves*, so that the theory could even be described as "the crystallisation of a point of view" (*O.S.*, II, 260). The real distinction between what Popper calls the "generalising" sciences (like physics or biology) and the "historical" sciences is not that the latter can find room for the element of a personal viewpoint, whereas the former cannot—in this respect the differences

between them are, ultimately a matter of degree—but rather that the 'generalising' sciences are ultimately interested in "universal laws or hypotheses" whereas the historical sciences are interested in "specific events" and in their interpretation as a means of elucidating the most urgent human problems of the day.

I would add that I cannot imagine any reader of *The Open Society* not being stimulated to a greater interest in, and enthusiasm for, the history of science, both ancient and modern. The importance of science as a dimension of the whole of human history, and its moral significance—both these things are emphasised again and again in Popper's work. For instance:

> In our day no man should be considered educated if he does not take an interest in science. . . . For science is not merely a collection of facts about electricity, etc.; it is one of the most important spiritual movements of our day. Anybody who does not attempt to acquire an understanding of this movement cuts himself off from the most remarkable development in the history of human affairs. . . . There can be no history of man which excludes a history of his intellectual struggles and achievements; and there can be no history of ideas which excludes the history of scientific ideas. . . . Only if the student experiences how easy it is to err, and how hard to make even a small advance in the field of knowledge, only then can he obtain a feeling for the standards of intellectual honesty, a respect for truth, and a disregard of authority and bumptiousness. [*O.S.*, II, 283-84]

This last sentence expresses one of Popper's most important recurrent themes. *Truth, so far from being manifest, is hard to come by.* And I think it is indeed highly important not only for the student, but also for the generality of citizens who are nonacademics, to realise just how hard it is "to make even a small advance in the field of knowledge." One cannot stress too often that the essence of university life is 'teaching in the atmosphere of research', and that it is this which makes universities distinct from all other institutions. Of course one also needs—unfortunately—to point out, nowadays (as I'm sure Popper himself would be the first to agree) that "a disregard for authority" is only a virtue in an institution where there is equally "a respect for truth"; in the words of Professor Julius Gould, "The Universities, however they be reformed, can never accept that standards of truth and reason are 'bourgeois' or 'empiricist' illusions."[3]

My only reservation regarding the above quotation is that I rather question whether it is sufficient to equate the history of science with the history of scientific ideas, or whether, in this context, it is right to leave out reference, also, to the history of technology and of engineering. We learn, in surveys of Mediaeval England, a great deal about the mediaeval cathedrals, but little or nothing—as a rule—about how they were actually constructed. And even now it is rare to come across a work on nineteenth-century British history which deals adequately with, say, the work and career of Brunel, or the way in which 'applied science' remained generally regarded as an alien element in our culture. Reading Popper is, for the nonscientist, such a stimulating lesson in what educationalists call "breadth" that one ends by wishing only that his scope could have been a little wider still.

2. I turn now from Popper's scientific philosophy to his philosophy of history. The unifying theme of *The Open Society* is Popper's critical examination of the origin and development of historicism: the view that we can discover laws of history which enable us "to prophesy the course of historical events" (*O.S.*, I, 3), and that "the story of mankind has a plot, (so) that if we can succeed in unravelling this plot we shall hold the key to the future." Popper's own attitude to historicism, he tells us, "is one of frank hostility, based upon the conviction that historicism is futile and worse than that" (*O.S.*, I, 34). "Prophetic wisdom," in Popper's view, is positively harmful: "the metaphysics of history impede the application of the piecemeal methods of science to the problems of social reform" (*O.S.*, I, 3-4). "History (itself) has no meaning" (*O.S.*, II, 269), but "we can impose (our own) ends upon it" (*O.S.*, II, 278).

It might be thought that Popper's antihistoricist arguments, set out so clearly and so urgently, would command general assent, at least on this side of the Iron Curtain. But, in fact they do not; they have never been satisfactorily answered, but they are quite frequently attacked. Thus Professor E. H. Carr, in his book, *What is History*, besides claiming (implausibly, as it seems to me) that "The historian of the past can make an approach towards objectivity only as he approaches towards the understanding of the future,"[4] also observes that Popper's writings on historicism "have emptied the term of precise meaning." I can't see that the definition I have already quoted is so very obscure; in fact, it seems to me considerably clearer than Carr's own dictum, two or three pages further on, that "all human actions are both free and determined, according to the point of view from which one considers them."

Then there is John Strachey's oddly intemperate attack on Popper at the very end of his thoughtful and impressive book *The End of Empire*. "I am aware," he says,

> that to suggest there may be something useful to be learnt from history; that history may be more than an unrelated jumble of facts and dates; that there may be connections between events, and so some pattern or meaning which it may be worthwhile to try to grasp, is to incur the full fury of . . . the now dominant antihistoricist school of thought.[5]

Two or three paragraphs later we learn that "Professor Popper does not dream of following his own preposterous advice"; we turn over the page, and learn that Popper "is fair compared at least to the pack of academic historians who yap at Professor Toynbee's heels." But the reprieve is only temporary. With a snarl at the "professional historians" who trace "the obscure placement of King George III's Parliament," Strachey concludes: "They assure us that history has no meaning whatever. Very well then, we will shut up their books and never, never open them again."[6]

There are, I feel, a number of comments worth making on this passage. First, no one—least of all Popper himself—is saying that history is simply "an unrelated jumble of facts and dates." On the contrary, Popper goes out of his way to refute the pretensions of any writer of history "who naively believes that he does not interpret, and that he has reached a level of objectivity permitting him to present 'the events of the past as they actually did happen' "; one should aim to avoid "unconscious and therefore uncritical bias in the presentation of the facts," but "in every other respect the interpretation" will stand or fall on merits like its ability "to elucidate the facts of history . . . [or] the problems of the day." "We want," says Popper, "to know how our troubles are related to the past, and we want to see the line along which we may progress towards the solution of what we feel, and what we choose, to be our main tasks" (O.S., II, 268). No one reading these words could possibly suppose that Popper was uninterested in learning from the course of history, or that he disapproved on principle of trying to trace "connections between events." But there is a real difference between these things, and the belief in what Strachey calls "some pattern or meaning which it may be worthwhile to try to grasp"; and I fully share Popper's preference for the rational question: "What, placed as we are, should we choose as our most urgent problems?" rather than the irrational question: "What is the part that history has destined us to play?"

Secondly, however concerned we may be to trace connections between events, and to pursue conscious aims, we must recognise that we can never resolve all the uncertainties even of the short term; and that the prudent politician, no less than the prudent historian must, in the well-known words of H. A. L. Fisher's preface to his *History of Europe*, "recognise in the development of human destinies the play of the contingent and the unforeseen".[7] As Fisher goes on to point out, these considerations need not lead us to cynicism, still less to despair: "The fact of progress is written plain and large on the page of history; but progress is not a law of nature. The ground acquired by one generation may be lost by the next"—the responsibility, as always, lies with *us*. I would agree wholeheartedly with this, adding only that, as Popper says, nothing (however cataclysmic) could ever count as annulling the facts of human achievement:

> Mankind, I believe, has not done so badly. . . . Many weak men have been helped, and for nearly a hundred years slavery has been abolished. . . . Even if all this should be lost again, this would not alter the fact that once upon a time slavery did disappear from the face of the earth. [O.S., I, 318]

No doubt for some of us it may sometimes *seem* as though history had a meaning, or as though we *really were* caught up in 'inevitable processes', and influenced by 'vast and impersonal historical forces'. And I am not forgetting the strength of conviction on the other side of the Iron Curtain that, even if (as will sometimes be conceded) Marx has been proved wrong about each of the capitalist nations so far, he must 'inevitably' be right about all of them in the end. But neither of these considerations weakens, for me, the cogency of Popper's antihistoricist arguments, and his concluding words on this theme still seem to me as convincing—and as noble—as when I first read them a quarter of a century ago:

> Neither nature nor history can tell us what we ought to do. Facts, whether those of nature or those of history, cannot make the decision for us, they cannot determine the ends we are going to choose. It is we who introduce purpose and meaning into nature and into history. Men are not equal; but we can decide to fight for equal rights. Human institutions such as the state are not rational, but we can decide to fight to make them more rational. [*O.S.*, II, 278]

3. Popper's philosophy of history does of course follow directly from his insistence that we cannot derive ethical *norms*, or *decisions*, from *facts*. "That most people agree with the norm 'Thou shalt not steal' is a sociological fact. But the norm 'Thou shalt not steal' is not a fact, and can never be inferred from sentences describing facts" (*O.S.*, I, 64). This "critical dualism of facts and decisions," as Popper calls it, is one of the key doctrines of *The Open Society*, and the arguments in its favour are set out fully in Chapter 5, entitled "Nature and Convention."

The clearest exposition of this doctrine is to be found early in the chapter at the point where Popper refutes the assertion that, because norms are "conventional," they can therefore be regarded as "merely arbitrary."

> Critical dualism merely asserts that norms and normative laws *can* be made and changed by man, more especially by a decision or convention to observe them or to alter them, and that it is therefore man who is morally responsible for them; not perhaps for the norms which he finds to exist in society when he first begins to reflect upon them, but for the norms which he is prepared to tolerate once he has found out that he can do something to alter them. Norms are man-made in the sense that we must blame nobody but ourselves for them; neither nature nor God. It is our business to improve them as much as we can, if we find that they are objectionable. . . . We can compare the existing normative laws (or social institutions) with some standard norms which we have decided are worthy of being realized. But even these standards are of our making in the sense that our decision in favour of them is our own decision, and that we alone carry the responsibility for adopting them. [*O.S.*, I, 61]

In the *Addendum* to the 1963 edition of *The Open Society*, Popper makes it explicit that this argument applies to "authorities" no less than to "standards": "It is I who must decide whether to accept the standards of any authority as (morally) good or bad" (*O.S.*, II, 385).

Popper bases his defence of this doctrine, both in Chapter 5 and elsewhere, on the surest of grounds, namely that he advances what seem to me unanswerable arguments for believing it to be true. He is particularly concerned to refute the "misunderstanding" of critical dualism, the belief that, "if we are free to choose any system of norms we like, then one system is just as good as any other"; there can be no justification, it should be stressed, for misrepresenting Popper's arguments as condoning ethical indifference: "Man has created new worlds—of language, of music, of poetry, of science; and the most important of these is the world of the moral demands, for equality, for freedom, and for helping the weak" (*O.S.*, I, 65). There is, however, another and, Popper thinks, "deeper" reason why 'critical dualism' is not adopted:

> It is based upon our fear of admitting to ourselves that the responsibility for our ethical decisions is entirely ours, and cannot be shifted to anybody else; neither to God, nor to nature, nor to society, nor to history. All these ethical theories attempt to find somebody, or perhaps some argument, to take the burden from us. But we cannot shirk this responsibility. Whatever authority we accept, it is we who accept it. We only deceive ourselves if we do not realize this. [*O.S.*, I, 73]

One may wholeheartedly endorse these words, and yet feel that they miss one rather crucial point. No doubt many of us, as individuals, are afraid of admitting to ourselves that "the responsibility for our ethical decisions is entirely ours." But the point about authoritarians, against whom the whole argument of *The Open Society* is directed, is that they are afraid of *other people* making this admission for themselves, and accepting the responsibility (indeed claiming the right) to decide for themselves what authority they will accept. Popper does indeed recognise, very truly as I believe, that "authoritarian principles are usually an expression . . . of an extreme moral scepticism, of a distrust of man and of his possibilities" (*O.S.*, I, 72); but such a distrust will usually go along with an unwillingness to accept that men and women should be encouraged to explore for themselves "the world of moral demands," or to recognise that no one else (nor God, nor society) can make this exploration for them. And, therefore, although (with one reservation which I mention later) I think Popper's arguments in favour of a critical dualism of facts and decisions are cogent and unanswerable, I don't think he has dealt fully adequately with the grounds of the "fear" that inhibits their more widespread acceptance.

In the later editions of *The Open Society*, and in reply to criticisms, Popper has suggested one or two amendments to his original statement. Thus he has added "proposals for a policy" to norms and decisions, on the grounds that "one can *discuss* a proposal, while it is not so clear whether, and in which sense, one can discuss a decision or a norm" (*O.S.*, I, 234). But there is, surely, an important distinction between a proposal that we *discuss*, and a decision that we actually *take* as an act of deliberate choice. Governments, in particular, cannot shirk choices; as M. Mendes-France once said in a famous phrase: *"Gouverner, c'est choisir."* And it seems to me important to stress that the responsibility for government decisions does indeed rest with ministers and "cannot be shifted to anybody else." It is one of the great merits of Popper's doctrine, in its simplest and strongest form, that it forces us to recognise that, precisely because there is no logical means of closing the gap between facts and decisions, we cannot help having 'a government of men and not of laws'.

My preference for Popper's first thought applies even more strongly in relation to a passage in the *Addendum* to the 1963 edition of *The Open Society*, where Popper seems to me to go much too far in the direction of his critics. "We may take," he says, "the idea of absolute truth—of correspondence to the facts—as a kind of model for the realm of standards, in order to make it clear to ourselves that, just as we may *seek* for absolutely true propositions in the realm of facts, so we may *seek* for absolutely right or valid proposals in the realm of standards—or at least for better, or more valid proposals (*O.S.*, II, 385). But this, surely, won't do. If, as I believe, Popper's original statement was correct, then it cannot be right to suggest that we should take the idea of "correspondence to the facts" as any kind of model for the "realm of standards." The notion of "absolutely valid proposals in the realm of standards" recalls, for me, those "objective values carrying the stamp of authenticity upon their faces" which Professor A. J. (Sir Alfred) Ayer dissolved so effectively in his splendid paper 'On the Analysis of Moral Judgments'.[8] One cannot, I feel, go beyond Ayer's conclusion that "to say that something which somebody thinks is right really *is* right is to range oneself on his side, to adhere to that particular standpoint"—a conclusion which incidentally reminds us that, although (in Popper's words) "the responsibility for our ethical decisions" is indeed "entirely ours," still, there is everything to be said for trying to unite our own wills with those of others.

What I think can be conceded to those who disagree with 'critical dualism' is something rather different. The point is that no one, especially if he has responsibility for a regular number of quite important decisions, can be thinking *about* his norms, and his standards, all the time. As a friend of mine in the Civil Service once said, "No Government department can derive every decision afresh from first principles," and anyone who bears important responsibilities, or who wishes actively to promote some cause, soon recognises the need in everyday life to think not *about* but *in terms of*, certain principles and objectives. Surely this is just what we mean when we speak of "commitment"; or, as another friend once put it, "Unless one recognises there are some principles whose violation makes life not worth living, life *isn't* worth living."

But a follower of Popper would none the less insist that we must always be prepared, from timé to time, to think *about* our principles and objectives in the light of new facts and greater experience. And he would wish us especially to take into account *other people's* experience of the consequences of our decisions.

4. Popper's sustained and eloquent assault on Plato has always been the most controversial part of *The Open Society.* But I doubt whether any of Popper's critics has fully succeeded in repulsing this assault; few of them have even spotted its precise direction. Thus it is no answer to Popper to claim, like G. C. Field, that Plato would certainly not have approved of Fascism or Nazism (though he might have had some sympathy with Russian Communism). Field goes on to say that it is a "profound fallacy" to suppose that Plato would have approved of absolute authority being conferred on any select group of rulers; "on the contrary, it was only because they were ideal rulers that the guardians were fit to be entrusted with absolute powers."[9]

But this is precisely the point at which Popper's assault is directed. If we admit, he says, "that political rulers are not always sufficiently 'good' or 'wise', and that it is not at all easy to get a government on whose goodness and wisdom one can implicitly rely, then we must ask whether political thought should not face from the beginning the possibility of bad government. . . . But this forces us to replace Plato's question: *Who should rule?* by the new question: *How can we so organize political institutions that bad or incompetent rulers can be prevented from doing too much damage?*" (*O.S.*, I, 121). This, surely, is the crucial point. If one regards Plato's question: Who shall rule? as fundamental, then no doubt one will applaud the purpose of the Platonic system of education which "establishes a barrier between the rulers and the ruled" and hands down wisdom "largely for the sake of establishing a permanent political class rule" (*O.S.*, I, 148). But if we, feel, rather, the force of Popper's alternative question, then we shall prefer the "humanitarian and universalistic" emphasis of Pericles' funeral oration (which Sir Richard Livingstone called "the greatest speech in literature"):

> Our administration favours the many instead of the few: this is why it is called a democracy. The laws afford equal justice to all alike in their private disputes, but we do not ignore the claims of excellence. When a citizen distinguishes himself, then he will be called to serve the state, in preference to others, not as a matter of privilege, but as a reward of merit. . . . Although only a few may originate a policy, we are all able to judge it. We do not look upon discussion as a stumbling block in the way of political discussion, but as an indispensable preliminary to acting wisely.

As Popper most aptly comments, these words recognise that democracy "must be based on faith in reason, and on humanitarianism. At the same time they are an expression of true patriotism, of just pride in a city . . . which became the school, not only of Hellas, but, as we know, of mankind, for millenia past and yet to come" (*O.S.*, I, 187).

It is worth remembering that Popper's views on Plato are not without support from scholars whose interests lie primarily in very different directions from his own. Nearly forty years ago, Sir Maurice Bowra wrote that

> At times it is hard not to feel that Plato's life was a gigantic mistake. . . . He decried the great men of the fifth century, but his imaginative life was spent in their company. He attacked the arts with the fury of a great artist and fought poetry with its own choicest weapons.[10]

What cannot in any case be questioned is the eloquence and cogency with which Popper advocates the creed of what he calls the 'Great Generation'—the creed not only of Pericles, but of Democritus, and the school of Gorgias, and

> perhaps the greatest of all, Socrates, who taught the lesson that we must have faith in human reason, but at the same time beware of dogmatism; that we must keep away both from misology (i.e., the hate of rational argument), the distrust of theory and of reason, and from the magical attitude of those who make an idol of wisdom; who taught in other words, that the spirit of science is criticism. [*O.S.*, I, 185]

"Although only a few may originate a policy, we are all able to judge it." It was Popper who first made me realise that of all human "rights," the most essential is *the right to criticise one's rulers*; and it is interesting to note how often in the course of history dictators—even relatively benevolent dictators like Napoleon III—have traded on blurring the distinction between *the right to criticise one's rulers* and *the right to absolute freedom of speech*, which is another matter. Criticising the powers-that-be must never *in itself* count as an offence; that is the essential point. How right Sir Winston Churchill was when he cited the Vote of Confidence debate after the fall of Tobruk, as the proof that Britain really did remain a parliamentary democracy, even in wartime.

5. I come, lastly, to the best known and most influential aspect of Popper's philosophy: his distinction between "Utopian" and "piecemeal" social engineering:

> The Utopian approach may be described as follows. Any rational action must have a certain aim. . . . Only when this ultimate aim is determined, in rough outline at least, like a blueprint of the society at which we aim, only then can we begin to consider the best ways and means for its realization, and to draw up a plan for practical action. . . . I wish to outline another approach to social engineering, namely, that of piecemeal engineering. It is an approach which I think to be methodologically sound. The politician who adopts this method may or may not have a blueprint of society before his mind, he may or may not hope that mankind will one day realize an ideal state, and achieve happiness and perfection on earth. But he will be aware that perfection, if at all attainable, is far

distant, and that every generation of men, and therefore also the living, have a claim; perhaps not so much a claim to be made happy, for there are no institutional means of making a man happy, but a claim not to be made unhappy, where it can be avoided. . . . The piecemeal engineer will, accordingly, adopt the method of searching for, and fighting against, the greatest and most urgent evils of society, rather than searching for, and fighting for, its greatest ultimate good. [*O.S.*, II, 157-8]

Popper emphasises that the differences between the two approaches are very far from being entirely verbal: "It is the difference between a reasonable method of improving the lot of man, and a method which, if really tried, may easily lead to an intolerable increase in human suffering." Two points on which Popper, very rightly, lays stress are, first, the importance of *learning from our mistakes*, and secondly, the error of supposing that social experiments must be on a large scale.

"We must learn to do things as well as we can, and to look out for our mistakes" (*O.S.*, II, 280). This is almost the very last sentence of *The Open Society*, and it is interesting to note that Popper returned to this theme, as the kernel of his political philosophy, in a recent broadcast discussion with Mr. Bryan Magee.[11]

> The readiness to learn from our mistakes, and to look out for them, I call the rational attitude. It is always opposed to authoritarianism. In the field of politics the method of learning from your mistakes is a method based on free criticism and discussion of the actions taken by the government.

By contrast, the Utopian approach is one which demands the "strong centralised rule of a few," and "authoritarianism must discourage criticism." Accordingly "the benevolent dictator will not easily hear of complaints concerning the measures he has taken. But without some such check, he can hardly find out whether his measures achieve the desired benevolent aim" (*O.S.*, I, 160). This seems to me admirably said. Incidentally it is precisely because "free criticism of discussion of the actions taken by the government" is so important that I think one should not be squeamish about recognising that the most important distinction in politics is always not the distinction between political parties—but the distinction between *the government and everybody else*. We only darken counsel by speaking, as we so frequently do in Britain, about 'Shadow Ministers' as though they, too, 'acted' like members of a government.

Popper is equally firm in his dislike of the prejudice, "as widely held as it is untenable," that social experiments must be on a 'large scale'—that "they must involve the whole of society if they are to be carried out under realistic conditions."

> But the kind of experiment from which we learn most is the alteration of one social institution at a time. For only in this way can we learn how to fit in-

stitutions into the framework of other institutions, and how to adjust them so that they work according to our intentions. [*O.S.*, I, 163]

Popper's clear-sighted understanding of the crucial role of institutions in promoting social and political advance is particularly valuable at a time when they have only recently been under severe attack from the antirational, radical 'left'. But *The Open Society* gives no comfort, either, to the traditionalist 'right' that tends to approach institutions in a spirit of unthinking deference. As Popper coolly observes, "Institutions are inevitably the result of a compromise with circumstances, interests and so on, though as persons we should resist influences of this kind" (*O.S.*, I, 159).

I should also like to underline, and to endorse, what Popper says about "the living" having a claim. Whenever a policy of radical change is proposed, it is always important to ask what will be the implications of this policy for the short term as well as the longer term; for example, when a local education authority in England or Wales is proposing to introduce a far-reaching proposal for the reorganisation of its secondary schools, it is important to be clear what this will mean for the *present* generation of children who are educated at those schools—not only the next generation, after the plan has been completed, or the generation after that. "No end," says Popper, "could ever justify all means . . . (but) a fairly concrete and realisable end may justify temporary measures as a more distant ideal never could" (*O.S.*, I, 161).

Thus the merits of 'piecemeal' social engineering, as an approach to social policy which is methodologically sound, seem to me very great. But it is only right that I should refer also to one or two of the criticisms that have been advanced against it. One criticism—that this is sentimental conservatism in disguise—is, I think quite unfair; Professor E. H. Carr gives a signally false impression of the whole trend of Popper's thought when he represents him as wanting "to keep that dear old T-model on the road."[12]

But there is, I think, rather more substance in Carr's point that Popper, for all his advocacy of reason, doesn't sufficiently allow for "the bold readiness of human beings . . . to present fundamental challenges in the name of reason to the current way of doing things and to the avowed or hidden assumptions on which it rests."[13] But for that annoying word "fundamental," which arouses all my most Popper-ish instincts, I should agree with Carr here. For the weakest point in Popper's political philosophy is, surely, his presupposition that the sole purpose of social engineering should be to eliminate avoidable evils. Can we be content with this? Granted that "there are no institutional means of making a man happy," isn't it true that there are means of increasing possibilities of happiness? Don't we—most of us—regard the preamble to the Declaration of American Independence as an important milestone in the history of the human race, with its insistence that all human beings ought to be free and happy?—Susan Stebbing wrote finely on this topic in her little book *Ideals and Illusions*.[14]

And even if we are sceptical about the pursuit of happiness for others, it is surely true that the deliberate encouragement of economic growth must result in increased freedom of choice for others; isn't this obviously a good thing? (It would come high on my own list of priorities.) And what about the purposes of our education policy? Surely when we speak of enabling each individual to achieve a sense of fulfillment, or of giving every child "the same opportunity for acquiring measured intelligence," we are thinking in terms of objectives which go a long way beyond "fighting . . . the most urgent evils of society."

Again (and here I admit I've somewhat modified my own views since first reading The Open Society in the 1940s) I think some may feel that Popper's definition of 'Justice' (*O.S.*, I, 89) hardly goes far enough. Popper's criteria include "equal treatment of the citizens before the law, provided . . . that the laws shown neither favour nor disfavour toward individual citizens or groups or classes." But such a criterion might be thought to rule out legislation like the British Race Relations Act of 1968 which (whatever its flaws) did raise the important question whether it was sufficient for the *law* not to discriminate between one citizen and another, and whether it ought also to be made unlawful for *persons* to discriminate. (For a fuller discussion of this point, including some comments on Mr. Enoch Powell's much-publicised Birmingham speech of April 1968, see my Eleanor Rathbone Lecture, *Race Relations and Education*.)[15] I have the feeling that the key concept, in this context, is *equal citizenship*, that this is a concept whose precise content has to be argued out afresh in each generation—and that it will take clear-sightedness, readiness to speak out, and sometimes to stand up and be counted on the part of older members of any democratic society, if the argument is to remain purely verbal and to be conducted at a rational level.

Thus, whereas I am in wholehearted support of Popper's views on the *means* of achieving social progress, I should personally wish to be rather more ambitious with regard to *objectives*. And I have no doubt that, in a democracy, the objectives of social and economic policy ought to be not merely freely discussed but rigorously analysed. They are nothing like so easy to formulate as the plain man is apt to suppose—though, of course, it is his voice which merits the most attention when it comes to judging not the theory but the practice.

However, I should not wish to end on a note of criticism. Popper is a great and humane thinker, who has devoted his intellectual life to a rigorous examination of the conditions of scientific and social progress. He is in the great tradition of those thinkers, and those writers, who are not utopians, nor pessimists, but *meliorists*—spurred on not by the love of fame, but by the determination to do their best with whatever is to hand; knowing that

> it is possible to combine an attitude of the utmost reserve and even contempt towards worldly success in the sense of power, glory, and wealth, with the attempt to do one's best in this world, and to further the ends one has decided to adopt with the clear purpose of making them succeed; not for the sake of success or of one's own justification by history, but for their own sake. [*O.S.*, II, 275]

"Progress," Popper reminds us once more, "rests with us, with our watchfulness, with our efforts, with the clarity of our conception of our ends, and with the realism of their choice" (*O.S.*, II, 280). And, I should like to add, with our realisations that moral demands cannot be politicised, that they cannot be subordinated to political orthodoxies or *diktats*. These are all of them, beliefs that I hold for myself and seek to justify to others. And therefore I feel a profound gratitude to Karl Popper for having defended them so cogently, never shirking a difficulty, and never refusing to meet a critic. For much of the power and the impressiveness of *The Open Society* depends, not merely on the humaneness and rationality of Popper's outlook, but also on his rigour and honesty; he is truly a thinker for whom, in Whately's fine words, "it makes all the difference in the world whether we put Truth in the first place or in the second place."

EDWARD BOYLE
(LORD BOYLE OF HANDSWORTH)

UNIVERSITY OF LEEDS
LEEDS, ENGLAND
MAY, 1971

NOTES

[1] K. R. Popper, *The Open Society and Its Enemies,* 2 vols. (London: Routledge & Kegan Paul, 1963). Hereinafter cited as *O.S.*

[2] K. R. Popper, *Conjectures and Refutations: The Growth of Scientific Knowledge* (London: Routledge & Kegan Paul, 1963; New York: Basic Books, 1963). Hereinafter cited as *C.&R.*

[3] Julius Gould, *The Observer* (London), March 2, 1969.

[4] E. H. Carr, *What is History* (New York: Knopf, 1962), p. 118.

[5] John Strachey, *The End of Empire* (New York: Random House, 1959).

[6] *Ibid.*, pp. 341-42.

[7] H. A. L. Fisher, *History of Europe* (London: E. Arnold & Co., 1937), p. vii.

[8] A. J. Ayer, "On the Analysis of Moral Judgments," in *Philosophical Essays* (New York: St. Martin's Press, 1954), pp. 231-49, esp. pp. 242-48.

[9] G. C. Field, *Plato To-Day* (London: Oxford University Press, 1949), p. 202.

[10] Sir Maurice Bowra, *Ancient Greek Literature* (London: Oxford University Press, 1933), p. 189.

[11] See Bryan Magee et al., *Modern British Philosophy* (London: Seeker and Warburg, 1971), p. 80.

[12] Carr, *What is History*, p. 151.

[13] *Ibid.*, p. 150.

[14] L. S. Stebbing, *Ideals and Illusions* (London: Watts, 1941), pp. 55-58.

[15] Edward Boyle, *Race Relations and Education* (Liverpool: Liverpool University Press, 1970), pp. 18-21.

John Wild †

POPPER'S INTERPRETATION OF PLATO

Approximately the first two hundred pages of *The Open Society and Its Enemies*, together with about 150 pages of notes (pp. 467-612),[1] are devoted to the elaboration and defence of an interpretation of Plato as an enemy, perhaps *the* enemy of the open society. Since the time of publication, this interpretation has been subjected to careful criticism in reviews and in more lengthy studies of Plato. So far as I know, Professor Popper has not as yet published any reply. Within the limits of space at my disposal here, I shall not be able to cover them all. I shall restrict myself, with only a few exceptions, to a selection of certain criticisms which appeared in my book, *Plato's Modern Enemies and the Theory of Natural Law*[2] and in Ronald Levinson's work *In Defence of Plato*,[3] of which the latter contains the most thoroughgoing examination of Professor Popper's views on Plato that has so far been made. They are concerned with three aspects of his interpretation: (1) Plato's basic philosophy; (2) his social and political views; and (3) his relation to Socrates. In this paper I shall summarize major criticisms falling under these headings as I now understand them.

I. PLATO'S BASIC PHILOSOPHY

In the first place, let me make it clear that I am not a Platonist, and that I am by no means prepared to defend all the doctrines he put forth in ontology and in political philosophy, nor all the attitudes he assumed towards Socrates, his teacher, and the democratic Athenian government of his time. I agree with Professor Popper that these doctrines and attitudes have exerted a predominant influence on the course of Western thought, that has often been passively accepted without sufficient criticism. They now call for such criticism in the freer atmosphere of our time. But I respect Plato as a genuine philosopher, and I believe that whatever criticisms are made, must in turn be judged by their philosophical depth and by their scrupulous focusing of what is said in the texts. It is with these standards in mind that I shall now proceed

---

† Because of his untimely death, on October 22, 1972, Professor Wild had no opportunity to make any corrections in the galleys of his essay, which is printed here therefore as he had submitted it—EDITOR

to examine Professor Popper's views about Plato, as he has expressed them in his book.

In Chapter 5 Professor Popper argues (p. 65) that "it is impossible to derive norms or decisions or proposals from facts," and he refers to this position as "critical dualism." He says that Plato and those who have followed him in recognizing natural norms or natural laws, as they have been called, have violated this principle. They have confused natural regularities, which are factually true and cannot be violated, with normative prescriptions which ought to be true (according to some person or group), and can always be violated. Since Plato recognized not only biological needs common to all men but nonbiological needs as well, Popper calls him a "spiritual naturalist" (p. 73). His attack on this position is very basic, and underlies many of his other criticisms of Plato.

He defends the opposed view that norms are "man-made," in the sense that "we are free to choose any system of norms we like" (p. 65). Professor Popper recognizes that a chief difficulty confronting this view is its apparent arbitrariness. If norms are in no sense derived from facts and factual laws, even those concerning man, then it is hard to see how they can escape from being arbitrary, and even capricious. Certainly this was one reason which led Plato to adopt his natural law theory. But according to Popper (p. 65), "the belief that 'convention' implies 'arbitrariness' " is due to a "fundamental misapprehension." Now I am not clear as to the precise nature of this misapprehension. He says at one point "that there will be a certain element of arbitrariness involved," and then he mentions "mathematical calculi," "symphonies" and "plays" as being artificial and yet not arbitrary in the sense that one is just as good as any other. But he does not explain why they are not arbitrary. He concludes (p. 66) "that the view that moral decisions rest with us does not imply that they are entirely arbitrary." In what respect are they not arbitrary, with reference to what? I wish that he would clarify his position on this point.

Of course, he suggests an answer to this question a few pages before (pp. 62-63) where he argues that decisions "pertain to facts." He says "it is perfectly true that our decisions must be compatible with the natural laws (including those of human physiology and psychology)." Otherwise they cannot be carried out. Here, I think, he is admitting that facts and laws of nature pertain to moral decisions. If children are not properly fed and cared for, they will sicken and die. This is an unalterable fact of nature, and any normative legislation which fails to take account of it, or tries to alter it, will be unsound. As he says (p. 63), "if the fact in question is unalterable . . . then any decision to alter it will be simply impracticable . . ." This may be what he means by the nonarbitrariness of moral norms.

But if so, he is in essential agreement with Plato and the natural law philosophers, since natural facts and laws cannot rule out certain norms as "impracticable" without suggesting others in accordance with them as practicable. The difference between Popper and these philosophers will then be reduced to a matter of degree. They attach more importance to the normative suggestions of natural facts and laws; he attaches less. They restrict the range of flexibility in taking account of these facts; he expands it. But this is only a difference in emphasis, which might be settled by disciplined discussion. From Popper's emphatic statements that norms can in no sense be derived from facts of any kind, and from his strictures against what he calls "biological naturalism" as well as "spiritual naturalism," I cannot believe that this is his meaning. But if not, I do not see what he can mean by the non-arbitrariness of "man-made" norms that are wholly divorced from the facts. I hope, therefore, that he will clarify his meaning on these points.

His conception of Plato as a "historicist" is the ground for other basic charges. By historicism Popper apparently means the claim of a philosopher to know the basic trends, or laws, of history, so that the concrete future may be predicted or prophesied (p. 11). This, he says, minimizes the importance of free choice, and is "apt to relieve men from the strain of their responsibilities" (p. 6). That this charge may be legitimately raised against Hegel and Marx I would not wish to deny. But his raising it against Plato, even in a qualified sense (p. 27), leads to certain doubts that have been explored by his critics. For example, he accuses Plato in other parts of his book (cf. Chap. 9) of entertaining vast ambitions for the utopian transformation of individual and social life. Plato is a "Utopian engineer," inspired by "the conviction that nothing short of a complete eradication of the offending social system will do . . ." (p. 161). Whatever else it may be, this hardly looks like an evasion of personal responsibility. Are these two charges of "historicism" as well as "Utopian engineering" really consistent?

The special brand of *historicism* which Popper attributes to Plato involves two theses that are worthy of comment. In the first place, he seems to think that the first example of an ideal form, or pattern (*eidos*), in time, is necessarily closer to the "original" and, therefore, more perfect than those which follow it. But he gives no textual references to support this view, which, I believe, is open to serious question. He is anxious to show that, according to Plato, the first human society was a Golden Age followed by a process of increasing degeneration, and, on pages 487-88 of his book, he has gathered many texts which speak favorably of past times. But as Levinson has shown, at least as many other texts can be found which speak of an advance from earlier and more primitive conditions.[4]

There is, no doubt, some development in Plato's understanding of human history. But his final view seems to have been that it is dominated neither by an inevitable law of progress nor by one of decline. It runs back into a very distant past and is characterized in different areas by cycles of successive development and decline (cf. *Laws* III). Every appearance of an *eidos* in time is imperfect and subject to destruction. But Plato's ontology makes no requirement that the first embodiment of an ideal form in the realm of change should be more perfect than its later successors.

Nor does it require any law of inevitable decline, as Popper maintains. IIis argument for this conclusion involves a use of texts which calls for a special comment. For example, he interprets Book VIII of the *Republic* as an account of a concrete historical decline from a perfect state, through inferior forms, down to tyranny. But, as I have argued in my book,[5] this is not the most probable interpretation of the text. It is not the account of any concrete history, but rather of an ideal decline—of what would happen if an ideal community were approximately realized, and if it were then to degenerate continuously into the worst state. *Laws* III, on the other hand, is an attempt on Plato's part to give a summary account of past history. But at *Laws* 680-684, where the various early forms of settlement are described, no original ideal "first settlement" is described. The constitutions of the early Dorian states are all defective, and the final Spartan constitution is said to have been arrived at only after constant improvements (cf. 684E-686A). This text, and, indeed, the whole of *Laws* III, do not support Popper's statement (p. 41) that "The *Laws* (i.e., Books III and IV) present the story of the decline and fall of human society as an account of Greek prehistory merging without any break into history." This is a one-sided oversimplification of the text. There is no clear reference to an original perfect state, and the course of change described is marked just as much by advances as by declines.

Professor Popper has interpreted *Laws* 904C ff. as a support for his thesis that Plato maintained an inevitable and progressive degeneration in the souls of men.[6] This interpretation has been exhaustively criticized by Levinson in his book.[7] After reading this text of the *Laws* in context, I must say that I find no ground for Popper's interpretation. The young man who has denied that the gods concern themselves with human affairs is being exhorted to the pursuit of virtue. The passage is not dominated by any sense of inevitable decay, which would be out of place. Time after time he is told that goodness brings movement upwards towards happiness, while evil brings movement downwards towards the abyss. There is no limitation of the upward movement to the exceptional soul whom Popper identifies with Plato himself. This is all part of a constructive theory, with no ground in the text itself. So I am curious to know if Professor Popper still thinks that this whole passage (*Laws* 903D-905A) is the clear expression of a law of inevitable decline in human history?

II. Plato's Social and Political Views

1. Holism

Popper has pressed the charge of what he calls *holism* against Plato. In certain passages, this is defined in a very vague and general way. Thus on page 99, he says that, according to Plato, "the individual should subserve the interests of the whole, whether this be the universe, the city, the tribe, the race, or any other collective body. . . ." It is true, as we have noted, that Plato believed in an ordered universe, pervaded by natural laws having a normative significance. For example, if a community takes no adequate precautions for the education and care of its children, it will suffer from the natural sanction of disease and ignorance. Both the individual and the state are subject to natural laws and sanctions of this kind. If they are to attain justice, harmony, and happiness, they must act in accordance with this universal moral order. In this sense, Plato can be called a holist.

But this universal *holism* is very different from the Nazi glorification of the state which Popper then proceeds to read into Plato. According to him, Plato held "that the state itself can never be wrong in any of its actions, as long as it is strong," and "that the state has the right, not only to do violence to its citizens, should that lead to an increase of strength, but also to attack other states, provided it does so without weakening itself " (p. 106). This Fascist doctrine is altogether foreign to Plato, who often attacks both external and internal actions of the state as unjust, and never defends wanton aggression. The greedy luxurious state of *Republic* II (375A-376E), for example, is condemned as unjust because of its failure to control those desires for wealth and material possessions "which are the most fruitful source of evils both to individuals and to states" (373E). The purification of this militant and expanding state, dominated by limitless desire, is a major concern of the remaining books of the *Republic*.

Popper also attributes to Plato the "organic" theory of the state as a superindividual thing, or organism, living a life of its own, independent of its individual members. This view is found in Hegel and his followers. But its attribution to Plato is a mistake which cannot be supported by any careful reading of the texts. It is true that Plato was not an *individualist* in Popper's sense. The aim of legislation, as he saw it, was not merely to turn the individual members over to themselves, and to protect them in doing whatever they pleased. He identified this with anarchy and irresponsibility; and in his strictures against it, he may have gone too far. But this does not mean that he accepted an "organic" theory of the social whole.

As I have argued in some detail,[8] Plato's view lies between these extremes. The aim of legislation is to achieve what was later called "the common good." This is more than the sum of the goods of the individual members, but it nevertheless includes these goods. Social structure arises from the characters of the individual citizens (*Republic* 544E), and the rationale, or *logos*, of the human community must be present, not in a group spirit (*objectiver Geist*), but in the souls of intelligent individuals (*Republic* 497C8). The individual is not "nothing but a cog."[9] Like Socrates, even in the midst of a degenerate society, he may resist corrupting tendencies, and may struggle for what is really right (*Republic* 496B).

2. Racialism

Popper has attacked Plato as a racialist whose ideal republic is based on the rule of a "master race" in the sense of the Nazi doctrine. This charge can be broken down into four parts. First, "the ethical category of 'humanity', as something that transcends the distinction of nations, races, and classes, is entirely foreign to Plato" (p. 149; cf. n. 50). Second, he correlated "the natural inequality of Greeks and barbarians to that of masters and slaves" (p. 150). Third, the three classes of the *Republic,* symbolized by the metals in the myth at *Republic* 414 are distinguished by hereditary, and, therefore, by *racial* characteristic. In Popper's words (p. 138), "these metals are hereditary, they are racial characteristics." Finally, fourth, the fall of the ideal state will be due to the guardians' "loss of interest in eugenics, in watching and testing the purity of the race, and in their ignorance of the mysterious 'nuptial number',", described at *Republic* 546A ff., of which Plato alone knew the secret (p. 150; cf. n. 52). Let us now consider these charges one by one.

With respect to Popper's first charge that the feeling of universal humanity "is entirely foreign to Plato," one counterinstance would be sufficient to refute it. But many such instances can be found. If we look at Plato's mythical accounts of the origin of mankind, we find no assertion of any original distinction between races. In the myth of the *Phaedrus* (247B ff.), it is said that some souls follow the divine forms only with difficulty. But this is not due to any racial handicap. It is due rather to a failure to exercise their faculty of insight, and to control their passions. The account of human prehistory and history, given in *Laws* III, is characterized by a strict philosophical neutrality between Greeks and other races (cf. esp. 699E).

Plato's discussions of the soul and of moral philosophy are pervaded by a universal feeling. Thus, taking one of his key doctrines at random, with which Popper has concerned himself, the philosopher-king thesis (*Republic* 473) asserts that until philosophers are kings there will be no end of troubles *for all mankind.* Popper calls this an "afterthought of comparatively minor importance" (p. 149), but the idea occurs again and again in different dialogues. Thus, at *Republic* 499C, he says that the *ideal* republic may at that very moment be approximately realized in some distant *barbaric* land! In a passage of the *Phaedo* (78A), Socrates urges his hearers to seek wisdom for quieting the fear of death, not among the Greeks alone, but among the barbarians as well.

Republic 469B-471 has attracted the attention of many commentators besides Popper. Plato here maintains that Greeks should not enslave Greeks but, remembering the common danger, permits the enslavement of barbarians. It is in connection with this passage that Popper makes his statement about the Greeks as natural masters and the barbarians as natural slaves. There is no doubt that Plato here is speaking as a Greek, who feels the danger of enslavement by military conquest on the part of his traditional cultural enemies. In his mature years, the Greek cities of Ionia were subjected to Persia in a humiliating manner. This is, no doubt, far from the modern ideal of a world community. But Popper has confused a feeling of cultural superiority and traditional enmity with the notion of a biological master race which is not present in Plato. He is not a pacifist, but he never defends aggressive war. Nor does he ever state that the barbarians are natural slaves. This is a Nazi doctrine that Popper is reading back into Plato.

With respect to the third charge I shall have to be more brief, in referring to the argument I have given in my book.[10] Plato does believe that the guardians of his ideal republic should be intelligent, able to learn quickly, and physically graceful and strong. He also believed that these were inherited traits, and that the breeding of children of this kind should be encouraged. But to believe in the importance of hereditary traits is not the same as to be a racialist, or most biologists at the present time would be racialists. This is clearly a *non sequitur*.[11] Furthermore, virtue, as Plato conceives of it, is certainly neither racial nor hereditary. It must be learned. It can be taught.[12] Popper pays little or no attention to these basic Platonic theses. The guardians are not a hereditary caste, or class, as he supposes. Their hereditary aptitudes are only necessary, not sufficient conditions. They are to be selected on the basis of examinations which test their intellectual and moral qualities (*Republic* 412E ff.). Children of guardians who fail to meet these tests are to be demoted. Children of artisans who meet them are to be promoted. These examinations are also mentioned later on in Book IV (429E9). Popper discounts these statements, and maintains that they are rescinded in later passages. But, in my opinion, a careful reading of the texts (*Republic* 546A and 435C) fails to confirm this view.

As to the fourth charge that Plato himself is the philosopher king with the secret of the nuptial number, that he is ready to apply it at once, but not eager, I think it is best to let Popper speak for himself. "He (Plato) is not eager; but as a natural ruler and savior, he is ready to come. The poor mortals need him. Without him the state must perish, for he alone knows the secret of how to preserve it—the secret of arresting degeneration . . ."[13] Levinson has shown that the elaborate web of argument which Popper has devised to support this weird but fascinating fabrication is without a real foundation in the text.[14] I shall return to this theory at a later point in my paper.

3. Class Rule

According to Plato's conception, the guardians (*phulakes*) of the ideal community work not for their own special interests, but for the common good in which they and all the citizens participate. They are able to accomplish this difficult and burdensome task because of their knowledge of the basic needs of man, and the hierarchical order of the values satisfying these needs. Thus, as Socrates held, the welfare of the soul is more important than that of the body, and physical health is worth more than the possession of external things (cf. *Laws* 870). In the light of this knowledge, the guardians are able to govern justly, giving to each need and desire its proper due, and to attain not only the real welfare of the whole community, but that of each individual as well. There is no necessary conflict between these two goals. When adequately understood, they coincide.

In my opinion, this version of natural law philosophy, which has played an important role in our Western history, cannot be summarily dismissed as a disguised form of tyranny. Nevertheless, it is subject to basic criticisms which need to be carefully worked out in the light of viable alternatives. Popper calls his alternative *protectionism* (pp. 108 ff.). "What I demand from the state," he says, "is protection for my own freedom and for other people's." I believe that this view, which subordinates the state to individual freedom, is worth exploring. But, in his book, Popper does not explore it very far. According to him, "it says nothing . . . about a natural right to freedom" (p. 110). But this raises the question as to whether man is really free, and if so, in what sense? What kind of an answer is to be given to those who do not believe in human freedom?—and there are many of them. Are these questions simply to be settled by a peremptory decree? If the individual in some sense possesses freedom, what are its limits?

According to Popper, the state should protect only that freedom "which does not harm other citizens" (p. 109). But is this harm limited to physical injury and murder? Do I harm a fellow citizen when I allow him to remain in poverty, when I fail to see that he is properly cared for and educated as a child? Do I harm my fellow citizens when I refrain from struggling against tyranny, which almost always emerges as a way of protecting the interests of the people?[15] Am I responsible for the state and its policies? What is the nature of this state, and how am I, as a free individual, related to it? It would be interesting to see Popper dealing with these questions, and working out a responsible criticism of the actual political philosophy of Plato, in the light of his answers. So far he has not done so.

Instead of this, he simply lays down his demand for freedom without saying what he means, and then, by slanted translations and epithets, suggests that Plato's guardians are imposing an irrational tyranny in the guise of reason. They are a "master race" (p. 138), a "ruling class" (p. 83), and herders of "human cattle" (p. 52). We need not deal with the racial connotations of these epithets, for as we have noted, the guardians, while originally intelligent, are not racially distinct from the other members of the ideal community. Neither are they a "ruling class" in the modern sense of this phrase, a privileged group exercising power for the satisfaction of their own special interests, which is denied to others. In Plato's conception, governing for the common good is not a "privilege." It is rather a burdensome responsibility. The guardians live a rigorous life, and are provided with no material goods beyond their necessary needs (*Republic* 419). This is not what we now mean by a *ruling class*.

Neither are these guardians the masters of unwilling slaves. In the *Republic,* the guardians are said to be "friends and supporters of those whose freedom they had been guarding" (547C1), "helpers of their fellow citizens" (417B1), "saviors and helpers" (463B1-2). It is only with the coming of the timocratic state that violence and class feeling enter the picture. These timocratic rulers "enslave their own people who formerly (in the ideal republic) lived as free men under their guardianship . . . and holding them as slaves and drudges, devote themselves to war (as in Sparta) and to keeping these subjects in bondage (like the helots)" (*Republic* 547C ff.). Plato's notion of the guardian is subject to many criticisms. But in these attacks, Popper is tearing a straw man to pieces.

4. Lying Propaganda

Popper works out a violent attack on Plato's allegory of the metals at *Republic* 414B. He follows certain others in translating the Greek phrase *gennaion pseudos* as "noble lie," which at once suggests to a modern reader the most glaring and debased deceptions of mass propaganda. Popper takes up this suggestion of a very dubious translation, and builds upon it a web of interpretation with invidious implications for Plato (pp. 138-141). He claims that this is a "big lie," consciously imposed upon the working drudges by their masters, like the lies of the Nazi Propaganda Bureau. In the second place, he maintains that the primary purpose of the lie is to infuse racialist doctrines of blood and soil, and the master race into the innocent inhabitants of the republic. I believe that both of these charges rest upon serious misunderstandings.

In the first place, it is a mistake to translate the Greek term *pseudos* here

by the English word *lie*. The range of *pseudos* is much wider. It covers works
of the imagination, fictions, and stories of any kind. Popper's procedure here
is like calling *Alice in Wonderland*, or *Pilgrim's Progress* a mass of lies. That
Plato's purpose is not to impose a gross deception on the main body of the
population is clearly indicated by his hope (414D1) that the rulers themselves
may be persuaded to believe in it, as one may come to believe in the truth conveyed by a certain parable in mythical form. Cornford, in his version of the
Republic,[16] translates the phrase as "a single bold flight of invention" in
order to avoid this misunderstanding. This story is not a *lie* at all. It is a truth
conveyed in fictional or mythical form. What is this truth?

According to Popper, of course, it is a divisive lie. Its purpose is to persuade the slaves that they ought to be ruled by a different and superior *master
race*. This again is a misunderstanding. Of course, individual souls are not
gold, silver, or bronze. They were not fashioned and educated under the
earth. But the truth conveyed in this traditional, mythical language is not
divisive but rather unifying. In spite of their different hereditary endowments
and the different functions that they perform, they are racially the same and
the earth (their land) is their common mother. The aim is to elicit loyalty to a
common community which transcends differences of intelligence and social
function. Does Professor Popper think that such communal loyalties should
be completely rooted out of human life? Does he believe, against Cornford,
that the Greek term *pseudos* in this context should be translated as *lie*? Does
he still think that the sense of this story is a propaganda deception imposed by
unscrupulous masters on a community of slaves?

III. Plato and Socrates

I shall now conclude with a few historical questions concerning Popper's
opinions about Plato and his teacher, Socrates. He has tried to strengthen his
case against Plato as a racialist totalitarian by building up another case for
what he calls "the Great Generation" of Athenian democratic and egalitarian
liberals of whom Socrates was perhaps "the greatest of all" (p. 180). According to Popper, the last of this "Great Generation" was Antisthenes, the "only
one worthy successor" of Socrates (p. 189), who is mentioned in the
Phaedo as being present with Socrates at the time of his death. Wilamowitz
in his book on Plato[17] has warned against the tendency of certain nineteenth-
century scholars to build up overly imaginative interpretations of Antisthenes
on the basis of the very limited evidence. But Popper has revived this line of
argument, and developed it even further.[18] According to him, Antisthenes
believed in "the equalitarian creed" to which Plato was "hostile" (p. 149); he
"developed the fundamental tenets of anti-slavery, of a rational protec-

tionism, and of anti-nationalism, i.e., the creed of the universal empire of men" (p. 180); and "believed in the brotherhood of Greeks and barbarians" (p. 562).

In his *In Defence of Plato*, Levinson has examined the chain of arguments by which Popper tries to justify these conclusions, and the weak, or nonexistent, links in this chain.[19] In the light of this careful criticism, I should like to ask Mr. Popper if he still believes that the evidence now at our disposal is sufficient to justify his assertions about the "protectionism" of Antisthenes, and about Plato's personal enmity towards him. If so, how does he fit into this interpretation Antisthenes' endorsement of the principle of leadership in the case of the elder Cyrus, his contempt for the Athenian democracy, and his admiration for Sparta.[20] These "facts" are not certain. But they are no more dubious than many of those on which Professor Popper has built his enthusiastic case.

He has identified certain polemic passages in the *Republic*, where Antisthenes' name is not mentioned and where the supporting evidence is very slim or nonexistent, with personal attacks on this author.[21] Other passages concerned with logical and metaphysical issues, like *Sophist* 251B, which are widely accepted as concerned with the atomistic views of Antisthenes, are ignored. In the light of these passages, and of what is known from other sources about his attacks on definition and the attribution of the many to the one, I find it impossible to accept Popper's idea that Antisthenes was Socrates' "one true disciple." Both Plato and Aristotle tell us that Socrates was passionately concerned with the finding of definitions of the different virtues. In Popper's language, this would seem to make him an *essentialist*, and I find his defence against this criticism (p. 32) unconvincing. But in any case, Socrates was seeking for moral definitions. Antisthenes, on the other hand, seen in the light of the little we know, seems to have denied the possibility of any real definition. This certainly sets a major gulf between them.

I am, in general, sympathetic with those who have maintained that there is a basic contrast between the attitudes of Socrates and those of Plato. But Popper's contrast is too simple, and flies in the face of too much evidence. He maintains, for example, that the Socratic attitude is "agnostic" (p. 127) and that he represented the "true scientific spirit" (*ibid.*). I believe, as I have argued in my book,[22] that this is grossly inaccurate. Popper accepts the *Apology* as an accurate account of Socrates' trial. In this dialogue, he expresses several basic convictions which are hardly scientific in their range and spirit. First, there is a divine being higher than man, and possessing a wisdom compared to which human wisdom is as nothing (23A; cf. 30-31); second, the evils of the soul, vice and injustice, are worse than the evils of the body, sickness and death (29B, 39A); third, tending the soul is more important than tending the body (30A, 41E); fourth, virtue depends primarily on knowledge

(26A); and fifth, it is not so evil to suffer injustice as to do it (30D). I do not see how one who holds these doctrines, and lives in accordance with them can be properly called an *agnostic*. Furthermore, Plato himself, in his own way, accepted all these doctrines.

Similar statements may also be made about the *Gorgias* which Popper holds to be, in general, authentically Socratic.[23] In this dialogue, Socrates presents an elaborate defence of the distinction between true and false art, and the relations of the arts to one another (463 ff.); argues at length in defence of his conviction that doing injustice is worse than suffering it (467-80); analyzes the virtues as they are analyzed in Book IV of the *Republic* (506C); argues that human goodness is radically distinct from pleasure (495-503); expresses a definite belief in the immortality of the human soul, and paints a mythical picture of the destiny of the soul in the afterlife (523-end). Is this agnosticism? And is this rather far-ranging body of doctrine radically opposed to what we find in the Platonic philosophy? Popper is right, I believe, in seeking for a basic contrast between the life and thought of Socrates on the one hand, and of Plato on the other. But it does not lie in a Socratic agnosticism and concern for science as over against a Platonic gnosticism and hatred of science. Socrates says in the *Apology* that he has no interest in theories about physical nature (19B-D).

Similar remarks may be made about Popper's other points of contrast. According to him, Socrates is an *equalitarian*, whereas Plato is an *elitist* who believes in a racially superior ruling class. Socrates is against slavery (because he argues with a slave boy in the *Meno*), whereas Plato not only accepted slavery, but openly defended it, and worked actively to set up a slave society. Socrates was a universal humanist who led the Great Generation of Fifth Century Athenians, including Antiphon and Antisthenes, in striving to clarify and establish a universal empire of mankind. Plato, on the other hand, was devoted to the ideal of a frozen, provincial society. Socrates was one of the great individualists of all time, whereas Plato was a collectivist who believed that the nation could do no wrong, and that the individual should be reduced to a mere cog in the machinery of the state.

These supposed oppositions are oversimple, and far too extreme. Sometimes, as we have already noted, they rest on misinterpretations of the texts. Thus the guardians of the *Republic*, while they may be superior in native intelligence and training, are not a racial, ruling class. When properly understood, it is difficult to see anything radically non-Socratic in this idea that the more intelligent and better trained should govern. In general, as Popper admits, Socrates had the deepest respect for knowledge, and for genuine proficiency in all the arts. In the *Gorgias*, he states that it is more of a challenge and far more difficult to convince a single intelligent partner in a dialogue, than to face a great crowd in the democratic assembly (*Gorgias*

472). It is hard to infer from passages like this that he would oppose the rule of those who are more intelligent and better qualified for rational rule.

The question as to whether there is slavery in the ideal republic of Plato is dubious and controversial, though to a competent scholar, like Levinson, the arguments against this conclusion seem stronger.[24] The institution of slavery is certainly recognized in the *Laws*, as in ancient society in general. The fact that Socrates argued with a slave boy in the *Meno*, however, can hardly be used to illustrate a basic opposition to Plato who wrote the dialogue. Furthermore, in no dialogue which Popper recognizes as historically Socratic, does Socrates ever attack the institution of slavery. These facts simply do not justify the notion that there was a basic conflict between Socrates and his pupil on this issue.

Turning now to the topic of universalism, we have already shown that Plato's versions of the creation myths, as well as his accounts of the human soul, the human virtues, and the philosopher-king thesis, apply universally to mankind, and are not racially restricted, as Popper supposes. He also places great emphasis on Socrates' "intellectualism, i.e., his equalitarian theory of human reason as a universal medium of communication . . ." (p. 184). This is certainly true. But the statement applies equally well to Plato, who believed that rational argument could reveal the orderly forms and patterns (ideas) which are always and everywhere the same. I do not see any fundamental opposition here.

According to Popper, Plato stands for a totalitarian collectivism completely opposed to the "individualism" of Socrates (p. 601 e4), who "believes in the self-sufficiency of the human individual" (p. 601 e4), meaning by this his intellectual and moral self-sufficiency. We have already considered some of the misunderstandings which underlie Popper's collectivist interpretation of the *Republic* (pp. 7-9). We need add here only a brief comment on the extraordinary way in which he has dealt with a passage from the *Laws* concerning military organization and exercises (942A-D). In his text, where the passage is quoted, Popper first rightly states that it is concerned primarily with "military discipline," which is true, but then complains about the manner in which "Plato leaves no doubt" that these military principles are to apply to the whole of civilian life in peace as well as in war. As Levinson has shown,[25] this rests on a misunderstanding. The prohibition of independent action applies to military maneuvers in time of war and to military games and contests in time of peace. Popper has translated the Greek *en paidiais*, in play, or in games (i.e., *military games*) by the phrase "even playfully," which is a distortion of the meaning.

Furthermore, he has mistranslated certain military terms in such a way as to slur over their technical military sense and to convey a more general meaning. Thus *poreuesthai, march,* is rendered as *move,* and *archon, com-*

mander, or *official*, as *leader*. In this way, regulations for military exercises and games are turned into a general political program. In addition, Professor Popper has torn certain sections of this passage from their context, omitting those with a specific military reference, and printed them, together with a sentence from Pericles' Funeral Oration on the title page of Part I of his book. Thus the unsuspecting reader, before he turns to Chapter 1, is encouraged, by a supposed translation, to regard Plato as a Fascist totalitarian who wishes to run the whole of life as a military camp.

When these misunderstandings of Plato are removed, there is no ground in the texts for building up any basic opposition between Plato and Socrates with reference to the intellectual and moral independence (*autarchy*) of the individual. According to the *Republic*, it is the individual alone who can resist the "great beast" of public opinion, and can discover for himself what is really good and bad, and right and wrong (*Republic* 492-3). In the same work, as we have noted, Plato argues that even in a diseased society, it is possible, at least for a few individuals to think for themselves and to arrive at the truth (*Republic* 495-6). After all, it is Plato who has preserved the most living image of Socrates that we now possess, and who has, to this degree at least, undone the work of the hemlock. Can we infer from this that he had no respect for the intrinsic worth and independence of the individual?

Popper regards Plato as a dogmatist and an authoritarian (pp. 131 ff.). But Cherniss has offered evidence[26] to show that Plato, in his Academy, did not try to teach an "orthodox metaphysical doctrine," nor to impose his own doctrines on his students. What does Professor Popper think of this evidence?

He lays great emphasis on the opposed attitudes of Plato and Socrates toward the actual Athenian democracy. "Socrates," he says, "was, fundamentally, the protagonist of the open society, and a friend of democracy . . ."[27] Plato, on the other hand, was a bitter enemy of democracy who "was led to defend lying, political miracles, tabooistic superstition, the suppression of truth, and ultimately, brutal violence" (p. 194). Not only did he attack all democratic aims and ideals in his writings; he was himself personally involved in an at least half-conscious plan to overthrow the democratic government of Athens during his life, to arrest its development, and to replace it with the closed institutions of the *Republic*. "The philosopher king is Plato himself, and the *Republic* is Plato's own claim for kingly power."[28] These striking assertions deserve a brief comment.

Popper, of course, recognizes that Socrates was sometimes rather critical of the democratic government that finally put him to death (pp. 184 ff.); but, as he sees it, this was a "friendly" criticism "of the kind that is the very life of democracy" (p. 184). He was in no sense basically opposed, and "had never intended to undermine democracy" (p. 188), as is shown by the attitudes Plato attributes to him in the *Crito*, which reveal his "loyalty to the state as well as to democracy" (p. 188). This is hard to reconcile, however, with Popper's view of the *Gorgias* as genuinely Socratic "in parts," aside from its Pythagorean elements which are Platonic (p. 593, n. 45). The attacks on the ports and shipyards and walls of Athens, Popper says, "are certainly Plato's," though he thinks "it quite possible that Socrates may have made similar remarks."

But these attacks are not restricted to such details as he mentions. They penetrate to the irrational sources of Athenian policy in the whims of the assembly, and they bitterly denounce the great heroes of Athenian history (*Gorgias* 515C ff.) as imposters. Socrates calls Pericles, whom Popper admires as a representative of "the true spirit of the Great Generation" (p. 182 *et passim*), a dishonest quack (*ibid.*). According to the tradition, this scathing attack, written by Plato, attracted considerable attention at the time, and led to the publication of pamphlets on the other side. If Socrates made remarks "similar" to these, it is hard to believe that the Athenians of his time would have regarded them as "friendly" to democracy.

One source of misunderstanding, I believe, is Popper's tendency to treat as essentially similar all the various political formations, ancient or modern, to which the term "democracy" is commonly attached. But, as I have tried to point out in my book,[29] this usage covers many differences to which we should attend. The present American "democracy," for example, involves a divided sovereignty with checks and balances, and a principle of judicial review, which were wholly absent in fifth-century Athens. The often emotional decisions of the assembly were final, and from the decision of five hundred citizens condemning Socrates to death, there was no appeal. The tradition of natural law philosophy, which Plato probably founded in the West, has made an important contribution to the establishment of these innovations. One cannot infer that, because Socrates and Plato made critical comments on the tyranny of the majority which defaced the democratic government of their time, they would, therefore, say the very same things about the "democracies" and "open societies" of our time.

I agree with Popper that, in spite of his basic disagreement with the irrationalism of Athenian politics, Socrates was still loyal to the Athenian community and to his own people who had nurtured him and, until the time of his trial, had tolerated his independent views. This is shown by the *Crito*. But I see no reason in the textual evidence for denying a similar attitude in Plato, who, after all, actually wrote the dialogue. At the end of the great war, he may have witnessed drunken rhetoricians clothed in armor, mounting the rostrum to persuade the popular assembly, by impassioned oratory, to embark on acts of mad aggression. Like Socrates, he was certainly opposed to mass tyranny of this kind. Nevertheless this was the city which had nurtured him, and he owed it a basic allegiance and respect. That this was not just a temporary attitude, abandoned in later life, is shown by the first part of the Seventh Epistle, now generally accepted as genuine. In this letter, the forceful overthrow of one's own native city is compared with patricide, and the earlier "democracy" is referred to as a Golden Age in comparison with the rule of the Thirty Tyrants in which Plato's uncles participated.

There is no evidence in the texts to support Popper's theory that Plato supported the oligarchic plots against Athens during the great war. This war seemed to him an absurdity, and he could give his full allegiance neither to the one side nor the other. From his point of view, both states and parties were degenerate. Hence, as he states in the letter (326 ff.), after watching the mad course of events until his head was in a whirl, he decided to abandon the active career in politics which he had planned, and to devote his life rather to the study and the teaching of philosophy. The textual evidence, when carefully read, gives us no firm ground for imagining any basic difference between Socrates and Plato in their ambivalent attitude towards their mother city.

As to Plato's "secret dreams" (p. 152), his "quest for power" (p. 153), and his half serious plan to become the philosopher king of Athens in his own time, I shall not argue. I know of no competent scholar who has, as yet, been persuaded by the elaborate mixture of dubious interpretation and clairvoyance by which Professor Popper attempts to justify this sensational thesis. Any argument against the fantastic becomes itself involved in the fantastic. Instead of this, I shall simply address a final question to him. Does he still think that the single text on the nuptial number (*Republic* 546) can bear the weight that his thesis places upon it? Does he still believe that, from his vantage point in the twentieth century, he can discern a secret plot in Plato's mind without any clear support from the relevant texts or the witness of his contemporaries? Does he now believe that Plato was seriously considering a project to become the philosopher king, and to establish the ideal republic in the Athens of his time?

As I have said, I am not a Platonist, and I do not believe that the Greek philosopher remained fully true to the teachings of Socrates. But, if he "betrayed" his master, he did not do this by developing the twentieth-century, totalitarian doctrines with which Professor Popper is directly acquainted from his own experience, and which he rightly condemns. There certainly is a contrast. But this contrast is less simple, and involves something deeper than the doctrinal, where there is a large measure of agreement. It involves a different way of life, and a different feeling for the sense of existence. With Socrates, we find the feeling for a more radical transcendence and mystery, a deeper sense of personal freedom and responsibility. In his book, Professor Popper has raised the problem of Socrates vs. Plato again with great force, and for this he should be praised. But he has not solved it. This task still remains to be done.

JOHN WILD

DEPARTMENT OF PHILOSOPHY
YALE UNIVERSITY
MARCH, 1964

Notes

[1] K. R. Popper, *The Open Society and Its Enemies* (Princeton: Princeton University Press, 1950). My page references will be to this edition. Hereinafter cited as *O.S.*

[2] John Wild, *Plato's Modern Enemies and the Theory of Natural Law* (Chicago: University of Chicago Press, 1953). Hereinafter cited as *M.E.&N.L.*

[3] Ronald Levinson, *In Defence of Plato* (Cambridge: Harvard University Press, 1953). Hereinafter cited as *D.P.*

[4] *D.P.*, pp. 622-29.

[5] *M.E.&N.L.*, pp. 23 ff. and nn. 89-92.

[6] *O.S.*, pp. 38 and 487.

[7] *D.P.*, pp. 624-25.

[8] *M.E.&N.L.*, pp. 19-25.

[9] *O.S.*, p. 107.

[10] *M.E.&N.L.*, pp. 26-27.

[11] Cf. E. M. Manasse, *Bücher über Platon* (Tübingen: J. C. B. Mohr, 1961), Vol. 2, pp. 214-17 for a consideration of this and other charges of Popper against Plato; also M. J. O'Brien's review of this work in *Gnomon,* **35** (1963), 765 ff.

[12] Cf. *Meno*, 88 ff. and *Protagoras*, 361A7-C2.

[13] *O.S.*, p. 152.

[14] *D.P.*, pp. 450-59, 615-17.

[15] Cf. Plato, *Republic* 565D-E.

[16] Francis Cornford, *The Republic of Plato* (London: Oxford University Press, 1952), p. 106; cf. his notes *ad loc.*

[17] Wilamowitz and von Moellendorff, *Platon*, 2d ed. (Berlin, 1920), p. 263.

[18] *O.S.*, pp. 149, 180 and esp. n. 48 to Chap. VIII, pp. 562-64.

[19] Cf. *D.P.*, pp. 201-12 and 592-96.

[20] Cf. *D.P.*, pp. 210-11.

[21] *D.P.*, p. 592.

[22] *M.E.&N.L.*, pp. 11 and 55.

[23] *O.S.*, p. 593, n. 45.

[24] *D.P.*, pp. 167-77.

[25] *D.P.*, pp. 530-32, n. 71.

[26] H. Cherniss, *The Riddle of the Early Academy* (Berkeley and Los Angeles: University of California Press, 1945), pp. 81-83.

[27] *O.S.*, p. 186; cf. p. 595, n. 53.

[28] *O.S.*, p. 150; cf. pp. 569-70, nn. 59-60.

[29] *M.E.&N.L.*, pp. 43-48.

H. B. Acton

MORAL FUTURISM AND THE
ETHICS OF MARXISM

I

The major part of Volume II of *The Open Society and Its Enemies* is given over to an exposition and criticism of Marx's social theory. These chapters are too well known to need recapitulation here, and in my opinion nothing published during the twenty years or so that have elapsed since they appeared requires any radical modification to be made in them. Karl Popper held that Marx was primarily concerned with achieving freedom for individual men and women, and this libertarian interpretation is borne out by study of the unpublished manuscripts that have been so widely discussed in recent years.[1] Again, Popper argued that Marx's own views differed from what is known as Marxism-Leninism in that Marx considered that politics and ideas are relatively inert factors in social change, whereas Soviet Marxists and their sympathisers have undertaken to transform society in terms of their own version of Marxist theory. By now such Marxists as Professor Marcuse have accepted a similar view about Marxism-Leninism.[2] Popper also argued that Marx's humanitarian outlook was to some extent obscured by a false conception of morality which he had inherited from Hegel. This moral outlook is called by Popper "moral positivism" and "moral futurism". This conception is only in part Hegelian, for Hegel, unlike Marx, did not claim to foresee a future civilisation. In what follows I shall call attention to some features of Marx's ethics which Popper has not commented upon, in the hope that I may add to the account and criticism of Marxist morality that he has given.

By "moral positivism" Popper means the view "that what is, is good, since there can be no standards but existing standards; it is the doctrine that *might is right*".[3] By "moral futurism" he means the view that *coming might is right*",[4] so that "the most reasonable attitude to adopt is *so to adjust one's*

system of values as to make it conform with the impending changes".[5] According to Popper, it was because Marx and Engels believed that they could
foresee the fall of the bourgeoisie, the triumph of the proletariat and the coming of communism with the system of morality appropriate to post-capitalist
society, that they considered it reasonable to reject bourgeois morality and to
work for socialism. Popper argues, however, that even if it could be foreseen
that the moral standards of the future would be of such and such a sort (and
he holds, of course, that this would not be possible), this could provide no
compelling reason for falling in with them. For a man might choose to go
against the moral standards which he regretfully expects will prevail in the
future. As examples, Popper imagines a contemporary of Voltaire who,
knowing that Napoleon III's standards will be, rejects them in advance, and a
man of our own time who foresees the coming of a slavish morality and rejects that too.[6] Popper argues, again, that in its "theoretical structure" moral
futurism is like moral conservatism and moral modernism, since like them it
consists in accepting the prevailing standards without criticism. Thus, the
moral conservative sides with the powers that have been, the moral modernist
with the powers that be, and the moral futurist with the powers that will be.
Popper thinks that, although moral futurism is a consequence of Marx's
sociological theories, Marx himself "took the ideals of 1789 seriously", had
an independent regard for freedom and equality,[7] and obtained support for
his views on account of the *moral* criticisms of capitalism implied by them.[8]

Thus on the moral issue Popper sees Marx as a mixed-up man, confident
that he has a scientific conception of human society and human history, con-
temptuous of preaching and of moralising, yet generously devoted to ideals of
freedom and equality and to the interests of those whom capitalism was exploiting. I see Marx (and Engels) in this way too, but I should like to draw
attention to another aspect of their moral outlook associated with their moral
futurism which calls for separate discussion. This I call their *antimoralism.*
Marx's antimoralism includes the rejection of preaching and moralising
which Popper has called attention to, but it includes more than this. I shall try
to explain what this is and to show its importance for the Marxist outlook
and for the "scientific" humanitarianism of our day.

Marx and Engels gave an account of their antimoralism in some detail in
The Holy Family (Frankfurt, a.M., 1845),[9] the first of the many writings in
which they collaborated. There are three main topics in this book that are
relevant to our theme. (1) In *The Holy Family* Marx expatiates on his
preference for self-expression and fulfilment over repression, renunciation
and expiation. (2) He supports this preference by reasons which show that he
knew and accepted Fourier's attacks on moral philosophy and on what he
called "moralism". (3) Marx argues that socialism and communism are the
outcome of "French materialism". He writes that Fourier "proceeds directly

from the doctrines of the French materialists", and that "the scientific French communists, Dezamy, Cay, etc., develop, like Owen, the doctrine of materialism as the logical basis of communism".[10]

II

Chapters V and VIII are among those chapters of The Holy Family written by Marx himself.[11] They are directed against an article in a journal which supported the views of those "Young Hegelians" with whom Marx had until recently been in agreement. The author of that article, Franz Szeliga (he was a Prussian officer, Franz Szeliga Zychlin von Zychlinsky, who lived until 1900), had discussed in detail Eugène Sue's novel Les Mystères de Paris. This book had been first published as a feuilleton in the Journal des Débats in 1842-43 and had had an enormous success, largely on account of its melodramatic treatment of poverty and crime. It was indeed the most popular novel of a genre that has since been described as "social romanticism".[12] In The Holy Family Marx ridicules Szeliga's attempts at interpreting the novel in Hegelian terms, and makes his own comments on the novel itself.

The main plot of the novel concerns the attempts of Prince Rodolphe of Geroldstein to intervene as a kind of Providence in order to rectify some of the evils and injustices manifested in the low life of Paris. (Before writing the book Sue had gone about the slums of the Ile de la Cité disguised as a workman.) Rodolphe "rescues" Fleur de Marie, a prostitute indeed but through no fault of her own, and makes her acknowledge and repent of her sins. It is subsequently discovered that she is Rodolphe's long-lost daughter. She refuses the opportunity of marriage ("J'aime trop le Prince Henri pour lui donner une main touchée par les bandits de la Cité"), takes the veil, becomes abbess of the convent, and dies a holy death. Marx quotes from the novel to show that, to begin with, Fleur de Marie had energy and gaiety and was not obsessed by the past. ("Enfin, ce qui est fait, est fait", she had said.) Then she was humiliated by being made to repent of her past behaviour, and finally she exchanged the possibility of a fulfilled life on earth for an imaginary life in heaven. Rodolphe, says Marx, has transformed Fleur de Marie first into a repentant sinner, then into a nun, and finally into a corpse.

Another character discussed by Marx is the Ripper (le Chourineur). Rodolphe first knocks him down as he attempts violence against Fleur de Marie, gains his respect, and then reforms him. What does this reform amount to, asks Marx. In effect, he answers, Rodolphe progressively ruins the man. To begin with, the Ripper, though criminal, was strong and brave. The process of reform consisted in turning him first into a stool pigeon, then into a "moral bulldog" who fawns on his master, and then into a prudent petit bourgeois. Marx also argues that Rodolphe's alleged acts of retributive justice are in fact "hypocritical justifications" for his personal antipathies. Any good that Rodolphe does—and this is not much—is brought about by his vast wealth. Without this wealth he would be regarded as a criminal himself, as he ignored and flouted the law.

That Marx rejected otherworldly Christian morality hardly needs saying. These passages show, however, that he believed that remorse for past offences is dangerous if not always bad, that the demand for retribution is a disguise for hatred, and that the human values to be fostered are strength, courage, gaiety, independence and fulfilment of the natural powers.

III

From *The Holy Family* it is apparent that Marx was much impressed by Fourier's views on morality. Fourier had held that all repression of the natural instincts (or passions, as he called them) is bad, and that repression of them only takes place because society is badly organised. In a "harmonious" society, Fourier believed, the passions would not be repressed but would be indulged in so as to bring about satisfaction for everyone. The method of "moralism", as Fourier called the repressive system, was bound to fail. "All these philosophical caprices called *duties*", he wrote, "have no connection with nature".[13] Moralists require people to do what is impossible, and hence have little or no effect upon what is actually done. "What is it [morality] in the body of the sciences", Fourier asks, "if not the fifth wheel of the coach, powerlessness in action? Whenever morality fights on its own against a vice, one can be sure that it will be defeated".[14] According to Fourier, morality "boasts that it makes a study of man and does the opposite. Morality has studied nothing but the art of taking man's nature from him (*l'art de dénaturer l'homme*), of suppressing the springs of his soul on the pretext that they do not fit in with the social order, *instead of seeking a social order fitted to the nature of man*".[15]

These views are reproduced by Marx in *The Holy Family*, where he praises Fourier's insight and quotes the phrase about morality as "powerlessness in action" (*l'impuissance mise en action*). What is the powerlessness of morality? One aspect of it is the alleged ineffectiveness of blame and punishment. People steal, assault and murder in spite of the police and of the moral law, and it would therefore be better to find out why they do these things rather than attempt the futile task of annulling what has been done.[16] What has been done cannot be undone (*ce qui est fait, est fait*), and remorse, with its backward look, draws attention away from the present and the future. Can, then, blame and punishment affect the future in the ways desired by police and judges? Marx seems to have thought that they cannot. A reason he had for this was that blaming and punishment are the offspring of hatred and are hence destructive ("they take man's nature from him", as Fourier had put it). They are also hypocritical in that the blamer or punisher condemns in the criminal the hatred and destructiveness which inspire his own acts of blaming or punishing. Presumably the remorseful man would be hating and destroying himself. Then, it is futile to blame the poor or punish them for committing crimes to alleviate their poverty, for as long as they are not cowed (and hence "denatured"), they will continue to do these things. To teach them that it is their *duty* to respect the rights of property is to expect them to suppress their natures, whereas they have every reason to want alterations in the laws of property and in the structure of society. Pressure for such alterations is to be expected from those who have most to gain from them, that is, from the proletariat. The regeneration of society, therefore, cannot occur as a result of moral exhortation, or of more efficient enforcement of the law, but only when the proletariat understand what they will gain from bringing it about. It is along such a line of argument, I suggest, that Marx came to adopt his antimoralistic view of social revolution. The view calls for a number of comments.

There is an important ambiguity in Fourier's and in Marx's antimoralism, for it is not clear whether it is morality as a whole that is held to be at fault, or whether moralism is merely a defective form of morality, the form in which remorse, blame and retribution and the sense of duty are thought to play their "denaturing" roles. Marx's references to Prince Rodolphe's *hypocrisy* in instigating, allegedly in the interests of justice, the punishment of men who had in fact injured him personally, suggest that Marx regarded hatred as intrinsically bad, both the hatred of the criminal and the hatred of the punisher. Marx also seems to hold that the maintenance and development of human capacities is morally paramount, and that diminution and destruction of them is intrinsically evil. Marx believed, of course, that industrial and economic forces beyond the control of individuals would bring about the collapse of the sort of society in which moralism prevails. Hence he did not think that appeals to the superiority of fulfilment over repression will ensure the regeneration of society. Appeals to the advantages of nonmoralistic, nonrepressive morality will do no more to bring this about than appeals to duty, and therefore morality, even in the acceptable sense, is a "fifth wheel of the coach" as well.

We see here an important difference between Marx and Fourier. Whereas Fourier thought that moralism was powerless, he did not think that the spreading of knowledge of "the attractive system" would be powerless too, for he believed that this appealed to men's "natural" desires. Furthermore, Fourier hoped that those who wished to operate the attractive system would voluntarily combine to do so. Marx, on the other hand, thought that industrial and economic forces would inexorably lead to social cataclysm, and that, until this happened, voluntary socialism was out of the question. Although, therefore, Marx was opposed to repression, he favoured encouraging whatever forces were opposed to capitalism, whether or not they themselves utilised repressive measures. It looks as if Fourier had greater faith than Marx in the morality of fulfilment. At any rate he was less anxious to put it into cold storage.

We must now consider more closely what it is that constitutes Marx's moral futurism. The Marxist moral futurist, Popper says, sums up his position as follows:

> My fundamental decision is not (as you suspected) the sentimental decision to help the oppressed, but the scientific and rational decision not to offer vain resistance to the developmental laws of society. . . . I adopt the facts of the coming period as the standards of my morality. And in this way, I solve the apparent paradox that a more reasonable world will come without being planned by reason; for according to my moral standards now adopted, the future world must be better, and therefore more reasonable.[17]

The aspect of moral futurism I should like to examine is expressed in Popper's phrase "the scientific and rational decision not to offer vain resistance to the developmental laws of society". This is an idea which non-Marxists have adopted when they put forward moral futurism as the rejection of moral quixotry. It would be absurd or pointless, the argument may be developed, to stick to a code that was formed in one set of circumstances when quite a new set of circumstances is coming into being. To attempt thrift, for example, when inflation prevails, would be ridiculous as well as unprofitable. Those who think that thrift is an important virtue might reply, of course, that they are opposed to inflation because of the injustice it gives rise to, and intend to try to stop it. But suppose they fail in their endeavour to do so? A point may well come when thrift is seen to be nothing but a meaningless gesture, and there is nothing for it but to submit to the trend that had hitherto been deplored. Thrift, of course, is a subordinate virtue and in part prudential, although not wholly so, and whatever it was that made thrift worthwhile in the past, may still be maintained in the new society. "Not to offer vain resistance" may be morally acceptable, therefore, when basic moral standards are still kept intact. There is a sense, therefore, in which it is right for moral standards to be modified in the light of social changes, for morally subordinate rules and aims may be rendered irrelevant by new circumstances. But this is not something, I suggest, to be done *before* the circumstances have altered. To abandon thrift before inflation has got under way may be to help it to take hold.

We must distinguish, however, between altering or abandoning a derivative moral rule because it is no longer relevant to the new circumstances and doing so because it is difficult to adhere to it in the new circumstances. "Difficult" here would mean that adhering to the rule in the new circumstances is likely to be detrimental in a nonmoral sense of the word, is likely, perhaps, to lead to unpopularity or material loss of some sort. But these are not reasons that would justify giving up a moral rule. To advocate giving up a moral rule for nonmoral reasons is in effect to advocate demoralisation. Another "difficulty" in the way of observing a moral rule could be that no one else accepts its authority. Such a situation might arise because the rule had lost its point, but if one man only thinks that it still has point, then it should be possible for him to explain why. He may be wrong, of course, or he may just be defeated.

However, it is one thing to abandon a derivative moral rule and quite another thing to abandon a moral principle or a whole moral code. Even a principle such as that requiring the truth to be told might become irrelevant if human beings all acquired telepathic powers. Abandonment of the Golden Rule, however, might be regarded as abandonment of morality itself. If not, the word "morality" is being used for any rules or institutions that may be extant. The extremest possible form of moral futurism, therefore, would be the acceptance, in complete ignorance of what they would be, of rules and institutions that will only come into existence many years hence. We might call this blank cheque moral futurism. This would indeed be strange morality, for it would involve rejecting the morality of one's own society in favour of a morality or of a system of rules that does not yet exist. If no date and no details are supplied, this morality would have no content whatsoever. Perhaps the people who come nearest to accepting it are those who, in the face of contemporary forms of corruption or destruction, say: "You can't stop progress". If it is not mere silliness, it is the sort of cunning reported of Hindenburg by General von Schleicher, according to whom Hindenburg said at a meeting of the German Cabinet: "Gentlemen, let us wait to see which way, with God's help, the cat will jump". But it is not really a moral view at all, for a moral view must at the very least accept some rules or guiding aims. To reject all such rules or aims except those that will prevail, say, fifty years hence, whatever they may be, is not to accept or profess anything. Moral modernism, if it is to involve anything specific, must be the acceptance of whatever rules or aims are in vogue or are just coming into vogue. Difficulty could arise, of course, in trying to decide what was in vogue, but one thing would be certain—rules and aims that were being abandoned by the majority would have to be given up. The moral modernist would therefore regard the moral conservative as quixotic for holding on to rules and aims that were passing out of vogue. The moral conservative, it seems to me, would have this much more of morality in him, in that his rules and aims, not being identical with the prevailing ones, allow for criticism of the existing state of affairs.

Marx's moral futurism, however, was no blank cheque moral futurism. As we have seen, it was specified to the extent of requiring conditions of life that promote enjoyment and fulfilment. Now Popper quotes[18] a passage from the *Anti-Dühring* in which Engels says that the proletarian morality is the morality which will last and "represents the future". Engels thought that proletarian morality already existed in capitalist society, and although he does not say what its tenets are, he did think that it presaged the morality of the future. For he and Marx had adopted the Saint-Simonian view that future forms of society begin their growth within the society they are going to supplant. This view is really an attempt to break down the difference between the past and the future by saying that the future is somehow *in* the present. But does it follow from the fact that there are traces of the past in the present, that there are signs of the future in the present? It might be thought so, because of the way in which "germs" (to use Saint-Simon's word) of present-day institutions can be found in institutions of the past. But the will and inventiveness of the past have ceased to function, whereas in the present they are still at work. Although it is correct to say that the past was once a future, it does not follow from this that the future future has the same status as past futures. Traces of the past, therefore, are not wholly analogous to signs of the future, and hence Saint-Simon has not provided a means of assimilating the two.

To return now to Engels's account of the morality of the future, we notice that he believed that the "Utopian socialists" came too early to be able to discern the lineaments of the future in the early capitalism of their day,[19] but that he and Marx had come at the right time to do so. The future, that is, was already there. Furthermore, although the proletarian morality was a pointer to the morality that would come with communism, it was nevertheless a class morality and hence in some degree repressive. However, "a truly human morality"[20] would ultimately emerge. This would be nonrepressive[21] and it would so operate that "the government of persons is replaced by the administration of things and the direction of the processes of production".[22] Thus Marx and Engels were at one about the central feature of the morality of communist society, its nonrepressiveness.

IV

We now come to Marx's view that materialism is "the logical basis of communism". The materialism that is "the logical basis of communism" is the view that men are originally good and endowed with equal intelligence, that the differences between them arise from their experience and from habit and education, that "external circumstances" influence men, that industry is of great importance, and that enjoyment is justified (*Berechtigung des Genusses*). These things show materialism's "necessary connection with communism and socialism". Marx claims to demonstrate this necessary connection by arguing that, if the circumstances in which man lives and experiences shape him, then he must shape them so that they become human (*So muss man die Umstände menschlich bilden*). It is not a question of man's becoming free in the negative sense of being able to avoid this or that, but in "the materialist sense" of acquiring "the positive power of asserting his true individuality" (*die positive Macht, seine wahre Individualität geltend zu machen*). This should not be achieved by punishing crime, but by "destroying the antisocial source of crime", so that "to each is given the social space for the essential manifestation of his life". Marx also takes it as established that the principle of all morality is "interest properly understood" (*das wohlverstandene Interesse*), and concludes that each man's private interest coincides with the interests of man generally. Man is held to be social in nature, and Marx argued that from this it follows that the power of human nature "must be measured not by the power of the particular individual, but by the power of society".[23] At the end of the section of *The Holy Family* [Chap. VI(d)] in which these arguments occur, Marx reproduced some passages from Helvétius, d'Holbach and Bentham to support his view. These passages are from writings in which social questions are being discussed, and it is clear that by "materialism" Marx here means a conception of human life as determined by natural and social circumstances which can be controlled or ordered (notably by industry) so as to obtain the maximum satisfaction for each individual. The morality—of this word is appropriate here—of enjoyment (*Genuss*), of self-interest (*das wohlverstandene Interesse*) and of essential self-expression (*wesentliche Lebensäusserung*) is necessarily connected with the view that man is a natural being whose powers can be diminished or heightened by the nature of the circumstances that surround him. In this context, "freedom" means the power of manifesting human individuality through controlling natural and social circumstances.

From all this it is clear that Marx was not asserting that communism and socialism are necessitated by materialism in the sense of metaphysical or reductive materialism. I have elsewhere[24] described what I take to be the nature of Marx's materialism, arguing that he was an epistemological realist, a naturalist (and antisupernaturalist), an empiricist, a pragmatist and an opponent of psychophysical dualism. I do not suppose that Popper disagrees with these characterisations, except perhaps the last, for he describes Marx as having "a certain leaning towards a dualism of body and mind"[25] and as being "a practical dualist" holding "that we are spirit *and* flesh, and, realistically enough, that the flesh is the fundamental one of these two".[26] Let us, then, give some further attention to Marx's views on the relation of mind and body.

We have already called attention to Fourier's idea that the passions or instincts exist to be indulged rather than to be repressed. We have considered, too, Marx's statement that the materialist philosophy justifies "enjoyment". Like Fourier, Marx held that the fundamental human instincts should be fulfilled in the satisfaction of desire. This suggests that Marx believed that "spiritual" goods are not obtained by renouncing the flesh, but as a result of gratification and self-fulfilment. Repression of the natural instincts leads to their mere shadow-fulfilment in imagination. Marx and Engels have something to say about this subject in *The German Ideology* (1846), in the course of their long polemic against Max Stirner's book *Der Einzige und sein Eigentum* (1845). Here Marx and Engels make fun of Stirner's idea that men can be slaves to their minds and thought as well as to their bodies and desires. The Christian, Marx and Engels say, regarded himself as one being, in that he regarded his body and his instincts as foreign to him, and his soul as his true nature.[27] Stirner, on the other hand, was a *chrétien composé*, upholding both body and soul.[28] In the course of this discussion, Marx and Engels say that certain bodily needs, e.g., food and sex, are ineluctable, and they jibe at what they call Max Stirner's "insurrection" against the fixity of desires and thought which, they say, "ends up in the impotent moral command of self-mastery".[29]

In this passage, of course, it is *Stirner's* dualism that is criticised, not all forms of body-mind dualism. Furthermore, the passages that Popper quotes[30] to support his view that Marx was a "practical dualist" occur in *Capital*, a much later work. Even so, it is in these early writings that Marx discusses philosophical and ethical topics in detail, and I do not think he changed his views about them in any fundamental way. Their emphasis, it seems to me, is on the unity of the human individual. Christian dualism, at any rate, was regarded as leading to individual and social repression, whereas Marx thought that no good could come from repression, which would be unnecessary once society was organised so as to allow the basic bodily needs to be satisfied. Within an essentially naturalistic view of man it would have been possible to argue, as Freud did later in *Civilisation and its Discontents*, that repression of some natural desires could lead to the production of valuable things and the maintenance of civilisation. Marx, however, like Fourier, held that the civilisation that depended upon repression was bad. Fourier, indeed, held that civilisation itself is bad, just because it calls for repression of the instincts. Hence, freedom itself is given a "materialistic sense" and is defined as the expression of "true individuality". In a society of free men, the argument is, conflicts would not take place, either within the individual or within the society, but only between the socialised individuals and external circumstances both material and social. Persons would not have to master themselves, for this, as we have seen, would be to submit to an "impotent moral command". Instead, they would make society responsive to their harmonised collective requirements. "Government over persons", "*Regierung*", with its implication of rules, commands and superior authority, would be banished and replaced by "administration" (*Verwaltung*) and direction (*Leitung*).

These expressions of Engels combine extracts from various passages in the writings of Saint-Simon. In the *Catéchisme des Industriels* (1823-24) occurs the phrase, possibly written by Comte, "The government of things replaces that of men . . .", and earlier in *l'Organisateur* (1819), Saint-Simon had written that "the desire to command men is transformed little by little into the desire to make and remake nature according to our desires".[31] Individuals do not have to control themselves and one another, but unite to control nature and the recalcitrant features of social organisation. It is interesting to notice that Saint-Simon put forward two versions of his thesis about domination. According to one version, "the love of domination" is "indestructible in man", but is, in the course of progress, transferred from man to nature. This is the version given in *l'Organisateur* and in the *Catéchisme des Industriels*. According to the other version, that given in *de l'Organisation Sociale* (1825), it is a mistake to suppose that men are best governed by force and that "persuasion and demonstration" are only secondary means. On the contrary, "these are the only means employed by administrators".[32] Engels's version is a combination and modification of these. "Domination" is dropped out altogether, and even the idea of administering persons seems to have been repugnant, so that it is things or states of affairs that are administered, and seemingly impersonal "productive processes" that are directed or guided. No doubt the impersonal terms *"Sachen"* and *"Produktionsprozesse"* were used because Engels was unwilling to think of the application to persons even of such relatively gentle pressures as administration and direction.

Like Marx, Engels looked forward to a time when force and repression had been altogether eliminated from human society, but this time, he thought, would come only after the forcible transformation of the corrupt social order. Many non-Marxist social reformers, however, especially those who think in terms of scientific humanitarianism, accept the view that even in society as it exists now, "administration" in the form of "persuasion and demonstration" is *more effective* than force or domination. The antimoralism and antirepressiveness which Saint-Simon and Fourier, Marx and Engels, had thought would prevail in some society transformed by revolution, are increasingly to be found in twentieth-century "capitalist" or "mixed" economies. The trend towards this is especially encouraged by penal reformers, who seek, with some success, to establish methods of prevention and cure to replace retributive punishment. It is a prominent feature, too, of industrial relationships, where many of the "experts" regard it as simple-minded to expect industrial agreements to be kept or trades unions to be subjected to legal sanctions. That part of the process of administration called "persuasion" by Saint-Simon is too prominent a feature of our society to need comment. The part called "demonstration", the part, that is, that sets out to base policy upon the facts of the case, is largely effected through the work of committees of enquiry of various kinds, and plays a considerable part in the public life of the twentieth century.

H. B. ACTON

DEPARTMENT OF PHILOSOPHY
UNIVERSITY OF EDINBURGH
JUNE 3, 1966

NOTES

[1] "The Economic and Philosophical Manuscripts of 1844", published in *Karl Marx, Friedrich Engels: Historisch-kritische Gesamtausgabe*, ed. by D. Riazonov, I, III (Berlin, 1932). Hereinafter cited as *MEGA*. There is an English translation by Martin Milligan, *Economic and Philosophic Manuscripts of 1844* (Moscow and London, 1959), and by T. B. Bottomore, *Karl Marx: Early Writings* (London, 1963). These views were discussed by Jean Hyppolite in articles published in 1946-47 and reissued in *Études sur Marx et Hegel* (Paris, 1955), and in Eugene Kamenka, *The Ethical Foundations of Marxism* (London, 1962; New York: Praeger, 1962).

[2] Herbert Marcuse, *Soviet Marxism* (London, 1957; New York: Columbia University Press, 1958).

[3] K. R. Popper, *The Open Society and Its Enemies* (London: Routledge & Kegan Paul, 1962), Vol. 2, p. 41. Hereinafter cited as *O.S.*

[4] *O.S.*, Vol. 2, p. 206.

[5] K. R. Popper, *The Poverty of Historicism* (London: Routledge & Kegan Paul, 1957; Boston: The Beacon Press, 1957), pp. 53-54.

[6] *O.S.*, Vol. 2, pp. 205 f.

[7] *O.S.*, Vol. 2, p. 207.

[8] *O.S.*, Vol. 2, p. 211.

[9] This is reprinted in *MEGA* I, 2, and in *Karl Marx und Friedrich Engels Werke* (Berlin, 1962), Vol. 2, pp. 1-223. Hereinafter cited as *MEW*. There is an English translation by R. Dixon, *The Holy Family* (Moscow, 1956; London, 1957).

[10] *MEW*, Vol. 2, p. 139.

[11] The table of contents indicated which chapters were by Marx and which by Engels.

[12] See Georges Jarbinet, *Les Mystères de Paris d'Eugène Sue* (Paris, 1932). I have discussed Marx's criticisms of Szeliga in *The Illusion of the Epoch* (London, 1955; Boston: Beacon Press, 1957), pp. 206-23.

[13] *Théorie des Quatre Mouvements* (Leipzig, 1808), p. 108. In spite of the mention of Leipzig on the title page, the book seems to have been published at Lyons.

[14] *Ibid.*, pp. 262 ff.

[15] E. Silberling, *Dictionnaire de Sociologie Phalanstérienne* (Paris, 1911), p. 284, quoting from Fourier's *Théorie de l'Unité Universelle* (1822).

[16] See Marx's discussion of suicide in a review of a book on that subject in the *Gesellschaftsspiegel* in 1845. Instead of blaming men, he says, we should try to understand them. A society in which men kill themselves in despair and loneliness is not a society but a desert. *MEGA*, I, 3, pp. 391-407.

[17] *O.S.*, Vol. 2, p. 204.

[18] *O.S.*, Vol 2, p. 205.

[19] *Anti-Dühring*, trans. by Emile Burns (London, 1934), p. 292. *MEW* (1962), Vol. 20, p. 247.

[20] *Ibid.*, p. 108. *MEW*, Vol. 20, p. 88.

[21] *Ibid.*, p. 308. *MEW*, Vol. 20, p. 266.

[22] *Ibid.*, p. 309. *MEW*, Vol. 20, p. 262. "An die Stelle der Regierung über Personen tritt die Verwaltung von Sachen und die Leitung von Produktionsprozessen".

[23] *MEW*, Vol. 2, p. 138.

[24] In "Karl Marx's Materialism", *Revue Internationale de Philosophie*, Nos. 45-46 (1958), Fas. 3-4.

[25] *O.S.*, Vol. 2, p. 102.

[26] *Ibid.*, p. 103.

[27] *MEW*, Vol. 3, p. 237.

[28] *Ibid.*, p. 240.

[29] *Ibid.*, p. 238.

[30] *O.S.*, Vol. 2, pp. 102 f.

[31] *Oeuvres de Saint-Simon et d'Enfantin* (Paris, 1869), Vol. 38, p. 131, and Vol. 20, pp. 126 f. (footnote). Cf. Vol. 39, pp. 144 f., where Saint-Simon says that "persuasion and demonstration" are "the sole means employed by administrators".

[32] *Oeuvres de Saint-Simon et d'Enfantin*, Vol. 39, pp. 144 f.

Peter Winch

POPPER AND SCIENTIFIC METHOD IN THE SOCIAL SCIENCES

I

Sir Karl Popper's account of society and of the scientific understanding of social life has two poles. The first of these is his general account of scientific method, as developed in his *Logik der Forschung* and subsequent writings assembled in *Conjectures and Refutations.*[1] I shall be able only to glance at this account, though a full analysis of Popper's social philosophy would doubtless demand a much more extended examination of his ideas on scientific method in general. The second pole is his account of ethics, the fullest presentation of which is to be found in *The Open Society and Its Enemies.*[2] There are two sides to this: (i) a philosophical analysis of what it is to hold an ethical position; (ii) the development and articulation of a distinctive ethical position of Popper's own, special emphasis being placed on his attitude to questions of social policy.

There are interesting and difficult questions about the relation between (i) and (ii), which I shall try to touch on, though no more than that. The same holds of the relation between (ii) and Popper's views on scientific method. It is quite clear that his own ethical views are decisively influenced both by his ideas on scientific method and by his philosophical treatment of the nature of ethics, though the exact nature and extent of these influences is by no means easy to discern and clarify.

Before turning to these matters I wish to make a preliminary remark about something else, which is certainly germane to them, but which I do not propose to examine directly—Popper's position in social philosophy is developed in a polemical way, in the context of a sustained criticism of a connected structure of doctrines to which Popper is violently opposed: 'Historicism', 'Holism', 'Essentialism', 'Tribalism', 'Totalitarianism', etc. In very large measure his stature in the field of social philosophy derives from the negative force of these criticisms and from the damage they have done to 'isms' like those mentioned. This remark is, *of course*, not intended in any belittling sense; and Popper himself, I feel sure, would not take it in that way, given his emphasis on the importance of *falsification* in the development of knowledge and understanding. I shall make no direct attempt to assess the conclusiveness of these negative criticisms; instead, I want to articulate the positive view of social life and of its study which grows out of them and to isolate and discuss what seem to me some of the main sources of difficulty in that view. This is the doctrine of 'social engineering' and the 'technological theory of institutions' on which it is based. My discussion will start from the first of the two 'poles' in Popper's thought, which I mentioned at the outset: his account of scientific method.

Scientific method, according to Popper, is the method of 'trial and error'. It consists in formulating hypotheses which are susceptible of falsification and in then attempting to falsify them. When any hypothesis has been falsified, a new one is formulated in the light of the resulting epistemological situation. For our present purposes two aspects of this procedure have to be emphasized. First, no hypothesis is put forward *in vacuo*: it springs from a context of existing theories regarded as provisionally established and it is intelligible only in that context. Second, a hypothesis is always advanced in a form which makes it possible for the investigator to learn from his mistakes: he does not have to start absolutely afresh each time, but puts forward his new hypothesis in the light of what he has learnt *not* to be the case.

The foregoing is the main hinge on which Popper's attack on 'utopian', 'holistic' engineering turns. The utopian engineer takes the view, which he supports with historicist arguments, that the only real change that can be 'engineered' in social conditions is a *complete* change; that any attempt to make partial improvements is doomed to failure, owing to the organic dependence of any particular aspect of social life on the 'social whole'. Correspondingly, the above conception of scientific method is the main support for Popper's contrasting view that the properly 'scientific' attitude to questions of social policy is that of 'piecemeal engineering', which consists in concentrating on one social problem at a time, 'making little changes and adjustments', and modifying one's subsequent interventions in the light of the outcome of one's previous interventions. Hence, too, Popper's emphasis in this connection on particular institutions rather than on society as a whole: we can deal with these *one at a time*, leaving the rest of social life alone—at least for the time being.

So far, so good. I think that the first real difficulties begin to accumulate when we enquire into Popper's account of the point of view from which these piecemeal changes will be initiated, of the ends which the engineer will have in view. Two conceptions enter into Popper's exposition of the matter at different points and it is not altogether easy to assess the relation between them: viz.

A. the conception of *improving the institution* in question;

B. the conception of *improving our understanding* of the institution.

Now it is manifest that there are important interrelations between these conceptions. For one thing, if our ultimate aim is to improve an institution, we might expect to be able to do this more effectively, the better we understand its mode of operation and its relations to other institutions. I do not think that Popper would disagree with this statement as it stands. He does, it is true, argue against the view (in its 'historicist' form) that, if we are to take 'a truly scientific attitude towards the problems of war and peace, . . . *we must first study the causes of war*'.[3] This, he says, is 'as if one insisted that it is unscientific to wear an overcoat when it is cold; and that we should rather study the causes of cold weather and remove them. Or, perhaps, that lubricating is unscientific, since we should rather find the causes of friction and remove them'.[4] But Popper's point here is that it is not 'scientific' to refrain from doing anything about an undesirable phenomenon until the causes of that phenomenon are *completely* understood. He is not, I think, denying that the more adequate our understanding of the causes of the phenomenon, the better chance our countermeasures have of being successful. In terms of his own examples: a greater understanding of mechanisms of heat-transference in various media may lead to the manufacture of more effective insulating materials for overcoats; a greater understanding of how friction produces heat may lead to the invention of more effective lubricants (though, of course, more effective overcoats and lubricants may also be hit upon in *other* ways). There is nothing in Popper's argument to rule out the possibility that a greater understanding of the conditions under which wars break out may lead to more effective countermeasures designed to prevent them: the point is that there are measures we may take, which may have some chance of success, *prior* to such understanding.

But I think that Popper wants to go further than this: he wants to say that a concern with practical problems is needed if our theoretical understanding of social institutions is to be advanced, that we shall improve our understanding of institutions by trying to improve the institutions. Sometimes he states this point in a way which implies a real distinction between these two concepts. 'Practice is not the enemy of theoretical knowledge but the most valuable incentive to it'.[5] Stated thus, Popper's claim is an empirical hypothesis; and, while its author's historical knowledge of the instances against which it would have to be tested far transcends my own, it seems to me reasonably clear that, while there have indeed been many occasions on which a concern with practical, technological improvements of various kinds has resulted in an improvement in theoretical understanding, there have *also* been many occasions when it has diverted attention from the investigations which would have needed to be carried out in order to advance such understanding. The technologist

> follows the intimations, not of a natural order, but of a possibility for making things work in a new way for an acceptable purpose, and cheaply enough to show a profit. In feeling his way towards new problems, in collecting clues and pondering perspectives, the technologist must keep in mind a whole panorama of advantages and disadvantages which the scientist ignores. He must be keenly susceptible to people's wants and able to assess the price at which they would be prepared to satisfy them. A passionate interest in such momentary constellations is foreign to the scientist, whose eye is fixed on the inner law of nature.[6]

At other times, though, Popper states the point in what is, perhaps, a less cautious way, which suggests that he regards the relation between theory and practice as a much closer conceptual one than my previous quotation from *The Open Society* implies. Modern science, he says 'enforces upon our intellect the discipline of practical tests. Scientific theories can be tested by their practical consequences';[7] and he clearly wants to use the word 'practical' here in a way which will reinforce his views about the relation between science and technology. But this, surely, is to use the word equivocally. The fact that a scientific theory has consequences which are 'practical', in the sense that experimental conditions can be devised which will put them to the test, has nothing intrinsically to do with the question whether they are 'practical' in the sense of being *useful* or relevant to the concerns of practical life.

Our theoretical understanding of an institution, or of an aspect of social life, may be increased by a successful, or unsuccessful, attempt to eradicate evils therefrom. But, equally, our theoretical understanding may be increased by our study of developments which we regard as constituting a serious, and perhaps permanent, *deterioration* of the aspects of social life that are in question. And there seems to be no reason to suppose that there are not cases in which this increased understanding could not have been achieved in any other way.[8]

II

To go deeper into this whole question we must look more closely at each of the two concepts whose interrelations we are trying to understand: what is it (a) to improve an institution; (b) to improve our understanding of an institution? I shall start with question (a); and this brings me to Popper's account of ethics.

The word 'improvement' obviously introduces the concept of *value*.

Popper's account of values is characterized by him as a 'dualism of facts and decisions'. Facts are expressed in statements, whereas values are expressed in norms, which in turn are embraced as the result of individual decisions. Facts are what they are, irrespective of what any man may happen to think, whereas norms '*can* be made and changed by man, more especially by a decision to observe them or alter them, and . . . therefore man . . . is morally responsible for them'.[9] Speaking rather more rhetorically, Popper sometimes expresses the same view in the words 'Man is the master of his fate'.

Now in an earlier paper[10] I have tried to state what seem to me some of the main difficulties in this sort of view. I shall not here repeat my earlier arguments; but one of the main upshots of those arguments is germane to my present subject. It is this. Whether a particular state of affairs obtains or not is certainly something to be discovered, and the investigator's interests, values and desires are irrelevant to whether it *does* obtain or not. A decision, on the other hand, has to be *made*: that is, it depends on the will of the decider in a way in which a fact does not. But if we now ask: what are the conditions under which we can speak of a man finding out that something is the case and what are the conditions under which we can speak of a man making a decision?—we find that the concepts of saying that something is so and of making a decision are related to each other in a way which Popper's account does not bring out and which is very relevant to his whole account of social engineering. Factual investigations are made in the course of particular kinds of human activity; what will *count* as a fact is something that depends on the kind of activity in the context of which the question is raised. I do not at all mean that it is, in general, up to the individual to *decide* what is thus to count: on the contrary, that is for the most part something which he is committed to *qua* participant in that particular kind of enquiry—if his conception of what is to count as a fact is eccentric beyond certain limits (though these may not be easy to specify), that will at least count against saying that he really is engaged in that sort of enquiry. Now the human activities in the context of which it is often necessary to make factual investigations *also* often create the necessity for individuals to make decisions. Given that an individual is in a situation where a decision is required from him, it is up to him what decision he makes. But it is *not* up to him whether what he does counts as making a decision, and there are limits to what considerations can be taken as relevant to the decision he makes—limits, again, which are not themselves decided on by him, but which are a feature of the activity within which we can understand the possibility of decisions of that sort being made at all. Durkheim's aphorism about the notion of contract—'everything in the contract is not contractual'[11] can be adapted to make this point: not everything in a decision is a matter for decision. To understand what is involved in making a decision of a certain sort, we must understand the limits to what can count as a consideration relevant to a decision of that sort; and this may well involve understanding something about the values which may be generated in the life of the ongoing activity in the context of which such decisions have to be made.

Now Popper would, I suppose, strongly object to this way of putting the matter. The form which his polemic against moral historicism takes commits him to rejecting the view that values can be 'generated in the life of an ongoing activity'. The position he wants to refute is that questions of value can be settled by looking at actual historical trends and that 'history' is the ultimate judge in questions concerning moral worth. I certainly agree that this is a position to be avoided. But in order to reject it, it is not necessary to embrace what seems to me the equally mistaken view that an individual's values can intelligibly be ascribed to him quite apart from the forms of social life in the context of which he lives his life. I am not making the point that such forms of life *as a matter of fact* have an influence on the values of individuals—I expect Popper would agree with that; I am saying that the conception of an individual's having values is unintelligible outside such an institutional context. And Popper is, I think, rejecting the view when, for example, he insists, 'It rests with us to improve matters. The democratic institutions cannot improve themselves. The problem of improving them is always a problem for *persons* rather than for institutions. But if we want improvements, we must make clear what *institutions* we want to improve'.[12] This view is expressed in the same context in which Popper compares institutions to fortresses, both of which, he says, must be 'well designed *and* manned'.[13] One of the main points of this analogy, as I see it, is to suggest that we have on one side the designer of the fortress (social engineer), who has decided *what* he wants to aim at, and, on the other side, the fortress (institution) which is his *instrument* for achieving the aim; but the aim is something that can be understood quite apart from the existence of the fortress (institution) and we could, in principle, think of that aim as being achievable by the use of some quite different instrument. As against this, the view I am urging is that there is an internal relation, in questions of social policy, between the aims that people adopt in the context of institutional life and their position *in* that context of institutional life.

The word 'aim' and its near synonyms are used in a variety of different ways, and I think there is a danger of confusion in discussions of the present sort if this variety is not taken account of. There are two connected complexities in particular which I will say something about. There is, first, a complexity about the way in which aims are ascribed to individual men on particular occasions and the relation of this to the way in which aims are ascribed to kinds of human activity and to institutions. And second, the means-end relation, which is implied by talk about aims, takes different forms: sometimes the relation is what I shall call an 'extrinsic' one, sometimes it is 'intrinsic'.

What is the relation between the aims which individual men have in what they do on particular occasions and the aims ascribable to the forms of activity in which individual men participate? Now for considerations related to those which lead Popper to espouse 'methodological individualism' it is tempting to regard the aims of individual men as primary and the aims ascribable to activities as a more or less complex construction out of these individual aims. What does seem clearly true is that there are plenty of aims that men (and animals) do have quite apart from the existence of any social institutions, e.g., eating and drinking, keeping warm, and mating (though even here of course the *form* which these aims take with humans is very closely dependent on institutional factors). It seems equally true that there would not be institutionalized forms of activity to which we could attribute aims, unless there were individual human beings who performed actions with particular aims in view. All the same, there are also aims which are attributable to individual men only insofar as they live in a society which contains institutions, ways of doing things and ways of thinking, forms of life. For example, a man may arrange to keep an evening free with the aim of playing chess, or take a certain examination with the aim of being admitted to a university. Now aims may be attributed to such activities and institutions too. In order to see what is involved in such an attribution it is necessary here to introduce the distinction between the 'extrinsic' and the 'intrinsic' means-end relation, to which I referred a short space back.

Suppose someone asks me: 'what are your aims in playing chess?'. According to the context in which the question is asked, two quite different kinds of answer may be appropriate. I may say: 'my employer attaches a lot of importance to proficiency at chess and I want to impress him'. Or I may say: 'to capture my opponent's king'. The first answer illustrates the extrinsic means-end relationship, the second answer the intrinsic. The second type of answer would be appropriate if my questioner were someone who had just come across the game for the first time and wanted to know how it was played. It is obvious that, in this case, my answer does not refer to any further aim, over and above chess-playing, which it may achieve; it would be natural to say that the answer explains something of what is *involved in* chess.

Now it seems to be that nearly all—perhaps all—social institutions can sometimes be spoken of in terms of this intrinsic means-end relationship. They can sometimes *also* be spoken of as being used to further aims in the extrinsic sense. When speaking about aims in respect of institutions, it is important to be clear which of these kinds of thing one is saying. It seems to me that Popper is not always clear about this. The official doctrine implied by his comparison of institutions to machines is that institutions are usable to achieve ends in the extrinsic sense; and his critical dualism of norms and statements of facts may well require that this is the only proper way to speak of aims in respect of institutions. In this vein Popper speaks in several places of the ultimate aims of all human institutions, including science, as being humanitarian ones.

The analogy with chess, with which I introduced the 'intrinsic' notion of aims must not, of course, be pressed too far. Social institutions, of the sort that interest Popper, are complex in a variety of dimensions and this complexity makes it very easy to become confused in talking about their 'aims'. Consider the institution of university education, for instance. In the first place, universities obviously embrace an enormous variety of activities of all kinds, such that any attempt to specify an 'aim' which they all have in common, comparable to the aim of capturing one's opponent's king in chess, could result in nothing better than a platitudinous generalization. And even if most people engaged in one or the other form of university work could be made to agree on such a generalization, radical disagreements would become apparent as soon as there was any attempt to interpret it. But perhaps even more important than this diversity of activities engaged in within the universities is the diversity of the different *conceptions* of university work held by people engaged in it, as well as by outsiders. Let me expand this point.

Education, being one of the principal vehicles by means of which what is regarded as valuable in the life of a society is preserved, developed and handed on, is obviously a very powerful social force. The way it is carried on will have important ramifications in other sectors of social life and it, in its turn, will be powerfully affected by movements in other social fields—religious, industrial, political, military, etc. Just now I used the phrase 'what is regarded as valuable in the life of a society'. But, one should ask, regarded *by whom*? People disagree about questions of value. Some, for example, will value military preparedness above material prosperity; some will have a strong interest in promoting a particular religious view of life, others with promoting different such views, and yet others will strongly oppose the promotion of any religious view. And so one might go on. The views people have about such matters will affect the views they have about education: about what subjects are most important and about how they should be studied and taught. So the question of the 'aims' of education is controversial in a way in which that of the aims of chess is not; or rather, there *is* such a question in the one case, and not in the other.

Now it is easy, as a result of attending to this sort of consideration, to come to think of educational institutions as simply a cockpit, as it were, in which rival values, springing from elsewhere, are fought out and furthered or opposed. And, since similar considerations, though not always so obviously, apply in the case of other social institutions as well, it is easy to come to think of all such institutions as simply instruments, by means of which values of a noninstitutional nature may be furthered. But this misses the point that educational institutions, to stick to my original example, are a source of social and cultural values of their own. University work, for example, has a distinctive character and generates distinctive values. Indeed, it is by virtue of this very fact that there is something there which *can* sometimes be made to further extraneous aims. In trying to specify its own distinctive character, we may indeed talk about the 'aims' of university education. But we are not always, in this case, talking about anything lying outside university work itself, which it furthers. This is not, of course, to say that university work is carried on in a vacuum or to deny that it has all kinds of important relations with other social activities.

But, besides requiring that the aims of the social engineer should be ascribable to him apart from any particular institutional context (although, of course, they will be *directed at* the improvement of existing institutions), the dualism of facts and decisions also has important consequences for the account Popper gives of the *rationality* involved in social engineering. In the first place, because the engineer's aims fall on the 'decision' side of the dualistic gulf, there can be no question of 'establishing' them by reference to any facts: they are cherished as a result of the engineer's personal commitment. Scientific reasoning comes in when it is a question of testing hypotheses about possible ways of achieving these aims and of studying possible consequences of adopting various means which the engineer might not intend and which might, therefore, make one sort of means less desirable than another, even though both are equally well adapted to achieving the original end. A situation might clearly arise in which the engineer wished to give up altogether an aim he had had, because he saw no way of achieving it which would not have consequences the undesirability of which appeared to him to outweigh the desirability of the original aim. So, here is one way in which scientific reasoning may react on the engineer's decisions about ends, and not merely govern his choice of means.

But Popper's argument also suggests more far-reaching implications than this about the aims that a rational social engineer will have. Because his rationality (I think Popper would say: *any* rationality) consists in using the method of trial and error, the engineer must be committed to 'piecemeal' rather than 'utopian' engineering. Because Popper's arguments to this effect must be sufficiently well known, I shall not retail them here. The point I want to make is that, although the dualism of facts and decisions requires that aims can only be decided on, not proved, nevertheless the account of rationality in terms of means to ends and unintended consequences of actions sets limits to the ends which a rational social engineer can have. They must be ends which are such that their appropriate means can be studied in a scientific way; and this is true of the piecemeal, but not of the utopian engineer. Although in no way internally inconsistent, this account does lead to tensions between the different things Popper says about rationality in connection with the ends of the social engineer. At times he wants to speak as if these are a matter purely of personal commitment (and therefore not of rationality); but at others it is quite clear that he thinks of the piecemeal engineer as more rational than his utopian rival and that this judgement *is* in part justified by Popper by reference to the kind of aim which each respectively has, though only via the possibility of rationally investigating the means to them.

A different aspect of Popper's account of rationality limits further the kind of aim that it is rational for a social engineer to have: his emphasis, namely, on the importance of criticism and discussion. Popper sees an analogy[14] between the scientific institutions which make possible the communication, discussion and free criticism of hypotheses within the scientific community and the political institutions of a democracy, which make possible the discussion, criticism and modification of social policies. Now discussion and criticism are possible only if there is agreement amongst the participants about *what* hypotheses or policies are to be discussed. But the hypotheses formulated by the social engineer as worthy of discussion will be those which have a bearing on the achievement of the ends which he has. So, unless his ends are shared by a large number of other people, he is unlikely to arrive at hypotheses which others will be willing to discuss with him and he will thus not have the benefit of criticism which is essential if his activities are to be carried out in a rational way. Hence there is a premium—deriving from the nature of rationality—on having social aims which are likely to be widely shared. In Chapter 9, of *The Open Society*, Popper claims that this is more likely to be true of policies which attack urgent evils in institutions as they exist, than of policies which aim at 'the greatest ultimate good'; because suffering and happiness, contrary to the doctrine of the classical utilitarians, are not 'ethically symmetrical' and human suffering, unlike the promotion of happiness, 'makes a direct moral appeal'.

Hence I think we must say the following about Popper's commitment to humanitarianism in relation to his account of social engineering. Whereas many things he says suggest that the rationality of a social engineer consists solely in the methods he uses to achieve his aims, the nature of the aims themselves not being discussable in terms of rationality, he *also* says many other things which suggest that he thinks that humanitarian aims are more consistent with a rational policy of social engineering than any other. Moreover, putting this point together with my earlier remark that Popper is committed to the view that the social engineer's aims are held by him as a person, rather than growing out of the workings of the institutions for which he has these aims, we find that Popper is led to say that, from a social engineering point of view, the point of all institutions (explicitly including science) is a humanitarian one. That is, the question of how any institution is to be improved is always a question of how it may best be made to further humanitarian aims.

The point here is that, if we take the view that the values guiding the social engineer's operations on institutions cannot themselves be institutional values, there seems nothing left to appeal to beyond certain values, interests and concerns which belong to men as such—what is left over, as it were, when we cancel out the differing and often opposed interests that we find being promoted within various institutions themselves.

Now it seems to me mistaken to suppose that, as a matter of fact, men will be inclined to agree on the greater desirability of furthering general humanitarian aims, when these are in conflict with aims which they have by virtue of their commitment to institutional values. Consider, for example, Georges Sorel's portrayal, in *Reflections on Violence*, of the anarcho-syndicalist attitude to the general strike, as contrasted with the attitude of the parliamentary socialists of his time. The latter attitude was essentially Popperian: the strike was a means to an end, the end of 'improvement' of the workers' condition. For Sorel, however, the strike was valuable for what it *was*, rather than for anything further that it might achieve: as an expression of the dignity and independence of the workers. For him no 'results' of such action were necessarily to be expected and in any case would not affect its point one way or the other.[15]

Now Popper might say, concerning this example, that his own conception of humanitarian values should not be *opposed* to the syndicalist emphasis on their dignity as members of the working class, but that the 'relief of suffering' would *include* conceptions like the preservation of dignity and independence. However, I do not think this move would entirely overcome the difficulty, as I shall try to bring out by putting my point in a slightly different way.

Instead of saying that men may oppose the general humanitarian end of relieving suffering with particular ends which they have by virtue of their attachment to particular institutions and movements, let me say that it is an illusion to suppose that there is such a general humanitarian aim at all. Opposition to the humanitarian policies of Popper's social engineers may sometimes be expressed by saying that there are, in *this* situation, values more important and urgent than the relief of suffering. But sometimes it will be better to say that what *constitutes* human suffering in the situation at hand cannot be understood apart from the institutional context in which it is being asserted to exist. That is, the conceptions and values inherent in, and inseparable from, the life of the institution that is in question, enter into what is *counted* as suffering. Take, for example, the sufferings of an oppressed religious minority. These *may*, of course, take the form of material deprivation: starvation, lack of opportunity for employment, imprisonment, and so on. Even where this is the case, the peculiar poignancy of the suffering involved could not be grasped by someone who did not realise that it was being inflicted for the holding of certain religious beliefs. And the suffering need not take such a form at all, of course. It may take the form of lack of any opportunity to pray and worship according to the demands of the religion, even though there is no lack of material welfare. I suppose that few would deny that this might indeed constitute a very severe form of human suffering; but its very nature depends on the character of the religious institutions and traditions which are under attack.

The emphasis that I have been placing on 'institutional values' does not commit me to the sort of moral historicism that Popper wants to oppose. (i) There is no question here of 'history deciding who is right'. (ii) The point of reference is not 'history' or 'society as a whole', as it is for the historicist. Nor is it, as it often seems to be for Popper, 'man' (a position which can easily lead to totalitarian tendencies of exactly the same sort as Popper wishes to oppose). Rather, the point of reference is particular institutions, traditions, forms of life. (iii) It must be emphasized that there is a *multiplicity* of such forms, which interpenetrate each other both in society at large and also in the lives of particular individuals. This means that there is genuine room for individual decisions in questions of social policy: decisions about where one's allegiances lie, what considerations one is going to take as most important, and so on. (iv) Indeed, this situation does not merely make room for individual decisions; it is what makes the very notion of such decisions possible. A man can decide what he is going to regard as most important[16] only insofar as he can attach some meaning to the word 'important'. *This* is not something that can be 'decided upon'; and not just any thing that anyone cares to mention can be *counted* as important. There are limits to what can intelligibly be said, here as elsewhere. To put the point another way: the institutional context does not decide what line must be taken on any particular issue; but it does determine what is to count as an issue. No limit on human freedom and responsibility is imposed by this situation, which constitutes, rather, the circumstances in which such freedom and responsibility can intelligibly be spoken of at all.

III

I turn now to Popper's account of what it is to *understand* (as distinct from *improve*) the workings of a social institution. Let me begin by again briefly stating his view about what is involved in coming better to understand anything whatever; I shall then examine how this view is applied to the special case of social institutions. In general, then, Popper thinks that we come to understand something by advancing explanatory hypotheses, capable of falsification, and by replacing with new hypotheses such as *are* falsified.

There is an important ramification of this general position, which needs to be made explicit at this point: namely, Popper's emphasis on the need for established social traditions and institutions, devoted to the exchange of views, results and criticism. In 'Towards a Rational Theory of Tradition',[17] a lecture delivered to the Rationalist Press Association, Popper discusses the importance of the tradition of scientific thought, and the development of habits of criticism, stemming from Ancient Greek times. He is here rightly concerned to emphasize that this is a particular tradition amongst others: one which had had to fight to establish and maintain itself in the face of opposing tendencies. The connection between this and Popper's emphasis on falsification is obvious. Falsification is possible only where it can be agreed *what* hypotheses are in question and where experiments are repeatable and do not have to be accepted simply on the say-so of the author of the hypothesis which is being examined. It is in the same lecture that Popper develops most explicitly the application of his general view of scientific method to the particular case of social institutions. He does this by claiming to find a close analogy between the function of *scientific theories* and that of *traditions* or *institutions*. Both, he argues, make possible a rational reaction to our environment by enabling us to *predict* to some extent, what is likely to happen under given conditions. 'If there is no possibility of our predicting what will happen in our environment—for example, how people will behave—then there is no possibility of reacting rationally. Whether the environment in question is a natural or a social one is more or less irrelevant'.[18] In science this possibility is created by the formulation of theories, which are 'instruments by which we try to bring some order into the chaos in which we live so as to make it rationally predictable'. Traditions and institutions have a similar function in social life, in that they 'may give people a clear idea of what to expect and how to proceed'. Popper presses this analogy in order to strengthen the parallel he wants to draw between rational methods in science and in social engineering. Like theories, traditions are 'something that we can criticize and change'. Just as the scientist works in a context of accepted theories, so the social engineer works in a context of existing traditions and institutions; and both proceed by 'making little adjustments and changes', using the method of trial and error.

Now this analogy is open to one obvious objection.—When the physicist formulates a theory, this may indeed make certain phenomena more 'rationally predictable', but it does not do so by affecting the behaviour of the phenomena: rather, it affects the physicist's intellectual grasp of the phenomena. In social life, however, if people's behaviour in a certain area of their lives comes to be governed by traditional standards where none existed before, then it is the behaviour itself that is changed, not an observer's grasp of it. Of course, if an observer wants to achieve an intellectual grasp of the behaviour, he is more likely to be successful if he discovers the existence of the tradition than if he overlooks it. But, unlike the case of scientific theories, the tradition exists whether any observer detects it or not. This confusion, I think, encourages Popper's tendency, noted and criticized by Rhees,[19] to con-flate practical social problems with theoretical problems: a tendency which is essential to his parallel between scientific method and democratic procedures. It is also relevant to his criticism of 'essentialism' in *The Poverty of Historicism*, where he compares social institutions to theoretical models—a comparison which I have criticized elsewhere.[20]

But there is another aspect of this analogy to which I wish to draw atten-tion and which is more immediately germane to my present concerns. I think that Popper is clearly right in insisting that the concept of rationality in social life cannot be understood except in relation to the existence of certain traditions of behaviour. But it seems to me that the account he gives of this relation is inadequate. I could express my dissatisfaction in general terms by saying that, for Popper, rationality has to be understood in relation to the ex-istence of *some tradition or other*, the *qualitative content* of the tradition be-ing more or less irrelevant. This, of course, is in accordance with his persist-ent attempt to equate rational thought with his account of the hypothetico-deductive method in science. It is true that in 'Towards a Rational Theory of Tradition' he does single out the beginnings of the scientific tradition in An-cient Greece as particularly important for the development of rational thought. Nevertheless, in his theoretical analysis of the general connection between tradition and rationality, what is important is not the specific nature of any tradition, but the general character of all traditions as being settled modes of behaviour and therefore as making rational prediction possible.

As against this, it is important to point out that standards of rationality are involved *in* traditions of behaviour and that they may be in mutual con-flict. A tradition of behaviour does not simply consist in habitually perform-ing certain sorts of action on certain sorts of occasion, but also in a *habit of thinking* in a certain way, in a disposition to appeal to certain standards rather than others. That is, the sense in which a mode of behaviour is settled, what makes it a 'mode of behaviour' at all, cannot itself be seen except in terms of the relation between what men do and the kinds of reason they may have for doing it. That reasons of a certain sort for acting in a certain way are possible at all is internally related to the possibility of *describing* what men are doing as a case of acting in that way. And it is only in terms of certain descriptions of behaviour that it is possible to talk of regularities in that behaviour. Even what people will regard as problems requiring solution will depend on such habits of thought; what will be a problem—let alone a solution—for one person may not even raise any question for another. The example of Sorel, which I discussed earlier, will serve here too. Within the anarcho-syndicalist movement there was just as much giving of reasons for and against particular policies as in the opposing parliamentary socialist camp; though what an anarchist would regard as a reason for doing something might well be seen by his opponent as a reason for doing precisely the opposite. The point that is important here is that the force of these 'reasons' could be understood only by someone who was familiar with the particular character of the movement within which it was offered. Merely to note that it was offered within *a* tradition, involving a 'settled habit of behaviour' would not be enough.

What this suggests is that there is a dimension to our understanding of the social life of human beings, which Popper's formal schema of hypothesis and falsification fails to illuminate. It may be all very well to say that improvements in our understanding and in the quality of our social life must come about *via* methods of trial and error. But this tells us little, unless we are clear what is to count as 'trial' and as 'error' in a particular context. The difficulty is essentially the same as that which faces any account of true propositions as 'corresponding to facts'. We can talk in this general way; but we still have not tackled the real problem: that of understanding what such correspondence amounts to in the case of propositions of particular kinds.

Designing a machine and then putting faults right; formulating a hypothesis and then revising it in the light of experiments; trying out a new form of government—these may all be spoken of as cases of 'trial and error'. But the considerations which enter into such trials and into one's views on whether there has been success or failure are very different in kind. And in the last case—that of trying out a form of government—people will tend to *disagree* on what constitutes a success. There may, of course, be disagreements in the other cases too; but in matters of political and social policy such disagreements are characteristic. Where it takes place, it does not necessarily follow that there has been any failure in communication; the disagreement may express different values, springing from diverse social movements, interests and institutions, which the people concerned are caught up in in different ways. To understand such situations, we have to understand the peculiar character of these institutions and people's participation in them. This is something we have to understand before we can attach any sense to the idea of 'trial and error' in such a context. I believe it is a kind of understanding quite different from anything that Popper gives an account of.

PETER WINCH

DEPARTMENT OF PHILOSOPHY
KING'S COLLEGE, LONDON
MAY 4, 1966

Notes

[1] K. R. Popper, *Conjectures and Refutations: The Growth of Scientific Knowledge* (London: Routledge & Kegan Paul, 1963; New York: Basic Books, 1963). Hereinafter cited as *C.&R.*

[2] K. R. Popper, *The Open Society and Its Enemies,* 2 vols. (London: Routledge & Kegan Paul, 1957). Third newly revised edition of 1952(a) with a new *Addendum* (Plato and Geometry) to Vol. I. Hereinafter cited as *O.S.*

[3] *O.S.,* Vol. I, p. 290.

[4] *Ibid.,* p. 291.

[5] *O.S.,* Vol. II, p. 242.

[6] Michael Polanyi, *Personal Knowledge: Towards a Post-Critical Philosophy* (London: Routledge & Kegan Paul, 1958), p. 178. Polanyi's whole discussion of the relations between science and technology in the section from which the above is quoted, is very illuminating.

[7] *O.S.,* Vol. I, p. 243.

[8] This is strikingly illustrated in Bruno Bettelheim's *The Informed Heart* (London, 1961), in which the author claims to throw light on certain features of life in modern industrial societies by drawing on his study of life in Nazi concentration camps while he himself was an inmate of Dachau and Buchenwald.

[9] *O.S.,* Vol. I, p. 61.

[10] Peter Winch, 'Nature and Convention', *Proceedings of the Aristotelian Society* (1959-60); also in *Ethics and Action* (London: Routledge & Kegan Paul, 1972).

[11] Emile Durkheim, *The Division of Labor in Society* (Glencoe: The Free Press, 1960), p. 211.

[12] *O.S.,* Vol. I, p. 127.

[13] *Ibid.,* p. 126.

[14] Powerfully criticised by Rush Rhees, 'Social Engineering', *Mind* (October, 1947); also in *Without Answers* (London: Routledge & Kegan Paul, 1969). Hereinafter cited as 'Soc. Engr.'.

[15] Cf. Rhees, 'Soc. Engr.': 'In proportion as men do participate in running their own affairs, they will come in conflict with humanitarians and with the reasonableness of social engineers'. Of course, the point here at issue is not whether one shares Sorel's or Popper's values, but whether values are connected with questions of social policy in the way Popper says they are.

[16] The conception of 'importance' seems to me to give Popper some difficulty in his exposition of critical dualism. See especially, *O.S.,* Vol. I, pp. 64-65.

[17] *C.&R.,* pp. 120-35.

[18] I have contested the claim made in the last sentence of that quotation—though not with direct reference to Popper—in my *The Idea of a Social Science* (London: Routledge & Kegan Paul, 1958; and New York: Humanities Press, 1958).

[19] Rhees, 'Soc. Engr.'.

[20] Winch, *The Idea of a Social Science*, pp. 126-28.

Alan Donagan

POPPER'S EXAMINATION OF HISTORICISM

1. Historicism and Historismus

Sir Karl Popper has recorded that he completed the main outline of *The Poverty of Historicism* in 1935, and that in the following year he read two papers of the same title: one privately to a group of philosophers and friends at Brussels, and later another to Professor von Hayek's seminar in London.[1] Soon afterwards, he prepared his results for publication; but, having been refused by the philosophical journal to which it was offered, the article embodying them was not published until 1944-45, when it appeared in three parts in *Economica*, **11** (1944) and **12** (1945).

Popper supplied only a brief explanation of his use of the term 'historicism', which he described as an 'unfamiliar label', deliberately adopted in the hope of 'avoid[ing] merely verbal quibbles':

> It will be enough [Popper wrote] if I say here that I mean by 'historicism' an approach to the social sciences which assumes that *historical prediction* is their principal aim, and which assumes that this aim is attainable by discovering the 'rhythms' or the 'patterns', the 'laws' or the 'trends' that underlie the evolution of history. [*PH*, p. 3]

He reserved more thorough analysis for the body of his book.

Although he thought the label 'historicism' unfamiliar, Popper did not think the approach it labels to be so. That approach, he remarked, 'is often encountered in discussions on the method of the social sciences; and it is often used without critical reflection, or even taken for granted' (*PH*, p. 3).

Popper was disappointed in his hope of avoiding merely verbal quibbles. Nothing in his criticism of what he named 'historicism' has been more indignantly denounced than the name he gave it. Professor Hans Meyerhoff has been his severest critic.

> To have a target to shoot at, Mr. Popper has set up a false image of historicism. What he has criticized as "the poverty of historicism" is a parody of historicism. It has nothing to do with the movement of historicism as defined and analyzed in the classic work of Friedrich Meinecke nor with the modern historicism of Dilthey and his successors.[2]

Even on its face, this charge is perplexing. For it turns out that Meyerhoff does not deny that Popper had a target to shoot at, a target which Meyerhoff prefers to describe, not as 'historicism', but as certain 'religious and philosophical interpretations of history'.[3] He has, then, no other ground of complaint than that the name Popper chose may mislead readers into imagining that his criticisms apply either to 'the movement defined in Meinecke's classic work',[4] or to the views of Dilthey and his successors.

Yet even this objection is curious, although it is more than a verbal quibble. Since both Meinecke on one hand, and Dilthey and his followers on the other, wrote in German, the word 'historicism' will not be found in their writings. The word they used was '*Historismus*'. By using the word 'historicism' as he did, Popper could have 'set up a false image' of *Historismus* only if at the time he published, that is, in 1944-45, the word 'historicism' had become established as the normal rendering of '*Historismus*'.

It is not difficult to show that it had not. Meyerhoff himself has recorded that even in 1959 'most of the standard works on the European tradition of historicism [were] not available in English'.[5] In the absence of translations of standard works, evidence of whether there was an accepted English rendering of '*Historismus*' must be sought in critical comments on the standard works, and in dictionaries.

The only dictionary containing an English equivalent of '*Historismus*' that was likely to have been available to Popper is J. M. Baldwin's *Dictionary of Philosophy and Psychology* (1901-1905; last corrected edition, 1925), which gives 'historism' as that equivalent. The word 'historicism' does not appear in it at all. It is true that in D. D. Runes's *Dictionary of Philosophy* (New York, 1942) this situation is reversed: 'historism' is absent and 'historicism' present. But 'historicism' is defined as a theory that is applicable to natural as well as to historical processes,[6] and that is not what Meinecke or Dilthey's followers meant by '*Historismus*'.

In the earliest discussions of Meinecke's *Die Entstehung des Historismus*,[7] by Charles A. Beard and Alfred Vagts in 1937, and by Eugene N. Anderson in 1938, '*Historismus*' was rendered by 'historism'.[8] The word 'historicism' had been used before that: by Guido de Ruggiero, in the article 'Idealism' in the *Encyclopaedia of the Social Sciences* (New York, 1932), Vol. 7; and by the translator of Croce's *History, Its Theory and Practice*, in rendering Croce's translation, '*Elementi d'Istorica*', of the title of Droysen's book *Historik*. This might have been expected: 'historicism' is a natural anglicization of the Italian '*storicismo*', as it is not of the German '*Historismus*'. Neither Lee and Beck, Rand, nor Iggers cite any authority before 1940 as rendering the German word '*Historismus*' by the English 'historicism', except Karl Mannheim in his article on Ernst Troeltsch in *The Encyclopaedia of the Social Sciences* (New York, 1935), Vol. 14, and in the

English translation of his *Ideology and Utopia* (London, 1936).[9]

Although Mannheim was the only supporter of *Historismus* whose work Popper discussed in detail, Mannheim's use of 'historicism' in *Ideology and Utopia* throws no light on Popper's use of it. Popper's most extended criticism of Mannheim, in *The Poverty of Historicism*, was confined to *Man and Society in an Age of Reconstruction* (London, 1941);[10] and his references to *Ideology and Utopia* in *The Open Society* were to the German edition of 1929.[11] What Popper had to say about Mannheim is nevertheless crucial. He described Mannheim's position in *Ideology and Utopia* as 'a theory of the social determination of scientific knowledge', which went 'under the name of "sociologism" or "the sociology of knowledge" ' (*O.S.*, II, p. 213). Of such theories he wrote:

> A theory of this kind which emphasizes the sociological dependence of our opinions is sometimes called *sociologism*; if the historical dependence is emphasized, it is called *historism*. (Historism must not, of course, be mixed up with historicism.) [*O.S.*, II, p. 208]

It is reasonable to conjecture that Popper considered Mannheim to be a representative supporter of the sociological counterpart of German *Historismus*; that he took the primary tenet of *Historismus* to be—in Mannheim's words about Troeltsch's position—that ideas are only 'reflex functions of the sociological [or historical] conditions under which they arose';[12] and finally, that he regarded 'historism' as the natural English word for the German '*Historismus*'.

Two additional pieces of evidence are difficult to explain on any other hypothesis. First, from Troeltsch to Meinecke the literature of *Historismus* is thick with references to a 'crisis' arising from the recognition that, if all institutions and ideas are to be understood historically, then the value of each is relative: there can be neither absolute value nor absolute truth. This conclusion, as Iggers observes, Troeltsch, 'like many of his German contemporaries, rejected emotionally but was never successful in refuting'.[13] Popper professed to refute it by showing that it was self-destructive:

> [T]he socio-analysts [i.e., the practitioners of the 'sociology of knowledge,'] invite the application of their own methods to themselves with an almost irresistible hospitality. . . . Can we, then, take seriously their claim that by their sociological self-analysis they have reached a higher degree of objectivity; and their claim that socioanalysis can cast out a total ideology? . . . [W]e could even ask whether the whole theory is not simply the expression of the class interest of this particular group; of an intelligentsia only loosely anchored in tradition, though just firmly enough to speak Hegelian as their mother tongue. [*O.S.*, II, p. 216]

Although Mannheim was Popper's immediate target in this passage, its deliberate generality, taken together with his earlier coupling of 'historism' with 'sociologism', shows that Popper had others besides Mannheim in mind. And whom does the cap fit except the supporters of *Historismus*?

Secondly, while he regarded 'historicism' as an 'unfamiliar label' to which he might assign what sense he pleased, Popper on several occasions spoke of 'historism' as a term with an accepted use. For example, he remarked that the project of 'analysing and explaining the differences between the various sociological doctrines and schools, by referring   to their connection with the predilections and interests prevailing in a particular historical period' is 'an approach which *has sometimes been* called "historism", and should not be confused with what I call "historicism" ' (*PH*, p. 17; italics mine.)[14] When Popper wrote, what name but '*Historismus*' had ever been given to such an approach?

Although I think that Popper's attack on the relativism implicit in *Historismus* is decisive, I do not deny that *Historismus* has sides that Popper did not consider at all. I contend only that it is anachronistic to take his account of historicism as a false image of *Historismus*. It is true that, since Popper wrote and published *The Poverty of Historicism*, the word 'historicism' has replaced 'historism' as the usual rendering of '*Historismus*': Friedrich Engel-Janosi's *The Growth of German Historicism* (1944)[15] was perhaps the turning point. But Popper cannot be blamed for lacking second sight. He explained clearly what he proposed to label by the word 'historicism'; and, in his few remarks about *Historismus*, the word he used for it was the natural anglicization 'historism', which, whether he knew it or not, not only had the authority of Baldwin's *Dictionary*, but also had been adopted by Anderson, Beard, and Vagts, who were writing at the same time as he.

Why did Meyerhoff and other critics fail to perceive this? I can think of three possible reasons. (1) They may, like Lee and Beck, consider that Popper 'does not make clear the distinction' between historicism and historism.[16] This perplexes me. Readers must judge whether the passages I have quoted from Popper make it clear or not. (2) In the twenty years after 'The Poverty of Historicism' appeared in *Economica*, 'historicism' became the accepted rendering of '*Historismus*'. Popper's critics may not have known either that there was no accepted rendering of it when he wrote, or that the natural rendering, 'historism', was then at least as common as 'historicism'. (3) Finally, Popper's account of 'historicism' is admittedly partly factitious: 'I have tried', he wrote, 'to perfect a theory which has often been put forward, but perhaps never in a fully developed form' (*PH*, p. 3). In perfecting it, Popper incorporated into it more than one idea from the ample store of *Historismus*, and among them the characteristic doctrine that the proper method of inquiry in the social sciences is intuitive understanding ('*Verstehen*', in Dilthey's term). It was, I believe, a mistake to do this. The historicism of Marx, for example, is not 'perfected' by adding the method of intuitive understanding to its impedimenta. And any critic, finding that Popper's 'historicism' is committed to the method of intuitive understanding, may be excused for confounding it with *Historismus*.

2. Antinaturalistic Historicist Doctrines

Popper's own philosophy of the social sciences was what he called 'naturalistic', that is, favourable to applying in the social sciences the methods of physics.[17] For convenience, I shall call Popper's naturalistic position on this matter 'naturalism', which Popper did not, presumably because he wished to avoid confusion with ethical naturalism, a position he strongly denounced (*O.S.*, I, pp. 69-73). Since many historicists developed their views by conscious reflection on how far the methods of physics are, and how far they are not, applicable in the social sciences, Popper chose to analyse historicism by comparing each of its characteristic doctrines with what historicists have taken to be its naturalistic counterpart. In this way he laid the foundations for his subsequent critique of historicism; for he became convinced that, both when they professed to reject the methods of physics and when they professed to accept them, the historicists misunderstood what the methods of physics are (*PH*, pp. 2-3).

The ten antinaturalistic historicist doctrines that Popper enumerated may be divided into (A) doctrines about the subject matter of the social sciences, and (B) doctrines directly about method.

(A) Antinaturalistic Doctrines about the Subject Matter of the Social Sciences
Of these, the first two are fundamental.
(A1) According to naturalism, laws of nature hold for all times and places; and the fact that a state of affairs has occurred once does not obviate its occurring again. Historicists, on the other hand, conceive social development as periodized. The laws that hold for society in one period may not hold in another; and, although social situations may recur, the fact of human memory tends to prevent it. However similar two social situations may be, if some participants in the latter have memories or even opinions about the earlier, then the two are not the same; and, since memories and opinions affect action, the difference may be decisive. Popper sometimes called this the 'Oedipus effect' (*PH,* p. 13). Hence, as opinions about the past accumulate, it becomes less likely that past critical situations will recur. Unlike situations in nature, social situations may be radically novel. I shall call this historicist doctrine the *principle of radical novelty*.
(A2) Physical structures or 'natural wholes', as historicists conceive

them, are no more than the 'sum of their parts, together with their geometrical configurations' (*PH*, p. 18). According to historicism, social wholes are altogether different. A social group cannot be specified, as a planetary system can, by listing and describing, for some specified date, its members and all the personal relations that obtain between them. Such historical facts about a social group as that it had a certain founder may be essential to its nature; but no historical fact can be essential to the nature of a natural whole. Moreover, whereas changes in a natural whole like a planetary system can be explained 'atomistically', according to physical laws, given the relative positions, masses, and momenta of its component parts, changes in a social group must be explained 'holistically', considering the group as a whole, and taking account of its history (*PH*, p. 19). Popper acknowledged that this distinction between genuine wholes and the mere atomistic 'heaps' found in nature is 'exceedingly vague' (*PH*, p. 83); and, as we shall see, he considered its vagueness to be irremediable. But vague or not, the principle that the social sciences have to do with wholes, which must be both described and explained historically and *as* wholes, is fundamental to historicism (*PH*, pp. 17-19). Following Popper, I shall refer to it as the *principle of holism*.

(A3) The principles of radical novelty and of holism are antinaturalistic in principle. But historicists also argue that even if naturalism were true in principle, it would be impracticable as a programme of research. Even in the physics of the solar system, where the forces that must be considered in explaining the paths of the planets are comparatively few, and the relevant laws fewer still, to compute with any exactitude the deviations caused in a planet's orbit by the varying gravitational fields through which it passes is extremely complicated. The courses of few large-scale natural processes can be calculated with comparable precision. Yet social processes appear to be enormously more complex than such natural processes. In addition, it is not possible, as it is in the case of large-scale natural phenomena, experimentally to isolate specimens of the various forces involved. Hence, historicists argue, even if naturalism were true, which they deny, the subject matter of the social sciences is so complex that naturalistic methods are impracticable in them (*PH*, p. 12).

(B) Antinaturalistic Doctrines Directly about the Methods of the Social Sciences

Most antinaturalistic historicist doctrines about method in the social sciences derive fairly straightforwardly from the foregoing antinaturalistic doctrines about their subject matter. A brief statement of each will therefore suffice.

(B1) Generalizations in the social sciences cannot apply to all historical periods. This follows from (A1) (*PH*, pp. 6-8).

(B2) Significant artificial experiments are rarely, if ever, possible in the social sciences. This is partly because social changes sometimes exhibit radical novelty (A1), and partly because, by (A2), discoveries about changes in artificially isolated parts of a social group are irrelevant to the problem of explaining processes in the group as a whole (*PH*, pp. 8-9).

(B3) Predictions in the social sciences are inexact. It follows from (A3) that the social sciences cannot employ the methods of prediction of physics; and, when they make predictions by their own less exact methods, the Oedipus effect mentioned in stating (A1) may invalidate them in part if not altogether (*PH*, pp. 12-14).

(B4) Predictions in the social sciences are impure. They have a practical as well as a theoretical function: either to bring about or to prevent what is predicted. The possibility of using prediction as an instrument is implicit in the statement of (A1); and Popper observed that 'most historicists have very marked tendencies towards "activism" ' (*PH*, p. 49; *PH*, pp. 14-17).

(B5) The quantitative and mathematical methods employed in sociological analyses of the nature and composition of social groups, cannot be employed in arriving at laws of social change. 'As there is no known way of expressing in quantitative terms the qualities of [such] entities [as 'states, or economic systems, or forms of government'] no quantitative laws can be formulated' (*PH*, p. 26). Historicists propound this as a commonplace about the present state of the social sciences; but its connection with (A3) is evident.

Each of the historicist doctrines (B1)-(B5) asserts that the methods of the social sciences differ from those of the natural sciences in some respect; and every one of them has been held by the principal modern historicists whom Popper names as his adversaries: by Hegel, by Marx, and, with the exception of (B1), by Toynbee.[18] Popper also included in his factitious historicism two doctrines that are contraries, rather than contradictories, of naturalistic positions. The first, which he described as 'a doctrine traditionally called "realism" ', he renamed 'essentialism' (*PH*, p. 27); the second, originally elaborated by Dilthey, but adopted by most adherents of *Historismus*, was the doctrine that the characteristic method of social inquiry is intuitive understanding *(Verstehen)*[19] (*PH*, pp. 19-24). Since few or no philosophers have ever accepted both these doctrines together, and since Marx, the greatest of Popper's modern historicists, would not have countenanced either of them, Popper was, I think, mistaken in trying to 'perfect' the theory of historicism by adding them to it. Each has, no doubt, been held at some time by some historicists. But neither is necessary to historicism; and, since on some interpretations they are incompatible with one another,[20] to add both together may even introduce a contradiction into it. I therefore disregard both.

3. Pronaturalistic Historicist Doctrines

Although historicism contradicts naturalism on many points, two naturalistic principles are fundamental to historicism itself, and are accepted by all modern historicists. The first is that the social sciences are *empirical*, in that they corroborate their hypotheses by empirically testing deductions made from them. The second is that the social sciences are *theoretical*, in that their function is to explain and predict social situations by discovering universal laws according to which such explanations and predictions can be deduced (*PH*, pp. 35-36).

Historicists, of course, apply these principles in conformity with their antinaturalistic doctrines. They acknowledge that the social sciences are theoretical, but not in the naturalistic sense. Hence they deny that the social sciences rest either on a naturalistic individual psychology, as J. S. Mill held, or on any other theoretical natural science; and equally they deny that the social sciences are independent natural sciences, with their own observational and experimental techniques. Since they hold that the only source of empirical evidence in the social sciences is history, historicists argue that 'sociology is theoretical history' (*PH*, p. 39). Furthermore, since all predictions made by the social sciences are historical too, historicists conclude that the laws of the social sciences must be such that, given historical initial conditions, historical predictions can be deduced in accordance with them. Predictions in the social sciences, historicists believe, are inexact (cf. B3), and neither the laws nor the statements of initial conditions from which they are derived can be stated in exact quantitative terms (cf. B5). It follows that in every prediction in the social sciences 'there must be a margin of uncertainty as to its details and timing' (*PH*, p. 37). Hence precise short-term predictions in the social sciences cannot be scientific: a prediction of details that is confessedly inexact in its details must be scientifically pointless (*PH*, p. 38). Historicists, therefore, infer that in the social sciences scientifically acceptable predictions must be stated qualitatively and in a measure vaguely, and must be sufficiently long-term for their margin of uncertainty in timing not to matter.

For these reasons, historicist predictions treat of qualitative social changes of large scope: national prosperity or depression; war and peace; the growth and decline of political or economic systems, or of religious communions; and, above all, the revolutions, peaceful or otherwise, by which one historical period is succeeded by another. Predictions of this kind, that is, 'long-term predictions whose vagueness is balanced by their scope and significance' Popper called 'large-scale forecasts' (PH, p. 37). Large-scale forecasts must be distinguished from forecasts that are merely long-term, like astronomical predictions of eclipses of the moon, which are neither inexact nor of great scope and significance.

The naturalistic historicist doctrine that the social sciences can and should attempt large-scale forecasts resting on qualitative historical laws, on its face, contradicts both the principle of radical novelty (A1), and its corollary that no generalization in the social sciences can apply to all historical periods (B1). The classic historicist resolution of this difficulty, which was adopted by Marx, may be given in Popper's words:

> . . .[T]he only universally valid laws of society must be the laws which *link up the successive periods*. They must be *laws of historical development* which determine the transition from one period to another. [PH, p. 41]

An example of a simple law of this kind would be the Marxist formula that feudalism is inevitably succeeded by capitalism, and capitalism by socialism.

Marx, of course, did not claim to establish his law of development by producing historical evidence that capitalism had ever before in history been succeeded by socialism. And, like Marx, historicists generally desire to find laws of development by which they can predict states of society before they come into existence. How can they possibly establish such laws, while adhering to their doctrine that the only evidence for them is historical? Popper has suggested that historicists 'might' draw an analogy between the social sciences and physical dynamics. (He does not name any historicist who has done so.) A social dynamics would 'analyse the forces which produce social change' (PH, p. 40). An historicism that accepted the analogy

> [would] demand the recognition of the fundamental importance of historical forces, whether spiritual or material. . . .To analyse . . . this thicket of contending tendencies and forces and to penetrate to its roots, to the universal driving forces . . . of social change—this [would be] the task of the social sciences. . . . [PH, pp. 40-41]

Yet inasmuch as it seeks *universal* driving forces of social change, the programme of social dynamics contradicts both the historicists' antinaturalistic doctrine that no generalization can apply to all historical periods, and the quasi-naturalistic doctrine to which it gave rise, that 'the *only* universally valid laws of society must be the laws which link up the successive periods' (PH, p. 41; italics mine). On the other hand, if the programme of social dynamics should be abandoned, how would it be possible, before the later periods, to establish by historical evidence laws linking up successive periods? This deadlock cannot be broken within historicism.

4. Activist Historicism

Although historicism is at bottom a theoretical position, most historicists have been 'activists', and Popper's most passionate disagreements with historicism are over its implications for practice. But, inasmuch as most of Popper's attacks on the practical consequences of historicism are directed against named adversaries—in *The Poverty of Historicism* Karl Mannheim above all, in *The Open Society* Hegel and Marx—it is of the last importance to distinguish what the practical implications of historicism are in truth from what this or that historicist has believed them to be. Popper did not always make that distinction clear.

It undoubtedly follows from the principles of historicism that 'only such [practical social and political] plans as fit in with the main current of history can be effective' (*PH*, p. 49). Utopianism, the planning of new social structures in accordance with nothing but abstract criteria of desirability, is irrational. The desires of individuals, it is true, are social forces; but the resultant of all the operative social forces, individual desires among them, will be what it will whether it is desired or not. Popper quoted the following classic historicist statement of antiutopianism from the preface of Marx's *Capital*:

> When a society has discovered the natural law that determines its own movement, even then it can neither overleap the natural phases of its evolution, nor shuffle them out of the world by a stroke of the pen. But this much it can do: it can shorten and lessen the birth-pangs. [*PH*, p. 51]

Yet some social reformers, who despise utopianism as much as historicists do, nevertheless maintain that social conditions can be improved by deliberate effort. They dream neither of constructing an ideal society, nor of lessening society's birth pangs at the delivery of the next stage of its historical development; they hope merely to remove or at least reduce specific social evils. Their sociology does not profess to lay down laws of large-scale social change, but only laws according to which limited technological predictions can be made: predictions 'intimating the steps open to us *if* we want to achieve certain results' (*PH*, p. 43). Nor does their sociology profess to furnish them with ends for social or political action: all it can say about ends 'is whether or not they are compatible with each other or realizable' (*PH*, p. 64). Hence both the social 'technology' of such reformers, and its application, which Popper calls 'social engineering', is *piecemeal* (*PH*, p. 64). And, although far-reaching programmes of piecemeal reform have been proposed

> the piecemeal engineer knows, like Socrates, how little he knows. . . . [H]e will avoid undertaking reforms of a complexity and scope which make it impossible for him to disentangle causes and effects, and to know what he is really doing. [*PH*, p. 67]

The principles of historicism imply the possibility of social engineering of a very different kind, which Popper, turning against it one of its own expressions of opprobrium, has called '*utopian*'. Utopian social engineering

> aims at remodelling the 'whole of society' in accordance with a definite plan or blueprint; it aims at 'seizing the key positions' and . . . at controlling from [them] the historical forces that mould the future of the developing society: either by arresting this development, or else by foreseeing its course and adjusting society to it. [*PH*, p. 67][21]

Popper himself acknowledged that, since he had placed no limits on the scope of piecemeal social engineering, he could not 'draw a precise line of demarcation' between the two methods (*PH*, p. 68).[22] The difference between them is in their point of view. At bottom, Popper rejected utopian social engineering, because it presupposes historicist theoretical sociology, which he believed he could show to be impossible (*PH*, p. 69). His practical objections to it, for example, his contention that "while the piecemeal engineer can attack his problem with an open mind as to the scope of the reform, the holist cannot do this; for he has decided beforehand that a complete reconstruction is possible and necessary" (*PH*, p. 69), all proceed from his fundamental theoretical objection, and must all be dismissed, if the possibility of historicist sociology can be vindicated.

Besides decrying their schemes for utopian social engineering, Popper accused historicists of opposing all projects of piecemeal social engineering (*PH*, p. 74). It is true that many historicists have done so. For example, as Popper has pointed out, even as late as the Great Depression of the 1930s, Marxist leaders disdained to elaborate serious practical programmes, and Marx himself had justified such disdain in a remark of astonishing silliness (*O.S.*, II, pp. 144-45). But, as a theoretical position, historicism cannot be jeopardized by the follies of individual historicists.

What are the implications of theoretical historicism for piecemeal social engineering? First, since, except for the laws of succession linking one historical period with another, there are no sociological laws applying to all historical periods, there can be no laws according to which technological predictions can be made for all periods. Yet it does not follow that generalizations applicable to specified periods cannot be discovered according to which technological predictions may be deduced by means of which piecemeal improvements may be made in social conditions. It is simply not true, even if some historicists have thought it is, that historicism implies that 'the real outcome [of the struggle to carry out a project of piecemeal social engineering] will *always* be different from the rational construction' (*PH*, p. 47; italics mine). It implies only that the outcome will be different if the rational construction neglects the results of historicist social science.

A second implication of historicism is that 'piecemeal tinkering' (cf. *PH*,

p. 67) cannot be more than palliative: it cannot affect the occurrence or the form of any major social change. Yet it no more follows from this that historicists should disparage minor piecemeal improvements than it follows from Christ's remark, 'The poor ye have always with you', that Christians should not give to the poor. Only when piecemeal improvements will prolong the birth pangs of a social revolution can historicists reasonably refuse to support them; and revolutionary situations are by nature rare.

5. *The Errors of Theoretical Historicism*

The distinctive theoretical doctrines of historicism, whether antinaturalistic or pronaturalistic, rest on two fundamentals: the principle of radical novelty (A1), and the principle of holism (A2). Popper claimed that both spring from confusions about the nature of the natural sciences.

His criticism of the principle of radical novelty draws upon his analysis of the causal explanation of individual events, which is too familiar to call for extended exposition. Popper himself stated it succinctly:

> To give a *causal explanation* of an event means to deduce a statement which describes it, using as premises of the deduction one or more *universal laws*, together with certain singular statements, the *initial conditions*.[23]

The causal explanation of a regularity described by a universal law must be distinguished from this.

> At first sight, one might think that the case is analogous and that the law in question has to be deduced from (1) some more general laws, and (2) certain special conditions which correspond to the initial conditions but which are *not* singular, and refer to a certain *kind* of situation. This, however, is not the case here, for the special conditions (2) must be explicitly stated in the formulation of the law which we wish to explain; for otherwise this law would simply contradict (1). [*PH*, p. 125; cf. *L.Sc.D.*, pp. 71-72]

The principle of radical novelty, in Popper's view, contradicts these analyses in two respects: it confounds novelty of initial conditions with novelty of laws; and it recognizes as laws of historical development statements that are not universal, and hence not laws at all.

The principle of radical novelty is advanced, at least partly, on the historical ground that regularities have obtained in certain societies in certain periods which have not obtained in other societies in other periods (*PH*, p. 99). Popper, however, pointed out that this is not peculiar to social regularities. Numerous natural regularities, for example in climate, obtain in some regions of the earth, and in some geological periods, but not in others (*PH*, p. 100). Novelties in natural regularities are explained, not by supposing that natural laws are confined to certain regions or periods, but by finding novelties in initial conditions. Historicists have advanced no tenable reason why novelties in social regularities should not be explained in the same way. The assertion that human nature itself changes is not such a reason; for, if it does change, why should its changes not be explicable from initial conditions according to universal laws (*PH*, p. 102)? Even the phenomenon of the Oedipus effect, which Popper fully acknowledged, implies only that past initial conditions are unlikely to recur, not that sociological laws cease to obtain.

A yet deeper confusion is betrayed by the historicist inference from the principle of radical novelty, that the only universally valid laws of society must be the laws which link up the successive periods (*PH*, p. 41). Popper denied the very existence of such laws on the ground that the development of human society, like the evolution of life on earth, is an individual historical process.

> Such a process [he freely conceded] . . . proceeds in accordance with all kinds of causal laws . . . Its description, however, is not a law, but only a singular historical statement. [*PH*, p. 108]

Historicists may deny this on either or both of two grounds: (1) that since the process of historical development is cyclical or repetitive, its description will at least provide evidence for formulating the laws of its cycles or repetitions; and (2) that even if the process of history is nonrepetitive, it nevertheless has 'a trend, a tendency, or direction', the statement of which would be a law linking up successive periods (*PH*, p. 109).

Popper's objection to both these positions was at bottom the same. What some historicists suppose to be repeated in history are trends. Hence both historicist positions presuppose that statements of certain historical trends would be laws. But a statement of a trend—that is, of an individual process following a describable pattern—cannot be a law. Laws are hypothetical, statements of trends are existential; laws are unconditionally and timelessly true, trends occur only under certain conditions, and they characteristically have a temporal beginning and end (*PH*, p. 115).

Since the continuation of trends depends on the continuation of the conditions that give rise to them, it would be unscientific, merely on the ground that a trend has existed up to a certain point, to predict that it will continue after that point; for there would be no reason to assume that the conditions that have given rise to it will continue. 'A trend (we may . . . take population growth as an example) which has persisted for hundreds or even thousands of years may change within a decade, or even more rapidly than that' (*PH*, p. 115). This holds whether the trend whose continuation is predicted is the repetition up to a point of an earlier one, or whether it has, so far as is known, occurred only once (cf. *PH*, pp. 110-11, 115).

Popper acknowledged the existence of trends in nature, which he called 'natural periodicities', that afford secure grounds for prediction because they depend on conditions that prevail throughout long periods. '[T]he seasons, the phases of the moon, the recurrence of eclipses, or perhaps the swings of a pendulum' are examples (*PH*, pp. 116-17). Even so, statements of such trends are at best 'quasi-laws', because they hold only during the periods, which may be very long, in which certain conditions prevail. They are not, like laws, universal statements (*PH*, p. 126).

> [A]lthough we may assume that any actual succession of phenomena proceeds according to the laws of nature, it is important to realize that practically *no sequence of, say, three or more causally connected concrete events proceeds according to any single law of nature.* [*PH*, p. 117]

If no sequence in nature of three or more causally connected events proceeds according to a single law, and if, as historicists themselves assert, social processes are far more complex than natural ones, then it would seem to follow that no such sequence of events in history will proceed according to a single historical or sociological law.

With some diffidence, I submit that on this point Popper is mistaken about natural sequences. In biology there are numerous statements about the stages through which the embryos of the various biological species pass in normal circumstances. Since these statements explicitly specify all the special conditions involved (what circumstances are normal can be specified), by Popper's own definitions, they are laws and not merely quasi laws or statements of natural periodicities. If I am right about this, the natural sciences provide no ground for an argument by analogy against the possibility of Toynbeean laws of social development.

The distinction between laws and trends is logically sharp; but its sharpness is hypnotic. Popper has established that mere statements of trends cannot furnish what historicists seek: namely, laws of historical development according to which large-scale forecasts can be made. But can historicists obtain nothing better than mere statements of trends? Why may they not aspire to find something like what Popper has called 'explained trends' (*PH*, p. 126)?

What Popper meant by an 'explained trend' may be elucidated by an imaginary example he himself gave. Suppose that in our solar system all the planets were tending progressively to approach the sun; and suppose the explanation of this trend to be that interplanetary space was filled with a certain gas (*PH*, p. 126). The structure of such an explanation would be

> (*I*) *Initial Conditions*: (a) the configuration of the sun and planets, their relative distances, momenta, etc., at a given time; (b) the pervading of the solar system by a certain gas.
> (*L*) *Laws*: the Newtonian Laws of Motion and Gravitation.
> Therefore, (*T*)*Trend*: the planets move in gradually contracting or-

bits with the sun as one focus.

The logical form of this explanation may be rendered: I and L, therefore T. Now it should be evident, according to a procedure described by Popper in his analysis of the causal explanation of laws,[24] that from an explanation such as this it is possible to construct a statement of the form: If a planetary system satisfies the conditions (I), then it will exhibit the trend (T). The form of this statement may be rendered: If I, then T. Now if

> I and L, therefore T

is a valid deductive argument, then

> L, therefore if I then T

is also a valid deductive argument. Hence, if the explanation of the trend (T) was sound, then the constructed statement, *If a planetary system satisfies the conditions (I), then it will exhibit the trend* (T) must logically follow from the laws (L), that is, from the Newtonian Laws of Motion and Gravitation. And that constructed statement must be a genuine law; for, since it 'incorporates all the conditions of its validity', it can be asserted universally or unconditionally (cf. *PH*, p. 125).

Suppose that an historicist influenced by Toynbee's *Study of History* should maintain that, provided a human society satisfies the conditions that would constitute it a Toynbeean civilization, then it will pass through certain phases of growth and decay. What *philosophical* reason would Popper have for denying that such an historicist had advanced a law of historical development of the form, *If* I *then* T, a law presumably derivative from more general laws as yet unknown? Popper would no doubt deny (and I would agree with him) that any historicist has formulated a putative law of this kind that is consistent with available historical evidence; but he would be the first to acknowledge that such an objection would be historical, and that it would not show that no historicist will ever formulate a law that is historically acceptable.

In the course of distinguishing between laws and quasi laws (statements of natural periodicities) Popper advanced a doctrine which, if true, would support an argument by analogy against the possibility of such historicist laws. It is this:

In the passage in *The Poverty of Historicism* in which he mentioned the analogy drawn by historicists like Toynbee between the development of civilizations and the life cycles of animals (*PH*, pp. 109-12), Popper offered no opinion about whether there could be biological laws of life cycles. But, in a lecture delivered in 1948 to the International Congress of Philosophy at Amsterdam, he observed that since 'the life-cycles of organisms are part of a semi-stationary or very slowly changing biological chain of events', it is possible to make scientific predictions about them only 'insofar as we abstract from the slow evolutionary changes, that is, insofar as we treat the biological system in question as stationary'.[25] Now it might be argued (Popper did not do so) that no universal hypothesis that under certain conditions animals of a certain species pass through a certain life cycle, can strictly be true. Any such hypothesis would presuppose the animals classified under that species to be strictly of the same kind; and that, owing to slow evolutionary changes, they cannot be. I would rejoin that, although there may be unclassifiable borderline cases, individual animals may be of the same species, even though there are small evolutionary differences between them. When classifying biological species, it is not unscientific to abstract from such differences. Hence the above argument affords no ground for denying that a statement about the life cycle of, say, the frog or the mosquito, may be a law in Popper's sense.

The argument against historicist laws advanced in *The Poverty of Historicism* is far less radical.

> This [Popper wrote] is the central mistake of historicism. Its 'laws of development' turn out to be absolute trends; trends which, like laws, do not depend on initial conditions, and which carry us irresistibly in a certain direction into the future. [*PH*, p. 128]

Here Popper was unquestionably right. The concept of an absolute trend is logically monstrous; for trends are scientifically explicable only as depending on conditions. But what had he to say of historicists 'who see that trends depend on conditions, and who try to find these conditions and formulate them explicitly' (*PH*, p. 128)? Although Popper confessed that he 'had no quarrel' with anybody who adopted such an approach, he charged that it is alien to the historicist mind:

> . . . in our search for the true conditions of a trend [he wrote] we have all the time to try to imagine conditions under which [it] would disappear. But this is just what the historicist cannot do . . . [C]onditions under which [his favourite trend] would disappear are to him unthinkable. The poverty of historicism is at bottom a poverty of imagination. [*PH*, pp. 129-30]

Such poverty of imagination, however, is not essential to historicism as Popper has analysed it. Would Popper, then, have no philosophical quarrel with an enlightened historicist who had set himself to think about conditions under which his favourite trend would disappear, and reached the conclusion that those conditions would not be realized in the period covered by his predictions? Of course any such conclusion could be disputed, by historicists and antihistoricists alike, on historical grounds.

Although, in *The Poverty of Historicism*, Popper advanced no philosophical argument against an enlightened historicism of the kind I have described, in his 1948 Amsterdam lecture (*C.&R.*, pp. 336-46), he did argue against it; and, in a preface added to the 1957 edition of *The Poverty of Historicism*, he offered a formal refutation (*PH*, pp. ix-xi).

His argument in the Amsterdam lecture was simple:

> [The historicist] cannot possibly [derive his historical prophecies from conditional scientific predictions] because long-term prophecies can be derived from scientific conditional predictions only if they apply to systems which can be described as well-isolated, stationary, and recurrent. These systems are very rare in nature; and modern society is surely not one of them. [*C.&R.*, p. 339]

I do not know why Popper considered that long-term predictions can only apply to recurrent systems. It is true that the long-term scientific predictions that are most familiar are of natural periodicities. Yet, provided that a system is stationary (that is, that its elements or members remain the same) and isolated (that is, that no new elements enter it or no outside forces are exerted upon it), there is no objection in principle to the possibility of a long-term conditional prediction about the course of a nonrecurrent process.

Furthermore, although it is true that modern society is not stationary in the simple way in which the solar system is, is it certain that it cannot be analysed into sociological elements that will remain the same over a long period? And is it certain that modern society as considered by historians and sociologists is not an isolated system? The population of the earth considered as a single society will remain socially isolated until there is interstellar communication; and it is not obvious that lesser social units may not be effectively isolated, as Toynbee thought his civilizations were. In sum: even if long-term sociological predictions are possible only about stationary and isolated social systems, it does not follow that long-term predictions of the course of modern society are impossible.

Popper's formal refutation of historicism in the 1957 Preface to *The Poverty of Historicism* may be stated as follows (cf. *PH*, pp. ix-x):[26]

(i) The course of human history is strongly influenced by the growth of human knowledge.
(ii) The future growth of scientific knowledge cannot be scientifically predicted.
(iii) Therefore, the future course of history cannot be predicted.
(iv) If there could be a theoretical history of the kind sought by historicists, then the future course of history could be predicted.
(v) Therefore, by (iii) and (iv), a theoretical history of the kind sought by historicists is impossible, 'and historicism collapses'.

The decisive premises of this argument are (i) and (ii). That (i) is true, Popper took to be conceded even by materialist historicists like Marx. That (ii) is true he believed to be capable of proof by demonstrating that no scientific predictor can predict, by scientific methods, its own future results (*PH*, p. x). Both (i) and (ii) are, in my opinion, true.

It does not follow from Popper's argument that no predictions in the social sciences are possible, but only that they cannot be expected to prove true if an unpredictable advance in human knowledge should change the initial conditions upon which they were based. However, since the forecasts with which historicists concern themselves are all large-scale, it is manifestly impossible to exclude the possibility that they will be invalidated by unpredictable advances in knowledge.

Paradoxically, although I accept Popper's refutation as valid, I judge it to be less damaging to historicism than his earlier analysis. For if historicists could produce large-scale forecasts, made in accordance with well-corroborated historical laws, that those forecasts would be invalidated if an unpredictable advance in knowledge should change the initial conditions upon which they were based, might reasonably be considered of secondary importance. Who would not desire to know such a forecast? But Popper's earlier analysis established that the historicist programme as commonly propounded is thoroughly confused; and that, when rendered coherent, it has never been carried out, and presumably never will be. It was more important to show that historicism is 'a method that will not bear any fruit' (*PH*, p. ix) than formally to refute it.

In expounding Popper's objections to historicism, I have dwelt upon his demolition of those points in it which spring from the principle of radical novelty, because they are, in my opinion, cardinal. The other fundamental principle of historicism—that of holism—is not only much vaguer, but its chief bad consequences are for practice rather than for theory. Popper's criticism of holism ought nevertheless to be mentioned. It is that it depends on an equivocal use of the word 'whole', as meaning both *(a)* the totality of the properties or aspects of a thing, and *(b)* the thing considered as an organized structure, as opposed to a mere heap (*PH,* p. 76). Historicists accuse naturalists of refusing to study societies as wholes in either sense. In charging naturalists with refusing to study society as a whole in sense (*a*), that is, as the totality of all its aspects, they are right in fact but wrong in criticism; for it is impossible to study anything as such a totality: 'all knowledge, whether intuitive or discursive, must be of abstract aspects' (*PH*, p. 78). In alleging that naturalism excludes the study of societies as organized structures, holists are simply wrong in fact. Although atomic physics is presumably 'atomistic', it studies atoms, not as 'heaps' of particles, but as particle systems which are wholes in sense (*b*) (*PH*, p. 82).

6. Conclusion

The results of Popper's examination of historicism were not all negative. His exploration of where historicism had gone wrong led directly to two positive conclusions of great importance, the theory of situational logic in history, and the institutional theory of progress, to discuss which would prolong this essay intolerably.[27] Yet his negative results were those for which Popper contended most passionately. When he wrote, historicist theories abounded; and the idea that mankind was being 'swept into the future by irresistible forces' (*PH*, p. 160) was common. In the Western intellectual world it is now disreputable; and no man has done more than Popper to make it so. Sir Isaiah Berlin's tribute to *The Poverty of Historicism* was no more than just: In it, Popper 'exposed . . . "historicism" with such force and precision, and made so clear its incompatibility with any kind of scientific empiricism, that there is no further excuse for confounding the two'.[28]

ALAN DONAGAN

DEPARTMENT OF PHILOSOPHY
UNIVERSITY OF CHICAGO
SEPTEMBER, 1967

NOTES

[1] K. R. Popper, *The Poverty of Historicism* (London: Routledge & Kegan Paul; Boston: The Beacon Press, 1957), p. vii. Hereinafter cited as *PH*.

[2] Hans Meyerhoff, ed., *The Philosophy of History in our Time* (New York, 1959), pp. 299-300.

[3] *Ibid.*, p. 300.

[4] Presumably Friedrich Meinecke, *Die Entstehung des Historismus* (Munich, 1936), which is still untranslated.

[5] *Philosophy of History*, p. 346.

[6] The entry reads: 'HISTORICISM: The view that the history of anything is a sufficient explanation of it, that the values of anything can be accounted for through the discovery of its origins, that the nature of anything is entirely comprehended in its development, as for example, that the properties of an oak tree are entirely accounted for by an exhaustive description of its development from the acorn. The doctrine which discounts the fallaciousness of the historical fallacy. Applied by some critics to the philosophy of Hegel and Karl Marx'.

[7] The information in this and the following paragraph is derived from three sources: Dwight E. Lee and Robert W. Beck, 'The Meaning of "Historicism" ', *American Historical Review,* **59** (1954), 568-77; Calvin G. Rand, 'The Meanings of "Historicism" in the Writings of Dilthey, Troeltsch, and Meinecke', *Journal of the History of Ideas,* **25** (1964), 503-18; and a forthcoming book by G. G. Iggers, *Historicism in Germany*. [After this essay was written, *Historicism in Germany* was published as *The German Conception of History; the National Tradition of Historical Thought from Herder to the Present* (Middletown, Conn.: Wesleyan University Press, 1968), xii + 363.—EDITOR] I thank Professor Iggers for his kindness in providing me with a copy of the pertinent chapter of his book; and both him and Professor Rand for commenting in correspondence on some of my conjectures. Neither is responsible for the conclusions I have drawn from the information they supplied.

924 ALAN DONAGAN

8 Charles A. Beard and Alfred Vagts, 'Currents of Thought in Historiography', *American Historical Review*, **42** (1937), 460-83; and Eugene N. Anderson, 'Meinecke's *Ideengeschichte* and the Crisis in Historical Thinking', *Medieval and Historiographical Essays in Honor of James Westfall Thompson* (Chicago, 1938), pp. 361-96.

9 The information in this paragraph about the use of 'historicism' by Mannheim and his translators, I owe to Iggers, *Historicism in Germany*.

10 I have verified this for the ten references to Mannheim indexed in *PH*, p. 164.

11 *The Open Society and Its Enemies*, 3d ed. (London: Routledge & Kegan Paul, 1957), Vol. II, pp. 351-52. Hereinafter cited as *O.S.*

12 'Troeltsch, Ernst' in *The Encyclopaedia of the Social Sciences*, Vol. XIV. I owe this reference to Iggers, *Historicism in Germany*.

13 *Historicism in Germany*.

14 Again, referring to the doctrine that the development of man's reason must coincide with the historical development of his society, Popper remarked that 'this theory of Hegel's, and especially his doctrine that all knowledge and all truth is "relative", in the sense of being determined by history, is sometimes called "historism" ' (*O.S.*, II, p. 214).

15 *The Johns Hopkins University Studies in History and Political Science*, Series 62, No. 2 (1944).

16 'Meaning of Historicism', p. 575.

17 *PH*, pp. 130-35; for the word 'naturalistic', *PH*, p. 2.

18 *O.S.*, II, pp. 37-38, 47-48, 101-09, 251, 319, 361.

19 That the method of intuitive understanding is legitimate, when employed in order to arrive at hypotheses, but not to verify them, was acknowledged by Popper, *PH*, p. 138.

20 The method of intuitive understanding was developed in order to study individuals as distinguished from kinds; and an individual has an essence only as belonging to a kind.

21 Popper quoted the expression 'seizing the key positions' from Mannheim's *Man and Society in an Age of Reconstruction*, which he described as 'the most elaborate exposition of a holistic and historicist programme known to me' (*PH*, p. 67 n.).

22 He wrote that he would not attempt to draw such a line; but I take him to have intended to imply that such a line cannot be drawn.

23 K. R. Popper, *The Logic of Scientific Discovery* (London: Hutchinson; New York: Basic Books, 1959), p. 59. Hereinafter cited as *L.Sc.D.*

24 Quoted above, p. 916.

25 K. R. Popper, *Conjectures and Refutations: The Growth of Scientific Knowledge* (London: Routledge & Kegan Paul; New York: Basic Books, 1963), p. 340. Hereinafter cited as *C.&R.*

26 My statement of steps (iv) and (v) deviates slightly from Popper's.

27 In *History and Theory*, **4** (1964), 17-23, I began such a discussion; but I could not there discuss Popper's sketch of a method of logical or rational reconstruction, which he sometimes called 'the zero method' (*PH*, pp. 140-1).

28 Isaiah Berlin, *Historical Inevitability* (London: Oxford University Press, 1954), pp. 10-11 n.

E. H. Gombrich

THE LOGIC OF VANITY FAIR

ALTERNATIVES TO HISTORICISM IN THE STUDY
OF FASHIONS, STYLE AND TASTE

I. The Problem Situation

In the spring of 1936 I attended the meeting of Prof. von Hayek's London Seminar in which Karl Popper (not yet Sir Karl) presented the arguments which he later published under the title *The Poverty of Historicism*.[1] This deadly analysis of all forms of social determinism derived its urgency from the menace of totalitarian philosophies which nobody at that time could forget for a moment. But it also had a bearing on my own field, the history of art and of civilization. Indeed, one of Popper's main opponents had a foot in both camps, that of political utopianism and of historical holism; I am referring to Karl Mannheim, whose early studies on the sociology of art and of style[2] had made a considerable impression on those students of the subject who were eager to refine their methods and to substantiate the intuition that works of art do not emerge in isolation but are linked with others and with their time by many elusive threads. From my student days in Vienna I had shared this concern, but I had become increasingly sceptical of the solutions offered by Neo-Hegelian *Geistesgeschichte* and Neo-Marxist Sociologism.[3] This scepticism was not very popular with some continental colleagues, proud of being in the possession of a key that revealed the "essence" of past ages. On the other hand, it may have seemed exaggerated to my new English friends who found the whole issue remote.

Today, after thirty years, it is perhaps less the "poverty of historicism" that needs pointing out, than the need for an alternative. The solutions offered by historicist theories are rarely taken very seriously in academic art history, but nothing very interesting has taken their place.[4] In contrast to the situation in my student days the prevailing mood is a desire for facts, a hope to get on with the business of cataloguing items without much interference from theorisers. No one acquainted with Popper's methodology need be told why this positivist attitude must be self-defeating. Not even a chronicle of art, let alone a history of styles, could ever be based on the collecting of uninterpreted data. This being so the theories of previous generations are less discarded as taken as read. They often form the unexamined framework of teaching and research. Thus what we need is new and better theories that can be tested against the historical material as far as such tests are ever possible.

Such alternatives cannot be pulled out of a hat. But I have at least tried in my book on *Art and Illusion*[5] to explore the limited problem of the history of pictorial representation and to find more convincing reasons for the existence of period styles than the Hegelian "spirit of the age". I referred in its Introduction to a passage from the *Poverty of Historicism* which I should like to quote once more in slightly more extended form:

> . . . .I have not the slightest sympathy with these 'spirits'; neither with their idealistic prototype nor with their dialectical and materialistic incarnations, and I am in full sympathy with those who treat them with contempt. And yet I feel that they indicate, at least, the existence of a vacuum, of a place which it is the task of sociology to fill with something more sensible. . .there is room for a more detailed analysis of the *logic of situations*. . . .Beyond this logic of situations, or perhaps as part of it, we need something like an analysis of social movements. We need studies, based on methodological individualism, of the social institutions through which ideas may spread and captivate individuals. . .our individualistic and institutionalist models of such collective entities as nations, or governments, or markets, will have to be supplemented by models of political situations as well as of social movements such as scientific and industrial progress.[6]

The fourteenth chapter of the *Open Society and Its Enemies* entitled *The Autonomy of Sociology* explains a little more fully what Popper had in mind when he speaks of these models. It is here that he endorses Marx's opposition to "psychologism" and analyses in some detail the reasons that lead him to reject the "plausible doctrine that all laws of social life must be ultimately reducible to the psychological laws of human nature".[7]

Art and Illusion was mainly concerned with such psychological laws. It did not (or only marginally) concern itself with the genuinely sociological problem of the unintended social repercussions of intentional human actions. A simple illustration of such a problem is taken by Popper from economics:

> If a man wishes to buy a house, we can safely assume that he does not wish to raise the market price of houses. But the very fact that he appears on the market as a buyer will tend to raise the market price.[8]

It is the purpose of this paper to apply the tool of situational logic to some recurrent problems of the history of fashion, style and taste.[9] If I have subsumed these in my title under the name of Vanity Fair it was not to "debunk" art. It is true that today the element of fashion in the alterations of movements stares the historian in the face.[10] "Pop" today and "Op" tomorrow—they justify the joke in the *New Yorker* of the long-haired man's remark at the cocktail party "I don't know anything about art, but I know what is 'in' ". Needless to say this assimilation of art to fashion should not tempt us to think less highly of the great artists of the past or of today. It only makes it easier to recognize the poverty of those historicist philosophies which scrutinize all manifestations of style as the expression of the innermost essence of the "age"—ours, or another.

II. Competition and Inflation

The latest versions of historicism current in the critical jargon of the press seeks for the sources of changing style and taste somewhere in the dark recesses of the Collective Unconscious. It may be all the more profitable, therefore, to start this investigation by testing the opposite approach, advocated by Popper where he recommends

> what may be called the method of logical or rational construction, or perhaps the 'zero method'. . .the method of constructing a model on the assumption of complete rationality (and perhaps also on the assumption of the possession of complete information) on the part of the individuals concerned, and of estimating the deviation of the actual behaviour of people from the model behaviour, using the latter as a kind of zero-coordinate.[11]

Popper was thinking in the first instance of economic behaviour and the type of deviation from rationality represented by the "Money Illusion", people's preference for a larger wage packet, even if it does not buy more than the smaller one. Now this model of inflation extends beyond the problems of money values to all tokens of value recognized in society, including fashion, language and art. The way, in fact, in which competition leads to unintended consequences is of prime concern to the student of fashion. All we need for an abstract model of such movements is the assumption that departure from a norm will arouse attention. Given the desire of a member of this group to focus attention on himself, the rational means for that purpose are therefore at hand.

There are closed societies where this game is institutionalised and almost ritualised, and where the auction for attention is confined to a particular area such as the number of heads hunted, or some other token of prowess. The ruinous expenditure on Potlatch feasts among the American Indians, the prestige attached to the possession of many heads of cattle regardless of the danger of overgrazing in certain African societies illustrates the departure from rational behaviour that Popper has in mind. These competitions have brought the societies concerned to the brink of destruction, and yet it is hard to see how the individual, caught up in the situation, can avoid these unintended consequences of his bid without foregoing the necessary prestige. We are only too familiar with a similar threat summed up in the word "escalation".

What characterises the situation on Vanity Fair is rather the fluidity of the game of "watch me" that may be characteristic of Open Societies. For here there is no predicting what departure from norm will become a focus of attention. There are the notorious "crazes" that sweep a school, of collecting cigarette cards or stamps, the performance of daring dos, or the flaunting of provocations, that are as remarkable for their intensity as for their volatility.[12] Satirists have inveighed against what they call the Follies of Fashion; but the folly of the game does not preclude rationality on the part of the players. For fashion can be described in terms of a rarity game. At one time it may be the display of rare lace that arouses attention and competition, at another a daring décolleté, the height of the coiffure or the width of the crinoline.[13] At various times competition has driven fashion to notoriously foolish "excesses"—though what we call an excess here is harder to tell. Whatever rationalisation we may be able to produce for our habit of shaving, to bearded nations or periods this fashion must surely look as unnatural and excessive as the wearing of powdered wigs looks to us. In all these matters some departure from the norm of apparel and appearance must at first have drawn attention for its rarity. If a game of display was in progress the choice in front of the other players was obviously whether to dismiss this particular move as an unprofitable eccentricity that should be allowed to remain one, or to emulate and top it. Once the battle is joined it lies in the logic of the situation that the particular departure from the norm must be trumped if attention is to be kept up.

As long as these games of "one-up-manship" are played within a small section of people who have nothing better to do than outdo each other, fluctuations are bound to be rapid, so rapid perhaps that the rest of society will not be caught up in these superficial ripples. But occasionally the game catches on and reaches a critical size where all join in. Whether we have our hair cut or put on a tie, whether we drink tea or go skiing, we all join in the game of "follow my leader". Given time and sufficient documentation each of these social fashions could of course be traced in its spread from the habits of a few to the custom of the majority. It would be tempting to attribute this spread of imitation to psychological causes, to man's desire to identify with leader- or father-figures. No doubt such a tendency exists and sometimes accounts for the wish of young people to model themselves on the idols of the screen in their "set". But, within the context of this section, it is more relevant to point out that even conformism is partly rooted in the logic of the situation. We have looked at fashion as a "rarity game" played by some in order to attract attention. But there is usually also an opposite team whose aim is to avoid attention. At first of course this team has an easy time. It just refuses to join in. Often, as we have seen, this refusal will do the trick and will leave only the players exposed to that gaze they coveted. But the more members of that society imitate the move in order to attract attention, the more its original purpose will be defeated. Leaders of fashion will have to think up a new gimmick. But the opponents of the fashion will discover to their chagrin that now it is they who are conspicuous in the rarity game, they attract unwelcome attention by their refusal to fall in. In most cases there will be a point when even the diehards and last-ditchers will give in. They, too, will powder their hair or wear a wig, will shave off their beards or put on a black tie to avoid being stared at.

It is true that by this time fashion will generally have been shorn of its most impracticable extreme. The waves will have been somewhat levelled, but it is still a fact that a move made by a fop to impress his fellow-fops may start a trend that imposes itself on society.

That there is a competitive element in art which aims at drawing attention to the artist or his patron needs no lengthy demonstration. The following figures about the height of French Gothic cathedrals speak for themselves.

> In 1163 Notre Dame de Paris began its record construction to result in a vault 114 feet 8 inches from the floor. Chartres surpassed Paris in 1194, eventually reaching 119 feet 9 inches. In 1212 Rheims started to rise to 124 feet 3 inches, and in 1221 Amiens reached 138 feet 9 inches. This drive to break the record reached its climax in 1247 with the project to vault the choir of Beauvais 157 feet 3 inches above the floor - only to have the vaults collapse in 1284.[14]

The figures strongly suggest a game of "watch me"—each city must have known what the previous record had been. They also remind us of the important fact that competition in art is not necessarily a "bad thing". There are beautiful structures on Vanity Fair which were stimulated by the desire to outdo the neighbour and there are great achievements in art which certainly were stimulated by the desire of artists to vie with their peers and to do even better than the best of them.[15] It is again part of the logic of the situation that where standards are high they may become even higher. After all not even all the excesses of fashion are unbecoming, whatever moralists may say; and, if tradition attributes a natural "chic" to the Parisian woman, this is precisely because she has learned to care about her looks. Once more we are up against the limits of prediction. For it is clear that competition for attention can lead to the unintended consequence of simply lowering the value of what you have been doing before. This is particularly so where methods of emphasis are concerned, and emphasis is after all a special case of soliciting attention. Decoration is a frequent victim of such inflation. It is well known that within the tradition of Gothic ornament this need to outdo previous work in the admired feature of intricacy gradually led to the "excesses" of the flamboyant Gothic style, much as the Renaissance tradition was driven—if that is the word—towards the "excesses" of Baroque and Rococo exuberance in ornament.

In the nineteenth century attempts were made to explain these regularities in psychological terms, that is through the blunting of sensibilities in repetition, the fatigue aroused by forms that are seen so often that they are no longer noticed so that a stronger stimulus is required.[16] There is no need to deny that such psychological tendencies may exist. The instance of the drug addict who needs more and more of the stimulant for its effect to be noticeable provides the illustration. But even in this instance there may be a logical element that forms the background to this tragedy. The habit creates a level of expectation, a fresh norm, but the desire is for "more".

However that may be, there are many instances of inflation outside the field of art which illustrate the purely situational element. Take the case of titles and decorations. No one has felt fatigue at receiving a rare honour in a stable society; but once inflation sets in, the whole system is running downhill. The fuss made in England when the "Beatles" received a decoration sprang from fear of such a precedent.

Hitler's war witnessed a particularly rapid inflation of this kind. At its start the German decoration for bravery was still the Iron Cross. Soon it was topped by the Iron Cross with Swords, which had to yield pride of place to the Iron Cross with Swords and Oakleaves, which was finally outshone by the Iron Cross with Swords and Diamonds. Every new move, of course, pushed the recipient of the previous top award down the ladder and probably made the next wonder what more additions were in store for his successor.

The example sums up the dilemma that is involved in all striving for extra emphasis. It thus serves to introduce the crucial problem of this kind—that of the corruption of language. In this corruption, I believe, both elements we saw at work and a few more can be discerned. If we use Bühler's terminology[17] distinguishing between the functions of symptom, signal and symbol, we may assign the ordinary influence of fashion primarily to the first function of drawing attention to the speaker. Affectations of every kind in the use of rare words fall under this category. We have all witnessed certain expressions becoming "okay words", being adopted by increasing numbers till they are either replaced by others or become part of the ordinary vocabulary. The turnover of words is rapid in all urban speech. In the Rome of Horace the rights and wrongs of coining words must have been much debated:

> If it should be necessary to refer to recondite things by recent terms. . .permission will be granted if it is done with modesty. . . . It has ever been permitted and always will be to issue a word stamped with the mint mark of the day. As the woods change their leaves when the year declines and the earlier ones fall, so the

old age of words comes to an end and like the newborn children they bloom and thrive. . . all man-made things will perish, nor will the honour and splendour of language endure. Many will be reborn that have fallen, and those words will fall in their turn which are now honoured, if Usage so wants it, the arbiter judge and norm of speech. . .[18]

In this drift of language, of course, the fashion element of "showing off " plays only a minor part. The signal function, too, can be corroded, witness the fable of the boy who cried "wolf " once too often. His fate, however cruel, concerns the student of situational logic less than that of the other shepherd boys whose signals he had rendered ineffective. How could they convince the villagers that their cry for help was not a hoax?

Inflationary debasement usually takes its departure from that need for increasing emphasis which we saw at work in the story of the iron crosses. Here the process of inflation really has more than a superficial resemblance to the debasement of currency. Words originally coined as the rarest tokens of exceptional emphasis rapidly sink down to the small change of the advertiser and the schoolboys' slang. It matters little here whether we class the advertisements of "unprecedented offers", of "gigantic successes" and "tremendous sensations" as signals trying to outshout each other and blunting their own effect in the process, or as descriptions. In either case they are the victims of their own erosion neatly illustrated by the true instance of a toothpaste that is sold in three containers—"large", "jumbo", and "mammoth" size. "Large" has come to mean the smallest. And yet one thing is sure. In such an environment it is pointless to try and shout even louder. The only chance for the judicious is negative emphasis, an attempt to return to the original gold standard.[19] If we decide only to call a large thing "large" we may reestablish a level where communication is again possible.

Popper has often stressed the responsibility of the individual to maintain the standards of clarity in language which, as a social institution, is as vulnerable as any to the seeds of corruption.[20] What makes it so vulnerable is the fact that strictly speaking, the introduction of any new word or meaning subtly affects the whole instrument of language.[21]

Any such word will inevitably introduce an alternative, and thus increase the range of choice for the speaker of the language. To use one word (even the old one) thus implies rejecting another, and our appreciation of any statement will be affected by this novel element. When the word automobile received a competitor in the word car the earlier term did not change its meaning, but in England its use began to sound a little precious and affected. When barbers became hairdressers, and ratcatchers rodent operatives, the earlier word began by contrast to sound a trifle vulgar. One of the reasons why it is so hard to know a language well enough to appreciate style is precisely that we must always be able to assess the connotations of the writer's choice between existing alternatives. It is not enough to look up the German word "Haupt" in the dictionary and find there that it means "head". We must also know that the more frequent word for head in German is "Kopf" and that "Haupt" is therefore poetic diction or elevated language. The degree to which we feel it to be a justified or a stilted word must depend on long familiarity with usages of every kind. But this familiarity will let us down when we do not know the region, the period or the set of the speaker. As new words come into use, therefore, they leave eddies of uncertainties behind and threaten that feeling for nuance on which civilized speech so largely depends. No wonder, therefore, that some of the greatest lovers of language have also been the most intense haters of neologisms. Every new coinage somehow debases the value of the old mintings. However, it is easier to preach purism than to enforce it; and so we frequently find the purist or classicist in language on the side of authoritarianism.

Nobody has explored the links between fear of change and authoritarianism more convincingly than Popper. From the time when Plato inveighed against change in music there is indeed a tendency of conservativism in language and art to ally itself to restrictive governments. The cry, "this lowers the tone", "this should be forbidden", may not be commendable, but it is understandable when we find our language threatened. Academies under royal tutelage were the outcome of this desire to arrest the flux of language and of art. They had a case; but the price they wished to exact for the stabilisation of currency was too high—as it so often is.

We find the same in all attempts to stem the tide of fashion and competition in a free society, the antiluxury laws of medieval cities which make such curious reading, the restriction on building heights or other items of "conspicuous waste". These, it seems, can be curbed only at the cost of a police state.

Granted the "poverty" of historicism where it proclaims immutable laws of history, situational logic and the zero method may thus indeed fill something of the void which Popper's formidable axe has created in the study of movements and trends.

The study of language offers itself as the best testing ground. We need only return to those subtle students of speech, the ancient writers and orators, to find a storehouse of illuminating examples of inflation and its consequences. Discussing the pleasure of novelty and change in oratory Quintilian diagnoses its source correctly:

> Novelty and change are pleasing in oratory and the unexpected gives more delight. Hence we have exceeded all bounds and have exhausted the charm of the effect by too much straining after it *(est enim grata in eloquendo novitas et emutatio, et magis inopinata delectant. Ideoque iam in his amisimus modum et gratiam rei nimia captatione consumpsimus).*[22]

Quintilian wrote in a situation when the introduction of verbal fireworks was a much discussed problem in the art of rhetorics. Some teachers were so disgusted with this so-called Asiatic fashion that they advocated a return to Attic purity.[23] The extremists among these critics did, in Quintilian's words "shrink from and shun all pleasing effects in their language and approve of nothing except the plain, the simple and the unstrained". He compares them to people who are so afraid of falling that they are always lying on the ground. Is a good epigram such a crime? he asks—True, the ancients did not use this device. But from what time on do you call an orator "ancient"? Even Demosthenes introduced innovations. How could we approve of Cicero if we think there should be no change from Cato and the Gracchi? Before these, however, speech was even simpler.

> As for me, I regard these highlights of speech as something like the eyes of elo-quence. I would not like the body to be full of eyes, however, for then the other parts of the body would cease to function. If I really had to choose I should prefer the roughness of ancient speech to the new license. However, there is a kind of middle way here as well as in the style of life. . . .[24]

There is an even more telling passage in which Quintilian comments on the similarity between language and fashion with urbanity and wit and draws his own conclusion from this situation.

Writing more than one hundred years after Cicero, he still considered Cicero the model orator. He was ready to concede, however, that Cicero's critics had a case in one respect. A few more "epigrams" than the master used might even increase the pleasure a speech could give.

> This is not impossible even without interfering with the argument and the authority of our pronouncement, provided these highlights are used sparingly and not continuously, when they destroy their own effect. But having conceded so much, let nobody press me further. I give in to the times in not wearing a shaggy toga, but not in wearing one of silk; in having my hair cut, but not in arranging it in tiers and locks. . .[25]

Do tempori, I give in to the times, I yield to fashion. In this pregnant phrase Quintilian has posed the problem of any individual caught up in the situation created by the "age". Of course he did not have to yield. He could have refused to insert "epigrams" in his speeches, worn a shaggy toga and left his hair uncut. But he was afraid that this course of action would have made him even more conspicuous; he feared the charge of affectation more than any other, and so he chose the "middle road", not running after every innova-tion but not resisting those that had become generally current. It was a rational course to take.

III. Polarising Issues in Art

Quintilian's problem, the problem of change and of the self-consciousness to which it can give rise may be a problem of "Open Societies". Not that the closed societies of tribal cultures never witness alterations of style. But, generally speaking, these alterations are gradual and imperceptible, they do not give rise to discussion and do not force the individual to take sides. Where Custom is King and standards are uniform innovation will generally be frowned upon and if togas are worn shaggy by one generation, they will continue to be so worn, at least new styles will not be introduced with a flourish.

It is precisely any departure from the accepted norms of tradition that can turn into an "issue". We are all familiar with the dilemmas posed by the logic of certain situations. We would not mind, maybe, on a cold day to call the dustman in to join us for lunch; we are certainly not held back from this charitable act by the same kind of social tradition that would make such an idea unthinkable to a Brahmin. What may hold us back is rather the knowledge that, having done it once, we would have to do it again even when we have no time or inclination. A failure to call him in a second time would make him wonder whether he had made some blunder. If, to avoid this unintended impression we call him once more, we are on the way towards a tradition which becomes increasingly hard to break, for now not to ask him becomes a withdrawal.

To some extent we all constantly act like the timid civil servant who would like to do a certain thing but refrains for fear of creating a precedent. The trouble is that this fear is often quite justified within the logic of his situation. If you depart from the norm in one case, however deserving—for instance in admitting a student to the University without the required paper qualification—you make it correspondingly harder for yourself and your successor to apply the existing rules. No wonder that such concessions are so often accompanied by the request not to talk about it to anyone. The knowledge of a rule broken is the knowledge of it being breakable. What is worse, the knowledge that you did relent once makes any future refusal to relent look doubly harsh. Where there was no alternative, there could be no complaint. Where one has been shown to exist, the complaint is only too justified.

At this point a psychological consideration comes in—an expectation unfulfilled seems to register more violently than one fulfilled. This special weight attached to the negative instance may well be connected with the survival value of negative tests which Popper has taught us to see.

There are many idiomatic expressions referring to the danger of creating a situation from which there is therefore no easy way out. "Where would we get to?" asks the reluctant bureaucrat, "we cannot have that". "Once you start it, you are in for it". German (or Austrian) parlance is even more explicit: "Fang' dir nichts an, du kannst dir das nicht einführen", ("Do not start things, it must not become an institution").

The "it" which is to be avoided is always in such cases the emergence of a new tradition which will exact the repetition of an act or a favour which was intended to be taken in its own right.

The link between this problem and that of inflation is obvious. What was to make an effect as an exception becomes a norm and has to be outbid if the effect is to remain. Start writing to someone once at Christmas and he will be expecting that card and get worried or annoyed if it fails to come. The same might be true if you wrote every mouth, every week or every day. It is the relation to the norm that matters, not the objective frequency of writing.

Our reactions to art are particularly closely bound up with the fulfilment and denial of expectations.[26] Hence the relevance of norms and the dangers of inflation discussed in the last section. But however much this consideration may support the case for classicism and conservativism in art, new moves will be made and precedents will be set which alter the situation irretrievably.

It is not surprising, therefore, that such moves can arouse real passions both on the part of those who wish to preserve the norm as on that of the innovators who want to establish a new tradition. The historian of art concerned with the changing styles of Open Societies is familiar with typical situations of this kind. A banner is raised and the world of art is ranged for or against the "revolution".

The hostility and mutual contempt with which these warring camps look at each other sometimes recall the fervours of religious wars. For a French classicist it was an outrage which stamped the perpetrator a barbarian to break the Aristotelian Unities of place, time and plot in a play: to the admirers of Shakespeare determined to break this bastion of conservatism the Aristotelian Unities were as the red rag to the bull. For a champion of Ideal Beauty in painting the *"naturalisti"* who followed Caravaggio[27] were dangerous subversives; the Spanish writer of the seventeenth century who called Caravaggio the anti-Christ of art[28] did not want to be funny. In Vienna, towards the end of the last century, the followers of Wagner and of Brahms were irreconcilable. When Hugo Wolf heard somebody at a party praise Brahms he sat down on the keyboard with the words "That is how I play Brahms".[29]

All these and similar battles in the arts were fought for or against certain principles which I propose to call "polarising issues". Not every challenge to tradition becomes such an issue. Some remain unnoticed or are shrugged off, others may be so successful that they rout the opposing party before it can

make a stand. If we can believe historians of literature this is what happened
when Cervantes published *Don Quixote,* that deadly satire of Amadis of
Gaul and similar Romances of Chivalry. It certainly might have happened
that the literary world had been split for and against Amadis. But it appears
that this literary survival of a medieval tradition was killed outright, and that
no further imitation of the Amadis novels came out after *Don Quixote,* but
plenty of continuations and imitations of Cervantes. A new bandwagon was
rolling on Vanity Fair.

There certainly is an aspect of all stylistic history that can be described in
terms of such triumphs, whether with or without a preceding fight. The
spread of the Renaissance was the submission of Europe to the banner of *"all'
antica".* The victory of Neoclassicism was the triumph of the standard of
"noble simplicity" championed by Winckelmann over the playful complexity
of the Rococo fashion. Classicism in its turn, of course, succumbed to the
bandwagon of Romanticism flying the flag of variety and originality, only to
be trumped by Realism and Impressionism enlisting the support of "scientific
truth".

What should interest the historian who tries to track down these changes
is to observe the polarising issues in *statu nascendi.* The type of documentation I have in mind is exemplified by a passage in the memoirs of an English
painter who mixed with the avant garde in Paris before the First World
War. It need not be taken as gospel truth to remain a neat illustration of the
Vanity Fair aspect of stylistic change:

> When I used to visit Paris at the beginning of the present century my artist
> friends in the Latin Quarter would explain that what seemed strange to me in
> their pictures was due to my own slovenly habits of vision. If I suggested that
> shadows were grey and not purple they would say, "That is because you do not
> use your eyes"; and when we were walking along the boulevards. . . .I discovered
> that they were right and I wrong. . .
>   But ten or a dozen years later I found that the young artists of Paris had
> totally altered their attitude towards art. All references to vision were impatient-
> ly brushed aside with the remark, "Yes, yes; but the important thing is not to
> paint what you see, but to paint what you feel". . . .
>   My friends spoke little of things seen; but they were full of ideas, full of
> theories. A new phrase was an inspiration, a new word a joy. One day a painter I
> knew accompanied a friend of his, a student of science, to the Sorbonne and there
> heard a lecture on mineralogy. He returned from an improving afternoon with a
> new word—*crystallization.* It was a magic word, destined to become a talisman
> of modern painting. Some nights later while sitting with some friends in the
> Closerie des Lilas, on the Boulevard Saint-Michel, I incautiously let drop a con-
> fession that I admired the work of Velazquez. "Velazquez!" said the most ad-
> vanced of our party promptly, "but he has no crystallization!". . . .a new theory
> of art was being constructed, based on the idea of the crystal being the *primitive
> form* of all things. Velazquez, I was given to understand, was a Secondary
> Painter because he employed rounded—that is to say secondary—forms. A

Primary Painter, I was told, would preserve sharpness in the edges of his planes and accentuate the angles of his volumes.[30]

The author is not unprejudiced and his suggestion that it was this chance encounter with a word that led the young painters to Cézanne need not be taken seriously. On the contrary, it was their desire to find an alternative to Impressionism that led them to discover Cézanne and sent them in search of a fresh theory and a fresh slogan.[31] And yet this little snapshot from Vanity Fair seems to me to illuminate the situation more clearly than many a more pretentious history of modern art which describes the rise of Cubism as a symptom of a New Age.

I believe that here, too, the historian's first concern should be with what Popper calls the logic of the situation. Popper called for "individualistic and institutionalist models"[32] which allow us to look at such a situation in purely sociological rather than psychological terms. I believe that an almost ideal model of such a "polarising issue" lies at hand. It is to be found in Jonathan Swift's famous account of the war between Lilliput and Blefuscu.

> It began upon the following occasion: it is allowed on all hands, that the primitive way of breaking eggs before we eat them, was upon the larger end: but his present Majesty's grandfather, while he was a boy, going to eat an egg, and breaking it according to the ancient practice, happened to cut one of his fingers. Whereupon the Emperor his father published an edict, commanding all his subjects, upon great penalties, to break the smaller end of their eggs. The people so highly resented this law, that our histories tell us there have been six rebellions raised on that account; wherein one Emperor lost his life, and another his crown. These civil commotions were constantly fomented by the monarchs of Blefuscu; and when they were quelled the exiles always fled for refuge to that empire. It is computed, that eleven thousand persons have, at several times, suffered death, rather than submit to break their eggs at the smaller end. Many hundred large volumes have been published upon this controversy: but the books of the Big-Endians have been long forbidden, and the whole party rendered incapable by law of holding employments. During the course of these troubles, the Emperors of Blefuscu did frequently expostulate by their ambassadors, accusing us of making a schism in religion, by offending against a fundamental doctrine of our great prophet Lustrog, in the fifty-fourth chapter of the Blundecral (which is their Alcoran). This, however, is thought to be a mere strain upon the text: for the words are these: *that all true believers shall break their eggs at the convenient end:* and which is the convenient end, seems, in my humble opinion, to be left to every man's conscience, or at least in the power of the Chief Magistrate to determine.
>
> Now the Big-Endian exiles have found so much credit in the Emperor of Blefuscu's court, and so much private assistance and encouragement from their party here at home, that a bloody war has been carried on between the two empires for six-and-thirty moons, with various success; during which time we have lost forty capital ships, and a much greater number of smaller vessels, together with thirty thousand of our best seamen and soldiers; and the damage received by the enemy is reckoned to be somewhat greater than ours.[33]

Swift no doubt intended his story as a parable of human folly, a castiga-
tion of stupidity explicable in psychological terms. But he has done more. He
has devised a convincing caricature of a social situation with a logic of its
own. For the purpose of our analysis we can disregard the story of terror and
persecution Swift unfolds. For even without these outward means of compul-
sion the situation allows of no easy escape. It is not only the foolish Lilliputian who is caught up in this quarrel over eggs. Even the most intelligent of his
countrymen who wants to eat a boiled egg has to open it somehow—and try
as he may, he cannot empty his action of significance. If he opens it at one
end he will either show himself to be pro-Lilliput or pro-Blefuscu and if he
laboriously opens it at the side to display his neutrality he will have been compelled by a foolish situation to perform a foolish act. The same applies if he
decides to give up boiled eggs altogether, which is a poor solution, particularly if he likes them. Moreover, there may be social situations such as communal breakfasts in which the withdrawal would be interpreted as an act of
disloyalty by both sides. His best hope, maybe, would be to act the madman
and thus to deprive his actions of any social significance, but the need for such
a desperate course only underlines the power of a situation from which there
is no opting out.

Of course, we must be careful, lest this analysis prove too much. If it
were quite correct, polarising issues could never loosen their grip, and the war
over the eggs would be doomed to last for ever. Perhaps it is here that psychology comes in; for people do get tired of issues, particularly if a new ex-
citement diverts attention from the old one. It would not be true, moreover,
that the wise Lilliputian could not contribute to this breaking of the deadlock,
particularly if he had the talent of a Jonathan Swift in showing up the
ludicrous side of such quarrels. But attend to it in one way or another he
must, if he is caught up in his society.

There are historians who will deny the relevance of the issue. The story
of the eggs, they will argue, was a mere pretext, an irrelevant frill in the long
chronicle of strife between Blefuscu and Lilliput. Their *real* dispute was over
issues of power, not over the ludicrous myth told to the populace. Though the
secret archives of both islands appear to be irretrievably lost, we must grant a
certain plausibility to this hypothesis. Had the Blefuscudians not hated the
Lilliputians they would not have made an issue of the enemy King's decree,
by aiding and abetting its opponents. But this is precisely what our analysis
would have led us to expect anyhow. The existence of this hostility does not
prove that there was not also an autonomous social situation deriving from
the polarising issue of where to open the egg. Moreover no amount of investigation of the conflict of interests between the two islands would allow us
to predict that this particular issue would arise, let alone which side would
favour which solution. What could be predicted is only that, if there was any

issue, the camps would be likely to divide along party lines.

Actually Swift tells another story earlier in the same chapter, about the internal politics of Lilliput, which confirms this interpretation. The two opposing parties—modelled of course on the Whigs and Tories, or cavaliers and roundheads—are marked by a badge of allegiance that cannot but be fortuitous in its absurdity:

> For above seventy moons past there have been two struggling parties in this empire, under the names of Tramecksan and Slanecksan, from the high and low heels on their shoes, by which they distinguish themselves. It is alleged indeed, that the high-heels are most agreeable to our ancient constitution: but however this be, his Majesty has determined to make use of only low heels in the administration of the government, and all offices in the gift of the Crown, as you cannot but observe; and particularly, that his Majesty's Imperial heels are lower by at least a *drurr* than any of his court; (*drurr* is a measure about the fourteenth part of an inch). The animosities between these two parties run so high, that they will neither eat nor drink, nor talk with each other. We compute the *Tramecksan*, or High-Heels, to exceed us in number; but the power is wholly on our side. We apprehend his Imperial Highness, the Heir to the Crown, to have some tendency towards the High-Heels; at least we can plainly discover one of his heels higher than the other, which gives him a hobble in his gait.

It will be noticed that the two stories do not duplicate each other entirely. In foreign politics, as with the opening of eggs, there is only the stark choice between two alternatives, in internal politics there is a spectrum extending between the two extremes. But this gradualness of transition does not materially change the logic of the situation. A Lilliputian ordering a pair of shoes will still be presented by the cobbler with the awkward and inescapable question how many *drurrs* he wants his heels to be. Even if, like Quintilian, he opts for the middle way, he has to place himself somewhere along the scale.

We need not go far to find an application of these models in the field of art. The most conspicuous polarising issue in contemporary painting is a case in point. I refer to the issue of "abstraction". Whether he wants to or not, the artist today is compelled to attend to this issue. He is of course quite free to shun exercises in what is called "nonobjective" painting; but he cannot avoid the result that the representational paintings he produces in this situation will be "non-nonobjective". He might long for the lost age of innocence, where to paint an apple and a jug meant precisely painting an apple and a jug. But, while the polarising issue looms over him, this innocence is not to be had. Painting a still life becomes, among other things, an affirmation in a situation not of his making. And, though he can preach against the artificiality of the issue, even this will only increase the attention he has to pay to it. In this situation, too, it is easy to ascribe the resulting tension to underlying conflicts of power. For, by and large, we find that the geographical distribution of the most vocal partisans pro and con abstract art coincides with the cold war frontiers. There are exceptions, but they confirm the rule. It is of political rather than artistic interest that abstract art is cultivated in Poland and Yugoslavia as an affirmation of independence from the party line that still enforces "social realism" in Russia and in China. But, though the polarising issue has been thus drawn into the political arena, it would still be misleading to identify the two. There is no intrinsic reason why Communists should side against abstract art rather than for it. However much they may at present rationalise their hostility in terms of Marxist aesthetics, the fact remains that, at an earlier phase, it was in Soviet Russia that extreme abstract experiments were launched (by Malevich), to be promptly denounced by the Right as *"Kulturbolschewismus"*.

Of course, the fact that the constellation of parties in such an issue can be fortuitous does not mean that it must always be fortuitous, even less that it must be felt to be fortuitous. Reasons can be given for the switch of Soviet art policy from modernism to socialist realism no less than for the official backing "experimental" art is receiving on the other side of the iron curtain.

It may have been hard to predict which party in Lilliput would wear the high heels, but it is quite intelligible that it was the middle class party in the English Civil War which had no use for the long hair of the cavaliers and became the "roundheads" just as their extremist successors in France became the *"sans culottes"*.

It is for this kind of intelligibility that the Hegelian looks in the formation of styles. He wants to identify Gothic elegance with courtly aristocracy and the realistic reaction with the hardheaded middle class. He is sure that the frivolity of the Rococo expressed the decadence of the doomed aristocracy and the severity of Neoclassicism the ideals of the classes which triumphed in the French Revolution. The historian can be forgiven if the crudity and triviality of such interpretation provoke his scepticism;[34] but, though the Hegelian and Marxist theories of determinism are as fallacious here as in other fields, there is no harm in conceding that even in artistic preferences the dice will sometimes be loaded. There are occasionally elements in an artistic issue that will become fused with a social or political tension.

One style of church building was felt to be appropriate for Protestants, another for Catholics, and, though the idea of a Jesuit style used for propagandist purposes has been exploded,[35] the fact remains that the very austerity of the Protestant camp in matters of art created an issue that made the Catholic camp all the more eager to exploit the effects of images and lavish ornament.

It is even possible that the young men in 1912 who rallied round the slogan of crystallisation were dimly attracted by the glamour of a scientific term and by some unformulated identification of such hard and cold forms with an antiromantic bias in other spheres of life. In other words, it is possible that the polarised issue becomes a symbol or a metaphor for other issues which are less articulate. Possible, but not necessary. Hence it is better at this point to break off this particular trend of thought, lest we are led from a logic of situations into the swamps of psychological speculations.

IV. Art and Technical Progress

In language and in art we feel entitled to deplore innovations that turn into issues (though this will not help us much); in other fields we are not, for in some innovations may be real improvements that save lives and diminish suffering, in others (and I refer to science) they may bring us nearer to the truth we wish to find. Given these aims (about which there can be little quarrel) it is often easy to say which departure from tradition will be adopted in a rational society. The history of technological progress and of scientific advance is thus to some extent the history of rational choices within an open society. Once bronze was shown to cut better than stones, iron better than bronze and steel better than iron, these alternatives had only to be invented and presented for rational men to use them for their cutting tools.[36] Similarly, Popper has discussed the progress of science, and has asked what social conditions would stop or impede such progress—for instance a ban on free enquiry.[37] The refusal of certain societies to adopt technical improvements is an equally topical problem, for it has turned out to be far from easy to introduce, for instance, better methods of farming in the so-called underdeveloped countries. The reasons have been frequently discussed. To quote the words of a recent broadcast:

> They have not passed the first intellectual hurdle, the great innovation which is acceptance of the idea of innovation itself. The annual agricultural round is part of a whole pattern of existence, and it is often religiously sanctioned. The seeds have to be blessed this way; the ploughing should not begin until after a certain saint's festival; only men may prune the olive trees; only women may gather the olives—and so on. Deviation means anxiety about the possibly fearful consequences. And it is not impossible to appreciate this point of view even for a product of a scientific Western culture. A fertility rite usually does look much more impressive than a dressing of ammonium sulphate, besides usually being more fun.[38]

The detailed analysis of any such situation in which improvements are resisted might be an excellent way to test the capacity of Popper's "zero method" to lead cultural studies out of its reliance on organicistic holism. To put it briefly, any tool or action that serves a great multiplicity of purposes will be much harder to change and therefore to improve than anything that serves only one particular aim. A cutting tool, as we have seen, can certainly be improved by sharpening and hardening the cutting edge. A knife one also wishes to use as a paper-knife should not be too sharp, for, if it is, it tends to slash the pages. Improvement in one respect makes it useless in another. If this is true of such simple and perfectly rational aims, the situation becomes more marked where some of the purposes are strongly charged with emotions. We are told that for a time Picasso never shaved without drawing lines in the lather and turning his face into the mask of a clown. As long as this habit lasted he would not have been a likely customer for an electric razor, however much the new device may be superior to the older ones. There can, of course, be few technological improvements that do not disrupt some habit and threaten some aspects of a way of life.

In many cases, therefore, technological change is at first confined to strictly utilitarian functions, while other spheres even in our society tend to respond more slowly or resist them altogether. The ceremony of Knighting is still performed by the Queen with the technologically obsolete sword, not with the butt of an automatic rifle. Candles are still lit in church, and cumbersome seals are still appended to important documents, though one could think of many means of achieving their purpose more easily and more lastingly.

But this special aura that for us surrounds the technically obsolete and the archaic, the judge's wig, the don's gown and the guardsman's gala uniform, only serve to confirm the influence which an increase in alternatives has on the gamut of expressive symbols. It was the invention of paper that made vellum look solemn.

Some idea of progress (as a possibility rather than as an impersonal force) is inseparable from the Open Society. Its members must believe that things and institutions can be discussed and improved. Its champions, therefore, can be forgiven when they look with exasperation at their opponents who fight for the status quo at any price. For good or ill this issue of "progress" has become the dominant problem of Western Society ever since the Enlightenment proclaimed its faith in the perfectibility of man and society. The French Revolution notoriously consolidated this issue in the "polarisation" of politics with the "radicals" on the left, the "reactionaries" on the right. And just as eggs and heels in Lilliput were turned into issues with the camps aligned according to these dominant tensions, so art has been caught up in the political problem of the nineteenth century and become "polarised" in progressivist and conservative schools. It is not surprising that even the advocacy of technical innovations in art was seen as a symptom of radicalism and that a resistance to such innovations tended to brand the critic as a stick-in-the-mud. What is more surprising is rather that the fit is far from perfect.[39] Artists of the "avant garde" (such as Degas and Cézanne) were sometimes found on the political right while their medievalizing opponents (such as William Morris) were on the political left.

The poverty of the kind of historicism that applies the idea of progress to art, has often been castigated but never been exorcized. Maybe the logic of situations and the zero method can help here, too, to clarify this all-important matter.

What we call "art" in primitive societies is obviously so deeply embedded in the ritual and life of the community that its multiple purpose makes change very precarious. Painting and carving for instance may have a magic or religious as well as a decorative and prestige function. The age of these traditions is often felt to be the guarantee of their value and efficacy; and since no rational criteria can exist to decide which image is more efficacious such changes as occur must be due to accidental "mutations".

But this ritualistic conception of painting and sculpture may be losing its grip in a society that is exposed to many influences from outside. The travelling merchant may come home with tales of images seen elsewhere that surpassed, in his judgement, anything his native craftsmen had ever done. In stressing this role of culture clash in the emergence of open societies I am of course following Popper's lead.[40] Where art is thus prized loose from its multiple allegiances, the question of standards can come up with new force.

I have tried to argue elsewhere that in the first Open Society, that of Greece, a technological and even scientific element did indeed enter art, as can always happen where one rational purpose is regarded as overriding. I have suggested the hypothesis that for the Greeks this aim was the representation of a sacred story as it might actually have looked to an eyewitness.[41]

Granted a specific demand of this kind, technical progress towards its achievement is certainly possible.[42] The stylistic changes in Greek art from the archaic representations of the sixth century to the illusionistic illustrations of the third constitute the most famous advance of this kind, which was recapitulated in the Renaissance development from Giotto to Leonardo da Vinci. It is true that, in postulating such an underlying purpose that would explain the successive innovations of these styles, we are using our hindsight. We cannot prove that the sculptors of the Temple of Aegina wanted to render the human figure as naturalistically as did their successors on the Parthenon pediments, nor can we give evidence to show that Giotto would have admired Leonardo. All we can demonstrate is that naturalistic inventions spread with the same rapidity as did other technical innovations. The mastery of the nude in Greek art impressed sculptors as far as Afghanistan and Gandhara; the invention of perspective in Florence conquered France and Germany within a century.

Even in a case like this the disruptive effect of this improvement on other functions of art was very serious indeed. The illusion of depth threatened the decorative unity of painting that displayed its lucid pictograph on a ground of gold. The mastery of the nude in Greek art led away from that simplicity and grandeur of form we admire in Egyptian statuary.

Speaking more generally, the technical innovations threatened the artist's tasks of creating a rich and satisfying order with his well-tried elements.[43] It is in this way that progress creates a polarising issue in art, for it presents the painter or sculptor with a choice of priorities. Are you ready—for instance—to risk disruption for the sake of this increase in naturalism or would you rather confine your art to the traditional game? Art is not a game; but there are important elements these two pleasures share—in both activities there are rules and there is mastery. The mastery is achieved within the rules through years of practice that explores the possible initial moves and their potentialities for further achievements. This mastery depends to no small extent on the exact knowledge of means. The weight and size of tennis balls is fixed and so are the dimensions of the field and of the net. It is within these fixed conventions that the champion develops his capacity to calculate and predict. Of course, a good player may take some change in these conventions in his stride; but the idea of "improving" tennis by giving his balls more bounce or his racket a boosting device would strike him as silly.

The champion's fans, in their turn, who flock to Wimbledon would certainly stare in incomprehension, if it were suggested to them that times had changed and that they should learn to appreciate a new game. If one struck their fancy and they wanted to understand its finer points, well and good; but where was their obligation to do so?

If art were nothing but a game this comparison would completely dispose of all historicist arguments in criticism. Neither players nor connoisseurs are interested in changing rules, let alone games. It is possible that only in such situations art can blossom to real refinement. The Chinese scholar looking at a painting on silk of some bamboo stems shares with the connoisseur of games something of this developed pleasure in *finesse*. The suggestion that this art could be improved by changing tools or media he would probably dismiss as barbaric.

But, for good or ill, as we have seen, art as it is functioning in our society is not only a game of this kind. It derives from its functions a technical component that is intrinsically unstable and shares with language the drift towards inflation. These two sources of instability may well belong together. At any rate, each of them can result in that disturbance I have called a "polarising issue". What appears as an improvement to one side, may be felt as a disruption by the other. But, once the initiative is with the innovator, the defence of the status quo becomes increasingly difficult. When more and more artists have gone over to more naturalistic methods, the old game will acquire a precious or a musty look. More and more gifted artists will be attracted by the challenge of the new one, and the old playgrounds will be increasingly deserted of players and spectators. The game may survive for a time as an archaising ritual played by defiant outsiders who may have all the right arguments but meet with no response. Their decision to keep up their little cult will impress their contemporaries as preciousness and affectation. When this moment comes, two equally undesirable things may happen according to the logic of Vanity Fair—either that the game dies out, or that the preciousness will attract the snobs and will bring the game back into fashion, but with very different social overtones. And, whether we want it or not, we cannot easily disregard these overtones.

V. Social Testing and the Plasticity of Taste

During the last few years of the nineteenth century the polarising issue in architecture was the question of the use of iron. Was the Eiffel Tower to be admitted as a work of architecture or was it just a feat of engineering? More was involved in this dispute than a mere verbal quarrel. The architects felt that the integrity of their art was threatened by the new material. Perhaps their attitude becomes more understandable if we look at it in the light of the first section. For architecture as an art also works with accents of emphasis. A high tower, a vault of wide span are the high-points of the architect's vocabulary. We still marvel at the lofty vaults built by the Romans and by the cathedral builders. These famous buildings established the scale within which the tradition of architecture worked. Now the use of iron threatened this scale and upset the whole hierarchy of values. Any railway station could boast of a wider span than the most "monumental" of classical interiors. No wonder that architects tried to resist this dislocation which upset their whole game. Let the engineers construct what they liked, but let architecture retain its established vocabulary.

In this situation before the turn of the century, a German critic and historian wrote a passage that seems to me to sum up the most important problem which concerns us:

> It is not much use to dismiss the impression (made by iron constructions) as inferior. After all, it looks as if the majority of people and a large section of the architects were increasingly accepting these impressions as satisfying. If the others, who are trained in the theory of art, continue to disapprove, this may easily bring them into an opposition to the progress of the world, in which they will certainly be the losers. The question therefore is not how to mould iron to make it conform to our taste, but the much more important one, how to mould our taste to make it conform with iron?[44]

At first blush this looks a cynical pronouncement. "Jump on the bandwagon and learn to like it". Indeed, when I once quoted it to a group of architects, they became downright abusive. Not that they disliked iron, but they were rightly suspicious of the relativism this advice seemed to imply. It appears to challenge the belief in objective solutions which are "liked", because they are good. It undermines the idea of art as an autonomous realm achieving values which are and remain independent of technical change. As an admirer of Popper's social philosophy my immediate reaction to this pronouncement was equally hostile. It seemed to me the embodiment of historicist opportunism. Moreover, I remembered an important passage in the *Poverty of Historicism* in which Popper takes issue with Mannheim in a related context. Mannheim had suggested that the political problem was to organize human impulses in such a way that they will direct their energy to the right strategic points and thus lead to the transformation of society in the desired direction. Popper points out to the

> well-meaning Utopian that this programme implies an admission of failure. . .for. . .the demand that we 'mould' these men and women to fit into his new society. . .clearly removes any possibility of testing the success or failure of the new society. For those who do not like living in it only admit thereby that they are not yet fit to live in it; that their 'human impulses' need further 'organizing'. But without the possibility of tests, any claim that a 'scientific' method is being employed evaporates. The holistic approach is incompatible with a truly scientific method.[45]

As an admirer of Popper's methodology, however, I have also learned from him that one must be critical of one's own reactions. Maybe there is something in the German critic's formulation that we can and sometimes must mould our taste. If it is, this would prove to be a source of weakness in art, but it may not be uninstructive to probe this possibility.

Clearly, architecture is one of those multiple purpose activities in which the artistic aim is only one of many. If the use of iron allows us to house many people better, it would be criminal to reject it for aesthetic reasons. We still have a right to regret the passing of the timber age and of the beautiful stone buildings of the preindustrial era; but our regrets are irrelevant to the architect working today. But, should we not rather accept it as a necessary evil, should we not face the fact that art had to be sacrificed to efficiency and hygiene? Not, surely, if we are architects. To an architect the new material does present a challenge, and an exciting one; he must try to subdue it into order and beauty, to create a new game that can be played with iron, and the greater the problem, the more he will perhaps come to "like it". He must discover the potential of the new material and, when he has found it, we too may see the point and "like it" too, provided we share in his adventure. Thus the plasticity of our aesthetic reaction which the critic's pronouncement implied, may be a fact, although a disturbing one. Is all taste acquired taste?

These questions may lose some of their sting if we return to the difference between the problems of technology and science on the one hand, and those of art on the other. In technology progress can be specified once aims are stated; in science the aim is implicit in the search for truth. If there were something corresponding in art, it should be precisely the creation of something we can "like". There have, indeed, been attempts to describe art in some such terms as a technology for the achieving of certain pleasures, the creation of that "aesthetic experience" about which we read so much.[46] One would like this to be true; for, if it were, our spontaneous reactions to works of art would be the sole and safe criterion of their excellence. I would still defend the position that Mozart has found means of giving real pleasure to human beings which are as objectively suited to this purpose as are aeroplanes for flying, that Fra Angelico has discovered ways of expressing devotion or Rembrandt of hinting at mysteries which anybody can learn to see because they are "there".

And yet we know from history and from our own experience that there were and are large groups of people who never "liked" Mozart, Fra Angelico or Rembrandt and who totally failed to appreciate their miraculous achievements.

It is perhaps important at this point to stress that a belief in the objectivity of artistic standards is not necessarily refuted by the undoubted subjectivity of likes and dislikes. Clearly those who do not like a game will not become good judges of players, and those who do not want to touch wine for whatever reason will not become connoisseurs of vintages. With most people, at least, liking is a preliminary condition of appreciation. Only if certain types of art hold a promise of pleasure for them will they make the effort of attending to the individual work. They may find they like ballet and dislike opera, enjoy eighteenth-century music but avoid the Romantics, or prefer Chinese to Indian art. Naturally, they would not claim to be able to distinguish excellence from mediocrity in the products of art forms or schools that "leave them cold". The professional critic, it is true, can attempt to surmount this subjective reaction. He may, on occasion, be able to appreciate artistic achievement in an artist or period that does not much appeal to him. He may for instance find Rubens not very sympathetic but come to admire his verve, skill and imagination. Or he may fail to respond to Poussin and still learn to understand what his champions see in him.

And yet it may be argued that this "cold" appreciation of what we really do not like is a poor substitute for the experience a work of art can give us. This experience is bound up with love. There is an element of initial yielding in this response that can perhaps be compared with what psychoanalysts call transference. It includes a willingness to suspend criticism and to surrender to the work of art in exploring its complexities and its *finesse*. If we try to be merely unprejudiced in our approach we shall never find out what the work can offer us.

We know from Popper, moreover, that this demand for unprejudiced objectivity represents altogether an impossible and erroneous methodological position. The objectivity of science does not rest on scientists being free of preconceived views and theories, but on their readiness to test them and to listen to arguments leading to their refutation. But, if I am right that as far as the testing of artistic excellence is concerned, such a critical attitude may impede the test, it becomes clearer why dogmatism and subjectivism is so prevalent in artistic matters. In this respect artistic creeds are indeed closer to religion than to science. The awe and consolation connected with religious experience also depends on such an initial readiness on the part of the worshipper and this readiness he mostly derives from tradition. In growing into the group he learns what to revere and what to abhor, and, whenever he is doubtful, he will anxiously look to other members to see whether he adores the right thing and performs the right ritual. The places of worship of rival sects may not only leave him cold, but appear to him as abominations. But the only test he has to distinguish between the holy and the unholy is the reaction of his group.

It is the probing of this reaction that I propose here to call "social testing". It need not take the form of a formulated question—we soon learn to feel how our actions or utterances are "taken" by those around us. It is well to remember, moreover, that this kind of "social testing" is the rule rather than the exception not only where religious beliefs are concerned, but also in matters of behaviour and even of ordinary beliefs. The child will try out an opinion and search the face of his mother or, later, of his companions to find out whether he has said something silly. In most cases, in fact, there is little else he could do to form his opinions. It is through social testing that most of us have arrived at the opinion that there are no witches; just as our ancestors arrived at theirs, that there are. Even the rationalist, as Popper has pointed out, must take a lot on trust in what passes for knowledge.[47] He only differs from the dogmatist in his awareness of limits, his own and those of others. He is at least ready in principle to test any opinion and to ask for credentials other than social ones.

It is here, of course, that the difference between scientific beliefs and artistic taste is crucial. For, in art there are no credentials that could be probed in the same systematic way. Debates about artistic merit, though I do not consider them empty, tend to be laborious and inconclusive. What wonder, therefore, that there are few areas where "social testing" plays a greater part than in aesthetic judgements? The adolescent soon learns that the group can be a dreadful spoilsport if he confesses to liking something that has fallen under a taboo. Imagine a young Spaniard in the first decade of the seventeenth century meeting his friends after a longish absence abroad and mentioning casually that Romances of Chivalry are his favourite reading. Suddenly he finds himself the centre of mocking attention; he is called Don Quixote, or the Knight of the Sorry Countenance, and may never live this down. It would need a strong character indeed in a similar situation to stick up for Amadis of Gaul and to discourse on its artistic merits which, after all, had recently been apparent to everyone. Even if our imaginary victim would try, the defence would die on his lips. He would find in his heart that maybe Amadis was all a lot of nonsense and that he was silly to have been taken in by that bombast.

The more seriously art is taken by any group, the more adept will it be in such brainwashing; for to enjoy the wrong thing in such a circle is like worshipping false gods; you fail in the test of admission to the group if your taste is found wanting. In the light of these solid facts it is curious to reflect on Kant's opinion that the aesthetic judgement is entirely "disinterested", entirely free, grounded only in the conviction of what every developed human being would enjoy. One wonders whether that was true even of the Sage of Koenigsberg. Whether not even he was influenced in his preferences by his group and by its ideas of "good taste". He probably never observed the nexus between aesthetic and social appeal, because he lived in a relatively closed milieu and because he was not very much involved in artistic matters. Had he been, he might have had occasion to see the pathetic desire of the socially insecure to "like" the "right thing", and the feeling of anxiety that can arise in a situation where an unlabelled and unconnected work of art is displayed that does not seem to fit any preexistent aesthetic pigeonhole. Contrary to Kant's opinion, it sometimes looks in such situations as if the expression "I like it" really implied, "I believe that is the kind of thing my group accepts as good. Since I like my group, I like it, too".

Here are the roots of the unholy alliance between snobbery and art that no observer of our social scene can have missed. There is every reason to combat the attitudinising to which it leads; but not everything is snobbery that is sometimes branded with this stigma.

Much has been written and talked, for instance, about the way art lovers have been known to enthuse about forgeries which they then have discarded ignominiously, once the fraud had been exposed. The suspicion is always voiced that this transformation of liking into disliking reveals the first as mere sham and the outcome of snobbery. It is an understandable suspicion and one which may not be totally off the mark in many cases, but, insofar as it implies that hidden postulate of an entirely unprejudiced appreciation, it is mistaken. We are never uninfluenced by our previous experience and expectations. We cannot approach all works of art without a theory, nor can we set out independently to test every reputation. There is just no time, nor, perhaps the fund of emotional response, to enter into every encounter with a work of art with such a mixture of readiness and critical detachment. Tradition, even where it is not accepted dogmatically, presents a tremendous economy. It is something to be told that among the countless items in our heritage the works of Homer, of Shakespeare or Rembrandt have given much enjoyment to those who surrendered to their magic. If I am told, therefore, that a drawing is by Rembrandt, I shall approach it with the expectation of finding a masterpiece. I shall look for the signs of mastery to which I have responded before in Rembrandt and will surrender myself to the promised pleasure. This means no more than that I have learned to have confidence in Rembrandt and that I take his lines on trust even where I may find them at first a little puzzling. Can I be blamed if my enjoyment turns into embarrassment and disgust on finding that my trust has been betrayed?

Take the case of "Ossian's" poems, which were hailed with such enthusiasm in the eighteenth century not only by snobs but by people who cannot be accused of ignorance of poetry—Goethe, for instance. Surely it does make a difference to our attitude whether we read them as the genuine creations of a primitive and heroic tribe or whether we know them to be little more than a literary fraud concocted by a sophisticated antiquarian. The uncritical acceptance of this fraud, incidentally, is instructive within the present context. It was perpetrated within a situation created by a polarising issue. Reaction against the dominance of the classical dogma in poetry was the overriding problem of poetry, particularly in the non-Latin countries which resented the pretensions of the French to be the guardians of the one and only classical standard. The rejection, by this standard, of Shakespeare as "barbarian" naturally invited the retort that, maybe, the French were not barbaric enough? Rousseau had provided enough ammunition for such an attack. And was not Homer the expression of an heroic age still ignorant of rules and polite conventions? Were not folk songs pure poetry? It was this debate that explains not only the forgery of a large body of barbaric poetry from the wilds of Scotland but also its reception. Ossian was a godsend, a confirmation of the theory that the anticlassicist camp was in the process of formulating. Moreover, it bolstered the self-respect and self-confidence of those nations that could not boast of a Roman lineage. What wonder that the champions of this movement "liked" Ossian and failed to notice the false notes of inflated pathos and overemphasis that strike us today as obviously jarring?

Such are the perils and pleasures of Vanity Fair. The classicists who had been conditioned to respond to Vergil, Racine and Poussin never explored the alternative traditions for they were "put off"—as the excellent idiom has it—by certain external irregularities. And, though some of them might have had the satisfaction of not having "fallen for" the Ossian fraud, they might have paid for it in not appreciating Shakespeare either.

We have here come back to the problem of polarising issues from another angle.[48] The situation tends to create self-confirming aesthetic theories. Each side in such a dispute will tend to look first at the badge on any work of art that comes its way. How does it stand with regard to the dominant dispute? If they find signs that it comes from the "right camp", they will receive it with a warm glow which in itself will be pleasurable to experience and will be productive of more pleasure as the work unfolds its qualities. A work of art would have to be very poor indeed not to be "likeable" in such favourable conditions. If, on the other hand, the work comes in the hated wrappings of the hostile camp, the partisan art lover will scarcely bother to cut the strings and have a look. In this climate of opinion even a good work will be likely to wither and die. It is true that history records enjoyable exceptions to this rule. Hugo Wolf who treated Brahms with such contempt, was heard to mutter at a first performance of a Brahms symphony: "Hell, I like it". *(Teufel, mir gfallts.)*[49] What was said of the influence of the planets also applies to social pressures—"they incline, but do not compel".

If this analysis has been correct, the situation in aesthetics is not dissimilar to the one in ethics. In both areas of value the standards of the group influence our decisions, in both they become internalised in the voice of the conscience or what psychoanalysts call the superego. There is an anxious creature hidden in us that asks "may I do this", or "may I like this"? Yet in one respect there is surely a great difference between ethics and aesthetics. Where moral issues are concerned we must obviously battle against conformism and preserve our critical independence in the face of these social pressures as far as is humanly possible. For ethics is not part of Vanity Fair.

Art, too, is important; and those of us who believe that it is must certainly do their best to remain as honest in their own reactions as Hugo Wolf could be. They must try what they can to ignore their fond prejudices and to see the possibilities of achievement on the other side of the fence. A distaste for the devotional art of nineteenth-century pseudo-Gothic should not prevent us from looking at such church furnishings and glass with a certain awareness that our rejection of this kind of product is socially conditioned; nor should our readiness to admire children's art make us incapable of remembering adult standards. But there clearly is a limit to this process of self-criticism in matters of taste, and it may well be that we may have to accept this social element in our reactions as the price we pay for untroubled enjoyment. Hugo Wolf's—as we have seen—was not untroubled. We may have to admit, in other words, that something of this enjoyment belongs to the pleasures of the Fair. I do not think (to repeat) that such an admission would have to destroy our belief in standards. Nor is it necessarily good for art to be set up on a pedestal high above the market place. *Ernst ist das Leben, heiter ist die Kunst.*[50] Too much moral solemnity may kill it.

VI. Historicism and the Situation in Music

I have left the problem of music to the last, not only because it lies largely outside my competence, but also because music presents a special case. It is a game and an art that relies on the listener's memory for what has gone before, for only this recollection will allow him to build up expectations, and experience delight at the transformation and elaboration the composer introduces. Small wonder that for the less musical a work gains in beauty on several hearings and that for many familiarity is a condition of complete enjoyment. If not familiarity with the individual work (which is the ideal case) then at least familiarity with the composer's idiom which allows the listener to "follow" more easily, even though he may not know the name and function of the various conventions which he has learned to recognise. But if music is in this respect a special case, it is also one that for this very reason shows the mechanism of self-reinforcement particularly clearly at work. Few music lovers want to attend to a work of which they do not know and like the idiom; fewer would want to give it a second hearing. Hence it is the constant complaint of professional critics that the public boycott new music, that they only flock to hear what these critics contemptuously dismiss as the "old war horses", such as Beethoven's symphonies or Handel's "Messiah", and that the presence of an unknown work by a modern composer on the programme means the risk of financial failure.

As one who still likes Beethoven symphonies and is likely to stay away when a modern work is announced, I must confirm the existence of this situation, though I resent the critic's tone. If he hears these symphonies too often, this is an occupational hazard which is pretty irrelevant to the general argument. Moreover, the argument he generally uses or at least implies is pure historicism of the brand Popper should have disposed of for good and all. We are told that we must go with the time, that each age has its own idiom or style, and that Beethoven, who may have been very well for the early nineteenth century, has nothing to offer to the second half of the twentieth.

In conversation Popper has often drawn my attention to the devastating effect that Wagner's Hegelian futurism has had in this respect on the theory of music. It is Wagner who is largely responsible for this "polarising issue" of musical thought in the last century. It was he who wedded the historicist belief in progress and evolution, which so preoccupied the nineteenth century, to the genius worship of the Romantics and turned himself into the exemplar of the genius who is spurned by the multitudes but worshipped by the elect. I remember an old lady in Vienna who was born in the fifties of the last century telling me how Wagner's writings and prophecies had impressed her and her friends in their youth and how she had become a "Wagnerian" before having had an opportunity of hearing any of his music. She still remembered how shocked and bemused she felt when the Valkyrie was at last performed in Vienna and the prelude contained no recognisable tune. Were the critics who attacked Wagner perhaps right after all, or was she possibly a philistine herself? It is an unpleasant situation to be in, and as far as I know she quickly climbed out of it. Being disposed to like Wagner, she looked for the features she could like and so she could again feel happy in the company of those brilliant people she respected and loved. Brainwashing in art is quite possible; and if one makes the effort one can no doubt make oneself like something that one did not care for before. We conservatives in music (and I know I can include Popper here) find it hard to get rid of the suspicion that many critics and other partisans of serialism have undergone a similar forced conversion. They were first converted to historicism and futurism, to the Hegelian creed of the march of the mind to its predetermined goal, and then considered it their duty to side with contemporary experiments. The more their self-respect depended on their liking what they approved of, the more they invested in efforts at appreciation. If they now had to confess that really, after all this effort made for extraneous reasons, they found the game not worth the candle, they would feel traitors to their cause. I have spelt out this suspicion of the antihistoricist in music, but I admit that it is both libellous and self-reinforcing. I cannot disprove the claim that people really like Schoenberg; in fact the evidence is that some really do. What would be open to me is to taste and test a serialist piece by Schoenberg myself more seriously and more earnestly. But here my suspicion stands in the way. Not that I have never tried to listen; but by and large such efforts as I have made flagged after a time when I was "put off " by a specially ugly sound or a particularly historicist defence. Popper, I know, has made greater efforts in his youth when he was well acquainted with Schoenberg's circle, and has still found his suspicion confirmed that the moving ideology behind these innovations was historicism. Maybe his and other people's personal accounts have "brainwashed" me in my turn and made it harder for me to see (or rather hear) the other side of the issue. Theoretically I must grant the possibility that, despite the historicist nonsense talked by Schoenberg's champions, there are fascinations in the serialist game which long effort and familiarity would reveal. And I must concede it to my opponents that I do not make the effort because I am dogmatically convinced that Mozart will be more worthwhile every time. At the same time I must admit that one of the unintended consequences of my dogmatism is in fact a worsening of the situation for composers writing now. For, if my arguments in this paper hold, it is not only the historicist creed that prevents them from writing now in Mozart's or Beethoven's idiom. They may curse or at least deplore the changes Wagner or Schoenberg introduced into the language of music, but they cannot wholly undo them. To be sure, it is open to anyone today to write in a classical or preclassical idiom, and I hope I am not betraying any secret if I mention that Popper has taken this course, writing fugues in the strict style of Bach. I do not know whether he would do so if he were a professional composer rather than a philosopher. At any rate, whether he would, or not, he could not prevent his choice to mean something different from what it meant in Bach's time. Not that Johann Sebastian himself was a vanguard or fashionable composer. On the contrary. He was certainly somewhat out of touch with latest developments. But he did not try to write like Lassus or Palestrina.

I cannot write fugues in any case; but I am not sure that, if I could, I would not be swayed by the consideration summed up in the Latin proverb "si duo faciunt idem, non est idem". In other words I would find it a problem how far to "give in to the times".

It is this logic of the situation that makes artists and critics so susceptible to the historicist's message. If the past cannot be retrieved, why not enjoy the drift to the future? The Hegelian theories they like to appeal to are, from this point of view, little more than what psychoanalysts call rationalisations. They provide a grand excuse for what Quintilian did with a shrug of his shoulders. They neither have his wisdom nor his humility to use his argument; for to "make concessions" is the worst sin in their code, "to be committed or engaged" the greatest virtue.

It is here, I think, that the nonhistoricist could help to break the deadlock by pointing out that life consists in making concessions and that situations in art may exact them from the participants, not, indeed, as virtues but neither as terrible vices.

All artists must be opportunists if we mean by "opportunism" the desire to be liked, to be heard and considered, especially by their friends and their friends' friends. It is in this way that the polarisation of opinion will generally react on the artist who is reluctant for his work to appear in a garb that will "put off" his friends. The difference here between the genuine artist and the mere time server is not, therefore, that the one forges ahead regardless of anyone, while the other wants to please the right people. It is that for the real artist concessions will be mainly matters of avoidance. He will instinctively turn away from methods or styles that have come to sound hackneyed or unpromising; but he will leave all these considerations aside once he has found his problem and has started to wrestle with his material. In other words, the real artist will obviously do his best in a situation in which the plasticity of taste and the corruptibility of his medium will have deprived him of any firm standards except those provided by his artistic conscience. He will neither eat out his heart in nostalgia, nor set his sights on a future which may never come, but will use the material at hand. As a painter once said to me who was himself critical of abstract painting and had succumbed—one must go where the fighting is! Rationalisation or not, it is hard to see how this reaction can be wholly avoided in the situation in which artists find themselves. Even after the hoped-for demise of historicist creeds the whirlygig of fashion will turn on Vanity Fair. It lies in the logic of the situation, as I have tried to show, that those arts which are no longer anchored in practical functions will be most easily drawn into this giddy movement. This is one of the unintended consequences of that emancipation from utilitarian ties for which so many great artists strove. No wonder artists today tend not only to be historicists but also romantics longing for a return to the shelter of a closed society, past or future. But if that is the choice, the fair is preferable to the barrack square.

The results to which I have come in this paper are a little distasteful to my own inclinations and prejudices. I certainly would not want them to provide ammunition for those who talk of the "inevitability" of any particular development in modern art, nor would I want to cheer the trimmers and opportunists on their way to success. I would therefore not have ventured to draw such dangerous conclusions from the flimsy premises of Vanity Fair, if I did not hope that they may provoke Sir Karl Popper to a critical reaction that will restore the independence of art from social pressures and vindicate the objectivity of its values.

SIR ERNST GOMBRICH

THE WARBURG INSTITUTE
UNIVERSITY OF LONDON, ENGLAND
NOVEMBER, 1965

NOTES

[1] K. R. Popper, *The Poverty of Historicism* (London: Routledge & Kegan Paul, 1957). Hereinafter cited as *PH*.

[2] Karl Mannheim, "Beiträge zur Theorie der Weltanschauungs-Interpretation", *Jahrbuch für Kunstgeschichte* (Vienna, 1921/22), I, p. 237-74.

[3] Cp. E. H. Gombrich, "Art and Scholarship" reprinted in *Meditations on a Hobby Horse & Other Essays on the Theory of Art* (London: Phaidon Press, 1963). Hereinafter cited as *MHH*.

[4] For an informative survey of the situation see James S. Ackerman and Rhys Carpenter, *Art and Archaeology*, in *Princeton Studies on Humanistic Scholarship in America*, ed. by R. Schlatter (Englewood Cliffs, N. J.: Prentice-Hall, 1963).

[5] E. H. Gombrich, *Art and Illusion* (New York: Pantheon Books, 1960; London: Phaidon Press, 1961).

[6] *PH*, p. 149.

[7] K. R. Popper, *The Open Society and Its Enemies*, 2 vols., 2d ed., rev. and enl. (London: Routledge & Kegan Paul, 1952), Vol. II, p. 89. Hereinafter cited as *O.S.*

[8] *O.S.*, Vol. II, p. 96. See also (for a similar formulation) "Theory of Tradition", in K. R. Popper, *Conjectures and Refutations: The Growth of Scientific Knowledge* (London: Routledge & Kegan Paul, 1965), esp. p. 124. Hereinafter cited as *C.&R.*

[9] I have dealt with some of these questions in an article on "Style", *International Encyclopedia of Social Science* (New York: Macmillan Co., and Free Press, 1968), Vol. 15, pp. 352-61. The present contribution hopes to supplement rather than to duplicate that entry where, however, a fuller bibliography will be found.

[10] For a discussion of this aspect see the last chapter of my book *The Story of Art* (London: Phaidon Press, 1965.

[11] *PH*, p. 141.

[12] See my review of Thomas Munro, "Evolution in the Arts", in *The British Journal of Aesthetics*, **4**, No. 3 (July, 1964).

[13] Dwight E. Robinson, "Fashion Theory and Product Design", *Harvard Business Review*, **36**, No. 6 (1958), 126-38.

[14] Jean Gimpel, *The Cathedral Builders* (New York: Grove Press, 1961), p. 44.

[15] Cp. my paper, "The Renaissance Idea of Artistic Progress and its Consequences", *Actes du XVIIme Congrès International d'Histoire de l'Art 1952* (The Hague, 1955), 291-307. (Now reprinted in my *Norm und Form* [London: Phaidon Press, 1966]. Hereinafter cited as *NF*.)

[16] Adolf Göller, *Zur Ästhetik der Baukunst*, 1887, as summarised in Cornelius Gurlitt, *Die deutsche Kunst des Neunzehnten Jahrhunderts* (Berlin: Georg Bondi, 1899), p. 491.

[17] Karl Bühler, *Sprachtheorie* (Jena: Gustav Fischer, 1934).

[18] *Ars Poetica*, verse 46 ff. My translation is based on that by H. Rushton Fairclough in the Loeb Classical Library (London: Heinemann, 1947), pp. 455-57.

[19] Cp. my paper, "Ritualized Gesture and Expression in Art", *Philosophical Transactions of the Royal Society in London*, Series B, *Biological Sciences*, **251**, No. 772 (1966), 393-401.

[20] *O.S.*, Vol. II, pp. 307-8, 357 and "Theory of Tradition", in *C.&R.*, esp. p. 135.

[21] Cp. my *Art and Illusion*, pp. 375-76.

[22] *Institutio Oratoria*, VIII, vi, 51. My translation here and in the subsequent quotations is based on that by H. E. Butler in the Loeb Classical Library (London: Heinemann, 1959).

[23] J. F. d'Alton, *Roman Literary Theory and Criticism* (New York: Russell, 1931). I have discussed some of the influences of this quarrel in "Mannerism: The Historiographic Background", *Studies in Western Art, Acts of the XXth International Congress of the History of Art*, II (Princeton: Princeton University Press, 1963).

[24] *Institutio*, VIII, v, 34.

[25] *Institutio*, XII, x, 47.

[26] Cp. my *MHH*, Index s.v. "Avoidance" and "Expectancies".

[27] The term is applied to the followers of Caravaggio by G. B. Bellori in his *Idea*, 1672, translated in Elizabeth Holt, *A Documentary History of Art* (New York: Doubleday, 1958), Vol. II, p. 103. This seems to be the first application of an "ism" term to a movement in art.

[28] Vicenzio Carducho, *Dialogos de la pintura*, Madrid, 1633. The passage is also translated in Elizabeth Holt, *Documentary History of Art*, Vol. II, p. 209.

[29] As I was told by my mother who witnessed this incident.

[30] Frank Rutter, *Evolution in Modern Art* (London: Harrap, 1926), pp. 82-84.

[31] Cp. my "Psycho-Analysis and the History of Art" in *MHH*.

[32] *PH*, p. 149.

[33] Jonathan Swift, *A Voyage to Lilliput* (1727), Chap. IV. (I have used the text of the Oxford Edition [Oxford: Oxford University Press, 1919].)

[34] Cp. my review of Arnold Hauser, "The Social History of Art", in *MHH*.

[35] Francis Haskell, *Patrons and Painters* (London: Chatto & Windus, 1963), Chap. 3.

[36] Cp. my review of T. Munro, *Evolution in the Arts* quoted above.

[37] *PH*, Chap. 32.

[38] R. P. Dore, "The Special Problem of Agriculture", *The Listener* (London, September 9, 1965), 367.

[39] Geraldine Pelles, *Art, Artists and Society* (Englewood Cliffs: Prentice-Hall, 1963).

[40] *O.S.*, Chap. 10.

[41] *Art and Illusion*, Chap. 4.

[42] Cp. my lecture, "Visual Discovery through Art", *Arts Magazine* (December, 1965). (Now reprinted in *Psychology and the Visual Arts*, ed. by J. Hogg [Harmondsworth: Penguin Books, 1969].)

[43] Cp. my "Norma e Forma", *Filosofia*, **14**, No. 3 (July, 1963). (Now translated and reprinted in NF.)

[44] Gurlitt, "Die deutsche Kunst", p. 466 (see footnote 16, above).

[45] *PH*, p. 70.

[46] Thomas Munro, *Evolution in the Arts* (The Cleveland Museum of Art, 1963), Chap. XX.

[47] "On the Sources of Knowledge and of Ignorance", in *C.&R.*, esp. pp. 22 ff.

[48] Cp. my paper, "The Vogue of Abstract Art", in *MHH*.

[49] I believe I read this story in a Feuilleton of the Viennese critic, A. F. Seligmann, who was presumably present.

[50] The line from Schiller's prologue to *Wallenstein* is as untranslatable as all such epigrams; its meaning lies somewhere between "Life is serious, art is gay" and "Life is business, art is play".

PART THREE

THE PHILOSOPHER REPLIES

Karl Popper

REPLIES TO MY CRITICS

I. INTRODUCTION

1. Aristophanes and the Socratic Legend

Nobody could be more impressed than I by the importance and excellence of Professor Schilpp's suggestion that a philosopher should be given a platform from which to reply to at least some of his critics.

But does it help? In Plato's *Apology*, Socrates replied to Aristophanes; and it certainly did not help him.

I have held for many years that this reply of Socrates' should, together with the rest of the *Apology,* be regarded as essentially historical. My arguments were compressed into the jumbo footnote 56 to Chapter 10 of *The Open Society,* and they were based on reasons which I have never seen criticized. (They were accepted by one outstanding Platonic scholar, Richard Robinson.) They make it possible to solve a cluster of historical problems in whose centre is the Socratic problem—a problem which, if soluble at all, can be solved *only* in the way in which this footnote solves it. Also entangled with it is the problem of "Plato's Progress" (as Gilbert Ryle calls his book), a problem which I have also tried to solve (in the n. 56 just referred to), though in a manner different from Ryle's.

The Socratic problem is, essentially, the problem of what is known about Socrates. (It is the problem of his historicity.) If we reject Plato's *Apology* as an essentially valid historical testimony then, even if we admit that a man named Socrates lived in Athens between 470 and 399, we are driven to the view that we simply know nothing about him. His immense influence must be explained as the influence not of Socrates but of the Socratic legend: the Socratic problem becomes insoluble because of our lack of knowledge. If, on the other hand, the *Apology* is regarded as essentially historical, then not only can we tap many other valuable sources, especially in the writings of Plato and to a lesser degree of Xenophon, which provide much corroboration, but we shall acquire a great possession: a Socrates full of life, a Socrates whose personality makes his influence comprehensible.[1] Moreover, we shall also be able to understand the genesis of the Socratic legend, created early in Socrates' life by Aristophanes.

These, in brief, are the credit and debit sides of accepting the *Apology* as historical. Why then has it so often and so emphatically been claimed to be unhistorical? The answer is, essentially and *almost* exclusively, that this testimony of Plato's in the *Apology* cannot be squared with the alleged testimony of Aristophanes.

This argument, however, was well known to Plato, and he therefore went out of his way to say explicitly and emphatically that Aristophanes' jokes were valueless as a testimony, and that they would have been fraudulent had he intended them to be taken seriously.

To this, the following two counterarguments are usually offered:[2]

(1) Plato's rejection of the testimony of Aristophanes is not Socrates' rejection.

(2) There must be some truth behind the jokes, otherwise they would not have been funny; Aristophanes was too experienced a jester and a craftsman to run this risk.

The answer to (1) is obvious. Socrates was not a writer; and had he been a writer, there was as yet no *Library of Living Philosophers*. The court of 501 jurymen before which Socrates was tried was by far the best platform open to him.

The answer to (2) is simple enough: nobody who has read Aristophanes can think that Aristophanes shared these fears about verisimilitude. Like some other great propagandists, he was never afraid of the big lie. Of course, there had to be some grain of verisimilitude; but the obvious fact that Socrates was in many, though not in all, respects a Sophist, or a near Sophist—that he was well known as one of the most powerful combatants in the verbal battles of the Sophists—gave Aristophanes all the verisimilitude he needed for creating the Socratic legend.[3]

It will be seen that about the historicity of Plato's *Apology* and Aristophanes' *Clouds* I am in agreement with W. K. C. Guthrie and his great *History of Greek Philosophy*.[4]

I regard myself as a disciple of Socrates, that is, of the speaker of the *Apology*,[5] and I love the man. This is why I am so interested—indeed almost passionately interested—in the Socratic problem. Moreover, I am in the fortunate position of being not only an admirer but also a critic of Socrates: I am a critic of his essentialism, including his essentialist theory of induction, just as I am an admirer of his self-critical search for truth. I am also an admirer of Plato's thought, and at the same time I am repelled by his ethics; and I conjecture that he never intended his Socratic dialogues (apart from the *Apology*, in which he explicitly refers to himself as an eyewitness) to be read as historical reports, though he may have intended some of them as parts of a composite personal portrait. All this helps me, I think, to uphold my conjecture about the historical character of the *Apology* without being dogmatic about it.

The fact that I love the man may make my position suspect to some. My reply to this suggestion is that without a strong personal interest, whether admitted or not, nobody is likely to get involved in this problem. In consciously admitting my involvement I am more likely to retain my critical attitude than if I were to think of myself as unbiased.

2. The Popper Legend

Nothing could be further from my mind than comparing myself to Socrates. But by showing that even the teaching of such a person as myself has given rise to a legend—and to a legend which is a perverse distortion of the truth—I may perhaps make a contribution to the destruction of the Socratic legend due to Aristophanes. For the existence of the Popper legend shows how easily a legend can arise, even under less favourable circumstances than those which gave rise to the Socratic legend. There was no Aristophanes who wanted, deliberately and frankly, to make fun of me. And there were books in which I had protested against the various parts of the legend,[6] and older books and papers[7] to which I referred in these protests, and which needed only to be read to disprove the legend. Nevertheless, the legend grew, and it continues to grow. What are the main facts, and what is the legend?

(1) I have always been a *metaphysical realist*.[8] Consequently, I upheld the view that, though some metaphysicians did perhaps talk nonsense, as did also some antimetaphysicians, the meaningfulness of some metaphysical ideas (such as realism or atomism) can be shown by their historical influence on the growth of scientific theories. Thus I always opposed those who declared that all metaphysics is meaningless pseudotalk, and I especially opposed the attempts of the Vienna Circle positivists who tried to back their views by developing a criterion of meaningfulness or literal significance.[9]

(2) I criticized in general as a form of dogmatism the enterprise of trying to set up such a criterion of meaning, and I criticized in particular as "too narrow and too wide" the proposed verifiability criterion of meaning; for it excluded unintentionally the theories of science and included as meaningful, just as unintentionally, some typical existential statements of metaphysics.

(3) I pointed out that this whole enterprise was an attempt to solve a pseudoproblem (an attempt to kill rather than to recognize metaphysics), and that this pseudoproblem had usurped the logical place belonging to a serious and real problem, whose significance had impressed itself on me years before I ever heard about the Vienna Circle. I mean the problem of demarcating between empirical statements or statements of the empirical sciences on the one hand, and nonempirical statements on the other; examples of which are the statements of a pseudoscience like astrology, and also logical and metaphysical statements. This problem I called the problem of demarcation

between science and nonscience, and I explained how it was the real problem hidden behind the positivists' (pseudo-) "problem of meaningfulness" or "significance". I showed that the positivists were convinced a priori that metaphysical talk was meaningless, and they therefore assumed *uncritically* that the problem of demarcation between science and metaphysics was to be solved by the formulation of a criterion of meaningfulness.

(4) I also suggested a solution of the problem of demarcation (but of course *not* of the pseudoproblem of meaning or significance), that is, the criterion of testability or refutability or falsifiability. And I argued that, whereas the criterion of meaning suggested by the positivists, that is, verifiability, leads to paradoxical consequences and to a wrong demarcation, my criterion of falsifiability—if taken as a criterion *not* of meaning, but of demarcation—has a number of fruitful consequences; more especially, it prepares the way for a theory of testability and content, and for a solution of the problem of induction. (I also pointed out that, if falsifiability were substituted for verifiability as a criterion of *meaning*, rather than of demarcation, it would lead, like verifiability, to absurd consequences.)

Now the Popper legend affirms the opposite of every one of these points

(1') The legend has it that Popper was (and perhaps still is) a positivist and perhaps also a member of the Vienna Circle.

(2') Accordingly, says the legend, Popper was also in favour of a criterion of meaningfulness or literal significance, in order to exclude metaphysics as meaningless.

(3') The legend is completely blind to the (for me) vitally important distinction between the problem of finding a criterion of meaning and that of finding a criterion of demarcation.

(4') The legend has it that Popper undertook a kind of rescue operation for the meaning criterion of "conclusive verifiability" (which somebody had shown to be too narrow and too wide) by introducing in its stead, as a new meaning criterion, falsifiability. Thus we can read in a recent and in many respects excellent paper on the subject by an American philosopher of the highest standing: "The difficulty presented [for] the principle of . . . verifiability . . . Prof. Karl Popper tried to circumvent [here there is a footnote reading 'Logik der Forschung 1935.'] by a new criterion, namely: that a statement counts as meaningful if it is in principle *falsifiable*."[10] And it is further often pointed out[11] that this leads to the new difficulty that purely existential statements like "Atoms exist" or "Unicorns exist" (though they are, after all, in principle verifiable) become meaningless, according to my legendary proposal; which, and I would hardly disagree, establishes the absurdity of this alleged proposal of mine.

The legend, in all its points, is clearly implicit in the quoted paper, which is fairly recent (1967). It is still implicit in the latest book (1970)[12] on the positivists' problem of meaning to have come to my notice; here the mistake is hardly excusable because the author refers several times to my "Demarcation" paper in Schilpp's *Carnap* volume ([1955(g)], [1964(b)]; also [1963(a)], Chap. 11) where I defended at length, in section 2, my view that among the meaningful theories of a language, "[there] will be well-testable theories, hardly testable theories, and non-testable theories. Those which are non-testable . . . may be described as metaphysical". (Schilpp's *Carnap* volume, p. 187; and *C.&R.*, p. 257.) And a little later on the same page I wrote: "beginning with my first publication on this subject," (there is here a reference to [1933(a)]; that is [1959(a)], pp. 312-14) "I stressed the fact that it would be *inadequate* to draw the line of demarcation . . . so as to exclude metaphysics as nonsensical from a meaningful language." One can hardly be more explicit.

It seems to me that the legend is widespread, although it is difficult to explain why a doctrine so obviously mistaken and indeed silly, should be so frequently referred to. The explanation is, no doubt, that the legend seems to have the highest authority to back it: it can be read into A. J. Ayer's *Language, Truth and Logic* (although not all of it is explicitly there, except for the identification of my refutability criterion with a criterion of meaning);[13] it can be read into some remarks by Rudolf Carnap; it can be read into some remarks by C. G. Hempel (the hints or reservations added by Hempel turned out to be insufficient to prevent misinterpretation); and it is almost unambiguously stated by Jørgen Jørgensen in his authoritative historical narrative in the *International Encyclopedia of Unified Science*.[14]

I shall say more about Carnap's and Hempel's remarks in the next section. Here I will only point out that we can learn from this not to put too much weight on the testimony even of learned professional witnesses: not a trace of Aristophanean intention to caricature my views can be found in the reports of any of the authorities mentioned.

We should therefore sift very critically even what Plato and Aristotle have to say about Socrates; but Aristophanes as a witness need not be taken seriously at all, especially in view of the explicit rejection of his testimony that can be found in the *Apology*.

3. The Background of the Legend: Criterion of Demarcation versus Criterion of Meaning

Why is it important to distinguish between my criterion of demarcation and a positivistic criterion of meaningfulness?

It was the central dogma of the positivists of the Vienna Circle that metaphysics is sheer balderdash: that its assertions are not false, but no assertions at all—just senseless babble. They originally thought that the natural grammatical rules of meaningful language excluded every possibility of talking correctly—grammatically correctly—about anything but observable or empirical facts; for they believed that the denotation of a word was always an empirical object, and the meaning of a sentence a verifiable empirical fact.

It is to be admitted, of course, that some metaphysicians did utter pronouncements which could fairly be suspected of being balderdash. For example, there exists, I believe, no commentary to Plato's *Parmenides* which succeeds really satisfactorily in dispelling the suspicion that some of it is pointless or even meaningless. But the *Parmenides* is in this respect unique in Plato's work, and, should it contain some meaningless (as opposed to merely invalid) arguments, then this is probably due to the inherent difficulty of saying what Plato wanted to say. Metaphysical formulations are often clumsy and unfortunate (such as the positivists' standard example "The Absolute is perfect") rather than ungrammatical (such as "Socrates is identical"—an example due to Wittgenstein).

It is quite possible that those who say "The Absolute is perfect" wish to say that the world, if properly understood, could not be better. This seems to me false, but not meaningless; for the statement, "A world in which there are concentration camps, torture, and war is highly imperfect", seems to me perfectly true, and its negation false, and therefore at any rate meaningful.

Like many other philosophers—and many positivists among them—I dislike high-sounding jargon. But I believe that the positivists were wrong when they thought that high-sounding jargon was peculiar to metaphysics, or typical of it. And I was always convinced that realism—commonsense realism—was a most important metaphysical doctrine. In holding this view I stood of course in contrast to all those Machians who thought that only subjective experiences ("sense data") were real and that things, and selves, especially "other selves", were "mere logical constructions" out of experiences (or "potential experiences"). In fact, this talk about "mere logical constructions" always repelled me as high-sounding jargon, jargon almost as bad as "The Absolute is perfect".

Realism—that is, commonsense realism—is a metaphysical theory, but it seems to me of the utmost importance for epistemology (it can be "based", though not established, on a criticism of epistemological arguments); and also for methodology, which can be or, I think, even has to be, to a great extent based on realism. As it entails the existence of other minds, it is also of the utmost importance for ethics (which is of no interest if we regard the suffering of other people as merely apparent), and altogether for any sane outlook on human life. I think that certain forms of positivism, on the other hand,—Mach's "neutral monism", for instance—are not only false, but bordering on nonsense. It is not that they are ungrammatical; but they make nonsense of our lives, since they reduce to irrelevance all human activity, including science and their own scholastic discussions of epistemology.

Since I was a convinced adherent of a certain kind of metaphysics, I was of course of the opinion that the positivists' use of meaningfulness as a criterion of demarcation between science and metaphysics was a grave error; for they asserted that only the statements of the natural sciences were meaningful. Consequently even what I regarded as the *true* statements among the talk of the metaphysicians were, according to the positivists, merely meaningless pseudotalk.

Of the contributors to the present volume Paul Bernays has, to my great relief, seen the point very clearly, as a glance at the second paragraph of the first section of his paper will show. His paper is mainly devoted to a different problem; but, referring to my paper "The Demarcation Between Science and Metaphysics" (*C.&R.*, Chap. 11) Bernays writes: "In this paper Popper explains the main point of his highly effective criticism of positivism. Positivist philosophy declares to be meaningless everything that is not scientific. *In a convincing argument Popper insists that it will not do to identify the distinguishing criterion of what is scientific with the criterion of what is meaningful.* The restricting criteria for meaningfulness proposed by the positivists are all shown to be inadequate, and Popper presents a criterion of demarcation between scientific and unscientific statements which is quite independent of the question of meaning. . . . " (Italics mine.)

Nothing could be clearer and further removed from the Popper legend than this description given by Bernays of my position. But then, Bernays was never a positivist; he started, like myself, as a Kantian. (For his present philosophical position he largely credits the influence of Professor Ferdinand Gonseth.)

But the fact that the positivists used their criterion of verifiability and meaningfulness also as a criterion of demarcation made them deaf and blind to the fact that I used falsifiability as a criterion of demarcation, but never of meaningfulness.

In a way one can explain the Popper legend as the almost necessary consequence of two things: (1) the almost incredibly warm reception and the almost complete acceptance which my criticism of the Circle received from a number of its leading members: from Feigl at my first meeting with him (according to him in 1929), from Victor Kraft and Heinrich Gomperz even a little earlier (but these two were themselves critically inclined towards some of the main dogmas of the Circle), from Carnap, from Waismann, and for a time also from Hempel;[15] (2) the fact that, although converted by most of my arguments—Carnap was even prepared to sacrifice the view that metaphysics was necessarily meaningless in every consistent language—they tried to rescue the dogma of the meaninglessness of metaphysics in a modified form:

Carnap hoped that it would be at least possible to construct some artificial language which contained science but excluded metaphysics. At least relative to this projected new language—*relative to "the language of science"* —metaphysics could still be described as meaningless.

This is the historical background of Carnap's and Hempel's unsuccessful attempts to construct such a "language of science". These attempts were continued for many years but remained, for reasons explained in the foregoing section, unsuccessful. The first of them was made in Carnap's famous paper "Testability and Meaning" (1936-37),[16] in which Carnap proposed, in essence, to construct a language of science which excluded metaphysics. A most influential report about the lack of success of the enterprise was Hempel's almost equally famous paper "Problems and Changes in the Empiricist Criterion of Meaning".[17] Essentially, the Popper legend springs from these sources, and from the books by Ayer and Jørgensen mentioned in the preceding section (see nn. 13 and 14).[18]

These are the outlines of the story. The details are as follows.

When I stayed with Carnap and Feigl in the Tyrol, in 1932,[19] I had with me the MS of my still unpublished first book, *Die beiden Grundprobleme der Erkenntnistheorie* (*The Two Fundamental Problems of the Theory of Knowledge*), which dealt with the problems of induction and demarcation. Its contents were briefly outlined in the first chapter of *The Logic of Scientific Discovery.*

In our daily conversations in the Tyrol, one of the main points was my contention that the idea of (absolute) "meaningfulness" or "meaninglessness" was dogmatic and untenable. I admitted that *"Socrates ist identisch"* ("Socrates is identical") was meaningless in current German (or English). But I asserted that some metaphysician may at any time make it meaningful by identifying the predicate "is identical" with the predicate "is self-identical", explaining "self-identical" perhaps as "conscious of where he belongs—to which country, or group of people". In this way most, if not every, meaningless phrase of a given language may be made meaningful within a slightly more expansive language. As a consequence, I asserted, the problem of meaning was relative to a given language (and context); and even if a metaphysician could be shown to speak nonsense with respect to the language L_1, this need not trouble him at all, or kill his metaphysics. For he could always explain that he was talking in a slightly different language L_2, and that in this language his talk was meaningful. There was not even any need for him to be able to translate his talk from L_2 to L_1, or to define his terms in L_2 or in L_1, as may be shown by the following examples: you cannot fully translate the language of (typefree) axiomatic set theory into, say, the language of Whitehead and Russell, or vice versa; nor can you demand (as did Wittgenstein in his *Tractatus,* 6.53) that we define or "give meaning" (ostensively) to all our terms, for in every language there necessarily are undefined terms, and in most ordinary languages used in science there are[20] undefined terms with nonostensive meanings (like point, mass point, electron, gene). I thus argued against the *"positivistic intolerance"* which I felt was implicit in their search for a general criterion of meaning. (As I heard a little later from Karl Menger, he had used independently, and apparently before me, quite similar arguments against Carnap's linguistic intolerance.)[21]

It seems to me that this criticism convinced Carnap. At any rate, in an important paper "Über Protokollsätze" ("On Protocol Sentences"),[22] Carnap stressed, in a reply to Neurath, the possible *multiplicity of methods of constructing the language of science*. He says, against Neurath, "it is not a clash between two conflicting dogmas which is here at stake but rather *two different methods of constructing the language of science, which are both possible and justifiable*. In what follows here, both methods shall be explained in some detail".[23]

Thus Carnap approaches here very closely to what he described later in his *Logical Syntax of Language*, section 17, as his "Principle of Tolerance".[24]

In the article itself, two "forms of the language of science" are discussed and compared. They are called on page 223 "Procedure A" and "Procedure B". Starting at the bottom of page 223, Carnap explains in some detail "Procedure B", which he attributes to me, and of which he ultimately says (p. 228), that "Popper, proceeding from different initial assumptions arrives one step further than Neurath". And after a lengthy comparison of Neurath's protocol sentences with my procedure of testing and testability, Carnap sums up as his final judgement: "Weighing all the various points considered, it seems to me that the second form of language, with procedure B [i.e. Popper's procedure] is the best among the at present competing forms of the language of science (which are usually not presented as suggestions for a form of language, but as a 'theory of the building up of knowledge')."[25]

Carnap had not told me that he was writing this article, and the first I knew about it was when he sent me offprints, only three months after our meeting in the Tyrol.

I was of course encouraged and made proud by Carnap's judgement of my work. Carnap had described in detail my way of interpreting experiments, and of the testing of experiments in their turn, as a fundamentally *objective* procedure in which subjective experiences play a totally inferior role, so that personal convictions (perceptions) never decide the outcome of an experiment. This was in sharp contrast to Neurath's view of "protocol sentences". Nevertheless, Carnap did not see how great the contrast was. And although he characterized my view, quite rightly, by saying "everything proceeds in the intersubjective, physicalistic language",[26] he also remarked that "in practice" we "shall frequently stop with the perceptual statements of the protocol-writing subject. This has no fundamental significance, but it happens only because the intersubjective testing of statements about perceptions (brain processes) is *relatively complicated and difficult* . . . ".[27] (Italics mine.)

This was a characteristically subjectivist mistake in the presentation of my theory; for according to my theory we stop the sequence of tests at the most easily intersubjectively testable experiments, such as a meter reading or a photographic plate, on which everybody can make up his mind, rather than at statements—such as protocol statements or perception statements—whose intersubjective tests are "relatively complicated and difficult". I pointed out the mistake, very briefly, in my *Logik der Forschung*;[28] too briefly, I think, for anybody to notice it. (That Carnap made this mistake was clearly part of his failure to free himself from the myth that perception statements or "protocol statements" normally play an important role in experimental science.)

I was thirty at the time, and though I had written my first book, I had no publisher for it;[29] and so far I myself had published nothing whatever on the subject in question. Yet here I was faced with great praise and the actual acceptance, by the leading proponent of the subject, of my antipositivist and objectivist views! It was an exciting but also a difficult situation.

It made me, of course, want to emphasize as soon as possible and with sufficient clarity that I was opposed to the thesis that metaphysics is meaningless. I did this both in my letter to the Editors of *Erkenntnis*[30] and, when it ultimately came out, even more sharply in my *Logik der Forschung*. The task was not a very easy one, owing to my own hostility to several forms of metaphysics, especially to the still ruling Hegelian form. (Even Otto Neurath, the leading anti-Kantian of the Circle, expressed great sympathy with Hegel.)

Carnap's paper of 1932, "On Protocol Sentences", created in Vienna a certain local sensation; I was invited to lecture to various philosophical groups, such as Edgar Zilsel's, and in time I was labelled, by Otto Neurath, as "the official opposition of the Vienna Circle". There were, among the members of the Circle, two groups: those who accepted many or most of my ideas and those who felt that these ideas were dangerous and to be combated. To the first belonged (in alphabetical order) Carnap, Feigl, Frank, Gomperz, Hahn, Hempel, Kraft, Menger, R. von Mises, and Waismann. (It should be remarked that some of the members of this group differed from each other radically on various important points, especially Waismann from Carnap.) The most important members of the other group were Otto Neurath, Reichenbach, and Schlick.

Trying to look back to those days from a distance of almost forty years, it seems to me that only Neurath and Schlick took my attitude towards metaphysics seriously, and thus realized that I really was not a positivist and, in some sense of the word, not even an empiricist, but close to a position Neurath called "rationalism" or "pseudorationalism".[31]

Carnap merely concluded his long and otherwise most positive review of *Logik der Forschung* with the remark that "in trying to explain clearly his [Popper's] point of view, Popper is frequently seduced to an overemphasis of the differences to other views, especially to those most closely related [i.e. positivism] . . . . Seeing that Popper speaks mostly in a highly derogatory way about conventionalism and positivism, and even about empiricism, while he treats for example Kant in a less derogatory way, and seeing also that he treats even metaphysics in a moderately favourable way, a careless reader might think that Popper must be, if not a metaphysician at least an apriorist and an anti-empiricist. His actual discussions show, however, that he is an empiricist and an opponent of apriorism."[32]

This last statement was certainly correct; I was, and still am, an empiricist of sorts, though certainly not a naive empiricist who believes that "all knowledge stems from our perceptions or sense data". My empiricism consisted in the view that, though all experience was theory-impregnated, it was experience which in the end could decide the fate of a theory, by knocking it out; and also in the view that only such theories which in principle were capable of being thus refuted merited to be counted among the theories of "empirical science".

Hempel reviewed my *Logik der Forschung* as favourably as Carnap did;[33] and in his last paragraph he criticized me, as Carnap did, for my critical attitude to the positivism of the Vienna Circle "from whose members he has undoubtedly received suggestions of many kinds, and to whom he has from his side made important contributions"; and he criticized me for "exaggerating the existing differences of opinion", and for "stressing certain views he holds in common with metaphysically orientated thinkers".

It will be seen from Carnap's and Hempel's reviews that they did not like my prometaphysical remarks, but that they were not impressed by them, and did not take them very seriously. *As a consequence, they did not take very seriously my distinction between my criterion of demarcation between science and metaphysics and their criterion of the meaninglessness of metaphysics.*

This, I think, explains the origin of the Popper legend, and of the fact that Carnap and Hempel, who had in their reviews described my criterion of demarcation very clearly, both stressing that it was not intended as a criterion of meaning, nevertheless forgot this point, and continued to identify empirical character with meaningfulness. Carnap had indeed described my position with approval in his review of 1935: "*Testability forms the criterion of demarcation between empirical science and metaphysics*; or more

precisely, falsifiability."[34] But a year later he published his famous paper
"Testability and Meaning"[35] in which, essentially, the proposal was made to
accept testability not only as a possible criterion of demarcation, but in
addition as a possible criterion of meaning, for a new language of science, still
to be constructed.

I think that the very name of the essay "Testability and Meaning" sealed
the fate of the legend, especially as Carnap had taken over from me, with
small adjustments and ample references to me, the theories of the
relationship between testability, falsifiability, and falsification, *"Bewährung"*
and *"Bewährbarkeit"* (which he translated by "confirmation" and "confir-
mability", while I later preferred the terms "corroboration" and "corroborability").[36]

It is interesting that in "Testability and Meaning" Carnap had not yet
forgotten my strictures. He says: "It is not the aim of the present essay to
defend the principle of empiricism against apriorism or anti-empiricist
metaphysics. Taking empiricism for granted, we wish to discuss the question,
what is meaningful."[37] And to the word "empiricism" in the last sentence is
added the footnote: "The words 'empiricism' and 'empiricist' are here
understood in their widest sense, and not in the narrower sense of traditional
positivism or sensationalism or any other doctrine restricting empirical
knowledge to a certain kind of experience."

It is clear that Carnap was most anxious to avoid any kind of dogmatic
narrowness, and I was greatly impressed by his generous acceptance of my
criticism in *Logik der Forschung*, and with his admission of mistakes earlier
committed. He now described the task of solving "the problem of a criterion
of meaning" as that of constructing an artificial model language in which all
the statements of science could be expressed but not "perhaps most of the
sentences occurring in the books of metaphysicians".[38] In other words, the
old problem of meaning, and of the meaninglessness of metaphysics, was
resurrected as the problem of constructing a language in which, in the main,
only scientific statements, not metaphysical statements, would be admitted,
or "meaningful".

As I say, I was greatly impressed by Carnap's new antidogmatic
attitude, and by his readiness to conciliate his opponents. I even did not see at
once why the new programme of constructing a metaphysics-free language
of science should not be realizable. Moreover, the problem of meaning and
meaninglessness had never been one of my own pet interests. As a
consequence, for many years I wrote nothing about Carnap's new theory of
meaning, although I did write in the first edition of *The Open Society* in 1945
quite a bit against the possibility of positivistic theories of meaning in
general, and of Wittgenstein's theory in particular.[39] (However, I saw clearly
that the exclusion of metaphysics from a specially constructed language of

science would infect, in part, its *terminology*, and therefore, for reasons already indicated, be impracticable: we always need undefined theoretical terms.)[40]

Yet I found out fairly soon that Carnap's programme of a language of science which "naturally" excludes metaphysics was impossible. First, because we could always extend it by new undefined terms; there was no natural criterion that distinguished between scientific and metaphysical undefined theoretical terms. (Berkeley and Mach had regarded "atom" and "corpuscle" as metaphysical terms.) Secondly, because the most obviously metaphysical ideas, such as the idea of an omnipotent, omniscient, and omnipresent God, could be defined within Carnap's language, as I have shown.[41]

Thus, even Carnap's very liberal programme for the construction of a language of science in which metaphysics became ungrammatical or meaningless could not be carried out.[42]

This seemed to me to clinch the issue; the linguistic elimination of metaphysics was no genuine problem. And since there was a host of genuine and urgent philosophical problems which interested me, I was not sorry to find this out.

In 1950, fourteen years after Carnap's suggestion to construct a language of science free of metaphysics, Hempel first published his famous historical survey article, "Problems and Changes in the Empiricist Criterion of Meaning".[43] In this article, Hempel introduces his problem by first formulating what he calls the "fundamental tenet of modern empiricism",[44] and he at once continues: "Contemporary logical empiricism has added to it the maxim that a sentence makes a cognitively meaningful assertion . . . only if it is either (1) analytic or self-contradictory or (2) *capable, at least in principle, of experiential test*."[45]

Thus the fate of the testability criterion of meaning (proposed as we have seen by Carnap in "Testability and Meaning") is taken to form the main problem of this survey article.

Hempel discusses first the "requirement of complete verifiability in principle", which, he says, "has several serious defects": it excludes universal laws, as "pointed out by various writers"; what is worse, though this and other "defects . . . do not seem to have been widely noticed", it admits their negations, the purely existential statements. For it is unacceptable to say that a sentence is meaningful and its negation is meaningless (or vice versa).

In the second place, Hempel discusses "the requirement of complete falsifiability in principle". This requirement of meaningfulness he ascribes, somewhat halfheartedly, to me, in a footnote[46] which says: "The idea of using theoretical falsifiability by observational evidence as the 'criterion of demarcation' separating empirical science from mathematics and logic on the one hand and from metaphysics on the other is due to K. Popper." Hempel gives some references and concludes his footnote with the words: "Whether Popper would subscribe to the proposed restatement of the falsifiability criterion, I do not know."

Thus Hempel is aware of the fact that there is a dispute here. But nowhere does he explain the dispute—demarcation criterion against meaning criterion.

It is not surprising therefore that even a careful reader of Hempel's survey will interpret it as confirming the Popper legend.

Incidentally, no explanation is given by Hempel of why Carnap's programme was unsuccessful.

In conclusion, I want to repeat why I regard the difference between positivism (or phenomenalism) and a point of view like mine as crucial: it is the problem of the admissibility of commonsense realism. This was debarred by Machian positivism and the logical positivism of the Vienna Circle as metaphysical. Even Feigl, who later became a realist, argued at our first meeting that realism must not be admitted. Against this, I regard the existence of bodies, of forces, of fields of forces, of selves, of various degrees and levels of consciousness and of other selves, and of objective ideas (contents of thoughts which may survive the original thinker), as obviously legitimate tenets of any sensible philosophy. The attempt to exclude them as ungrammatical balderdash seems to me balderdash, though not ungrammatical.

4. Kraft on My Relation to the Vienna Circle

Victor Kraft in his contribution gives a crisp intellectual history of me, seen from the point of view of a leading member and historian of the Vienna Circle. I enjoyed his contribution greatly, although I sometimes see things, necessarily, in a different light.

Not only was I not a member of the Circle, knowing next to nothing about it beyond what could be found in publications, but I never even heard anything about it from any of its members until perhaps in my first meeting with Feigl. For me it remained something almost like a secret society, though one which was receiving great publicity. Members of the Circle, especially those who felt that my ideas were not uncongenial to their own and that I should be admitted to the Circle, may have looked upon me as a kind of near-member, as did Kraft and Feigl, and perhaps Carnap, Hempel, and Waismann. Yet in fact I never thought that I was as close to the Circle as that.

I had been an admirer of Schlick's work before I even heard of the Circle. Although I did not think that Schlick's *Erkenntnislehre* solved all the problems he set out to solve, I admired it tremendously for its clarity, for the novelty of some of its arguments, and above all for its uncompromising realism. When later, under the influence of Wittgenstein and Carnap and, I suppose, the Ernst Mach Society, Schlick and Feigl gave up realism and adopted something like "neutral monism" (Feigl, of course, later returned to realism), I was greatly disappointed.

It was this issue, realism, which divided me most strongly from the Vienna Circle; and I do not think that Kraft has stressed this point (though he mentions it in his section II, part 5).

It is connected most closely with my rejection of a criterion of meaningfulness, discussed in the foregoing section; and in this connection it is interesting that Kraft, in his summary, says of the development of the Circle, "The meaning-criterion of scientific knowledge was given up and Popper's criterion of testability was taken over", implying very clearly that my criterion of testability was not a meaning criterion. I do not doubt that this historical statement of Kraft's was true of himself and perhaps a few more members of the Circle; but that it did not hold for some of its leading members, especially for Carnap and Hempel, has been shown in the foregoing section: they did not give up the meaning criterion.

It was my anti-inductivism which induced Gomperz to draw my attention to Victor Kraft's most admirable book, *Die Grundformen der wissenschaftlichen Methoden*.

When I first arrived at the view that neither animals nor men—nor, especially, scientists—proceed by anything like induction, I did not think that this view was new; and, in a way, it was not. I found that "Liebig (in *Induktion und Deduktion*, 1865) was probably the first to reject the inductive method from the standpoint of natural science", as I put it in my *Logik der Forschung*.[47] But at first I failed to find any other empirically minded critics of induction. It was then that Heinrich Gomperz drew my attention to Victor Kraft's *Die Grundformen der wissenschaftlichen Methoden*, a unique work which developed with great force and clarity a noninductive methodology of science. Kraft did not draw any anti-empiricist conclusions from his deductivist approach. I referred to him as one of the few deductivists I had been able to find.[48] I was greatly cheered by Victor Kraft's book, and Gomperz encouraged me to write to Kraft and ask for a meeting. Kraft suggested that we should meet in a park near the University, and we met there two or three times. In this way I met my first member of the Vienna Circle (unless Gomperz was a member—but opinions are divided on whether he was a member or not; Neurath I had known slightly, before there was a Circle).

But as to influence, I think that I was more strongly influenced by Karl Bühler, the psychologist and member of the school of Külpe, than by any member of the Circle; except, that is, Richard von Mises, whose theory of probability I tried to remodel.

I see Victor Kraft, and also Schlick, Carnap, and Feigl as philosophers of outstanding achievement.

II. THE PROBLEM OF DEMARCATION

5. The Centre of the Dispute: The Problem of Demarcation

I have told in Chapter 1 of *Conjectures and Refutations* how the problem of demarcation between science and nonscience, including logic, metaphysics, and pseudoscience (*not* between true and false scientific theories) became fundamental for my whole intellectual development. I did not at first think of it as a philosophical problem: I was only a little over seventeen, and although I had read some philosophy, I did not dream of making a contribution of my own to it. But it was for me an urgent personal problem, and its solution helped me immensely in my personal decisions, such as my rejection of Freudian and Adlerian psychoanalysis and of Marxism.

Only after some years did I find to my surprise that there was a close connection between this problem and the classical problem of induction; and it was only then that I began to take it seriously. Looking back I can say that the problem of demarcation and my solution of it have proved fertile in many fields of philosophy. There are, so far as I am aware, only two other ideas which have become quite as important for my philosophy: indeterminism (the openness of the physical world, which I shall discuss when I come to reply to John Watkins's paper), and Tarski's theory of truth.

Since a number of contributors to this volume (and noncontributing critics) have attacked the idea of a criterion of demarcation, I shall discuss this idea anew in some detail. For I do not think that anybody can have even the most superficial understanding of my main ideas unless he understands this simple and straightforward idea in its simplicity, as well as in its complexity, for certain complications have to be introduced.

As an introduction I wish to announce an important principle and a few corollaries.

1. *All good science consists, and all good philosophy consists, of lucky oversimplification* or, if you prefer the term, *idealization*.

Comments: (a) our objects of study, whether swans or stars or philosophies, are complex—perhaps infinitely complex—but all we can say in a finite life and in as few words as practicable are simple things, which may nevertheless throw light on the world around us: the more light and the greater the simplicity, the better;

(b) some oversimplifications are very much better than others;

(c) obscurity is due either to incompetence or to the attempt to impress people by words.

2. It lies in the nature of the method, of oversimplification (or idealization) that we have to approach our problem *in stages*. Nearly every solution raises new problems. And very often the new problems produce their own peculiar oversimplifications which often turn out to be very fertile.

3. What we must avoid, like great artists, is the bad taste of a finicky scholasticism—getting tied up in little assertions or minor criticisms for the sake of criticism.

4. Criticism, as we shall see more clearly later, is the lifeblood of all rational thought. But we should criticize any theory always in its best and strongest form; if possible, repairing tacitly all its minor mistakes and concentrating on the great, leading, and simplifying ideas. Otherwise we shall be led into the swamp of scholasticism—of clever questions and answers which have a tendency of multiplying endlessly; a swamp from which there is no escape once we have slipped in; a swamp over which the paralysing vapours of the publication explosion hold an eternal sway.

To put it briefly: never lose sight of the main idea. Never get involved in little side issues if they can be avoided or solved in a simple straightforward way.

I now turn to my *problem of demarcation*, and to explaining how this problem is related to the problems of empirical content and of testability.

The great scientists, such as Galileo, Kepler, Newton, Einstein, and Bohr (to confine myself to a few of the dead) represent to me a simple but impressive idea of science. Obviously, no such list, however much extended, would *define* scientist or science *in extenso*. But it suggests for me an oversimplification, one from which we can, I think, learn a lot. It is the working of great scientists which I have in my mind as my paradigm for science. Not that I lack respect for the lesser ones; there are hundreds of great men and great scientists who come into the almost heroic category.

But with all respect for the lesser scientists, I wish to convey here a heroic and romantic idea of science and its workers: men who humbly devoted themselves to the search for truth, to the growth of our knowledge; men whose life consisted in an adventure of bold ideas. I am prepared to consider with them many of their less brilliant helpers who were equally devoted to the search for truth—for great truth. But I do not count among them those for whom science is no more than a profession, a technique: those who are not deeply moved by great problems and by the oversimplifications of bold solutions.

It is science in this heroic sense that I wish to study. As a side result I find that we can throw a lot of light even on the more modest workers in applied science.

This, then, for me is science. I do not try to define it, for very good reasons. I only wish to draw a simple picture of the kind of men I have in mind, and of their activities. And the picture will be an oversimplification: these are men of bold ideas, but highly critical of their own ideas; they try to find whether their ideas are right by trying first to find whether they are not perhaps wrong. They work with bold conjectures and severe attempts at refuting their own conjectures.

My criterion of demarcation between science and nonscience is a simple logical analysis of this picture. How good or bad it is will be shown by its fertility.

Bold ideas are new, daring, hypotheses or conjectures. And severe attempts at refutations are severe critical discussions and severe empirical tests.

When is a conjecture daring and when is it not daring, in the sense here proposed? Answer: it is daring if and only if it takes a great risk of being false—if matters could be otherwise, and seem at the time to be otherwise.

Let us consider a simple example. Copernicus's or Aristarchus's conjecture that the sun rather than the earth rests at the centre of the universe was an incredibly daring one. It was, incidentally, false; nobody accepts today the conjecture that the sun is (in the sense of Aristarchus and Copernicus) at rest in the centre of the universe. But this does not affect the boldness of the conjecture, nor its fertility. And one of its main consequences—that the earth does not rest at the centre of the universe but that it has (at least) a daily and an annual motion—is still fully accepted, in spite of some misunderstandings of relativity.[49]

But it is not the present acceptance of the theory which I wish to discuss, but its boldness. It was bold because it clashed with all then accepted views, *and* with the prima facie evidence of the senses. It was bold because it postulated a hitherto unknown hidden reality behind the appearances.

It was not bold in another very important sense: neither Aristarchus nor Copernicus suggested a feasible crucial experiment. In fact, they did not suggest that anything was wrong with the traditional appearances: they let the accepted appearances severely alone;[50] they only reinterpreted them. They were not anxious to stick out their necks by predicting new observable appearances.

To the degree that this is so, Aristarchus's and Copernicus's theories may be described in my terminology as unscientific or metaphysical. To the degree that Copernicus did make a number of minor predictions, his theory is, in my terminology, scientific. But even as a metaphysical theory it was far from meaningless; and in proposing a new bold view of the universe it made a tremendous contribution to the advent of the new science.

Kepler went much further. He too had a bold metaphysical view, partly based upon the Copernican theory, of the reality of the world. But his view led him to many new detailed predictions of the appearances. At first these predictions did not tally with the observations. He tried to reinterpret the observations in the light of his theories; but his addiction to the search for truth was even greater than his enthusiasm for the metaphysical harmony of the world. Thus he felt forced to give up a number of his favoured theories, one by one, and to replace them by others which fitted the facts. It was a great and a heartrending struggle. The final outcome, his famous and immensely important three laws, he did not really like—except the third. But they stood up to his severest tests—they agreed with the detailed appearances, the observations which he had inherited from Tycho.

Kepler's laws are excellent approximations to what we think today are the true movements of the planets of our solar system. They are even excellent approximations to the movements of the distant binary star systems which have since been discovered. Yet they are merely *approximations* to what seems to be the truth; *they are not true.*

They have been tested in the light of new theories—of Newton's theory and of Einstein's—which predicted small deviations from Kepler's laws. (According to Newton, Kepler's laws are correct only for two-body systems.)[51] Thus the crucial experiments went against Kepler, very slightly, but sufficiently clearly.

Of these three theories—Kepler's, Newton's, and Einstein's—the latest and still the most successful is Einstein's; and it was this theory which led me into the philosophy of science. What impressed me so greatly about Einstein's theory of gravitation were the following points.

(1) It was a very bold theory. It greatly deviated in its fundamental outlook from Newton's theory which at that time was utterly successful.[52]

(2) From the point of view of Einstein's theory, Newton's theory was an excellent approximation, though false (just as from the point of view of Newton's theory, Kepler's and Galileo's theories were excellent approximations, though false). Thus it is not its truth which decides the scientific character of a theory.

(3) Einstein derived from his theory three important predictions of vastly different observable effects, two of which had not been thought of by anybody before him, and all of which contradicted Newton's theory, so far as they could be said to fall within the field of application of this theory at all.

But what impressed me perhaps most were the following two points.

(4) Einstein declared that these predictions were crucial: if they did not agree with his precise theoretical calculations, he would regard his theory as

refuted.

(5) But even if they were observed as predicted, Einstein declared that *his theory was false*: he said that it would be a better approximation to the truth than Newton's, but he gave reasons why he would not, even if all predictions came out right, regard it as a true theory. He sketched a number of demands which a true theory (a unified field theory) would have to satisfy, and declared that his theory was at best an approximation to this so far unattained unified field theory.

(It may be remarked in passing that Einstein, like Kepler, failed to achieve his scientific dream—or his metaphysical dream: it does not matter in this context what label we use. What we call today Kepler's laws or Einstein's theory of gravitation are results which in no way satisfied their creators, who each continued to work on his dream to the end of his life. And even of Newton a similar point can be made: he never believed that a theory of action at a distance could be a finally acceptable explanation of gravity.)[53]

Einstein's theory was first tested by Eddington's famous eclipse experiment of 1919. In spite of his unbelief in the truth of his theory, his belief that it was merely a new important approximation towards the truth, Einstein never doubted the outcome of this experiment; the inner coherence, the inner logic of his theory convinced him that it was a step forward even though he thought that it could not be true. It has since passed a series of further tests, all very successfully. But some people still think the agreement between Einstein's theory and the observations may be the result of (incredibly improbable) accidents. It is impossible to rule this out; yet I shall say more about it later when I come to discuss the problem of induction in sections 13-19.

The picture of science at which I have so far only hinted may be sketched as follows.

There is a reality behind the world as it appears to us, possibly a many-layered reality, of which the appearances are the outermost layers. What the great scientist does is boldly to guess, daringly to conjecture, what these inner realities are like. This is akin to mythmaking. (Historically we can trace back the ideas of Newton via Anaximander to Hesiod,[54] and the ideas of Einstein via Faraday, Boscovich, Leibniz, and Descartes to Aristotle and Parmenides.)[55] The boldness can be gauged by the distance between the world of appearance and the conjectured reality, the explanatory hypotheses.

But there is another, a special kind of boldness—*the boldness of predicting* aspects of the world of appearance which so far have been overlooked but which it must possess if the conjectured reality is (more or less) right, if the explanatory hypotheses are (approximately) true. It is this more special kind of boldness which I have usually in mind when I speak of bold scientific conjectures. It is the boldness of a conjecture which takes a real risk—the risk of being tested, and refuted; the risk of clashing with reality.

Thus my proposal was, and is, that it is this second boldness, together with the readiness to look out for tests and refutations, which distinguishes "empirical" science from nonscience, and especially from prescientific myths and metaphysics.

I will call this proposal (D): (D) for *"demarcation"*.

The italicized proposal (D) is what I still regard as the centre of my philosophy. But I have always been highly critical of any idea of my own; and so I tried at once to find fault with this particular idea, years before I published it. And I published it together with the main results of this criticism. My criticism led me to a sequence of refinements or improvements of the proposal (D): they were not later concessions, but they were published together with the proposal as parts of the proposal itself.[56]

6. Difficulties of the Demarcation Proposal

(1) From the beginning I called my criterion of demarcation a *proposal*. This was partly because of my uneasiness about definitions and my dislike of them. Definitions are either abbreviations and therefore unnecessary, though perhaps convenient ("right-to-left definitions", as I called them in *The Open Society*) or they are Aristotelian attempts to "state the essence" of a word, and therefore unconscious conventional dogmas.[57] If I define "science" by my criterion of demarcation (I admit that this is more or less what I am doing) then anybody could propose another definition, such as "science is the sum total of true statements". A discussion of the merits of such definitions can be pretty pointless. This is why I gave here first a description of great or heroic science and then a proposal for a criterion which allows us to demarcate—roughly—this kind of science. Any demarcation in my sense *must* be rough. (This is one of the great differences from any formal meaning criterion of any artificial "language of science".) For the transition between metaphysics and science is not a sharp one: what was a metaphysical idea yesterday can become a testable scientific theory tomorrow; and this happens frequently (I gave various examples in *Logik der Forschung* and elsewhere; atomism is perhaps the best).

Thus one of the difficulties is that our criterion must not be too sharp; and in the chapter "Degrees of Testability" of *Logik der Forschung* I suggested (as a kind of second improvement of the criterion (D) of the foregoing section) that a theory is scientific to the degree to which it is testable.

This, incidentally, led later to one of the most fruitful discoveries of my *Logik der Forschung*: that there are degrees of testability (or of scientific character), which can be identified with degrees of empirical content (or informative content).

(2) The formula (D) of the foregoing section is expressed in somewhat psychological language. It can be considerably improved if one speaks of *theoretical systems* or *systems of statements*, as I did throughout *Logik der Forschung*. This leads at once to the recognition of one of the problems connected with the falsifiability criterion of demarcation: even if we can apply it to *systems* of statements, it may be difficult if not impossible to say which particular statement, or which subsystem of a system of statements, has been exposed to a particular experimental test. Thus we may describe a *system* as scientific or empirically testable, while being most uncertain about its constituent parts.

An example is Newton's theory of gravitation. It has often been asked whether Newton's Laws of Motion, or which of them, are masked definitions rather than empirical assertions.

My answer is as follows: Newton's theory is a system. *If we falsify it, we falsify the whole system.* We may perhaps put the blame on one of its laws or on another. But this means only that we *conjecture* that a certain change in the system will free it from falsification; or in other words, that we conjecture that a certain alternative system will be an improvement, a better approximation to the truth.

But this means: attributing the blame for a falsification to a certain subsystem is a typical hypothesis, a conjecture like any other, though perhaps hardly more than a vague suspicion if no definite alternative suggestion is being made. And the same applies the other way round: the decision that a certain subsystem is not to be blamed for the falsification is likewise a typical conjecture. The attribution or nonattribution of responsibility for failure is conjectural, like everything in science; and what matters is the proposal of a new alternative and competing conjectural system that is able to pass the falsifying test.

(3) Points (1) and (2) illustrate that however correct my criterion of bold conjectures and severe refutations may be, there are difficulties which must not be overlooked. A primitive difficulty of this kind may be described as follows. A biologist offers the conjecture that all swans are white. When black swans are discovered in Australia, he says that it is not refuted. He insists that these black swans are a new kind of bird since it is *part of the defining property* of a swan that it is white. In other words, he can escape the refutation, though I think that he is likely to learn more if he admits that he was wrong.

In any case—and this is very important—the theory "All swans are white" is refutable at least in the following clear logical sense: it must be declared refuted by anybody who accepts that there is at least one non-white swan.

(4) The principle involved in this example is a very primitive one, but it has a host of applications. For a long time chemists have been inclined to regard atomic weights, melting points, and similar properties as *defining properties* of materials: there can be no water whose freezing point differs from 0° C; it just would not be water, however similar in other respects it may be to water. But if this is so, then according to my criterion of demarcation "Water freezes at 0° C" would not be a scientific or an empirical statement; it would be a tautology—part of a definition.

Clearly, there is a problem here: either my criterion of demarcation is refuted, or we have to admit the possibility of discovering water whose freezing point is other than 0° C.

(5) I plead of course for the second possibility, and I hold that from this simple example we can learn a lot about the advantages of my proposal (D). For let us assume we have discovered water with a different freezing point. Is this still to be called "water"? *I assert that the question is totally irrelevant.* The scientific hypothesis was that a liquid (no matter what you call it) with a considerable list of chemical and physical properties freezes at 0° C. If any of these properites which have been conjectured to be constantly conjoined should not materialize then *we were wrong*; and thus *new and interesting problems open up*. The least of them is whether or not we should continue to call the liquid in question "water": *this* is purely arbitrary or conventional. Thus my criterion of demarcation is not only not refuted by this example: it helps us to discover what is significant for science and what is arbitrary and irrelevant.

(6) As I explained in the very first chapter of *Logik der Forschung*, we can always adopt evasive tactics in the face of refutations. I called these tactics (for historical reasons) "conventionalist stratagems [or twists]", but my friend Professor Hans Albert has found a much better term for them. He calls them *"immunizing tactics or stratagems"*: we can always immunize a theory against refutation. There are many such evasive immunizing tactics; and if nothing better occurs to us, we can always deny the objectivity—or even the existence—of the refuting observation. (Remember the people who *refused* to look through Galileo's telescope.)[58] Those intellectuals who are more interested in being right than in learning something interesting but unexpected are by no means rare exceptions.

(7) None of the difficulties so far discussed is terribly serious: it may seem that a little intellectual honesty would go a long way to overcome them. By and large this is true. But how can we describe this intellectual honesty in logical terms? I described it in *Logik der Forschung* as *a rule of method*, or a *methodological rule*: "Do not try to evade falsification, but stick your neck out!"

(8) But I was yet a little more self-critical in *Logik der Forschung*: I first noticed that such a rule of method is, necessarily, somewhat vague—as is the problem of demarcation altogether. Clearly, one can say that if you avoid falsification *at any price*, you give up empirical science in my sense. But I found that, in addition, supersensitivity with respect to refuting criticism was just as dangerous: there is a legitimate place for dogmatism, though a very limited place. He who gives up his theory too easily in the face of apparent refutations will never discover the possibilities inherent in his theory. *There is room in science for debate*: for attack and therefore also for defence. Only if we try to defend them can we learn all the different possibilities inherent in our theories. As always, science is conjecture. You have to conjecture when to stop defending a favourite theory, and when to try a new one.

(9) Thus I did not propose the simple rule: "Look out for refutations, and never dogmatically defend your theory." Still, it was much better advice than dogmatic defence at any price. The truth is that we must be constantly critical; self-critical with respect to our own theories, and self-critical with respect to our own criticism; and, of course, we must never evade an issue.

This, then, is roughly the *methodological form* of (D), of the criterion of demarcation. Propose theories which can be criticized. Think about possible decisive falsifying experiments—crucial experiments. But do not give up your theories too easily—not, at any rate, before you have critically examined your criticism.

As Professor Ayer blames me (cp. n. 56 to my section 5) because I "found it necessary to modify", in the manner described here, my principle of falsifiability "in the course of this very book [*L.d.F.*]" (in fact, in the course of its very first chapter; see the penultimate paragraph of its section 6) I gladly accept the blame: it turned out to be more fertile than sticking dogmatically for years to a (long ago refuted) sterile criterion of meaningfulness.

7. Empirical-Scientific and Nonscientific Theories

The difficulties connected with my criterion of demarcation (D) are important, but must not be exaggerated. It is vague, since it is a methodological rule, and since the demarcation between science and nonscience is vague. But it is more than sharp enough to make a distinction between many physical theories on the one hand, and metaphysical theories, such as psychoanalysis, or Marxism (in its present form), on the other. This is, of course, one of my main theses; and nobody who has not understood it can be said to have understood my theory.

The situation with Marxism is, incidentally, very different from that with psychoanalysis. Marxism was once a scientific theory: it predicted that capitalism would lead to increasing misery and, through a more or less mild revolution, to socialism; it predicted that this would happen first in the technically highest developed countries; and it predicted that the technical evolution of the "means of production" would lead to social, political, and ideological developments, rather than the other way round.

But the (so-called) socialist revolution came first in one of the technically backward countries. And instead of the means of production producing a new ideology, it was Lenin's and Stalin's ideology that Russia must push forward with its industrialization ("Socialism is dictatorship of the proletariat plus electrification") which promoted the new development of the means of production.

Thus one might say that Marxism was once a science, but one which was refuted by some of the facts which happened to clash with its predictions (I have here mentioned just a few of these facts).[59]

However, Marxism is no longer a science; for it broke the methodological rule that we must accept falsification, and it immunized itself against the most blatant refutations of its predictions. Ever since then, it can be described only as nonscience—as a metaphysical dream, if you like, married to a cruel reality.

Psychoanalysis is a very different case. It is an interesting psychological metaphysics (and no doubt there is some truth in it, as there is so often in metaphysical ideas), but it never was a science. There may be lots of people who are Freudian or Adlerian cases: Freud himself was clearly a Freudian case, and Adler an Adlerian case. But what prevents their theories from being scientific in the sense here described is, very simply, that they do not exclude any physically possible human behaviour. Whatever anybody may do is, in principle, explicable in Freudian or Adlerian terms. (Adler's break with Freud was more Adlerian than Freudian, but Freud never looked on it as a refutation of his theory.)

The point is very clear. Neither Freud nor Adler excludes any particular person's acting in any particular way, whatever the outward circumstances. Whether a man sacrificed his life to rescue a drowning child (a case of sublimation) or whether he murdered the child by drowning him (a case of repression) could not possibly be predicted or excluded by Freud's theory; *the theory was compatible with everything that could happen—even without any special immunization treatment.*

Thus while Marxism became nonscientific by its adoption of an immunizing strategy, psychoanalysis was immune to start with, and remained so.[60] In contrast, most physical theories are pretty free of immunizing tactics and *highly falsifiable to start with.* As a rule, *they exclude an infinity of conceivable possibilities.*

The main value of my criterion of demarcation was, of course, to point out these differences. And it led me to the theory that the empirical content of a theory could be measured by the number of possibilities which it excluded (provided a reasonably nonimmunizing methodology was adopted).

8. Ad Hoc *Hypotheses and Auxiliary Hypotheses. The Falsifiability of Newton's Theory*

There is one important method of avoiding or evading refutations: it is the method of auxiliary hypotheses or *ad hoc* hypotheses.

If any of our conjectures goes wrong—if, for example, the planet Uranus does not move exactly as Newton's theory demands—*then we have to change the theory*. But there are in the main two kinds of changes; *conservative and revolutionary*. And among the more conservative changes there are again two: *ad hoc hypotheses* and *auxiliary hypotheses*.

In the case of the disturbances in the motion of Uranus the adopted hypothesis was partly revolutionary: what was conjectured was the existence of a new planet, something which did not affect Newton's laws of motion, but which did affect the much older "system of the world". The new conjecture was auxiliary rather than *ad hoc*: for although there was only this one *ad hoc* reason for introducing it, it was *independently testable*: the position of the new planet (Neptune) was calculated, the planet was discovered optically, and it was found that it fully explained the anomalies of Uranus. Thus the auxiliary hypothesis stayed within the Newtonian theoretical framework, and the threatened refutation was transformed into a resounding success.

I call a conjecture "*ad hoc*" if it is introduced (like this one) to explain a particular difficulty, but if (in contrast to this one) *it cannot be tested independently*.

It is clear that, like everything in methodology, the distinction between an *ad hoc* hypothesis and a conservative auxiliary hypothesis is a little vague. Pauli introduced the hypothesis of the neutrino quite consciously as an *ad hoc* hypothesis. He had originally no hope that one day independent evidence would be found; at the time this seemed practically impossible. So we have an example here of an *ad hoc* hypothesis which, with the growth of knowledge, did shed its *ad hoc* character. And we have a warning here not to pronounce too severe an edict against *ad hoc* hypotheses: they may become testable after all, as may also happen to a metaphysical hypothesis. But in general, our criterion of testability warns us against *ad hoc* hypotheses; and Pauli was at first far from happy about the neutrino which would in all likelihood have been abandoned in the end, had not new methods provided independent tests for its existence.

Ad hoc hypotheses—that is, at the time untestable auxiliary hypotheses—can save almost any theory from any *particular* refutation. But this does not mean that we can go on with an *ad hoc* hypothesis as long as we like. It may become testable; and a negative test may force us either to give it up or to introduce a new secondary *ad hoc* hypothesis, and so on, *ad infinitum*. This, in fact, is a thing we almost always avoid. (I say "almost" because methodological rules are not hard and fast.)

Moreover, the possibility of making things up with *ad hoc* hypotheses must not be exaggerated: there are many refutations which cannot be evaded in this way, even though some kind of immunizing tactic such as ignoring the refutation is always possible.

In this section, and in the previous three (5 - 7), I have tried to say very carefully what I had to say, not because I have not said it before, perhaps more concisely, but because a number of my critics appear not to have understood it. I shall reply to the contributions of two of these critics—Professor Putnam and Professor Lakatos—in sections 11 and 12 respectively. In some ways their contributions are very similar. In particular, they both assert, though for different reasons, that Newton's theory (his laws of motion plus his law of gravitation) is not falsifiable; and they both refer—Putnam explicitly, Lakatos only indirectly—to the example given above of the discovery of the planet Neptune. According to both Putnam and Lakatos, *all putative refutations of Newtonian theory can be thwarted just as the threat posed by Uranus's deviant orbit was thwarted.*

This point, as both these critics rightly recognise, is crucial for my philosophy. Consequently I feel obliged to say again, before I proceed to examine their arguments, that *Newtonian theory is a falsifiable theory* just as "All swans are white" is a falsifiable theory. That is, it is falsifiable in the simple logical sense of being logically incompatible with some basic statements. It has "potential falsifiers".

9. Kneale on My Alleged Exclusion of Nonuniversal Hypotheses

Professor William Kneale, whom I greatly admire for much of his work, attributes to me, correctly, in his section II, the view that the demarcation between science and nonscience has nothing whatever to do with talk about meaninglessness. He also attributes to me, incorrectly, the view that only *universal statements* fall within the province of science. My discussion of Kneale's very interesting contribution I must therefore devote, reluctantly, and a little sadly, to clearing up this grave misunderstanding.

My criterion of demarcation between the theories or statements of *empirical science* and those that do not belong to it (but perhaps to pseudoscience, logic, and metaphysics) is *testability, or falsifiability*. By this I mean: *the possibility of a clash with test statements* (basic statements, singular statements describing observable events).

It follows from this that, for example, universal statements of laws can belong to science, provided they are testable; but it certainly does not follow that *only* universal statements can belong to science: singular statements especially can also belong to it, and all singular test statements (basic statements) *do*.

Not only is this a consequence of my criterion of demarcation, but I have said so explicitly many times. On the very page (*L.Sc.D.*, p. 41) to which Kneale refers (in his section I) I say that, as a consequence of my criterion of demarcation, "the [tautological] statement 'It will rain or not rain here tomorrow' will not be regarded as empirical [that is, as belonging to empirical science], simply because it cannot be refuted; whereas the [singular] statement, 'It will rain here tomorrow' will be regarded as empirical"; for we may find tomorrow that it clashes with test statements which we "accept". (The words "here tomorrow" were, of course, meant to be short for something like "on March 12, 1933, in Vienna".) Statements capable of clashing with a singular test statement (basic statement) I described as "falsifiable" or "testable"; and since singular test statements—all of which are falsifiable and so belong to empirical science—are historical statements, it follows that many historical statements satisfy my criterion, and belong to empirical science. The statement "It rained in Vienna on March 12, 1933" is an example of such an historical *and* empirical (or empirical-scientific) statement.

Very unfortunately, Kneale has misunderstood me. He believes that it was my intention to say, and that I did say, that *only* universal statements are scientific. (See especially the first and last paragraphs of his paper.)

I blush at the thought that he could think me capable of a view which I can only describe as outrageously silly. He quotes me (in his section I) as saying (in *L.Sc.D.*, p. 41) that my proposal to accept falsifiability (or testability) as a criterion of demarcation "is based upon an *asymmetry* between verifiability and falsifiability; an asymmetry which results from the logical form of universal statements". But this does not say, of course, that I admit *only* universal statements. On the contrary, this quotation from *The Logic of Scientific Discovery* continues as follows: "For these [the universal statements] are never derivable from singular statements, but can be contradicted by singular statements. Consequently it is possible . . . to argue from the truth of singular statements to the falsity of universal statements."

It is clear that I use here the ability of clashing with singular statements as a touchstone of the empirical or scientific character of other statements. And since two singular statements can clash with each other, singular test statements (that is, "basic statements")—and therefore a large class of historical statements—fall, as mentioned, within the province of empirical science, according to my criterion of demarcation.

It is also clear that *some* statements which may be called "singular" and "historical" do not fall within this province. Take the singular historical statement: "Napoleon dreamt vividly, on the night before Waterloo, of his impending defeat, but when he woke up he could not remember anything of his dream, and he never recalled it; nevertheless, unconsciously, his vivid dream shook him so badly that he was not himself during the battle." I do not see any possibility of ever testing this statement, and I should regard it as untestable, at least in our present state of knowledge; but I could *imagine* (though I do not for a moment believe it will ever happen) an advancement of our knowledge which could turn even this wild statement into a testable statement.

As mentioned already, Kneale thinks, seriously, that I regard all historical statements as "metaphysical". I might call the above statement about Napoleon's dream "metaphysical", though I should not attach any particular significance to this term. But I can well understand why Kneale finds my use of "metaphysical" hard to swallow if he believes that I am committed to calling *all* historical statements "metaphysical".

I cannot imagine how Kneale's misunderstanding has arisen. It is true that I suggest at various places that we test singular statements always in connection with universal theories. It is also true that I have said that our language is theory-impregnated: even a singular statement like "Here is a glass of water" is testable only because we assume that glasses, and water, "exhibit a . . . *law-like behaviour*". (*L.Sc.D.*, pp. 94 f.) But although these arguments tend to put singular statements nearer to universal ones than is usually assumed, they are far from suggesting that only universal statements are testable and thus empirical; on the contrary, they all tend to explain the testability of singular statements, and thereby to stress their empirical and scientific character.

As a consequence of this misunderstanding of Kneale's, his essay fails to offer a criticism of my actual views: I am entirely with him in rejecting such narrow positivistic views of science and of metaphysics as those which he here attacks; and this was my position in *Logik der Forschung*.

This misunderstanding apart, Kneale's essay is of considerable interest; but it has very little directly to do with my philosophy. It saddens me that my reply has had to dwell almost entirely on a straightforward misunderstanding.

10. *Quine on My Avoidance of the "Paradoxes of Confirmation"*

I was extremely pleased about W.V. Quine's remarks. He has fully appreciated the simplicity of my ideas on demarcation and on evidence, and he has seen that they avoid Hempel's so-called "paradoxes of confirmation".

I am in complete accord with his first five paragraphs; but I disagree a little with the sixth.

Let me, like him, explain my point "along vaguely logical lines", as he well describes this kind of argument.

In *The Logic of Scientific Discovery*, note *1 to section 28 (p. 101), I elaborated a remark made in *Logik der Forschung*, to the effect that nothing like an observation statement follows from a universal law alone, without additional initial conditions. I showed that "instances" of a universal law do not follow from it and cannot be regarded as corroborating it or confirming it: they can always be had for the asking, whether the law is true or false, and are therefore irrelevant to the question of the validity of the law. The reason is as follows.

First of all, from a universal law, of the form "If something has the property *F* it also has the property *G*", for example, *nothing observable* follows. (*L.d.F.*, section 28. This is a consequence of the well-known fact that universal statements have no "existential import".) Let the universal law be "All swans are white". The fact that nothing observable follows from this is seen at once when we realize that it is compatible with "All swans are black": these two laws contradict each other *only* on the assumption that at least one swan *exists*; together therefore they entail the statement "No swans exist". *This statement cannot be "confirmed" or "verified" by any experience*: it can *only* be refuted, by finding a swan.

Thus no "empirically verifiable" statement follows from a purely universal theory. (There are theories, such as the atomic theory, which contain existential statements; and from these "empirically verifiable" statements *may* follow.)

We can therefore write a universal law such as "All swans are white" also in the equivalent form "Either there are no swans or all of them are white". In this form it becomes quite clear that no existential or empirically verifiable statement follows from it.

Nevertheless, some universal laws may be said to have *instances*. For example, we may say that "Within the spatiotemporal region *k* there is a white swan" is a "positive instance" of "All swans are white". It is clear from what has been said that these *instances cannot be deduced* from the universal law.

Moreover, *these positive instances cannot be used either as test statements or for the purpose of corroboration*. For a positive instance would also be: "Within the spatiotemporal region *k* there is either no swan, or else a swan that is white."

This shows that instances can always be had for the asking—whether the law in question is true, as is perhaps "All ravens are black", or false, as is "All swans are white" (or "All swans are non-white"). In fact, almost every instantiable purely universal law I know of, whether true or false, is instantiated *almost everywhere* (within almost every spatiotemporal region), simply because the universe is almost empty. (It is not that there are merely infinitely many instances; the measure of the noninstances is zero.)

This shows that positive instances are completely *valueless and uninteresting*. Only negative instances—refutations—are of interest, and such "positive" instances which are, in fact, negative instances of a competing theory: but these derive their interest from being crucial experiments or crucial cases, rather than from being positive instances. Crucial cases are attempted refutations of the theory. Thus they are part of its critical discussion.

This clears up completely, it seems to me, the famous "paradoxes of confirmation" of C. G. Hempel and of Nelson Goodman. For these paradoxes arise from the attempt to show that positive instances must be corroborating or "confirming" instances.

The realization that positive instances are as such without value, and merely part of the inductivist approach, and that all corroborating cases are, really, attempted negative instances, and attempted refutations, shows not only that but also why these paradoxes are indeed refutations of the "positive", the verificationist or inductivist approach.[61]

It is interesting that Hempel in a paper published in 1966 still argues that the paradoxes of confirmation are only apparently paradoxical, and that the first task of a theory of induction is the definition of "positive instance" or "confirming instance".[62] It seems that Goodman agrees with this, and that he sees in this task "the new riddle of induction"

The riddle is solved by the realization of the complete irrelevance of the problem.

All this may be regarded as a reply to—or rather an elaboration of—the sixth paragraph of Quine's paper, and especially to his remarks on Goodman, and his remark "I do not despair over Hempel's paradox". I certainly do not despair either; but Quine's remark indicates, it seems, that either he does not realize that Hempel's problem is simply the problem of defining "positive *instance*", a problem here shown to be pointless, since a positive *instance* is not positive *evidence*; or else that, in spite of his agreement with me, Quine still hankers after some "better" supporting *evidence* than that provided by attempted refutations.

Let us look for a moment at how this popular fancy that positive instances provide positive evidence could have arisen. I suggest that it derives from the so-called "inductive syllogism":

Socrates is a man and a mortal.
Plato is a man and a mortal.
Crito is a man and a mortal.

.
.
.

_____

Conclusion: All men are mortal.

Now each of these premises may be regarded as an *"instance"*; moreover, they have often been regarded as "supporting evidence" for "All men are mortal". So by using the "inductive syllogism" itself we could conclude: All instances are supporting evidence.

This, I suppose, is historically the basic mistake. It is a mistake since, by the symmetry of "and", the same instances should also be supporting evidence for the *conclusion*: All mortals are men.

Why do we not accept this conclusion? Because we have counterexamples: my neighbour's bulldog Socrates died two years ago: it was mortal but no man.

This is why I suggest that it is not the instances but solely the absence of counterexamples which is *evidence* for the conclusion "All men are mortal" (where "mortal" appears in the sense of "bound to die after a well-known though somewhat inexact period"; see section 13 below). But obviously, the mere absence of a counterexample is very unimpressive unless we have actually made some effort to find one. (Doing so indeed leads to the dismissal of the Aristotelian theory of which "All men are mortal" is a part; see section 13, below.)

Let us say "is a Greek" means the same as "is an organism born in Greece". We have:

Socrates is a Greek and a man.

.
.
.

Nobody would say that ever so many such premises are evidence for the *Conclusion*: All organisms born in Greece are men.

Indeed, no one but a learned inductivist would even feel inclined to look on the premises as supporting evidence.

No, supporting evidence consists solely of attempted refutations which were unsuccessful, or of the "knowledge" (it does not matter here how it was obtained) that an attempted refutation would be unsuccessful. The idea that a positive instance is supporting evidence should be discarded.

But there is a little more to be said about this sixth paragraph of Quine's paper.

Quite apart from all questions of "projectibility", I do agree with his view that "our native primitive intuition of natural kinds" can be accounted for "by Darwinian natural selection". Yet my way of looking at this fact is a little different from his. First, I do not think that it has much to do with predicates ("projectible" or otherwise), but with expectations and then with theories: in my view, predicates, or concepts, are the result of the formation of expectations and theories rather than the other way round. (This is one of my many reasons for disagreeing with Goodman's way of looking at these problems.)

Moving on to Quine's seventh paragraph, in which he discusses the symmetry between universal and existential statements, I can only say that I have discussed these questions in great detail in *Logik der Forschung*, and also since; and further, that I have pointed out that, if (as Quine says) "All ravens are black" is "the very paradigm . . . of an empirical law", an isolated existential statement (that is, one which is not part of a theory which also contains universal statements) such as "There exists a black raven" (or "There exist devils") is the very paradigm of a metaphysical assertion.

Quine also discusses "All men are mortal", but he takes "x is mortal" to mean "there is a time t such that x dies at t". This is how I myself have analysed some (but not all) "all-and-some statements" in *Logic of Scientific Discovery* (see n. *2 on p. 193), that is, as of the form $(x) (Ey) F (x,y)$. I have also pointed out not only the consequences drawn by Quine but also how mistaken it would be to assume (as Hempel did at the time I wrote this criticism, following up a somewhat carelessly formulated remark of mine) that statements of this kind are never falsifiable. For example, the statements "All brothers have sisters" and "All primes are twin primes" can both be falsified. The question—as I noted—depends upon whether F does or does not impose a finite limit upon the range of the y relative to every given x.

With Quine's final remarks I agree completely.

11. Putnam on "Auxiliary Sentences", Called by Me "Initial Conditions"

I

I enjoyed reading Professor Hilary Putnam's paper because it is crisply and clearly written. But Professor Putnam's conclusions are all wrong.

Professor Putnam is a leader of the younger generation of logicians, while I am a tottering old metaphysician.[63] This is perhaps the explanation of why he found it unnecessary to do his homework.

Putnam's criticism is based on two arguments; a major and a minor, as it were.[64]

(1) The minor argument is that I have observed the existence of natural laws, *but overlooked that of certain "auxiliary sentences"*; but Putnam's "auxiliary sentences" are well known to my readers under the name of "initial conditions" (or "statements of initial conditions"). No reader of *Logik der Forschung* can possibly have avoided my repeated discussion of initial conditions (for an example, see the first three paragraphs of section 12, [1959 (a)], pp. 59 f.). From this and the indubitable identity of at least some of Professor Putnam's "auxiliary sentences" with my initial conditions it seems to follow almost syllogistically that Professor Putnam has not read my *Logic of Scientific Discovery;* though he quotes several passages from it, and undoubtedly believes he has read it sufficiently well to criticize it in his paper. I admit that in this way he has saved himself from the tiresome experience of reading over and over again my analyses of his "auxiliary sentences" (see the *Index* to *L.Sc.D.* under "initial conditions") and my analyses of the relationship between universal laws and these initial conditions, as I call them.

(2) Putnam's major thesis is the outcome of his attempts to analyse (as I did forty years ago) the logical relationship between these two kinds of statements (universal laws and initial conditions), especially with regard to the notorious question of falsifiability. Putnam finds that universal laws alone, without the support of additionally assumed "auxiliary sentences", cannot be falsified. Despite the triviality of the logical situation, and despite his competence as a logician, Professor Putnam's result is wrong.

These are the two central theses of Professor Putnam's paper. They are imbedded in all sorts of talk about "induction". It is clear that, if one uses the word "induction" widely and vaguely enough, any tentative acceptance of the result of any investigation can be called "induction". In that sense, but (I must emphasize) in no other, Professor Putnam is quite right to detect an "inductivist quaver" in one of the passages he quotes (section 3).[65] But in general he has not read, or if read not understood, what I have written, some of which happens to be very similar to (but older than) a very interesting paper of Putnam's to which he refers in his footnote 1.[66] For example, he is hardly right to attribute to me without the slightest justification views which "are . . . [as he says in section 13], to speak impolitely, *ridiculous*": "all the formal algorithms", he writes, "proposed for testing [theories], by Carnap, by Popper, by Chomsky, etc., are, to speak impolitely, *ridiculous*". Now it is perhaps true that Carnap proposed a formal algorism (the *Oxford English Dictionary* gives this as the correct spelling) for induction (though scarcely for testing theories); I do not know whether Chomsky did. But I know that I have all my life denied the existence of such algorisms. No doubt, Professor Putnam has seen a formula (for corroboration) in my *Logic of Scientific Discovery*. But one of the functions of this formula is to show that no algorism of probability theory can be interpreted as an algorism for corroboration or "for testing". In fact, our choosing one of a set of competing theories, far from being an application of an algorism, is an act of preference; and any preference of a theory over another is in its turn a conjecture (of a higher order). The fact that Putnam has not noticed any of this seems to me an excellent corroboration of my conjecture that, although he picked here and there sentences from my *Logic of Scientific Discovery*, he does not seem to know what its contents are, and that my views on theories are very similar to his, though admittedly much older.[67]

Thus Putnam puts forth a priority claim about theories with the words (section 9): "Recently a number of philosophers have begun to put forward a rather new view of scientific activity. I believe that I have anticipated this view about ten years ago [a reference points here to a publication in 1962] when I urged that some scientific theories cannot be overthrown by experiments and observations *alone*, but only by alternative theories." If he ever reads my *Logic of Scientific Discovery*, he will find that the view was anticipated there in 1934, when I wrote (for example, on pp. 86 f.) that theories can be overthrown in practice *only* by what I there called "a falsifying hypothesis". I have elaborated this view since on many occasions and I have for many years—beginning with my *Logik der Forschung*—spoken of the struggle for survival of competing hypotheses. (Not that I agree in the least with most of what Putnam calls the "new view of scientific activity"—Kuhn's view, that is. See especially my [1970(w)] and my reply to Kuhn in section 39 below.)

Another point of Putnam's is "the remarkable fact" that my *Logic of Scientific Discovery* "contains but a half-dozen brief references to the *application* of scientific theories" (section 2), and that what I say can be partly explained by my oversight of the pragmatic aspects of the problem of induction. This point is treated elsewhere in this volume (in section 14 of my *Replies*).

Yet another point that needs to be mentioned is Putnam's assertion that Kepler's Laws are derivable from Newton's theory (sections 9 and 12). In fact, as Duhem knew, Kepler's Laws and Newton's theory contradict one another in the presence of a few uncontroversial singular statements (see, for example, [1963 (a)], n. 28 on p. 62). Thus to say, as Putnam says, that Newton's theory was not corroborated until a long time after publication, "because Kepler's Laws were already known to be true", and so could not provide "a 'test', in Popper's sense" is just historically false. Newton's theory *corrected* some Keplerian predictions. (See also [1957 (i)], [1969 (k)], now Chap. 5 of [1972 (a)], and Lakatos's note 57 above.)

But Putnam's whole criticism turns out to be a false alarm. He believes that I am denying that "[we] are concerned in science with trying to discover correct ideas: Popper to the contrary, this is not *obscurantism* but *responsibility*" (section 13). Since I have said many times (Putnam to the contrary) that we are trying to discover *true* ideas, these remarks, like so many in Putnam's paper, only show that we hold very similar views without his noticing either this fact or the dependence of his ideas on mine (not on what he has read of me, but what has leaked through and become part of the general "spirit of the age": I suppose that those who speak about "truth", "obscurantism", and "responsibility" in science may be reminded that these words are also applicable to the history of ideas). And at the end of his section 13 we even read: "*In general, and in the long run, true ideas are the ones that succeed. . . .* " (Italics mine.) I should agree with this if for the word "true" we substitute the word "good" or the word "valuable"; for false ideas often succeed even in long runs—until they fail. (Moreover, I should not want to be suspected of holding a pragmatic theory of truth.) But I have gone beyond the mere statement that *good ideas are the ones that succeed.* What *Logik der Forschung* did was very simple. It explained how a theory could score a *success.* It pointed out that astrologers too are often, in a sense, successful, and that *"success"* counts in science only when a theory succeeds *in spite of the risk it takes of being refuted.* Scientific success consists of unsuccessful attempts at refutation. Thus I do not exactly disagree with Putnam; only I went a little further. My analysis has, unbeknown to Putnam, been very successful in leading to the solution of many problems, among them to a real solution of Putnam's problem (in his section 13) of the alleged circularity of alleged inductions (see my section 13 below). But this is all of little importance. What is important is that Putnam has not got my very simple point: success in science counts the more the harder we test the theory, and this means: the harder we try to falsify it. That Putnam missed this simple point can only be explained either by my bad writing or by his bad reading.

In the second part of my reply I shall concentrate on some logical points mentioned at the beginning, which can be rationally discussed. There is no need to say more about Putnam's minor argument (1), that I neglect "auxiliary sentences" (initial conditions); so I shall discuss only (2) Putnam's thesis that a theory like Newton's cannot be falsified unless it is strengthened by "auxiliary sentences".

II

After a paragraph in his section 4 in which Putnam says: "Popper regards these further conditions as anti-Bayesian" (with a footnote 4 in which Putnam explains Bayes's theorem, but gives no evidence whatever of a passage in support of his assertion that I regard certain "conditions as anti-Bayesian"),[68] Putnam comes to the assertion that "the heart of Popper's schema is the theory-prediction link" and that I say that "theories imply basic sentences in the sense of 'imply' associated with deductive logic—because basic sentences are DEDUCIBLE from theories. . . . And this same link is the heart of the 'inductivist' schema. Both schemes say: *look at the predictions that a theory implies; see if these predictions are true*."

"My criticism", Putnam continues, "is going to be a criticism of this link, of this one point on which Popper and the 'inductivists' agree. I claim: in a great many important cases, scientific theories do not imply predictions at all. In the remainder of this paper I want to elaborate this point, and show its significance for the philosophy of science."

Now we are at the heart of the matter, at Putnam's major argument; it is here that Putnam makes use of Newton's theory of gravitation as an illustration. Astonishingly, it turns out that (i) he ignores completely what I have said about this point long ago, and (ii) he proposes a thesis which is false in elementary logic.

(a) Putnam asserts that I, like the "inductivists", believe that "basic sentences are DEDUCIBLE from theories". But the truth is that I have pointed out dozens of times that no basic statements are deducible from any universal theory.

What I have asserted is that basic statements may, sometimes, *contradict* a theory. This means that the negations of these basic statements will be "DEDUCIBLE" from that theory; and I pointed out that in general, negations of basic statements are not in their turn basic statements.

(Incidentally, the term "basic statement" or "basic proposition" was introduced by me in *Logik der Forschung* in connection with this problem; but it is clear from his text that Putnam is not aware of this fact.)

(b) What is the true situation? It is very simple. In almost all cases in which we wish to deduce a "*prediction*" from a theory, we need in addition to the theory (Newton's, say) further statements, which I have called initial conditions and which Putnam calls (in his section 5) "auxiliary statements (A.S.)". For example, in order to "*predict*" where the moon will be situated tomorrow night at 10 P.M., we need not only Newton's theory, but initial conditions giving us (at least) the position of the moon and the earth at, say, 10 P.M. yesterday. Thirty-five years after I said so in the book which he criticizes, Putnam believes and asserts that I am unaware of the need for these statements. Yet oddly enough, he acknowledges later on that "Popper recognizes that the derivation of a prediction from a theory may require the use of auxiliary hypotheses" (see his section 11). But he seems to suppose that I have to treat these auxiliary hypotheses as "part" of the theory under test. This mistake is due to his mistaken major argument (2).

(c) For although without initial conditions we obtain no *positive* predictions, a certain unusual kind of negative prediction can be derived from any theory; for example, from the theory "All swans are white" we obtain the unusual prediction "You will not encounter at 10 P.M. tomorrow a black swan".

Putnam has overlooked the existence of these *two different kinds of predictions*. The first kind can be put in the form of "At such and such a space-time region, there exists such and such an object"; these I have called "basic statements"; the second kind can be rendered in the form of a nonexistential proposition, "There does not exist such and such a thing, at such and such a space-time region".

If we look at the last example, then we see that it is nothing but a specialization of a universal law in its "There does not exist" form (a form which I have discussed at some length) to a particular space-time region; it can therefore be called a (negative) "prediction", but not a basic statement.

Now what has Putnam done? He says that we do not obtain basic statements from theories alone without initial conditions; this is true. He says that I did not know this; this is false. And he says that we cannot derive predictions from theories alone, which is also false, for it *is* a prediction, though a negative one, if I tell you what you will not encounter tomorrow at 10 P.M.

He concludes that a theory like Newton's theory cannot be refuted, that "astronomical data can *support* U.G. [Universal Gravitation], but they can hardly *falsify* it" (see his section 8). This quotation clearly formulates a point of view that my criterion of demarcation was intended to combat. Yet it is woefully wrong. *Newton's theory can be refuted without the use of initial conditions.*[69]

Of course, we often need as well idealizing assumptions, "auxiliary hypotheses" (in the sense of my section 8 above), for some sophisticated tests of a highly informative theory. But some tests are quite crude. If the force of gravity were to become a repulsive force Putnam would soon notice the difference; indeed, he considers this sort of possibility himself, saying in his section 9: "Newtonian physics would probably have been abandoned . . . if the world had started to act in a markedly non-Newtonian way." I cannot see what (auxiliary) assumptions would be needed in such unambiguous cases.

If we do make auxiliary assumptions, then of course we cannot be certain whether one of them, rather than the theory under test, is responsible for any refutation. So we have to guess. But as I said some time ago: "Though this . . . may turn a verificationist [or inductivist] into a sceptic [or, I should have added, a dogmatist], it does not affect those who hold that all our theories are guesses anyway".[70] Thus my position anticipates Putnam's summarizing remark in his section 8 that since we are very unsure of the auxiliary statements "we cannot regard a false prediction as definitively falsifying a theory".

This is my reply to the only logically relevant part of Putnam's paper—the part which he himself considers to be the heart of the matter.

12. *Lakatos on the Equal Status of Newton's and Freud's Theories*

I have always had much admiration for Professor Lakatos's achievements as a historian and philosopher of mathematics, and I have greatly enjoyed reading his work in this field, and referred to it where I was indebted to it. It is with regret, therefore, that I feel that I have to divide my reply to him into two parts, of which the first (subsection I) will deal with certain world 2 problems which are forced upon me by Professor Lakatos's paper. The second (subsections II to VI) will deal with some of the world 3 problems raised by his paper, particularly with his suggestion that Newton's theory of gravitation is no more open to refutation than is Freud's theory of psychoanalysis.

I

I find Professor Lakatos's contribution difficult to reply to. Unlike Professor Putnam, he has certainly read a great deal of what I have written, including some unpublished writings of mine, such as the *Postscript* [1959(n)]. After having been my student, he became my colleague in 1960, and he is now one of my successors at the London School of Economics. It is for this very reason that I feel, unfortunately, obliged to warn the reader that Professor Lakatos has, nevertheless, misunderstood my theory of science; and that the series of long papers in which, in recent years, he has tried to act as a guide to my writings and the history of my ideas is, I am sorry to say, unreliable and misleading.

It would not have been difficult for Professor Lakatos to find out whether he was right in his various historical and interpretative speculations: he could have asked me. For while he was working on these papers, we were both at the London School of Economics. For many years he attended my lectures and seminars, at which criticism was invited as a matter of course; and I made myself regularly available for him to discuss—if he so wished—any problems or criticisms that he might have. When Professor Lakatos was writing the paper which he refers to as [1968b] he asked that I should "never" read this paper, and I have complied with his wish; since then I have read only passages of his works to which my attention was especially drawn, either by some students or colleagues of mine, or by his present contribution. The only occasion on which he took up my invitation to discuss with me his criticism of my position led to a conversation about corroboration and verisimilitude to which he refers in section II (*b*) (iii) of his contribution. In this conversation I said roughly the same as what I had already said in *Conjectures and Refutations*, page 234, quoted in subsection v below.

Now that I am called on to reply to his views, I am disturbed to find that the argument which appears to be crucial for his criticism of my views on demarcation must, in my opinion, be rejected as totally unsound; that among his criticisms he raises points which I would not have expected from one who is well acquainted with my work; and that his examination of my views seems to have left him—and, unfortunately, large numbers of people who have read his papers—with an interpretation of my theory of falsifiability that makes nonsense of all my views.

The points which I have mentioned above are ones which I will discuss in subsequent parts of my reply. In the present subsection, I am concerned with a different problem which faces me when attempting to reply to Professor Lakatos's contribution.

In reading his contribution I was again and again surprised by the views which he attributes to me and by the nature of the quotations and references which he uses to back up his interpretations. Passages, and extracts from passages, are frequently taken out of context; minor remarks, sometimes of the nature of asides, and mere allusions to some view, given when I am discussing something else, are taken as if they were representing my position on the question in hand; and my major discussions are frequently ignored. Moreover, his quotations and references are not always correct and are often highly misleading, as I shall indicate.

But this is not my only problem. Professor Lakatos has, in the course of his discussion of my work, introduced a large number of complications, distinctions, and epicycles; technical terms abound, and everything Professor Lakatos touches seems to sprout numbered subdivisions. All this is regrettable, for it will make it difficult for people to comprehend and to criticize what were originally some simple ideas of mine. Moreover, although in the course of what he writes Professor Lakatos raises some points which, if tenable, would have serious consequences for my work, I find it difficult to get to the heart of his arguments. For he raises in quick succession many points of very unequal merit, some of them important, some at best asides, and he often omits to present arguments for these points in any detail. I was also surprised by the aggressive and even arrogant tone of certain parts of his lively paper, particularly his postscript, entitled "*Added in 1971*", and by the fact that Professor Lakatos's contribution contains, more or less veiled in its body and quite explicit in that postscript, some priority claims which seem to me obviously untenable.

In view of all this, I suppose that only somebody who knows my work well, or who takes the trouble to check Professor Lakatos's references carefully, will be able to appreciate fully my objections to his contribution. I therefore feel that it is particularly important for me not to be dragged into too many details, and also to keep my reply as simple and as clear as possible. Thus I shall not reply in detail to many of his points, not even to many of those which badly misinterpret my views; not only because it would take up too much space, but also because such a discussion is bound to be "minute" (to use Berkeley's term), finicky, and scholastic. Instead I shall confine myself to a few of the more important points, such as Professor Lakatos's view that Newton's theory is no more falsifiable than Freud's, the question of the rejection and falsification of theories, the problem of the status (the criticizability) of my methodology, and the relation between corroboration and verisimilitude.[70a]

In the present subsection, my main point is the analysis of *one* case of Professor Lakatos's interpretations of my views in some detail. (There are too many for me to deal with them all.)

In section I (*b*) of his contribution, when discussing my views on the aim of science, Professor Lakatos puts forward a historical thesis concerning my intellectual development. This historical thesis is that my taking the aim of science to be truth was a comparatively late development; he asserts that "The idea that the *aim* of science is *truth*, occurs in his [Popper's] writings for the first time in 1957. In his *Logik der Forschung* the quest for truth may be a psychological *motive* of scientists—it is not a rational *purpose* of science." (The italics are by Professor Lakatos.)

I am not clear why Professor Lakatos is interested in establishing the (untenable) thesis about my intellectual history that "The idea that the *aim* of science is *truth*" (in itself a somewhat trite idea) occurs in my writings for the first time in 1957. And I am surprised by the detailed discussion in his later section, II(*a*), in the course of which he says: "The whole of *Logik der Forschung* is in an important sense a *pragmatic* treatise; it is about *acceptance* and *rejection* and not about *truth* and *falsehood*" (Lakatos, n. 73); especially since he admits, in section II(*a*), just a few lines before, that "it is abundantly clear that Popper's *instinctive* answer [in the *Logik der Forschung*] was that the aim of . . . science *was* indeed the pursuit of Truth". At any rate Professor Lakatos's discussion implicitly declares an explicit statement of mine to be untrue. This statement was added in 1959 (*L.Sc.D.*, p. 274, n. *1 and slightly elaborated in 1968). My statement runs " . . . although my views on formal logic and its philosophy were revolutionized by Tarski's theory [of truth], my views on science and its philosophy were fundamentally unaffected, although clarified." I still think that this is so.

When I wrote *Logik der Forschung*, I was unhappy about the uncritical use of the notion of truth, because there existed criticisms of it that I was not able to meet. Nevertheless, I said there as much about truth and falsity as I was able to do with a good conscience. Not only did I constantly operate with the notions of falsity and falsification (and I, of course, recognised that the term "false" was equivalent to "non-true", and "true" to "non-false"), but I actually dedicated a whole section of that work—section 84—to "The Concepts 'True' and 'Corroborated' ". In the course of that section I did say (though not "proudly"): "In the logic of science here outlined it is possible to avoid using the concepts 'true' and 'false'." But I also said, after an elaboration of the first quotation, "This certainly does not mean that we are forbidden to use the concepts 'true' or 'false', or that their use creates any particular difficulty." Indeed my point was not that we should avoid using these terms, but, on the contrary, that their use was *innocuous* and not open to objection.

I have always stressed that Tarski's rehabilitation of the idea of absolute or objective truth came to my notice after the publication of *Logik der Forschung*, and that it was for me most important because it contained answers to the criticisms of truth which I could not give myself.[71] I made reference to Tarski's theory of truth as soon as I could—in my lectures at Bedford College in 1935, and in print in the first edition of *The Open Society* in 1945.[72] And I used this theory at once in a manner which Professor Lakatos does not discern in my work before 1957. This may be seen from the following passages, written before 1942 and published in 1945:

> First, although in science we do our best to find the truth, we are conscious of the fact that we can never be sure whether we have got it. . . . Thus we can say that in our search for truth, we have replaced scientific certainty by scientific progress.

(The quotation is from [1945(c)], p. 10; = [1966(c)], Vol. II, p. 12.) In the same volume ([1945(c)], p. 250; = [1966(a)], Vol. II, p. 263) I wrote:

> In the case of the so-called theoretical or *generalizing sciences* . . . we are predominantly interested in . . . universal laws or hypotheses. We wish to know whether they are true, and since we can never directly make sure of their truth, we adopt the method of eliminating false ones.

But there are, in fact, certain quite clear statements in *Logik der Forschung* itself of my views on truth (and content) as the aim of science. One is actually quoted by Professor Lakatos in his footnote 27, but unfortunately not in its original form. His footnote (which also includes a cross reference which I do not quote here) reads:

> He calls the search for truth "the strongest [unscientific] motive" ([*L.Sc.D.* 1934*b*], section 85).

The word "unscientific" which Professor Lakatos inserts in square brackets occurs in my text two lines below the quoted passage, in a different context and in a different paragraph. And without this insertion (which robs it of its force), my passage ([1959(a)], p. 278), constitutes a refutation of Professor Lakatos's historical thesis. I now quote my passage in context:

> Science is not a system of certain, or well-established, statements; nor is it a

system which steadily advances towards a state of finality. Our science is not knowledge (*epistēmē*): it can never claim to have attained truth, or even a substitute for it, such as probability.

Yet science has more than a mere biological survival value. It is not only a useful instrument. Although it can attain neither truth nor probability, the striving for knowledge and the search for truth are still the strongest motives of scientific discovery.

This passage in section 85 is preceded by my section 84 whose topic is truth, and which argues for an *objectivist* interpretation of truth. Thus the passage here quoted cannot be interpreted as "pragmatic", as Professor Lakatos has it nor, incidentally, as subjectively motivated.

But the matter is put even more prominently in the same section 85, at the end of the penultimate paragraph of the text (of the first edition, 1934).

The wrong view of science betrays itself in the craving to be right; for it is not his *possession* of knowledge, of irrefutable truth, that makes the man of science, but his persistent and recklessly critical *quest* for truth.

It should, I think, be clear that my own historical statements on this matter are true, and that Professor Lakatos's historical thesis, which runs contrary to what I have said, is simply false.

I am sorry that I was forced into this long analysis. It is much ado about nothing—at least I cannot see the point of Professor Lakatos's thesis concerning my intellectual history. It was necessary, however, to pick one out of a score of similar theses and to pursue it to the bitter end. The present section belongs to world 2 insofar as I use this example to show that Professor Lakatos's historical theses—and his use of quotations to support them—are not reliable.

Before leaving this section, and before leaving world 2, I will briefly draw attention to another of his misinterpretations. In his section II(*a*) Professor Lakatos writes about my views of corroboration. (The italics are his.)

But the *only* function of high corroboration is to challenge the ambitious scientist to overthrow the theory.

At the end of the passage quoted, Professor Lakatos has a footnote, footnote 75, which is to my *Logic of Scientific Discovery*, page 419. But this page does not say "*only*" this. On the contrary, it even mentions "the positive side". My passage runs:

What we do—or should do—is to *hold on, for the time being* . . . to the one [theory] that can be most severely tested. We tentatively 'accept' this theory—but only in the sense [of 'accept'] that we select it as worthy to be subjected to further criticism, and to the severest tests we can design.

On the positive side, we may be entitled to add that the surviving theory is the best theory—and the best tested theory—of which we know.[73]

After this, I will now turn to the discussion of Professor Lakatos's *arguments*; and thus to world 3.

II

The Alleged Equal Status of Newton's Theory and Freud's Theory. Of the various criticisms of my work that Professor Lakatos raises in his contribution, the most important is undoubtedly his suggestion that Newton's theory and Freud's theory are equally nonfalsifiable, for example in his section I(*c*). Here is an extract from his discussion:

> Popper's basic rule is that *the scientist must specify in advance under what experimental conditions he will give up even his most basic assumptions*: "Criteria of refutation have to be laid down beforehand: it must be agreed which observable situations, if actually observed, mean that the theory is refuted. But what kind of clinical responses would refute to the satisfaction of the analyst *not merely a particular clinical diagnosis but psychoanalysis itself*? And have such criteria even been discussed or agreed upon by analysts?". [A footnote here gives the source of this quotation—[1963(a)], p. 38, n. 3—and mentions that the second set of italics are Lakatos's.] ... But what if we put Popper's question to the Newtonian scientist: "What kind of observation would refute to the satisfaction of the Newtonian not merely a particular Newtonian explanation but Newtonian dynamics and gravitational theory itself? And have such criteria even been discussed or agreed upon by Newtonians?". The Newtonian will, alas, scarcely be able to give a positive answer.

In this second subsection, I will give an answer to the questions Professor Lakatos poses at the end of this quotation. (His conflation of refutation and rejection when discussing my work on methodology will be discussed below in subsection III.)

I will start by considering his first question "What kind of observation would refute to the satisfaction of the Newtonian not merely a particular Newtonian explanation but Newtonian dynamics and gravitational theory itself?" The answer is very simple. Disregarding the possibility of immunizing stratagems,[74] the answer to the question is: *there is an infinite number* of simple and quite different sets of possible observations (or potential falsifiers) which if accepted would refute Newtonian theory. And this is the heart of the matter, for my criticism of Freud's theory was that it simply does not have potential falsifiers.

Suppose that our astronomical observations were to show, from tomorrow on, that the velocity of the earth (which remains on its present geometrical path) was increasing, either in its daily or in its annual movement, while the other planets in the solar system proceeded as before. Or suppose that Mars started to move in a curve of the fourth power, instead of moving in an ellipse of power 2. Or assume, still more simply, that we construct a gun that fires ballistic missiles which consistently move in a clearly non-Newtonian tract. . . . There are an infinity of possibilities, and the realization of any of them would simply refute Newton's theory. In fact, almost any statement about a physical body which we may make—say, about the cup of tea before me, that it begins to dance (and say, in addition, without spilling the tea)—would contradict Newtonian theory. This theory would equally be contradicted if the apples from one of my, or Newton's, apple trees were to rise up from the ground (without there being a whirlwind about), and begin to dance round the branches of the apple tree from which they had fallen, or if the moon were to go off at a tangent; and if all this were to happen, perhaps,[75] without any other very obvious changes in our environment. (Of course, there are immunizing strategies, but these do not concern us here.) As opposed to this, I cannot describe any state of affairs concerning Mr Smith—say about his behaviour—which would need immunization in order not to clash with Freudian theory. It is just this feature of the "impressive and all-explanatory theories" to which Professor Lakatos refers in footnote 1 of his contribution that I have pointed out.

In what way does Professor Lakatos disagree with my analysis of the difference between psychoanalysis and Newtonian theory? Since he gives no arguments in his present contribution, but refers us, at the end of the passage quoted above, to his "Falsification and the Methodology of Scientific Research Programmes",[76] and since he says in his footnote 2 that reference to that paper may be "necessary . . . for more detailed expositions", I had to turn to it in order to examine his discussion there.

Professor Lakatos begins this discussion with a formulation in italics (Lakatos, "Scientific Research Programmes", p. 100) which is the *thesis* to be established: "*exactly the most admired scientific theories simply fail to forbid any observable state of affairs*". Note that he writes "observable state of affairs" not "observations": this implies that at least one vast class of immunizing strategies is excluded—those that blame the observation for not representing the actual state of affairs.

Now, before I proceed to discuss his argument, I want to make clear three things about what appears to be his thesis.

(1) The italicized thesis would be pointless unless it assumed the exclusion of immunizing stratagems or any of the other difficulties which I have so elaborately discussed in the preceding sections of my *Replies*.

(2) Were the thesis true, then my philosophy of science would not only be completely mistaken, but would turn out to be completely uninteresting.

(3) Lakatos bases the most far-reaching criticisms on his thesis; *in fact almost all his criticisms depend on it and collapse if this thesis collapses*. This is the reason why I have to discuss his arguments in support of this thesis in some detail.

Immediately after his italicized thesis, Lakatos continues as follows: "To support this last contention, I shall first tell a characteristic story and then propose a general argument."

This is a typical proof-sketch: the "characteristic story" is to introduce the idea of the proof and the "general argument" is to clinch it. The characteristic story, of course, is not intended as a proof: its purpose is only to prepare for it. The proof, clearly, is to consist of the "general argument".

The "characteristic story" turns out to be an "imaginary" but simple variation of the often told (for example by Professor Putnam in sections 7 and 10 of his contribution above), and so often by myself elaborated,[77] story of the discovery of Neptune. A "misbehaviour" of a planet p is discovered and the Newtonian astronomer investigates why: "He suggests that there must be a hitherto unknown planet p' which perturbs the path of p. He calculates the mass, orbit, etc., of this hypothetical planet and then asks an experimental astronomer to test his hypothesis." (Lakatos, "Scientific Research Programmes".)

Professor Lakatos's "characteristic story" is by no means at an end. He continues as follows: "The planet p' is so small that even the biggest available telescopes cannot possibly observe it: the experimental astronomer applies for a research grant to build yet a bigger one. . . ."

I will not go on with Lakatos's "characteristic story" because of its repetitive nature (involving a cosmic dust cloud that hides the planet from the new telescope and the construction and launching of a satellite to detect the cloud). Instead I will proceed to the "general argument".

The general argument opens ("Scientific Research Programmes", p.101) with the words (which refer back to the "characteristic story"):

> This story strongly suggests that even a most respected scientific theory, like Newton's dynamics and theory of gravitation, may fail to forbid any observable state of affairs.[78] Indeed, *some scientific theories forbid any event occurring in some specified finite spatio-temporal region (or briefly, a 'singular event') only on the condition that no other factor* (possibly hidden in some distant and unspecified spatio-temporal corner of the universe) *has any influence on it.*

Lakatos now switches his attention entirely to such theories, "theories . . . containing a *ceteris paribus* clause". But finally he draws the lesson from his "characteristic story" in the form of the bare assertion that "it is exactly the most important, 'mature' theories in the history of science which are *prima facie* undisprovable in this way [through having *ceteris paribus* clauses]" ("Scientific Research Programmes", p. 102). So we find, in the end, that the "characteristic story" provides Lakatos's only argument in support of his "contention" (which I have called his "thesis").[79]

But this story is "characteristic", and generalizable, only if it is assumed that all movements of a planet which are prima facie non-Newtonian are perturbations which may be interpreted as caused by *some* planet; or in brief that all possible prima facie falsifications would be similar to the "characteristic story". Lakatos ignores the fact that almost all possible kinds of mis-behaviour—that is, all except a set of measure zero—would *not* be explicable by postulating the existence of a planet p'. Thus Lakatos's "characteristic story" is in fact an *extremely exceptional* case. Adams's and Leverrier's success in pinpointing the planet p' (Neptune) was by no means a trivial or expected success; it was a far from straightforward calculation, and the actual discovery of Neptune was a priori improbable in the extreme. (Putnam anyway makes this clear in his analysis of the discovery; see his section 10 above.)

Let us look at this in more detail. As already noted, the story (more especially what I have called his "thesis") refers to "*observable* states of affairs" rather than to, say, "*observations*", thus ruling out those immunizing stratagems that blame observations for not representing correctly the actual state of affairs. It is also clear from the example with which Professor Lakatos works that the problem of immunizing stratagems is not involved in his discussion. For it concerns the misbehaviour of the orbit of a planet, and this is to be accounted for by postulating the existence of some new planet which would account, in detail, for the deviation from the expected path.[79a]

Professor Lakatos's view is clearly that we can generalize from the case of the discovery of Neptune to show that Newton's theory cannot be refuted.

But this is completely unacceptable. While it is of course true that cases of the sort that Professor Lakatos discusses could exist, it is also true that vast numbers of observable orbits could not possibly be dealt with by such auxiliary hypotheses. Assume we were to accept that a planet moves on the same geometrical orbit as at present, but with constant velocity. Or assume that the velocities of some planets were to decrease rather than increase when approaching their perihelion. Or assume the orbit of Mars were, in every fourth Mars year, *not* to show any perturbations (and thus none of those we attribute to Jupiter). Or assume the orbit of some planet were to be approximately rectangular. None of these cases could be dealt with and explained away by a method similar to the one suggested by Professor Lakatos within Newtonian theory. Thus we have many, many, potential falsifiers; and Professor Lakatos's story is not in his sense "characteristic".

I have discussed this trivial example in some detail, for if what I have called Professor Lakatos's thesis were true, then (as I have said above) my philosophy of science would be completely mistaken. Because of this, I may be excused if I carry my counterargument a bit further, even though I feel that what I have said so far clinches my criticism.

First, Lakatos's argument does not, as he seems to think, bring Newton's theory near to Freud's; rather, the argument is one about the possibility of avoiding falsifications with the help of auxiliary hypotheses.

As to Newton's theory of gravitation, two different theses may be meant:

(a) All bodies in interplanetary space (like the moon, or the planets) not only move according to Newtonian dynamics, but their movements can also be explained by an appeal to *gravitational forces alone.*

(b) As just stated under (a), but *omitting* "in interplanetary space (like the moon, or the planets)". That is, we assert that *all the forces* (or *all the attractive forces*) are gravitational.

Now in the form (b), Newtonianism has long been known to be refuted. We had to introduce electrical and magnetic forces. Admittedly, the attempt was made, by Newtonians, to *explain* these forces (with the help of various theories involving the ether) in terms of Newtonian mechanics. But even if those attempts had fully succeeded, they would not have explained electrical or magnetic forces as being due to *gravitation.* If I rub the end of my fountain pen and pick up a small paper pellet, then I am faced with one of the countless cases which refute Newtonianism in the sense of (b).

But if Professor Lakatos were right—if all apparent deviations from Newtonian gravitation could be explained away by postulating (hidden) masses—then (b) would be acceptable, and we could explain magnetic and electrical attraction by gravitation plus postulated masses. But this is obviously not the case.

Of course, Newton himself knew that magnetic or electrical attraction was not identical with gravitational attraction. Thus one can say that, owing to *"observable states of affairs"*, (b) was probably never held by anybody; certainly not by Newton. It was refuted before Newton ever thought of explaining *by the same force* a falling apple and the failure of the moon to move off at a tangent.

But just as (b) is falsified, and thus falsifiable, then so is (a): almost all conceivable states of affairs would refute (a). (Nobody doubts that a moon rocket that moves into a new orbit cannot be moving under gravitational forces alone.)

It is well known that Newton postponed the publication of the *Principia* because he feared that it was falsified by data about the moon; he thereby made it clear what kind of "observable states of affairs" would refute his theory to his own satisfaction. Similarly Einstein repeatedly pointed out what kind of results he would regard as crucial refutations of his theories.

When Professor Lakatos, as quoted, asks "have such criteria [of refutation] even been discussed or agreed upon by Newtonians?", the answer is: "agreed upon"—yes; "discussed"—perhaps no, because of their triviality—discussion was no more necessary than in the case of the black swan.

To sum up, Professor Lakatos's example is not only incapable of generalization; it is rather an attempt to turn a series of brilliant scientific successes (the discoveries of Neptune, of Pluto and other planets) into a series of trivialities. The discovery of Neptune was a corroboration or a success of Newtonian theory *only because it was the failure of the threatening falsification.*

III

Falsification and Rejection. While Professor Lakatos's criticism that I have discussed in subsection II is crucial from a logical point of view, one of his more confusing moves is his repeated contention, when discussing my ideas, that I conflate the refutation of a theory with its rejection; that is, with the necessity for people to abandon the theory, and more especially to abandon working on it. Indeed, while the former is, given the acceptance of a refuting state of affairs, a matter of logic, the latter is a question of methodology, and will depend among other things, on what alternative theories are available. (I have often stressed the need for working with more than one hypothesis in connection with both falsification ["falsifying hypotheses"] and the growth of science in general).[80]

It is true that I have used the terms "elimination", and even "rejection" when discussing "refutation". But it is clear from my main discussion that these terms mean, when applied to a scientific theory, that it is eliminated as a contender for the truth—that is, refuted, but not necessarily abandoned. Moreover, I have often pointed out that any such refutation is fallible. It is a typical matter of conjecture and of risk-taking whether or not we accept a refutation and, furthermore, of whether we "abandon" a theory or, say, only modify it, or even stick to it, and try to find some alternative, and methodologically acceptable, way round the problem involved. That I do not conflate even admitted falsity with the need to abandon a theory may be seen from the fact that I have frequently pointed out[80a] that Einstein regarded general relativity as false, yet as a better approximation to the truth than Newton's gravitational theory. He certainly did not "abandon" it. But he worked to the end of his life in an attempt to improve upon it by way of a further generalization.

I fear that I cannot, at any rate in the space here available, sort out everything that Professor Lakatos has to say about my views on falsifiability. I hope, however, that what I say above, and what I have said earlier in these *Replies* in sections 5-8, will have made my views fairly clear. As to the interpretations that Professor Lakatos puts forward which are in conflict with what I have said here, I suggest to the reader that he should look closely at the passages of my writings to which Professor Lakatos refers and read the various passages in their context; and I also wish to refer to my discussion of these matters in *The Logic of Scientific Discovery*, and in Chapter 10 of *Conjectures and Refutations*.

I might mention, however, that I have never operated in a context like this with such vague ideas as "the very heart of the system" (or of the theory), or with its "*most basic* assumptions" (see the text to Lakatos's nn. 10 and 11). On the contrary, I have indicated that it is a matter of risky conjecture to which part of a theory we attribute the responsibility for a refutation (see, for example, the end of section 18 of *L.d.F.*, and *C.&R.*, pp. 112 and 238-39).

What I have said here might also dispel any confusion that may have arisen about the fact that I have said that the dogmatic defence of a theory has a positive methodological role to play. I repeat that it has.

IV

The Question of the Falsifiability of my Methodology. I select for my next reply, Lakatos's section I(*b*).

A question that I am almost regularly asked by intelligent students on their first acquaintance with my work is the following: "But is your own theory of falsifiability (and of scientific method in general) falsifiable?" Now while this is a very natural question, it should not be asked by anybody familiar with my work. For the answer is that my theory is not empirical, but methodological or philosophical, and it need not therefore be falsifiable. Falsifiability is a criterion of demarcation, not one of meaning. (If it were one of meaning then the question *might* be fatal.) Thus, trivially, the criterion of demarcation must not be applied to it.

In fact, I devoted a whole chapter—Chapter 2—of *Logik der Forschung* to the problem of the status of a theory of scientific method. In this I took the view that methodology was not an empirical science (the opposite view I described as "naturalistic").

I have later, in Chapter 8 of *Conjectures and Refutations*, discussed how one can criticize and reject a philosophical theory. And in my lectures when discussing this matter, I usually asserted that I would be willing to give up my theory of scientific method if certain conditions were to be realized.[81]

Surprisingly, Professor Lakatos asks "Under what conditions would you give up your demarcation criterion?" (see the text to his n. 30) as if I had never dealt with this question. But here I can give a new reply. I shall give up my theory if Professor Lakatos succeeds in showing that Newton's theory is no more falsifiable by "observable states of affairs" than is Freud's.

V

Corroboration and Verisimilitude. Professor Lakatos writes (section II[*b*]): "While he [Popper] now talks freely about the metaphysical ideas of truth and falsity, he still will not say unequivocally that the positive appraisals in his scientific game may be seen as a—conjectural—sign of the growth of conjectural knowledge; that corroboration is a *synthetic*—albeit conjectural—measure of verisimilitude."

My position is as follows:

(1) Since meeting Tarski in 1935 I have always talked freely about truth and falsity. See my subsection I above.

(2) I am sorry that I ever used the word "game" in the context "game of science". This metaphor originated in my *Logik der Forschung* [1934(b)], section 11. But Professor Lakatos has taken this metaphor so seriously, and has overworked it so cruelly, that I now regret having coined it.

(3) I *did* suggest in *Conjectures and Refutations*, Chapter 10, that the degree of corroboration may be taken as an indication of verisimilitude; I wrote (p. 234)

> ... we have again to distinguish between the question "What do you intend to say if you say that the theory t_2 has a higher degree of verisimilitude than the theory t_1?", and the question "How do you know that the theory t_2 has a higher degree of verisimilitude than the theory t_1?"
>
> We have so far answered only the first of these questions. The answer to the second question depends on it, and is exactly analogous to the following (absolute rather than comparative) question about truth: "I do *not* know—I only guess. But I can examine my guess critically, and if it withstands severe criticism, then this fact may be taken as a good critical reason in favour of it."

Thus I *did* say, even if in slightly different words, that we may *guess* that the better corroborated theory is also one that is nearer to the truth. This is a conjecture, a guess (and "synthetic"); *not* the appraisal which states the degree of corroboration (which may be said to be "analytic"). (See also section 16 of my *Replies*, below.)

(4) What I certainly have *not* said (and I do not want to say) is that "corroboration is a ... measure of verisimilitude". I have indeed not said so because I do not think that it is so. Nor would I admit what I regard as even worse—that my "methodological appraisals are interesting primarily because of the hidden *inductive assumption* that, if one lives up to them, one has a *better chance* [my italics] to get nearer to the Truth than otherwise" (see the text following Lakatos's note 87).

Let me quote briefly from my [1963(a)], page 235 (written for a Conference in 1960); note the words "*good indication*" in the second paragraph which I have now italicized):

> ... I think that my theory of testability or corroboration by empirical tests is the proper methodological counterpart to this new metalogical idea [verisimilitude]. The only improvement [in introducing verisimilitude] is one of clarification. Thus I have often said that we prefer the theory t_2 which has passed certain severe tests to the theory t_1 which has failed these tests, because a false theory is certainly worse than one which, for all we know, may be true.

To this we can now add that even after t_2 has been refuted in its turn we can still say that it is better than t_1, for although both have been shown to be false, the fact that t_2 has withstood tests which t_1 did not pass may be a *good indication* that the falsity-content of t_1 exceeds that of t_2 while its truth-content does not. Thus we may still give preference to t_2, even after its falsification, because we have reason to think that it agrees better with the facts than did t_1.

(5) What we demand of a theory t_2 in order that it should be better (or nearer to the truth) than t_1 is (a) that it contains t_1 as an approximation in a way that explains the success of t_1 and (b) that it explains all those cases where t_1 failed at least better than did t_1. (This is a kind of—revolutionary—principle of continuity.)

VI

Reply to Lakatos's Postscript "Added in 1971". Professor Lakatos's contribution now contains a postscript, entitled *"Added in 1971"*. It is his response to a paper of mine, "Conjectural Knowledge: My Solution of the Problem of Induction" ([1971(i)]; now Chap. 1 of [1972(a)]).

Before I received this postscript, I had written my reply (later amended) to Professor Lakatos's contribution (which reached me in a series of different versions late in 1970). In my reply I said, after acknowledgements to Lakatos's papers on the history and philosophy of mathematics, that I did not think that he had understood my theory of science, and that I therefore did not think that he was properly equipped to expound the history of my ideas. The latter remark is strikingly corroborated by Professor Lakatos's new postscript, *"Added in 1971"*.

Professor Lakatos claims here without specific evidence that "large sections" of my paper ("Conjectural Knowledge") "consist of responses to" a paper of his (which he refers to as "[1968a]") and to his "present contribution". Though these claims are not important, I may say, in order to preserve historical accuracy, that he is mistaken. In my paper there is *one* critical footnote, quoted below, to pages 410-14 of his [1968a]; that is all. Moreover, I wrote several drafts of my paper "Conjectural Knowledge" before ever having received Professor Lakatos's contribution, and I do not think that apart from footnote 23 of that paper of mine, there is even the slightest influence of Lakatos's [1968a] or of his present contribution.

Professor Lakatos's next point is a priority claim. He says:

> I was interested to see that *on some minor points* Popper has now adopted some of my earlier suggestions. For instance, he now equates boldness with non-adhocness, that is, with excess content rather than content.

At the end of this passage he refers to page 181 of my paper "Conjectural Knowledge" where I write: "The idea of *adhocness* and its opposite, which may perhaps be termed 'boldness' is very important."

As anybody knows who has read *Logik der Forschung* or, say, my paper "The Aim of Science" ([1957(i)] now Chap. 5 of my book [1972(a)]), I constantly operate with the opposition between (on the one hand) "bold", "audacious", "adventurous", or "highly testable" conjectures, or theories of "great content" which are "logically improbable", or "anticipations", "rash and premature prejudices", and so on; and (on the other hand) "*ad hoc* auxiliary hypotheses", "low level generalizations" which are of "low content" and of comparatively "low testability".[82]

Thus in the passage alluded to by Lakatos I simply used my forty-year-old terminology; and Professor Lakatos's suggestion that I "now" equate boldness with non*adhocness* is pointless.[82a] His claim that I have "now" adopted" some of his "earlier suggestions", and especially his idea of "excess content", is incorrect. I would not dream of using any of those many new terms of epicyclic refinement which Professor Lakatos has added to my theory, and which I have never even attempted to keep track of.

The third point of Professor Lakatos's postscript is his assertion that I "misquote" him. But I did not even quote him: I referred to him only once, in a footnote ([1971(l)], n. 23) which I will quote here in full.

> It appears that Professor Lakatos suspects that the actual contribution of numbers to my "degree of corroboration", if possible, would render my theory inductivist in the sense of a probabilistic theory of induction. I see no reason whatever why this should be so. (Cp. pp. 410-412 of *The Problem of Inductive Logic*, I. Lakatos and A. Musgrave, eds., North-Holland Publishing Co., Amsterdam, 1968.)

Thus I have not quoted Professor Lakatos and thus could not misquote him. However, I think it is out of place here to say more about the substantial issue of this passage, since anybody wishing to judge would have in any case to consult Lakatos's page 412, referred to in my note, and also my *L.Sc.D.*, pages 418 f. Yet I am glad to deduce now from Professor Lakatos's postscript that I must have misunderstood his intentions, and I have added a note to this effect to this passage in my [1972(a)].[83] I shall say no more about any other issue here.[84]

III. THE PROBLEM OF INDUCTION

13. My Solution of Hume's Problem of Induction[84a]

As I recounted at the start of section 16 of my *Autobiography* above, it took me a long time to put two and two together and to realize the connection between my demarcation criterion and the problem of induction. But since then, and especially since my unpublished *Die beiden Grundprobleme der Erkenntnistheorie*, I have regarded them as inseparable companions. So, apparently, do several of my critics regard them. Indeed, I find that I can no longer postpone a discussion of the problem of induction, and its importance for my philosophy.

Although I am fully aware of the fact that I may be mistaken, I think that I have solved the problem of induction, this major philosophical problem first raised by David Hume. Perhaps I should be more wary; I claim only to have solved the other half of the philosophical problem whose more fundamental half was already solved by Hume, in his early *Treatise on Human Nature*, 1739. With a little generosity the problem may even be described as the *problem of human knowledge*.

Despite the age of the problem and despite its philosophical abstractness, or perhaps even absurdity, I think that both Hume's and my own solutions are generally interesting and surprisingly fruitful. I am more or less alone in this opinion.

To solve a problem, nothing is as important as a proper formulation. To solve Hume's problem, I shall have to reformulate it.

Hume's problem of induction has almost always been badly formulated by what may be called the philosophical tradition. I will first give a few of these bad formulations, which I shall call the *traditional formulations of the problem of induction*. I shall soon replace them, however, by what I regard as better formulations.

I

Typical examples of formulations of the problem of induction that are both traditional and bad are the following.

What is the justification for the belief that the future will resemble the past? What is the justification of so-called *inductive inferences*?

By an inductive inference is here meant an inference from repeatedly *observed instances* to some as yet *unobserved instances*. It is of comparatively minor significance whether such an inference from the observed to the unobserved is, from the point of view of time, predictive or retrodictive; whether we infer that the sun will rise tomorrow or that it did rise 100,000 years ago. Of course, from a pragmatic point of view, one might say that it is the predictive type of inference which is the more important. No doubt usually it is.

There are various philosophers other than I who also regard as misconceived this traditional problem of induction. Some say that it is misconceived because no justification is needed for inductive inference; no more in fact than for deductive inference. Inductive inference is inductively valid just as deductive inference is deductively valid. I think it was Professor Strawson who was the first to say this.

I am of a different opinion. I hold with Hume that there simply is no such logical entity as an inductive inference; or, that all so-called inductive inferences are logically invalid—and even *inductively* invalid, to put it more sharply (see the end of section 14 below). We have many examples of deductively valid inferences, and even some partial criteria of deductive validity; but no example of an inductively valid inference exists.[85] And I hold, incidentally, that this result can be found in Hume, even though Hume, at the same time, and in sharp contrast to myself, *believed in the psychological power of induction*; not as a valid procedure, but as a procedure which animals and men successfully make use of, as a matter of fact and of biological necessity.

I take it as an important task, in replying to my critics, to make clear, even at the cost of some repetition, where I agree and where I disagree with Hume.

I agree with Hume's opinion that induction is invalid and in no sense justified. Consequently neither Hume nor I can accept the traditional formulations which uncritically ask for the justification of induction; such a request is uncritical because it is blind to the possibility that induction is invalid *in every sense,* and therefore *unjustifiable.*

I disagree with Hume's opinion (the opinion incidentally of almost all philosophers) that induction is a fact and in any case needed. I hold that neither animals nor men use any procedure like induction, or any argument based on the repetition of instances. The belief that we use induction is simply a mistake. It is a kind of optical illusion.

What we do use is a method of trial and of the elimination of error; however misleadingly this method may look like induction, its logical structure, if we examine it closely, totally differs from that of induction. Moreover, it is a method which does not give rise to any of the difficulties connected with the problem of induction.

Thus it is not because induction can manage without justification that I am opposed to the traditional problem; on the contrary, it would urgently need justification. But the need cannot be satisfied. Induction simply does not exist, and the opposite view is a straightforward mistake.

II

There are many ways to present my own noninductivist point of view. Perhaps the simplest is this. I will try to show that the whole apparatus of induction becomes unnecessary once we admit the general fallibility of human knowledge or, as I like to call it, the *conjectural character of human knowledge.*

Let me point this out first for the best kind of human knowledge we have; that is, for scientific knowledge. I assert that scientific knowledge is essentially conjectural or hypothetical.

Take as an example classical Newtonian mechanics. There never was a more successful theory. If repeated observational success could establish a theory, it would have established Newton's theory. Yet Newton's theory was superseded in the field of astronomy by Einstein's theory, and in the atomic field by quantum theory. And almost all physicists think now that Newtonian classical mechanics is no more than a marvellous conjecture, a strangely successful hypothesis, and a staggeringly good approximation to the truth.

I can now formulate my central thesis, which is this. Once we fully realize the implications of the conjectural character of human knowledge, then the problem of induction changes its character completely: there is no need any longer to be disturbed by Hume's negative results, since there is no need any longer to ascribe to human knowledge a *validity* derived from repeated observations. Human knowledge possesses no such validity. On the other hand, we can explain all our achievements in terms of the method of trial and the elimination of error. To put it in a nutshell, our conjectures are our trial balloons, and we test them by criticizing them and by trying to replace them—by trying to show that there can be better or worse conjectures, and that they can be improved upon. The place of the problem of induction is usurped by the problem of the comparative goodness or badness of the rival conjectures or theories that have been proposed.

The main barrier to accepting the conjectural character of human knowledge, and to accepting that it contains the solution of the problem of induction, is a doctrine which may be called the commonsense theory of human knowledge or the *bucket theory of the human mind.*[86]

III

I think very highly of common sense. In fact, I think that all philosophy must start from commonsense views and from their critical examination.

For our purposes here I want to distinguish two parts of the commonsense view of the world and draw attention to the fact that they clash with one another.

The first is commonsense realism; this is the view that there is a real world, with real people, animals and plants, cars and stars in it. I think that this view is true and immensely important, and I believe that no valid criticism of it has ever been proposed.

A very different part of the commonsense view of the world is the commonsense *theory of knowledge*. The problem is the problem of how we get knowledge about the world. The commonsense solution is: by opening our eyes and ears. *Our senses are the main if not the only sources of our knowledge of the world.*

This second view I regard as thoroughly mistaken, and as insufficiently criticized (in spite of Leibniz and Kant). I call it the bucket theory of the mind, because it can be summed up by the following diagram:

What allegedly enters the bucket through our senses are the elements, the atoms or molecules, of knowledge. Our knowledge then consists of an accumulation, a digest, or perhaps a synthesis of the elements offered to us by our senses.

Both halves of commonsense philosophy, commonsense realism and the commonsense theory of knowledge, were held by Hume; he found, as did Berkeley before him, that there is a clash between them. For the commonsense theory of knowledge is liable to lead to a kind of antirealism. If knowledge results from sensations, then sensations are the only *certain* elements of knowledge, and we can have no good reason to believe that anything but sensation exists.

Hume, Berkeley, and Leibniz were all believers in a principle of sufficient reason. For Berkeley and Hume the principle took the form: if you do not have sufficient reasons for holding a belief, then this fact is itself a sufficient reason for abandoning this belief. Genuine knowledge consisted for both Berkeley and Hume essentially of belief, backed by sufficient reasons; but this led them to the position that knowledge consists, more or less, of sensations on their own.

Thus for these philosophers the real world of common sense does not really exist; according to Hume, even we ourselves do not fully exist. All that exist are sensations, impressions, and memory images.

This antirealistic view can be characterized by various names, but the most usual name seems to be "idealism". Hume's idealism appeared to him to be a strict refutation of commonsense realism. But though he felt *rationally* obliged to regard commonsense realism as a mistake, he himself admitted that he was in practice quite unable to disbelieve in commonsense realism for more than an hour.

Thus Hume experienced very strongly the clash between the two parts of commonsense philosophy: realism, and the commonsense theory of knowledge. And although he was aware that emotionally he was unable to give up realism, he looked on this fact as a mere consequence of irrational custom or habit; he was convinced that a consistent adherence to the more critical results of the theory of knowledge ought to make us abandon realism.[87] Fundamentally, Hume's idealism has remained the mainstream of British empiricism.

IV

Hume's two problems of induction—the logical problem and the psychological problem—can best be presented, I think, against the background of the commonsense theory of induction. This theory is very simple. Since all knowledge is supposed to be the result of past observation, so especially is all expectational knowledge such as that the sun will rise tomorrow, or that all men are bound to die, or that bread nourishes. All this has to be the result of past observation.

It is to Hume's undying merit that he dared to challenge the commonsense view of induction, even though he never doubted that it must be largely true. He believed that induction by repetition was logically untenable—that rationally, or logically, *no amount* of observed instances can have the slightest bearing upon unobserved instances. This is Hume's negative solution of the problem of induction, a solution which I fully endorse.

But Hume held, at the same time, that although induction was rationally invalid, it was a psychological fact, and that we all relied on it.

Thus Hume's two problems of induction were:

(a) The logical problem:

Are we rationally justified in reasoning from repeated instances of which we have had experience to instances of which we have had no experience?

Hume's unrelenting answer is: No, we are not justified, however great the number of repetitions may be. And he added that it did not make the slightest difference if, in this problem, we ask for the justification not of *certain* belief, but of *probable* belief. Instances of which we have had experience do not allow us to reason or argue about the *probability* of instances of which we have had no experience, any more than to the *certainty* of such instances.

(b) The following psychological question:

How is it that nevertheless all reasonable people expect and believe that instances of which they have had no experience will conform to those of which they have had experience? Or in other words, why do we all have *expectations*, and why do we hold on to them with such great *confidence*, or such strong belief?

Hume's answer to this psychological problem of induction was:

Because of "custom or habit"; or in other words, because of the irrational but irresistible power of the law of association. We are *conditioned by repetition;* a conditioning mechanism without which, Hume says, we could hardly survive.

My own view is that Hume's answer to the logical problem is right and that his answer to the psychological problem is, in spite of its persuasiveness, quite mistaken.

V

The answers given by Hume to the logical and psychological problems of induction lead immediately to an irrationalist conclusion. According to Hume, all our knowledge, and especially all our scientific knowledge, is just irrational habit or custom, and it is rationally totally indefensible.

Hume himself thought of this as a form of scepticism; but it was rather, as Bertrand Russell pointed out, an unintended surrender to irrationalism. It is an amazing fact that a peerless critical genius, one of the most rational minds of all ages, not only came to disbelieve in reason, but became a champion of unreason, of irrationalism.

Nobody has felt this paradox more strongly than Bertrand Russell, an admirer and, in many respects, even a late disciple of Hume. Thus in the Hume chapter in his *History of Western Philosophy,* published in 1946, Russell says about Hume's treatment of induction: "Hume's philosophy . . . represents the bankruptcy of eighteenth-century reasonableness" and, "It is therefore important to discover whether there is any answer to Hume within a philosophy that is wholly or mainly *empirical.* If not, *there is no intellectual difference between sanity and insanity.* The lunatic who believes that he is a poached egg is to be condemned solely on the ground that he is in a minority . . .".

Russell goes on to assert that if induction (or the principle of induction) is rejected, "every attempt to arrive at general scientific laws from particular observations is fallacious, and Hume's scepticism is inescapable for an empiricist".

And Russell sums up his view of the situation created by the clash between Hume's two answers, by the following dramatic remark:

"The growth of unreason throughout the nineteenth century and what has passed of the twentieth is a natural sequel to Hume's destruction of empiricism."[88]

This last quotation of Russell's goes *perhaps* too far. I do not wish to overdramatize the situation; and although I sometimes feel that Russell is right in his emphasis, at other moments I doubt it.

Yet the following quotation from Professor Strawson seems to me to support Russell's grave opinion: "[If] . . . there is a problem of induction, and . . . Hume posed it, it must be added that he solved it . . . [;] our acceptance of the 'basic canons' [of induction] . . . is forced upon us by Nature. . . . Reason is, and ought to be the slave of the passions".[89]

However this may be, I assert that I have an answer to Hume's psychological problem which completely removes the clash between the logic and the psychology of knowledge; and with it, it removes all of Hume's and Strawson's reasoning against reason.

VI

My own way of avoiding Hume's irrationalist consequences is very simple. I solve the psychological problem of induction (and also such formulations as the pragmatic problem) in a manner which satisfies the following *"principle of the primacy of the logical solution"*, or, more briefly, the *"principle of transference"*. The principle runs like this: the solution of the logical problem of induction, far from clashing with those of the psychological or pragmatic problems, can, with some care, be directly transferred to them. As a result, there is no clash, and there are no irrationalist consequences.

The logical problem of induction itself needs some reformulation to start with.

First, it must be formulated in terms not only of "instances" (as by Hume) but of universal regularities or laws. Regularities or laws are presupposed by Hume's own term "instance"; for an instance is an instance *of* something—*of* a regularity or *of* a law. (Or, rather, it is an instance of many regularities or many laws; see my reply to Quine above.)

Secondly, we must widen the scope of reasoning from instances to laws so that we can take heed also of counterinstances.

In this way, we arrive at a reformulation of Hume's *logical problem of induction* along the following lines:

Are we rationally justified in reasoning from instances or from counterinstances of which we have had experience to the truth or falsity of the corresponding laws, or to instances of which we have had no experience?

This is a purely logical problem. It is essentially merely a slight extension of Hume's logical problem of induction formulated here earlier, in subsection IV.

The answer to this problem is: as implied by Hume, we certainly are not justified in reasoning from an instance to the truth of the corresponding law. But to this negative result a second result, equally negative, may be added: we *are* justified in reasoning from a counterinstance to the *falsity* of the corresponding universal law (that is, of any law of which it is a counterinstance). Or in other words, from a purely logical point of view, the acceptance of *one* counterinstance to "All swans are white" implies the falsity of the law "All swans are white"—that law, that is, whose counterinstance we accepted. Induction is logically invalid; but refutation or falsification is a logically valid way of arguing from a single counterinstance to—or, rather, against—the corresponding law.

This shows that I continue to agree with Hume's negative logical result; but I extend it.

This logical situation is completely independent of any question of whether we would, in practice, accept a single counterinstance—for example, a solitary black swan—in refutation of a so far highly successful law. I do not suggest that we would necessarily be so easily satisfied; we might well suspect that the black specimen before us was not a swan. And in practice, anyway, we would be most reluctant to accept an isolated counterinstance. But this is a different question (though one which I have dealt with extensively). Logic forces us to reject even the most successful law the moment we accept one single counterinstance.

Thus we can say: Hume was right in his negative result that there can be no logically valid positive argument leading in the inductive direction. But there is a further negative result; there are logically valid negative arguments leading in the inductive direction: *a counterinstance may disprove a law.*

VII

Hume's negative result establishes for good that all our universal laws or theories remain forever guesses, conjectures, hypotheses. But my own negative result concerning the force of counterinstances by no means rules out the possibility of a positive theory of how, by purely rational arguments, we can *prefer* some competing conjectures to others.

In fact, we can erect a fairly elaborate *logical theory of preference*—preference from the point of view of the search for truth.

To put it in a nutshell, Russell's desperate remark that if with Hume we reject all positive induction, "there is no intellectual difference between sanity and insanity" is mistaken. For the rejection of induction does not prevent us from preferring, say, Newton's theory to Kepler's, or Einstein's theory to Newton's: during our rational critical discussion of these theories we *may* have accepted the existence of counterexamples to Kepler's theory which do not refute Newton's, and of counterexamples to Newton's which do not refute Einstein's. Given the acceptance of these counterexamples we can say that Kepler's and Newton's theories are certainly false; whilst Einstein's may be true or it may be false: that we don't know. Thus there may exist *purely intellectual* preferences for one or the other of these theories; and we are very far from having to say with Russell that all the difference between science and lunacy disappears. Admittedly, Hume's argument still stands, and therefore the difference between a scientist and a lunatic is not that the first bases his theories securely upon observations while the second does not, or anything like that. Nevertheless we may now see that there *may be* a difference: it *may be* that the lunatic's theory is easily refutable by observation, while the scientist's theory has withstood severe tests.

What the scientist's and the lunatic's theories have in common is that both belong to *conjectural knowledge*. But some conjectures are much better than others; and this is a sufficient answer to Russell, and it is sufficient to avoid radical scepticism. For since it is possible for some conjectures to be *preferable* to others, it is also possible for our conjectural knowledge to improve, and to *grow*. (Of course, it is possible that a theory that is preferred to another at one time may fall out of favour at a later time so that the other is now preferred to it. But, on the other hand, this may not happen.)

We may *prefer* some competing theories to others on purely rational grounds. It is important that we are clear what the principles of preference or selection are.

In the first place they are governed by the idea of truth. We want, if at all possible, theories which are true, and for this reason we try to eliminate the false ones.

But we want more than this. We want new and interesting truth. We are thus led to the idea of *the growth of informative content,* and especially of *truth content.* That is, we are led to the following *principle of preference:* a theory with a great informative content is on the whole more interesting, even before it has been tested, than a theory with little content. Admittedly, we may have to abandon the theory with the greater content, or as I also call it, the bolder theory, if it does not stand up to tests. But even in this case we may have learned more from it than from a theory with little content, for falsifying tests can sometimes reveal new and unexpected facts and problems.

Thus our logical analysis leads us direct to a theory of method, and especially to the following methodological rule: try out, and aim at, bold theories, with great informative content; and then let these bold theories compete, by discussing them critically and by testing them severely.

Perhaps I may conclude this section by showing that three standard examples of "inductively valid" laws are all false in the sense in which they were originally meant. The laws are:

(a) that the sun will rise and set once in 24 hours (or approximately 90,000 pulse beats);
(b) that all men are mortal;
(c) that bread nourishes.

(a) The first was refuted when Pytheas of Marseilles discovered "the frozen sea and the midnight sun". The fact that (a) was intended to mean "Wherever you go, the sun will rise and set once in 24 hours" is shown by the utter disbelief with which his report was met, and by the fact that his report became the paradigm of all travellers' tales.

(b) The second (or more precisely the Aristotelian theory from which it follows) was also refuted. The predicate "mortal" is a bad translation from the Greek: *thnētos* means "bound to die" or "liable to die", rather than merely "mortal", and (b) is part of Aristotle's theory that every generated creature is bound to decay and to die after a period which, though its length is part of the creature's essence, will vary a little according to accidental circumstances; but this theory was refuted by the discovery that bacteria are not bound to die, since multiplication by fission is not death, and later by the realization that living matter is not in general bound to decay and to die (cancer cells can go on living), although it seems that all can be killed by sufficiently drastic means.

(c) The third—a favourite of Hume's—was refuted when people eating their daily bread died of ergotism, as happened in a catastrophic case in a French village not very long ago. What (c) originally meant was that bread properly baked from flour properly prepared from wheat or corn, sown and harvested according to old-established practice, would nourish people rather than poison them. But it did poison them.

14. The Psychological and Pragmatic Problems of Induction

I have so far tried to show that Hume's logical problem of induction, if a little generalized, yields the following two results.

(a) All scientific or theoretical knowledge is conjectural.

(b) There can be rational preferences for some of the competing conjectures: some can be better than others, at least in two senses: they can be more informative and thus more interesting, more bold; and they can be better in standing up to more severe tests.

Let me turn now to Hume's second problem, the psychological problem of *why* we nevertheless all have expectations, or of why we believe that the future will be like the past. Here I disagree with Hume entirely. Not only do I regard the problem as inadequately analysed; I also regard as mistaken Hume's reply—that our beliefs are conditioned by association or repetition.

Before proceeding to details, I should recall the difference between Lamarck and Darwin. Lamarck explained adaptation as the result of more or less direct *instruction* given (through repetition) by the environment to an aim-seeking organism. Darwin explained it as the result of *selection*. He showed that the result of selection may look like a result obtained by instruction. One can put this by saying that Darwin showed that selection may *simulate* instruction.

Hume's reply to the psychological problem of induction is Lamarckian. But it can be replaced by a Darwinian reply, and by one which, at first sight, looks similar to Lamarckism; it *simulates* it.

It is, I think, hardly open to serious doubt that we are fitted with an immensely rich genetic endowment which, among other things, makes us most eager to generalize and to look out for regularities; and also, to apply the method of trial and error. Now I assert that all learning of *new* things is by the *selective* elimination of error rather than by instruction. (I do not deny that there exists what Konrad Lorenz calls imprinting;[90] but this is very different from inductive instruction through repetition.) I assert, moreover, that this is an application of what I have called the *principle of transference from logic to psychology*—the principle that what is true in logic must, by and large, be true in psychology.

My *solution* of the logical problem of induction was that we may have *preferences* for certain of the competing conjectures; that is, for those which are highly informative and which so far have stood up to eliminative criticism. These preferred conjectures are the result of selection, of the struggle for survival of the hypotheses under the strain of *criticism, which is artificially intensified selection pressure.*

The same holds for the psychological problem of induction. Here too we are faced with competing hypotheses, which may perhaps be called beliefs, and some of them are eliminated, while others survive, anyway for the time being. Animals are often eliminated along with their beliefs; or else they survive with them. Men frequently outlive their beliefs; but for as long as the beliefs survive (often a very short time), they form the (momentary or lasting) *basis of action.*

My central thesis is that this Darwinian procedure of the selection of beliefs and actions can in no sense be described as irrational. In no way does it clash with the rational solution of the logical problem of induction. Rather, it is just the transference of the logical solution to the psychological field. (This does not mean, of course, that we never suffer from what are called "irrational beliefs".)

Thus with an application of the principle of transference to Hume's psychological problem Hume's irrationalist conclusions disappear.

In talking of preference I have so far discussed only the theoretician's preference—if he has any; and why it will be for the "better", that is, more testable, theory, and for the better tested one. Of course, the theoretician may not have *any* preference: he may be discouraged by Hume's, and my, "sceptical" solution to Hume's logical problem; he may say that, if he cannot *make sure* of finding the true theory among the competing theories, he is not interested in any method like the one described—not even if the method makes it reasonably certain that, *if* a true theory should be among the theories proposed, it will be among the surviving, the preferred, the corroborated ones. Yet a more sanguine or more dedicated or more curious "pure" theoretician may well be encouraged, by our analysis, to propose again and again new competing theories in the hope that one of them may be true—even if we shall never be able to make sure of any one that it is true.

Thus the pure theoretician has more than one way of action open to him; and he will choose a method such as the method of trial and the elimination or error only if his curiosity exceeds his disappointment at the unavoidable uncertainty and incompleteness of all our endeavours.

It is different with him *qua* man of practical action. For a man of practical action has always to *choose* between some more or less definite alternatives, since even *inaction is a kind of action.*

But every action presupposes a set of expectations, that is, of theories about the world. Which theory shall the man of action choose? Is there such a thing as a *rational choice?*

This leads us to the *pragmatic problems of induction,* which to start with, we might formulate thus:

(a) Upon which theory should we rely for practical action, from a rational point of view?

(b) Which theory should we prefer for practical action, from a rational point of view?

My answer to (a) is: from a rational point of view, we should not "rely" on any theory, for no theory has been shown to be true, or can be shown to be true (or "reliable").

My answer to (b) is: we should *prefer* the best tested theory as a basis for action.

In other words, there is no "absolute reliance"; but since we *have* to choose, it will be "rational" to choose the best tested theory. This will be "rational" in the most obvious sense of the word known to me: the best tested theory is the one which, in the light of our *critical discussion,* appears to be the best so far; and I do not know of anything more "rational" than a well-conducted critical discussion.

Since this point appears not to have got home I shall try to restate it here in a slightly new way, suggested to me by David Miller. Let us forget momentarily about what theories we "use" or "choose" or "base our practical actions on", and consider only the resulting *proposal* or *decision* (to do *X;* not to do *X;* to do nothing; or so on). Such a proposal can, we hope, be rationally criticized; and if we are rational agents we will want it to survive, if possible, the most testing criticism we can muster. *But such criticism will freely make use of the best tested scientific theories in our possession.* Consequently any proposal that ignores these theories (where they are relevant, I need hardly add) will collapse under criticism. Should any proposal remain, it will be rational to adopt it.

This seems to me all far from tautological.[91] Indeed, it might well be challenged by challenging the italicized sentence in the last paragraph. Why, it might be asked, does rational criticism make use of the best tested although highly unreliable theories? The answer, however, is exactly the same as before. Deciding to criticize a practical proposal from the standpoint of modern medicine (rather than, say, in phrenological terms) is itself a kind of "practical" decision (anyway it may have practical consequences). Thus the rational decision is always: adopt critical methods that have themselves withstood severe criticism.

There is, of course, an infinite regress here. But it is transparently harmless.

Now I do not particularly want to deny (or, for that matter, assert) that, in choosing the best tested theory as a basis for action, we "rely" on it, in some sense of the word. It may therefore even be described as the *most* "reliable" theory available, in some sense of this term. Yet this is not to say that it is "reliable". It is "unreliable" at least in the sense that we shall always do well, even in practical action, to foresee the possibility that something may go wrong with it and with our expectations.

But it is not merely this trivial caution which we must derive from our negative reply to the pragmatic problem (a). Rather, it is of the utmost importance for the understanding of the whole problem, and especially of what I have called the traditional problem, that in spite of the "rationality" of choosing the best tested theory as a basis of action, this choice is *not* "rational" in the sense that it is based upon *good reasons in favour* of the expectation that it will in practice be a successful choice: *there can be no good reasons* in this sense, and this is precisely Hume's result. On the contrary, even if our physical theories should be true, it is perfectly possible that the world as we know it, with all its pragmatically relevant regularities, may completely disintegrate in the next second. This should be obvious to anybody today; but I said so[92] before Hiroshima: there are infinitely many possible causes of local, partial, or total disaster.

From a pragmatic point of view, however, most of these possibilities are obviously not worth bothering about because we cannot *do* anything about them: they are beyond the realm of action. (I do not, of course, include atomic war among those disasters which are beyond the realm of human action, although most of us think just in this way since we cannot do more about it than about an act of God.)

All this would hold even if we could be certain that our physical and biological theories were true. But we do not know it. On the contrary, we have very good reason to suspect even the best of them; and this adds, of course, further infinities to the infinite possibilities of catastrophe.

It is this kind of consideration which makes Hume's and my own negative reply so important. For we can now see very clearly why we must beware lest our theory of knowledge proves too much. More precisely, *no theory of knowledge should attempt to explain why we are successful in our attempts to explain things.*[93]

Even if we assume that we have been successful—that our physical theories are true—we can learn from our cosmology how infinitely improbable this success is: our theories tell us that the world is almost completely empty, and that empty space is filled with chaotic radiation. And almost all places which are not empty are occupied either by chaotic dust, or by gases, or by very hot stars—all in conditions which seem to make the application of any physical method of acquiring knowledge impossible.

There are many worlds, possible and actual worlds, in which a search for knowledge and for regularities would fail. And even in the world as we actually know it from the sciences, the occurrence of conditions under which life, and a search for knowledge, could arise—and succeed—seems to be almost infinitely improbable. Moreover, it seems that if ever such conditions should appear, they would be bound to disappear again, after a time which, cosmologically speaking, is very short.

It is in this sense that induction is inductively invalid, as I said above, in section 13, subsection I. That is to say, any strong positive reply to Hume's logical problem (say, the thesis that induction is valid) would be paradoxical. For, on the one hand, if induction is the method of science, then modern cosmology is at least roughly correct (I do not dispute this); and on the other, modern cosmology teaches us that to generalize from observations taken, for the most part, in our incredibly idiosyncratic region of the universe would almost always be quite invalid. Thus if induction is "inductively valid" it will almost always lead to false conclusions; and therefore it is inductively invalid.

15. Objective and Subjective Knowledge

Many philosophers interested in the theory of knowledge are highly interested in belief. For they usually characterize knowledge as a special kind of belief—belief for which we possess sufficient reason, and of which we can therefore be certain. (Thus Locke says that immediate or intuitive knowledge and demonstrative knowledge are the only kinds of knowledge —everything else "is but faith or opinion"; and this is, essentially, Aristotle's view, or Berkeley's, or Hume's; for which reason Hume prefers to speak of "demonstration"—in contrast to "probability"—rather than of "knowledge"; or else of "belief"—rational belief in contrast to nonrational belief.)

I strongly disagree with this view. Human knowledge at any rate, and especially scientific knowledge, is made up to a large extent of *linguistically formulated theories.* And I contend that there is a world of difference between a belief and a linguistically formulated theory. (The belief is in world 2; the theory is in world 3.)[94]

A subjective belief which I hold, or which an animal holds, is in a fairly clear sense a part of me or of the animal. Neither of us can objectively criticize it. Only if I *formulate it in language,* or in *writing,* or still better *publish* it, can it become an object of critical discussion—of objective criticism. There seems to be little difference between the feeling that it is very late for lunch and saying "It is very late for lunch". But I hold that the difference is immense. Once formulated in words, the belief may be criticized and refuted.

Thus I do not look upon human conjectural knowledge as a subspecies of subjective belief. (Even animal knowledge can be regarded [from the outside] as objective or interpersonal. It is, I think, better understood as part of the organism; and it is criticized not *by* the organism, but, for example, by changing or destroying the organism.)

The traditional theories of knowledge (from Plato's *Theaetetus* to Wittgenstein's *On Certainty*) fail to make a clear distinction between objective and subjective knowledge. As a consequence they constantly get into trouble. For can we call an unjustified and unjustifiable belief (a belief in a conjecture, say) by the name of "knowledge"? Or perhaps an uncertain belief? Clearly we cannot. Thus we are faced with the difficulty of having to say, either, that only self-evident (intuitive) knowledge—and what follows from it—is real knowledge, that is, Aristotle's *epistēmē* and Locke's demonstrative knowledge (this is difficult because self-evidence has so often been wrongly claimed for false theories such as that of the flat earth at rest); or that there is no knowledge (or certainty); or else that we have beliefs which amount to knowledge, even though it is not so clear whether we have beliefs which are (absolutely) certain.

All these problems assume an entirely different character if we realize that the theory of knowledge was in truth always groping for objective knowledge; that objective knowledge is not founded on subjective knowledge; and that the study of subjective knowledge belongs to psychology (though logic may show psychology the way).

An interesting illustration of this may be found in a recent discussion[95] between W. C. Salmon and J. W. N. Watkins about the question of whether or not I have solved the problem of induction. It is worth looking at here because particular emphasis is laid on the pragmatic problem of induction.

As Salmon says,[96] he originally confronted my theory with the following dilemma: either science embodies *knowledge* of the unobserved [the future, say], in which case it is inductive; or it does not, in which case it is barren.

Against this, Watkins points out that the hypotheses of science (conjectures, guesses) do embody assertions about the unobserved. (In the terminology of the present section, they are objective knowledge about the unobserved, although those who "know" these hypotheses do not possess subjective knowledge about the unobserved even if they happen to believe in those hypotheses; for they cannot "justify" their belief.) Watkins also points out that a corroboration statement only sums up the *logical relation* between the theory and the test statements. Thus if in a corroboration statement the theory and the test statement are explicitly referred to, the corroboration statement might be called "analytic". However, the statement that the theory t_1 had a lower degree of corroboration than theory t_2 at the time when their degrees of corroboration were last compared by critically discussing them, is of course a "synthetic" statement.

In his reply to Watkins, Salmon speaks again about *"knowledge"*. "When someone is said to *know* physics", Salmon says (italics mine), "most of us would suppose he *knows* some general laws. . . . Taken at face value, such laws or theories make statements about unobserved matters of fact. [But according to Popper] . . . we cannot claim to *know* any such things . . . [and thus according to Popper] science does not embody *knowledge* beyond observation."

But it is clear that, according to my views, science does embody *objective* knowledge (of a hypothetical character) although of course *it does not embody knowledge that is certain* (which means that we cannot claim to *know* in the sense of certain rational belief). Nevertheless we can claim that in deciding to prefer one theory to another (say, because of its higher degree of corroboration), we proceed in a perfectly rational way—in the way of the searcher for truth, though not in the way of the possessor of truth.

Salmon sums up this part of his discussion by stating my views in a way which makes it very clear that he has understood them fairly well—except that he is still puzzled about their relation to "knowledge" (the italics are mine): " . . . the hypotheses themselves form no part of the *corpus of our knowledge,* and the corroboration statements merely reformulate the content of our observations." I should say, yes and no. The theories do form part of the corpus of our *objective* knowledge (which is what is under critical discussion); that is, they belong to the realm of ideas produced by us (world 3). But they do not, of course, form part of the corpus of knowledge in the sense of Salmon—of subjective, justified knowledge—even if such a corpus exists. (It is of minor importance that the corroboration statements assess the *relationship* between what Salmon terms "the content of our observations" and the various competing theories, rather than merely stating that content.)

In this context it is crucial that it is not our corroboration statements but our *theories* which allow us to make predictions (in the presence of observed "initial conditions", of course), with the consequence that these predictions may be as hypothetical as the theories. *Thus our theories do have predictive import.* Our corroboration statements have no predictive import, although they motivate and justify our *preference* for some theory over another.

Salmon, however, writes: "Watkins acknowledges . . . that *corroboration* does have predictive import in practical decision making", quoting Watkins, who says of some agent who has a limited number of theories to choose from: " . . . it would be rational for him to choose the better corroborated one . . . since he has nothing else to go on." (Italics mine.)[97]

Yet nothing whatever of a predictive nature follows from a corroboration statement or even from the (synthetic) statement that yesterday t_1 was found to be less well corroborated than t_2. On the other hand, in deriving the prediction nothing is involved except the chosen theory (and the initial conditions). In fact it may well happen that an agent chooses between two equally well corroborated theories, in which case his choice may be a toss-up (rather than "rational" in the sense of preferring the logically better theory). It should be obvious that this toss-up as such has no predictive import whatever: it is only the chosen theory which has. Thus the reference to Watkins's quoted statement is certainly not sufficient to allow Salmon to reformulate his original statement of what he regards as the dilemma in which I am involved: "Either corroboration has an inductive aspect or there is no logic of prediction." The situation is in fact quite different. Corroboration has no inductive aspect; and the logic of prediction consists, simply, in deducing predictions from hypotheses plus initial conditions. In other words, the logic of prediction is the ordinary deductive logic and nothing else.

16. Reply to Medawar on Hypothesis and Imagination

> The belief that great discoveries and little everyday discoveries have quite different methodological origins betrays the amateur. Whewell, the professional, insisted that the bold use of imagination was the rule in scientific discovery, not the exception. . . .
>
> PETER MEDAWAR

Sir Peter Medawar's essay does not fall among those which criticize my philosophy or among those which expound it. Rather, he takes my theory of science as read and approved, and draws attention to some of those scientists and philosophers who held fundamentally the same views. This is of course fascinating to anybody interested in the history of ideas. In particular, Medawar's contribution made me read Claude Bernard's *Introduction to the Study of Experimental Medicine*[98] and I am immensely grateful for this. Not only was Bernard a great and revolutionary scientist, but all his fascinating examples illustrate the passage from Medawar that I have taken for my motto. For Bernard, revolutions in science were a matter of course. He constantly faced the ever-repeated overthrow of theories on all levels of universality and importance, from the solving of minor puzzles to the overthrow of major theories which he himself had accepted (such as the theory that sugar is produced in plants but never in animals). It was all in a day's work—though the day's work was not of a routine character, but always demanding the highest inspirational and critical powers.

Medawar's contribution has made me see, to my surprise, how many of my ideas have been anticipated by others; for these ideas not only came to me without my having read or heard about them, but in some cases were developed in conscious opposition to my elders and betters.

I

The first section of Medawar's paper has the following structure: he first allows an "educated layman" (or a philosopher?) to "set down his understanding" of science; and then he gives a summary of five objections which "a critic" (such as Medawar himself, or I myself) would make to the lay view. These objections are:

(1) There is no such thing as a Scientific Mind.

(2) There is no such thing as The Scientific Method.

(3) The idea of naive or innocent observation is philosophers' make-believe.

(4) Induction is a myth.

(5) The formulation of a natural law begins as an imaginative exploit and imagination is a faculty essential to the scientist's task; and it is an unhappy usage that treats a "hypothesis" as an adolescent "theory".

To point (1) I have nothing to add to Medawar's objection.

To point (2)—that there is no such thing as The Scientific Method—I wish to add something.

The idea that great scientists are master practitioners of a special method—a special way which, if followed faithfully, must lead to success, that is, to a discovery—seems to me mistaken. It is refuted by the fact that some great scientists (such as Max Planck) made only one great discovery; and though they continued in a life devoted to science, and did not stop producing work of considerable merit, they did not repeat their one outstandingly brilliant performance. The phenomenon is not rare, and this shows that their great success was not explicable by their mastery of a method (whether or not its rules are consciously understood or followed unconsciously). This, however, is not to deny that all or most successful scientific activities have something in common: a flair for the important (and soluble)[99] problem; the imagination which produces not one but many competing hypotheses, and, above all, that critical attitude which, alone, might helpfully be described as a "method": the method of severely criticizing one's own ideas.

To point (3)—that the idea of naive or innocent observation is untenable—I should also like to add something. Claude Bernard, as Medawar shows in his section IV, was not merely a great scientist but a man of deep insight into those questions of method which Medawar here discusses. Yet in *An Introduction to the Study of Experimental Medicine,* Bernard laid great stress on the distinction between experimenting and observing; and he taught that, while experiment is always inspired by an idea and should be designed to test a hypothesis, observation ought to be, in Medawar's terminology, "naive and innocent". A close reading shows that Bernard had seen too many cases in which people observed what they "knew" must be there. This he wanted to exclude. But it did not occur to him that observational neutrality is impossible, and that something approaching it can be realized only by an attitude which is consciously critical of the "idea" or "hypothesis" which the observation is to test. We are always inclined to observe what we know, unless we are awake to the fact that we should look for a refutation of what we think we know. This, I think, is the only precept that can lead to results like those which Bernard's "naivety" or "neutrality" or "detachment" was intended to achieve. As opposed to Bernard I hold (and I think Medawar and I are at one in this) that what Bernard calls an "observation" is as much inspired and influenced by theoretical assumptions as what he calls an "experiment", and therefore that the distinction between them is less significant than he suggests.

To point (4)—induction is a myth—I wish to add only that nothing depends upon words. If anybody should write, as did Peirce, "The operation of testing a hypothesis by experiment . . . I call induction", I should not object, as long as he is not misled by the word. But Peirce *was* misled, as were many others. This is why I prefer to use the word "induction" to stand for the myth that the *repetition* of something—"observations" or "instances", perhaps—provides some rational basis for the acceptance of hypotheses. Peirce, in spite of the flawless explanation he sometimes gave of the method of hypotheses and tests, at other times defended precisely this myth; for example, when he compared natural laws with habits (acquired by repetition) and when he tried to give a *probabilistic* theory of induction.

It is induction by repetition (and therefore probabilistic induction) which I combat as the centre of the myth; and in view of the past history of induction from Aristotle and Bacon to Peirce and Carnap, it seems to me appropriate to use the term "induction" as standing, briefly, for "induction by repetition".

Indeed, I agree with Dugald Stewart, as quoted by Medawar: "No hypothesis . . . can completely exclude the possibility of exceptions or limitations hitherto undiscovered". But I do not think that this is equivalent to Jevons's, or Peirce's remarks, quoted by Medawar in the same context, that no hypothesis is more than probable (unless, indeed, we assume that the word "probable" has nothing to do with the probability calculus but means no more than "rationally preferable").

It may be interesting to add to Medawar's historical remarks that Claude Bernard reached this anti-inductivist or deductivist position, or at least came as near to it as did anybody.

To point (5)—in brief, to Whewell's remarks that good hypotheses are "felicitous strokes of inventive talent" or "happy guesses"—I may perhaps add that "lucky guesses" seems to me even more adequate than "happy guesses": in addition to a rich and active imagination, luck is needed to make a *good* hypothesis. Luck is needed *and* familiarity with the problem, deriving (as a rule) from those many imaginative guesses which failed to solve the problem, but brought home its peculiar difficulties. Whewell's "happy guess" is undoubtedly one of the many anticipations of my ideas which can be found in his work; another is that both he and I accepted from Kant that a hypothesis is an attempt to impose a man-made idea upon nature. Where we seem to differ is in my stress on the fact that we usually fail in this attempt, discovering the errors of our ways; and that even when we are lucky and hit upon a true idea, we can never know this for certain. Whewell on the other hand had a theory of the progress of an idea from the status of a tentative hypothesis or happy guess to that of a necessary truth. This progress (which is the result of our repeated use of the idea, of our increasing familiarity with it and understanding of it) takes the place, within Whewell's scheme, of the induction process.

II

In his second section, Medawar comments in a most interesting way on "the history during the eighteenth and nineteenth centuries of some of the central ideas of the hypothetico-deductive scheme of scientific reasoning". He considers especially:

(1) The uncertainty of all "inductive" reasoning and the probationary status of all hypotheses.

(2) The need for hypotheses and their heuristic significance.

(3) The value of false hypotheses and the asymmetry between proof and disproof: only disproof is logically conclusive.

(4) The obligation to put a hypothesis to the test.

All these are views which are central to my way of seeing things. I will confine myself to some comments on points (3) and (4).

To point (3) I wish to add that in my opinion some unnecessary fuss has been made by those who have criticized Medawar's remark that it is "one of the strongest ideas in Popper's methodology, that the only act which the scientist can perform *with complete logical certainty* is the repudiation of what is false". (Italics mine.)

I have no serious objection to this formulation, even though it is perhaps not quite as explicit and cautious as might be wished.

The situation is quite simple. From the point of view of pure logic, it is not possible for us to hold, at the same time, some universal theory and an observation statement (or any other kind of statement) which contradicts it. Take the hypothesis that "the two categories of nerve cells, excitatory and inhibitory, are quite distinct", and that "in the mammalian brain, there are no known examples of cells having an excitatory action by one set of their synapses and an inhibitory action by another set".[100]

It is clear that once the existence in a mammalian brain of a nonspecific nerve cell, that is one that has *both* types of synapses, has been accepted, the hypothesis of the exclusive character of these two specialized types of nerve cells would have indeed to be given up and repudiated with *"complete logical certainty"*.

Now let us make quite clear what would be certain here and what would be uncertain.

It would be completely logically certain that we cannot admit the existence of a nonspecific nerve cell and, at the same time, uphold the hypothesis of exclusive specialization: otherwise we would contradict ourselves, and to do so is indeed forbidden with "complete logical certainty". On the other hand, the existence of a nonspecific nerve cell cannot be established with "complete logical certainty". But this is almost a platitude: since it is an empirical question, we may always be victims of a more or less subtle experimental mistake. Yet the methods of identifying excitatory and inhibitory synapses are well developed; and if a scientist claims to have found a nonspecific nerve cell, his claim might be of a kind which can be easily tested, especially if he shows how his experiment can be repeated; say, by describing the localization of such nonspecific cells in the brain of a cat, thereby proposing a universal hypothesis which contradicts the hypothesis of specificity.

In such a simple case, the refutation of the hypothesis of the specificity of nerve cells would obviously not be achieved by purely logical argument, or "with complete logical certainty", since empirical questions can be raised about it. Still, the refutation would be final, even if we should later discover that the falsifying hypothesis about the localization of nonspecific nerve cells was not universally true for all cats, and that it held, say, only for cats of a particular kind. Although, of course, our whole theoretical interpretation of the "facts" may change with our theories.

We have here three points:

(a) A refutation can be logically conclusive in the sense that, if we accept a refuting instance, we are logically bound to reject the hypothesis.

(b) The refuting instances are never statements of formal logic; they are empirical statements and therefore open to all kinds of empirical mistakes.

(c) There are cases, such as those involving a well-tested falsifying universal hypothesis, in which the original hypothesis remains refuted even if the falsifying hypothesis should, in its turn, not be universally true, but open to exceptions. In these cases we may well say that the original hypothesis has been refuted anyway, even though the falsifying hypothesis is also refuted.

Other cases are still more complicated. As was first pointed out by Duhem, and later by myself and especially by Quine, all empirical tests involve theoretical assumptions, so that we do not really test single hypotheses but, more or less, whole systems of theories. (*L.d.F.*, sections 19-22.) It is thus, in principle, possible to question the refutation of any hypothesis by asking whether responsibility for the outcome of the refuting experiment might not be attributable to one or more of the cooperating hypotheses.

All this is always possible, and in some cases it may be the right thing to do. But these cases must be exceptional and we must have special reasons for them. Were they not, no test would count as a real test (since the hypothesis could escape refutation), and so we would have no science and no progress in science.

And anyway, it is frequently perfectly clear which results would refute, and which would call background knowledge into question. Consider, for example, Eddington's eclipse experiment as a test of general relativity. There were certain possible results which, it was agreed in advance, would refute Einstein's theory—for example, a result indicating a zero deflection of the light rays. But there were, no doubt, also results which would have led first to a scrutiny of the experimental arrangement, and perhaps even to the overthrow of some of the more speculative auxiliary hypotheses. For example, had the deflection appeared to be hundreds of times the value predicted by Einstein; or had it been a deflection in the wrong direction; or had there been no light visible at all: in all these cases we might have felt it necessary to test again some of the items of our background knowledge. But this does not mean that we should do this on every occasion when a refuting instance is observed.

I have here gone into some detail in order to comment on a passage in Medawar's section II, point 3. But in so doing, I have merely tried to clarify what I have said before (cp. [1959(a)], pp. 42, 50, and 81-87; and also [1963(a)], Chap. 10). Although one accepted observational proposition may refute a theory (this is just a logical fact), we should not, as a rule, regard a good theory as refuted merely because it appears to be in conflict with a few observations which (we may even know) can be explained in other ways.

To point (4) I wish to add that even though the demand that hypotheses should be tested has often been raised, as Medawar shows, he does not refer to any anticipation of my suggestion that testability or falsifiability should be regarded as a criterion of the empirical character of a hypothesis. It seems that neither has the idea of degrees of testability been anticipated, nor the idea of identifying these degrees with degrees of empirical content. Claude Bernard speaks of the growth of scientific knowledge, but nobody, it seems, suggested that the growth of knowledge should be identified with the growth of the empirical content of our theories.

III

In his section III, Medawar pays a just tribute to Whewell, and points out that others (whom I had never heard of before), such as Neil Adamson, were also quite clear about the method of hypothesis and testing. I greatly admire the thoroughness that has led to these historical discoveries which were entirely new to me. I hope to be able to read soon the authors to whom Medawar refers.

IV

Medawar begins his section IV by saying that in methodology we attempt "to find out exactly what scientists do or ought to do".

I am inclined to say that we should attempt to find out what they "ought" to do. This "ought" is not a matter of ethics, of course (though ethics comes in too) but rather the "ought" of a *hypothetical* imperative. The question is: "How should we proceed if we wish to contribute to the growth of, scientific knowledge?". And the answer is: "You cannot do better than proceed by the critical method of trial (conjecture) and the elimination of error, by trying to test, or refute, your conjectures". The argument supporting this reply belongs to situational logic. I do not think that we should turn to the (sociological) question of what scientists actually do or say, except perhaps to refute certain competing answers. Newton *did* say, as Medawar points out, *"Hypotheses non fingo"* (or " . . . *non sequor"*); yet he did use hypotheses.

I do not think that the theory of knowledge, or of scientific knowledge, is in its turn an empirical science, and testable or falsifiable in the sense in which, I hold, empirical theories are testable.

Yet I can conceive of empirical circumstances which would lead me to revise my theory of science. If, say, drinking coffee, or the taking of a certain (otherwise harmless) drug, could be shown to stimulate the output not only of scientific theories, but even of successful scientific theories (reducing, say, the output of theories which are refuted), then this, I admit, would force me to give up my views; but since I do not regard the theory of scientific knowledge as an empirical theory, I do not look out for empirical refutations.

Yet factual questions do come in, especially questions of the history of science. Medawar comments in the last two paragraphs of his essay on a factual question which it is difficult to answer: what are the resemblances and differences between artistic and scientific inspiration? I personally should have been inclined to stress the resemblances (as does Bronowski, to whom Medawar refers). Medawar points out certain differences which, so far as I am aware, have not been pointed out before. However, his concluding sentence makes it clear that he too regards the resemblances as very great indeed.

17. Maxwell on Demarcation and Induction

Like Professors Putnam and Lakatos, Professor Maxwell thinks that "many, perhaps most, important scientific theories are not falsifiable"; and he argues this in the first part of his paper. "But", he says, "the main thrust of the paper is intended to be less negative" (both quotations are from the Introduction to his contribution); Maxwell accepts, more or less, my solution of the problem of induction, despite the fact that he rejects my criterion of demarcation (this is in part II of his paper). However he seems to hanker after positive evidence of some sort, and in part III he attempts to provide a theory about such evidence.

Since, then, the main portion of Maxwell's paper is devoted to induction, and since, in my opinion, his discussion is more or less independent of his attack on the criterion of demarcation, I have decided to place my reply to him here, rather than earlier. However, it is necessary for me to make some rejoinder to the first part of his contribution, to his attack on my demarcation criterion, and this I now proceed to do.

I

Unfortunately, like Professor Putnam (see section 11 of my *Replies* above), Professor Maxwell has misread the role of initial conditions in the testing procedure. For after a brief and fairly accurate statement of my general intentions he goes on at once to say that, in my view, a theory is refuted by deducing from it an "(observation) statement inconsistent with [a] . . . potential falsifier . . . [which] turns out to be true". This is not my view. According to me the "falsifier" is the *conjunction* of Maxwell's "(observation) statement" and his "potential falsifier"; in other words, the "falsifier" on its own *contradicts* the theory (*L.Sc.D.*, sections 22 and 28). *Initial conditions are not needed for falsification.*

In the context of Professor Maxwell's paper, admittedly, this point might seem to be largely a verbal one. And I admit also that Maxwell has not here committed any logical mistake; he completely agrees with me that many theories can, *logically speaking,* be falsified. He would, I am absolutely sure, agree that "All swans are white" can be falsified. On the other hand, he has qualms about existential statements and all-and-some statements.

Here is perhaps the best place to answer Maxwell's Appendixes I and II. In the latter appendix Maxwell tries to show that "All men are mortal" (in the sense of (x) (Ey) (x dies at time y); but see my section 10 above for another interpretation), though not falsifiable, can have a positive degree of corroboration, according to my definition; and even that its degree of corroboration can be increased by "instances". His proof, I regret to say, is fallacious. For he disqualifies as statement of evidence the statement "Jones dies on October 5, 1969" (which would be highly improbable relative to the conjunction of "All men are mortal" and "Jones is a man"; and thus unable to sustain the proof); and opts instead for the much weaker "Jones dies", which is an *existential statement,* and so has probability 1. But Maxwell's proof, I fear, depends on its being given a probability of less than 1.

(It might be thought that it is possible to avoid giving "Jones dies" probability 1. It is; for it can be construed as a singular rather than as an existential statement. But then "All men are mortal" becomes falsifiable.)

Quite apart from this, we can well ask what authority permits the discarding of part of the evidence (the date of Jones's demise). For, firstly, as I have always insisted, test statements must be themselves testable (this is really the previous objection in a nonquantitative form). This means that, as indeed is the case in Maxwell's example, when existential statements are verified this is done by means of *stronger falsifiable* (though perhaps still existential) statements. "Jones dies", for example, might be verified by "Jones dies before his 150th year". Consequently the totality of evidence "confirming" "All men are mortal" in fact confirms a much stronger, and *falsifiable,* statement; for example, "All men die before their 150th year".

What this means is this. Whenever a pure existential statement, by being empirically "confirmed", appears to belong to empirical science, it will in fact do so *not on its own account,* but *by virtue of being a consequence of a corroborated falsifiable theory.* Thus the discovery of the neutrino (see part I of Maxwell's paper) not only "confirmed" the until then metaphysical assertion "For every beta emission there is a neutrino emitted from the same nucleus"; it also provided a test of the much more significant *falsifiable* theory that such emitted neutrinos could be trapped in a certain way.

I have perhaps not stated this as clearly before; and I am grateful to Professor Maxwell for stimulating me to say it, and also to David Miller who has greatly helped me to do so. I feel that it completely clears up the status of "isolated" existential statements, some of which, as I always admitted, sometimes appear to belong to empirical science.

Professor Maxwell's main argument for the thesis that few scientific theories are falsifiable is that in order *"to derive statements . . . inconsistent with . . . 'basic statements,' in most cases it is necessary . . . to use as premises . . . singular . . . initial conditions involving unobservables"* (part I); that is, essentially, that my "material requirement" for basic statements (*L.Sc.D.*, p. 102) is not usually satisfiable.

Maxwell supports this contention with an example from thermodynamics, and also with a discussion of the neutrino hypothesis. I do not greatly disagree with what he says about the latter (see my section 8 above), and I shall not discuss it further. Of the former, however, something must be said. And what must be said at once is that I disagree.

The thermodynamic theory in question eventually, after some discussion, boils down to "For every pure solid substance . . . there is at most one . . . *equilibrium* liquefaction . . . point". It is not falsifiable, says Maxwell, because "in order to falsify [it] . . . , it would be necessary to *verify* . . . [that two liquefactions at different temperatures] are *equilibrium* processes. And such statements while *confirmable,* are not *verifiable*." Let us suppose that this is so. But we need not also suppose that the theory Maxwell discusses is unscientific. After all, although a statement asserting that certain processes are at equilibrium may not be verifiable, it is *falsifiable;* and therefore, as Maxwell says, *confirmable* (I should prefer to say "corroborable"). Maxwell actually tells us how. Disturb the system mechanically; should it "solidify throughout almost instantaneously", then the statement is falsified. But this means of course that the theory at issue is a consequence of the (stronger) hypothesis "For every pure solid substance . . . there is at most one . . . liquefaction . . . point [at which mechanical disturbance has an insignificant effect]". This is falsifiable; it belongs therefore to empirical science. And so—as with certain existential statements, discussed above—do some of its consequences.

(In reply to this it might be argued that by these means *every* statement can be shown to be scientific—for *every* statement is the consequence of some scientific—that is, falsifiable—theory. But I would submit that to show a statement scientific it is not enough to subsume it under an *ad hoc* strengthening. Rather, the strengthened theory must belong to science in its own right; as indeed in Maxwell's example it does. And I might even turn the accusation round and say that since every area of science obviously abounds with unfalsifiable hypotheses—weakened versions of falsifiable ones, such as "All schizophrenic swans are white", which is a consequence of "All swans are white"—nothing much is shown by pointing their existence out.)

II

In the second part of his contribution Professor Maxwell discusses my views on induction. He is very kind and generous in his praise of what I have done. But he settles for an extremely sceptical position: there are no empirical reasons for preferring one theory to another, for there will always be in-definitely many theories equally well corroborated by the evidence. (That there cannot be *empirical* reasons is a corollary of Maxwell's disapproval of my criterion of demarcation.)

I am not sure that I understand why the infinity of possible theories should make it impossible for us to prefer one of those theories to some other one. But, on the other hand, I am not sure that I need worry. For Maxwell goes on to endorse most warmly what I have called the "critical approach". He realizes, what all too few of my critics have realized, why we can hardly expect to do better than eliminate some of our errors; and why this nevertheless allows us to progress. On the method of conjectures, weeded out by severe criticism, we are agreed. Where we are not agreed is that I emphasize the importance of empirical falsification as a mode of criticism; whilst Maxwell is so unimpressed by it that he has begun to believe that it does not exist.

On one other point we disagree. Maxwell is worried that we "still 'feel in our bones' that we *do* have *positive* reason to believe that the sun will rise tomorrow", and tries to give a "justification for this feeling"; I, on the other hand, believe that the feeling is there but must not be taken too seriously (see my section 14 above). But Maxwell's argument is interesting, and I now turn to it.

III

Perhaps I may be permitted to cut unceremoniously through some com-plications, and also through what I feel are several unfortunate formulations. The gist of Professor Maxwell's part III seems to me to be this. *If* we are well adapted to our environment then it is highly improbable that there is much serious divergence from the truth in those well-tested theories we have con-structed to help us live in that environment. Admittedly, there is no hope of supplying positive reasons for the assertion that we *are* well adjusted in this way. "*Some* theory or other [, however,] is called for to explain the fact that we have acquired knowledge . . . ". And the best available is undoubtedly the one which says that we are well adapted. If we accept this theory, we do have *good (positive) reasons* for supposing that our theories, if well tested, are somewhere near the truth.

I do not deny a certain plausibility to this argument, and even a kernel of truth. (See my reply to Professor Campbell.) But I cannot regard it as successful. In my opinion the plausibility is at bottom produced by a confusion of objective and subjective knowledge (see my section 15 above); in fact, two such confusions. For, firstly, although *subjectively* we may need to accept (if only tentatively) some explanation of our success, *objectively* we should (as I explained towards the end of my section 14 above) reject all such explanations, for they all prove too much. We cannot explain our success. The "justificatory" theory that Maxwell proposes—a sort of evolutionary epistemology—does not explain it; it explains our *success so far* by our survival so far. (Thus we are faced with the same old problem.) So even if (in some objective sense) we accepted this theory, we would still have no *objective* positive reasons of the sort Maxwell envisages. And if we accept it subjectively (believe it), we may perhaps "feel in our bones" that we have positive reasons for believing what we in fact do believe. But this is no justification; for the belief points to a future which we may never reach.

As I said long ago, "the metaphysical faith in the existence of regularities in our world . . . [is] a faith . . . without which practical action is hardly conceivable".[101] I might have added that we also need a little faith that we have actually discovered some of these regularities. But the (objective) content of this subjective faith is something to marvel at rather than to explain. And as I have shown above, for rational action we need criticism even more urgently than faith. In short, positive reasons are neither necessary nor possible.

One other point in Professor Maxwell's part III calls for comment. It is his use of *verisimilitude* rather than *truth* in connection with probability. He rejects—rightly in my opinion—any sort of view that holds that a well-tested theory could conceivably be probably true. For two theories which contradict one another may both be well tested (Maxwell does not quite say this, but I suppose that it underlies his discussion). However, this by no means rules out the possibility that a well-tested theory might perhaps be *probably near to the truth.* In fact this insight of Maxwell's seems to me to make some sense of (though not to warrant) an old argument, perhaps as old as Aristotle, of which Maxwell's own is, I think, a variant. The argument is, namely, that concatenations of accidents are very improbable; so that if a theory passes many varied tests it is highly improbable that this is due to an accident; highly improbable therefore that the theory is miles from the truth.

I agree that there is something to be said for this argument, which (though Professor Maxwell could not know this) I have recently discussed.[102] But I do not think that it can bear the weight that Maxwell puts on it. Rather than repeat, however, what I have said elsewhere, I may perhaps leave the problem here, and refer Professor Maxwell to my paper "Two Faces of Common Sense". (See now also n. 165b below.)

18. Levison's Critique of My Solution of the Problem of Induction

I

Professor Levison's plan (in his section I) is excellent: " . . . even if we should succeed in showing that Popper has failed to solve the problem of induction . . . we will see in just what respect Popper's theory of method does make a genuine advance . . . ", What is more, Levison clearly approached his task with the excellent intention of being fair and just to me, even should he succeed in showing that I have failed.

In spite of this, Professor Levison's criticism appears to be not quite right. He seems to have misunderstood my claim to have solved "Hume's problem of induction", as I call it. It never occurs to him that I have never tried to solve the traditional problem of induction, as he and I both call it; but that on the contrary, I have tried to solve Hume's problem by showing that as far as the logical problem of induction is concerned, *Hume was right.* (See section 13 above.)

Thus we read in Levison's section II "Hume could retort to Popper", as if Popper had tried to refute Hume; and we find an argument which makes sense only under the assumption that my solution to the logical problem of induction was an attempt to use the ideas of testing and of corroboration to solve the problem in a *positive* way: "Popper's claim", Levison writes, "could then be construed as the claim that our reason for preferring theories that have survived testing up to the present is . . . that the [second order] hypothesis that theories that have repeatedly survived testing continue to do so . . . ".

But I have repeatedly *rejected* this "claim"; for one thing, it is plainly false. But even if I thought it were true, I would, as I have in fact always done (see section 1 of my *L.d.F.*) totally repudiate this or any other attempt to fall back on a second order hypothesis. For, as Professor Levison quite rightly says in his section II (without realizing that he repeats my own argument), "this way of countering the original objection entails an infinite regress". I have done so because I genuinely reject induction, while Professor Levison's attempts to save my alleged claims clearly presuppose that I want to rescue induction.

II

I should however say that I appreciate Levison's efforts on my behalf. In the first place, I was impressed by the on the whole excellent summary of my views with which he starts his paper (though there are some minor misinterpretations and differences).[103] I was pleased that, like me, he has little time for the currently fashionable attempts to "dissolve" the problem of induction (see subsection I of my section 13 above). And I was struck by the fact that, although, as I say, Levison clearly imagines that I want to rescue induction, and have failed, he nevertheless makes such a handsome attempt to defend me against his own arguments, that he brings me (see his section II) to exactly the conclusion to which I have already brought myself: " . . . the only [positive] reason that . . . [Popper's theory] enables us to give for relying on a predictive consequence of a well-tested theory is that we have no reason for not relying on it."

Now I agree with every word of this; there *are* no such things as good positive reasons; nor do we need such things (see my section 14, esp. the text to n. 92). But Levison obviously cannot quite bring himself to believe that this is my opinion, let alone that it is right. He goes on as follows: "We may doubt, however, that this reconstruction of the rationale of applying physical laws in order to build bridges or airplanes is more satisfactory than Hume's, or even very different from his." (This is of course quite wrong.) But then he appears to abandon the whimsical thought that I really do adhere to this "reconstruction", and reverts to his previous interpretation, that I am at least as much of a justificationist as is anyone else: "Popper's difficulty is that he cannot consistently hold that [surviving tests] . . . makes it likely that a theory will continue to survive such tests. Thus, to be consistent, he must deny that the claim that a test can be successfully repeated can be justified by argument."

Quite so. I do deny it. There is no "difficulty".

III

The traditional problem of induction is the problem of rescuing induction by answering Hume.

What I call the problem of induction (see my section 13 above) starts from the conviction that Hume was right in condemning induction on logical grounds; and what I call the corroboration of a hypothesis is merely a summary report about the past performance of the hypothesis; it is *not* an attempt to justify any expectation that the hypothesis will *in future* prove successful if it was successful in the past. Rather, I hold with Hume that *nothing* can justify such an expectation.

But then, I have not solved the problem of induction, everybody will exclaim. Exactly: I have not solved—or even tried to solve—what you call the problem of induction, the problem I now[104] call (as does Levison) "the traditional problem of induction". This problem can be formulated: "How can induction be justified?". To this problem, my answer is: "It cannot" (wherefore some people have thought that I hold the problem of induction to be insoluble). But I have said more than "It cannot": I have said, in effect, *"It cannot and it need not"*.

Levison's paper has convinced me that my position is not easy to understand: what Professor Thomas Kuhn calls a "*Gestalt* switch" seems needed—a fairly complete break with the traditional way of looking at these things, and with the commonsense theory of knowledge (as I now call it);[105] and I am greatly indebted to Professor Levison, for it was largely his paper which persuaded me to insert in this book the three sections on induction (13-15). Professor Levison may say that these sections go in some places beyond my previous work, I hope so; they would not have been worth writing otherwise. But I can assure him that if they go beyond my previous work, they do so only in the spirit which he himself formulated in the programmatic passage which I quoted at the beginning of this reply.

19. Bar-Hillel on the Compatibility between Static and Dynamic Theories of Science

In the first paragraph of his essay, Bar-Hillel speaks of the controversy between Rudolf Carnap and me, and calls himself an "onlooker (and occasional participant)". I think it is only right if I remind him that his participation was not exactly occasional; that it was he who started the "controversy" and created most, if not all, of "the disturbing heat". To me, the other surviving participant, it is little consolation that Bar-Hillel writes now that the controversy "has been a constant source of wonder, embarrassment and frustration" to him. I am not to be induced by all this to start the controversy again.

I

I am therefore proceeding directly to Bar-Hillel's point 2.

II

Not "the least among the insights" Bar-Hillel has gained is that I am interested in the dynamics of the philosophy of science, Carnap in its statics. Be it so. I have said in Chapter 10 of *Conjectures and Refutations,* that "the repeated overthrow of scientific theories and their replacement by better or more satisfactory ones" (p. 215) is the heart of the matter, as I see it, and that "the study of the growth of scientific knowledge is . . . the most fruitful way of studying the growth of knowledge in general" (p. 216; see also for example my Preface to *The Logic of Scientific Discovery* [1959(a)]). Bar-Hillel is also right when he says that I have said many times that an excessive interest in formalization should be opposed and discouraged. He asks me whether this holds only for the scientist ("in which case" he is "ready to accept" my position) or for the methodologist (in which case he is not ready to accept my position). My answer is: for both. I am an enemy of uncalled-for complication and of all scholasticism. I know that this attitude leads me at times to formulate things not as carefully as they might be formulated. All right, I am sorry, but there are by now so many people working in these fields that one need not worry too much about one's formulations, and possible little slips (if any): they certainly will not remain unnoticed, but will be discussed and exploited many times.

III

In his section 3 Bar-Hillel writes: "Interestingly and strangely enough, not enough attention has been paid to what seems to me definitely to be a decisive prior question, . . . *for what purpose* [should theories be compared]? Neither Popper nor Carnap have ever, to my knowledge, explicitly posed this question." This is incorrect: I believe that Carnap did so when he said that probability is a guide of life (a remark with which I disagree); and I did so when I said that the better theory, or the theory to be preferred, is the one which is a better approximation to the truth. Bar-Hillel claims that I have said "with some implicit argumentation, that the comparison of theories is an essentially simple and one-dimensional affair". The opposite is true: in 1934, in *Logik der Forschung,* I said that only in the simplest cases—when one theory is logically stronger than another—is the affair simple and one-dimensional. Admittedly, I always stress the simple cases, because if one does not learn from the simple cases, one is bound to go wrong on tackling the more complicated.

To be quite frank, I regard Bar-Hillel's stressing the obvious (that theories can be compared from different points of view) as a kind of gambit to distract our attention from something else, which should perhaps also be obvious: all philosophical or scientific work is necessarily a matter of oversimplification and the complaint that somebody has oversimplified (unsupported by any specification of the serious problem thereby missed) is, a priori, always true, and therefore empty.

Bar-Hillel speaks (as sometimes does Lakatos) of acceptance$_1$ and acceptance$_2$, as if they had discovered that I sometimes unconsciously use the word in different senses. But the fact is that, without using this jargon, I have often explicitly drawn attention to the difference that the subscripts are supposed to mark. Consider, for example, "my first thesis" in section II of Chapter 10 of *Conjectures and Refutations* (p. 217), which is "that we can know of a theory, even before it has been tested, that *if* it passes certain tests it will be better than some other theory"; and my distinction between "potential satisfactoriness" (or "potential goodness") of a theory and satisfactoriness *"in fact".* (In n. 2 on the same page I give references to even earlier formulations of this distinction; thus the discovery that I am working with "acceptance$_1$" and "acceptance$_2$" is at best a typographical discovery.)

At the end of his section 3, and in his footnote 5, Bar-Hillel wants me to "present" "the answer" myself to a question concerning his interpretation of my views which, he says, imply that "theories should never be compared as to how they fare for the same evidence"; but tests "are undertaken for each theory at a time"; and so on. My answer is that I certainly never held such a view, a view which appears to me to be pointless; and I do not know how anybody can ascribe it to me. Bar-Hillel's footnote 5 quotes no passage from my writings from which such an interpretation could be constructed. Since Bar Hillel appeals to me to commit myself, I gladly do so, though I do not know how or why this appeal should have become necessary.

IV

In his section 4 Bar-Hillel begins by saying "let me make it first perfectly clear that, in my view . . . [Popper's conception] does not really stand in competition with Carnap's conception". He thereby forces me to repeat that I regard Carnap's *Logical Foundations of Probability* as completely mistaken in its treatment of "induction" and "degree of confirmation". Part of my criticism was accepted by Carnap in a later edition; but part of my criticism—in fact the oldest, since it was already contained in *Logik der Forschung,* in my criticism of Reichenbach—has been denied by Carnap in the latest utterance on this subject known to me. It concerns Carnap's "instance confirmation". In *Logik der Forschung,* section 80, I criticized[106] an idea which I thought Reichenbach might offer, in reply to my criticism, as a viable interpretation of what he had said. It was formally equivalent to what Carnap later called "instance confirmation", which, he asserted, could be used by engineers to estimate the reliability of a law. I showed that according to this conception (which I described as a form of "probability" that Reichenbach might possibly entertain), a law which is falsified in half of its tests obtains the degree of reliability or "probability" of 1/2; and I described this criticism as "devastating". However, in a book published in 1968 Carnap asserts, in a reply to "Popper's comment on instance confirmation": "In Popper's example, the law which is in the average satisfied by one half of the instances, has, on the basis of my definition, not the probability 1/2, as Popper erroneously believes, but 0."[107] Thus Carnap denies the validity of my criticism of the doctrine of instance confirmation; a criticism which I had thought was unanswerable. (Carnap's reply is true if we take literally the phrase "on the basis of my definition of probability", but false if we substitute for "probability" the words "instance confirmation"; but this we must do, since this was the object of my criticism.) In view of this and many similar cases, it seems to me wrong to suggest that Carnap's and my views do not clash; but this suggestion seems to me made by Bar-Hillel's remark that our views do not "really stand in competition".

The point here mentioned is most relevant since Bar-Hillel says, in the next (second) paragraph of his section 4, that "comparing theories from the . . . point of view . . . of full-blooded technological application" is as legitimate as comparing them "for the purpose of testing"; suggesting that Carnap's theory is right if applied to the "full-blooded technological application", while mine works for the purposes of "testing"; and that a clash is therefore only apparent. That Carnap defended his full-blooded technological concept of instance confirmation against my criticism shows that he anyway did not consider the clash to be only apparent.

Now to Bar-Hillel's criticism. Its central sentence is (see his discussion of point (2) in section 4 of his paper): "I am not at all sure that the notion of standing in competition has been or could be sufficiently well defined . . . [for theories] to be of much use." I have, however, tried to argue that two theories stand in competition if they both contain solutions of the *same problems*. (Bar-Hillel speaks not only of "problems" but of "domains", but I do not think that this way of talking is of much help.)

Bar-Hillel writes in the next paragraph: "Is it or is it not possible to assign (initial) logical probabilities to theories, if only for the purpose of comparing the numbers attained, though not taking seriously the numbers themselves? I (in this respect departing from Carnap's views which are much more optimistic, unrealistically so, as I see it) regard this as practically utterly and totally hopeless. . . . "

Bar-Hillel seems to have forgotten that I assert (as did Carnap, by the way) that all theories have the logical probability zero, and that what we compare is the "fine structure of probability", which can sometimes be done by comparing their content, and at other times by comparing their "dimension"; that is, the degree of complexity of their simplest falsifiers.

Since Bar-Hillel has overlooked this point, his "schema" (section 4) is indeed a caricature if it comes to be applied, though it might pass if the fine structure of probability is taken account of. But even then we must remember that acceptance$_1$—preference for a theory before it has been tested—is for me not a formalized concept. The scientist who decides of a theory, before testing, that it is more promising (acceptable$_1$) than another, is as a rule *conjecturing,* even though his conjecture has a logical rather than an empirical character. Moreover (as the discussion between Einstein and Bohr shows)[107a] he will be largely influenced by what I have called (in my *Postscript*) a (metaphysical) research programme.

V

I shall not reply to subsection A separately in detail. It asserts that "none of Popper's two explicata, the ones I termed here 'accept$_1$' and 'accept$_2$', are helpful". No doubt; I am not interested in "explicata". But quite a number of successful scientists have found my advice helpful: be daring in your hypotheses, and test them severely. This is an oversimplification, but it is meant to be (and for some people is) a useful oversimplification. As to subsection B, I found the complications which Bar-Hillel tries to introduce into my simple approach unhelpful. Of course, I oversimplify. But as I see it, this is one of my main functions.

VI

Bar-Hillel's section 6 makes some disdainful comments on my concept of verisimilitude. They are wholly mistaken. However, they need not be answered here, since I have discussed the significance of verisimilitude elsewhere in this book.[108]

VII

For similar reasons Bar-Hillel's comments on Professor Lakatos's views need not be discussed here.

VIII

Bar-Hillel writes here in his first sentence that I have "clarified" the role played by theories and theorizing "in an unforgettable way". I think that this handsome compliment is refuted by his paper. "Popper's continued feud against the 'systematizers' seems to me no longer useful and a plain waste of time . . .", Bar-Hillel writes. Since I have not the slightest idea what he is alluding to, it would be neither useful, nor anything but a plain waste of time, if I were to defend myself against this attack. I hope that a glance at my list of publications will show how much time I have spent on controversies, and how much time I have saved by doing something more interesting; and that that balance will not be unfavourable.

IV. EVOLUTION AND WORLD 3

20. Introductory Remark

As I explained in my *Intellectual Autobiography,* there is a definite connection between Darwinism (despite its logical weakness, which inclines me to see in it not much more than an almost logically necessary metaphysical research programme) and my own theory of the evolution of knowledge through the competition and elimination of theories. Although I have written and lectured about this for a long time, it is only since about 1960 that I have actually suggested modifications to Darwinism. I might mention in particular my Herbert Spencer Lecture of 1961 and my Arthur Holly Compton Memorial Lecture of 1965. At about the same time I began to do more about the distinction of objective and subjective knowledge, and to develop a theory of objective knowledge which I called the theory of the "third world", and later (upon the suggestion of Professor Sir John Eccles) the theory of "world 3".

21. Eccles on World 3 and the Mind-Brain Liaison

I

Sir John Eccles's contribution is of the greatest significance to me. Of all the scientists in whose own work I had the privilege to participate, if only on the fringe, he, and my late friend Franz Urbach, are the ones from whom I learned most, because they took me into their confidence, explaining to me their work and their current problems in detail. They demanded much; I had to get close to the heart of the matter in a few days.

In the first section of his contribution Eccles speaks about the help I rendered to him in connection with the theory of synaptic transmission. I suggested to him in those days that his theory was sufficiently advanced to be formulated in a sharper, fuller, and more falsifiable form than it had been so far; and this enabled him later to force a decision, even though it was not favourable to his theory. Not long after, I heard a well-known physiologist say in Oxford: "Eccles? Quite a good man, but he must be a bit mad. Only think, he works to falsify his own theory." I did not reply, but I was very glad. It is certainly better to falsify your own theory than let others do the work for you.

From Urbach, Hans Thirring, and Schrödinger, and later from Eccles, Medawar, and others, I learned how important it is for a philosopher to keep in living contact with science, however inexpertly, and to learn what the work of a scientist demands. It is of very different character from the work of a philosopher, even from a philosopher who works on mathematics; for it is deeply inspired by a respect for hard facts, and the need to interpret respectfully facts which to start with are something of a muddle, and anything but hard. I suspect that only those who have experienced the tortuous decision of a scientist on what is the truth about a fact really appreciate what "truth" (I mean of course objective, Tarskian truth) means.

There are thinkers of various types. Deep thinkers can be fast or slow. Eccles thinks breathtakingly fast. In the days when he held his first chair of physiology, in the University of Otago, he invited me after some preliminary discussions to deliver a course of lectures on scientific method. These lectures were delivered (in 1945) to a large audience of staff and students mainly from the Medical School. I found Eccles thinking so fast that I could only with an immense effort of concentration keep pace with him.

II

It is characteristic of Eccles that he has gone deeply into a field far removed from his own. Almost alone among my friends, he has made a profound study of the third world or, as he prefers to call it, world 3—on which I read my opening paper in Amsterdam in 1967.[109] Like most of my thoughts, it goes back to some views in *Logik der Forschung,* but it was only approximately in 1960 that I devoted a paper to the subject. This paper, which I read in my seminar at the L. S. E., was not too well received, except by my former student, Professor Musgrave, who later wrote his Ph.D. thesis on the subject, as well as a contribution to the present volume.

Eccles has written several papers on world 3. In his latest book, *Facing Reality* (see n. 100 below), there are about three chapters devoted to it, and it is explained with the help of a number of highly illuminating diagrams.

Eccles is strongly in favour of my theory and there is little, if any, criticism of my views, either in this book or in his contribution to the present volume. In the main, Eccles enriches the theory by pointing out, with great clarity and in considerable detail, its relationship to neurophysiology. Nevertheless, there are one or two points on which we do not seem to agree fully, and on which a discussion seems necessary.

What I called "the third world" and now prefer to call, upon Eccles's suggestion "world 3" is, essentially, the world of the products of the human mind; but I include in it, and I hold it necessary so to include, the unintended interrelationships and interactions between these products. World 3 is to a remarkable extent autonomous.

Eccles, in his diagrams, describes world 3 as being encoded in world 1. It consists, he says, essentially in the storage of human achievement, it is a kind of physical memory for nonphysical world 3 objects.

I agree, but not entirely. When I speak, probably not clearly enough, about the autonomy of world 3, I am trying to convey the idea that world 3 essentially transcends that part of world 1 in which it is, as it were, materialized. Let us call the materialized, the stored-up part of world 3 "world 3.1". Libraries belong to it, and probably certain memory-carrying parts of the human brain. I then assert the essential and fundamental inequation

$$\text{world } 3 \gg \text{world } 3.1,$$

that is, world 3 transcends essentially its own encoded section.

There are lots of examples, but I will take a simple one. There can be no more than a finite number of numbers in world 3.1. Neither a library nor a human brain incorporates an infinite series of natural numbers. But world 3 possesses the lot, because of the theorem (or axiom): every number has a successor.

This theory must have belonged to world 3 almost from the beginning. In the remote past however it was in nobody's world 3.1 (or 3.2—that is, the part of world 3 which has been grasped or understood by some people); but one day the procedure of adding to an integer was *invented,* and then the theory became a theorem, and so achieved world 3.1 (and thus world 3.2) status.

In a similar way, world 3.1 may not at a certain time contain the notion of a prime number. But prime numbers (and of course also this notion) may be *discovered* as implicit in the series of numbers, and Euclid's theorem—"There is no greatest prime number"—may be proved.

Once discovered, Euclid's new theorem may start to belong to world 3.1. But before its discovery, it *existed* in world 3. Not only that; it was open to anybody to discover it, but nobody (or so it seems), however much he disbelieved it, could add its negation to world 3 (that is, to world 3.1), except as a falsehood.

I am far from wishing to exclude falsehoods from world 3. Although true theorems constitute an important section of it, conjectures not known to be either true or false constitute in my opinion an even more important section; and with every truth, there is a falsehood (the negation of the truth), or even an infinite number of falsehoods. ($0 + 0 = 0$ brings in its wake the infinite procession of falsehoods $0 + 0 = 1$, $0 + 0 = 2$, $0 + 0 = 3$, ...) In my way of looking at world 3, its theories contain essentially the *information content* which is conveyed by them. And two books which may differ widely as world 1 objects may be *identical* insofar as they are world 3 objects—say, if they contain the same coded information.

But I wish to go further. There are world 3 objects which possess no world 3.1 materialization at all. They are yet to be discovered problems, and the theorems which are already implied by the materialized world 3.1, but which have never yet been thought of. (Had they been thought of, then they would have belonged to the brain part of world 3.1.)

I am strongly opposed to making it impossible to say certain perfectly sensible things by confining world 3 to the world of eternal (or perhaps, more precisely, timeless) *true* theories. Such a world of nontemporal true theories is part of my world 3, but it is only a part. World 3, as I want to see it, is a product of the human mind, and therefore has a history. Part of this history consists in the discovery (and incidentally in the transfer into world 3.1) of previously unknown problems or critical arguments, and also of previously unknown solutions, by means of world 3.2 (that is, the world of thoughts consciously thought).

I fully admit that this turns what is left of world 3 when deprived of worlds 3.1 and 3.2 into a kind of shadow world. But even shadows exist in a physical sense—they can be photographed, they may function as a warning signal for an animal. I assert that this shadowy world—let us call it 3.3—exists. Proof: it interacts via world 2 with world 1.

A man who has an inkling that a solution of a problem in world 3.3 exists, may spend his life in tracking it down. (a) He may find it. Can we say that it was the direct influence of world 3.3 on his brain (world 1) that produced the solution? Is it not much nearer to experience to say that his wish, his hope, his half-baked ideas (world 2), which may or may not all have had a strictly corresponding analogue in his brain, were what produced the solution? (b) He may not find the solution, even though his hope that it existed was unimpaired. Why not? Because his brain was not good enough? Perhaps. But is it not possible that his brain was quite good enough for the purpose, but that a minor clue, which would have led him to *seeing a new possible way to a possible solution,* may have escaped him? Or that he may even have spotted that minor clue, but was discouraged by what turned out to be a minor mistake in it? And have we to assume that such a thing as a sudden discouragement is genuinely a part of the brain, with its afferent and efferent paths, rather than an effect of that minor mistake with quite different antecedents? Both in case (a) and in case (b), the really driving factor may have been the intuitive interest in the autonomous world 3.3 problem, a problem not yet existing in world 3.1 or 3.2, only suspected by the mind (the mind, but hardly the brain) of lurking somewhere in world 3. (c) And may not this world 3.3 problem be insoluble, at least with the historical material (stored in worlds 3.1 and 3.2) at his disposal at the time?

In all I have said so far, I was ready to assume that there is a one-to-one brain-mind liaison, and that it makes no essential difference whether we speak of the brain or of the mind. But what reason have we to make this assumption, except physicalism, in the sense that the physical world must be causally complete? Can we rule out a priori that there is a world 2 which really counts? Can we not imagine a world 2 which grasps and interprets the *world 3 situation as such*—not in one of its perhaps infinitely many physical codings, *but the problem as such,* in one of its *logically* essential forms?[110]

In fact, it is my conjecture that it is this which takes place. World 2, the world of understanding, may grasp (with great difficulty) the world 3 problem, and the liaison between world 2 and the brain may play either no role at all in this action or—more probably—a role analogous to a recording machine which definitely encodes a sound *after* the sound has been produced.

The conjecture I am here proposing has this very special advantage over all others I know: it seems to me the only one which gives a real and biologically significant function to the mind, consciousness, the experience of strenuous thought, and to the self. In all other cases these are epiphenomena, whether admitted or not. And I am averse to turning the greatest miracle we know of in this universe into an epiphenomenon. What is more, the function it allows world 2 is exactly that function which everybody except a cyberneticist ascribes to it as a matter of course. Can our grasp, our understanding, not be dominant? In other words, can world 2 not be the intellectual leader, even though its leadership may depend on the good functioning of the essentially recording pathways of the brain (just as a military leader's leadership may depend on the existence of efficient lines of communication to his troops)?[111]

Thus I am here disagreeing with Figure 36 (p. 167) in Eccles's book *Facing Reality:* and I am doing so for reasons which, I know, he and I share.

But there remains much in common. Eccles and I see the fully developed human world 2—the world of thought, reflection, self-consciousness, and of the tribulations involved in solving the most difficult problems—as having evolved with the specifically human world 3.[112]

No doubt there is such a thing as Eccles has called the brain-mind liaison. But both he and I are opponents of epiphenomenalism. If we wish to sustain our rejection of this theory, we must not make the brain-mind liaison too close. We both believe that, especially in intellectual matters, the mind leads, owing to its access to world 3. If we make this access too indirect—too dependent on world 3.1, and on the brain—then we are back at the position which we both want to reject. "Liaison" is a vague term, and this is all to the good. Let us interpret it dualistically, in such a way that sometimes the brain is paramount, and at others it is dominated by the mind.

I do not think that I should dare to say such things to a brain physiologist were I not confident that I formulate a view with which this particular great brain physiologist can agree.

22. Watkins on Indeterminism as the Central Problem of My Philosophy

I

John Watkins's contribution to this volume is one of the few which aims at a presentation rather than at a refutation of my ideas. In the terminology of the Table of Contents of the Carnap volume in *The Library of Living Philosophers,* it is a "descriptive" rather than a "critical" essay on my philosophy. I have found only *one* passage in Watkins's essay in which he criticizes me and none—not even this one—in which there is a serious divergence of opinion. Admittedly, I see the *"unity"* of my philosophy in a slightly different way: I should be inclined to regard my emphasis on *criticism* (or the doctrines of critical realism or critical optimism) as being more appropriate than indeterminism is to the unity of my theoretical and practical thinking. But I do not deny that Watkins has made out a brilliant case for his way of looking at the matter; and the fact that he succeeds in bringing a notable degree of coherence to my philosophy by his way of looking at it (which differs from my own) proves the originality and independence of his view.

II

However, the volumes of this Library are no place for mutual praise; and so I turn at once to the passage where Watkins criticizes me. He broaches a most interesting point: after discussing some comments I have made on the significant difference between a scientific reduction and a philosophical one, especially with reference to the reducibility of mind to matter, Watkins reports, correctly (in his section 4.2), that I concede "that it is at least conceivable that such a reduction might eventually be carried out, though he [Popper] obviously doubts that it ever will be". And Watkins continues:

> But it seems to me that his [Popper's] general account of scientific reductions means that *this* reductionist programme [that of reducing mind to body] *cannot* be carried out. For let us try to suppose that it will be carried out. Then those phenomena which we now regard as *experiences* are going to stand revealed as physical processes that *simulate* experiences but are *not* experiences. But it seems to me to be nonsense, and not just false, to say of somebody's toothache that it is not really an experience but only something simulating an experience.

This is an excellent argument; and since I do not believe in the success of the philosophical programme of reducing mind to matter any more than he does, I should perhaps acquiesce, and say that Watkins has overcome what few reservations I ever had.

But few though my doubts are, I am too much of a fallibilist to admit the *finality* of Watkins's argument that no *scientific* reduction of mind to matter (or of biology *cum* psychology to physics) will ever be possible. First of all, our idea of what is important about experiences and what is not (being perhaps merely physical) may undergo radical changes; for example, in the direction of panpsychism—the (Spinozistic) doctrine that all physical matter has the quality of consciousness, though perhaps no memory and thus no consciousness of consciousness. And it might be shown that these higher stages of consciousness—memory, expectation, consciousness of consciousness, which seem to me unavoidable ingredients of a toothache—arise necessarily with more complex and highly organized forms of matter. Although this might hardly constitute a *reduction by simulation,* it could, and would, still be claimed as a devastating victory for reductionism.

I personally do not believe that even this victory will ever be scored. But some theoretical physicists, such as Wigner, who on quantum-mechanical grounds have embraced a kind of solipsism have, by venturing the opposite reduction, shown that there may be unexpected routes by which we might arrive at a monistic theory of the world. And this is, I think, what is at stake. I admit that my own argument here is very weak, but I think it shares its weakness with all philosophical forms of reductionism; and this is indeed a reason why I combat philosophical reductionism, and why I feel some inclination to accept Watkins's argument. All I wanted to say—and I still want to say it—is that we should not regard such arguments as conclusive proofs: we know very little about the constitution of the world, and we must not be dogmatic[113] even about a miracle such as the emergence of genuine coherent consciousness, in the form of a toothache.

Looking at Watkins's essay as a whole, this point, though it touches on one of the greatest miracles of our world, is a very minor one; and so I do not want to end my reply here. Let me perhaps say a few words on indeterminism.

What I am going to say is not a defence of my views against criticism; still less is it a criticism of Watkins's presentation: it is, I think, best regarded as an attempt on my part to elaborate on some of the points he has made.

III

I have come more and more to the opinion that what is at stake, in the problem of indeterminism, is the problem of *the causal closure of world 1 against world 2*. Or in other words: is (the physical) world 1 (which may be deterministic or indeterministic) causally changed or causally influenced by (the mental) world 2? It is clear that if world 1 is completely deterministic, it will also be closed (and world 2, if existing at all, will be an epiphenomenal world). But even if world 1 is not deterministic—containing probabilistic propensities, for example—it still could conceivably be closed; the indeterminism of world 1 by no means implies that it is under the influence of world 2, even though indeterminism is, it seems to me, a necessary condition for there to be such an influence.

Now I admit that it is very dificult for a physicist or a physiologist to take to his heart the openness of world 1. It is much easier to think in terms of a parallelism between world 1 and world 2; that is, to suppose that any world 2 process which has influence in world 1 is accompanied in world 1 by a parallel brain process. But this brings us dangerously near to the causal closure of world 1, and to epiphenomenalism.

A way out seems to me the following: Perhaps indeed nothing can happen in world 2 without some "parallel" process in world 1; but this parallelism need not be a one-to-one correspondence. Let world 1 (our brain) be indeterministic; let world 2 processes, such as drawing a logical conclusion, be (more or less) determined within world 2 (and its grasp of world 3); let there be, while these world 2 processes take place, associated world 1 processes; but let these be to some extent undetermined in world 1, and perhaps not "parallel" in the sense of "the same" world 2 process's being always accompanied by "the same" world 1 process. This will obviously be satisfied if the world 2 process is creative, and therefore partially *unique;* for one can speak of a one-to-one correspondence between world 1 and world 2 processes only if these processes are repeated, and if sufficiently similar world 2 processes occur along with sufficiently similar world 1 processes.

So I suggest that some one-to-one parallelisms may exist, but also unique world 2 processes accompanied by indeterministic world 1 processes; these may or may not be unique. The world 1 process occurring in the invention of a piece of music, or of a poem, would lead ultimately perhaps to the writing down of the invented piece of music or poem, without its having been in any sense in one-to-one correspondence with the world 2 experience.

On the other hand, there is nothing against the assumption that repeated attacks of "the same" toothache are actually correlated one-to-one with "the same" brain processes. But I doubt it. It seems that the brain is rich enough sometimes to produce different world 1 processes which are nevertheless experienced as attacks of "the same" toothache; so that there need even be no parallelism in the actions of world 1 upon world 2.

(What we are inclined to interpret as a repetition in the physiological sense—for example, that characteristic dry cough which I had last week and which I now have again—may well have *some* physiological component in common with the earlier process; but though the central nervous system participates in both cases, its participation need not be a repetition: another part of the brain may have taken over.)

It is on such lines that interactionists (as opposed to parallelists) may have to think if they not only are dualists and interactionists but are prepared to admit the existence of a brain-mind liaison thanks to which all mental processes involve work from the brain at the same time.

In its role as mediator between world 3 and world 1, our mind (world 2) may depend on world 3 objects, such as melodies or arguments, which it "follows" and "grasps"; and the brain processes initiated by these world 2 processes may lead to actions in world 1 such as speech or writing whose coherence is explicable in world 3 terms (it is "anchored" entirely in world 3), and indeed cannot be explained causally in purely brain-physiological terms.

Far be it from me to see in such speculations a solution of the body-mind problem. All that I claim is that this problem has been changed when we allow world 3 to exist, and to interact with world 2.

IV

The indeterminism of world 1 is thus needed to prevent its causal closure. However, even a *"prima facie deterministic physics"* (such as classical physics, or the nonlinear field physics of Mendel Sachs)[114] is sufficiently *indeterministic* for this purpose, as I first tried to show in [1950 (b) and (c)], and as Watkins shows very convincingly, using arguments of his own, as well as arguments due to Landé and to myself.

I may perhaps add another similar argument to those already so attractively and clearly presented by Watkins. (Arne Petersen informs me that there is a similar argument due to Harald Høffding,[115] and another due to Edgar Tranekjaer Rasmussen.)

We can start from the activity of the draughtsman who draws a large plan of the room he is sitting in, including in his plan a plan of the plan which he is drawing. It is clear that he can never finish his plan: it will never contain in full the plan he is drawing, that is, up to the last touches he has made.

This argument perhaps deserves to be a little expanded and even developed into a kind of logical proof for the incompleteness of the physical world and of physical science. For our growing knowledge of physics is laid down partly in the form of an accumulation of physical bodies such as books and journals. A dynamical version of the map argument would show that the attempt to *describe* these books and journals (to say nothing of the attempt to explain them, say on the basis of the brain processes involved in their composition) is in principle incompletable. Thus there can be no complete description of the physical world and *a fortiori* no complete explanatory theory of it. To sum up: if the world contains an explanation of itself, this explanation can never be *complete*.

But this means that physics is, for logical reasons, necessarily incomplete as a description of the world, even if we assume that it is complete so far as universal laws are concerned; the idea that we can achieve a complete theoretical explanation or description of the world is absurd. In every theoretical description of the world, or more precisely, in every theoretical description of the making of such a description, there will be gaps. Thus our knowledge of the world is necessarily incomplete, and it is, more especially, necessarily too incomplete to predict its own growth (or to catch up with its own growth). Hence there is at least one thing beyond all possible scientific knowledge—the future growth of scientific knowledge. But since this future growth must strongly influence the shape of physical things to come (such as the making of new machines), our knowledge of the shape of physical things to come is necessarily incomplete. Thus a true theory of a "closed world 1" is impossible, even though a good approximation to the truth may be prima facie deterministic, that is to say, it may depict world 1 as a closed system. To sum up, all physical explanations and descriptions of the world are either prima facie deficient or, if prima facie closed or deterministic, at best merely approximations which ignore this aspect. (In Hegelian jargon one could say that the world, in becoming conscious of itself, becomes necessarily open and incompletable.) Somehow this is connected with the nonexistence of essentialist explanations, that is, of explanations which are neither capable nor in need of being further explained: for in both cases we can always renew (as small children are inclined to do) the question: "but why?".[116]

Over and above all this, however, prima facie *deterministic* physical theories do not seem to be even prima facie adequate theories for the description of our world, just because we can always build a randomizing machine which creates a local pocket (as Watkins calls it) of randomness; and then we can apply Landé's argument.

V

So far I have not, in my argument here against the causal completeness of world 1, made anything like full use of world 3. Yet our growing knowledge of world 1 is laid down, partly, in the form of an accumulation of physical bodies, such as machines, books, and scientific papers; and the essential incompleteness of world 3 (which is a consequence of our map argument) makes the physical prediction of this accumulation of physical bodies essentially incompletable.

Moreover, the fact that world 3 has a (plastic) control over much of our action shows, I think, that it has also some control over our brains; if this is so, then the essential unpredictability of world 3 enters world 1 along this path as well.

The theories which describe world 3 theories or developments—such as histories of problem situations—are necessarily metatheories, formulated in a (semantic) metalanguage. This leads us to another aspect of the incompletability of world 3—the (nonvicious) infinite regress of metalanguages, which alone would suffice to make any completion of world 3 impossible; even that part of world 3 which is confined to the description of world 1, and to the world 1 consequences of this description, would for this reason never be completed.

These factors enter the situation only with world 3: the existence of world 3 adds as it were a new dimension to indeterminism. The incompleteness described is thus part of what existentialists would call "the human situation". And so we arrive again, in a slightly different way, at the essential incompleteness of world 1 itself. Even if we could completely describe our organisms, as far as they do not depend on world 3, every physical description must fall short when it comes to describe those parts which interact strongly with world 3. Thus the indeterminism of world 1 in the presence of the man-made world 3 transcends the indeterminism at a prehuman stage: it is underlined by the peculiar human situation, by the existence of the peculiar human world 3.

VI

Now I conjecture that natural selection puts a premium on the evolution of a partial randomization of the connection (including cybernetic feedbacks) between stimulus and response. For a vitally relevant situation hardly ever corresponds in a one-to-one way with the physical stimuli: very similar stimuli sometimes represent very different vital situations, and so demand different responses—trials to be eliminated if unsuccessful. In other words, overrigid links between stimuli and responses would be fatal.[117] Thus there will be a premium on plasticity, at least in several regions of life processes, and especially in certain regions of behaviour: there will be a premium on "free" behaviour, exploratory behaviour, creative behaviour; that is, on behaviour not fully determined by genetics *plus* environment.

This, together with the old arguments from my Herbert Spencer Lecture[118] which Watkins reports, seems to me to offer some hope of explaining what Darwin tried to explain: the evolution of *higher* forms of life.

23. Campbell on the Evolutionary Theory of Knowledge

Professor Campbell's remarkable contribution is perhaps the one which shows the greatest agreement with my epistemology, and (what he cannot know) an astonishing anticipation of some things which I had not yet published when he wrote his paper. In addition, it is a treatise of prodigious historical learning: there is scarcely anything in the whole of modern epistemology to compare with it; certainly not in my own work. His historical references are all highly relevant; they are a real treasure house; and they often surprised me greatly.

For me the most striking thing about Campbell's essay is the almost complete agreement, down even to minute details, between Campbell's views and my own. I shall try to develop one or two of these points a little further still, and shall then turn to the very rare and comparatively minor points where there may be some difference of opinion.

I

In a paper, not yet published at the time I write this, "Two Faces of Common Sense",[119] I develop in considerable detail the relationship between my realism and my fallibilistic epistemology. Although I wrote this paper before reading Professor Campbell's contribution, there is the closest similarity (especially with his Summary).

I show in my paper that if we start from a critical commonsense realism (not from a naive realism, and even less from a direct realism which somehow attributes to us the ability to "see" that the world is real) then we shall take man as one of the animals, and human knowledge as essentially almost as fallible as animal knowledge. We shall suppose the animal senses to have evolved from primitive beginnings; and we shall look therefore on our own senses, essentially, as part of a decoding mechanism—a mechanism which decodes, more or less successfully, the encoded information about the world which manages to reach us by sensual means. There is some reason to think that our senses and our brain operate fairly well together in this business of decoding, but no reason at all to allow them or us any "direct" knowledge of anything immediately "given".

I think this is in complete agreement with Campbell's views; and with the views he attributes to me.

The next step is to look at the function and working structure of our apparatus for gaining knowledge about the physical world ("world 1"). Here we have, like some animals, the senses and the brain, which between them deliver us with knowledge that belongs, if conscious, to "world 2". But the characteristic thing about specifically human knowledge—*science*—is that it is formulated in a descriptive and argumentative language, and that the problems, theories, and errors which are embedded in this language stand in their own peculiar relations, constituting what I call "world 3".

Campbell does not say very much about my theory of world 3, and it is here that I should like to make some remarks in amplification of his.

A point which follows almost directly from this critical realism is what I have described as the *knowledge situation* of animals and men. So far as the knowledge is not, somehow, genetically built into them, animals and men can only gain knowledge if they have a drive or instinct for exploration—for finding out more about their world. Their very existence, to be sure, presupposes a world which is *to some extent* "knowable" or "explorable", but it also presupposes an innate disposition to know and to explore: we are active explorers (explorers by trial and error) rather than passive recipients of information impressed upon us from outside (Lamarckism, inductivism).

But we live in a complicated and partly mysterious world. We seem to know much more about it than the animals do—or anyway much more in a not entirely instrumental or utilitarian sense of "knowledge"; but there is no reason to think that our knowledge is not highly fallible and sketchy. It is only in the last three hundred years that we have begun to know much about the situation of the Earth on which we are living; and it is only one hundred years or a little less since we began to know more about the limitations of our natural senses as detectors, and to build detectors which reveal to us encoded information or messages about the world to which our senses would not be immediately responsive.

Thus it is an almost immediate consequence of critical realism (together with an evolutionary approach) to regard ourselves, and our knowledge, as continuous with the animals and with animal knowledge. This means in my opinion that we must abandon any approach which starts from sense data and the given, and replace it by the assumption that all human knowledge is fallible and conjectural. It is a product of the method of trial and error.

Part of our knowledge consists of innate dispositions and expectations (or of drives or instincts to explore, for example, or to imitate). What is so notable about human knowledge is that it has grown so very far beyond all animal knowledge, and that it is still growing. The main task of the theory of human knowledge is to understand it as continuous with animal knowledge; and to understand also its discontinuity—if any—from animal knowledge.

In all this there is, I believe, complete agreement between Campbell and myself.

II

A point in Campbell's theory seems to me to deserve special mention; it is a point on which I have had to say very little that is useful, if anything, and on which he has to say excellent and enlightening things. I am thinking of what he calls the *"blindness"* of the trials in a trial-and-error method.

I have sometimes compared the human situation in the quest for new knowledge with the proverbial situation of a blind man who searches in a dark room for a black hat which is—perhaps—not there. This is not saying much; but it indicates that the searcher at least acts as if he had a problem. I have often added that the trial movements of the searcher will not be completely random. There are various reasons for this, both positive and negative. The positive ones are in the main that the searcher has a problem to solve, and that this means that he has some knowledge, however fuzzy, previously acquired by essentially the same trial-and-error method; this knowledge serves as a guide, and eliminates complete randomness.[120] A negative argument is that randomness, and the associated idea of (probabilistic) independence in the sequence of trials, are hardly applicable: the tosses with a penny may be random, but only with respect to a definite property—heads or tails. There must be a definite, given *order* if we want to speak of randomness, such as the orderly sequences of tosses with a penny, considered from the point of view of which side comes up: here we have definite "elementary events", which may or may not yield a random sequence.

But although the blind man who searches for a black hat may *bring* some order into his trials, the order is not *given* to him; he may choose or invent one order (method) first, and a different order later; and these choices will be trials too—even though on a higher level. (They may, but need not, be influenced by his earlier experience in somewhat similar or in very different situations.) There is no definite or given order of "elementary events"; we do not even know what is the maximum activity that constitutes *one* trial (event) rather than two.

Nevertheless, the trials are *forays into the unknown.* Campbell, who explains why he does not call them random (see the text between his nn. 21

and 24), calls them "blind" (an excellent term) and insists on the fact that, so far as they are trials in a trial-and-error movement—that is, so far as they are forays into the unknown—they are blind; while to the degree that past knowledge enters, their blindness is only relative: it begins where the past knowledge ends.

I think this is very important. It means that we may at the beginning of an exploration be blinder than we are after even a short time, though after even a short time we may still be blind: we may still not know where the black hat is, but we may know (or think that we know) where it is not.

I regard this idea of the "blindness" of the trials in a trial-and-error movement as an important step beyond the mistaken idea of random trials,which in any case stand under the influence of a (changing) exploratory drive and (likewise changing) problem situation. (See esp. the text to, and following, Campbell's n. 57.)

Campbell comes to the conclusion that the trial-and-error method is essentially similar to the attempts of a blind man to feel his way with a stick. It is active. And he shows that our use of our sense organs is essentially of the same nature (see the text following Campbell's n. 28): "From the point of view of an evolutionary epistemology, vision is just as indirect as radar."

This shows that nothing is "given" to us by our senses; everything is interpreted, decoded: everything is the result of active experiments, under the control of an exploratory drive.

There is a point here, however, into which Campbell does not go, but which I regard as important. The blind trial stands not only under the influence of the exploratory drive or instinct, but also under the influence of the experience of error—the experience that this is wrong, that this is *not* the solution. This point (which he of course would concede) seems to me so important because it becomes on the human level the basis of our *criticism* of the results of our trials.

III

Campbell's paper touches (though from a very different direction) some of the points discussed by Professor Watkins, who also deals with questions of evolution. Some of the points mentioned in my reply to Watkins belong also here, and vice versa.

There is especially the question of the decoding (itself yielding an interpretation subject to trial and error) which is partly undertaken by our sense organs and partly by our brain. I conjecture that the deepest basis of this decoding operation is a genetically based, innate drive to find out, to understand, to correlate. This is perhaps the strongest reason why blindness is so different from randomness.

When blind and deaf Helen Keller's teacher "spelt" the word "water" into the hand over which water was running, and Helen Keller "understood"—when she knew that this *meant* water—there must have been at work not only a dispositional ability to learn a language (an "unnatural" language, and one which was hardly "social" at all), but also a deepseated dispositional *need,* an unconscious *desire* for symbols and for the understanding of symbols.

I conjecture that it is so with all our decoding instincts—for example with vision, including the vision of colour. I conjecture that a child who is colourblind (say, red-green blind), but otherwise as healthy and active as Helen Keller, would make use of any help to decode colours and to learn to distinguish red from green. I suggest that if such a child is fitted, for example, with a red lens before the right eye and a green lens before the left eye, he would soon learn not only how to make use of his peculiar experiences in order to distinguish red from green: he would actually learn to *see* red and green; that is, he would, under the influence of his healthy nervous system and its *needs* and *drives,* learn to make use of the distinct experiences available to *decode the encoded messages correctly* ("correctly" according to the guidance of his inborn needs).[121] It is, I think, some support of my hypothesis that a former pupil of mine, the psychoanalyst Dr Noel Bradley, reports that colourblind children may deeply suffer from their deficiency (which they should not, one would think, experience, unless some instinct is not satisfied), and many even develop a neurosis in connection with it.[122]

IV

I come now to two points where I may possibly slightly deviate from Campbell.

The first is connected with his psychological analysis of Kant's a priori categories. In this connection, Campbell first quotes at length a passage from me (see the text to his n. 98) and then continues: "This insight is the earliest and most frequently noted aspect of an evolutionary epistemology", referring to Herbert Spencer, Harald Høffding, Wallraff, Lange, Baldwin, and Konrad Lorenz.

However, I may perhaps say that in the long passage quoted by Campbell from me there are, I hope, several "insights", and that the insight denoted by Campbell as "this insight" is not the one which I wished to bring out as important.

It is a clear and an almost obvious insight that Kant's idea of a priori knowledge can be psychologically interpreted (and has sometimes been so interpreted; sometimes even by Kant himself, and certainly by Fries). That is, our interpretation of events in terms of causality (for example) may be merely psychological, or due to the structure of our brain, without being necessarily *valid* in Kant's sense; valid, that is to say, not only for all possible rational beings, but in the sense that it must be true for the world as we know it. This latter meaning is not psychological but raises a claim to absolute *objectivity;* and the fundamental meaning of Kant's teaching was that his categories (and principles) were *a priori valid*—and *objectively valid*—in this sense, and not merely a priori in the sense that they factually preceded our experiences, and were needed for our experiences.

All writers here quoted by Campbell, including myself, have pointed out that we may reinterpret Kant's a priori so as not to mean *"objectively valid"* but "prior to sense experience". (I have pointed out too that in some way or other all hypotheses *(H)* are psychologically prior to some observation *(O)*, since observation presupposes an interest, a problem, a conjecture; see the text following Campbell's n. 97, and his reference to my *C.&R.*, p. 47.) But in the long passage quoted by Campbell and referred to when he speaks of "this insight", I said, I think, several other things besides this, things which had to my knowledge not been said before by any of the authors whom Campbell quotes. However, I leave it to the interested reader to find out what these other insights are.[123]

V

I come now to my last comment. It is, I think, an important one, and it is related to the difference between man and animal, and especially between human rationality and human science and animal knowledge.

Campbell speaks very interestingly of the language of the bees (text to his n. 65), and he also mentions my stress on criticism; but he nowhere seems to allude to my view that human descriptive language differs from all animal languages in being also argumentative, and that it is human argumentative language which makes criticism possible, and with it science.

There is a world of difference between holding a belief, or expecting something, and using human language to *say* so. The difference is that only if spoken out, and thus objectivized, does a belief become criticizable. Before it is formulated in language, I may be one with my belief: the belief is part of my acting, part of my behaviour. If formulated, it may be criticized and found to be erroneous; in which case I may be able to discard it.

The language of the bees may resemble human language in that it can be said (up to a point) to be descriptive. But so far as we know, a bee cannot lie, and another bee cannot deny what the first bee asserted.

I think that the first storyteller may have been the man who contributed to the rise of the ideas of factual *truth* and *falsity,* and that out of this the ideal of truth developed; as did the argumentative use of language.[124] I do not sense any difference in opinion in what Campbell says concerning truth and instrumentalism. But there seems to be a slight difference in emphasis: in my stress on the idea of truth, on the argumentative function of the human language, and on criticism—in brief in my predilection for world 3. But it is very likely that there is no difference here: Campbell's beautiful essay covers a great many things; he may have been reluctant to say more.

24. Freeman and Skolimowski on Peirce's Anticipations of Popper

Professor Freeman justly assesses my more radical fallibilism as "one of the fundamental disagreements between Peirce and Popper"; Peirce believes (at least sometimes) that "it is the nature of truth that it will hit us sooner or later, given enough time. Popper, on the other hand, . . . denies this" (see the text to their n. 2). This is a very fair remark. But what is the reason for this great divergence? The Einsteinian revolution. Peirce wrote before Einstein shattered our belief in Newton's most wonderful and most successful theory. Newton's theory had been, it is true, criticized by Mach; but his philosophical arguments, originally due to Berkeley,[125] impressed few physicists, especially as Berkeley and Mach rightly accepted Newtonian theory as the best in existence. To be a fallibilist at all in those days was no mean achievement; and it is greatly to Peirce's credit that he was one. My more far-reaching fallibilism, on the other hand, is the direct result of Einstein's revolution.

Freeman also points out another basic difference: Peirce "accepts the empirical axiom that nothing can be in the intellect which was not first known through the senses, from which it follows that unless generality is given in perception, it can never be known at all". Freeman, like myself, does not believe that universals are given in perception. But my disagreement with Peirce goes somewhat deeper: I think that *nothing* is "first known through the senses". The senses themselves interpret and theorize, they are fallible: they are, literally, only the feelers of the central nervous system, which is a problem solver. However the gap between Peirce and myself is narrowed by Freeman's remark that "perceptual judgement" is "on Peirce's view, . . . to some extent an interpretation by the subject". But it is also "a process which [we are] utterly unable to control and consequently . . . unable to criticize". (This is Freeman quoting Peirce 5.157.) This I do not agree with; as soon as a "judgement" (a term I rarely use) is linguistically formulated, it becomes part of world 3 and can be criticized. Perhaps Peirce's "judgement" is the un-formulated "impression" or "belief" which (according to my view) is indeed part of myself and out of my critical control; just as the expectation of an animal is out of its control. But I do not think so, since Peirce (5.157; quoted by Freeman) indicates that a perceptual judgement, though not "inferred from any premise", is like one of those things which may be inferred. If this is so, then it widens the gulf between his "no control thesis" and my thesis of our critical control of world 3 objects.

Another big gulf between Peirce and myself is his thesis (quoted by Freeman) that "all reasoning is diagrammatic", while I am inclined to say "all reasoning is critical". (But see Bernays's contribution, and my reply to him in section 28.)

This brings me to Freeman's generous—too generous—remarks about my principle of falsifiability. I am greatly indebted to Freeman for pointing out what a difference my negative formulation makes. I could only wish he had emphasized that my criterion, though it may be called a "pragmatic criterion for objectivity" (as he does call it), is one of demarcation; and though perhaps one of "meaning" in Peirce's sense, it is not a criterion of "meaningfulness" in the positivists' sense. Professor Freeman then quotes Peirce (1.120) as saying that "the best hypothesis, in the sense of the one most recommending itself to the inquirer, is the one which can be the most readily refuted if it is false".

Professor Freeman's last comparison but one is devoted to Peirce's "Tychism", which indeed is more similar than Freeman could possibly have known to the "Metaphysical Epilogue" which I developed fifteen years ago in the last chapter of my as yet unpublished *Postscript.* As for the similarities and dissimilarities of Peirce's realistic position and my own—my theory of world 3—I should only like to stress that my realism is not (like Plato's) one of essences—of concepts or natures which neither are in need of, nor permit, any further explanation; nor are all the denizens of my (man-made) world 3 man-made: the theories usually are, and so are the world 3 mistakes, but not the world 3 problems: they are internally generated, and perhaps discovered.

Reply to Professor Skolimowski

Professor Skolimowski's paper surprised me by the degree of his understanding of what has been so often misunderstood.

I

In his excellent first section *(Popper's Problem),* where he gives an exposition of my main interest, he proposes a conjecture which I must correct, since it does not correspond to historical fact. It is a conjecture about the opponents against whom I fought in what he calls my "metaphysical period". The conjecture is ingenious, but mistaken. The fault is, mainly, my continued failure to publish my *Postscript.* This *Postscript,* which was concluded in 1956 and has lain in galley proofs since February, 1957, will now, I hope, be published soon; and in it Skolimowski will find, as the last chapter, the "Metaphysical Epilogue" whose similarities with Peirce's "Tychism" I have just pointed out; here I outlined a theory of what Skolimowski calls "larger frameworks", and what I called "metaphysical research programmes". I think that so far there has been published, apart from "The Aim of Science",[126] only one passage from this book; a passage from this chapter, quoted by Professor Lakatos, who has had a copy of the galleys for many years.[127] Skolimowski's conjecture is that my "meta-physical period" was a reaction to Michael Polanyi's *Personal Knowledge* and to Thomas Kuhn's *The Structure of Scientific Revolutions*. But Polanyi's book was published in 1958; and Kuhn's still later, in 1962. No, my fight for objectivity (this is how I should describe what Skolimowski calls my metaphysical period) began much earlier. It started from my interest in quantum mechanics and indeterminism (see my [1950 (b) and (c)]) and took me to the propensity interpretation of probability, which I had worked on for several years before I published my first paper on it [1957 (e)]. But I freely admit that when in 1959 I published the first English edition of my *Logic of Scientific Discovery,* the end of my new Preface (where I referred to the "post-rationalist" and "post-critical" age) was a critical allusion to Polanyi's *Personal Knowledge.* (Polanyi himself described his philosophy as "post-critical".) But I saw in it only a symptom of a deadlier disease—the dissolution of the most objective of all sciences, physics.[128]

I think that these references will bear out my assertion that Skolimowski's ingenious conjecture is not correct, and explain why I mentioned neither Polanyi nor Kuhn but rather Niels Bohr, in whose work I had been interested since the early 1920s. But Skolimowski's guess, despite being wrong, is a good guess, for in all these places I argued against views which were later developed by the two thinkers Skolimowski mentions, Polanyi and Kuhn.

II

Again, Skolimowski's table in his section 2 is a surprisingly good summary of my "methodological period" (the topic of his section 2), and of my relation to logical positivism. I can recommend it to anybody interested in the issue; it is most informative and it is very simple. My only critical comment is that he might have added to his table a further issue:

ISSUE	LOGICAL POSITIVISTS	POPPER
What can we do about metaphysics?	It is just nonsense. Destroy it.	We are all metaphysicians; and science derives historically from metaphysics.

Such an addition would also have eased the transition from what Skolimowski calls my first period to my second. It is just a historical fact that, after the interlude of *The Open Society* and *The Poverty of Historicism*, I turned to other issues: first to logic (the logic of natural deduction), and then to the problem of the history of rationalism and its present dangers.[129] Only a little later in 1953 I discussed the body-mind problem—a paradigm metaphysical problem, which had long fascinated me—in two brief papers;[130] these papers are extremely brief, but I had lectured on it, and on its history, at some length before. If I were to speak of a metaphysical period in my interests, I would put two closely related problems in its centre: the fight against subjectivism, in quantum mechanics and elsewhere, and the body-mind problem, in which my theory of "world 3" plays so essential a part. (A far from finished book, based on my Emory lectures of 1969, is in existence on this subject; it has been read, and partly reported on, by Sir John Eccles.)[131]

Indeed Skolimowski is certainly right when he says (in his section 1) that one of my main interests was "to combat the peril of subjectivism" and that, in so doing, I "acquired new opponents". I might point out that I acquired them only by the way and that, with the exception of Niels Bohr, I could not take them, or their theories, very seriously. So I should appeal to Niels Bohr and nobody else if, as Skolimowski says (in his section 2) "in the 1960s, some radical changes occurred in . . . [Popper's] concept of objectivity". Whether these changes were radical I very much doubt (see my *L.d.F.,* sections 8, 10, 27, for example); but I agree with Skolimowski that there were changes. He asserts further (section 2) that for similar reasons "the whole focus [of Popper's work] has been shifted to problems of greater generality". But here I am less inclined to agree; for from the beginning I have always tried to see problems in their "greater generality"; so no external explanation is needed to explain any shift there may have been.

In this connection, I should perhaps also comment on Skolimowski's remark (in his section 2) "that the most interesting and novel ideas in the philosophy of science during the last decade came from the adherents of the dynamic concept of knowledge. . . . They have in a way carried on and developed various aspects of Popper's dynamic programme". With the exception of Polanyi the people whom Skolimowski lists either were pupils of mine or have written in some place or other that they were influenced by me. Referring to them, Skolimowski at once continues: "But sometimes they carried some of these aspects so far, radicalized some of the positions so much that Popper found it necessary to defend himself against other dynamic concepts of science."

I can well believe that this is the way the matter looks from outside. But to me it all seems rather different.

I have always encouraged my pupils to criticize my ideas, and some have done so, on one occasion or another, quite successfully. (I do not of course include in the category of successful criticism those attacks which use as arguments against me arguments which come from my own writing and teaching.) Yet I challenge Professor Skolimowski to give one example—apart from my brief criticism of some aspects of Kuhn's theory[132]—in any of my writings, prior to this volume, which shows that "Popper found it necessary to defend himself against other dynamic concepts of science". And I think that even this one brief paper hardly anywhere shows any spirit of self-defence. As far as my former pupil Feyerabend is concerned, I cannot recall any writing of mine in which I took notice of any writing of his. Lakatos is a different case. He originally worked in the field of the history and philosophy of mathematics, and I have in various places made acknowledgements of having learned from him, as he made various acknowledgements of having learned from me. Later, he turned to methodology. But except for writing a footnote[133] which was published a year after Professor Skolimowski's paper reached me I have said nothing about this until now.[134] I cannot recall a single publication of mine which could be said to have the character of a defence, least of all a defence against an overradical development of my dynamic conception of science.

I say all this only in order to prevent the emergence of yet another Popper legend, and not as a criticism of Skolimowski, who offers an ingenious historical conjecture. It might well have been as he thinks; but it did not happen in this way.

Skolimowski's summing up of my "methodological period" again seems to me excellent. It is true that, especially since about 1958 or 1960, "what is at stake is the very rationality and objectivity of science, the legitimacy of the distinction between science and nonscience". And it is true that some of the people listed by Professor Skolimowski seem now to be among those who attack this distinction; but although it has strengthened my conviction that my fight for rationality and objectivity is far from being a fight against windmills, none of this has much influenced my philosophy or my writing. It only supports the view which I formulated in the first section of my "Three Views" [1956(f)]: that Galilean science is threatened again by irrationalism.

III

Skolimowski's section 3, on my "metaphysical period", is extremely good, like the preceding sections; but a few points need to be corrected.

In his point 1 in section 3 Skolimowski suggests that Kuhn's "paradigms" are units which are necessarily *larger* than my "conjectures". But I have never put an upper or lower limit to the size of what I have called "conjectures". They may comprise a whole religion; they may refer to a footprint in the sand. What Kuhn calls a "paradigm", I might call, according to its character, a dominant theory or a ruling fashion. But if "paradigms" are so much bigger than conjectures then this very fact brings them dangerously near to Hegel's "spirit of a period" *(Zeitgeist);* and from this my "conjectures" are, I think, fairly far removed. But I have (in my lectures since about 1940 and also in print)[135] drawn attention to the fact that the idea of what is and what is not an acceptable scientific explanation changes in time; and in my *Postscript* I described these "big changes" as "metaphysical research programmes" for science. Thus I have no quarrel with the view that there are "big" *regulative ideas* for science, and that these may change.

When therefore Skolimowski writes (section 3) that "[in] order to counteract Kuhn, Popper had to ascend to a still higher level", then he tells a "fascinating" story, as he calls it himself; but not history.

From his story Skolimowski draws the conclusion that "we have considerable liberty to choose the framework we consider best"; and he further draws from this a consequence which he calls (with reference to my late friend Kasimir Ajdukiewicz) a radical conventionalism. He forgets that Ajdukiewicz's "radical conventionalism" definitely belonged to the "static" rather than to the "dynamic" type of metascience. But what is more important, and what I wish to make quite clear, is that I am not a conventionalist: I hold that although we build our own systems or frameworks, we do everything we can to let "nature" decide between them.[136]

IV

In his fourth section, Skolimowski tries to give a guide to my three worlds: world 1 (physical processes), world 2 (mental processes), and world 3 (problems, theories, and solutions, including mistaken solutions). Skolimowski is fairly successful in his description, which ends with the words: "Although [Popper's] effort is strenuous, it is not successful."

It seems to me that from this passage on, Skolimowski utterly fails to give a fair picture of my theory.

He quotes (in his section 4) a passage from a lecture of mine,[137] an introductory passage whose various allusions, regarded as unsatisfactory (and italicized) by Skolimowski, are explained more fully later in the same lecture. Skolimowski writes, in his comment on the quotation (italics again his): "All Popper's difficulties on this issue stem, in my opinion, from one source, namely from Popper's insistence that there is no similarity *whatsoever* 'on any level of problems between contents and the corresponding processes,' that is between the entities of the second and the third world."

Skolimowski supplies no reference to my work in this crucial passage; neither to the italicized *"whatsoever"*, nor to what looks, in view of the (here single) quotation marks, like a quotation from my lecture; but he says "This is emphatically pronounced on more than one occasion". I cannot recall any occasion on which it is "pronounced", to say nothing of "emphatically pronounced", in the sense which Skolimowski assumes. Nor can I see from Skolimowski's text what he means by "All Popper's difficulties". And Skolimowski who in other places is generous with references and quotations gives me no help in this one, though in his opinion it is crucial. (Of course, whether I have used the *words* that Skolimowski quotes is much less important than whether I have somewhere expressed the *content*.)

At the end of the section, however, Skolimowski announces (in italics) his own programme for overcoming my difficulties; and this seems to me to be just a summary of the lengthy descriptions and examples I have given. For he writes *"the processes of thinking in the individual mind . . . are carried through structural units of the third world"*. (I have omitted, as indicated by the three dots, a few words to which I do not fully subscribe because they seem to me to reduce the passage to a definition of the word "cognitive"; the omitted words are: *"become cognitive if and only if they"*.) To quote a not dissimilar passage of my own: "I admit that this subjective or dispositional state of understanding belongs to the second world. But I assert . . . that almost all the important things we can say about it [that is, about our second world understanding or grasping of the third world] consist in pointing out its relations to third-world objects."[138]

I admit that the brief passage just quoted, taken out of context, may sound not very clear. I have quoted it only because it is here that I begin my analysis of the relationship of a mind to the third world objects in its grasp; and this analysis seems to me not only quite different from what Skolimowski hints is my central mistake, but even an improved version of Skolimowski's own solution to "Popper's difficulties".

V

Skolimowski's section 5 is entitled "Language and Mind" and his section 6 is entitled "On the Concept of the Linguistic Mind". Both are largely about Chomsky and not about me. Although I am not very well informed about Chomsky, I disagree with the doctrines Skolimowski develops in these sections; and I should perhaps note that he takes no account of what I have said on the issues in question.

The issue is what Skolimowski calls (in his summary in section 7) Chomsky's "innatism", a point in which, judging by Skolimowski's criticism of Chomsky, I seem to agree to a considerable extent with Chomsky.

I conjecture that animals and men have what can be called "inborn knowledge", or more especially, "inborn expectations" and "inborn dispositions".[139] I should not greatly relish speaking of inborn "ideas" (as, I understand, Chomsky does), but this is a minor and largely terminological issue. The learning by the human child of an articulate, descriptive, and argumentative language is, I conjecture, based upon innate dispositions; it has a genetic basis. The genetic basis comprises dispositions to state, to describe, to agree or disagree with a description; to argue, to be critical of a statement; and countless more. All this has, of course, to be learned by the child in the course of its development; but the possibility of learning it is inborn, in the shape of inborn dispositions and inborn expectations.

Since I do not know Chomsky's work well enough to assert, or deny, that we agree on this point, it seems safest to conjecture that we agree; and there is nothing in Skolimowski's section to refute this conjecture. Skolimowski himself disagrees with Chomsky's doctrine of inborn ideas, but since he does not refer to my discussion of inborn dispositions and expectations, I do not know whether his disagreement would extend to my own doctrine. It seems to me that all that Skolimowski criticizes in Chomsky can easily be answered if we agree to use the term "idea" in so wide a sense that it comprises even dispositions and expectations.

VI

Skolimowski's last section is entitled "The Conceptual Net of Science and the Conceptual Structure of the Mind". This seems to me a weak section. It operates with the metaphor of "patterns of thought" in a manner which makes me doubt whether he appreciates the metaphorical character of the expression. But he uses it—and the no less metaphorical idea of a "similarity" between these patterns of world 3 objects—in order to solve all "Popper's difficulties"; difficulties which I have from the start had difficulty in identifying or locating.

These last three sections of Skolimowski's contribution seem to me the least instructive ones. But this is not to be wondered at since they treat, in a brief space, a really difficult problem: the problem of the relations of world 1, world 2, and world 3. I suspect that this problem contains components which will—if they are ever solved—not be solved before we know much more about the human brain and the human mind than we do now.

But these sections apart, Skolimowski's essay is a highly instructive one, and one that repays serious reading.

Reply to Professors Freeman and Skolimowski

To the third part, which is the common work of Professors Freeman and Skolimowski, I have hardly a comment to make; I should only like to express my gratitude to them for the many enlightening passages from Peirce, which show to what degree Peirce anticipated some of my central ideas.

25. Feigl and Meehl on the Determinism or Completeness of World 1

I

Professors Feigl and Meehl treat in their common contribution fun-

damentally the same problems as do Professor Sir John Eccles, Professor
J. W. N. Watkins, and to a lesser extent, Professor Alan Musgrave. For me,
the central problem is whether the physical world is closed or not; that is,
whether anything nonphysical can in some way or other influence the physical
world. Feigl and Meehl write as physicalists or physical monists, defending
the thesis of the closed physical world against my pluralist account, as given
in my Arthur Holly Compton Memorial Lecture "Of Clouds and Clocks".[140]

Feigl and Meehl have not been convinced by my arguments in this
lecture. It would have surprised me if they had been convinced: my lecture
was, after all, just one lecture, lasting just over one hour. As I said at the
beginning of another lecture ("Epistemology Without a Knowing Subject"):
"I have . . . no illusions about what I can convey in a lecture. . . . I shall
make no attempt in this lecture to convince you. Instead I shall make an
attempt to challenge you, and, if possible to provoke you."[141] If one looks at
the sheer size of Feigl's and Meehl's contribution and of an additional paper
by Meehl[142] (not contributed to the present volume) to which Feigl and Meehl
refer, one can hardly doubt that I succeeded in provoking them.

But I not only failed to convince them, I failed completely in getting my
argument across.

What I tried to show in "Of Clouds and Clocks", and what I developed
further in "Epistemology Without a Knowing Subject", is that the physical
world is not *closed,* but that *reasons* (which I regard as nonphysical) *can have
physical effects* (or physical "causal efficacy", to use Meehl's words), at any
rate *after having been grasped by some mind.*

If we call the physical world "world 1"; the world of mental experiences
"world 2"; and the world of problems, arguments, reasons (and also of works
of art and many other things) "world 3", then my thesis can be formulated:
world 3 can act (at any rate via world 2) upon world 1; therefore, world 1 is
not causally closed. This thesis is my answer to what I called "Compton's
problem" in "Of Clouds and Clocks". I developed it further in "Epistemology Without a Knowing Subject" and in "On the Theory of the Objective Mind",[143] and in other papers.[144] Although Meehl's paper (referred to in
my note 142) mentions my "Epistemology Without a Knowing Subject", the
joint contribution takes account only of the first of these papers, "Of Clouds
and Clocks". But what they present as their main arguments *against* my main
thesis I regard as amongst the strongest arguments *for* it: what they seem to
regard as my main thesis I do not so regard.

Let me explain this more fully. One of my central theses is that reasons
(or the validity of reasons), arguments, and even problems, can influence
human behaviour and therefore the physical world (world 1). For example, a
scientific argument between builders of bridges can lead to a change in the
plan for the construction of a bridge, and therefore influence the part of the
physical world represented by the completed bridge. Or to use Compton's

own example: a promise or an agreement to give a lecture in America on a certain date somehow caused him to return physically by boat from sunny Italy to a part of the United States to which he did not feel at all physically attracted. Many subsidiary physical events were involved (such as, perhaps, his going to a travel agency).

Using such examples I came forward with the thesis that the physical world (world 1) is not causally closed, but open to causal influences originating in world 2 and in world 3.

So far as I can see, there exists one main objection to my thesis. It is the denial of the real existence of world 3. What really exist are not reasons or arguments or objections, but physical entities (such as a typed memorandum of agreement, or a diary entry); thus there is no world 3, there are only pieces of paper with symbols on them; and these belong to world 1. We thus arrive at a dualism: only worlds 1 and 2 exist. Similarly, one can deny the existence of world 2: what exists is not an experience such as the grasping of a scientific argument; rather what exist are behaviour (or misbehaviour), and also brain processes. Thus we arrive at a world 1 monism, also called "physicalism".

As I understand Feigl's and Meehl's contribution, it is a highly undogmatic plea in favour of world 1 monism; the authors even admit the possibility of the existence of experiences (what they call "raw feels"), thereby leaving open the possibility of a certain dualism of body and mind. This shows their undogmatic approach; but they seem to prefer, by and large, the view that world 1, the physical world, is *closed.*

Far be it from me to claim that I have shown in "Of Clouds and Clocks" that either dualism or monism is logically untenable; in fact, my strongest arguments in favour of world 3 were only developed in [1968 (s)] and [1968 (r)], and even these arguments I do not regard as anything like conclusive proofs. What I have done in "Of Clouds and Clocks" is to offer some arguments—good, though inconclusive arguments—against monism and mere dualism; and my main argument is directed against the closedness of world 1.

In the course of my arguments, I made remarks like the following:

If world 1 is not closed, then it cannot be a deterministic world: its machinery for determination must have loopholes. Thus physical indeterminism is part of my thesis. Yet I stressed that *indeterminism is not enough:* world 1 may be indeterministic but, at the same time, closed. "Assume", I wrote, "that our physical world is a *physically closed* system" but one that contains "chance elements. Obviously it would not be deterministic; yet purposes, ideas, hopes, and wishes could not in such a world have any influence [because of the closedness of the physical world]. . . . Note that a deterministic physical system will be closed, but that a closed system may be indeterministic. Thus 'indeterminism is not enough' . . . ;"[145] not enough, that is, to make the causal efficacy of arguments, reasons, agreements, misunderstandings, and so on, understandable.

It is in this way that the problem of determinism versus indeterminism enters into my argument: it enters as a merely *subsidiary problem,* subsidiary to the problem of the closedness or openness of world 1.

"Of Clouds and Clocks" was a Compton Memorial Lecture, and I took care to quote and to discuss Compton's ideas. It is for this reason that the subsidiary problem of determinism and indeterminism takes up perhaps almost as much space as what I have called there "Compton's problem", the problem of the closedness or openness of world 1. Yet this was my main problem.

The situation has fatally misled Feigl and Meehl, as indicated by the very title of their joint contribution ("The Determinism-Freedom and Body-Mind Problems"; compare also the title of Meehl's own paper, "Psychological Determinism and Human Rationality").

Feigl's and Meehl's central argument is: Popper holds that rationality—the causal efficacy of reasons—clashes with determinism. But he must be wrong in this, since we can predict, for example, the linguistic behaviour of a logician if asked a question concerning a certain logical fallacy: he will react by saying "Illicit distribution of the major".[146]

Perfect predictability of behaviour would imply determinism. Here we have predictable behaviour linked to rational inference. Since reasoning is a standard example of mine against determinism, Feigl's and Meehl's example, so they argue, refutes my thesis.

But this is one big misunderstanding. As it happens, I dislike logical examples, and especially fallacies, because of their artificiality. But since my own central thesis is the influence of reasoning (worlds 2 and 3) upon the physical world 1, for example, upon behaviour, Feigl's and Meehl's example fits my case perfectly. It certainly cannot be used to illustrate the closedness of world 1. But it is the closedness of world 1 which is at stake.

It certainly cannot be used, either, to illustrate the determinism of world 1. Feigl and Meehl indicate that the predictability of the logician's behaviour speaks for determinism rather than against it. Perhaps, but not for the *precise* determinism of a closed physical world.

The thesis that some other form of determinism could be rescued by first admitting that world 1 as such is not closed, and then asserting that its loopholes are completely filled with "causes" originating in worlds 2 and 3, opens an entirely different and less important problem. There are in my paper some arguments[147] against this thesis—for example, the characteristic vagueness of psychological causation, compared with physical causation—but these arguments are neglected by Feigl and Meehl. Applied to their own example, these arguments would draw attention to the fact that we may be able to predict, in a case like theirs, what the logician will say; but we may be unable to predict the tone of his voice—whether for example he will speak with interest or disgust. This in fact they themselves admit. For they predict only that the logician will reply (Feigl and Meehl, section II) " 'Illicit distribution of the major, ' or some synonymous expression" ; so that the precise language he uses may not be predictable. But this is a world 1 matter, and what language is used may make a great deal of difference in world 1. Thus Feigl's and Meehl's arguments do not support the stronger thesis that world 1 is determined.

Since I assert the causal efficacy of reasons upon world 1, Feigl's and Meehl's central arguments against me all turn out to be arguments in favour of my thesis. The only explanation of the fact that they did not see this is that they took me, because of certain quotations from Compton (which they quote again), as arguing in a general and vague way against determinism; but this was not my point.

It should be mentioned, however, that although the Feigl/Meehl example of the predictability of the logician's verbal behaviour perfectly accords with my thesis, and is therefore not, as they think, an argument against me, I should not regard this kind of (almost perfect) predictability as characteristic of the way in which human rationality influences human behaviour. The more interesting examples are not the trivial ones such as a syllogism in Barbara or "$5+7=12$", but the nontrivial cases; and here predictability breaks down. I certainly was unable to predict anything of Feigl's and Meehl's highly rational contribution; I was, I frankly admit, moved and surprised by its complete absence of dogmatism, by the way in which they felt challenged by my arguments, and by their great friendliness and fairness; but also by some fundamental misunderstandings. Similarly it seems to me most improbable that they should have been able to predict the main contents of my reply to them: there is no trace of anticipation, in their paper, of the lines my reply follows. Yet both their paper, and mine, may be described as examples of rational behaviour; but these examples are very different from their own, the spotting of a typical fallacy in Aristotelian logic, or the correct thinking of a syllogism in Barbara (section II).

II

Feigl and Meehl seem to be impressed by the efficiency of computers, and to think (section I) that the fact that a computer could radically ab- breviate an elementary proof in Whitehead's and Russell's *Principia*, or that a chess-playing computer could beat its constructor in a game of chess, speaks for the possible creativity of physical machines.

I am unimpressed, for many reasons. First, mechanisms capable of "creating" something new—for example, new ornaments—are very old. And the created product may indeed be "new" in the sense that it was not explicitly built into the machine by its maker.

As far as the proof from *Principia Mathematica* goes, it is well known that some of the proofs of this pioneering work are very clumsy. I think that everybody who has produced some new mathematical proofs knows that his first successful proof of a theorem is usually unnecessarily complicated. Almost invariably it can be simplified. I have found this myself quite often. There seems to be no reason why a fast-working computer should not, for example, pick out the shortest of the proofs it produces. It can moreover be programmed to grind out *all* possible valid proofs (up to a certain length, say), perhaps ordered by some lexicographical schema; if no maximum length is given, the task is of course infinite; but after a sufficient time, short (perhaps even the shortest) proofs would be forthcoming.

Einstein once said, "My pencil is more intelligent than I",[148] meaning that armed with pencil and paper he obtained some results which he did not foresee. This is, I suppose, why he used pencil and paper. We use computers because they can do more than we can do without them, and more quickly. Otherwise, we should not spend enormous sums of money on them. In my view, a computer is nothing but a glorified pencil.

III

I have argued that world 3 is a changing world—a product of the human mind—and that the discoveries of open problems and their proposed solutions by way of new theories are among its most characteristic events. I am well aware of the fact that dualistic opponents of world 3 may therefore argue that world 3 only exists in the human mind; and physicalist monists may say that it only exists in the form of spoken words or printed books, and brain processes responding to them.

These are objections so obvious that I found it unnecessary to mention them: one is almost tempted to say that they represent the two most likely commonsense reactions to the thesis of the existence of world 3. I should even say that the interest of the thesis that there exists a world 3 depends entirely on the fact that there are these obvious objections to it.

My main argument is that world 3, though the product of human minds, develops its own autonomous problems. The series of natural numbers may be diagnosed as an invention of the human mind, or the human brain. Yet prime numbers are not things that anybody invented; they were discovered. This shows that our inventions may have unexpected and unwanted objective consequences. And an engineering decision—say, whether or not to build a bridge in a certain way—may depend on the result of a calculation no less difficult to decide or to predict than whether or not $2^{222} + 1$ is a prime number.

Thus many of our engineering decisions depend upon as yet unknown calculations, that is, on as yet unknown facts belonging to world 3. Of course, it is the *discovery* of the fact, rather than the fact itself, which is a cause of our decision, and thus of some effect in world 1. But given sufficient time, the discovery whether $2^{222} + 1$ is prime or not depends completely on whether it is prime or not; and thus objective facts belonging to world 3 *may* become causes of events in world 1. As far as I can see, they can become so only if grasped by a human mind, or by a machine constructed for the purpose by the human mind. It seems that the facts of world 3 cannot operate upon world 1 without the intervention of mental processes; and this seems to me a strong argument in favour of the existence of world 2 (*much* stronger than the appeal to *raw feels*) and against any monistic physicalism.

These arguments were (briefly) discussed in "Of Clouds and Clocks", and they were developed more fully in some of my later lectures. They seem to me very powerful. They are not discussed by Feigl and Meehl.

IV

Looking back at this controversy, it seems to me that the physicalists are epistemological optimists who think that we know a lot about our world, and that no completely revolutionary changes in our view of the world are to be expected. Yet while I think that it is true that there are no sharp limits between living and dead matter, I also feel that we are only at the very beginning of biology, and that with life there come into existence things entirely new: *problems, and problem solving.* Nothing of the kind seems to exist in the physical world before the emergence of life. World 3 is merely a belated outcome on the human level of the existence of problems, and of problem solving, which I regard as the most characteristic and specific property of life as we know it.

This is why I am not a physicalist, even though I think that it is perfectly compatible with my position that nothing—not even problem solving—exists in worlds 2 and 3 without a physicalist "basis" of some sort. But "basis" is a consciously vague term, and I regard it as possible that on the level of organisms, the relation between worlds 1 and 2, and between worlds 2 and 3, may be one of give-and-take; it may have the character of a genuine interaction.

I am not a vitalist, but I suspect that in one way vitalism is right and that physicalism is wrong: there are more things in physics and biology than are dreamt of in all our philosophies.

26. *Musgrave on My Exclusion of Psychologism*

I think that Professor Musgrave's paper shows that he understands my epistemology very well, and that there is hardly a point of disagreement between us. But there is what I must regard as a blemish.

He is perfectly right, I admit, that I have in a few cases used two words, one of which, if taken out of its antipsychologistic context, may sound like an echo of psychologism. He is also perfectly right in his explanation of what I really meant, which is free from that psychologism which I, and he, have tried so strenuously to avoid. I am grateful for his improved way of formulating these passages which can, as he himself stresses, easily be read in a non-psychologistic sense.

It can only be Musgrave's conscientiousness, I think, which has led him to regard my occasional use of slightly psychologistic terminology as worthy of critical comment; though in general in complete sympathy with my views, he did not wish to shrink from exposing and discussing what are at best prima facie instances of a lapse towards subjectivism. But though I admire his conscientiousness, I still have a slight grievance which is not psychological. As it happens, it is for stylistic reasons that I prefer the phrase "critical attitude" to "critical procedure" or to "critical policy"; I surely mean by attitude nothing more psychological (as Musgrave admits) than procedure or policy. I suppose that to Musgrave's ears (and perhaps to those of other people) it has a psychologistic sound, and perhaps in future I should be careful always to write "critical approach" instead of "critical attitude", as indeed I have often done in the past. After all I have no desire to mislead people by terminology, and I am sorry when it happens. But though I may use psychologistic terminology now and then, I can hardly be accused of having formulated any psychologistic thesis; and it is only this that would be serious. So I object to Musgrave's taking these verbal matters so seriously, even though he concedes that the points are minor. He knows my rule "Never quarrel about words", and that this rule is important in the present situation in philosophy; and I am afraid that in writing about words which were never meant by me in any psychologistic sense, he sins more against philosophy than I.

Having said something about "critical attitude", let me now say a word about "sincerity and severity of tests". Musgrave agrees that I did not mean to use the words "severe tests" other than in an objective sense. (See, for example, C.&R., p. 220 and Addendum 2 on pp. 388-91.) As for the word "sincerity", this too had, when I used it, an objective meaning; quite clearly an objective meaning, I should say, in view of footnote 8 on page 402 of my Logic of Scientific Discovery. A little later, on page 418 of that book, I explained it more fully. It was meant to contain an implicit criticism of Carnap's demand that we must use our total observational knowledge as our evidence before we apply his formula for degree of confirmation. What I wanted to point out was that (apart from being nonformalizable) this was asking both too much and too little. Too much, because it is an idealization to which nothing in scientific practice can correspond: in science we never mention explicitly more than the *relevant* evidence; the rest may appear as "background knowledge" (as I have called it), but only in a rough and implicit way: whenever an element of this "background knowledge" becomes problematic, it no longer counts as part of the background knowledge.

On the other hand, the requirement of total evidence also requires too little. Carnap thought that "total evidence" would give his formula some much needed security from misuse; that it would rule out situations where favourable or nonfavourable evidence had been carefully selected in order to obtain just the desired value for his degree of confirmation. I hoped to point out, with my reference to sincerity, that this is hardly an adequate safeguard against such "fixing"; that we need only shut our eyes at appropriate moments (when we fear the evidence may be unhelpful) to make this "total evidence" arbitrary and biased. Ruling such a strategy out is not "psychologism" in any sense—Musgrave's or mine—any more than are any of Musgrave's own references to "procedure" or "policy"; and "sincerity" therefore was obviously not meant in a psychologistic sense. I was proposing in fact a methodological rule.

What worries me is this. If I have used some words in a slightly misleading sense (not misleading enough ever to have misled anybody who tried to understand me) then anybody may say so; but he must distinguish this criticism *clearly* from a criticism of my philosophy. It is important in philosophy to speak clearly. But verbal usages are not to be put on a level with philosophical mistakes. This way leads to scholasticism.

Moreover, I have always tried to show that *sincerity in the subjective sense* is not required, thanks to the social character of science which has (so far, perhaps no further) guaranteed its objectivity. I have in mind what I have often called "the friendly-hostile cooperation of scientists".

But all these are minor matters as, I hope, Musgrave and I agree. I do not think that I have ever used an argument which can be interpreted (if properly interpreted) in a psychologistic sense; and I claim to have been as valiant a fighter against psychologism in philosophy as any philosopher ever has been. It is of little importance in comparison if I have once or twice used an expression which may be open to misinterpretation.

Much as I agree with practically everything that Musgrave writes, I am a little puzzled by the last sentence in his penultimate paragraph. I do not know what he means when he says: "Subjectivism may yet succeed in vindicating itself . . . ". I thought that he agreed with me that subjectivism in the theory of knowledge was a straightforward mistake. Since everything else in his contribution seems to support this view, I assume that the sense of Musgrave's last sentence manages for some reason to escape me.

V. RATIONALITY AND CRITICISM
AND SOME PROBLEMS IN LOGIC

27. Introductory Remark

Under this title I have collected my replies to Professors Paul Bernays, Jacob Bronowski, Czeslaw Lejewski, G. Schlesinger, Sir Alfred Ayer, and Joseph Agassi.

There is not much in common either in these papers or in my replies to them; unless, that is, one takes seriously, as I do, my view (see *C.&R.*, p. 64) that formal logic, which comprises metalogic, is not only the *organon of deduction,* or *proof,* but also—and especially in practice—the *organon of rational criticism.*

28. Bernays's Plea for a Wider Notion of Rationality

The paper by Paul Bernays discusses important points from fields which are far apart. It raises a number of profound problems. His central and final criticism of my views is formulated most clearly in the last sentence of his paper: he feels that *my view of rationality is too restricted.* He takes exception to an identification of rationality with the critical attitude, with a *merely selective function.* By contrast, he proposes to "ascribe to rationality a *creativity*".

So far I have no objection; but I feel a little uneasy when he continues: "not a creativity of principles, but a creativity of concepts".

My procedure in this reply will be to follow Bernays's own seven sections, whose content I will briefly summarize.

Section I of Bernays's paper—deadly destructive of what I call the Popper legend—is a beautifully crisp exposition of my views on demarcation and induction, leading up to what has been called my "critical approach".

Section II traces the relationship between this approach and Darwinism.

Section III raises an interesting difficulty in connection with Darwinism.

These three sections may be regarded as a preparation for the remaining four, which I regard as constituting the thesis of the paper.

Section IV sketches my theory of knowledge and then raises the central problem of the paper: is there a wider conception of rationality than the one which is encompassed by my critical approach? Bernays suggests a positive answer.

Section V makes an attempt to characterize rationality in general, and then proceeds to examine the creative role of rationality, as distinct from the critical role that I have stressed. It outlines six most interesting points which a theory of the creative aspects of rationality must cover.

Section VI is a fascinating discussion of certain important points belonging (I suggest) to the theories of truth and verisimilitude: Bernays discusses here the *kind of correspondence* between theory and reality which is characteristic of the sciences that employ mathematical methods. This is a vast and rarely discussed problem, and I am proud that it has been raised by Bernays on this occasion.

Section VII shows that something can be learned from this by the biological and social and political sciences.

I have started my discussion with this outline because this charming paper is very compressed, and a reader—especially a quick reader—who does not take great care may easily miss some of its most valuable points.

I

Part of Bernays's paper is not intended as criticism; rather, he explains my problems and views and adds to them important new problems and views. His first section especially is in complete agreement with my views on *demarcation*. It was a great relief to see that some of my fundamental ideas can be understood and explained in so straightforward and simple a manner.

II

In his section II, Bernays refers to my schema "$P_1 \rightarrow TS \rightarrow EE \rightarrow P_2$", as developed in *Of Clouds and Clocks* [1966(f)] (the idea was first formulated in my "What is Dialectic?" [1940(a)]). Bernays refers here first to a similarity between my views and those of Ferdinand Gonseth, the founder of *Dialectica,* whose profound influence on him is amply acknowledged by Bernays. I understand that Gonseth also stresses the change of the problem situation which is brought about by the very attempt to produce a solution, whether this solution succeeds or fails. Bernays also stresses the nonpsychological sense which I have given in [1966(f)] to the idea of a problem.

III

In his third section, Bernays raises the fascinating problem whether "all these novelties"—the various new solutions to problems being put forward—"occur purely at random, so that the ... formative element is ... error elimination", and nothing else.

It is here, I think, that Bernays's more critical considerations begin, and that his central and final criticism mentioned above is first foreshadowed: the question raised is well known: is everything—even our rationality—to be fully explained by two categories: chance and elimination?

This, I think, is the main problem of Bernays's paper. Its main value lies in a problem shift: in his linking of this problem to the problem of rationality as it arises in logic, mathematics, and in many other regions; even in politics.

But let me return to Bernays's section III. The problem so succinctly formulated by Bernays in this brief but brilliant section must have struck many Darwinists. Yet there is a Darwinian answer to the last sentence of the section: "The particular difficulty here is that the various problems solved by the hereditary apparatus are not immediate needs, but appear only if further evolution is, so to speak, anticipated as a goal."

The Darwinian answer would be something like this. Early forms of life will not have had a hereditary apparatus as specific as later forms. Or more precisely, the hereditary apparatus as we know it has provisions for what Bernays calls "further evolution", that is, for further change. These provisions may not improve the fitness of the individual to survive, but they may help the species to survive, by producing sufficiently varying individuals to make it possible for some to adjust themselves to environmental changes. Or in other words, it appears that great environmental changes were operative in the early stages of the evolution of life, and that these changes eliminated all the early forms except those which had (*accidentally,* perhaps) evolved a solution of the problem of *variation-cum-invariance* (invariance = heredity). It appears from all we know that only one solution was found to this problem, for there seems to be only *one* genetic code.

Natural selection selects not only for fitness but, in the long run, also for what may be called "selectability", or "selective sensitivity"; that is, a combination of variability with a mechanism for heredity.

We can see that, for example, a high degree of specialization may lead a species to great success in a stable environment, but also to almost certain destruction in case the environment should change.

This kind of Darwinian "explanation" is obviously not very satisfactory, for reasons which I have often pointed out (see, for example, [1966(f)]). But it is the "proper" Darwinian explanation: it gives a solution "in principle" (in the sense of Hayek).[149]

As for the question of the "accidental" character of the variations —"whether all . . . novelties occur purely at random"—the answer is that even if mutations occur at random, say by a kind of chemical roulette, this does not mean that no mechanism could develop which would explain orthogenesis. I have tried (in my Herbert Spencer Lecture of 1961—now Chapter 7 of my [1972(a)]) to show that a Lamarckian evolution may be *"simulated"* by a genuine Darwinian mechanism, and that for this reason Lamarck's theory may be regarded as an approximation to a special case covered by Darwin's theory, just as Kepler's laws may be regarded as an approximation to a special case covered by Newton's theory (which, in its turn, may be said to "simulate" Kepler's laws). Besides, I do not believe that *"purely at random"* is applicable here: see Professor Campbell's conception of "blindness" and my discussion of it in section 23, above.

The upshot of all this is that if we admit the possibility of the evolution by accident of living structures (which in their turn do not any longer react merely accidentally, but purposefully, for example, by anticipating future needs), then there does not seem to be any reason why we should reject the evolution of higher-order systems which simulate purposeful behaviour, by anticipating future needs or future problems.

Before leaving this subject however, I wish to say that, although I regard it as legitimate to give these answers to Bernays's problem, I should disagree with anybody who is *fully satisfied* by such an answer. Darwinism is the only workable theory (or research programme) we seem to have at the moment. It may even be true. But it has very little content and very little explanatory power, and it is therefore far from satisfactory. Thus we should try hard to improve upon Darwinism, or to find some alternative.[150]

IV

In his section IV, Bernays attributes to me "the hidden assumption that rationality must be *knowing*" ("knowing" *for certain* or "proving", rather than "guessing"); for he thinks that he has discovered in my work an "opposition of rationality and guesswork".

I am at a loss to see how anything resembling such a view could be found anywhere in my work. It is true that I always emphasized (and in view of some of Bernays's considerations, perhaps sometimes overemphasized) the *critical* character of rationality. But this has nothing to do with the alleged equation of *rationality* and *certain knowledge* and even less with the alleged opposition of *rationality* and *guessing*.

I could not possibly hold anything like this since I hold that *we have no certain knowledge* and that all so-called scientific knowledge is guessing.

I am quite unable to recognise either the equation or the opposition as views I could ever have held. As for the equation, I regard myself as a disciple of Socrates, and I am deeply aware of my, and more generally our, *lack* of knowledge. This seems to me to be a direct consequence of my critical attitude, which I identify with my rational attitude. As for the opposition, I have always held that all our alleged knowledge consists, in reality, of guesswork, and that the best of it consists of *guesswork controlled by rational criticism*. So here I am baffled.

All I can do is to take the blame for having perhaps gone too far in writing "only one" (and thus misleading Bernays) in a sentence quoted by Bernays: "There is only one element of rationality in our attempts to know the world: it is the critical examination of our theories."

I should have written instead: "There is at any rate this element of rationality. . . . "

I apologize and withdraw. But I suggest that the "only one" was not to be taken quite so seriously, since earlier in the same lecture ("Back to the Presocratics" [1958(e)]) I had written, in a most prominent place: "I want to return to . . . the simple straightforward *rationality* of the Presocratics. Wherein does this . . . lie? *The simplicity and boldness of their questions is part of it,* but my thesis is that the decisive point is the critical attitude. . . . "[151]

But even the paragraph in [1958(e)] that immediately precedes the "only one" passage quoted by Bernays seems to me to show that these two misleading words were not meant to be taken so seriously; for I wrote there:

> According to the theory of knowledge here outlined there are in the main only two ways in which theories may be superior to others: they may explain more; and they may be better tested—that is, they may be more fully and more critically discussed, in the light of all we know, of all the objections we can think of, and especially also in the light of observational or experimental tests which were designed with the aim of criticizing the theory.

It will be seen from these two passages that I did not mean the word "only" to be taken so seriously: there is more to rationality than just a narrowly understood critical attitude; an ingredient is, for example, the simplicity of both problems and solutions; another, the boldness of both problems and solutions. Even observation and experiment come in, since their role is largely one of being used in critical arguments. But I have always thought, and I still think, that the adoption of a critical attitude is the decisive point of rationality. This I wish now to defend.

I have a deeply ingrained fear of big words, such as "rationality". What I fear is being impressed by them, or impressing others with them. Yet I do think, at the same time, that men are capable of adopting a rational attitude, or an attitude of rationality, and that this capability is of the utmost importance. And I also thought so when I wrote *The Open Society;* I will quote the key passage at length.

> Since the terms "reason" and "rationalism" [I could have added "and rationality"] are vague, it will be necessary to explain roughly the way in which they are used here. First, they are used in a wide sense; they are used to cover not only intellectual activity but also observation and experiment. It is necessary to keep this remark in mind, since "reason" and "rationalism" are often used in a different and more narrow sense, in opposition not to "irrationalism" but to "empiricism"; if used in this way, rationalism extols intelligence above observation and experiment, and might therefore be better described as "intellectualism". But when I speak here of "rationalism", I use the word always in a sense which includes "empiricism" as well as "intellectualism"; just as science makes use of experiments as well as of thought. Secondly, I use the word "rationalism" in order to indicate, roughly, an attitude that seeks to solve as many problems as possible by an appeal to reason, i.e. to clear thought and experience, rather than by an appeal to emotions and passions. This explanation,

of course, is not very satisfactory, since all terms such as "reason" or "passion" are vague; we do not possess "reason" or "passions" in the sense in which we possess certain physical organs, for example, brains or a heart, or in the sense in which we possess certain "faculties", for example, the power of speaking, or of gnashing our teeth. In order therefore to be a little more precise, it may be better to explain rationalism in terms of practical attitudes or behaviour. We could then say that rationalism is an attitude of readiness to listen to critical arguments and to learn from experience. It is fundamentally an attitude of admitting that *"I may be wrong and you may be right, and by an effort, we may get nearer to the truth"*. It is an attitude which does not lightly give up hope that by such means as argument and careful observation, people may reach some kind of agreement on many problems of importance; and that, even where their demands and their interests clash, it is often possible to argue about the various demands and proposals, and to reach—perhaps by arbitration—a compromise which, because of its equity, is acceptable to most, if not to all. In short, the rationalist attitude, or, as I may perhaps label it, the "attitude of reasonableness", is very similar to the scientific attitude, to the belief that in the search for truth we need co-operation, and that, with the help of argument, we can in time attain something like objectivity.[152]

I do not think that I ever deviated from this position, although I have elaborated it greatly. I might even be said to have hinted, in this passage, that "the power of speaking" was related to reason or rationality just as "gnashing our teeth" was related to passion. What I later developed more fully is mainly the equation of our rationality with our ability to use human language in an argumentative way.

Bernays begins the last paragraph of his section IV with the statement: "What distinguishes guessing from proving is in fact not the absence of rationality. . . . " Since this occurs in a criticism of my views, it seems to imply that I hold that guessing is distinct from proving by the absence from guessing of the rationality which is present in proving. This agrees with Bernays's attribution to me of the equation "rationality [is] . . . knowing [or even demonstrative knowledge]", and of "the opposition of rationality and guesswork". For a rationalist like myself, who advocates guessing and holds that there are no proofs outside mathematics and logic, all this was very puzzling.

After some effort I think I have come to see how the misunderstanding has arisen. I do hold, and sometimes say, that there are two different components in the psychological processes which lead to new theories or guesses. One of them is creative imagination or, if you like, "intuition"; the other is rational criticism. But I hold that exactly the same is true of new mathematical proofs: there is first the intuitive and imaginative idea of how the proof might run; and then comes the critical testing of the various steps of the proof—a critical revision which, more often than not, reveals that the proof is not valid (a valid proof being a proof which would survive any searching and systematic criticism).

So I hold that the procedure is essentially the same for guesses and for proofs, as far as their genesis is concerned. Indeed, proofs which have not been thoroughly examined are just guesses; they may be called "proof-guesses" as opposed to "theory-guesses".

Thus Bernays no doubt misunderstands me when he attributes to me the view that proofs are rational, while guesses are not. I am inclined to say (with some oversimplification), that both are in a prerational stage as long as they are only propounded by our intuition, and rational the moment we turn to examine them critically.

But, Bernays asks in section IV, in the last sentence before the one just discussed, "do not the inner merits of a theory constitute for it something like its rational character?".

This is an entirely different kind of question: we must distinguish between *our* rationality—the question of the intuitive or irrational versus the rational elements in the processes of producing a proof or a theory—and the value of the produced structure (proof, or guess, that is, tentative theory) itself. A structure may be better or worse from a rational (critical) point of view. It is here that the clarity of the formulation may play a role; also important is the logical power of the idea produced—the depth of the proof, or the explanatory power of the theory.

Thus the question whether we produce a theory rationally must be entirely separated from the question of the value of the product.

I admit that I allow, in theory production, some scope for irrational imagination or intuition. But I do not attribute to it any reliability. "Intellectual intuition and imagination are most important [in the sciences]" I wrote, "but they are not reliable: they may show us things very clearly, and yet they may mislead us. They are indispensable as the main sources of our theories; but most of our theories are false anyway."[153] All this applies to the discovery of new theories (or proofs). Once they are produced, we examine them critically. And this critical examination is the rational part of theory production.

But all this is, of necessity, highly schematic. In reality, we constantly switch from intuition to criticism and back to intuition; besides, intuition often enters in the critical phase: we often learn to "see" without any detailed examination that something is wrong (and sometimes we "see" wrongly).

All this is quite interesting, I think, but much less so than the objectivist (or world 3) questions of the "inner merits of a theory", to use the excellent phrase of Bernays.

V

If asked the essentialist question, *What is rationality?*, I would be inclined to say that I do not know, and that I do not care to answer any *what-is?* questions. Nevertheless, I find what Bernays says in reply to this question extremely interesting, and I feel inclined to think that something of importance may emerge.

The question is raised by Bernays in his section V, in the form "What is the proper characteristic of rationality?". Bernays's answer is: "the *conceptual element,* which transcends perceiving . . . and which produces a kind of *understanding*". This answer shows that Bernays has now the objectivist or third-world question of "the inner merits of a theory" in mind.

With regard to Bernays's suggested answer, I was at first inclined to say "no" to his "conceptual element" and "yes" to his allusion to "understanding". On consideration, however, I am quite ready to say "yes" to the "conceptual element" also, provided we agree first that this means essentially the *formulation in an argumentative language.*

(I am disinclined to answer the question "What is rationality?" by "Rationality is operating with concepts". For this leads us straight into the swamp of "glossogon philosophy".[154] For we must go on asking: "What is a concept?". Answer, perhaps: a word with a definite meaning. With this we have arrived at the swamp; at the philosopher's morass par excellence: at meaning philosophy.)

But it is a fact that argumentative language uses words—or concepts—and that one may therefore attribute to it a conceptual character.[155] But the rational value of any theory will depend not on its conceptual elaboration, but on other things.

Of course we use abstract concepts. But I claim that our attitude towards concepts has undergone tremendous changes, especially in mathematics (to which Bernays refers). There was a time when a mathematician would have shuddered if he had realized that *different "meanings"* can be attached to the words "point", "plane", and "solid"; and when having realized it, his first reaction (after shuddering) would have been to add something (probably a definition, but perhaps an axiom) to keep the "meaning" of his "concepts" unambiguous. It is a great step from this attitude to model theory and nonstandard models; and in the development the original idea that concepts are words with definite meanings loses most of its significance.

Thus I am not entirely happy with Bernays's emphasis on concepts, and I feel that his analysis in section V, points (1) - (4), may perhaps be reformulated with advantage if we speak of languages and the degree of their articulation, instead of speaking of concepts. But the problems which Bernays raises in these points remain important.

Even more important, and of a different character, is Bernays's reference to the rational character of *the idea of a natural law* (section V, point (6)). Though this idea has undergone considerable refinements, its rational character is prima facie of a kind which Kant described as a priori.

I think that Bernays is clearly right when he argues (on lines similar to my own) against Hume that rationality need not entail certainty, and that the conjectural character of natural laws (and theories) does not detract from their character as *means of rational understanding*.

Here the objectivist or value aspect of rationality comes in: there is a rational evaluation of theories from the point of view of their content, their unifying power, their simplicity.

VI

In his section VI, Bernays reports first on what Ferdinand Gonseth calls the schematic character of all description.[156]

This is a point of great importance. I have described it in a slightly different terminology, pointing out, with reference to Kant, that every description (and even every perception), and therefore even every true description, is (a) selective, omitting many aspects of the object described, and (b) augmentative, in that it transcends its evidence by adding a hypothetical dimension. (See, for example, *L.Sc.D.* [1959(a)], end of section 25, pp. 94 f.) I have also often said that all rational description and argumentation must essentially *oversimplify* the situation: it must schematize it.

I fully agree with Bernays that this schematic character of all description is connected with the rationality of the description. I should also like to connect it with the *problem-solving character of rationality.* Even an apparently endless narration of uninteresting detail will always be schematic; but it is neither as schematic nor as "rational" as a narration designed to solve a problem—for example, the problem of the responsibility for the catastrophe of Britain's first and last government-produced airship, the R101.[157] What characterizes those higher levels of rationality in which we—Bernays and I—are interested is their systematic, problem-dependent, and problem-solving selectivity and transcendence.[158]

The last paragraph of Bernays's section VI is equally interesting. Here Bernays speaks of idealized theoretical structures and says that "their interrelations constitute an open domain of objectivity—an objectivity *sui generis*". I may perhaps suggest that this idea, so briefly sketched by Bernays, may turn out to have much in common with my "third world" (or, as Eccles prefers to say, "world 3") or, more precisely, its mathematical domain.

VII

In his last section, Bernays suggests briefly that the idea of rationality may be widened so as to include such prescientific distinctions as that between living and dead matter, or that between such different mental states as "wanting", "ambition", and "anger". He points out that by the use of these concepts—I should prefer to say, by the use of hypotheses involving these concepts—a "kind of understanding is achieved, which . . . cannot be replaced by any structural explanation, however elaborate it may be".

This is a very simple and most interesting remark, which cuts right through the discussion of the possibility of "reducing mental talk to physical talk" (that is, reducing psychological theories to physiological theories). I like the idea, but I think it needs much critical discussion. I can well imagine that an estimate of the amount of adrenalin in the blood may, *for the trained biochemist,* provide understanding *of the same kind* as, but of greater depth than, the psychological diagnosis of fear; and if such scientific terms become popular and part of general usage then they may replace some of the terms of prescientific popular psychology. Physiologists may prefer speaking of blood-sugar level to using psychological terms, and their language may become the fashion. That such things may happen is clear: an ideological explanatory term like "exploitation" may become more fashionable than, say, "poverty in the midst of riches"; and it may purvey intuitive "understanding"—though understanding of perhaps dubious validity from a rational and critical point of view.

Thus I find this idea of Bernays's attractive and important but, in the brief form presented, too sketchy for an assessment.

No such doubts assailed me when I read Bernays's proposal to regard "the *regulative idea of justice*" as "a prominent element of rationality", and as constitutive of "a domain of objectivity". Indeed, problems, tentative solutions, and critical evaluations, and states of affairs brought about by them, appear to me to belong to a domain of world 3 as clearly as does any physical theory.

I suggest that what characterizes those domains of world 3 which we may call rational is the possibility of there formulating *comparable and arguable standards,* and evaluating states of affairs by comparing them critically with these standards. Thus the possibility of the critical discussion of standards, and of the critical comparison of standards, may be said to characterize the domain (the essence?) of rationality in world 3. For there are, I believe, parts of world 3—such as works of art, and artistic standards—which are not, or rather, not fully, within the domain of rationality.

VIII

In conclusion I wish to stress again the distinction between the more personal or psychological or subjective sense of "rational", the sense in which it may be opposed to "emotional" or "passionate" or perhaps to "imaginative" or "intuitive", and the more objective sense in which "rational" may characterize certain kinds of products of our mental activity (world 3 objects). To me the first or subjective sense seems less important and in any case pretty vague. I gladly admit that one should not overemphasize here the purely critical attitude, and that there can be such a thing as rational creativity or creative rationality. Yet it still seems to me that in order to be creative, rationality will have to be composed of elements, as it were, *of imagination and of criticism*. There will have to be some product of our mind, some world 3 object, which we subject critically to some world 3 standards.

And there is a domain of world 3 which has the character of rationality in the objective sense. Mathematics is in the very centre of this domain; *not* because its propositions can be proved (here, as in many other places, Bernays and I certainly agree), but rather because they can be rationally, that is critically, discussed. The conjectures of natural science form another part of this domain, as do discussions of problems of justice and of ethical standards. In all these cases it still seems to me enlightening and clarifying to say that we speak of rationality wherever there is something which, in part, is the product of critical discussion, or rather the combined product of imagination and critical discussion.

In order to show that I am defending no narrow idea of rationality I may conclude by mentioning one kind of rational entity not especially mentioned by Bernays as rational or creative. I mean problems. The discovery of a new problem is a creative act, and yet as a rule it is the result of criticism. Thus it is rational in a high degree.

29. *Bronowski on the Impact of* Logik der Forschung *and on Tarski's Theory of Truth*

Bronowski's essay "Humanism and the Growth of Knowledge" is unique in this collection in several senses. Fundamentally, there is far-reaching agreement. There are several minor lines of cleavage between our opinions, and one major one. But there is complete agreement about which cleavages are minor and which one is major. It is only here—the applicability to scientific theories of the correspondence theory of truth—that I feel a strong urge to defend myself; elsewhere, there are cases where I accept Bronowski's criticism, and others where the difference between us is small and open; and one, which I shall discuss in a moment, where to a certain extent I disagree with him.

Let me make it clear that what I have here called "minor lines of cleavage" arise sometimes in connection with points of fundamental importance. For example, the problem which Bronowski calls that of the *"richness"* of a scientific theory is of the greatest importance. But I feel that I can accept all that Bronowski says on this point; and where what he says is critical of what I say I do not object to the criticism. Bronowski and I agree that scientific theories are to be looked at, fundamentally, as explanations. I can go further; I believe we agree that the main aim of science is to explain in order to *understand the world* (*L.Sc.D.*, p. 15)

The role of richness, or internal unity, or depth in a theory has been analysed by me in a not too satisfactory way, as Bronowski points out; but we both have practically the same idea of what scientific theories are for and of what we should expect from them. This is why I feel that the dissent between us on this major point is only a minor dissent. Let me perhaps quote from a paper of mine that Bronowski does not mention.

> The "depth" of a scientific theory seems to be most closely related to its simplicity and so to the wealth of its content. . . . Two ingredients seem to be required: a rich content, and a certain coherence or compactness (or "organicity") of the state of affairs described. It is this latter ingredient which, although it is intuitively fairly clear, is so difficult to analyse, and which the essentialists were trying to describe when they spoke of essences, in contradistinction to a mere accumulation of accidental properties. I do not think that we can do much more than refer here to an intuitive idea, nor that we need do much more. For in the case of any particular theory proposed, it is the wealth of its content, and thus its degree of testability, which decides its interest, and the results of actual tests which decide its fate. From the point of view of method, we may look upon its depth, its coherence, and even its beauty, as a mere guide or stimulus to our intuition and to our imagination.[159]

Before proceeding to discuss the major dissent on the major point I ought perhaps to make a comment on the asymmetry between verifiability and falsifiability. Bronowski recognises (section V) the importance for my criterion of demarcation of this asymmetry; yet he suggests (sections VII and VIII) that in the realm of probability statements the asymmetry evaporates. "Of course verification is only provisional; but the point is that in this scheme [in statistics], falsification is also only provisional" (section VII). Bronowski recounts correctly how, in order to render probability statements refutable—for no finite succession of heads is strictly incompatible with a coin's being fair—I had introduced in Chapter VIII of *L.Sc.D.* a methodological rule permitting us to neglect "extreme improbabilities". Bronowski has no quarrel with this rule as such; he just thinks that if it is indispensable then falsification "is no longer a rigorous and foolproof method . . . [and] what we have . . . is a stratagem for decision, but not a prescription" (section VIII). "So long as we are allowed to doctor the criterion of falsification when we need, we cannot . . . be forbidden to doctor the criterion of verification. . . ." (section VIII).

I think this is rather misleading. The criterion of falsification has not been doctored. For to refute even nonprobabilistic statements we need, as I have always said (*L.Sc.D.*, sections 9 and 20), methodological rules; so I am not smuggling in anything essentially novel in the statistical case. But, this apart, *there does not exist a similar rule that would make probability statements verifiable* despite what Bronowski says in section VIII; for we can never know that a coin will not begin to misbehave in an alarming manner. While this shows that the fairness of the coin can never be verified, it by no means shows that it cannot be falsified. Certain sorts of coin-behaviour are incompatible with the coin's being fair (given our rule) and that is that; future good behaviour can in no way affect, or redeem, this incompatibility.[160]

Throughout his paper Bronowski stresses many points of agreement, and he is very generous in his praise of what I have written, both in *The Logic of Scientific Discovery* and in *Conjectures and Refutations*. All this makes it important to concentrate on the major issue.

If I understand him correctly, Bronowski's criticism of the applicability of the correspondence theory of truth is this. "Snow is white" can correspond to the facts, for it is about a fact; but Newton's or Einstein's theories are not descriptions of *facts:* they are essentially *explanations* of facts. Thus their relation to facts is quite different from those simple descriptions which the correspondence theory, and Tarski, had in mind.

I believe that Bronowski has been misled by the word "correspondence" and by Tarski's oversimple example.

The statement "Snow is white" corresponds to the facts if and only if snow is white.

This example (I believe) has made Bronowski think that scientific theories are not like this: they do not describe simple facts. They are our own inventions, and they are good or bad according to whether they explain the facts (facts like the whiteness of snow) well, or less well.

This raises indeed a host of questions. First, I agree that scientific theories are our inventions; but this Kantian idealism is limited in my case (and I believe in Bronowski's too) by the anti-Kantian qualification that we cannot simply impose our inventions upon the world. Kant thought that our mind not only produces Newtonian theory, but forces it upon experience, thereby forming Nature. I think very differently. There is a world, and we try to understand it, by talking about it, and inventing explanatory theories; but although we are often unable to think otherwise than in the terms of these theories, there is a reality on which we cannot arbitrarily impose our theories. This reality, this world, was there before man, and our attempts to impose our theories on it turn out, in the majority of cases, to be vast failures: thus Kant's idealism is wrong, and realism is right.[161]

I suppose that Bronowski is just as good a realist as I am. But we differ over the interpretation of Tarski's theory of truth, and also over whether our explanatory theories might not, as well as explain facts, also describe facts; strange facts, highly abstract regularities of nature.

I conjecture that such strange regularities of nature do exist. But even if they do not—even if there should be exceptions to *all* scientific laws—this does not mean that the correspondence theory of truth is inapplicable to scientific theories; it would only mean that *all* scientific theories are false. It would mean that there are no exceptionless regularities in nature.

Although I do not believe this, I admit that my belief that there exist some exceptionless intrinsic regularities of nature is a metaphysical belief. It is a metaphysical belief which is perfectly compatible with the belief that these exceptionless intrinsic regularities of nature for which we are groping in science are too deep for us, and that we shall never discover them.

However, the applicability of the correspondence theory of truth, as I (following Tarski) understand it, would not be threatened—not even if all our explanatory laws are false. It only would mean that the world is much more complicated than it seems to be to most of us; and that our attempts to understand it are for ever illusory; that the enterprise of science (though not the world) is a dream, an illusion.

I can very well understand Bronowski's feeling that there are no *"facts"* corresponding to scientific theories: I have often considered this possibility. But I think that my opposite belief, although it is a metaphysical belief, can up to a point be supported by argument. The main argument is as follows.

Explanatory scientific theories seem to us to be vastly different from simple facts, such as the fact that snow is white. But this difference is only apparent. All the most simple and apparently "factual" statements like "Snow is white" are, in fact, deeply impregnated by theory. That there is such a thing as snow is not only a fact, it is also a theory. For South Sea islanders who have never seen it, it is even a fairly abstract theory. But even we who know snow so well might be puzzled by something that looks and behaves exactly like snow but does not, chemically, consist almost exclusively of H_2O in crystallized form. This indicates the abstract and theoretical content of "Snow is white".

For this reason I do not believe in the existence of a line which separates two kinds of statements: simple statements of fact, and sophisticated explanatory theories. I believe that apparent statements of fact are theory-impregnated, and that whether or not a theory is *explanatory* depends entirely upon the question whether it is being used to *explain,* that is, to solve an intellectual problem, a problem of understanding.

Once we admit that theories can describe facts as much as explain them we must beware of adopting too naive an attitude towards facts; we must not allow ourselves to suffocate the important processes of the world under an overwhelming plethora of facts. As I said many years ago:

> . . . that there is no elephant in this room is not one of the processes or parts of the world. . . . Facts are something like a common product of language and reality; they are reality pinned down by descriptive statements. . . . New linguistic means . . . in a way . . . even create new kinds of facts. In a certain sense, these facts obviously existed before the new means were created which were indispensable for their description. . . . But in another sense we might say that these facts do not exist *as facts* before they are singled out from the continuum of events and pinned down by statements—the theories which describe them.[162]

I therefore think that Tarski's theory of truth is applicable to explanatory theories, and that the success of science is best accounted for by the metaphysical belief that the growth of knowledge consists in progress towards the truth. Bronowski and I disagree here; but I would agree that there still is much that remains to be said.

30. Lejewski's Axiomatization of My Theory of Deducibility

I

Professor Lejewski's contribution is a very generous reconstruction of a number of formal-logical (or rather, metalogical) papers which I wrote in the years from 1946 to 1948. The amount of work devoted by Lejewski to these papers is great, and his criticism is admirable: it is always fair and always fully justified; and, I suppose, only too often it is too moderate.

Professor Lejewski has done his best for me—more than I thought possible. Taking up and developing further a suggestion of Bernays's, he has proved that a system which he denotes by P is inferentially equivalent to one which he denotes by T, where the two letters stand for Popper and Tarski. This he does by (a) first eliminating certain blunders from my system, and (b) formulating both systems "in the language which we owe to Leśniewski". He thus arrives at a result which does me more than justice, I fear, for nobody will question the interest of Tarski's system. I am immensely grateful to Professor Lejewski for this result, for it shows that what I wrote (with much enthusiasm) was not a complete failure.

II

However, much as I am indebted to Lejewski for thus saving my honour, as it were, he has not brought out, or even briefly hinted at, what my intentions were in writing these bad and ill-fated papers. By putting them in Leśniewski's language he has, in fact, done something extremely interesting, but at the same time something that goes contrary to my intentions. For my main intention was to simplify logic by developing what has been called by others "natural deduction". I suppose that as an effort to build up a simple system of natural deduction (a commonsense logic, as it were), my papers were just a failure. However, Evert Beth told me that he was inspired partly by them to build up his own logic (his "semantic tableaux"). He told me so after I had received much discouragement, which had depressed me and had made me give up the attempt at developing my ideas further.

III

My papers were, largely, the result of an attempt to reform the teaching of elementary logic—the propositional calculus and the lower functional calculus; and I had some encouraging results, especially in quantification theory, which Lejewski for lack of space was unable to discuss. But my papers were, at the same time, inspired by the hope of solving a problem which Tarski (in "On the Concept of Logical Consequence", a paper which I knew well in its German original: a paper different from those with which Lejewski shows that my papers can be compared) indicates as insoluble; rightly, I now suspect. This was the problem of distinguishing between logical (or as I prefer to call them, "formative") signs and descriptive signs. Logical or formative signs are words like "not", "or", "and", "all", "there is at least one". Descriptive signs are "atom", "dog", "green", and so on. The task of distinguishing between the two types of signs or words seems at first sight simple; but for example the phrase "is identical with" does not obviously belong to one group or the other. Tarski showed that the concept of logical consequence can be easily elucidated (with the help of the concept of truth or of a "model") once we have decided upon a list of logical or formative signs. My idea was very simple: I suggested we take the concept "logical consequence" as primitive and try to show that those signs are logical or formative which can be defined with the help of this primitive concept. Most of my work was an attempt to carry this out. It is only fair to say that my papers did not succeed in this (as emerges from Lejewski's analysis). But I should add that Lejewski works within an elaborate system—that of Leśniewski—which demands a degree of explicitness which few other logicians live up to; indeed, which few logicians ever mastered, or even know of in these days. And also that my papers were "essays" or "attempts", trying to sketch a way; I had little hope of finalizing it.

But I should make plain that I now think that Tarski's scepticism concerning a clear demarcation between logical and descriptive signs is well founded. Demarcations are needed; but they are usually not sharp. This seems always to be so, interestingly enough; and it is perhaps not to be regretted.

31. *Schlesinger on My Paper on Self-Reference and Meaning*

Professor Schlesinger says that his paper is a criticism of a paper of mine—a little dialogue entitled "Self-Reference and Meaning in Ordinary Language" ([1954(c)]; now Chapter 14 of *Conjectures and Refutations* [1963(a)]). But really it isn't, in spite of the strong words he uses quite frequently to express his disgust for my "loose arguments . . . [, which any] defender of the orthodox view would find very little difficulty in rebutting" (the quotation is from his first paragraph).

Why do I say that Schlesinger's paper is not a criticism? Because he has no idea what I intended to show in my dialogue. Let me state first what my intentions were.

(i) My dialogue is, as its title says, about *ordinary language,* and it criticizes "ordinary-language philosophy", which was much in vogue at the time I wrote. That this was my topic was made very clear in the dialogue, for example in the latter half of page 309 (the references are to [1963(a)]), down to the end of page 310: here I speak about the difference between the situation in ordinary language and in artificial formalisms.

Although the words "ordinary language" occur in the title of my paper, and the title is quoted by Professor Schlesinger, he ignores my *repeated emphasis on ordinary language.* Anyway, he does not confine himself to ordinary language, but uses some kind of logical formalism, akin to the calculus of predicates; I think he uses it in the wrong way, but I won't go into that here.

(ii) I indicate clearly on pages 309 f. that there has been, among the great mathematical logicians, an important discussion on the problem of avoiding paradoxes; and I refer by name to Gödel and Tarski. I suggest that this discussion is beyond the understanding of my "Socrates"—and of many other philosophers—and that I am restricting myself in this paper to the ordinary-language problem. But I also indicate that nobody can make any real contribution to the problem of these paradoxes who has not read Gödel and Tarski.

(iii) I now come to the thesis of my old paper. It is that within ordinary language the problem of avoiding the paradoxes is insoluble, unless we introduce rules which mar its character as ordinary language. This was stated by Tarski, and I did not and do not claim any originality for it. The thesis is to be found on page 309, where Theaetetus says that "paradoxes can be constructed in it [ordinary language], and are understandable", that is, "meaningful" in the most ordinary sense. That this is so I show with the help of examples of *indirect* self-reference.

(iv) I add that it does not matter much since most people who use ordinary language manage to avoid the paradoxes.

(v) I also point out that those who try to avoid the paradoxes by introducing *a rule forbidding all self-reference* (perhaps combined with the assertion that it makes the expressions meaningless) are departing from "ordinary language" since they introduce some *artificiality*.

This is all I wished to do in this paper. I did *not* wish

(a) to prove that you cannot or must not introduce a rule forbidding self-reference (though I tried to illustrate by examples that such a rule would be very artificial). Schlesinger apparently thinks that this was my main aim;

(b) to explain where to draw the line between permissible and impermissible self-reference. For I believe that this cannot be done without some considerable legislation and consequent artificiality.

On the other hand, it will be pretty clear to all who know something about Tarski's great paper on the concept of truth that, if we make the distinction between syntactical and semantical metalinguistic expressions, one way of solving the problem is this: syntactical self-referring statements are harmless, but semantical ones are prone to paradoxes. This does not, however, touch a paradox such as Russell's.

I think every reader of my paper will understand why I did not give this solution but referred to Tarski instead. Incidentally, my paper is partly a joke (demonstrating that a joke can be about itself)[163] and partly a reminder to some people who write about these matters to look at Gödel's and Tarski's work.

Schlesinger seems to think that I wanted in my paper to solve the problem here called (b). He is mistaken: I merely referred to Tarski instead; a reference whose significance has escaped him. At any rate, he never mentions Tarski or Gödel; and in view of what he writes, it hardly seems possible that he took up my references.

So much for my intentions.

I shall not say much about Schlesinger's paper. He tries to solve the problem (b), and he thinks he has succeeded ever so much better than I did. I really cannot deny this since I did not try to solve the problem (b). But I think that a good solution exists (thanks to Tarski) and that Schlesinger's solution, summarized in the last paragraph of his paper, is pointless, pragmatically and theoretically. I also think that it is inconsistent.

There are just three comments I should like to make about his paper.

Professor Schlesinger speaks in his first sentence of "the received view on the nature of self-referential sentences" and he again and again speaks of such things as "the traditional solution to the Liar's Paradox", and so on. But he never really makes clear just what this solution is supposed to be, and he appears to ignore some of the best—and best known—work on the subject.

According to what I should regard as the best view, the view that is held by most mathematical logicians, these semantical antinomies can best be avoided by assuming a hierarchy of (semantical) metalanguages; but moreover, most of these logicians would say that there is no "solution" of the paradoxes. From Schlesinger's text it never becomes quite clear what the "received" or "traditional" or "accepted" view is. I thought first that he meant the view that all self-referring sentences are meaningless. However, this is contradicted by his remark in section I that "Theaetetus *has committed no self-reference of the sort which has ever been ruled out as illegitimate*". This remark (which I have italicized) suggests that its author knows the literature well enough to know everything that has ever been ruled out as illegitimate; which makes his omission of reference to Tarski or Gödel even more surprising.

Now it is perfectly true that *indirect* self-reference has not been so much discussed in the literature as has direct self-reference. But there are many sweeping suggestions which forbid all self-reference, such as Wittgenstein's famous "No proposition can say anything about itself . . . this is the whole 'theory of types' " (*Tractatus,* 3.332). If this is to be "the whole theory of types"—that is, the solution of all paradoxes—it has clearly to be taken as covering indirect self-reference; and because of its sweeping character, it may be said to cover the case of Theaetetus's self-reference. *At any rate, Schlesinger never makes clear* what the "orthodox view" rules out as "illegitimate" and what not.

My second point is about Schlesinger's use of logical symbols. Here I can only say that I am completely baffled. He does not explain his formalism; nor why he introduces it.

My third point concerns the argument in his fourth paragraph. It is a passage which appears to make some sense. Yet it amounts to very little.

Suppose U is the utterance "U is false". (Schlesinger uses "S_1" for "U".) Then I argued in my dialogue that we could not just decree that U be meaningless; for that would imply that "U is false" is false, and so meaningful; that is, that U is meaningful. Schlesinger objects that whilst indeed it is false to assert that U is false, U does not assert this, even though it appears to do so. Thus "U is false" is not false, but meaningless.

This sounds plausible, yet it is mistaken. For one of the explicit assumptions of my argument was that every utterance falls unambiguously into one of the categories "true", "false", "meaningless". Thus if "U is false" sometimes means something (as Schlesinger admits it does, since in section I he says that it is false to say that U conveys a false proposition), it *always* means something. We cannot consistently maintain that it only *appears* to say something on some occasions.[164] But even if we did, nothing would really be changed by this criticism of Schlesinger's. After all, it is agreed that all (well-formed) utterances *appear* to say something; so the obvious thing to do is to substitute appearance of falsity for falsity, and thereby reconstitute the Liar as follows. Let X be the utterance "What X appears to say is false"; concede the "orthodox view" that X doesn't say anything; and ask for the truth value of what it appears to say. The paradox returns (and Schlesinger's solution to problem (b) above is shown to be inconsistent). For assume that Schlesinger's solution to problem (b)—see his (4) according to which "sentences . . . ought to be regarded as . . . meaningful if and only if . . . one can adduce some reason why they rather than their denial ought to be given a certain truth value"—rules out X as meaningless: it does not avert the paradox.[165]

Since Professor Schlesinger shows no reluctance to claim that my paper is bad and his much better, I may perhaps be excused for thinking that I have given reasons why the two papers cannot be compared.

32. Ayer on Empiricism and Against Verisimilitude

Sir Alfred Ayer's contribution gives me a welcome opportunity to see clearly where we differ, as well as an opportunity to reply to his various criticisms.

These criticisms culminate in an attack on "a new technical concept to which he [Popper] gives the name of 'verisimilitude' ".

It is this attack that I will try to parry first, because I can show that it is based on a misunderstanding; having got rid of it I will feel freer to concentrate on the other and more important issues, to do with truth and verification. And I shall conclude with an attempt to fathom the fundamental disagreement between Ayer and myself. Thus I will divide my reply into five sections: I Verisimilitude; II The Impact of Tarski's Theory of Truth on my Theory of Knowledge; III The Verification of Theories; IV The Verification of Basic Statements; V Subjective Experience and Linguistic Formulation.

I

Verisimilitude. Ayer's accusation is, essentially, that I introduce a "concept" that is entirely useless. My reply is, essentially, that I am not interested in concepts but in theories, and that I use this concept—the concept of verisimilitude—because I find it helpful for certain theoretical purposes. Ayer, unfortunately, has quite misconceived these purposes.

It is true that in *Conjectures and Refutations* [1963(a)] I have discussed the concept of verisimilitude at some length. I have even recounted some of its history—and more about this was added in [1969(h)]. But I did so mainly for two reasons: (1) because—like the notion of truth—it has been suspected of being meaningless (or useless) and I wished to rehabilitate it; and (2) it has repeatedly been confused, at least since the time of Plato, with probability. On neither of these points do I feel I have to say more here.

I think it is important to make clear in what sense Einstein, who to the end of his life remained convinced that General Relativity was not true, claimed that this theory was "better" than Newton's: that it was a better approximation to truth. If, as Ayer claims, the concept of verisimilitude is useless and unnecessary, then we could hardly make sense of the fact that Einstein regarded his General Relativity as false, but as a decisive improvement of Newton's theory of gravitation.[165a]

Long before [1963(a)] I had talked, without much explanation and perhaps rather naively, about one theory's being closer to the truth than another. So had Peirce. Indeed, it was only an adverse remark of Quine's which made me think of it more critically. And Ayer too, despite his unenthusiastic—and even incorrect—comments about verisimilitude, quite clearly makes use himself of essentially the same idea.

Ayer writes towards the end of his contribution: "Considerations of this kind lead Popper to assume that his concept of comparative verisimilitude will apply to all the cases in which we should be inclined to say of two theories . . . that one corresponded better than the other to the facts." Nothing of this is true. Nor are any of the technical remarks made by Ayer later in the same paragraph correct. They suggest that "the pursuit of verisimilitude may conflict with the principle" of preferring the more informative theory. The plain fact is that verisimilitude often increases with content. It *always* does, if the theories are true (and truth content always does; a slightly surprising theorem proved in [1966(g)]).

It is when he talks of "progress towards truth" (at several places in his contribution) that Ayer obviously uses an idea, a little vague to be sure, which cannot be much different from the idea I tried to make a little less vague in [1963(a)], calling it "increase in verisimilitude". That my making it less vague did some good service is seen by the fact that I could prove about it (or, more precisely, about truth content) in [1966(g)] the theorem mentioned above—a theorem which refutes a suspicion I had about it, and one which Ayer also had.

Thus Ayer in fact himself subscribes to my claim that to talk of verisimilitude is of some help in discussions of the growth of scientific knowledge. But this is really all I claim for it.

It is only if we look again at the beginning of Ayer's final paragraph that we see what has gone wrong. For Ayer writes: "In what way, then, does the concept of verisimilitude afford us a criterion for assessing our progress towards truth?"

But I never dreamt of offering the concept of "verisimilitude" as a "criterion" of anything. It is introduced by me not as "a criterion for assessing our progress towards truth" but simply as a clarification of what I think we mean when we use phrases such as Ayer's phrase "progress towards truth". What I suggested was that we should not be satisfied with mere progress towards truth—since this might be tautological truth, such as $1+1=2$. *Progress in science* involves *increase of truth content* (provided this can be had without a compensating increase of falsity content). This clarification introduced the new and interesting idea of truth content which, I showed, can be simply and unambiguously defined with the help of Tarski's calculus of deductive systems and Tarski's concept of truth: I defined the truth content of a theory A as the (in general nonaxiomatizable) deductive system which is the intersection of A with T, the system of all true statements of the language in which the theory is formulated. (See *C.&R., Addendum* 3, and [1966(g)]].)

Thus Ayer's understanding of "the concept of verisimilitude" as introduced by me with the aim of providing "a criterion for assessing our progress towards truth" is a sheer misunderstanding. No wonder he does not like the idea.

I claim that the responsibility for the misunderstanding is largely Ayer's. On pages 217-20 of the essay to which he here refers, Chapter 10 of [1963(a)] (he has complained of it before, in a review which I did not understand on this point—I now see why) I too speak, admittedly, of a "criterion". But the criterion is not one for "assessing our progress towards truth"; nor is "the concept of verisimilitude" offered as the criterion. (I do say on p. 226 of [1963(a)], in a passage quoted by Ayer [see the text to his n. 4], that "there are something like criteria of progress towards the truth"—and in [1969(h)] I even deleted the words "something like". But what I refer to here, of course, are my "three requirements for the growth of knowledge", discussed on pp. 240-48 of the same paper; I made it quite clear *on the same page* that to say that a theory has a greater verisimilitude than one of its competitors remains essentially a matter of guesswork.)

The only criterion for anything that I do offer is "a criterion of relative *potential* satisfactoriness, or of *potential* progressiveness, which can be applied to a theory [not to all theories] even before we know whether or not it will turn out, by the passing of some crucial tests, to be satisfactory *in fact*". ([1963(a)], p. 217; the italics are in the original text.)

Thus it is a criterion of satisfactoriness that is applicable to a theory—more precisely, to most *interesting* theories—before the theory is submitted to tests; and it is not even a new criterion. I stress ([1963(a)], n. 2) that the criterion—increase in information content—is the same as that proposed in my *Logik der Forschung;* only my analysis, in terms of verisimilitude, of the idea of progress towards the truth is new. I say this on page 217 and again on page 219; and on page 234 I warn the reader, especially, "again to distinguish between the question 'What do you intend to say if you say that the theory t_2 has a higher degree of verisimilitude than the theory t_1?', and the question 'How do you know that the theory t_2 has a higher degree of verisimilitude than the theory t_1?' ''. (The first of these, I say, is answered by my newly proposed definition of verisimilitude; the second must be answered by a guess.) And I say there, as I said above, that ''the idea of a higher or lower degree of verisimilitude seems less remote and more [easily] applicable . . . than the—in itself much more fundamental—idea of absolute truth itself ''.

This is all I claim for the idea of verisimilitude, or of an increase in verisimilitude.[165b] I do not think that I have ever really suggested any more.

II

The Impact of Tarski's Theory of Truth on my Theory of Knowledge. As recounted in section 20 of my *Autobiography,* it was not until after my *Logik der Forschung* was published that I became acquainted with Tarski's theory of truth, and with the fundamental idea of a hierarchy of (semantical) metalanguages. I had previously worked with an intuitive idea of truth, and I had even in *Logik der Forschung,* section 84, somewhat timidly offered the view that truth was a logical and, more precisely, a metalinguistic concept. But since I had had no inkling of the distinction, within metalanguages, between syntax and semantics, I suggested that the idea of truth was a syntactical idea.

I was of course aware of many attacks upon the idea of truth, but I was not greatly impressed by them. At the same time I was aware of my inability to answer these attacks, and of getting the matter right. I was therefore glad to be able to say that I could (in principle) do without the concept of truth. What I had in mind was, I suppose, that my whole investigation was based on such concepts as the relations of *deducibility* and of *contradictoriness.* What I did not realize was that these logical concepts were, in a sense, based on the semantic concept of truth.

Only after reading the German translation of Tarski's "On the Concept of Truth", which was then in proof, did I realize the depth of these problems, and how far I had been from understanding them; only then did I see, especially, the need for a hierarchy of metalanguages, if the semantical paradoxes were to be avoided. And I also realized of course that in my *Logik der Forschung* I had not, as I thought, been able to do without the idea of truth. In fact, my emphasis on the search for falsity in the service of truth should have made this obvious to me.

It is also obvious from my footnote 1 to section 84 that in *Logik der Forschung* I had little confidence in my own suggestion that the concept of truth was syntactical. (Carnap also favoured this idea at this time, though I was not aware of it: the German text of his *Logical Syntax,* 1934, did not contain sections 60*a*-60*d* of the English edition, 1937.) Indeed, it was my lack of confidence in my ability to produce a really satisfactory theory of truth which led me to try to do without it.

This is why Tarski's theory made so great an impression on me, leading to my lectures at Bedford College on his work. (See section 22 of my *Autobiography*.) Ayer was present at these lectures, but I doubt whether he will remember them; my English was much worse even than it is now, and I am far from certain whether it was at all understandable.

The main result of Tarski's theory of truth for my *Logik der Forschung* was, of course, that I could now say clearly that the aim of science was the search for informative content *and* truth. I had, indeed, said as much in my final section 85; but I had stressed it perhaps not sufficiently, for the reasons indicated. Now I could say it without hesitation.

I have told this story before, from a slightly different point of view; but I am telling it again here because it answers some of the points in Ayer's first few pages.

For example, Ayer begins his second paragraph by saying: "As Popper recognized, this treatment [in *L.d.F.*, before Tarski] of truth and falsehood brought him very close to pragmatism." But far from recognising this I even went out of my way, in section 84 (p. 276 of [1959(a)]) to point out "the contrast between my views and those of the pragmatists".

In his next paragraph Ayer criticizes my new footnote on Tarski in *The Logic of Scientific Discovery* ([1959(a)], p. 274; [1966(e)], p. 219) by saying: "This explanation would have been more to the point if Popper's original reason for dispensing with the concept of truth had been that he thought it unclear or defective, rather than that he simply had no need of it." But I had alluded in *Logik der Forschung* to the fact that *others* had found some "particular difficulty" in the concepts "true" and "false"; and I had, after all, argued explicitly against the pragmatists. At any rate, I hope I have now made clear that under the influence of Tarski I changed my mind on this very important issue. I am proud to have done so, and to have been (outside Poland) one of the earliest to realize the importance of Tarski's theory of truth. And, indeed, my previous treatment *was* "unclear and defective", to the extent that I was unaware of the existence of Tarski's theory. (Tarski had published his paper originally in Polish, a language I have never learned to read; the German translation was not published until more than a year after *L.d.F.*)

I may perhaps mention that Tarski's conception of a *metatheory* was for me important for a different reason.

In the discussions following some of my early lectures to the fringe of the Vienna Circle I had been heckled by some Wittgensteinians for speaking of "methodological rules": they indicated that, according to Wittgenstein, this must be nonsense, since such rules could not be truth functions of "elementary" (or "atomic") propositions. Obviously they were not Carnapian "syntactic" rules either. I had never accepted these prohibitions, which appeared to me arbitrary and even high-handed. Nevertheless I was not really happy about how to explain what I was doing until I learned from Tarski that we need even in logic a metatheory or metascience not confined to "logical syntax".

So much for the early impact on me of Tarski's theory of truth.

III

The Verification of Theories. Almost all philosophers since Kant agree with him that there can be no criterion of truth (*Critique of Pure Reason*, trans. by N. Kemp Smith [London: Macmillan, 1929], pp. 97 f.; 2d ed., pp. 83 f.); and with the help of Tarski's theory of truth it is even possible to prove that, for any but the most trivial languages, there can be no general criterion of truth, even of logical truth, to say nothing of empirical truth. (See Tarski, *Logic, Semantics, Metamathematics* [London: Oxford University Press, 1956], note on p. 254.)

By a criterion of truth is meant a kind of decision method: a method that leads either generally, or at least in a certain class of cases, through a finite sequence of steps (for example, of tests) to the decision whether or not the statement in question is true. Thus in the absence of a general criterion of truth it may easily happen that we possess true theories, and yet are unable to show, to our satisfaction, that they are true. What can also happen is that we are able to establish some statements as true, by a sort of lucky coincidence rather than an application of a criterion of truth (which may not exist in the case in question).

Thus to assert that we have a general criterion of truth is to assert very much more than to assert that certain statements are true.

Now the two crucial paragraphs of Ayer's paper, as far as the verification of theories is concerned, are the paragraphs beginning with "First, however," and ending with the words "empirical truth". The second paragraph is of particular importance.

"First, however," Ayer writes at the beginning of the first of these two paragraphs, "I want to examine his [Popper's] claim that, at any rate so far as empirical propositions are concerned, there are no general criteria by which we can recognize truth." Thus it is my claim which is examined here, and the term "criterion of truth" is clearly used in the sense explained here—a general criterion by which we can recognise truth.

Yet after a number of remarks in which he seems to agree with me (as well as a few pin pricks on the way), Ayer reaches at the end of the second paragraph a conclusion which is the precise opposite of mine:

"Accordingly, if we can lay down a general criterion for recognizing the truth of basic statements [test statements], there is a sense in which we shall after all have a general criterion for recognizing empirical truth."

By "empirical truth" Ayer means, especially, the truth of scientific theories; and the statement just quoted implies that, given an empirical method to decide on the truth or falsity of what I in *Logik der Forschung* called "basic statements" (and now prefer to call "test statements"), we can decide the truth or falsity of scientific theories.

It may be said that Ayer does not and cannot mean this, because in the first of these two paragraphs, and also in the second, he himself repeats most of the arguments by which I support my thesis of the one-sided refutability of universal theories. However, the last three sentences of the second paragraph are clearly designed to arrive at the conclusion they do arrive at, by an apparently smooth-running but quite invalid argument, leading off with a word—the word "Nevertheless"—that succeeds in invalidating all the preceding admissions.

Ayer's argument is, in brief:

Step (1) Admission: "Finding a counterexample proves the statement false, but failing to find one does not prove it true. . . ."

Step (2) "Nevertheless. . .the absence of any counterexample. . .is. . .a necessary and sufficient condition of truth. . . ." [This step is invalid, as I shall show, and it invalidates the argument; but even if we grant it, the argument does not become valid.]

Step (3) ". . .the only way in which any empirical statement can meet with a counterexample is by its coming into conflict with a basic statement [test statement]. . .[; thus] the truth or falsity of any empirical statement. . .is entirely determined by the truth or falsity of *some set* of basic statements." (Italics mine.)

Step (4) consists of the last statement of Ayer's second paragraph, ending triumphantly, as quoted above, ". . .we shall after all have a general criterion for recognizing empirical truth".

Is the argument valid, provided we admit step (2), as for the moment I am prepared to do? If it sounds so, it is because Ayer is a trifle indistinct about what set of basic statements is "some set of basic statements". For the set of basic statements actually necessary to "determine" the truth of a theory *A* would be the infinite *set of all test statements* which could be *relevant to A*, reporting on all possible tests undertaken *anywhere in the universe, in the past, present, or future.*

This is obvious; for by Ayer's own admission (see step (1) above), "failing to find [a counterexample] . . . does not prove . . . [the theory] true", *because* there may be unrecorded counterexamples. Thus only if that questionable set of basic statements includes complete reports about all possible counterexamples could the set "determine" the truth of the theory *A* (always provided we grant step (2), which will be discussed later), while *one* counterexample, *one* test statement, could determine the falsity of A.

But if this set of basic statements is infinite—one might even say "indefinite"—it is clear that we would need more than "a general criterion for recognizing the truth of basic statements" in order to obtain a "general criterion for recognizing empirical truth"; in just the same way, and for just the same reason, that we need more than a "criterion" for recognising the whiteness of swans in order to determine whether *all* swans are white. (This error is perhaps the gravest defect of Ayer's whole argument.) To "recognize" the truth of all the basic statements belonging to the set is clearly not an empirical process: it would involve a kind of omniscience—an omniscience with respect to basic statements.

Thus Ayer's argument establishes at best merely the thesis: "basic omniscience" (as I will call it) is involved in any "general criterion for recognizing empirical truth"; or *empirical omniscience involves basic omniscience.*

This thesis sums up, I suggest, all there is in this part of Ayer's criticism. It hardly needs saying that even if it were validly argued, it would not reveal any weakness in my views.

But even this somewhat unexciting thesis is invalid, owing to the invalidity of Ayer's step (2). I will discuss this step briefly, although it is somewhat subtle, and although its invalidity need not be established in order to show that Ayer's conclusion—his step (4)—is mistaken, and that there is *no* "general criterion for recognizing empirical truth".

Ayer contends that "the absence of any counterexample is a necessary and sufficient condition of truth". This view may be defended for theories like "All swans are white": if there exists (existed, will exist) no counterexample, that is, no non-white swan, then indeed the theory is true. But the view is untenable for all more abstract theories, such as Newton's. Non-white swans are observable; Newton's forces varying inversely with the square of the distance are not. (This is why Berkeley said that Newton's forces were "occult".) The idea that two theories which agree with respect to all testable consequences must be equivalent, is mistaken. Einstein's special theory of relativity and Lorentz's interpretation of it are two theories which contradict each other (Lorentz suggested the existence of an inertial system that is absolutely at rest). It does not help here to say that Lorentz's interpretation contains a metaphysical element that *has* to be omitted: Einstein's denial is just as metaphysical, or almost as metaphysical, because nothing observable follows from it. (It is not, in general, possible to split a theory into an empirical and a nonempirical part so that the "empirical part" constitutes a system which can be characterized by a finite number of empirical hypotheses; on the contrary, Craig's theorem can be used to show that the empirical part of a theoretical system will not in general be finitely axio-matizable. This, obviously, holds even for a comparatively simple theory such as Newton's theory of gravity.)

Thus there may be two theories which are incompatible, but have identical observational consequences; and one of them may even be em-pirically better than the other as it may suggest a further generalization (such as General Relativity) which has new and interesting empirical consequences.

But if A and B are incompatible, they cannot both be true, even if there is no counterexample to either of them; and this means that Ayer's suggestion (2), that the absence of counterexamples is a sufficient condition for the truth of a theory is mistaken.

So Ayer's deceptively smooth-running argument, consisting of the last three sentences of that second paragraph, is fallacious. It contains at least two steps each of which alone invalidates it. (Does Ayer perhaps realize this when he substitutes "empirical truth" for "truth" [of empirical theories] in the last step? Might he want to contend that incompatible theories A and B could both be "empirically true", even though only one could be true?)

I was so disturbed when I arrived at this result that I tried many ways to get away from it.

For a time I tried to interpret Ayer's argument quite differently; not as an attempted *reductio ad absurdum* of my thesis that there is no criterion of truth, but as a *reductio ad absurdum* of this thesis in conjunction with my theory of the role of test statements—a theory criticized by Ayer in the immediate sequel of those two crucial paragraphs. I thought, for a time, that Ayer wished to argue thus: since Popper says that basic statements are accepted or rejected by an act which he sometimes describes as a "conven-tion", we could "convene" a priori to reject the *set of all the basic statements*—even though this set is infinite—which are potential falsifiers of the theory A, thus (if Ayer's mistaken (2) is accepted) making the theory A true; and so we obtain a method of verification and something which may "in a sense" be called a criterion of empirical truth.

There is very little in Ayer's text to support this interpretation. On the contrary, he speaks of a criterion for *recognizing empirical truth*. But the method sketched would be one of laying down *conventional truth*. For the method is equivalent to a decision to treat A as irrefutable, or to decide about A by an a priori convention; and this I explicitly discussed and rejected in *Logik der Forschung* as a nonempirical method. And, again, such a method would mean deciding on test statements a priori, while I made it very clear that we decide about test statements only after the experiment, and indeed only after observing the experiment.

Indeed there is almost nothing in Ayer's paper to support this inter-pretation of what he had in mind, except perhaps this remark, in the paragraph following the two crucial ones: that "It may be objected that this way of putting it is unfair to him [Popper], since even in this case [the case of the basic statements] he does not equate truth with acceptance or falsity with rejection. He leaves open the formal possibility of our accepting a false basic statement or rejecting a true one." That Ayer mentioned this as a relevant reply is the only hint, and a small one, to support my hypothesis that he might have in mind the argument mentioned above.

But anyway this would not really improve matters; not only have I never said anything to support the kind of conventionalism mentioned, but I have discussed it at length, and have warned my readers against it. This fact speaks strongly against the conjecture, at best very weakly verifiable by Ayer's text, that the purpose of those two crucial paragraphs was to show that, *given my theory of basic statements*, we possess a criterion of truth for empirical theories: even this conjecture fails to make sense of those apparently smooth-running steps (2) to (4).

I shall very soon have to say a little more about my theory of the acceptance and rejection of basic statements, and Ayer's attitude towards it. At the moment I will turn back to the first of those two crucial paragraphs of Ayer's. For it becomes clear from this paragraph that Ayer sees the problem of induction in what I have called the traditional way. This is seen, for example, when he writes: "He [Popper] lays great emphasis on the need for testing hypotheses as rigorously as we can. . . .It is, however, not clear why we should make this effort if the hypotheses gain no credit from passing the test."

If by "credit" Ayer means (as apparently he does) reliability in future applications, then hypotheses do not, according to my view, gain credit. But in another sense they do gain "credit", according to my theory of corroboration explained in section 20 of my *Autobiography,* above: they are "better" than those of their competitors which fail the tests.

That Ayer has the traditional problem of reliability "in the future" in mind is seen very clearly when, further in the same paragraph, he quotes a statement of mine in which I use the words "attested by its tests" instead of "corroborated". (It was a silly pun. It seems that "test" in the sense of testing whether a coin is genuine gold comes from a root quite different from that of "testimony", "testament", and "attest".) Ayer comments: "I do not know what the word 'attested' means in this context if it carries no suggestion that we have acquired any reason at all to expect the statement to maintain itself in the future." My reply to this is to be found in my discussion of the pragmatic problem of induction in section 14 above.

In Ayer's book, *The Problem of Knowledge*, 1956, a formulation of the problem of induction can be found on page 74 which is I should say "traditional": "So far from approaching nature in the spirit of those gamblers at roulette who see in a long run of one colour a reason for betting on the other, we assume in general that the longer a run has been the more it is likely to continue. But how is this assumption to be justified? If this question could be answered, the problem of induction would be solved."

Obviously, this cannot be a serious problem since "this assumption" is *not* "justified", as has been explained in section 13 above. The problem of induction has to be formulated very differently.

I may perhaps mention here that at the same place in Ayer's book (p. 74) there is also a criticism of my theory in the form: "Why should a hypothesis which has failed the test be discarded unless this shows it to be unreliable. . .?" Answer: because if it has failed the test, it is false, independently of any pragmatic issue. Ayer also speaks of a possible world in which "a hypothesis which had been falsified was the more likely to hold good in future cases. Falsification might be regarded [in this world] as a sort of infantile disease which even the healthiest hypotheses could be depended on to catch." Yes, such a world is not contradictory. But there are many possible worlds in which not only the problem of knowledge but the problem of acquiring knowledge—such as scientific knowledge—would be insoluble. As explained above, knowledge as we know it is bound up with life as we know it, and this cannot exist in almost any region of the universe as we know it. (I use "almost any" in the sense of "measure zero".) It is therefore easy to construct worlds in which our method, the method of conjectures and refutations, would fail: he who wishes to solve the problem of induction must beware of trying to prove too much.

IV

The Verification of Basic Statements. It seems to me that Ayer's long discussion of the problem of the acceptance or rejection of basic statements completely misses my point. It concentrates on some expressions used by me such as "decision" and "convention", without due regard to the very full discussion of the procedure which can be found in *Logik der Forschung* (and which was to a considerable degree accepted by Ayer in *Language, Truth and Logic*, 1936).

What I suggested was that, logically considered, we cannot say that a test statement is "justified" by perceptions: it is, I suggested, more nearly like the "verdict" (*vere dictum* = spoken truly) of a jury, and it can therefore be said to be a decision or a convention.

It seems to me that Ayer's criticism is based completely upon the mistaken assumption that every decision or convention must be arbitrary. Indeed, in my *Open Society* (Vol. I, p. 64) I wrote on a similar issue: "Nearly all misunderstandings can be traced back to one fundamental misapprehension, namely, to the belief that 'convention' implies 'arbitrariness'."

That it does not should have been clear from my example of the jury, which plays such a role in *Logik der Forschung*, section 30. The jury decides about a fact—say, whether or not Mr A. killed Mr B. Its decision is the result of prolonged deliberation; much time is needed for coming to a common decision (which is the meaning of "convention" intended here). But who would say that a jury which has long and seriously debated the issue decides "completely arbitrarily"? Its decision is the result of a common effort to *find the truth*.

From a purely logical point of view, its decision may be called "arbitrary" insofar as the accepted statement (verdict) is in no way logically derivable from any other ("given") statement, as I explained in *Logik der Forschung*, section 30. The verdict plays a role comparable to a "primitive proposition" or a "postulate". It may be compared to the decision to accept or to reject Euclid's axiom of parallels, or the Archimedean axiom. In all these cases, the decision may be called "arbitrary" in the logical sense mentioned; but it is far from being "totally arbitrary": in all these cases it is motivated by the search for truth.

Let us now look at scientific tests and test statements, that is, reports of the results of tests. These statements are *not* "linguistic expressions of personal (or subjective) experiences" as was suggested by the logical positivists prior to my intervention (see section 3 of my *Replies*, above). Rather, they are perfectly *public* and impersonal statements about facts; and by "public" I mean that they can, in their turn, be tested. Thus even though they may be *singular* statements—say, about the positions of Mercury or of Uranus at certain instants of time—they have the character of *hypotheses* (*L.d.F.*, sections 8, 25-30). And the acceptance or rejection of them is a matter for something like a scientific jury—the scientific community (which may or may not come to an agreement).[166]

V

Subjective Experience and Linguistic Formulation. What is the fundamental difference between Ayer and myself? I suspect it is the following.

Ayer seems to me to accept the almost universally accepted theory which I have called the commonsense theory of knowledge; I believe this theory to be false, and to clash with a very different part of common sense, the commonsense theory of realism.

If this latter theory is right, then there is a reality about which we "know" (objectively and conjecturally) a great deal and fail to know still more. This reality has its invariants, and its organic life, and with it "knowledge" becomes possible provided the invariants play—locally—a sufficiently prominent role for the organisms to "adapt" themselves to them. What may be called the "subjective knowledge" of an organism is part of this organism's adaptation, and especially part of its anticipation of impending events ("expectations"). This subjective knowledge is, clearly, fallible, just as the organism is fallible. What may be called "subjective knowledge" in the widest sense is the organism's innate apparatus of expectations, including its ability to modify its expectations under the influence of environmental stimuli.

Sense organs, and sense observations dependent on sense organs, are something very special from this point of view. They are part of the decoding mechanism by which certain organisms—especially animals—interpret the state of their environment, and anticipate its impending changes: they are part of our expectational apparatus. This apparatus works, by and large, astonishingly well, although it is far from perfect: it is *fallible*. Most of its properties are inherited, and its momentary achievements—the single perception, the raising of a certain expectation—are incomparably less deeply seated than the inherited ability or disposition to produce these perceptions or expectations.

Nevertheless, most organisms act upon interpretations of the information which they receive from their environment; and the fact that they survive, for some considerable time, shows that this apparatus usually works well. But it is far from perfect. All organisms make mistakes in interpreting their environment, especially under unusual conditions.

I have described part of my realist's outlook upon the world. As living organisms, we constantly change and refute our interpretations of our environment, and have many complex and interrelated methods of checking and correcting our interpretations. Nevertheless, all interpretations remain fallible, and so do all expectations of impending events, which form part of these interpretations. The epistemic apparatus of a living organism is as a rule astonishingly good in these interpretations and in its anticipations of relevant impending events; but it is never perfect, and often fails to correct itself quickly enough.

This, I think, is a realistic though brief description of the function of the anticipatory and signal-interpreting organs with which organisms are fitted and which we usually call their sense organs. They are marvellously powerful and efficient as organs of adaptation; but they are fallible, especially in unfamiliar circumstances.

The development of human language plays a complex role within this process of adaptation. It seems to have developed from signalling among social animals; but I propose the thesis that what is most characteristic of the human language is the possibility of story telling. It may be that this ability too has some predecessor in the animal world. But I suggest that the moment when language became human was very closely related to the moment when a man invented a story, a myth in order to excuse a mistake he had made—perhaps in giving a danger signal when there was no occasion for it; and I suggest that the evolution of specifically human language, with its characteristic means of expressing negation—of saying that something signalled is not true—stems very largely from the discovery of systematic means to *negate* a false report, for example a false alarm, and from the closely related discovery of false stories—lies—used either as excuses or playfully.

If we look from this point of view at the relation of language to subjective experience, we can hardly deny that every genuine report contains an element of decision, at least of the decision to speak the truth. Experiences with lie detectors give a strong indication that, biologically, speaking what is subjectively believed to be the truth differs deeply from lying. I take this as an indication that lying is a comparatively late and fairly specifically human invention; indeed that it has made the human language what it is: an instrument which can be used for misreporting almost as well as for reporting.

But we may report (as might a bee) what is objectively untrue even if we believe that it is true. The real importance of the invention of lying is on the one hand the possibility of story telling, and the enhanced development of imagination; and on the other hand, that it leads to the *problem of truth or falsity*. It provides a stimulus to develop tests for finding out whether a report is not merely subjectively true but objectively true also. Thus we come to questioning, and to critical discussion, and to *decision making* on the truth or falsity of any given report.

It is here, I believe, that Professor Ayer and I are so strongly in disagreement. I assert that, however different, psychologically, lying may be from speaking what is subjectively felt to be the truth, it is not this psychological difference that science is ultimately based on, but the critical tests by which we try to discern the objective difference between truth and falsity. But these tests (a) are never fully decisive and (b) always contain an element of weighing reasons, an element of decision. From a purely logical point of view, this makes every scientific assertion a decision: a choice of one among two or more possibilities.

But these decisions are of course not "free" decisions; we do not decide for what we prefer, but for what we regard, in the light of the critical discussion, as objectively true, or as nearest to the truth. Our immediate sense experiences, our expectations, may play an important role in our decision. But in my view of the matter they do so only because our sense organs are in so many cases adequate for their task that they turn out, even on prolonged critical examination, not to lead to contradictions or any other symptoms of untruth. I admit that we often accept "the evidence of our senses", especially in cases in which we have learned to trust them. But I utterly deny that "the evidence of our senses" can ever be anything like a decisive or final or perhaps even defining criterion of truth; or that what we are looking for—the truth of our theories—can be in any way traced to the evidence of our senses. This is not only because they remain essentially fallible, but for a much more important reason: because truth—objective or absolute truth—is in principle irreducible to sense experience, whether the domain under discussion is empirical or not.

It would incidentally be a complete misunderstanding to assimilate my view to any form of "conventionalism": the "conventional" or "decisional" element in our acceptance or rejection of a proposition involves in general no element of arbitrariness at all. Our experiences are not only motives for accepting or rejecting an observational statement, but they may even be described as *inconclusive reasons*. They are reasons because of the generally reliable character of our observations; they are inconclusive because of our fallibility. Decisions which are somewhat arbitrary come in only when we have to make up our minds on whether our tests are, for the time being, satisfactory, and may be concluded; or whether we are to try another test. And even these somewhat arbitrary decisions are, if considered more closely, more conjectures than decisions—conjectures, that is, that further tests will not lead to any deviating result.

Thus realists have quite a good argument for relying, up to a point—the point of fallibilism—upon observations or even perceptions. They have even arguments for so relying, while uncritical empiricists and positivists must take this reliance as a fundamental (a priori) dogma, incapable of further explanation unless they are prepared to adopt a subjectivist idealism (in the last analysis a solipsism or Machean neutral monism).

I hardly need to stress here the difference between myself and those empiricists and positivists who think that all we know is "based" on or derivable from sense experience. "Derivable" in any logical sense it is certainly not; and "based" only in the highly indirect and fallible sense which has been here explained.

To put the matter in a nutshell: uncritical empiricists and positivists have been misled by the generally excellent working of our decoding apparatus into idolizing, or even deifying it. They have overlooked that the apparatus and its excellence are the result of "natural selection"; that we should not be here if the apparatus were much worse.

33. Agassi on a Modified Conventionalism

I am a realist, in both of the main senses of this philosophical term: I believe in the reality of the physical world ("world 1") which, I conjecture, existed long before man; and I believe in the reality of a world of man-made theories, problems, and mistakes, which I call "world 3".

By the term "essentialism" I understand a form of realism which I do not accept: essentialism in its Platonic version is the belief that world 3 consists mainly of concepts or ideal Forms. In its Aristotelian version essentialism is the belief that the things of world 1 are what they are by virtue of the forms or essences which are in them, like the spirit of wine or the essence of vanilla. Aristotelian essentialism is, I believe, a mistaken philosophy, but it seems to be not so bad an approximation for vanilla (though perhaps less so for wine), and for biology: modern genetics says that plants and animals are what thcy are by virtue of their genetic essences, the genes (or whatever may take their place as fundamental).

In my essay "Three Views Concerning Human Knowledge" ([1956(f)], Chap. 3 of [1963(a)]) I discussed (a) Essentialism, (b) Instrumentalism, and (c) a nonessentialistic form of realism in its "world 1" sense. (I hardly discussed worlds 2 and 3, although my pluralistic belief in them is, I think, implicit in the essay.) An anonymous reviewer in *The Times Literary Supplement* described my own realist position as a "modified essentialism"; and since it was that rare thing, a sensible review, I assumed that the reviewer, whoever he was, had understood me; and when the problem turned up in another essay of mine,[167] I admitted this in a footnote.

Thus the term "modified essentialism" is not my own term; moreover, I am not even quite sure whether I interpreted the unknown reviewer correctly when I expressed my agreement with him. I believe, but I am not sure, that he wished to characterize my *realism* when he called me a modified essentialist; my reasons are (a) that it was a perceptive review, and (b) that in my essay I discussed instrumentalism, essentialism, and the realistic "third view" which, I explained, was my own.

In his contribution Professor Agassi proposes the following thesis: of the two views which I combat, instrumentalism and essentialism, the latter can be modified, but not the former; but instrumentalism is closely related to conventionalism, and conventionalism *can* be modified. He then raises the question whether my own philosophy is not perhaps described better as a modified conventionalism than as a modified essentialism.

Before turning to this question, I wish to acknowledge that what Agassi says about the impossibility of modifying instrumentalism and the possibility of modifying conventionalism instead seems to me not only correct, but highly ingenious. But why should we raise the question about my philosophy which he then raises?

I have been reproached in the past for speaking much too often about "isms". I wish therefore to say what legitimate role, if any, "isms" have to play in philosophical discussions.

I think that most people, learned or otherwise, uphold unconsciously several philosophical views of some sort. These views are philosophical in the sense that they colour a whole variety of their opinions, turning them into something like a system, an "ism". (When an unlearned old man in Tyrol once said to me, during a thunderstorm, that the clouds must be very hard to cause such a noise by their collision, he gave expression to an unconsciously held primitive form of materialism.)

I suggest that the task of philosophy is, mainly, the critical analysis of the many "isms" which are held by various people. When I describe myself as a "realist" or a "critical rationalist" I feel unusually ill at ease. I do not want to hold an "ism" or to propagate an "ism"; but it is sometimes necessary to give a set of views a short name; so be it.

In my "Three Views" paper, I tried to show that two "isms" are widely held; and I criticized them. I called my own view "the third view", in preference to calling it "realism".

I therefore disagree with Agassi's way of posing his problem. The question whether one can modify conventionalism does not interest me greatly, although I admit the ingenuity of Agassi's remarks on this possibility and on the impossibility of modifying instrumentalism. But I am still less interested in the question whether such a modified conventionalism is nearer to or further from my own philosophy than is a modified essentialism. If "modified essentialism" is a kind of synonym for realism, then I have no objection to being called one of its champions. If, but only if, "modified conventionalism" in Agassi's sense is another kind of synonym for realism, I have no objection either. But the question of the proximity or otherwise of the one "ism" or the other to my philosophy fails to rouse my interest; in fact, I do not understand its point, in spite of having tried hard to do so.

It appears that in speaking of "conventionalism", Agassi has in mind not so much a position like that of Poincaré (discussed by me in section 19 of *L.Sc.D.*), but the fact stressed in Chapter 5 of the first volume of *The Open Society*, that social institutions are man-made, and therefore "conventional" in the sense of the old Greek opposition between "nature" and "convention". Agassi says that science must be treated, in some respects, as a social institution, and it is therefore not "natural" but "conventional" in this sense.

But I have never fully accepted the Greek opposition between "nature" and "convention" which, incidentally, is understood in somewhat different ways by different Greek authors; more especially, I have never identified "by nature" with "in truth", and "by convention" with "falsely" or "in fiction". I even dissociated myself sharply from a weaker position which identifies "by convention" with "by *arbitrary* convention" (*O.S.*, Chap. 5, the paragraph on pp. 64 f.; and *Addendum* I to Vol. II, which was added in 1961). Institutions are, I believe, man-made, and we are therefore greatly responsible for them. But they have a certain degree of autonomy: they belong to world 3. And just as mathematics is not wholly arbitrary (though different systems of mathematics are possible, for example, Euclidean and non-Euclidean geometries), so it is with social institutions. And if science is a social institution, so is its autonomous aim, the search for objective truth, for correspondence with the facts of nature, of reality; which makes me in this field more of a "naturalist" (or realist) than a conventionalist.

To sum up, if I follow Agassi into "ismism", and if I understand him rightly, then I cannot agree with him: I am not a conventionalist (whether modified or not) but a defender of the autonomy of the objective world 3, in which objective truth plays a major role.

VI. OBJECTIVITY IN PROBABILITY THEORY AND IN PHYSICS

34. Introductory Remark

There are a few related problems—the propensity interpretation of probability, objectivity in quantum mechanics, and objectivity in the theory of time—which have between them taken up a considerable part of my life's work. I am therefore particularly indebted to four contributors, Professors Settle, Margenau, Suppes, and Grünbaum for having given me the opportunity to clarify some points in these fields in which, it seems, I have sometimes been misunderstood. Settle's paper consists of two parts, the first of which is more concerned with the problem of induction than with the propensity interpretation; but in view of the fact that it is the *application* of the problem of induction which he has in mind, I found it easier to discuss his paper in the context of the propensity interpretation of probability, which is the topic of the second part of his paper.

After these four papers I go on to discuss those of Professors Kuhn and Wisdom, which both treat of my theory of scientific revolutions, and its contrast with Kuhn's.

35. Settle on Induction and the Propensity Theory of Probability

Professor Tom Settle's excellent contribution consists of two parts, each of which states very fully his views on a cardinal problem. The first part concerns my suggestion (criticized in Professor Bernays's contribution) to identify rationality, or the heart of rationality, with critical discussion. The second tackles my propensity interpretation of probability.

I

I think that everything that Settle says in the first part of his paper about rationality and criticism is exceptionally good, especially his analysis of the relationship between responsibility (I usually speak of "intellectual responsibility") and critical discussion. This topic is extremely well and carefully treated, and I hardly find worth mentioning any point on which I cannot accept what he says. Throughout his paper his opinions and mine are in real harmony. I had the feeling that he understands unusually well what I want, and what I wanted to say.

However, I ought to mention that I find Settle's criticism of my falsifiability criterion unconvincing, for reasons already given above. Settle devotes most of the fourth section of the first part of his paper to this criticism. But I need not say more about it here. Nor need I do more than refer to my reply to Peter Medawar above in response to some of the problems posed in part One, 1, B, of Settle's paper.

On the other hand, I was perhaps a little surprised by his implied (and very mild) criticism that I am unconcerned with the problems of practical application and of technology, and of "standards" (especially "standards of responsibility"). That he takes this as a fact is, I suspect, connected with the absence from both his text and his very many footnotes (there are more than 140) of any reference to the place where I discuss these questions briefly but comparatively fully; I mean the *Addendum* to the second volume of *The Open Society* ([1962(c)] and later editions) entitled "Facts, Standards and Truth: A Further Criticism of Relativism". Altogether I got the impression, probably a mistaken one, from Settle's criticism that he has neglected, or forgotten, both my *Open Society* and my *Poverty of Historicism* (esp. sections 19 and 20). These are works in which I say more about the relation of "pure" science to technology than seems to be indicated in those of Settle's remarks which depict me as austerely interested in pure science alone.

But I think that in these works I say only things which Settle could have referred to as supporting his own views on responsibility. And there is one little remark made in *The Poverty* which would actually have added to Settle's analyses, though these are mostly much fuller than mine: the remark is that theoretical problems can usually be traced back to and found to originate in practical problems.[168] A further reference that might to some purpose be made here is to a paper of mine which was not yet published when Settle wrote his contribution: "Conjectural Knowledge: My Solution of the Problem of Induction".[169]

II

The second part of Settle's contribution centres round my *axiomatizations* of the calculus of probability,[170] and my *propensity interpretation* of probability.

Settle draws attention to my axiomatizations, comparing the final ones with Kolmogorov's and Rényi's, and explaining some of their essential features. I think he is right that my axiomatizations have been neglected. I know only of one mathematician who has looked at them: Paul Bernays, and he has expressed to me his approval. I am therefore particularly grateful to Settle for breaking a lance for them. (On this, see also my reply to Professor Suppes in section 37 below.)

Settle's discussion of my propensity interpretation has, in its turn, two main topics. The first is whether or not I have been anticipated by Peirce. Here I must say that I do not know. I can claim independence, but not originality; moreover, I am not all that interested in the problem of originality: Peirce anticipated several of my ideas—ideas I had independently—, as has been shown by Professors Freeman and Skolimowski in this volume (and earlier by Professors W. B. Gallie and David Rynin in personal communications). I have never felt sorry for being thus anticipated; on the contrary, I feel proud of so eminent a predecessor.

But the question whether Peirce's and my propensity interpretations are really similar turns out, as Professor Settle shows, to be a taxing one. It is a subject to which I have not given any thought myself; thus unless some student of Peirce contradicts Settle, I shall accept, tentatively, Settle's view.

The question is, as Settle points out, connected with another: whether we should take absolute probability or relative probability as fundamental in our axiomatization.

Here I should perhaps add something to Settle's discussion. It is this. My own preference for relative probability as fundamental was decided, after many years of wavering, *before* I went over to the propensity interpretation. As long as I thought that the two concepts were mutually definable, I had a certain preference for absolute probability. I only decided in favour of relative probability when I realized that absolute probability is a special case of relative probability, *but not the other way round*. For we can introduce absolute probability into the calculus of relative probability by an axiom or an explicit definition, *but not the other way round*. (The definition of relative probability $p(a,b)$ in terms of absolute probability is conditional at best, the condition being that $p(b) \neq 0$.) Thus the theory of relative probability, and my axiomatization of it, are stronger and more interesting than the theory of absolute probability. This point was decisive for my choice. But it helped me greatly with the propensity interpretation (in a way which becomes quite clear from Settle's paper).

I do not think that there is anything from the point of view of interpretation to be said for choosing absolute probability instead; it is, of course, at our disposal in any case.

III

The last point I should like to make is a response to Settle's appeal in his footnote 135. It concerns the "occultness" or otherwise of propensities.

Settle writes there: "This posed the question, which I ask Sir Karl to answer, whether my 'improved' view is not what he intended after all, appearances to the contrary being the result of the specific context of his published discussions of propensity theory."

My answer is that Settle's view is not only what I "intended after all", but it is in all explicitness to be found in my published discussions of the propensity theory.

For Settle (and apparently also Bunge, who influenced Settle on this point, as Settle explains in his contribution) have apparently overlooked my main "published discussion of the propensity theory": only once in all his footnotes do I find a reference to my paper "The Propensity Interpretation of Probability", published in 1959 in *The British Journal for the Philosophy of Science*;[171] and this paper is nowhere mentioned in the text of Settle's contribution. But it is a paper which has a strong emphasis on an anti-instrumentalist and antiobservationalist point of view. It is a pity that Settle does not take any notice of this paper,[172] for it is quite unambiguous on the issue at stake: whether the propensity interpretation, as I understand it, contains an element of instrumentalism or operationalism, or not. (I would have thought that all I have written against instrumentalism and operationalism might have cleared me a priori of such a suspicion.) In the 1959 paper mentioned, I wrote for example on pages 30 f. (*"unobservable"* was on both occasions italicized in the original):

I . . . accept the suggestion [my own] that there is an analogy between the idea of propensities and that of forces—especially fields of forces. But I should point out that although the labels "force" or "propensity" may both be psychological or anthropomorphic metaphors, the important analogy between the two ideas does not lie here; it lies, rather, in the fact that both ideas draw attention to *unobservable dispositional properties of the physical world*, and thus help in the interpretation of physical theory. Herein lies their usefulness. The concept of force—or better still, the concept of a field of forces—introduces a dispositional physical entity, described by certain equations (rather than by metaphors), in order to explain observable accelerations. Similarly the concept of propensity, or of a field of propensities, introduces a dispositional property of singular physical experimental arrangements—that is to say, of singular physical events—in order to explain observable frequencies in sequences of repetitions of these events. In both cases, the introduction of the new idea can be justified only by an appeal to its usefulness for physical theory. Both concepts are "occult", in Berkeley's sense, or "mere words". But part of the usefulness of these concepts lies precisely in the fact that they suggest that the theory is concerned with the properties of an *unobservable* physical reality and that it is only some of the more superficial effects of this reality which we can observe, and which thus make it possible for us to test the theory.

I hope that this is sufficiently unambiguous; and it shows that in Settle's diagrams, Tables 3 and 4, I am wrongly placed; my position is right only in

Table 5; and this is the position of which Settle himself approves.

36. Margenau on Empiricism, Probability, and Quantum Mechanics

Professor Henry Margenau's gracious contribution may be divided into two parts. One is on my *epistemology*, which differs fairly radically from the epistemology of Professor Margenau; the other is on my *views on quantum physics*. For me, the latter part is the more important, because Margenau is one of the pioneers of quantum physics, and in this domain he does defend me (even though he disclaims the need) "[against] a host of vociferous critics who have attacked his [Popper's] position vis-à-vis the modern theories of physics".

I

Margenau lists first a number of epistemological points on which, as he says, my views and his concur: my indictment of positivism, logical and otherwise; my opposition to formalism and formalization, which he boldly describes as "the search for substance, not mere form"; I say boldly because, though I agree fully with what Professor Margenau means, I should not have ventured to use a historically-loaded expression like "substance". But it turns out at once that Margenau does not attribute to this term any of its dubious philosophical meanings. On the contrary, he is referring to investigations which have *substantial content,* and contrasting them with the emptiness of scholastic or "glossomorphic"[173] deliberations; for he at once indicates "the places where that substance is to be found, namely the sciences and mathematics". He goes on to list my acknowledgement of a moderate measure of conventionalism, of the inevitable flux of what is accepted in science as the truth; my indictment of the logic of induction, and my concern with probability.

This list of points of agreement is quite impressive. But there are also serious disagreements in the general field of the philosophy of human knowledge, and Margenau turns soon to a discussion of these.

II

The disagreement which Margenau refers to is fundamental and extremely interesting. I should say that both Margenau and I are commonsense realists. We are also both empiricists. But Margenau's empiricism is close to what I call the commonsense theory of knowledge (see my section 13, subsection III, above). He speaks of "*experiences* as the unique foundations of all science", and he remarks, rightly, that "neither words, nor sentences, nor propositions, nor logical rules can replace [these] *experiences*". With this last remark I fully agree as it stands, even though it is meant as a criticism of my views. But it seems clear that Margenau, when he feels that words, or sentences, or propositions, or logical rules play much too important a role in my theory of scientific knowledge, has put his finger on a point where there is a real disagreement between us. For though I am not a believer in words, or sentences, or other linguistic entities as such, I do regard as central the fact that world 3 largely controls world 2; and indeed I was of the same opinion long before I introduced the terminology of "world 1", the world of physical objects and states; "world 2", the world of our conscious *experiences*; and "world 3", the world of the products of our minds, especially the linguistically formulated products, and more especially the problems, theories, and logical arguments of science. This terminology has been introduced by me so recently[174] that Margenau could hardly have known about it when he wrote his paper. But the underlying ideas played a decisive role in my early work;[175] and when Margenau speaks of "*experiences* as the unique foundations of all science" then he and I diverge, quite certainly, over the relationship between what I call world 2 and world 3.

I am far from certain whether Professor Margenau would admit the existence of a world 3 in my sense. But he would agree, I am sure, that scientific problems, theories, and arguments find a kind of physical embodiment in books, journals, and libraries; and he would further agree, of course, that, together with certain scientific *traditions*, they play a big role in science.

Assuming harmony on this point, I can now state the difference between Margenau and myself as follows: Margenau says that world 2 experiences are fundamental for science, while I say that, despite its origin in world 2, world 3 (or if you do not believe in it, its embodiment in libraries and books) has so great an impact (or "feedback", if you like) on world 2 that world 2 experiences are utterly different after the development of (descriptive and argumentative) language, and of science, from what they were before.

The experimentalist may be at first reluctant to agree with this; he knows that he is *observing*, that he is looking intently through a telescope, or a microscope, and that his acceptance or rejection of a theory may depend on the result of his visual observations (on his "sense data"). But he forgets that it is a telescope, or a microscope, through which he is looking, and that he takes the whole theory of these instruments for granted (they form part of his "background knowledge"). And he further forgets that, in making his observations, he is trying to answer definite questions (that is, theory-impregnated questions), rather than just "looking hard" (as he might be inclined to say if he stresses experiences as the "unique foundations" of science).

What can my observationalist opponent answer? (I do *not* attribute these answers to Margenau; I only wish to carry on the argument one step further.) He could say that I am arguing about a very late and mature state in the development of science, and that, though these days all observations and experiences are theory-impregnated, they were not so in the early stages of our scientific development. Observations were made, and experiences were experienced, long before libraries, books, or journals existed.

To this my answer would be yes; but once a human language—a descriptive and argumentative language—existed, observations became something entirely different from what they were before. Before, they were part of ourselves, they were subjective, they were acted upon (or rather reacted upon) without any critical reflection. Not so those experiences and observations which came after human language developed; for these experiences could be reported, criticized, and investigated: *only they are "foundations" of science*. But they are irreducibly theory-impregnated, problem-impregnated. Thus the experiences which became the foundations of all sciences were in their turn postlinguistic; they were experienced in a world in which a language existed (though it may not yet have had books) and also myths, and primitive theories.

There is therefore no fundamental difference between observations using the invention of a telescope and observations made in the light of a myth, or a theory; that is, observations made after the invention of language.

Consequently, it is not quite sufficient to say, as Margenau does, that *experiences* (as opposed to words, propositions, and the like) are "the unique foundations of all science", and to criticize me, however mildly, for speaking of "theories" and "scientific statements". (I hardly ever speak of words, since I identify the *descriptive statement* as the unique foundation of human language, and the problem of its truth or falsity as the unique foundation of all science. Words—so far as they are not equivalent to statements—I regard only as instruments for the formulation of statements; but this is perhaps a minor point in the present context.)

No, I cannot agree with this part of Margenau's criticism; I think that the realization that world 2 experiences depend largely on world 3 problems—especially in science—is a major improvement on the kind of empiricism which Margenau prefers to my approach. But I agree that in my *Logik der Forschung* I wrote much too briefly on these points. And I acknowledge the value of Margenau's criticism, especially in a volume like the present one; for it encourages me to defend myself by restating my position in what is—I hope—a somewhat improved form.

III

From these considerations, all the points on which Margenau and I agree in the general philosophy of science, and those on which we disagree, follow almost immediately. Margenau is far from overlooking the role of theory in the higher development of science. Still, there are many minor disagreements, for example over the role of "rules of correspondence", of "conventions", of "constructs". But these differences are superficial compared with those discussed here in subsection II; they can, perhaps, be summarized by saying that in my opinion human language is something like a "construct", and this is why I do not use the word "construct"; for "constructs" are everywhere, while the term was meant to imply that they are not only not everywhere, but not "fundamental", since they are distinct from the (perhaps raw) *experiences*, the only things which are fundamental.

One point only can be taken up here: my agreement with Margenau that "theories are thought of as true or false" and not as "probable". But there is an important difference even here. Although we agree that theories are only true or false, and not probable, I assert that even of our true theories we cannot ascertain, by impressively successful "verifications", or by any other method, that they are, in fact, true. This fallibilism is the least we must learn from the fact that Einstein proved Newton's theory to be but one among perhaps many hypotheses that might explain the facts in an almost unsurpassedly excellent way. Connected with this point is Margenau's remark "that there is no absolute, ultimate or final truth in science" and "that the basis of science is not secure *knowledge*". I think that since he accepts this, Margenau must revise his rejection of my doctrine of the asymmetry between verification and falsification; for since I use the term "truth" in the absolute or final sense (of Tarski), my fallibilist doctrine that we cannot verify a theory agrees completely with Margenau's doctrine that there is no absolute or final truth in science. An important difference is indicated by Margenau's continuation in which he says that though we have no "secure *knowledge*", we have *"faith"*. It is not that I disagree. But in saying that we have no secure knowledge, I am talking logic, in the sense of world 3; while "faith" or "belief" is a world 2 concept.[176]

In Margenau's paper I find a paragraph in which he suggests that I ignore the "principle of invariance" of natural laws. This I must correct. I have discussed this principle at length in various places in my *Logik der Forschung*.[177]

IV

This brings me to the second part of Margenau's paper, the part which deals with probability and quantum mechanics. Here I can only say how gratifying it is for an old fighter in this curiously controversial field to read in a paper by a physicist of Margenau's eminence that "the area of agreement between Popper's interpretation of quantum mechanics and my own is very large. He was among the first philosophers to interpret Heisenberg's uncertainty principle as a statistical scatter relation". I did so in my *Logik der Forschung*, shortly before the publication of the celebrated paper of Einstein, Podolsky, and Rosen; and I did so in spite of the raised eyebrows of all the physicists I knew. Only Professor Hans Thirring gave me a hearing, by inviting me in 1934 to read a paper on the subject in his seminar. I am most grateful to Professor Margenau for endorsing these old ideas of mine after so many years—ideas which, at the time, as the mistake in section 77 of *Logik der Forschung* shows, were far from mature; amongst other things, I had not yet arrived, at that time, at the propensity interpretation (or dispositional interpretation) of probability.

But the decisive agreement between Professor Margenau and myself is our common "insistence on objectivity in quantum mechanical description", as he puts it. This point is *the* point of fundamental importance, especially for a philosopher. I am glad that more and more physicists are inclined to disagree with Heisenberg and Wigner, and to agree with Einstein and Margenau.[178]

37. Suppes's Criticism of the Propensity Interpretation of Probability and Quantum Mechanics

The main criticism in the first section of Professor Suppes's challenging and interesting contribution is directed against my propensity interpretation. Not that he dislikes this interpretation intuitively; what he objects to is my failure to give a formal account or a formal definition of it. I gladly admit the validity of this criticism, and I will now try to remedy my failure here; and though I might say a good deal about what I should describe as Suppes's overestimation of the value of definition and formalization, I want to stress that his challenge has led me to clarify my views, and I am grateful for it.

Suppes's second section I found even more interesting than the first. It is directed against all those who talk about quantum mechanics as a statistical theory without stressing that *qua* statistical theory it is most unusual. Suppes's final criticism, based on the work of Leon Cohen[179] is, it seems to me, particularly important. It culminates in the historical prophecy that the discrepancies between quantum theory and "standard" or "classical" statistical theories "will come to play the same fundamental role in the foundations of physics and probability that the three classical problems of the Greeks [trisecting an angle, squaring the circle and—I conjecture—doubling the cube; or perhaps proving Euclid's fifth postulate?] have played in the foundations of mathematics".

This is an interesting and impressive prophecy, and Suppes may well be right. My very different wager (that quantum theory will be reconstructed on a new statistical basis) will be explained in my second section.

I

The Plurality of Interpretations of Probability. Some fundamental discrepancy between Suppes and myself seems to lie in our metaphysics or set of values. To me it seems that formalization is an interesting technique for solving certain problems, but not something beautiful or meritorious in itself; though in this field, as in others, we may sometimes be struck by beauty and depth: the beauty and depth of some brilliant idea involved (example: Tarski's theory of truth) or even the beauty and depth of an originally hardly suspected symmetry (example: Boolean algebra). Suppes, on the other hand, seems to look upon formalization almost as if it were an end in itself. It seems that for him it can be something like the way through which a philosopher of science achieves his aim, or fulfils his destiny.

These are differences in general outlook. Of course I also make use of formalization if I wish to solve a problem—for example, a philosophical problem—which can be solved with its help; and in connection with probability theory I have done so since [1934(b)]. In such cases I am inclined to proceed with the formalization precisely so far as is needed for the solution of the problem in hand.

Take probability theory. Here the philosophical problem was, originally, *the problem of the meaning of "probability"*. However, as early as my *Logik der Forschung*, and even more explicitly from my [1938(a)] on, I replaced this by what I regarded and still regard as a better problem: *the problem of the various ways in which probability statements—the statements of the calculus of probability—can be interpreted.*

The difference is that while the older question is essentialistic and requires *one* correct answer, the question of interpretation allows many answers, all of which may be interesting and none of which may give us the "essence of what probability means".

Already in *Logik der Forschung* I distinguished *two main kinds of interpretations of probability: subjective and objective;* and I distinguished between the classical, the logical, the subjective or "psychologistic", and the frequency theories of probability. (I also distinguished from *all* of these the problem of interpreting another theory which is formally different from the theory of probability though it is usually mixed up with it; I mean the theory of corroboration.) A similar view of the plurality of interpretations of probability (in the sense of the probability calculus) was later very ably expounded by one of *Logik der Forschung*'s (at that time) enthusiastic reviewers, Ernest Nagel, in his *Principles of the Theory of Probability*.[180]

I mention these points for the following reason: I am a little uncertain whether or not Suppes agrees with my view that there are *several* interpretations of probability statements, or whether he believes in *one* essentially correct interpretation, that is, in "*the* meaning" of probability.

However this may be, I have a major quarrel with Suppes about what he says in connection with the three interpretations for which he offers formal definitions; that is, the classical definition of probability, and the frequency and the subjective interpretations.

I think that anybody who reads Suppes's first section will receive the impression that Suppes discusses these three interpretations in order to show the kind of thing he expects, and has a right to expect, from any decent interpretation of probability, but which he fails to find in my paper [1959(e)]—incidentally my only work on probability in general (as opposed to probability in quantum mechanics) to which he ever refers.[181] But it may be better to let Suppes himself formulate his very restrained complaint:

> In broad terms [Suppes writes], the issue is that of characterizing the explicit meaning of the propensity interpretation. To ask for the meaning of the interpretation without making any more definite statement of the methodology to be used . . . is to ask in philosophers' jargon the ordinary question, *What is the propensity interpretation?* However, in the case of probability, a strong intellectual tradition of analysis can be used. [Italics mine.]

To this I wish to make four comments:

(1) *What-is?* questions as here mentioned by Suppes have been rejected by me with the help of elaborate arguments, as have also questions of the meaning or definition of terms such as "propensity" (or "propensity interpretation").

(2) I pointed out long ago that, instead, we may demand of the various interpretations of probability that they satisfy an axiom system for the probability calculus.

(3) I think that, unknown to Professor Suppes, I have thereby made several contributions to the "strong intellectual tradition" which as he says exists "in the case of probability".

(4) I have always pointed out that, as long as we are concerned with interpretations, we cannot hope to distinguish them fully by formal rules alone: formal rules are just the kind of thing that always allow of *several* interpretations. But Suppes's paper seems to suggest that we can *formally* distinguish between the classical, the frequency, and the subjective interpretations; and he seems to ask: What is the formal basis for, or a formal definition of, the propensity interpretation?

In brief, it seems that Suppes's criticism may be summarized in this way: "Bruno de Finetti has offered us a formal definition of subjective probability, and having been offered this, I am prepared to accept it. Why do you not offer us the same for propensity?" (This is not a quotation.)

My answer is: All right, I will, although I must point out that I disagree with your interpretation of de Finetti's achievement, and it seems that you fail to notice the disanalogies between your three Definitions (3), (4), and (5) (of the classical, frequency, and subjective interpretations respectively) on which you base your criticism. In fact, the propensity interpretation is as good an interpretation of your third (de Finetti) definition (Definition 5), as is your own subjectivist interpretation. It can be related to de Finetti's formal rules in precisely the same way as is de Finetti's or your own subjectivist interpretation.

My thesis is simply this: Suppes's (or de Finetti's) formal definition, and the formal axioms of which it is composed, can be looked upon as *theorems of the calculus of probability* (or of a slightly specialized version of it). They have to be satisfied, therefore, by *every* admissible interpretation—whether subjective, frequency, classical, or propensity.

This remark contains in a nutshell, I think, a fairly complete reply to Suppes's main criticism. But it absolves me neither from explaining it more fully nor from trying to do a little more about axiomatizing propensity.

I will not dwell on certain defects of Suppes's paradigm definitions (3), (4), and (5), such as the absence of conditions of randomness (so that according to the definitions the swing of a pendulum is as good an object to apply these theories to as is the fall of a spinning coin). For he alludes (I think) himself to these defects (although only in connection with his Definition 3) and so we can perhaps neglect them for the present discussion. A defect of a different kind adheres to Suppes's Definition 5, the subjective interpretation: the one which he himself favours and the one which he sets up as the best of his models—as the ideal of which I fall short so badly. This definition incorporates equiprobable "atoms"; a fact which appears to me to confine or specialize the subjective theory to expectations concerning homogeneous dice or spinning coins (or, as just mentioned, swinging pendulums), and to exclude all numerically less cut and dried expectations such as would be connected with a *loaded* die. To my mind this specialization almost destroys the intuitive appeal of the subjective interpretation. But for argument's sake I am quite ready to overlook even this defect of Suppes's definitions, provided always that he reciprocates with comparable generosity and allows me in the present argument a similar degree of superficiality.

If this is taken for granted, then the following lack of symmetry between Suppes's three definitions becomes clear.

Theorem 1. If we confine ourselves to applications of Suppes's Definition 4 to symmetrical games of chance with equal "atomic" frequencies, then Suppes's Definition 5 is satisfied by objects satisfying his Definitions 3 and 4, but not vice versa.

Or more precisely, a system of equal "relative frequencies" (and their disjunctions and complements) relative to a fixed reference sequence X satisfies the qualitative relationship $A \geq B$ of Suppes's Definition 5, if we interpret "$A \geq B$" to mean "the relative frequency of A (given X) is greater or equal to that of B (given the same X)". An analogous theorem holds for a system of equal "possibilities" in the sense of Definition 3. But a system of subjective probabilities, or, as Suppes calls it in his Theorem 3 (in Definition 5 he omits the keyword "subjective") "a finite qualitative subjective probability structure with equal atoms", cannot be said to satisfy all the stipulations of either Suppes's Definition 3 or his Definition 4. The result can be generalized.

Theorem 2. Take any "structure" of objects $\mathscr{X} = \ <X, \mathscr{F}, P>$ which is a finitely additive probability space in the sense of Suppes's Definition 2.

Define $A \leq B$ if and only if $P(A) \leq P(B)$; assume *in addition* that the structure is atomic, and that for any two atoms X, Y

$$P(X) = P(Y);$$

then the conditions of Suppes's Definition 5 are theorems which are valid for this structure.

It will be seen that the assumption made *"in addition"* in this theorem is a defect; but this is the same defect which I pointed out above in Suppes's Definition 5, and I therefore am entitled to ask that it be overlooked here and in what follows.

My Theorem 2 says in brief that, formally considered, Suppes's Definition 5 consists of theorems; and that it imposes, contrary to his suggestion, no limitation whatever upon our choice of interpretation of probability theory. It holds for *all* interpretations (always overlooking the atomistic defect); and it must therefore not be claimed, as it is claimed by Suppes, that it characterizes the *subjective* interprctation. Or to put the same thing differently, Suppes's Definition 5 is of the nature of a representation theorem rather than a definition. It therefore holds for propensities just as well as for subjective probabilities.

Thus Suppes is mistaken as far as his arguments in favour of the subjective interpretation are concerned. But this does not mean that he is not right in claiming that more should be done in connection with the axiomatization of the propensity interpretation.

II

The Propensity Interpretation. The propensity interpretation of probability, like the Newtonian idea of force, may be described as a "metaphysical idea". Newtonian forces are dispositions that act upon the velocities of masses and change them. They may thus be regarded as measurable by the change of velocity, that is, by acceleration. Thus the question was raised (by Hertz) whether Newtonian mechanics may do without forces and simply deal with velocities and their changes. No doubt it can. Yet it seems to me that it is more fruitful not to be afraid of these metaphysical dispositions, but even to locate them in space. In this way we may arrive at the idea of a field of forces; and we may learn that not only matter can be real, but fields of forces also.

I suggest that propensities are real dispositions; dispositions that determine relative frequencies rather than accelerations. Relative frequencies of what? The answer to this question is: of any occurrences you may consider; for example, of accelerations; or else, of the absorption or emission of light (of photons) or of the creation of a pair of (positive and negative) electrons.

Propensities can, in the limit, become Newtonian forces. This is the "causal" limit of propensities equal to 1. If a propensity is less than 1, then it is a disposition to produce the effect not always but in a proportion of cases if the situation repeats itself.

Thus I see propensities as an indeterministic generalization of an (anti-Humean) view of causes, and more especially of forces (that is, causes of acceleration). Propensities are, like forces, "occult" entities. They are something like (a) indeterministic (or not fully reliable) "causes" of certain occurrences and (b) causes (of an almost-deterministic character) determining frequencies if the situation—for example, the experimental arrangement which gives rise to the propensity—repeats itself. They may be envisaged as determining virtual frequencies.

Suppes comments on my views about the analogies between propensities and Newtonian forces: "I would again raise the same question I have been raising. Already in the case of Newtonian forces there are explicit formal laws . . .: the laws of addition of forces. . .[and] the law that the force exerted by one particle on another be equal and opposite . . .[But] I find no systematic laws whatsoever that the propensity interpretation is to satisfy, except the formal laws of probability already embodied in Definition 2." (Definition 2 is Suppes's definition of probability.)

My reply to this criticism is as follows.

First, as I have explained, Suppes's criticism also applies to his own most favoured interpretation, the subjective interpretation.

Secondly, there is an addition law for propensities, as there is one for forces. That this law is part of the probability calculus is perfectly true, but this is so because the calculus of relative probability (as axiomatized, say, in my *L.Sc.D.*) is a good axiomatization of the general theory of propensity.

Thirdly, there is a fairly clear and very important idea, the idea of the *independence of two or more events*. This idea can be formalized, or defined, by a formal definition more or less in Suppes's style.[182] Yet *this does not explain* the cases which we regard as independent; for this purpose, examples are needed, and perhaps the two most important examples are these.

(1) Experiments conducted under conditions—for example, temporal and spatial separation—excluding any causal interference are independent.

(2) An experiment and its repetition are independent, provided the repetition reproduces the conditions of the original experiment with sufficient precision. (Examples for (2): most physical experiments of a causal character;

or dicing with the same or with a physically equivalent die, *whether loaded or not*, provided the beaker is properly shaken, which, we assume, ensures repetition of the conditions of the experiment.)

The theories of independence and of nonindependence of various kinds (especially of Markov processes) belong to those of greatest interest within probability theory. But while the formal definition of independence can of course be extended to the subjective and the frequency interpretations, the explanation of the idea of independence by way of examples, as here given, makes sense, I think, only within the propensity interpretation and what I call the logical interpretation. (The latter is never referred to by Suppes.) That is, no examples for independence can be given within the subjective inter-pretation—only examples for *irrelevance* (irrelevant information).

Thus if I am dicing with a die which is heavily loaded, then the results obtained by earlier trials with the same die are *not irrelevant* for betting on a new trial, while from the propensity point of view the new trial will indeed be fully *independent* of the old ones, provided only that the new trial was properly conducted—that is, provided the beaker was properly shaken. This we regard as sufficient to destroy any causal influence of the earlier experiments upon the new one, thus ensuring the new one's independence from its predecessors.

Now in view of the fact that independence can be formally defined, we have here a difference, amenable to formalization, between the propensity interpretation and the subjective interpretation.

I think that these three points would be sufficient as a reply to Suppes's criticism; but more can be said.

Suppes stresses the significance of Kolmogorov's axiomatization of probability theory and he mentions that in my paper [1959(e)] I "indicated some reservations about that axiomatization . . . , but [Suppes continues] those reservations are minor and not a serious issue here". It is a pity that, in spite of his interest in axiomatics, Suppes did not go a little deeper into this matter; for at the place he quotes I refer to my fairly full discussions in the new appendices to my *Logic of Scientific Discovery*; and I think that if Suppes had followed up this reference, he might have regarded the issue as serious.

For one of my several major reservations about Kolmogorov's ax-iomatization is that Kolmogorov operates with what I call "absolute" rather than "relative" probabilities; and he is followed in this by Suppes.

In my *Logic of Scientific Discovery* I tried to explain (see, for example, pp. 325 and 329-33; see also n. 12 on p. 346) why this point is important *formally*. Besides, it is of paramount importance for what I call the logical interpretation of probability, and it is of almost equal importance for the propensity interpretation.

In my axiomatization, it is demonstrable that all laws of Boolean algebra follow from my axioms even though any one of these axioms is "autonomously independent", that is, independent of the others even if they are strengthened by all the laws of Boolean algebra. This means that none of my axioms depends on a law of Boolean algebra—as would an axiom of commutation like $p(ab) = p(ba)$ or $p(ab,c) = p(ba,c)$ or some similar axiom—and that none of them formulates, perhaps in a hidden way, a law of Boolean algebra. But as the laws of Boolean algebra, and thus of propositional logic, are derivable, I can claim that my axiomatization of probability theory may be *interpreted as a genuine generalization of propositional logic* (or more precisely, of what Tarski calls "sentential algorithm"; see his *Logic, Semantics, Metamathematics*, 1956, p. 348).

It is usually assumed (and I once thought so myself)[183] that there is not much to choose between an axiomatization based on absolute probabilities, and one based on relative probabilities, since in the first case we can define relative probability by

DR   If $p(b) \neq 0$ then $p(a,b) = p(ab)/p(b)$,

while in the second case we can define absolute probability in various ways, for example, by

DA $p(a) = p(a,(aa')')$.

But this assumption is mistaken: DR is conditional; and the condition of DR, that is, $p(b) \neq 0$, is very important since it leaves $p(a,b)$ undefined if $p(b) = 0$. This means, among other things, that the so-called "general law of multiplication",

$$p(ab) = p(a)p(b,a),$$

is not generally and unconditionally valid, since $p(b,a)$ is undefined if $p(a) = 0$.

Three formulae which are particularly important for *the logical interpretation of probability* are not generally valid in an absolute system in which relative probabilities are introduced by the definition DR; they are:

(1) $a \leq b$ if, and only if, $p(a,c) \leq p(b,c)$ for every c;
(2) $a \geq b$ if, and only if, $p(a,bc) = 1$ for every c;
(3) $a \geq b$ if, and only if, $p(a,ba') = 1$.

To return now to the problem of the propensity interpretation, I suggest that the only adequate axiomatization is a system of relative probabilities in which (1), (2), and (3) are derivable. And although I do not claim that I can give a formal definition of propensities, I claim that I can add some laws to the axiom system which hold for the logical interpretation, but not for the propensity interpretation, and some others which hold for the propensity interpretation, but not for the logical interpretation. Note, however, that we have no right to say that these distinguishing laws are definitions; there may be hundreds of other interpretations which satisfy the one set or the other. They are, rather, of the nature of additional axioms or postulates; and I will call them so.

We begin by postulating the existence of a system S of elements a, b, ... on which (at least) two nonidentical valuations or measures are defined, $pl(a,b)$, the *logical probability* of a given b, and $pr(a,b)$, the (natural) *propensity* of a given b, or the propensity of a to occur in the situation described by the conditions b. We assume that S can be, ambiguously, interpreted as the *set of the statements* of some language, or as the set of the *corresponding states of affairs* described by those statements. The first interpretation is appropriate for the logical probabilities, the second for the propensities.

Our postulates amount to the metaphysical (or methodological) view that there exist laws of nature, and that these are either strictly deterministic or "causal", or indeterministic and probabilistic. However, I shall first state the postulates and discuss their significance later. (The system of postulates here given is not intended to be independent.)

Postulate 1. If a is in S, then its complement a' (read: "not-a") is in S; and if a and b are in S, then their intersection or conjunction ab is in S.

Corollary 1. If a and b are in S, then their union or disjunction $a \lor b$ is in S.

Postulate 2. The axioms A1-3, B1-2, C of the probability calculus in *The Logic of Scientific Discovery*, new Appendices *iv and *v, hold for $pl(a,b)$ and for $pr(a,b)$.

Postulate 3. There are elements a, b, in S such that

$$pl(a,b) \neq pr(a,b).$$

Corollary 2. There is a nonempty subclass L of S consisting of all those elements a of S which satisfy the formula

$$pl(a,a') = 1.$$

I call these the L-true elements ("tautologies") of S.

Corollary 3. There is a nonempty subclass Lr of S consisting of all those elements a of S which satisfy the formula

$$pr(a,a') = 1.$$

I call these the causal or deterministic lawlike regularities of S.

Postulate 4. If a is in S, and if $pr(a,a') = 1$, then a is true, in the sense of

Tarski; but not vice versa.

Postulate 5. L is a subclass of *Lr*, but not vice versa.

Clearly, Postulate 3 is not independent of Postulate 5; for the latter is obviously equivalent to the following

Corollary 4.

(a) If *a* is in *S*,

$$pl(a,a') = 1 \text{ entails } pr(a,a') = 1;$$

(b) Yet there is an *a* in *S* such that

$$pr(a,a') = 1 \text{ and } pl(a,a') \neq 1.$$

In view of the general theory of *The Logic of Scientific Discovery*, (b) entails further

Corollary 5. There is an *a* in *S* such that

$$pr(a,a') = 1 \text{ and } pl(a,a') = 0.$$

Postulate 6. There is a nonempty subclass *Ln* of *Lr* such that $L \neq Ln \subset Lr$, and such that for every *a* in *Ln*,
   if *b* and *c* are in *S*, then

$$\text{if } b \text{ is in } L \text{ and } pl(c, b) \neq 0 \text{ then } pl(a, c) = 0.$$

The class *Ln* may be called the class of (true) causal theories, or *deterministic laws of nature*.

Postulate 7. Let *a* and *b* be in *S*, and let *X* be a subclass of *S*; and then write "*pl(a,b,X)*" for "the logical probability of *a* given *b* assuming *X*", or "in the presence of the elements of *X*"; we then have:

$$pr(a,a'b) = 1 \text{ if, and only if, } pl(a,a'b,Ln) = 1;$$

or in other words, causal or deterministic propensities are *in the presence of the causal or deterministic laws of nature* equal to logical probabilities. (Note that the formula "*pl(a,a'b,Ln)* = 1" can be interpreted as "*a* follows from *b* in the presence of *Ln*", or as "*b* is a sufficient condition of *a* in the presence of *Ln*".)

We can therefore interpret

$$pr(a,a'b) = 1$$

as a *subjunctive conditional* with *b* as antecedent or condition and *a* as consequent. (It has I think all the properties of a subjunctive conditional or, in case *b* happens to be false, of a so-called "counterfactual conditional". The latter is a misleading term since it draws undue attention to a special case, the falsity of the sufficient condition *b*.)

So far we have discussed only cases of logical probabilities and propensities equal to 1 or to 0; in fact, we have confined our attention to cases in which the negation of the first argument occurred in the second argument, that is, to cases reducible to logical deducibility. (We used the rule of augmentation of the premises of an inference which says "whenever a follows from b, it also follows from bc for every c, and therefore follows from ba' "; thus augmentation of the premises by a' leaves the deducibility of a invariant, a fact which can be used as a kind of criterion of the deducibility relation.)

The first step in our generalization is to drop a' and to interpret

$$pr(a,b) = 1$$

as "the conditions b are at least almost sufficient to produce a". $pr(a,b) = 1$ is *merely* an "almost sufficient" condition of a if, in addition to $pr(a,b) = 1$, $pr(a,a'b) = 0$ holds. We interpret $pr(a,b) = 1$ as "the conditions b almost invariably produce a", where the word "almost" has the same meaning as it has in mathematics.

The next step is that we interpret

$$pr(a,b) = r \ (0 \leq r \leq 1)$$

as "the conditions b have a natural tendency or propensity of the degree r (or measure r) to produce a"; and we postulate:

Postulate 8.[184] If $pr(a,b) = r$, and if the conditions b are reproducible, then (a) the relative frequency of the result a upon reproduction of the conditions b will, if the number of repetitions is ("sufficiently") large, be close to r; and (b) any method of ordering the trials into a series independent of the outcome will be approximately independent in the probabilistic sense (or approximately ideally random in the sense of *L.Sc.D.,* Appendix *vi).

Thus far my attempt to supply what Suppes has found missing. It should be noted that in view of our postulates, the propensity interpretation differs formally from all the others discussed by Suppes *and* from the logical interpretation discussed here by myself.

The contrast with the subjective interpretation, in particular, is very clear and striking. Decisive is *Postulate* 4 in which truth is used. This ensures that propensities are something objective. And it turns out that in practice *all subjective guesses or estimates of probabilities are attempts to guess or estimate an objective propensity.*

Of course, in the absence of complete knowledge of what the value of the propensity of a given b is, we can only *guess* or *conjecture* what it is. But although these guesses are "subjective", *they are always conjectures about the objective world*, exactly like our other theories, especially those which we conjecture belong to *Ln*.

It is clear that the subject is a large one, and that our postulates merit detailed discussion. I shall have to leave this for another occasion, but I shall add a few odd comments.

(1) To the different propensities correspond different subjunctive conditionals; the following are possible examples.

$pr(a,a'b) = 1$. This is the case of the causal conditional, such as: "Should this piece of sugar be placed into water, it would definitely (or necessarily) dissolve."

$pr(a,b) = 1$. This is the case of a high propensity: "Should this piece of sugar be placed into water, it would (almost certainly) dissolve."

$pr(a,b) = r$. This is the general case for which the frequency interpretation becomes relevant: "Should this piece of sugar be placed into water, it would dissolve with probability r, and upon repetition of the experiment (that is, upon reproduction of b) we should get a relative frequency of positive outcomes a (dissolving) close to the number r."

This shows that we can generalize subjunctive conditionals, and that subjunctive conditionals expressing "natural or physical necessity" are only one special class.

Any of these examples can be a counterfactual without its truth value's being affected either way by the falsity of the antecedent. This is partly connected with the fact that a statement of relative probability has a very different structure from a conditional; in fact, we have the formula for the excess probability of the conditional over relative probability:

$$Exc(a,b) = p(b \supset a) - p(a,b) = (1-p(a,b))p(b').$$

See *Conjectures and Refutations*, page 396. Thus the excess is never negative, and it can reach unity. This holds for all interpretations. In case $a \lor b' \ \epsilon \ Lr$, the propensity excess is always zero.

(A good example for analysis is the statement: "Had I not thrown the loaded die, which I still had yesterday, into the fire, the probability of six turning up at the next throw, after proper shaking, would be about 0.20 rather than 0.166, as it would be with a homogeneous die." As a propensity statement, the truth or the falsity of this statement depends entirely on the structural physical properties of the die before it was thrown into the fire.)

(2) I do not very much like the term "natural [or physical] necessity", but there is no great harm in this terminology, and I have used it in *The Logic of Scientific Discovery*, Appendix *x. But our analysis shows that, in spite of great differences, there is an analogy between logical and natural necessity. This is brought out here very clearly by the analogy between

$$pl(a,a'b) = 1 \text{ and } pr(a,a'b) = 1;$$

or in other words, between the logical interpretation and the propensity interpretation of the probability calculus.

(3) It should be noted that—owing especially to *Postulate* 4—our theory of propensities is, as it stands, a physical and a metaphysical hypothesis. *It implies that there are true deterministic causal laws.* Note however that even if the class of elements a satisfying $pr(a,a') = 1 \neq pl(a,a')$ should be empty, there could still be propensities.[185] In this case we should have to weaken our system of postulates; here I tried to make it strong, in order to exclude formally as many other interpretations as possible, in response to Suppes's challenge.

(4) It should also be noted that the role of the second argument b of $p(a,b)$ is utterly different in $pl(a,b)$ and in $pr(a,b)$, and again different in the subjective interpretation. This point was strongly emphasized by me in a paper in *Dialectica* [1957(1)], but it seems that nobody has taken any notice of it.[186]

III

Propensities in Physics, Especially Quantum Physics. In his section 2, Suppes proceeds, after some very flattering remarks on my criticism of Birkhoff and von Neumann's famous paper on the logic of quantum mechanics, to point out a number of important difficulties which beset the statistical interpretation of quantum mechanics.

I propose to proceed differently. I will not say anything further about my paper on the proposals made by Birkhoff and von Neumann; I will merely record here that Suppes does not seem to object to my thesis that quantum mechanics needs *singular* probability statements (which have so far been explained either as subjective or, by myself, as statements of propensities); and I will proceed as quickly as I can to a survey of the situation in quantum mechanics as I see it.

If there exist propensities other than prima facie deterministic or causal ones then our world is essentially of an indeterministic character. (See my Compton Memorial Lecture, *Of Clouds and Clocks* [1966(f)], now Chap. 6 of [1972(a)].) I am inclined to conjecture that the opposite is also true: if our world is indeterministic—and I conjecture that it is—then there must exist genuine propensities. I will try to explain this.

The existence of propensities $\neq 1$ (or, to demand less, of propensities other than $pr(a,aa') = 1$) means the existence of lawlike dispositions which lead to randomlike sequences. This may be made clear with the help of several considerations, for example, the following five.

(1) We can assume that there are two categories of laws: laws of a causal or prima facie deterministic character, and laws which constantly operate on the microphysical initial conditions, changing them in a Gauss-like manner

so that, as a consequence, they will show a Gaussian scatter over the intervals within which they are confined (either by Markovian aftereffect or by our experimental arrangements). As a consequence, there is a tendency towards a statistical equilibrium (Second Law of Thermodynamics).

(2) We can assume that the "ether", or perhaps the "empty space", is a propensity field that acts upon particles in the way in which the molecular heat-motion (Brownian motion) acts upon suspended Brownian bodies.

(3) We could also assume that metrical space is intrinsically probabilistic (that it is a Menger space); for example, the distances between particles may not be sharp in themselves, but essentially of the character of a Gaussian distribution (due either to an intrinsic movement of the particles or to some intrinsic lack of sharp localizability of particles, which may thus behave essentially like Gaussian wave packets, or as if they were "smeared", as Schrödinger had it).

(4) We could also assume that in interaction, the fields of force are indeterminate or essentially fluctuating.

(5) Of particular interest are the theories of Imre Fényes, very clearly developed by Edward Nelson, and the new topological (and indeterministic) theory of David Bohm. Both are attempts to explain, and to supersede, the present quantum mechanics.

The theory of Fényes[187] and Nelson[188] starts from the assumption that particles perform a "trembling movement" (*Zitterbewegung*), that is a Markov process with a diffusion coefficient equal to $h/4\pi m$, where m is the mass of the particle. It is then shown that the Schrödinger equation holds for such a particle, and that Born's statistical interpretation—the square of the amplitude determines the probability—holds for the probability of its being in a certain *position* (though not necessarily for all other observables). This, as shown by Nelson, is sufficient to ensure that there cannot arise a discrepancy between observations predicted by this theory and those of ordinary quantum mechanics.

It is important to realize that the theory of Fényes and Nelson operates with *noncausal "hidden" variables*;[189] and it is especially important to realize that this theory, which differs mathematically from quantum mechanics, allows for a statistical interpretation of the Schrödinger equation in terms of noncausal hidden variables. It thereby destroys the usual philosophical morals drawn from von Neumann's proof; for example, by von Neumann himself and by many others. It would be most interesting to see the results of J. Bell,[190] and those of S. Kochen and E. P. Specker[191] discussed in the light of these findings.

Quantum theory contains much more, of course, than the Schrödinger equation, and it is not clear how the other results can be derived from this extremely simple and elegant statistical theory. But I am sure that nobody whose memory goes back to 1926-1927—to the reception of Schrödinger's theory, and of Born's statistical interpretation—can doubt that if this derivation of Schrödinger's equation had been available in 1927, quantum physics would have had a different history. The Copenhagen interpretation would never have been produced; it would have been totally unacceptable, and nobody would even have thought of it.

David Bohm's theory[192] is much more ambitious, and goes much deeper; it is the most impressive attempt towards a reform of quantum theory I have seen. And it does not merely reform quantum theory; it is a more radical departure from classical physics than quantum theory, and at the same time wholly realistic. It shares with the theory of Fényes and Nelson the "trembling movement" of the particles. But it does not assume it; it derives it from a new topological theory of space-time.

Both theories[193] establish the fact that it is not impossible to obtain something better than the Copenhagen interpretation of quantum mechanics, with its subjectivism and its many paradoxes.

Among the paradoxes are the ones connected with the problem of joint probability distributions of noncommuting observables.

Suppes says that he was "surprised not to find more explicit comment on these matters" in my writings. I am sorry for the omission, but the reason is that these matters seemed to me rather fluid and beyond my unaided powers. They were, I think, originally discussed by M. S. Bartlett and J. E. Moyal,[194] and more lately mainly by Henry Margenau and his school,[195] who achieved most important results.

These results are, as Suppes indicates, very surprising, if not paradoxical; or in the words of Park and Margenau, they are "historical, accidental, and extraordinary".

They are certainly all this. But if we accept, for example, the theory of Fényes and Nelson, then all these difficulties disappear.

The simple fact is that the constantly repeated claims of the orthodox quantum theorists are invalid. It is not true that there is only *one* consistent interpretation of the formalism—the Copenhagen interpretation—and that quantum theory, like Capitalism according to Marx, cannot be reformed but can only be destroyed. On the contrary, there seems to be a plurality of interpretations of the formalism and many possibilities of reforming the theory by *deriving it as an approximation.*[196]

I have of course never dreamt of being able to do this myself. I only fought against the orthodox denial of this possibility, and for the need to work for its realization. My wager, different from Suppes's, is that the Copenhagen spirits—the subjective observers—will be laid, and that with them will vanish most of the extraordinary joint distributions, and some at least of the other paradoxes of the present theory.

38. Grünbaum on Time and Entropy

Professor Grünbaum's most careful and closely reasoned paper is very difficult to reply to. On many of the questions he discusses I agree with him. (Our first disagreement in *Nature*[197] can, I think, be buried: it seems to me that what Grünbaum and Hill[198] actually wrote was open to the interpretation I put on it, but that my interpretation was incorrect in the sense of having been at odds with what they intended to convey.) About other questions, such as the usefulness or relevance of Reichenbach's "branch systems" (an idea originating in Schrödinger's attempt to find a sound and unquestionable basis for Boltzmann's cosmological hypothesis of the subjectivity of the arrow of time) we disagree; but I feel far from confident that this is the place for me to start a discussion of a topic which I find interesting but not central, and about which I cannot recall having committed myself in writing in the past.

I

Let me start perhaps by making clear why I am interested in the philosophy of time, and in that problem which can be presented with the help of the metaphor "The Arrow of Time".

I am a realist and an objectivist, in several senses of these terms, and an opponent of most forms of idealism and subjectivism. I think that there are good reasons to conjecture that this world of ours existed long before plants and animals existed, and that there are the incredible facts of emergence and evolution. These may be described as processes—perhaps even as irreversible processes, though I do not see any reason why life should not begin some day to revert to more primitive forms, and eventually disappear. If so, it would be a great pity, but it would not affect the direction of time. It is trivial that we can if we wish denote the time coordinate with the help of decreasing numerals—that we can undertake all kinds of transformations, among them $t' = -t$. But from my realistic viewpoint this does not alter the fact that *time has a direction, over and above being anisotropic*.

Let us consider a railway line, consisting of two horizontal sets of rails. There are two directions, and they are, we may assume, perfectly symmetrical. It is quite indifferent whether we count the distances from some arbitrarily chosen point with the help of the series of positive integers, $+1$, $+2, \ldots$, or whether we call the chosen point "$+2$" and count: $+2, +1, 0, -1$, $-2, \ldots$. Is time like this? Both Grünbaum and I say "No". It is anisotropic: that is, it is more like a railway line running up an incline: there is some asymmetry. So far we agree.

But is this all? If the railway line runs up in one direction, it runs down in the opposite direction: its asymmetry or anisotropy has no preferred or singled-out direction. It seems to me (but I may be mistaken) that this is the way Grünbaum envisages time: it is anisotropic, and there are thus two nonequivalent directions to it. But it has *not*, he seems to say, one inherent direction, as would have a one-way road, or a pair of rails on which trains only move upwards (whether or not there is another pair on which they only move downwards), or an escalator. I conjecture that it is part of the structure of our spatiotemporal universe that time is not only anisotropic but has in addition a direction; that there is not only the relation of betweenness in its topology, but also the relation of before and after. And that the *words* "before" and "after" are of course as conventional as the numerals by which we may characterize time, but that the relation denoted by these words is part of the structure of reality, so that time has an arrow.

It is clear, and we do not need to waste many words over it, that if we speak of time as if it were a physical object or a physical process, we are making a mistake. But it seems to me just as clear that (like all notions) time is a legitimate theoretical notion, and so is the direction of time. Let there be a physical system S which undergoes a completely reversible physical process P, beginning at time t_1 and ending at the time t_2. Let us reverse this process at t_2: this means that after a certain time S will revert to the state it was in at t_1; it will not mean that the time has returned to t_1; when the reversed process comes to an end the time will be t_3, where, if the reversal was perfect, both processes took the same amount of time, $t_3 - t_2 = t_2 - t_1$. But the time will have elapsed (or moved, or run down, or whatever metaphor you like best) *without* running back, or returning in the opposite direction, or changing its "arrow".

This is what I mean when I speak of the "reality" of the "arrow" of time—all very bad metaphors, no doubt. And my view of the universe, or my conjecture about the universe, is such that I should accuse a philosopher, even if he is a realist in other respects, of lapsing into idealism with respect to time if he does not admit the reality of the before-after relationship; its complete objectivity; that is, its independence of what humans or animals think; and thus the reality of the evolution of stars, and of the universe.

I know that Professor Grünbaum is not an idealist; but I suspect (I may be mistaken) that with respect to the arrow of time, he is an idealist.

The last great idealists and great innovators in this field were Boltzmann and Schrödinger. Boltzmann (as I already explained in section 35 of my *Autobiography*) suggested that the world had a time coordinate that was in most respects similar to a space coordinate; that almost always—that is, along almost the whole time axis—the universe was in a state of equilibrium or disorder, with smaller or greater fluctuations of its entropy here or there; and that unusually great fluctuations (or states of low entropy) provided the conditions under which life could arise. This, he thought, explains why in the presence of life there is a tendency for the fluctuation to die down (entropy increase, Second Law of Thermodynamics). And, he added, we experience

time as increasing in the direction in which the entropy increases; and we call
this the "true" direction of time; that is, we experience, and call, this direction the direction from "earlier" to "later". Yet these concepts are subjective,
anthropomorphic. Objectively there is no "sooner" or "later", no "before"
or "after", but there are directions (always two opposite ones) along the time
axis in which the fluctuation dies down; and whichever direction it is that our
fluctuation is dying down in, *that* direction we experience, and call the
direction from the past towards the future—the direction of time.

I am sure that this idealism of Boltzmann's is vastly different from
Grünbaum's view; but I do not know exactly how different. At any rate,
Boltzmann's theory was embraced by Schrödinger, who was thinking largely
along Schopenhauer's lines and saw in Boltzmann's theory the greatest
achievement of physics so far; for here physics invaded and even ruled
philosophy, especially the idealistic philosophy that time is an illusion.

II

It was to attack this view that I wrote that short letter to the editor of
Nature;[199] a letter of thirty-three half-lines that have given rise to much
controversy, leading ultimately to Professor Grünbaum's critical discussion
in the present volume of some of my views. My first argument was directed
against the subjectivism and idealism of Boltzmann's theory: if there existed
nonentropic physical processes which are irreversible, indeed "anything that
decides independently [of entropy] upon the arrow of time", then, as
Schrödinger admitted[200] "Boltzmann's beautiful building collapses".

Grünbaum's and Hill's letter to *Nature* was in support of mine, and this
is one reason why I believe what I hope, that Grünbaum is a realist and an
objectivist.

Professor Grünbaum generously agrees with some of my arguments, and
this should set my mind at rest, were it not that he argues for the connection
between the anisotropy of time and entropy, using a more sophisticated form
of an argument that originated with Schrödinger and was further developed
by Reichenbach and then Grünbaum himself. This is one reason for my
uneasiness. Another is that Professor Grünbaum seems to regard the notions
of "past", "present", and "future" as anthropomorphic; and I think, though
I am not quite sure (there is no suggestion in his present paper), that he once
defended this with the argument that the "present" or "now" plays no part in
objective science.

As I said, I do not wish here to enter into the argument concerning
branch systems, due to Schrödinger, Reichenbach, and Grünbaum. It is a
complex argument, and not of the type that I feel able to represent so simply
and clearly as to arouse genuine insight or conviction in the reader. But I shall
say something in defence of the usefulness of the notions of the past, present,

and future for the description of reality.

III

Like the word "I", the words "here" and "now" belong to the class of words which philosophers call "egocentric particulars"; and being egocentric, they are no doubt anthropocentric or anthropomorphic. Moreover, *they certainly do not occur in theoretical physics.*

All this is a reason to suspect them. And were we to place them somewhere in worlds 1, 2, and 3, we would be tempted to assign them without more ado to world 2, as typically subjectivist notions, not good for the description of world 1, and glaringly absent from the theories of world 3. What world 3 puts in the place of "here" and "now" are objective terms such as "Penn, Buckinghamshire, England", and "October 14, 1970".

All this is undeniable. Nevertheless words like "the past" and "the present" have a world 3 status of their own.

"The present state of the surface of the moon suggests that. . ." is a phrase which is fully legitimate in science, though it is not likely to occur in theoretical physics. "The present age of the universe" is a perfectly good term in cosmology, and one which it would be quite unnecessary and pedantic, if not downright misleading, to replace by "the age of the universe on October 14, 1970". In other words, the past, present, and future are perfectly good terms in cosmology and astronomy, two excellent examples of (to some extent historical) physical sciences. It is fully legitimate to remind the astronomer that what he observes, in certain cases, is the state of a star 1,000 years ago, or of a galaxy 100,000 years ago, where "ago" is just a synonym of "before the present". The fact that these notions do not occur in theoretical physics, and that we replace them by names and dates in history, does not show that they are to be expunged.

Nor are they expungeable. It is perfectly true that astronomers *can* use coordinates instead of speaking of the Great Nebula in Andromeda. But the coordinates go back to the axis and equator of the Earth, to here-and-now terms. (The Earth changes its axis in time; and although we may speak of the north pole of the sky on "October 14, 1970" we must not forget that "October 14, 1970", though in many respects preferable to "now", refers to a zero date which is highly conventional and anthropomorphic. Nobody claims to know even the precise year of the birth of Jesus Christ.)

Thus my thesis is that notions like "the present" are needed, if not in theoretical physics, at any rate in physical science. But I want to claim even more. Theoretical physics uses all the time spatiotemporal variables; and without applications in which these variables are specified (in the last instance with the help of "here and now"), they would have no reasonable function whatever.

IV

I am afraid these arguments have carried me far away from those of Professor Grünbaum's paper. But since it is the main task of the present volume to elucidate my philosophy, it was necessary to explain the broader philosophical context in which those letters to *Nature* are to be understood that started our little disagreement. I conjecture that our present theories of space and time, and our theory of the nature of entropy, will change a good deal in the near future. But I regard it as a philosophical mistake not to take time—the past, present, and future—in a serious spirit of realism. We live in a time of wars in which innocent people are losing their lives every day. True, the past was not better. But we must not cynically look at all this as an illusion, and dodge our responsibility for a better future. A realist theory of time is thus as absolutely essential for ethics as it is (in my view) for physics. Idealism, which once could be disregarded as a harmless fancy of philosophers, has been vaunted as a reason for not taking one's responsibilities seriously. (So far I agree with Lenin.) I know that Grünbaum too is a realist; only I am not sure whether he is fully a realist with respect to time. I am indebted to him for his wonderfully clear analyses, and for giving me the opportunity to say here a few things on time which I have not, to my knowledge, said elsewhere.

39. Kuhn on the Normality of Normal Science

I was for a time in doubt whether I should perhaps reply to Professors Kuhn and Wisdom together, because the main contents of Professor Wisdom's paper could be brought under the heading "Kuhn versus Popper". I decided however, to adhere to the method I adopted in every other case of replying to each contribution separately.

Professor Kuhn and I met first at one of the most exhilarating times of my life. It was in 1950, on the occasion of my first visit to the United States, as William James Lecturer at Harvard. I gave a series of lectures and seminars, and Kuhn was one of the most interesting members of a select group of students who attended the seminar. (He refers to this occasion in his n. 2.) Not very long after this he and his wife visited me in London; and years later I met him again when I came to Berkeley, where he was a professor.

Kuhn makes it very clear that our views of science have something in common. I agree with him on this point; and I think they have now more in common than they had when he first wrote his book, *The Structure of Scientific Revolutions*. I was pleased and surprised by Kuhn's remark, in the first paragraph of his contribution to the present volume, that he had "admired. . . [Popper's] work for too long to turn critic easily at this date": pleased *and* surprised because several remarks in *The Structure of Scientific*

Revolutions seemed to me to indicate that he did not know my work too well, and that he was somewhat influenced by that version of my views which I have called here the "Popper legend".[201] But I think I should forget, for the time being, all about this, and simply face the question of the similarity and difference between our views.

I

I will turn first to a point of difference with which I can deal briefly because I have discussed it more fully elsewhere.[202] Kuhn has discovered something which I failed to see, and I have derived considerable enlightenment from his discovery, even though my attitude to the phenomenon which Kuhn discovered is very different from his. Kuhn discovered what he has called "normal science" and the "normal scientist". This name refers to a phenomenon which in his opinion, as the name indicates, is "normal". I admit the existence of the phenomenon (which I had before overlooked or not seen in its full significance); but I do not admit the evaluation hinted at by the term "normal": I not only dislike the phenomenon, but I think that it has only recently become very important and, in my opinion, a danger to science.

But I have to admit, before saying anything else, that Kuhn is right when he says (section I) that, prior to his work, I have "ignored" what he calls "normal science": I gladly acknowledge that what he said about "normal science" was an eye-opener for me, even though I do not much care for what I see; one might say that I look at this phenomenon through spectacles very unlike those used by Kuhn.

II

In order to explain this difference, I must remind the reader that in Kuhn's view of the history of science there are two different types of historical periods to be distinguished: (1) *normal periods*, in which there is *an established "routine" of puzzle solving*; this routine unites the community of normal scientists, and their activities constitute "normal science"; (2) *extraordinary periods*, consisting of a crisis followed by a revolution, which consists in the overthrow of the old routine and in the establishment of a new one. The scientists responsible for the revolution are called "extraordinary scientists" and their revolutionary activities are called "extraordinary science".

I believe that this periodization picture is mistaken, even though there are, no doubt, quieter and less quiet, less and more revolutionary periods in science. But in my opinion, the quieter periods need by no means be periods of the application of a *"routine"*; nor are the more revolutionary periods periods in which a *"routine"* is overthrown and replaced by another.

I am prepared to admit now, following Kuhn, the existence of *"routines"* in science, and thus the existence of what he calls "normal science". But I think that the very idea of a routine is uncharacteristic of science, and consequently that "normal science" is not normal, but uncharacteristic. I think that the phenomenon of a "routine" in science has become more prominent only recently, along with the mass production of scientists; and I think that Kuhn is projecting a comparatively recent phenomenon, which he has personally experienced, not only upon earlier periods but upon the whole long history of science.

I believe that routine played very little role in science until this century, or more precisely, until the First World War. Kuhn believes that routine characterizes the essence of science. There can hardly be two opinions more diametrically opposed.

It will now be seen why I overlooked or "ignored" the phenomenon called by Kuhn "normal science" or "routine": I closed my eyes to it because it was a kind of modern blemish in my essentially routine-free picture of science. From the point of view of evolutionary theory, routines seem to me more characteristic of the way in which animals "know", or adjust themselves to their environment; man, in inventing human language, which is descriptive and argumentative, has begun to replace *routine* more and more by a *critical approach*; and I see in science the most advanced application of this critical approach to the growth of human knowledge.

That routine plays such a role in our century is to be explained by the sudden need for huge numbers of trained technologists; a consequence of the modern armaments race, perhaps.

But "routine" may well take over, may completely supersede science. This is a danger to which I was blind before Kuhn opened my eyes. We may soon move into a period where Kuhn's criterion of a science—a community of workers held together by a *routine*—becomes accepted in practice. If so, this will be the end of science as I see it.

III

Kuhn and I agree that astrology is not a science, and Kuhn explains why from his point of view it is not a science. This explanation seems to me entirely unconvincing: *from his point of view* astrology should be accepted as a science. For it has all the properties which Kuhn uses to characterize science: there is a community of practitioners who share a routine, and who are engaged in puzzle solving. ("Puzzles" are, so far as I can understand, minor problems which do not affect the routine, or the beliefs linked up with the routine.)

Once this has been seen we may find, in a couple of years' time, the great foundations supporting astrological research. From Kuhn's sociological point of view, astrology would then be socially recognised as a science.

This would in my opinion be only a minor disaster; the major disaster would be the replacement of a rational criterion of science by a sociological one.

IV

As I have said before, I see in science (whenever I look at it in an evolutionary context) the conscious and critical form of an adaptive method of trial and error.

This is why I say that we (from the amoeba to Einstein) learn from our mistakes. This is also why I say that science—that is, scientific discovery—is "revolution in permanence".

I do not mean by this that we cannot distinguish in science between periods of stagnation (as Watkins calls them) and more revolutionary and progressive periods; or that all periods are permanently "revolutionary" *in that sense in which we speak* of a Copernican, a Galilean, a Newtonian, and an Einsteinian "revolution".

I mean something very different. I mean that even a minor discovery (it may be made by an animal) is revolutionary. I mean that many engineers and technologists are minor or major revolutionaries. I mean, more precisely, that established beliefs (or routines) are overthrown every day. Sometimes these are major discoveries: more often they are very minor discoveries. The heating engineer who faces the problem of how to install a central heating system required to work under unusual conditions may just apply his established rules of thumb, and thus fail to solve the problem: in the face of this failure he may depart from his routine and (after eliminating several possible solutions) arrive at a critical solution of his problem. He will have acted as an applied scientist in my sense of the word, and he will have made a minor discovery by critical thinking, by the critical rejection of erroneous solutions.

I suspect that Kuhn would say that this is just puzzle solving in his sense, and that my heating engineer was a "normal" scientist. But I have stressed that he had to depart from his usual practice in order to find his solution; most of the time he may be a "normal" scientist in Kuhn's sense, since most of the time he is just following his routine. But when he works by trial and the elimination of error, and when he eliminates the error by a *critical* survey of tentative solutions, then he does not work in this routine manner; which for me makes him a scientist. But Kuhn, who takes the routine as essential for science, should either say that he was not a scientist, or an extraordinary one. But since the latter term is confined by Kuhn to those major revolutions in which *a new routine* is established, this would be going a bit too far.

V

Kuhn, in his criticism of my views, thinks that when I think of science I have only the extraordinary scientists, the major revolutionaries, in mind. Admittedly, I have them in mind; but not exclusively. I sometimes suspect that I have written too often that "from the amoeba to Einstein there is just one step" (the new step is the conscious and critical search for one's errors); but in view of Kuhn's attribution to me of the mistake of seeing only major revolutions as scientific, I have written it once again, for I clearly have not yet written it often enough.

VI

Of course, the central issue between Kuhn and myself is given in Kuhn's title "Logic of Discovery or Psychology of Research?". My answer to this has been given more than once in this volume. Science is part of world 3, and not of world 2; or more precisely, the psychological world 2 of the scientist is almost completely dependent upon the man-made world 3, the world of scientific theories and problems. The world 3 science can be investigated only logically. Thus any good psychology of research will have to depend on, and be guided by, the logic of discovery.

I must not conclude this reply without referring again to what is in my opinion a much better rejoinder to Kuhn's criticisms: John Watkins's.[203]

40. Wisdom on the Similarity between Kuhn and Popper

Professor Wisdom's contribution, entitled "The Nature of 'Normal' Science" is fundamentally an attempt to reconcile my views with those of Professor Kuhn. In fact, its title could well have been: "Kuhn and Popper: A Reconciliation".

I agree with much that Wisdom says, though not with all.

That Wisdom is right in seeing some similarity between Kuhn's views and my own may perhaps be illustrated by the following passage from a paper of mine, written early in 1963 (see [1963(h)]), which I wrote before I had seen Kuhn's book The Structure of Scientific Revolutions (1962).[204]

> The intellectual history of man has its depressing as well as its exhilarating aspects. For one may well look upon it as a history of prejudice and dogma, tenaciously held, and often combined with intolerance and fanaticism. One may even describe it as a history of spells of religious or quasi-religious frenzy. It should be remembered, in this context, that most of our great destructive wars have been religious or ideological wars—with the notable exception, perhaps, of the wars of Genghis Khan who seems to have been a model of religious toleration.
>
> Yet even the sad and depressing picture of religious wars has its brighter side. It is an encouraging fact that countless men, from ancient to modern times,

have been ready to live and to die for their convictions, for ideas—ideas which they believed to be true.

Man, we may say, appears to be not so much a rational animal as an ideological animal.

The history of science, even of modern science since the Renaissance, and especially since Francis Bacon, may be taken as an illustration. The movement inaugurated by Bacon was a religious or semi-religious movement, and Bacon was the prophet of the secularized religion of science. He replaced the name "God" by the name "Nature"; but almost everything else he left unchanged. Theology, the science of God, was replaced by the science of Nature; the laws of God were replaced by the laws of Nature; God's power was replaced by the forces of Nature; and at a later date, God's design and God's judgements were replaced by natural selection. Theological determinism was replaced by scientific determinism, and the book of fate by the predictability of Nature; that is to say, God's omnipotence and omniscience were replaced by the omnipotence of Nature and by the virtual omniscience of natural science.

But the paper goes on, and this is its main point, to defend rationalism in spite of the church of the religious movement founded by Bacon.

I

As far as Kuhn's explicit criticisms of my views in his *Structure of Scientific Revolutions* are concerned, I did not take them very seriously, since he was obviously influenced by misunderstandings (more precisely by the Popper legend). The only criticism which struck me as vital and deserved was—as I have said in my reply to Kuhn—my complete neglect of what Kuhn calls "normal science"; and I have fully accepted this criticism, though in a spirit which is barely compatible with Kuhn's own. For I see in the phenomenon called by Kuhn "normal science" a dangerous threat to what I cherish as "science".

Wisdom sees it otherwise, because he is struck by a neglect (both his own and mine) of certain scientific activities which fall into Kuhn's category of "normal science", and which, in my opinion, are scientific because they are critical (and thus in my sense "revolutionary", even though they may be far removed from those big revolutions which Kuhn has in mind). Wisdom's examples (section 1) are mostly of this kind. To determine with more precision the mass of the moon is critical if it neither accepts (confirms) the traditional value uncritically, nor follows slavishly the traditional (or orthodox) methods, but seeks to *improve* on that value by means of *improved* methods; and new methods are always the result of *critical and theoretical* thinking, the result of new ideas (possibly about new applications of well-known theories).

Splendid examples of such highly critical (and in my sense revolutionary) new ideas, ideas, however, which did not induce any big Kuhnian scientific revolution, are the work of the Braggs, and C. T. R.

Wilson's invention and use of the Wilson chamber. Another example of highly critical and revolutionary work that would presumably be classed by Kuhn as "normal" is that of A. H. Compton. But perhaps the best examples of revolutionary discoveries which failed to create at once a new "paradigm" are the work of Röntgen, Becquerel, the Curies, and (of course) Rutherford. This was work whose significance I never overlooked, and which I should have regarded no more as "routine" or "puzzle solving" than the work of Newton or Einstein.

When Wisdom says that he and I have neglected "normal science" in Kuhn's sense, I agree. But I disagree when Wisdom accepts Kuhn's application of "normal scientists" to all those scientists who did not immediately produce, by a "Gestalt switch", an extraordinary revolution. I completely agree, however, with the implications of Wisdom's section heading (in his section 1) " 'Normal' Science as Puzzle-Solving and as Daily Rebellion". I disagree only when Wisdom says that "there is no clash with Kuhn (in this area)".

II

After a very good description of "The Role of a Counterexample for Popper", in which Wisdom defends me against misunderstandings on Kuhn's part, and to which I see no cause to add anything, and after another visit to "normal science", Wisdom turns to a section "From Anomaly to Crisis", in which he tries to show that "the apparent difference between their views evaporates" if one presents them clearly. Here, however, I wish to add something.

I think that there have been "anomalies" in Kuhn's sense, such as X-rays, or Becquerel rays, which did not create on their own any crisis in Kuhn's psychological or sociological sense. This particular development did lead to the discovery of radium—a great discovery which was universally accepted without a feeling of crisis, and which led to a major revolution in experimentation. It also led to new theories; but although these theories were felt to be pretty incomplete, there was no theoretical crisis in anything like Kuhn's sense, no new revolutionary "paradigm", to use Kuhn's term. Nor was the Einsteinian revolution of Special Relativity dependent on anomalies and crisis. The asymmetries from which Einstein's first relativity paper starts were well known; yet nobody but Einstein looked on them as something to be exterminated. It may even be argued that Einstein did not look upon them as "anomalies" in Kuhn's sense: they did not endanger any of the current theories. He only felt that they were asymmetries which were ugly, and could be removed by his hypothesis of the absolute constancy of the velocity of light. In fact, I do not think that Kuhn's description really fits any of the better known major revolutions.

III

In his next section (section 3) Wisdom turns to "Kuhn's Sociology of Acceptance of New Theories". Wisdom says that "Kuhn gives the impression . . . that scientists who develop a new theory cannot be on speaking terms with scientists of the . . . [old] theory". Wisdom refers here to Kuhn's *The Structure of Scientific Revolutions* (pp. 145-50), and Wisdom comments: "to be specific, [Kuhn holds] that Einsteinian scientists could not really understand Newtonian physics, and the other way around".

Now I am prepared to grant "the other way around": that in order to understand Einstein, Newtonian scientists needed more mathematics than most of them had. So some were prevented from understanding Einstein. But that either Einstein himself, or an Einsteinian physicist, was unable to understand Newton, I deny; and if Kuhn says sometimes something that can be so interpreted, then I think he does not really mean it. Einstein was a great admirer of Newtonian physics, and he understood it probably better than any Newtonian scientist did. (Moreover, it is possible to formulate Newtonian physics completely in the mathematically richer language at the disposal of Einsteinian physicists;[205] Einstein himself, incidentally, was no mean historian of science.) Indeed I have often asserted that Newton's theory explains (and contains as a first approximation) both Kepler's laws and Galileo's law of falling bodies, while Einstein's theory contains, in a similar way, Newton's.

It is a strange way of "containing", for Newton's theory logically contradicts Kepler's and Galileo's, just as Einstein's logically contradicts Newton's. The relationships here are very interesting, and deserve closer study (such as the studies by Peter Havas quoted in n. 205); I have discussed them in many lectures; in "The Aim of Science";[206] and in various chapters of *Conjectures and Refutations*.

In any case, any lack of understanding between Newtonians and Einsteinians is completely asymmetric; and this should be stressed. As a consequence there can be *genuine progress* in science: human knowledge can grow.

As opposed to this, Kuhn sees scientists of the various periods caught in "incommensurable" paradigms; and "incommensurable", whatever it may mean, suggests a symmetrical relationship.

In order to complement what Wisdom says about this problem of mutual understanding, I may perhaps quote here briefly from a discussion of mine of the very popular but in my opinion *mistaken relativistic thesis that only those who accept the same basic framework can rationally communicate with or understand each other.*

I have dubbed this thesis *The Myth of the Framework*, and I have discussed it on various occasions. I regard it as a logical and philosophical mistake. . . .

I should like just to indicate briefly why I am not a relativist: I do believe in "absolute" or "objective" truth, in Tarski's sense (although I am, of course, not an "absolutist" in the sense of thinking that I, or anybody else, has the truth in his pocket). I do not doubt that this is one of the points on which . . . [Kuhn and I] are most deeply divided; and it is a logical point.

I do admit that at any moment we are prisoners caught in the framework of our theories; our expectations; our past experiences; our language. But we are prisoners in a Pickwickian sense: if we try, we can break out of our framework at any time. Admittedly, we shall find ourselves again in a framework, but it will be a better and roomier one; and we can at any moment break out of it again.

The central point is that a critical discussion and a comparison of the various frameworks . . . [are] always possible. It is just a dogma—a dangerous dogma—that the different frameworks are like mutually untranslatable languages. The fact is that even totally different languages (like English and Hopi, or Chinese) are not untranslatable, and that there are many Hopis or Chinese who have learnt to master English very well.

The Myth of the Framework is, in our time, the central bulwark of irrationalism. My counter-thesis is that it simply exaggerates a difficulty into an impossibility. The difficulty of discussion between people brought up in different frameworks is to be admitted. But nothing is more fruitful than such a discussion; than the culture clash which has stimulated some of the greatest intellectual revolutions.[207]

Kuhn has replied to my here quoted remark that "we can break out of our framework at any time . . . [into] a better and roomier one" by saying: "If that possibility were *routinely* available, there ought *to be no very special difficulties* about stepping into someone else's framework in order to evaluate it."[208]

But I did not suggest that this possibility is *routinely* available. Why does Kuhn have always *routines* in mind? Are only *routine* achievements real or practicable? In fact I said later in the same passage (though without italics), that the "Myth of the Framework exaggerates a *difficulty* into an impossibility". And I added (again in roman) that "The *difficulty* of discussion between people brought up in different frameworks is to be admitted".

But let us return to Wisdom's comments. He writes (in section 3):

Kuhn adds to the somewhat irrational flavor by suggesting that when a new theory is produced there is what I would call a bandwagon effect (though this expression somewhat exaggerates his sociological tendency). Somehow or other, the new theory becomes accepted, and the old one becomes rejected, as a result of a not fully rational change of attitude.

Wisdom comments, and I fully agree with his comments, that nothing among human beings ever proceeds fully rationally; not even in science. "This is a commonplace", is Wisdom's fair comment, and he continues: "The question is whether there is also a rational factor involved, and whether it is decisive." I think that it is not always decisive, but that it ought to be decisive: science, of all things, ought to be rational. And I think that if it ceases to be rational it ceases to be science, whether or not it may continue to be so called.[209]

To the latter sections of Wisdom's contribution I have little to add; and although I must say that I regard his distinction between "top-grade" and "rank and file" as highly problematic, I agree almost completely with his final summary; though I must say that I was a bit surprised by Wisdom's concluding thesis that Kuhn's theory and mine are, when correctly interpreted, "identical". But I agree that there is much in common, except for one point of importance: Kuhn's commitment to what I call the "Myth of the Framework".

VII. HISTORICAL AND SOCIAL PHILOSOPHY

41. Introductory Remark

Under this heading I have grouped my replies to six partly descriptive and partly critical essays concerned mainly with my *Poverty of Historicism* and my *Open Society*. Besides this, my final reply (to Sir Ernst Gombrich) takes up again problems which were discussed in my *Intellectual Autobiography* in connection with music: and I go back also to the problem of the final section of my *Autobiography*, the problem expressed by the title of Wolfgang Köhler's book *The Place of Value in a World of Facts*.

42. Lord Boyle on the Dualism of Facts and Decisions in The Open Society

Lord Boyle's most generous "personal appreciation" of my *Open Society* contains a small number of critical remarks. One of the last of them is very important and will require a full reply.

I

Early in his essay Lord Boyle writes: " . . . on the occasions when I myself venture to feel critical of Popper, it is often because I feel he has yielded too much to his critics rather than too little."

This is certainly a criticism, though a very mild one, and Lord Boyle is not the first to draw attention to what I fear may be an attitude of mine.

I plead guilty, but I ask that mitigating circumstances be taken into consideration. Serious rational criticism is so rare that it should be encouraged. Being too ready to defend oneself is more dangerous than being too ready to admit a mistake. Even if the mistake is only doubtfully a mistake, even if the criticism is based partly on a misunderstanding of what I have said, I try to work on the assumption that, if I have been misunderstood, it might be my own fault to some extent.

While it is hard to find a rational way to cope with criticism which is itself not entirely rational, especially if it has a personal edge, criticism which is not only entirely free of personal animosity but fundamentally as appreciative as Lord Boyle's is so rare that one should, I think, go out of one's way to accept what is right in it, even if it is not too easy to find something with which one can agree (which is *not* the case here). And one should always be conscious of the fact that nobody should attempt to be his own judge. Thus I have in the past identified the rational approach with the critical approach: but in the light of Professor Bernays's friendly though critical contribution to this volume, I am anxious to admit that this was perhaps going a little too far. On the other hand, Professor Bernays himself says that my mistake is not one which affects my philosophy in any important way. His essay is mainly devoted to reminding us of other aspects of rationality; and he would be prepared, I believe, to say that the critical approach, the readiness to listen to criticism and to correct one's mistakes, is of very central significance to rationality; and that I was right to stress its significance.

Lord Boyle himself is a critic whose criticism is not only rational but combined with the warmest personal appreciation. Shall I or shall I not defend myself against his criticism? Or shall I simply accept it?

The rational approach to this question is, clearly, that it depends on the merits of each case.

II

Of an explanation of mine why "critical dualism" is not more generally adopted, Lord Boyle says (in his section 3): "One may wholeheartedly endorse these words, and yet feel that they miss one rather crucial point." The point he has in mind is that "authoritarians, against whom the whole argument of *The Open Society* is directed", may be afraid of others' claiming the right "to decide for themselves".

This is obviously true, and I should be surprised if I have nowhere in *The Open Society* said it, or implied it. (I think I have implied it in *Conjectures and Refutations*, for example, on pages 6 and 374.) But although Lord Boyle may be right that I should also have made this point clear at the place of *The Open Society* to which he refers, I may perhaps explain why it did not occur to me there. For although it is true, as Lord Boyle says, that it is "authoritarians . . . against whom the whole argument of *The Open Society* is directed", I do not usually speak to the authoritarians, and I certainly do not do so there. Almost everywhere in the book it is the man whose values are similar to mine, the freedom-loving citizen, to whom I am speaking; I assume his good intentions, but I try to help him make up his mind on certain problems which are intellectually difficult. This is the reader to whom I address myself almost everywhere in the book. That authoritarians are afraid of the consequences of freedom is (I hope) made clear throughout my discussion of Plato: for example, in Chapter 4, on "Change and Rest". If it is not clear, then I am certainly to be blamed. But my problem in the place to which Lord Boyle refers was to explain the readiness of so many of the victims of authoritarianism to submit themselves to authority.

III

Lord Boyle's next criticism (in his section 3) is much more important and here I feel he is simply right. By putting in some of the later editions "proposals for a policy" on a level with "decisions" I certainly made a real mistake. I had been attracted by the fact that a *proposal*, and especially *a proposal to take a decision* can obviously be rationally discussed, while a *decision* can only be taken; as Lord Boyle rightly stresses, it can and should be critically discussed before it is taken, at the stage when it is still a proposal. (Of course a decision can also be discussed later, in the light of its consequences, and a new proposal may be made; for example, to rescind the decision.) I think that Lord Boyle is right to say that I should not, in stressing the rationality of proposals, have omitted to stress also, as he now does, that however rationally a proposal may be discussed—in committee, say—the decision to adopt it cannot, as a rule, follow from the discussion any more than a norm can follow from a fact: it has to be "taken". I should have said this, and at the same time stressed the difference between irrational decisions, taken without listening to critical arguments, and those more rational decisions which are taken after giving fair hearing to all the known arguments *against* them. I did stress that the rational politician will be on the lookout for unforeseen and unintended consequences of his decisions; but this is not quite enough in order to show that, unavoidably, *there is an element of freedom* in the taking of decisions. But this freedom does not nullify, or in the least interfere with, the distinction between the rationality of critical decision-making on the one hand and irrationalist "decisionism" on the other; that is, between favouring every effort to foresee and judge as far as possible what we are doing and, on the contrary, asserting that decisions, thanks to the impossibility of *deriving* them from rational discussions, are always, and equally, irrational.

IV

Lord Boyle's next point I am not prepared to concede. On the contrary, I feel I have a duty to defend myself, and to criticize Lord Boyle's own position as inconsistent with his general approval of my "dualism of facts and decisions": he accepts—perhaps under the influence of the persuasive presentation of Professor Ayer, which he quotes, and without fully realizing the gravity of the issue involved—a position which I have described as "moral relativism" and to which my "dualism of facts and decisions" is diametrically opposed.

Lord Boyle begins his criticism, in the spirit of friendliness which is so obvious throughout his contribution, with the conciliatory words: "My preference for Popper's first thoughts. . .". What he criticizes is "a passage in the *Addendum* to the 1963 edition [a reprint of the 1962 edition] of *The Open Society*, where Popper seems to me to go much too far in the direction of his critics". Now I regard this *Addendum* to Volume II (entitled "Facts, Standards, and Truth: A Further Criticism of Relativism") as a very important, though surely not completely successful, clarification of my "dualism of facts and decisions", of which Lord Boyle approves. It is an essay not on morality but on metaethics; and in order to reply to Lord Boyle's criticism, I will restate my position as clearly and concisely as I can.

I hold (and Lord Boyle agrees) that moral decisions or standards or norms cannot be derived from anything else; certainly not from facts, though they *pertain* to facts.[210] It is a fact that many men have a colour prejudice; but we can decide to lessen its consequences by legislation. (Lord Boyle alludes later to the British Race Relations Act, and there I agree with all he says, including his criticism of an inadequate formulation of mine.) As I wrote in *The Open Society*, and Lord Boyle fully approves (see his section 1): "Men are not equal; but we can decide to fight for equal rights." The nonequality is a fact; and we decide either to accept this fact, or to fight against it. I expressed this by saying that decisions, norms, and standards, though not derivable from facts, *pertain* to facts. If, for example, it could be established that some "races" have statistically a lower average I.Q. than other "races", then this might, and in my opinion it should, be taken as establishing their claim or their right to special consideration and help, rather than the right of those with a statistically higher I.Q. to a privileged position. But it is clear that this view of mine has the nature of a proposal for a decision: it is not the only possible view.

We are, as I actually explained in the first edition of *The Open Society*, free to accept or to reject decisions, norms, and standards; free in the sense that the responsibility for doing so remains with us. But I also explained that, although norms and standards are our own creations, *some can be better and some can be worse.* "It is our business to *improve* them as much as we can, if we find that they are objectionable", I wrote in *The Open Society*, and Lord Boyle concurs. And I go on to say, with Lord Boyle's approval: "Man has created new worlds—of language, of music, of poetry, of science; and the most important of these is the world of the moral demands, for equality, for freedom, and for helping the weak."[211]

In later writings (and also in the present volume) I have called this world of the products of the human mind "world 3", to distinguish it from the world of physical states, "world 1", and from the world of mental states or of our conscious experiences, "world 2". World 3 is man-made, but not entirely consciously: it is not an "expression" or "projection" of world 2. I call the fact that world 3 has its own unintended consequences the *autonomy* of world 3. I tried to make this clear in Chapter 5 of *The Open Society* ("Nature and Convention") when explaining my "dualism of facts and decisions": "The statement that norms are man-made . . . has often been misunderstood. Nearly all misunderstandings can be traced back to one fundamental misapprehension, namely, to the belief that 'convention' implies 'arbitrariness'; that if we are free to choose any system of norms we like, then one system is *just as good* as any other."[212]

In other words I stressed (with Kant) that our *freedom* makes us responsible for our *choices*; and that even though there are no *natural* standards (no standards derivable from world 1 or world 2), there are differences in worth, and that we *ought* to choose the best of the competing systems of standards, even though these systems, and the (higher) standards by which we judge them, are all our own creation.

To think that it is all "a matter of arbitrariness", at best "a matter of taste", is relativism. But even taste can be better or worse: we can cultivate our taste.

Relativism in morals is, very largely, the result of the true insight that there cannot be any normative science of morals. But more lately, historical and sociological relativism has even attacked science: every period, every "spirit of the age", has its own characteristic science (so say Hegel and Spengler): science is man-made and is therefore merely an expression of world 2. There is no really autonomous world 3.

What I tried to show in that new *Addendum* to the 1962 edition of *The Open Society* was that there is a kernel of truth in this relativistic view of science: science is man-made, and therefore fallible. But the idea of objective or absolute truth is also a man-made idea; and fallibility means that though truth is our supreme standard, we often fall short of it. Truth is therefore a regulative idea: we try to live up to our standards, even though we have *no criterion* by which we could decide whether we have reached them.

I wrote this because I felt that the recognition that truth is a man-made standard and that we are fallible, possessing no criterion of truth, would make it easier to see that moral standards (for which the word "goodness" is conventional) are also not arbitrary, though we are fallible and possess no criterion of goodness.

Nothing can be proved here. But even Bertrand Russell felt that the relativism of morals (which he vainly tried to find arguments against) is a typical philosophers' problem, and that relativism can hardly be accepted.

We *cannot* completely satisfy ourselves with Professor Ayer's contention (quoted by Lord Boyle in section 3) "to say that something which somebody thinks is right really *is* right is [or means] to range oneself on his side, to adhere to that particular standpoint". For this would make the Mafia adherent "right", who ranges himself on the side of criminals, and adheres to that particular standpoint: he would be "right" in the relativistic sense if we apply this sense of the term "right" to him, or to those who "unite their wills with those of the others" belonging to the Mafia.

The reason why we do not and cannot accept moral relativism is very simple: we all know that our moral decisions and our moral judgements are fallible (and sometimes even criminally so); that we may, and often do, fall short of the best, the "right", decision; that if we find out that we have made a moral mistake, or adopted a defective moral judgement, we may not be merely wavering (in world 2) but may be *improving* our moral decisions and our moral judgement (in world 3): we may have earlier fallen short of what we now more clearly realize is the "right" standard, the better judgement, or the better way. We may progress morally, in the world 3 sense.

This fallibilism was the main point of my *Addendum*, and the point of comparing moral values with truth values, or moral standards with truth standards: ". . . the idea of error implies that of . . . [a] standard of which we may fall short." If we can *fall short* in our moral decisions, it must be that we fall short of some man-made and insecure and yet objective standard.[213]

Nobody, I suggest, in practice accepts moral or even aesthetic relativism completely. Freedom of choice does not mean arbitrariness of choice. The meaning of words like "good" or "right" is no more identical with "I agree" or "I approve" than is the meaning of "true". (We may even say of a world 3 object that it is objectively valuable, but that we do not like it. This may hold for a scientific theory or for a work of art or for a moral value.) There *are* man-made values which transcend the maker; there is a world 3 of science, art, and morals, whose partly man-made and partly autonomous standards can grow with the growth of world 3. Our best creations are values which are freely created and yet go beyond merely human authority. What I wrote about truth in *Conjectures and Refutations* (p. 30) holds, *mutatis mutandis*, for other values:

> If we thus admit that there is no authority beyond the reach of criticism to be found within the whole province of our knowledge, however far it may have penetrated into the unknown, then we can retain, without danger, the idea that truth is beyond human authority. And we must retain it. For without this idea there can be no objective standards of inquiry; no criticism of our conjectures; no groping for the unknown; no quest for knowledge.

What I tried to do in the *Addendum* to *The Open Society* was to extend this to the field of morals. No doubt, I was not very successful, and the passage which Lord Boyle criticizes was, as his reaction proves, very badly formulated. But out of context it sounds a lot worse than in; and so I may close with another passage from the same *Addendum*, a passage which almost immediately follows the one rejected by Lord Boyle:

> Though we should seek for absolutely right or valid proposals [values, or standards, would have been better], we should never persuade ourselves that we have definitely found them; for clearly, there cannot be a *criterion of absolute rightness*—even less than a criterion of absolute truth.[214]

43. *Wild on Plato and* The Open Society

In the second sentence of his contribution Professor Wild speaks of the "careful criticism in reviews and in more lengthy studies of Plato" which the first volume of *The Open Society* has received, and continues: "So far as I know, Professor Popper has not as yet published any reply." I am far from expecting my critics to read everything I write, or to scrutinize every new edition of *The Open Society*. But it would, surely, have not been very difficult for Professor Wild to find out, before writing his contribution, that in 1961 I added an *Addendum* "Reply to a Critic" to *The Open Society*; this has been available since 1962 in several editions, paperback and otherwise. The criticism to which I replied in this *Addendum* was Professor Levinson's monumental work *In Defense of Plato*.[215] The reason why I selected this work for a reply is that it contains, to quote Professor Wild, "the most thoroughgoing examination" of my "views of Plato that has so far been made". Since Professor Wild clearly means it as a criticism when he remarks on my failure to reply, this first criticism of his is answered: I did not fail to reply to Levinson. Moreover, since Professor Wild says that his "page references to Popper's book will be to *The Open Society and Its Enemies, Princeton University Press, 1950*", it really seems unlikely that Professor Wild has made much attempt to find out whether, in the five editions published since 1950, I have replied to criticism or, perhaps, even modified my views, or expounded them more fully.

Professor Wild's method of criticism takes usually the form of a reference to some passage in my book, a brief comment, and then, as in his section I: "I wish that he [Popper] would clarify his position on this point." Quite a few of these requests are fair enough: there *are* treated in my book many difficult problems which are in need of further clarification. But quite a few of these problems have been further clarified by me since—either in the later editions of *The Open Society* or in other of my writings. Again, I hardly expect a busy philosopher to take heed of many of the things which I have published since 1950; but then, a careful critic might at least keep in mind the possibility that I may have written on some of these points; and therefore not put his questions in a form which implies that I have not done so. And here I ignore the fact that several of the clarifications Professor Wild demands were, in my opinion, adequately provided in the places which he finds so defective.

This concludes my complaint about Professor Wild's *method or procedure.* As far as I am concerned, I shall try briefly to satisfy his wish for further clarification. But it is obvious from his comments on my attempts in the 1950 edition to say as clearly as possible what I mean, that I can expect little success in satisfying Professor Wild: the manner in which he interprets my old attempts at clarification so often makes nonsense of what I have written that I cannot hope to do much better now.

Let me start with Professor Wild's first request.

On pages 64 f. of the first volume of *The Open Society*[216] I discussed the old and important distinction, made by several Presocratics and by Plato, between "Nature and Convention". I was, however, also expounding my own views on the matter. I wrote (p. 64):

> To sum up, *it is impossible to derive a sentence stating a norm or a decision or, say, a proposal for a policy from a sentence stating a fact;* this is only another way of saying that it is impossible to derive norms or decisions *or proposals* from facts.

In a footnote to this passage (pp. 234 f.) I argue against the positivist position that norms and imperatives are either meaningless, or expressions of emotions, and I say (at the end of point (1) of the footnote): "I may perhaps express here my opinion that the reluctance to admit that norms are something important and irreducible [irreducible to facts, that is] is one of the main sources of the intellectual and other weaknesses of the more 'progressive' circles in our present time."

After this footnote, I proceed in the text as follows:

> The statement that norms are man-made (man-made not in the sense that they are consciously designed, but in the sense that men can judge and alter them—that is to say, in the sense that the responsibility for them is entirely ours) has often been misunderstood. Nearly all misunderstandings can be traced back to a fundamental misapprehension, namely, to the belief that "convention" implies "arbitrariness"; that if we are free to choose any system of norms we like, then one system is just as good as any other. . . . Mathematical calculi, for instance, or symphonies, or plays, are highly artificial, yet it does not follow that one calculus or symphony or play is just as good as any other.

It is to the sentence before the last that Professor Wild alludes; and he seems to find it in need of further clarification. Now let us take a system of geometry such as Euclid's. It is, clearly, man-made. There is, as we know, even an element of arbitrariness in it: non-Euclidean geometries have been developed (for example, spherical geometry) in which the Euclidean theorem that the sum of the angles of every triangle equals two right angles no longer holds. But even though there is thus an element of arbitrariness to be found in Euclidean geometry, nobody who knows it will say that it is entirely arbitrary. Though we are free (in certain contexts) to choose between Euclidean and non-Euclidean geometries, our freedom of choice does not imply complete arbitrariness.

This was my point in the passage which Professor Wild judges so much in need of clarification.

Lest I be accused of dodging any reasonable demand for clarification, I will explain here more fully my reference to "symphonies". Nobody will deny that they are man-made and that a composer who writes a symphony is "free" in the sense that he can write almost anything. But a classical composer's freedom, though far from absent, was limited by certain norms, such as tonality, the preparation and resolution of dissonances, and so on. These rules or norms are, in their turn, man-made; and they have been severely changed by certain modern composers. But nobody who knows and loves classical music—not even the most modern composer—will say that its rules or norms are "entirely arbitrary".

It seems to me that all this is fairly clear, even though it leaves many questions open. But I never pretended that I had answered all questions, or that I could answer them. When Wild asks (section I) "In what respect are they [norms, moral decisions] not arbitrary, with reference to what?", it seems to me that his question makes less sense than the explanation I have tried to give.

Professor Wild quotes me in his next paragraph as arguing that "[norms and] decisions pertain to facts". The norm or imperative "Do not kill", and the decision to accept it, pertain to the fact that men can be killed and have been killed. But even a rule like "Do not write a symphony whose performance takes 12 hours" may be said to pertain to, or apply to, certain possible facts, by excluding them. Now it is characteristic that moral norms pertain always to alterable facts; "Do not treble your weight every day" is not a moral norm, at least not as long as no method is known by which we could treble our weight every day. Wild quotes me (section I) as saying: "if the fact in question [to which the rule pertains] is unalterable. . .then any decision to alter it will be simply impracticable. . .". This is a very trite remark of mine, and it simply means that norms, or decisions, pertain to facts which are "alterable" in the sense that we can do something about them. Wild's comment on this trite remark seems to me particularly unhelpful; for he writes (section I): "This may be what he [Popper] means by the nonarbitrariness of moral norms." I am afraid I meant by the nonarbitrariness of moral norms something totally different: that some systems of moral norms are better than others—morally better, more worthy to live by, than other systems of moral norms. And what systems I had in mind as preferable to others were indicated throughout the book: more tolerant, less authoritative systems; systems which (within the limits of mutual toleration) leave more freedom and initiative to the individual, and curb the power of tyrants, and of state officials.

Immediately after the last quoted sentence, in which Professor Wild conjectures (wrongly) what I meant, he continues: "But if so, he [Popper] is in essential agreement with Plato and the natural law philosophers. . . ." This leaves me gasping. Do Plato and the natural law philosophers merely assert that any decision to alter facts which are unalterable is impracticable?

Professor Wild concludes this paragraph with the words (section I): "I do not see what he [Popper] can mean by the nonarbitrariness of 'man-made' norms that are wholly divorced from the facts. I hope, therefore, that he will clarify his meaning on these points."

What *I* don't see is what Professor Wild can mean by "norms that are wholly divorced from the facts". I have never spoken of them; on the contrary, I said that norms, though not logically deducible from facts, pertain to facts. It appears from the context that "wholly divorced" is Professor Wild's reference to my "not logically derivable": I cannot recall having ventured anything stronger about the divorcedness of norms from facts than that norms are "not logically derivable" from facts.

I wish, however, to inform my readers that in my *Addendum* (1961) to Volume I of *The Open Society*, "Reply to a Critic", quite a number of the more substantial questions which Professor Wild opens up later (such as Plato's racialism, or class rule, or lying propaganda, or Plato's relation to Socrates) have been discussed and answered by me.

44. Acton on the Part Played by Repression in Karl Marx

Professor H. B. Acton's contribution, "Moral Futurism and the Ethics of Marxism", contains some agreement with, as well as a number of supplementations and corrections to, my treatment of Marxist ethics in *The Open Society*. When originally working on my criticism of Marxism, I did not intend to publish what I had written, and was satisfied with a criticism of the later writings of Marx and Engels (from the *Manifesto* onwards). And when working in New Zealand during the Second World War on *The Open Society*, I had no access to those early works of Marx and Engels which Acton makes much use of. No doubt, his analysis of Marxist ethical theory is vastly superior to mine.

I tried to defend Marx against the charge that his materialism implied, in the moral field, the idea of unrepressed fulfilment of desires. Acton shows that the young Marx (no less than the old Marcuse), did hold ideas such as this.

I accept this criticism, and Acton's correction, with one proviso: I think that it is quite possible that in his early days Marx held these views without much hesitation, while at least in his later days he believed in a society in which cultural values (and not only the unrepressed seeking of bodily satisfaction) would play a major role.

The key word of the debate seems to me the word "repression", with its many meanings, ranging from the repression exerted by a ruthless dictatorship to the legal devices through which a democratic state may attempt to protect its youth from being exploited by pedlars of drugs, and thus from unintended intellectual and perhaps physical suicide.

Social life without any kind of "repression" is an old dream; we find it in the story of Paradise, and in Hesiod's and Ovid's myth of the Golden Age. In holding up an anarchical ideal like this a certain immaturity is needed: there may always be bullies who might want to repress others; and what we should aim at, is to protect the nonbullies from the bullies by an equal distribution (as Kant said) of the minimum amount of repression of freedom compatible with the (approximate) equality of its distribution. Of the practicable ideals not greatly more repressive than anarchism, the least repressive would involve that minimum amount of state interference compatible with equality in the distribution of the burden of citizenship.

The level of this minimum depends very largely on such things as the density of the population and the productivity of industry. If there are many motor cars, then there must be a considerable amount of "repression", for motorists as well as for pedestrians. This is a trivial example, but it is a typical example. A society without repression is clearly impossible, and I believe that there are some indications that the older Marx, at any rate, realized this. That the younger Marx (like the old Marcuse) was largely motivated by a hostility to *all* "repression", in a very wide sense of this word, I am very ready to admit.

Repression in this sense is a result of clashes of interests. My interests as a lover of quiet surroundings clash with the interests of the people who use motor cars to pass the house in which I live, or jet airliners to fly over it. But such a clash of interests is not a clash of class interests. I myself use from time to time a car or an airliner. The example is typical. Moreover, most of us are consumers as well as producers, and our interests as consumers clash with our own interests as producers. All this makes heaven on earth and freedom from all repressions impossible.

In that Marx—certainly the younger Marx—was more naively inclined to attack "repression" than I described him in *The Open Society*, I plead guilty of having idealized the picture of Marxism, and I accept Acton's criticism. But apart from ignorance I plead as an excuse that one ought to treat one's opponents—Marx in this case—not only fairly but generously;

and one should *not only overlook* stupidities which are not essential to their teaching, but actually try to *repair* them.

One point, perhaps a minor point, on which I would like to defend myself a little against Acton's criticism is my claim that Marx and Engels were "moral futurists". Acton makes a good point when he shows that "moral futurism" may be an empty idea. But I do not think that it was so for Marx or Engels. As I see it, they tried to free themselves from any ethical theory, and to base all their views on what they regarded as "science"—more especially, social and economic science. Their science told them that the coming of socialism was a historical necessity; and so they believed that they could be socialists without a moral basis. (They even believed, a little inconsistently, that it was "criminal" to resist the coming of socialism, since such resistance could only make its coming less smooth.)

Against this view I argued along three different lines.

(1) The "scientific" prophecy of the necessary coming of socialism was without foundation.

(2) A prophecy, if valid (or say, scientifically accepted), may play an important part in our ethical considerations; but if I regard that which is coming as evil, I am not bound to give up all resistance to it because its coming has been prophesied.

The two points are, of course, closely connected. But they are, I think, independently valid. Point (2) may be much strengthened if one holds, as I do, that

(3) All human knowledge, and especially all foreknowledge, is fallible.

I do not think that Acton and I would disagree on any of these three points. But I think that they can be used as a defence of my criticism of moral futurism.

I admit, of course, what is stressed by Acton, that future facts may change the moral situation, and that morality is always strongly dependent upon the situation, since it is the situation which determines the moral problem.

Example 1: When atom bombs or biological weapons are easily produced in every kitchen, then we will probably be faced with a situation in which an open and democratic society is an empty dream. However, we may try to prevent such a situation from arising.

Example 2: There is perhaps no more important social issue today than population control. But if we succeed in making this control effective, then this will change our life immensely; not only our morals, but our aesthetic values.

I plead guilty to not having sufficiently explained the way in which our morality may be dependent upon things to come. But having made this plea, I think that there is quite a bit left in my criticism of moral futurism; and I am confident that Acton would agree with this.

45. *Winch on Institutions and* The Open Society

I find Professor Peter Winch's contribution puzzling. He seems to think that he is criticizing me from a point of view radically opposed to mine; and even to feel satisfied that his own point of view is supported by the discovery (or what he believes to be a discovery) of serious weaknesses in what I have written. This feeling permeates the essay. It is expressed, for example, in his concluding sentence: "I believe it is a kind of understanding quite different from anything that Popper gives an account of."

But this feeling, which, as I say, permeates the essay, and quite naturally communicates itself to the reader, has simply no basis in the actual points of criticism made by Winch. Almost all these points—so far as they are not simply mistaken—seem to me quite trivial. I invite the reader to consider—it is a glaring example—the following remark (from his section II), which is quite unrelieved by its context: "A man can decide what he is going to regard as most important only insofar as he can attach some meaning to the word 'important'."

Now what can one say to this remark? If it means that we can speak only if we understand the language we are using—this language being of course a social institution—then the remark is trivial, and its triviality, I contend, is unrelieved by the context. If it means—and, as it stands, this seems the only proper interpretation—that a man cannot make up his mind as to what is, at any time, most important, without understanding the meaning of the word "important", then the remark is obviously false: when the house is on fire, one is prone to make up one's mind as to what is most important without having time to use the word even in silent speech.

Thus I suggest that a reader should be ready to correct his impression if, like myself, he felt in first reading Winch that in the passage just quoted Winch had something significant to say.

In a footnote appended to the first occurrence of the word "important" in the quoted passage, Winch writes: "The conception of 'importance' seems to me to give Popper some difficulty in his exposition of critical dualism." He then refers the reader to pages 64 f. of *The Open Society*, Volume I. This footnote of Winch's, I must say, does "give Popper some difficulty", for the following reason. I use certain expressions and words when they are convenient or useful for stating theories or arguments or problems, and I try to avoid words which are inconvenient or unhelpful; but I am not at all acquainted with any experience which could be described by saying that a "conception" like "importance" has given me "some difficulty". This is a kind of philosophers' talk which does not convey anything to me.

Nevertheless I took up Professor Winch's reference, and I reread pages 64 and 65, to find out what was the "difficulty". I can only think that Professor Winch's reference is a slip. Or can it possibly refer to my warning, on page 65, not to carry the analogy "between moral decisions and decisions in the field of art" too far? "Many moral decisions [I wrote] involve the life and death of other men. Decisions in the field of art are much less urgent and important." It would have made no difference to my argument had I replaced the last sentence perhaps by "In the field of art, few decisions do". Thus there was no need to use the "conception of 'importance' ". Have I not said often enough that nothing depends on words, or on "conceptions"?

As some of my readers may know, I am intensely interested in human language—which is, I believe, one of the things which makes us human. But I am *not* interested in talk about words and their meanings. (See section 7 of my *Autobiography* above.) To discuss words and meanings seems to me *unimportant*; and I can hardly see that I need explain what I mean by this. Nor, surely, do I open up any "difficulty" by recording my opinion that the problems discussed in my *Open Society* are more important and urgent than problems of words and their meanings. I have often described human language as a social institution—the most important and universal of all human institutions. And as to institutions in general, I quoted (on p. 66 of *The Open Society*, Vol. I) with approval Protagoras, and Burnet's interpretation of Protagoras's views, that "institutions and conventions were what raised men above the brutes".

This brings me to what I think is Winch's central criticism of my *Open Society*.

Professor Winch's central criticism reads like a sustained argument, but I found it difficult to unravel what the point was, and what Professor Winch was objecting to. After many readings and rereadings, I conjecture it is the following.

Winch, who relies almost exclusively on the first volume of *The Open Society* and neglects Chapter 14 of the second volume, thinks that I regard social institutions *only* as means to ends and, more precisely, to ends which are *extraneous* to these institutions. Moreover, so Winch says, all social institutions should be regarded by the "social engineer" (as allegedly I envisage the social engineer) only from the point of view of humanitarian aims, that is, from the point of view of minimizing misery.

But, Winch suggests, institutions have a life of their own, and intrinsic aims of their own, and he suggests that I overlook this; and he also suggests that I overlook the fact that human values are often not abstract or extrinsic or extraneous "humanitarian" values like the minimizing of misery, but intrinsic values. Universities, for example, may, by educating doctors and by furthering medical research, serve humanitarian aims, but I am committing a gross mistake (Winch suggests) in overlooking the many and diverse intrinsic values which a university creates, such as contributions to knowledge and scholarly standards.

If this is what Winch wishes to convey, then in order to make his criticism effective he would have to establish more than he tried to do. For he merely shows that I say here and there that the social engineer (another word for politician or administrator) should look at certain institutions from a humanitarian point of view: he would have to show that I overlook all those other points. In order to establish his negative thesis a few quotations about humanitarian aims are clearly insufficient.

In fact, I discuss all those problems which, according to Winch's suggestion (if I interpret him rightly), are missing in my account of social institutions and of values. I discuss them many times, even in passages adjacent to some of those that Winch quotes. (But, as I have had occasion to remark elsewhere in these *Replies*, no one should be expected to say all the time, at the same time, everything that is to be said.)

Winch thinks that the failure he ascribes to me is an inherent consequence of what I have called "the dualism of facts and decisions"; that is to say, of the impossibility of reducing decisions to facts. And he seems to think that this dualism makes no allowance for the possibility that values may belong not only to the realm of decisions but also to the realm of facts: that they may be incorporated in social institutions. Yet I wrote, for example, at the very place, referred to by Winch (*The Open Society*, Vol. I, p. 64), where I introduce this dualism: "That most people agree with the norm 'Thou shalt not steal' is a sociological fact. But the norm 'Thou shalt not steal' is not a fact, and can never be inferred from sentences describing facts."

In the first of these two quoted sentences of mine I say clearly enough that a norm—and thus a value—may be an intrinsic part of a social institution, such as a religion, or a legal system. And I say similar things many times, especially in parts of the second volume, such as Chapter 14, and also in *The Poverty of Historicism*.

In Chapter 14 of *The Open Society*, for example, Winch will find (on p. 93 of the edition to which he refers) the following statement: "Men—i.e. human minds, the needs, the hopes, fears, and expectations, the motives and aspirations of human individuals—are, if anything, the product of life in society rather than its creators." This is only a summary of a lengthy argument. I think that it is a clear and unmistakable statement, and a refutation of Winch's criticism (if this is his criticism) that I fail to see the values which are "internal" or "intrinsic" to an institution. At the same place in *The Open Society* I quote my own earlier remark from *The Poverty of Historicism* [1944(b)], page 122: "Only a minority of social institutions are consciously designed, while the vast majority have just 'grown', as the undesigned results of human actions." In the book edition of *The Poverty* [1957(g)], page 65, I italicized this passage, because it had been overlooked by several of my critics. In a footnote to the same passage I refer to "the instrumental character of undesigned institutions (such as language)". I mention this here because, like Winch, I look upon language as a social institution, but unlike him (or so it seems) I regard it as extremely important not only to study the "intrinsic" values of words within a given language, but also the (no doubt less "intrinsic") functions of human language in general, and especially its descriptive and argumentative functions (and to a lesser degree also the hortative and command functions, and so on). And as I have said here and elsewhere, I regard human language as the institution which has made man transcend the animals—which has made us human. (See sections 15 and 40 of the *Autobiography* above.)

This view is, surely, incompatible with Winch's criticism. But perhaps it is also incompatible with the passages of *The Open Society* which Winch has in mind? This is certainly not asserted by Winch, although if true it would explain Winch's criticism.

However, there is no incompatibility of this sort. My view, in brief, is this. At any moment of time we, and our values, are the products of existing institutions and past traditions. Admittedly, this imposes some limitations on our creative freedom, and on our powers of rational criticism. Yet it also provides our critical and creative powers with stimuli and with objects; though we are the products of institutions and traditions, our rationality consists in our being able to criticize and reshape institutions and traditions. And although the regulative values which enter into these critical activities are, largely, derived from these institutions and traditions, they are themselves criticizable, and changeable. These, I think, are facts. (See also my reply to Kuhn, section 39 above, and *C.&R.*, p. 28, point 5.)

There is a second criticism of Professor Winch's—second, I think, to the central criticism mentioned above.

Winch contrasts Sorel's "anarcho-syndicalist attitude to the general strike" with "the attitude of the parliamentary socialists of his time" (in his section II). The latter Winch declares as "essentially Popperian: the strike was a means to an end", while for Sorel "the strike was valuable for what it *was* . . ."; it was, in brief, valuable in itself or intrinsically valuable—just as war was regarded by Hegel and others as valuable in itself.

I wonder whether I should regard it as a criticism of my defence of democracy to be told that my views are incompatible with Sorel's somewhat more violent views. Of this kind of incompatibility I was intensely conscious, of course, and I referred to it in several places, especially in my Hegel chapter. Fundamentally, Sorel's attitude towards the general strike, or towards revolution, is just that romantic and irrational attitude which I combat—*by rational arguments*—from a rational and democratic point of view.

I do not in the least deny that even the greatest evils, such as murder, may for some people incorporate values in themselves: there are, unfortunately, people who enjoy murder for its own sake, and there are some who enjoy war for its own sake—just as I myself greatly enjoyed, when young, climbing mountains, and still enjoy reading about it. Is this fact seriously to be considered as an argument against legislation aimed at protecting people who do not wish to be murdered? Let's have art for art's sake and science for science's sake, but not (for heaven's sake) war for war's sake or social revolution for social revolution's sake. If this anti-Sorelian attitude is what Winch calls "essentially Popperian", then I am, for once, a Popperian.

But I do not think that Winch is aware of what he is criticizing, because he refers in this context to R. Rhees, who criticizes me for being too much of a "social engineer", and for endangering individualism. "In proportion [so runs the passage quoted by Winch from Rhees] as men do participate in running their own affairs, they will come in conflict with humanitarians and with the reasonableness of social engineers." The kind of social engineering attacked here by Rhees seems to be precisely the kind which I also attack. (That Rhees thinks otherwise—I believe because, like Winch, he misreads me—does not concern us here.) It seems to me quite clear that the kind of "social engineering" which Rhees wishes to attack is not the kind that would interfere, say, with wars, although his wording does not exclude it; for wars interfere with "men . . . [who] participate in running their own affairs" at least as much as, say, peace treaties, or collective security pacts do. Neither Rhees nor Winch seems to see that what I call piecemeal social engineering is intended to make men free to run their own affairs, unless this should interfere with the freedom of others to do likewise. (See my *O.S.*, Vol. I, Chap. 6, section VI, esp. pp. 110 f.) And when Winch writes, in the same footnote in which he quotes Rhees, "Of course, the point here at issue is not whether one shares Sorel's or Popper's values, but whether values are connected with questions of social policy in the way Popper says they are", then it again becomes clear that he does not realize what the issue is which he has opened up by his example. For my book is in part an attempt to show how we might do better (in a value sense) than Sorel and the Hegelians; better in a humanitarian sense which would lay stress on that individualism implicitly advocated in Rhees's criticism. This *is* a very important and difficult problem. The problem of preventing wars, for example, is important enough to warrant reading books like mine carefully; and to warrant clear and careful criticism of my proposals. Generalities and vague insinuations that I am *not* doing this or that (claims which are mistaken anyhow) are not enough. They should be replaced by more responsible discussions.

In his last section, Winch returns from practice to theory, and he becomes, for me at least, very hard to understand. One thing is clear: he is highly dissatisfied with what I say, and he thinks he has important objections. Thus in his section III a sentence (quoted below) begins with the words "This confusion", apparently referring to a confusion of mine which Winch has just analysed; but although I have read the preceding paragraphs of Winch's essay at least ten times, I have not been able to detect even a claim that a confusion of mine has been analysed. I did find the claim that some "analogy is open to one obvious objection", but not even a claim that it is I who has confused anything.

According to my views which Winch reports—very badly—at this point, men live in a world of nature which consists, from the point of view of their subjective knowledge, in expectations or *theories*. (This holds for men in general, not only for scientists; and among the theories are trivial ones such as, for example, that the chair on which they are settling down will not suddenly evaporate.) These expectations are very important, and they reflect, of course, certain "natural regularities" in our environment. Now all I say in the place criticized by Winch ([1949(b)], p. 49; that is, [1963(a)], p. 130) is that it is very important for us that there are also regularities in our *social* environment, such as traditions of behaving in certain ways; without such regularities there would be social chaos and we should be lost.

These views of mine are pretty trivial. But Winch says: "unlike the case of *scientific* theories, the tradition exists whether any observer detects it or not. This confusion, I think, encourages Popper's tendency . . . to conflate practical social problems with theoretical problems: a tendency which is essential to his parallel between scientific method and democratic procedures." (Section III; italics mine.)

I can only say that in my analogy, it was not *scientific* theories but ordinary expectations which were said to be analogous in nature and social life. True, I regard these expectations of the ordinary man (and also of animals) as, in their turn, analogous to scientific theories. (But if *A* is in some sense analogous to *B*, and *B* is in some sense analogous to *C*, then we are not committed to saying that *A* must be analogous to *C*.) This, however, is not the point. *The "confusion" of which Professor Winch speaks, and from which he draws such far-reaching consequences*, is clearly not mine: "unlike the case of scientific theories, the tradition exists whether any observer detects it or not" was Professor Winch's criticism of my alleged confusion. But the natural regularity also exists, like the tradition, whether any observer detects it or not. (Incidentally, so do the scientific theories, in what I call "world 3".) And our ordinary expectations (or "theories") are, *in both cases*, essential to our rational actions.

On the same page, Professor Winch attributes to me a view I find simply staggering. "I could express [he writes] my dissatisfaction in general terms by saying that, for Popper, rationality has to be understood in relation to the existence of *some tradition or other*, the *qualitative content* of the tradition being more or less irrelevant." (Section III) By this Winch means that, according to Popper, rationality in social life is connected with tradition as such—with all tradition more or less equally—so that it does not matter much whether the tradition is that of the Royal Society or of the Royal Society for the Protection of Birds: these, according to Winch's reading of Popper, are more or less equal from the point of view of rationality in social life. (Or so it appears from the passage I have quoted.)

This is not my view. It is true that, in order to explain the role of traditions in social life, I suggested that without them there would be chaos, and no rational action would be possible. But I cannot imagine how anybody can ascribe to me on this evidence the absurd opinion that, in their relations to rationality, all traditions are more or less equal, or that their differences are "more or less irrelevant", from a rational point of view.

> Nevertheless [Winch writes], in his theoretical analysis of the general connection between tradition and rationality, what is important [for Popper] is not the specific nature of any tradition, but the general character of all traditions as being settled modes of behaviour and therefore as making rational prediction possible.
>
> As against this, it is important to point out that standards of rationality are involved *in* traditions of behaviour and that they may be in mutual conflict.

Really—have I not by rational arguments criticized *as endangering rationality* the Platonic and Aristotelian tradition of essentialism, and its barely argumentative modern developments such as those of Hegel and Wittgenstein? That anybody who has read either *The Open Society* or *Conjectures and Refutations* can saddle me with the opinion Winch ascribes to me, and think that it follows from my theory, merely because I have said that traditions are *necessary* for acting rationally, is beyond my comprehension. Necessary conditions are not necessarily sufficient conditions.

It is my essay "Towards a Rational Theory of Tradition" (*not* perhaps "Towards a Traditionalist Theory of Rationality") which Professor Winch criticizes here. I have said quite a lot on rationality not only elsewhere in this essay but also elsewhere in the volume in which this essay appears. In fact Professor Winch would only have had to read on in this essay to see that his "dissatisfaction", quoted above, was due to his not having read to the end. For this end—like the whole of *The Open Society*—is an attack on the various traditions of the enemies of reason:

> Even more precious [I say] . . . is the tradition that works against the ambivalence connected with the argumentative function of language, the tradition

that works against that misuse of language which consists in pseudo-arguments. . . . This is the tradition and discipline of clear speaking and clear thinking; it is the critical tradition—the tradition of reason.

The modern enemies of reason [I continue] want to destroy this tradition. They want to do this by destroying and perverting the argumentative [function] . . . of language. . . . We see this tendency very clearly at work in certain types of . . . philosophy—in a philosophy which does not argue because it has no arguable problems.

Who can say that I do not insist—too passionately as I am now inclined to think—that the differences between the various intellectual and moral traditions are decisive?

46. *Donagan on* The Poverty of Historicism

Professor Donagan's contribution can be classed among the "descriptive essays" on my philosophy, like those of Professors Campbell, Eccles, Watkins, and Wisdom. But it differs from all of these (even from Wisdom's essay) in containing a defence of my views against certain unfounded misrepresentations.

In addition, Donagan's essay is critical. In a number of places he shows that my arguments are invalid, or in need of revision. But in spite of these criticisms (which are always fair and just), he agrees that my argument succeeds and (quoting Sir Isaiah Berlin) that it has actually destroyed historicism. I can hardly conceive of a fairer and more favourable comment.

I think that I can promote the purpose which the present volume and the Library set out to serve if I make here a few comments on points which Donagan does not mention, and if I corroborate his findings on another point, which he has with great ingenuity cleared up: my use of the term "historicism".

I

During my studies in Vienna, the climate in right-wing and left-wing circles was strongly historicistic. "History is with us" was a cry you could hear from National Socialists and the many closely related groups, as well as from the Social Democrats to whom I and my friends belonged. "Scientific socialism" was the scientific proof that socialism was bound to come, whatever may happen. But the opponents on the right had similar ideas about history. The various nationalist and fascist parties took over much of the Marxist (especially of the Communist) ideology and turned it, dialectically, into a strikingly similar mirror image. Early leaders in this development were Georges Sorel, Vilfredo Pareto, and Oswald Spengler. But especially with Mussolini's break away from socialism, the nationalist groups, unfortunately quite correctly, saw that "History" was on their side: we were in, they thought, for a nationalist and authoritarian upsurge.

It was in 1919 and in the early 1920s that I began to disbelieve in all this: I discovered for myself that all this "social science" was spurious, and possibly most damaging. I remained an (inactive) member of the Social Democratic Party, because it was the only democratic one, and because I was deeply attracted by the socialist ideal of a just and more fraternal society. But I became an anti-Marxist. I felt, however, that I must not tell anybody but my closest friends, for Social Democracy was Marxist ("Austro-Marxist") and every weakening of its ideology would play into the hands of its terrible and violent enemies.

This is part of the background of *The Poverty of Historicism*. (I have told it in more detail in section 8 of my *Autobiography* above.) It is the reason why, when the Social Democrats had been decisively defeated, I argued not only against historicism but against Marx and against some of the Marxist "intellectuals", such as Mannheim.

II

With regard to the term "historicism" and its introduction into my book Donagan is simply right. But I may perhaps add a few words about the connection between the historists or historical relativists and those I call historicists.[216a]

There was in those days a closer connection between some historists and the nationalist historicists than Donagan sees. They were the days of the immense popularity of Spengler; and Spengler clearly was both a historist in the sense of, say, Dilthey ("understanding" in Dilthey's sense played a major role in Spengler's work) and a historicist in the sense of my terminology (for he predicted the Decline of the West). Of course, Spengler represented a variant of the many national-socialistic splinter groups, most of which were, in the end, destroyed by Hitler.

He was, like Dilthey, a historical relativist, but he was also, like Dilthey, what I called an essentialist. I think that one of the very few mistaken sentences in Donagan's paper is in section 2 (B) where he suggests that "few or no philosophers have ever accepted both these doctrines together", namely essentialism and the method of intuitive understanding. On the contrary, both go back to Aristotle and his *nous*, as I pointed out; and both were reborn again out of Hegelianism. Dilthey, though he gave essentialism a kind of psychological twist, was an essentialist; and so was Marx, as I have tried to show in *The Open Society*.

III

It was only after the victory of fascism in Austria that I wrote down the first version of *The Poverty of Historicism:* there was no danger any longer of damaging Austrian democracy, since it no longer existed; and the truth (or what I thought was the truth) had to be told.

My special emphasis on Mannheim was a reaction to Mannheim's influence on minds with whom I still felt essentially akin: the antifascists, and those who hoped for a better order.

IV

It was only after the publication of my book that I realized how great the influence of historicism still was in the English-speaking world. It was great in politics, but greater still in art and music, where a completely senseless idea of progress and novelty played a most destructive part.

I wish that historicism were no danger any longer. I think it is, and I am grateful to Alan Donagan for fighting this danger so forcefully.

Donagan mentions at the end the more positive results of my *Poverty of Historicism*, especially my theory of "situational logic". Readers of this volume will find a brilliant exposition, or rather a most original application, of this in Professor Gombrich's contribution.

47. *Gombrich on Situational Logic and Periods and Fashion in Art*

> I sometimes wonder how it was that the mischief done was not more clearly perceptible, and that the young men and women grew up as sensible and goodly as they did, in spite of the attempts almost deliberately made to warp and stunt their growth. Some doubtless received damage, from which they suffered to their life's end; but many seemed little or none the worse, and some almost the better. The reason would seem to be that the natural instinct of the lads in most cases so absolutely rebelled against their training, that do what the teachers might they could never get them to pay serious heed to it.
>
> SAMUEL BUTLER

Sir Ernst Gombrich's paper is exhilarating in its originality and brilliance. But at the very end there enters a somewhat depressing tone of pessimism. He expects an optimistic reply from me. This is a challenge indeed, and I will attempt to live up to it as well as I can. I shall try to be optimistic and I shall model my optimism on that of Samuel Butler, as expressed in my motto from his wonderful *Erewhon*.[217]

I

The essays of the contributors to this volume are supposed to be either descriptive of my philosophy, or critical, or both. In a way, Gombrich's essay belongs to the category of descriptive essays; but it radically transcends description. What Gombrich does is to start from certain suggestions which I have made on how to replace historicist method by a better one: he starts from my suggestions for what I call *"situational logic"*. And he develops these suggestions in a brilliant and original way, and applies them to a host of important and largely new problems. A few of these problems—the elimination of historicism in favour of something better, and the problem of the spread of fashions—have been perhaps briefly mentioned before, by him and by me. But most of the problems, and more especially the theory of the polarization of opinion and its logic, are startlingly new. Gombrich's development of my ideas not only surprised and delighted me by its excellence and by its wealth of new suggestions; it is also an application of my ideas far outshining what I ever hoped or dreamt would be possible, even after the sparkling applications made earlier by him in various of his works.

There is nothing which I can add to these applications: indeed, Gombrich deploys the method of situational logic with a skill which I can only enjoy and admire. I have nothing to say by way either of criticism or expansion.

II

In his last paragraph, Gombrich addresses to me, somewhat unexpectedly, a most formidable challenge. I will first restate his challenge in a slightly different form and then try as well as I can to meet the challenge.

The situational logic of the social life of a composer—or of any other artist—contains a kind of hidden mechanism which is analysed by Gombrich especially in his section VI, "Historicism and the Situation in Music". He points to aspects of this situation which in both his and my opinion constitute a serious menace to art. For although the situational mechanism he has in mind is inherent in almost any competitive field, it is especially dangerous in a field in which objective standards are either controversial, or ignored, or altogether missing.

The spur of competition makes the artist look for something striking, for something outstanding, for something new to adorn his work; it leads easily to "polarization", as Gombrich calls it: to partisanship, and to fashions. The situation, he shows, makes it practically impossible for those who have the fate of the arts at heart, to remain neutral. They have to take sides, he argues; and they thereby contribute to the danger.

The danger I am speaking of consists of the eclipse of the purely artistic standards or values by standards or values—perhaps admirable ones—extraneous to art itself.

This danger has of course something to do with my theory of art or, more generally, with my theory of world 3. The great thing about world 3 is that, in our efforts to do our work well, we can transcend ourselves, taking the work itself, and the standards which it represents, as more significant than our own feelings and ambitions. It is not that a great artist or scientist will be or should be without ambition; but his first ambition will be to perfect his work; and he will sense his shortcomings, though appreciating at the same time the immense help which he is receiving from the objective work he is trying to create—the world 3 object. In this he will lean very heavily on the wealth of objective standards which are, as the result of the efforts of other workers, incorporated in world 3.

Compared with these standards and values, personal ambition, and even the wish for personal recognition, though perhaps unavoidable, will seem like an intrusion, an impurity. This is part of the explanation of how we can lift ourselves by our own bootlaces (as I have often described it): in doing our best, knowing it is not good enough, we learn, while we are doing it, what the standards are which we aspire to meet. And in this way we transcend ourselves.

These standards are objective in more than one sense. They are shared, and they can be criticized. They can change (and far be it from me to say that they should not). But alterations should not be arbitrary, and even less should they be hostile to those great old standards by which we once grew, and outgrew ourselves. It is, after all, these "old" standards which represent art, and by which art must be judged at any moment in its development; and an artist who hates all the old standards is hardly an artist: what he hates is art.

Thus standards in art may change. But they can change in various ways and they may perhaps proceed to transcend themselves, and ourselves. And it is a mistake to believe that the great artists are always, or usually, the great revolutionaries, or enemies of the old order: these are historicist fables.

III

Gombrich tries to show with his examples—such as Quintilian, or the artist who felt he had to be at the spot where the actual battle was fought—how difficult it can be for the artist to escape social and personal pressures inherent in the logic of the situation. This may be so. But the tremendous influence of popular (but mistaken) theories of art, such as the expressionist or the historicist theories, can be combated, and so can the influence of similar theories of art criticism. It is not true that, in the past, the greatest artists were those who created a new style or a new way of expression. Originality and novelty are great values, but they are much greater if they come unsought. Not every good artist can be a genius, and styles are not standards. The style in which a work is conceived is part of that work, as is the language; but it is almost irrelevant to the quality of the work in which style—or in which language—it is written.

These are truisms, in my opinion (and, I suppose, in Gombrich's too); but they run counter to the prevailing atmosphere among artists, and especially among art critics. I am enough of an optimist to hope that these doctrines (which are purely intellectual) will one day be recognised for what they are, and that the atmosphere will change; for at present, I fear, it is debilitating, and in it art and music are bound to decline. Admittedly, we cannot "restore the independence of art" or free it of "social pressures": I suspect that Gombrich is not wholly serious in his last paragraph when, in these words, he demands from me suggestions of how to achieve the impossible. But we can fight the arrogant and clever stupidities of historicism, and of modernism, in the field of art and music, and if we are lucky we may perhaps win this fight. And we can hope, in this way, to establish a new atmosphere of modest appreciation and of tolerance in art and in music. Then we must wait patiently for the worker who has learned from others' and from his own work, and whose work shows that he owes everything to his submission to objective standards, standards engendered by the work of the uncounted workers who came before him, together with his own.

IV

Even though Gombrich's contribution was written some years ago, it contains, in its final challenge especially, references to my theory of world 3. World 3 comprises amongst other quite disparate things (such as social institutions) especially the sciences and the arts, and it has its own nonarbitrary domain of autonomy. My favourite example—much laboured in this volume—is that though we have invented (along with the invention of a highly developed language) the sequence of natural numbers, we did not invent the sequences of odd or even or prime or perfect numbers, which existed, even if for long unnoticed, as soon as the natural numbers did: prime numbers were actually there, to be *discovered rather than invented*. Although in its origin and growth world 3 is a product of the human mind, it is one of my theses that the human mind in its turn is also largely a product of world 3. World 3 creates its own problems; and without these, our intellectual activities—activities that belong to world 2—are incomprehensible, since they are attempts to solve problems which are, largely, world 3 problems. Thus world 3, as I see it, is in flux, partly in response to the changes it has itself provoked in world 2; changes induced, that is to say, by feedback from the autonomous problems of world 3.

This feedback effect is at least as important in art as it is in science: most of the problems of the sciences and the arts arise within the sciences and the arts themselves. It is the *tradition* of the sciences and the arts that is, quantitatively and qualitatively, by far the most important source of our problems—and of our knowledge, or craftsmanship. As I wrote some years ago:

> Most things we know [and also most things we reject] we have learned by example, by being told, by reading books, by learning how to criticize, how to take and accept criticism, how to respect the truth [and, more generally, how to recognise and take seriously a promising new solution of a problem].
> ... The fact that most of the sources of our knowledge are traditional *condemns anti-traditionalism as futile. But this fact must not be held to support a traditionalist attitude:* every bit of our traditional knowledge [and craftsmanship] (and even our inborn knowledge) is open to critical examination, and may be overthrown. Nevertheless, without tradition, knowledge [in science and in art] would be impossible.[218]

It is this tradition, historical continuity, together with revolutions which overthrow "bad" traditions, which builds and nurtures the sciences and the arts. Without a tradition, or with a complete break in tradition, we would have to start again where Adam started—or the Peking man—and who can say we should do as well as they did?

As Gombrich says, and I fully agree:

> an artist ... works within a medium that is preshaped by tradition. He has before him the benefit of countless experiments in creating orders of a similar kind and value. Moreover, in setting out to create another such ordered and meaningful arrangement ... he will discover new and unintended relationships during the process of creation, which his watchful mind can exploit and follow up, till the richness and complexity of the work transcends in fact any configuration that could be planned from scratch.[219]

Art changes; but great art always changes under the influence of its own autonomous problems: the great artist is an original genius, much more in the sense of Newton and Einstein, who tried to *solve problems* which they discovered (but which existed anyway), than in the sense of those musicians (I have named some of them in my *Autobiography*) who were influenced by the historicist view of progress in music as a value in itself, and by the not very original wish to be original; that is, to be different.

These views are presented in his own inimitable way, and with a reference to my "third world" (now "world 3") in an address by Gombrich entitled "Art and Self-Transcendence".[220]

I have not asked Professor Gombrich about the history of this address, but I like to think that it was a wish—perhaps unconscious—to see his challenge to me (by then a few years old) taken up and answered that made him write what he wrote in this address: it contains what I now suspect he wanted me to say in reply to his contribution to the present volume.

I hardly need to say that I could never have done it half as well. I am not, as Professor Gombrich is, rich in examples of world 3 problems from the history of art. Thus he mentions "an elementary artistic problem that may go back to the dawn of history: the decoration of a pot with an evenly spaced row of marks". The similarity with the invention of natural numbers, and the autonomous emergence of the problems of odd and even numbers, and of prime numbers, is striking.

Gombrich shows here (and elsewhere)[221] that an analysis of the work of the artist in terms of the solution of his *problems* can be most rewarding, and fatal to the expressionist theory of art, even if applied to the so-called "expressionists". Thus he quotes van Gogh speaking of

> the mental effort of balancing the six essential colours, red, blue, yellow, orange, violet, green. This is work and cool calculation, when one's mind is utterly stretched like that of an actor on the stage in a difficult part, when one has to think of a thousand different things at a time within half-an-hour. . . . Don't think I would ever artificially work myself into a feverish state. Rather remember that I am engrossed in a complicated calculus . . .[222]

Einstein once said "My pencil is more intelligent than I".[223] It is clear what he means: his pencil, the writing down of his equations, helped him to solve problems, equations, whose solution he could not anticipate. Van Gogh speaks not very differently. Even though, being less happy and more dissatisfied with his work, he perhaps might not have said that his brush was cleverer than he, he did stress the objectivity of his problem, and of the need to wrestle with it, in order to obtain his solutions.

I will not quote more from Gombrich's most interesting address (except to conclude my reply), but instead strongly recommend it to those who were struck by the challenge in the last paragraph of his contribution.

Let me, rather, briefly summarize.

The arts (like the sciences since the Foundations made them lucrative) are exposed to serious temptations. In the sciences there is at least one sovereign regulative idea which determines the rationality of its critical discussions; I mean the idea of objective truth. Nevertheless the sciences themselves are threatened, and may succumb: the tradition of problem solving may give way to that of puzzle solving; and the idea of scientific progress (however revolutionary) through problem solving may have to yield to that of the succession of a number of more or less incoherent periods which hardly understand each other. The idea of self-liberation through knowledge—of breaking out of our prison, not "routinely", but through a great revolutionary effort—may give way to the idea that we are condemned to prison life, and that there is not much to choose between a Ptolemaic prison and an Einsteinian prison. The same historical relativism threatens us in the field of art, though with a totally inverted emphasis. Here we are also told of revolutions, and even of the irrelevance of an older art for the needs of our present historical period. But the massively inappropriate emphasis here is upon advance (not to say progress), or art as an expression of the spirit of the changing times.

I know that I am at one with Professor Gombrich in thinking that these theories of art are intellectually less than half-digested, and that when put up against the objective standards of truth and falsity, they are seen to be just false. In fact, Gombrich calls these theories "total nonsense". Their problems arise from a misconceived sociology, they are mischievous intellectualist froth, which is utterly extraneous to the problems of art.

This "movement" may kill art, just as the other "movement" may kill science. But as long as we can fight them with good reasons, there is no need for despair. We may succeed in showing that these mistaken intellectualist theories of art, both that of art as the expression of the age and that of art as self-expression, are intellectually empty; and we can hope that there will arise again young artists who are gripped by the great problems of art itself, and who will, like Samuel Butler's lads, be gifted and sane enough to be deaf to the preaching of their fashionable teachers and critics.

For art has a place in this world of facts: and I can do no better than end with that moving passage from Gombrich's address which he himself chose as the conclusion of "Art and Self-Transcendence".[224]

> the title . . . "The Place of Value in a World of Facts" is of course taken from a book by . . . the late Wolfgang Koehler. . . . In the first months of Nazi rule, while he still held his chair in Berlin, he dared to write a newspaper article against the purges of the Universities. When I was fortunate to meet him again in Princeton, shortly before his death, conversation fell on this episode, and he described how after the publication of his protest he and his friends spent the night waiting for the fatal knock on the door which fortunately did not come. They were playing chamber music all night long. I cannot think of a better illustration of the place of value in a world of fact.

Karl Popper

NOTES

[1] Ryle's conjecture that the *Apology* is not Socrates' but Plato's own apology when accused of a similar crime seems to me insufficiently supported; and it is but one of its major drawbacks that it renders the Socratic problem insoluble. Cp. Gilbert Ryle, *Plato's Progress* (Cambridge: Cambridge University Press, 1966), esp. pp. 154-92.

[2] The only impressive argument of which I am aware, other than (1) and (2), that may be used against my thesis, seems to go back to my teacher, Heinrich Gomperz, *Sophistik und Rhetorik* (Leipzig: Teubner, 1912; reprinted, Stuttgart: Teubner, 1965); see esp. pp. 9-11. This argument contends that the Platonic *Apology* cannot be historical because of certain parallels with the *Apology of Palamedes*, of which there is extant a manuscript ascribed to Gorgias (and printed in Diels/Kranz, *Fragmente der Vorsokratiker*, Vol. II, pp. 294-303). Let us admit the ascription and the similarities, and let us even assume that it belonged to a literary *genre* to which Aeschylus and Euripides also contributed. (These points are argued by A. H. Chroust, *Socrates, Man and Myth* [Notre Dame, Ind.: University of Notre Dame Press; London: Routledge &

Kegan Paul, 1957], esp. pp. 116-19; in n. 1439 on p. 321, Chroust lists his predecessors, among whom the earliest is Gomperz, *Sophistik und Rhetorik*.) How does this bear on the historicity of the *Apology?* If Plato was influenced—consciously or unconsciously—by an alleged "Palamedean literature", could not Socrates have been influenced by it also? Moreover, the dissimilarities are as significant as the similarities; and precisely those aspects which one who holds the same views as I hold would wish to attribute to Socrates belong to the dissimilarities. The similarities, on the other hand, may well belong to what every educated Athenian would expect, consciously or unconsciously, as proper to a defence against an accusation of this kind—and something similar may hold for the indictment.

³ At least seven early dialogues of Plato, *Charmides, Lysis, Hippias Minor* and *Major, Laches, Euthyphron,* and *Protagoras* are "sophistical" in the sense that they are mainly disputatious (eristic). They differ from sophistic teaching largely through the self-critical and modest attitude of Socrates. But, although Socrates does not try to make the worse case sound the better, he makes it very clear that his arguments carry him often to conclusions which he regards as unacceptable. (Cp. *Charmides* 175 E; *Lysis* 216 C; *Hippias Minor* 372 D; *Major* 304 C, and elsewhere; see Svend Ranulf, *Der Eleatische Satz vom Widerspruch* [Copenhagen: Gyldendalske Boghandel, 1924], esp. pp. 117-22—a book to which my attention has been drawn by Dr Flemming Steen Nielsen.) It seems that Socrates' message—or at least his first message—was: I can play the argumentative game as well as anybody, but although I can refute much, I cannot prove anything positive in this way; in brief, I know that I don't know, and I have no wisdom to sell.

⁴ See W. K. C. Guthrie, *A History of Greek Philosophy* (Cambridge: Cambridge University Press, 1969), Vol. III. I am not sure whether Guthrie would approve of the n. 56 (*The Open Society*, Chap. 10) mentioned above, or of my somewhat pointed methodological opposition of *The Apology* to *The Clouds*. But I agree with practically everything he says on the historicity of *The Clouds*; compare with my next section especially his striking quotation from an unpublished lecture of Cornford's on p. 362. *The Open Society* will hereinafter be cited as *O.S.*

⁵ I had better, perhaps, make it quite clear that I admire Socrates in spite of the fact that in some respects he may justly be interpreted as a forerunner of language philosophy. I look upon this aspect of Socrates as something to be explained, and even to be excused, by historical considerations.

⁶ See [1957(a)], now Chap. 1 of *Conjectures and Refutations* (hereinafter cited as *C.&R.*), esp. section III (*C.&R.*, pp. 39-41); and [1955(g)], now Chap. 11, esp. section 2 (*C.&R.*, pp. 255-58).

⁷ See esp. my *Logik der Forschung* ([1934(b)] and later editions) hereinafter cited as *L.d.F.;* my letter to the editors of *Erkenntnis* [1933(a)]; and my paper [1935(a)], now all in the later editions of *L.d.F.* and in my *Logic of Scientific Discovery* ([1959(a)] and later editions), hereinafter cited as *L.Sc.D.*

⁸ See [1934(b)], p. 186; [1959(a)], p. 252; [1966(e)], p. 199. Since then I have considerably developed my metaphysical realism into a rationally arguable theory. (See [1950(b)]; [1958(f)], now Chap. 8 of [1963(a)]; [1970(1)].)

⁹ See [1933(a)] and [1966(e)], pp. 254-56, and the translation in [1959(a)], Appendix *i, pp. 312-14.

¹⁰ The quotation and the footnote are taken from p. 56 of a paper by Alice Ambrose, "On Criteria of Literal Significance", *Crítica, Revista Hispanoamericana de Filosofia,* 1 (1967), 49-72.

¹¹ For example in the paper just quoted.

¹² The book I am alluding to is Lothar Krauth, *Die Philosophie Carnaps* (Vienna and New York: Springer-Verlag, 1970); see esp. p. 85: "Karl Popper war vielleicht der erste, welcher an die Stelle des Verifikations-prinzips ein anderes Sinnkriterium setzte: das Falsifikationsprinzip." ("Karl Popper was perhaps the first to suggest that we should substitute for the principle of verifiability an alternative criterion of meaningfulness: the principle of falsifiability.") See also the end of the following paragraph on p. 86. (Added after completion: A still more recent book is

Leszek Kolakowski, *Positivist Philosophy* [Harmondsworth: Penguin Books, 1972]; see esp. pp. 209 and 216.)

In this context I should also mention R. W. Ashby's article "Verifiability Principle" in *The Encyclopedia of Philosophy*, ed. by Paul Edwards (New York: Macmillan Co. and Free Press, 1967; London: Collier-Macmillan, 1967), Vol. VIII, pp. 240-47. On p. 242 the author asserts that it was "sometimes suggested that conclusive falsifiability rather than conclusive verifiability should be the criterion of a cognitively meaningful statement". However, I am not mentioned, and neither is the problem of demarcation, even though many of my criticisms, both of verifiability and of criteria of meaning, are discussed (in a somewhat offhand way). Nor is *L.d.F.* recorded in the long list of references on p. 241.

On the other hand, an Italian Encyclopedia has an article *"Falsificabilità"* in which the idea of falsifiability is attributed to me. See Nicola Abbagnano, *Dizionario di Filosofia* (Turin: Unione Tipografico-Editrice Torinese, 1961), p. 368.

[13] See A. J. Ayer, *Language, Truth and Logic* (London: Victor Gollancz, 1936), pp. 24 f.; 2d ed., 1946 (and later editions), p. 38. Here we read after arguments against the adoption of "conclusive verifiability" as a criterion of meaningfulness or factual significance: "Nor can we accept the suggestion that a sentence should be allowed to be factually significant if, and only if, it expresses something which is definitely confutable by experience"; to which a footnote is added: "This has been proposed by Karl Popper in his *Logik der Forschung*." Much later this error has been more or less repeated in Ayer's Editorial Introduction to *Logical Positivism* (Glencoe, Ill.: The Free Press, 1959); see pp. 13 f.

[14] Jørgen Jørgensen, "The Development of Logical Empiricism", *International Encyclopedia of Unified Science*, Vol. II, No. 9 (1951), p. 72. Jørgensen differs from Ayer in explicitly attributing the criticism of the verifiability criterion to me. He then raises the problem of what could be done to save the situation, and he continues: "This could be done only by amending the theory. A first proposal in that direction was made by Popper in his *Logik der Forschung* (1935) where, as the criterion of the meaningfulness of a sentence, he uses not the verifiability but the falsifiability of the sentence."

[15] See section 16 of my *Autobiography* above.

[16] Cp. Rudolf Carnap, "Testability and Meaning", *Philosophy of Science*, **3** (1936), 419-71; and **4** (1937), 1-40; reprinted with Corrigenda and Additional Bibliography by the Graduate Philosophy Club (New Haven, Conn.: Yale University, 1950); and (with omissions) on pp. 47-92 of Herbert Feigl and May Brodbeck, eds., *Readings in the Philosophy of Science* (New York: Appleton-Century-Crofts, 1953).

[17] Cp. C. G. Hempel, "Problems and Changes in the Empiricist Criterion of Meaning", *Revue Internationale de Philosophie*, **4** (1950), 41-63; reprinted on pp. 163-85 of Leonard Linsky, ed., *Semantics and the Philosophy of Language* (Urbana: University of Illinois Press, 1952); and on pp. 108-29 of Ayer, ed., *Logical Positivism* (see n. 13 above).

[18] Ayer's book seems to have been the first printed report in which my criterion of demarcation was presented as one of meaning. But I had previously to argue orally against this misinterpretation at some of the lectures I gave in Vienna between 1932 and 1935.

[19] The story is briefly told in *C.&R.*, pp. 253 f.

[20] William Craig has shown that we can eliminate these terms from our theory, but only if we have a sufficiently rich metatheory at our disposal; thus the metatheory would become "metaphysical" in place of the object-language theory. See also n. 42 below.

[21] Cp. Karl Menger, "Die neue Logik", *Krise und Neuaufbau in den Exakten Wissenschaften* (Leipzig and Vienna: Franz Deuticke, 1933), pp. 93-122, esp. pp. 117-19.

[22] Rudolf Carnap, "Über Protokollsätze", *Erkenntnis*, **3** (1932), 215-28. It is not quite understandable why this crucial (and in a manner final) paper was omitted from Professor Ayer's comprehensive collection *Logical Positivism*, which treats precisely these problems.

[23] Carnap, "Über Protokollsätze", p. 215.

24 Cp. Rudolf Carnap, *The Logical Syntax of Language* (London: Routledge & Kegan Paul, 1937), pp. 51, 164, and esp. p. 321 with the references to Carnap's article "Über Protokollsätze" and (at the bottom of the page) to me: "A detailed criticism of the view according to which laws are not sentences is given by Popper."

25 Cp. Carnap, "Über Protokollsätze", p. 228. See also the text following n. 115 in section 17 of my *Autobiography* above.

26 "Über Protokollsätze", p. 225.

27 *Ibid.*, pp. 225 f.

28 *L.d.F.* [1934(b)], p. 61; [1966(e)], p. 70; *L.Sc.D.* [1959(a)], pp. 104 f.

29 Heinrich Gomperz had sent the MS of my book to the great publishing house J.C.B. Mohr in Tübingen who, very understandably, declined it. But thirty years later the same house undertook the publication of the 2d German ed. of my *L.d.F.*, whose first chapter is an outline of the still unpublished book which was rejected.

30 Cp. my letter in *Erkenntnis*, **3** (1933), 426 f., republished in English in *L.Sc.D.*, pp. 312-14, and in German in the second (and later) editions of *L.d.F.*, pp. 254-56. The letter is brief, but it is clear enough: "For our criterion of falsifiability distinguishes with sufficient precision the theoretical systems of the empirical sciences from those of metaphysics . . . , without asserting the meaninglessness of metaphysics (which from a historical point of view can be seen to be the source from which the theories of the empirical sciences spring)."

31 Cp. Otto Neurath, "Pseudorationalismus der Falsifikation", *Erkenntnis*, **5** (1935), 353-65. This was the third review article of my *L.d.F.* (entitled "Pseudorationalism of Falsification") which appeared within two consecutive numbers of *Erkenntnis*, **5**: Reichenbach's long negative criticism and Carnap's positive ("official") review had both appeared in the preceding number of the same volume. In his last section, Neurath speaks quite correctly of my "metaphysical tendencies" which make me "friendlier towards Kant and other metaphysicists than towards the group of thinkers whom he . . . describes as 'the' positivists" (p. 364). (Neurath was hostile to Kant but friendly to Hegel. Perhaps I may repeat here that I am a realist who makes the following concession to idealism: all our knowledge is theory, and our theories are our inventions, as Kant saw; we try to impose them upon the world. Where Kant was wrong, under the influence of Newton's success, is that he did not see how often we err, and fail to impose our theories on the world.)

32 Cp. Rudolf Carnap, *Erkenntnis*, **5** (1935), 293.

33 C.G. Hempel, *Deutsche Literaturzeitung*, **58** (1937), 310-14.

34 (Italics mine.) Cp. Carnap's review of *L.d.F.* in *Erkenntnis*, p. 290: "Die Nachprüfung bildet das Kriterium der Abgrenzung zwischen empirischer Wissenschaft und Metaphysik; genauer: die Falsifizierbarkeit."

35 See Carnap, "Testability and Meaning", 3, pp. 419-71, and 4, pp. 1-40; reprinted (with omissions) in Feigl and Brodbeck, eds., *Readings in Philosophy of Science*, pp. 47-92 (see n. 16 above).

36 See esp. my *L.Sc.D.*, the n. *1 on pp. 251 f., where I tell the story of these terminological muddles.

37 "Testability and Meaning", **4**, p. 2; *Readings in Philosophy of Science*, p. 72.

38 "Testability and Meaning", **4**, p. 5; *Readings in Philosophy of Science*, p. 75.

39 See my *O.S.*, Subject Index (3d and later editions) under "positivism, logical".

40 See my *O.S.*, Vol. II, Chap. 11, pp. 9-31 and nn. 39-54 to this chapter (pp. 290-301). See, for example, n. 47 (p. 295): "Thus . . . a definition shifts the problem of *meaning* back to the defining terms, without ever being able to solve it."; and the next, n. 48: "But we can say that it is impossible to 'constitute' [define] universals in terms of particulars. (With this, cp. my *L.d.F.*, esp. section 14, pp. 31 ff., and section 25, p. 53 [*L.Sc.D.*, pp. 64-68 and 93-95]. . . .)".

41 See my *C.&R.*, pp. 275-77.

42 William Craig's famous theorem merely shows that *if we have at our disposal* a language of science of arbitrary richness, we can with the help of an interesting metalinguistic method purify it of any class of terms we dislike. Thus within the purified sublanguage the disliked terms would indeed be "meaningless". But in order to construct the purified sublanguage, we have first to have the nonpurified (theoretical) language and its metalanguage at our disposal. See also n. 20 above.

43 Cp. Hempel, "Problems and Changes in the Empiricist Criterion of Meaning", pp. 41-63. Here quoted from the reprint of Linsky, ed., *Semantics and Philosophy of Language*, pp. 163-85 (see n. 17 above).

44 Hempel's fundamental tenet is: "all non-analytic knowledge is based on experience". I prefer my "principle of empiricism" of [1933(a)] ([1966(e)], p. 254), translation [1959(a)], p. 312: "only 'experience' can decide about the truth or falsity of a factual statement", since it avoids the vagueness of the idea of "knowledge based on experience".

45 Cp. Hempel, "Empiricist Criterion of Meaning", p. 41; *Semantics and Philosophy of Language*, p. 163. (Italics mine.) Hempel has a footnote to the word "added", referring to W. T. Stace, "Positivism", *Mind*, **53** (1944), 215-37, who pointed this out. In fact, the "addition" of "testability" as a criterion of *meaning* was made by Carnap, though it was a little earlier wrongly ascribed by Ayer to me.

46 "Empiricist Criterion of Meaning", n. 1 on p. 48; *Semantics and Philosophy of Language*, p. 170.

47 [1934(b)], [1959(a)], [1966(e)], n. 5 to section 1.

48 In the same passage of *L.Sc.D.* mentioned in the preceding footnote.

49 See *C.&R.*, p. 110: "From the point of view of general relativity, . . . the earth rotates . . . *in precisely that sense in which a bicycle wheel rotates*."

50 What I say here is an oversimplification as far as Copernicus is concerned, but it is almost certainly true of Aristarchus.

51 For a detailed discussion see "The Aim of Science" [1957(i)] and [1969(k)]; now Chap. 5 of *Objective Knowledge* [1972(a)].

52 The small deviation of the perihelion of Mercury did not seriously trouble anybody in the light of its other almost incredible successes. Whether it should have done is another matter.

53 Cp. *C.&R.*, Chap. 3, nn. 20 and 21, pp. 106 f.

54 Cp. the Index of *C.&R.*, 3d ed., under these names.

55 Cp. [1961(h)]; now Chap. 1 of [1974a].

56 I must stress this point, because Professor Ayer has asserted on pp. 583 f. of "Philosophy and Scientific Method", *Proceedings of the XIVth International Congress of Philosophy, Vienna: 2nd to 9th September 1968* (Vienna: Verlag Herder, 1968), Vol. I, pp. 536-42 that "In modern times, two theses have held the field. According to one of them, what is required is that the hypothesis be verifiable: according to the other, that it be falsifiable." And after outlining very briefly a history of the verifiability criterion, he writes: "In its current form, all that it requires of a scientific hypothesis is that it should figure non-trivially in a theory which is open to confirmation when taken as a whole."

"In the case of the principle of falsifiability", Professor Ayer continues, "the process of adaptation has been less explicit. Some of its adherents still talk as if the formulation which was given to it by Professor Popper in the opening chapters of his *Logik der Forschung* continued to hold good. The fact is, however, that Professor Popper himself found it necessary to modify it in the course of this very book." To this I can only reply that (1) it seems to me better to introduce the necessary modifications in "this very book" in which the proposal was made; (2) I introduced falsifiability as a criterion of demarcation in *L.d.F.*, section 6, p. 12 (*L.Sc.D.*, p. 40) and "I found it necessary to outline all the various objections" on the next page, p. 13 (*L.Sc.D.*, p. 41), in the same section, announcing my intention to discuss each of them more fully later; (3) the one difficulty which I postponed for later—the formal nonfalsifiability of probability statements—was solved by a methodological proposal.

[57] Cp. *O.S.*, Vol. II, 3d and later editions, pp. 14 f.

[58] This is an old story but there are many new instances. I once met a very famous physicist who, although I implored him, declined to look at a most simple and interesting experiment of a professor of experimental physics in Vienna. It would not have taken him five minutes, and he did not plead lack of time. The experiment did not fit into his theories, and he pleaded that it might cost him some sleepless nights. And I know more than one philosopher who refuses to look at a simple proof or disproof.

[59] For a fuller discussion see my *O.S.*, Vol. II, 3d and later editions, pp. 108 f.

[60] Cp. *C.&R.*, esp. pp. 35-38.

[61] This case has been elegantly and, I think, unanswerably argued by J. W. N. Watkins, "Confirmation, the Paradoxes, and Positivism", in *The Critical Approach to Science and Philosophy*, ed. by Mario Bunge (New York: Free Press of Glencoe, 1964; London: Collier-Macmillan, 1964), pp. 92-115. See also P. K. Feyerabend, "A Note on Two 'Problems' of Induction", *The British Journal for the Philosophy of Science*, **19** (1969), 251-53.

[62] C. G. Hempel, "Recent Problems of Induction", in *Mind and Cosmos*, ed. by R. G. Colodny (Pittsburgh: University of Pittsburgh Press, 1966), pp. 112-34.

[63] I am even said by Putnam to be at times an *apriorist* (see his section 13). This remark mystifies me.

[64] These are the arguments of a logical character. Putnam also shows—and admits—affinities with Kuhn; but because I shall later discuss Kuhn (section 39 below) I shall here leave aside (except for a minor remark in the text following n. 67 below) this aspect of his paper.

[65] Quoting the concluding sentence of Appendix *ix of [1959(a)] (p. 419; in German, [1966(e)], p. 373), namely "On the positive side, we may be entitled to add that the surviving theory is the best theory—and the best tested theory—of which we know", Putnam asks: "...am I mistaken, or do I detect an inductivist quaver? What does 'best theory' mean? Surely Popper cannot mean 'most likely'?". Referring to the same sentence, Lakatos inquires (p. 412 of "Changes in the Problem of Inductive Logic", in *The Problem of Inductive Logic*, ed. by Imre Lakatos [Amsterdam: North-Holland Publishing Co., 1967], pp. 315-417): "But what is the 'best theory' *apart* from being 'best tested'? The one which is most 'trustworthy'?". And he concludes: "There is no answer." But there is an answer, not only to this second rhetorical question of Lakatos's, but also to Putnam's second question. The answer is "No". I should have thought that this was obvious, considering what I say on the previous page (p. 418) of *L.Sc.D.* There too I answer Putnam's first question, and Lakatos's as well. But see also my section 14 below.

[66] Hilary Putnam, "What Theories are Not", in *Logic, Methodology and Philosophy of Science*, ed. by Ernest Nagel, Patrick Suppes, and Alfred Tarski (Stanford: Stanford University Press, 1962), pp. 240-51.

[67] Consider, for example, the other paper of his own that he mentions in n. 1, namely "How Not to Talk About Meaning", in *Boston Studies in the Philosophy of Science*, ed. by Robert S. Cohen and M. W. Wartofsky (New York: Humanities Press, 1965), Vol. II, pp. 205-22. In his n. 2 Putnam refers us to this paper (originally read in December, 1963) for "a discussion of 'approximate truth' ". It seems that Putnam is not aware that much of what he says there (pp. 206 f.) had already been said by me when I discussed "verisimilitude", first at the Stanford Congress in 1960 [1962(h)], and later, much more comprehensively, in *C.&R.* [1963(a)]. Thus Ayer's dislike (see his contribution, above) of my "verisimilitude" would presumably extend to Putnam's "approximate truth".

[68] Bayes's theorem is derivable in every classical calculus of probabilities, and I, for one, have never doubted it. But it is not generally applicable to hypotheses which form an infinite set—as

do our natural laws. I am as little an anti-Bayesian as I am an anti-1+2=3 man or an anti-the-sum-of-two-numbers-is-infinite-if-either-of-them-is-infinite man. But I do not think that these two theorems are applicable to the same cases.

[69] For straightforward ways of doing this, see the first part of subsection II of my reply to Lakatos.

[70] C.&R., p. 239.

[70a] (Added in proofs.) I admit that I sometimes introduce terminological distinctions, such as between corroboration and verisimilitude (and also probability). But I do so only reluctantly and if forced by a pressing problem situation. In general I try to live up to the rule (not a dogma) that we should avoid fine terminological distinctions, and that we should not stick even to a definite terminology. It is the context, and the problem under discussion, which should elucidate, in each case, what is at stake. I believe that this rule is important: we should not, like Aristotelian essentialists, worry too much about the meanings of words; and we should recoil from the danger of introducing another esoteric jargon. There is also my old thesis that precision—itself only a means to an end—cannot be achieved by introducing a precise terminology, and that trying to do so leads to pseudo precision and to scholasticism. (Compare the motto from F. P. Ramsey to Chap. 11, section II of my O.S.; also section 7 above of my Autobiography.)

This will explain why I do not want to enter here into Professor Lakatos's distinctions between $Popper_0$, $Popper_1$, and $Popper_2$. However, he discusses, in his "Note", which he adds to the end of his section I(a), the question whether I should be identified with his "$Popper_1$" or his "$Popper_2$", and there confesses that he is "at a loss" and makes a direct appeal to me to dissolve his "puzzlement". In view of this appeal I may say that I conjecture that his puzzlement arises from the fact that he unconsciously saddles me with the obligation of using terms always in the same sense, and with the intention of being "precise". This, and the attempt to live up himself to that supposed obligation, makes him tie himself up in a Gordian knot which I shall not attempt to untie. For were I to admit that I am $Popper_2$ (that is, his "sophisticated methodological falsificationist"), I too should become entangled in terminological minutiae.

I may perhaps add the conjecture that the tendency to overrate terminological distinctions might also be one of the reasons why there are many mistaken assertions about my intellectual history in Professor Lakatos's papers.

[71] I have discussed these criticisms—and the way in which Tarski's theory contained answers to them—on many occasions. See esp. the first part of subsection II to my reply to Ayer above, and section 20 of my Autobiography above. In addition, see section 4 of my paper "A Realist View of Logic, Physics, and History", [1970(l)], now Chap. 8 of [1972(a)], and also the new Chap. 9 of [1972(a)], "Philosophical Comments on Tarski's Theory of Truth".

[72] Alfred Tarski recently told me that he was "slightly shocked" to find himself indexed in O.S. almost as often as was Marx. While this is an exaggeration, it does emphasize my interest in his work at that time.

[73] At this point I added an Addendum in 1968 to the German edition, p. 373, and a similar one in 1972 to the latest English edition, p. 419. In these Addenda I tried to clarify further the distinction between "the best theory" and "the best tested theory". The best theory is the one among the surviving theories which has the greatest explanatory power, the greatest content, and so is the least ad hoc. The best theory in this sense need not necessarily be the best tested theory.

[74] If immunizing strategies (such as the arbitrary rejection of well-tested and corroborated observations, or the ad hoc hypothesis that our telescopes are all suffering from defects which systematically deceive us) are adopted, then Newtonian theory cannot, according to my L.d.F., be refuted, and so there is no case to answer. See also n. 79a below.

[75] No ceteris paribus clause is necessary. I do not want to get involved in the morass of a discussion of these clauses; but I must say that I hold that most of the discussions of ceteris paribus clauses and all of the appeals to them are misleading. As a condition or antecedent, the clause "ceteris paribus" (all other things being the same) is, of course, never satisfied in this world. Such an antecedent would therefore empty a theory to which it was attached of any empirical content. Where use is made of such clauses in the social sciences, what is intended is to say that the relevant circumstances should not change. Yet what is relevant or irrelevant is a matter of risky conjecture (and such conjectures will be the more interesting the more specific they are, and the more

testable they render the original theory). I therefore suggest that *ceteris paribus* clauses should be avoided and, more especially, that they should not be imported into the discussion of the methodology of the natural sciences.

[76] "Falsification and the Methodology of Scientific Research Programmes", in *Criticism and the Growth of Knowledge*, ed. by Imre Lakatos and Alan Musgrave (Cambridge: Cambridge University Press, 1970), pp. 91-195. This paper is hereinafter cited as "Scientific Research Programmes".

[77] For a discussion of this story, see section 8 of my *Replies* above. I have discussed it many times in my lectures, and it is mentioned in *L.Sc.D.* [1959(a)], section 30, n. *3 ([1968(a)], *4) on p. 108 (*L.d.F.* [1966(e)], p. 73). See also the text following n. 35 in my *Autobiography* above.

[78] It is at this place (p. 101), in a footnote, that Professor Lakatos puts almost the same rhetorical question that he puts in section I(c) above. He writes: "Popper asks: 'What kind of clinical responses would refute . . . not merely a particular diagnosis but psychoanalysis itself?' ([1963(a)], p. 38, footnote 3). But what kind of observation would refute . . . not merely a particular version but Newtonian theory itself?" My answer follows immediately: almost any kind of observation.

[79] There is perhaps in Lakatos's next paragraph (the parenthetical one) on p. 102, the ghost of a "general argument" which starts ". . . *one can easily argue that ceteris paribus clauses are not exceptions, but the rule in science*". But since his (essentialist) argument leads to the conclusion that "All swans are white" is not refuted by a black swan (see his "Scientific Research Programmes", p. 102), we have good reason to reject it. See also my n. 75, above.

[79a] If immunizing stratagems are to be allowed, the example, as I have said before, is no criticism of my views, because in *L.d.F.* I discussed at some length the possibility of making laws such as Newton's true by convention, by means of adopting a methodological policy involving the use of immunizing stratagems. See also n. 74, above.

[80] The idea of theoretical pluralism is no novelty. Under the name "The Method of Multiple Hypotheses", its methodological importance was stressed by the geologist T. C. Chamberlin at the end of the nineteenth century. See, for example, his article "The Method of Multiple Working Hypotheses", *The Journal of Geology*, 5 (1897), 837-48.

I owe the reference to Chamberlin to my late friend the geologist Professor R. S. Allan of Christchurch, New Zealand, who drew my attention to certain similarities between Chamberlin's views and my own.

[80a] (Added in proofs.) See, for example, the following passage from my [1963(h)], p. 969. "Einstein proposed his theory of general relativity; . . . he defended it patiently against violent criticism; . . . he suggested that it was an important advance, and that it should be accepted as an improvement on Newton's theory; yet . . . he never accepted it [accepted it, that is, in the sense of accepting its truth] himself".

For recent criticisms and improvements of the formal or technical definition which I proposed in my attempt to defend the intuitive use of verisimilitude, see n. 165a below which refers to David Miller and Pavel Tichy.

[81] For a discussion of one such condition, see subsection IV of my reply to Medawar.

Incidentally, the criticisms Professor Lakatos makes of my views in his n. 28 are vitiated by the fact that he ignores most of what I say about the conventionalists in *L.d.F.*, section 19, especially about the differences between their and my views of the aims of science; and also what I have since said (for example, *L.Sc.D.*, section 4, n. *5 and *C.&R.*, Chap. 8, first published in [1958(f)]) about the possibility of discussing such aims rationally.

Professor Lakatos's own attempts to solve the question of the criticizability of a methodology I will not discuss in detail. For I do not think that his "quasi-empirical approach" has any advantages; indeed, it involves solving difficult (and perhaps insoluble) problems such as "Who are the scientific élite?". Professor Lakatos himself does not accept his own original suggestion (see the text between his nn. 33 and 34); and in the end, after many pages of discussion, he himself admits, of his improved criterion (see the text to his n. 63): "I . . . can easily answer the question when I would give up my criterion of demarcation: when another one is proposed which is better on my metacriterion. (I have not yet answered the question under what circumstances I shall give up my metacriterion; but one must always stop somewhere.)". My own criterion of demarcation, however, is not threatened by an infinite regress.

[82] Cp. *L.Sc.D.*, sections 31-46; and also pp. 80 (the last three lines of the first paragraph for *"ad hoc"*; the second paragraph for "bold"), 273, 278-80.

[82a] Professor Lakatos's attempt to show that our best theories are nonfalsifiable destroys, among other things, my *theory of the empirical content* of a scientific hypothesis, which I suggested we regard as the class of its potential falsifiers. It thereby would make nonsense of my distinction between risky or bold theories (like Newton's or Einstein's) and theories which take no risk (as Freud's or Adler's) since they can "explain" every conceivable event in their field. This is the reason why I find Professor Lakatos's priority claim concerning boldness not only historically untenable, but philosophically absurd. He does not seem to have realized that his destruction of my ship (that is, falsifiability) if successful, would leave him hopelessly afloat in the sea, and without any boldness.

[83] I will note only in passing Professor Lakatos's remark " . . . he now gave up his long held and tenaciously defended doctrine that the degree of corroboration of an unrefuted theory cannot be smaller than the degree of corroboration of any of its consequences". What can one really say about such a world 2 expression as "tenaciously defended"? The fact is that I always held the view that *theories* are *systems* of statements and that it is the *theory* that is corroborated—that is to say the whole system of statements. A weaker theory t_1 which follows from a stronger theory t_2 will be, as a system of statements, because of its weakness, more weakly corroborable than t_2; but if it is regarded as part of t_2 then it shares the corroborability of t_2. (The passage referred to by Professor Lakatos—*L.Sc.D.*, p. 270—is devoted to a different problem; more precisely, to the question whether degrees of corroboration can possibly satisfy the probability calculus. Admittedly I do not explain, in the particular passage referred to by Professor Lakatos, what I have explained in the present footnote and in "Conjectural Knowledge". But nobody can say, at every place, all things at once.)

[84] But see nn. 91 and 93 below.

[84a] This section is a ruthlessly pruned version of a lecture I gave to the Royal Society of Edinburgh in June, 1971; the lecture itself was a much shortened and revised variant of my [1971(i)], now, with minor alterations, Chap. 1 of my [1972(a)], which should be consulted for further references.

[85] See, for example, [1968(i)], sections 10 and 11; and section 32 of my *Autobiography* above.

[86] The term was first used in *O.S.*, [1945(c)] and later editions, pp. 213 f.; and in [1949(d)], a lecture given in Alpbach in 1948 and now translated as an appendix to my book *Objective Knowledge* [1972(a)]. For the commonsense theory of knowledge see esp. Chap. 2 of *Objective Knowledge*.

[87] David Hume, *A Treatise on Human Nature*, ed. by L. A. Selby-Bigge (London and New York: Oxford University Press, 1941), Book I, Part IV, the last paragraph of section II on p. 218. David Miller has pointed out to me that by establishing and experiencing the contrast between what he believed (realism), and what he thought was true (idealism), Hume made here—no doubt unwittingly—a first step away from his own (commonsense) characterization of knowledge as a form of belief; a step, that is, towards recognizing the profound gulf between world 2 and world 3 (as I call them; see, for example, section 15 below; sections 20-26 below; and section 38 of my *Autobiography* above). Unfortunately, this discovery of Hume's itself remained almost entirely in world 2, as an irritation, rather than appearing in world 3, as an objective problem.

[88] The three quotations are from Bertrand Russell, *A History of Western Philosophy* (London: George Allen & Unwin, 1946), pp. 698 f.; new ed. (1961), pp. 645-47. (Italics mine.)

[89] See p. 21 of P. F. Strawson, "On Justifying Induction", *Philosophical Studies,* **9** (1958), 20 f. See also Hume, *Treatise*, Book II, Part III, section III (Selby-Bigge ed., p. 415): "Reason is, and ought only to be the slave of the passions. . . ."

[90] For a much fuller discussion see section 10 of my *Autobiography.*

[91] Professor Lakatos, in a postscript *"Added in 1971"* to his contribution, dubs my claim that "it will be 'rational' to choose the best tested theory" a "well-worn tautology" (see his n. 127).

[92] See *L.d.F.* [1934(b)], section 79; *L.Sc.D.*, pp. 253 f.

[93] Professor Lakatos, in his n. 127 (referred to in n. 91 above), cites this disapprovingly and asks: "What then should a theory of knowledge attempt to explain?" How [not Why] we make progress is one thing I have tried to explain. But I do not feel that this is the place to start an inventory of epistemological problems.

[94] See n. 87 above for Hume's partial appreciation of this difference, and for further references.

[95] The discussion is a discussion of W. C. Salmon's paper, "The Justification of Inductive Rules of Inference", in *The Problem of Inductive Logic*, ed. by Lakatos, pp. 24-43 (see n. 65 above). See J. W. N. Watkins, "Non-inductive Corroboration", *ibid.*, pp. 61-66, and pp. 95-97 of W. C. Salmon, "Reply", *ibid.*, pp. 74-97.

[96] "Reply", p. 95.

[97] "Reply", p. 97; Salmon quotes from Watkins, "Non-inductive Corroboration", p. 66.

[98] Claude Bernard, *An Introduction to the Study of Experimental Medicine*, trans. by Henry Copley Greene (New York: Henry Schuman, 1927 and 1949).

[99] In his book, *The Art of the Soluble* (London: Methuen & Co., 1967), Sir Peter Medawar stresses this point (pp. 7 and 87): "If politics is the art of the possible, research is surely the art of the soluble." This is perhaps the only point of importance in the book with which I do not agree completely: both Einstein and Schrödinger devoted much of their lives to heroic attempts to solve problems which they did not succeed in solving; although it is of course true that they succeeded in solving *other* problems. Admittedly, many great scientists have solved a problem they set out to solve, yet others solved important problems which were not identical with the problems they wished, but failed, to solve. (Example: general relativity and the so-called "Mach Principle".) Indeed a problem may attract a scientist by its difficulty, and even by its apparent insolubility. I am inclined to think that the body-mind problem is insoluble. But I think it can be shifted, so that the problem becomes different from what it is usually taken to be; and this may be interesting, especially if the problem is insoluble.

[100] J. C. Eccles, *The Inhibitory Pathways of the Central Nervous System* (Liverpool: Liverpool University Press, 1969); and J. C. Eccles, *Facing Reality, Philosophical Adventures by a Brain Scientist* (New York, Heidelberg and Berlin: Springer-Verlag, 1970), p. 150.

[101] *L.Sc.D.*, section 79, p. 252.

[102] See section 32 of "Two Faces of Common Sense", Chap. 2 of [1972(a)], esp. pp. 101-3.

[103] For example, what Professor Levison calls "Hume's problem of induction" (introducing it in the text to his n. 8 by saying that the "latter, it will be recalled, arises when Hume asks") is not identical with what I have called Hume's problem in my *L.Sc.D.* Levison refers (in his n. 8) to a passage in the *Enquiry*, which can be interpreted as pretty close to what I call the traditional problem of induction; while I refer mainly to the *Treatise* (Selby-Bigge ed., p. 89); see, for example, my *L.Sc.D.*, p. 369.

[104] See my paper "Conjectural Knowledge: My Solution of the Problem of Induction" [1971(i)], esp. section 12. The paper forms now Chap. 1 of my book *Objective Knowledge* [1972(a)]; and parts of it reappear, considerably modified, in section 13 above.

[105] See Chap. 2 (not previously published) of my book *Objective Knowledge*, cited in the preceding footnote; and also subsection III of section 13 above.

[106] Cp. [1934(b)], p. 191; [1966(e)], [1969(e)], p. 203; [1959(a)], [1968(a)], p. 257.

[107] Rudolf Carnap, "Reply to K. R. Popper", in *The Problem of Inductive Logic*, ed. by Lakatos, pp. 309-11; see esp. pp. 309 f. (see n. 65 above).

[107a] Niels Bohr, "Discussion with Einstein on Epistemological Problems in Atomic Physics" and Einstein's response to Bohr's essay, both in Paul A. Schilpp, ed., *Albert Einstein: Philosopher-Scientist*, pp. 201-41 and 668-76 respectively (now Open Court, La Salle, Ill.)—EDITOR.

[108] See subsection I of my reply to Ayer. (I have now discussed verisimilitude in more detail in Chap. 2 of [1972(a)].)

109 "Epistemology Without a Knowing Subject" [1968(s)]; now Chap. 3 of [1972(a)].

110 See also my reply to Feigl and Meehl, esp. the text between nn. 143 and 145.

111 I owe this military simile to David Miller.

112 I must defend myself against a minor misunderstanding. I am well aware that the human world 3 is specifically human, and like man himself, a product of the higher functions of language—especially of the argumentative function. When I compare, in places, the human world 3 to animal products—to bees' honey or spiders' webs—then I do it not in an attempt to identify the human world 3 with an animal world 3, but in order to show that even the greatest novelties and emergent steps in evolution have analogues in some of the preceding steps. In creating a different impression I must have expressed myself very badly. But I am not sure whether Eccles has really misunderstood me here. (Feyerabend has. See n. 1 on p. 219 of his "Consolations for the Specialist", in *Criticism and the Growth of Knowledge*, ed. by Lakatos and Musgrave, pp. 197-230 [see n. 76 above]; I owe this reference to David Miller.)

113 I do not, of course, wish to suggest that Watkins is dogmatic.

114 See Mendel Sachs, "Is Quantization Really Necessary?", *British Journal for the Philosophy of Science*, **21** (1970), 359-70.

115 I have quoted the passage from Harald Høffding which contains this argument in n. 203 of my *Autobiography*.

116 See Chap. 3 of [1963(a)]; and also the text to n. 203 of my *Autobiography* above.

117 See also my discussion of coding, decoding, and the actions of the senses, in my reply to Campbell in the next section; Campbell's paper deals, in places, with problems similar to those discussed by Watkins.

118 [1961(j)]; now Chap. 7 of my *Objective Knowledge* [1972(a)].

119 Chap. 2 of *Objective Knowledge* [1972(a)].

120 David Miller has drawn my attention to the parallelism here with Plato's *Meno* 80 D f. The existence of vague or "fuzzy" knowledge (hardly possible of course for Plato) indicates, I think, how Meno's problem is to be solved.

121 There are many variants of this suggested experiment, such as the use of contact lenses, and especially of two contact lenses which are both vertically divided into a red and a green side.

122 This neurosis may, of course, be due to the discovery that they do not see like normal human beings; that is to say, its origin may be a social inferiority rather than a dissatisfied innate drive to decode. I conjecture, however, the latter.

123 I may perhaps mention another minor point here: I completely agree with what Campbell has to say about chance discovery. I do not know which unfortunate remark of mine may have created a different impression. (See Campbell, text to n. 72.)

124 I have expanded a little on this towards the end of my reply to Professor Ayer.

125 See my [1953(d)], now Chap. 6 of [1963(a)].

126 [1957(i)], [1969(k)]; now Chap. 5 of [1972(a)].

127 See Lakatos and Musgrave, eds., *Criticism and the Growth of Knowledge*, p. 183, n. 3 (see n. 76 above). There is also my [1957(l)], which is an abstract from a chapter of the *Postscript*.

128 See also my "Towards a Rational Theory of Tradition" [1949(b)] and my "Three Views Concerning Human Knowledge" [1956(f)], now Chaps. 4 and 3 of *C. & R.*

129 [1949(b) and (d)]; [1952(b) and (c)]; and so on. ([1949(d)], a lecture given in Alpbach, has now been translated under the title "The Bucket and the Searchlight: Two Theories of Knowledge", and included as the Appendix to my [1972(a)].)

130 [1953(a)] and [1955(c)].

131 In his *Facing Reality* (see n. 100 above).

132 In [1970(w)].

133 In [1971(i)].

[134] See now my reply to Lakatos in section 12 above.

[135] See particularly "The Aim of Science" [1957(i)], [1969(k)]; Chap. 5 of [1972(a)]; and also my [1949(d)], now translated as the Appendix to my [1972(a)].

[136] See my reply to Agassi below.

[137] [1968(r)]; Chap. 4 of [1972(a)].

[138] [1968(r)], p. 31; I have since expanded this passage in [1972(a)], see p. 163.

[139] See my [1957(a)], section v; [1963(a)], pp. 47 f.

[140] [1966(f)]; now Chap. 6 of [1972(a)].

[141] [1968(s)]; now Chap. 3 of [1972(a)]. The paper is mentioned on p. 68 of Paul E. Meehl's paper referred to in the next footnote; a paper which, in its turn, is referred to in Feigl's and Meehl's contribution.

[142] Paul E. Meehl, "Psychological Determinism and Human Rationality: A Psychologist's Reactions to Professor Karl Popper's 'Of Clouds and Clocks' ", cyclostyled, 105 pages. (Received by me in the autumn of 1969.)

[143] Respectively [1968(s)] and [1968(r)], ([1972(a)], Chap. 3 and Chap. 4). It seems unlikely that Feigl or Meehl knew the second of these two papers when writing their contribution.

[144] Cp. [1969(j)], [1970(h)], and [1970(l)], ([1972(a)], Chap. 8). See also sections 38 and 39 of my *Autobiography* above.

[145] Cp. *Of Clouds and Clocks*, n. 29; cp. also *ibid.*, sections VII and X.

[146] Feigl and Meehl, section II.

[147] See esp. *Of Clouds and Clocks*, section VIII.

[148] Quoted in n. 39 of *Of Clouds and Clocks*.

[149] F. A. von Hayek, "Degrees of Explanation", *The British Journal for the Philosophy of Science,* **6** (1955), 209-25; reprinted in F. A. von Hayek, *Studies in Philosophy, Politics and Economics* (London: Routledge & Kegan Paul, 1967), pp. 3-21. See also the second chapter of this book, entitled "The Theory of Complex Phenomena", first published in Bunge, ed., *Critical Approach to Science and Philosophy*, pp. 332-49 (see n. 61 above).
Since it is my appointed task in this place to answer criticism I may perhaps mention that Hayek's n. 21 on p. 31 of his *Studies* (though doubtless fully justified in view of some insufficiently clear formulations in my *Poverty* [1957(g)], pp. 106 f.) is critical of a view I have never held. I only wished to characterize *the evolutionary hypothesis as such* as historical, but not, to be sure, Darwin's mechanism of natural selection. But I do not think that there is really any disagreement on this point between Hayek and myself.

[150] I have tried to offer some slight improvement of Darwinism (of the theory of the Baldwin effect) in the "genetic pluralism" which is explained in part 3 of, and the "Addendum 1971" to, my Herbert Spencer Lecture of 1961, now published as Chap. 7 of my [1972(a)], and in some remarks (to which Bernays refers) in my Arthur Holly Compton Lecture *Of Clouds and Clocks* [1966(f)] now Chap. 6 of my [1972(a)].

[151] "Back to the Presocratics", section 1, *C.&R.*, p. 136. (The second set of italics are not in the original.)

[152] *O.S.*, Vol. II [1945(c)] and later editions, Chap. 24, section I, pp. 224 f.; there is a footnote, omitted here, attached to this passage.

[153] See *C.&R.*, p. 28 (point 8).

[154] The terms "glossogon philosophy" (and "glossomorphic") are due to Adolph Stöhr; see Felix M. Cleve, *The Giants of Pre-Sophistic Greek Philosophy* (The Hague: Martinus Nijhoff, 1965), Vol. I, p. XXXI for "glossogon philosophy", Vol. II, p. 539 for "glossomorphic".

[155] One might think, perhaps, that it would help to speak rather than of "concepts", of "symbols (with some meaning attached)". I do not think that this would improve matters, especially for the present discussion. For there are many symbols which are not related to rationality, as the role of symbols in animal languages shows. (For that matter, consider the role

of swearwords in human languages.) I think that human rationality and the argumentative or critical use of human language have evolved together, and are, in fact, hardly distinguishable.

156 See esp. Ferdinand Gonseth and Henri-Samuel Gagnebin, *Determinisme et libre arbitre* (Neuchâtel: Griffon, 1944).

157 See Nevil Shute's autobiography, *Slide Rule* (London: Heinemann, 1954), Chaps. 2-7. (Pan Books ed. [London: Pan Books, 1968], pp. 54-135.)

158 Compare *C.& R.* [1969(h)], Chap. 10, p. 241, n. 24.

159 "The Aim of Science" [1957(i)], p. 29; [1969(k)], p. 135; [1972(a)], p. 197.

160 A slightly different way of putting the matter is this. Mere statements of convergence of frequencies are not falsifiable (or verifiable), and cannot even be made so by the adoption of a methodological rule of the kind suggested. Consequently, if probability statements are falsifiable, they must be stronger than, and say more than, statements of convergence. What I tried to do in *L.Sc.D.*, by means of my construction of *finite* random sequences, was to explain in what this additional strength consisted. (One might even say that I tried to increase the content of these convergence statements, in order to make them falsifiable.) But any such strengthening in this way is bound to *render the statements in question even less verifiable than they were before*. Thus the asymmetry remains. (See *L.Sc.D.*, sections 64-66, and esp. n. *2 to section 68, and text.) I am grateful to David Miller for the formulation of this note.

161 See esp. Chap. 2, "Two Faces of Common Sense", of my book *Objective Knowledge* [1972(a)]. Compare also *C.& R.*, pp. 116 f.

162 See [1946(b)], pp. 59 f.; or [1963(a)], p. 214.

163 See also section 13 of my *Autobiography*, n. 73 and text.

164 The remainder of this paragraph was suggested to me by David Miller.

165 This formulation saves us the trouble of distinguishing between sentences, statements, propositions, and so on. Schlesinger in his section I tries to use such a distinction to show that one of my arguments "proves nothing". But in fact Theaetetus's utterance "I said: 'I am now speaking so softly that dear old Socrates cannot make out what I am saying.' " obviously refers to the "proposition he has asserted", as well as to the "sentence conveying it"; for Socrates would hardly have made out what was said had he not understood it, at least a bit. Thus Schlesinger's own (inelegant) counterexamples (in his section (2)) are superfluous. (Incidentally his example referred to my reply as *U* is patently *semantical*, for it contains the phrase "correctly stating". Thus Schlesinger's distinction between "form" and "content" cannot coincide with the syntax/semantics distinction. At any rate we are left in the dark what his distinction is.)

165a (Added in proofs.) Note that Ayer does *not* criticize the particular formal definition which I have proposed (in [1963(a)] and in [1972(a)]), but that he condemns any employment of the idea of verisimilitude or nearness to truth as useless. As to the particular formal definition I have proposed, I have been shown its formal inadequacy by David Miller and, independently, by Pavel Tichy. Yet they are both convinced not only of the usefulness of the idea of verisimilitude but also of its being indispensable; and both have, in different ways, proposed new formal definitions. Compare David Miller, "The Truth-likeness of Truthlikeness", *Analysis*, 33 (1972), 50-55, and another as yet unpublished paper. Pavel Tichy's paper is also unpublished at the time of writing.

165b Truthlikeness or verisimilitude is very important. For there is a probabilistic though typically noninductivist argument which is invalid if it is used to establish the probability of a theory's being true, but which becomes valid (though essentially nonnumerical) if we replace truth by verisimilitude. The argument can be used only by realists who not only assume that there is a real world but also that this world is by and large more similar to the way modern theories describe it than to the way superseded theories describe it. On this basis we can argue that it would be a highly improbable coincidence if a theory like Einstein's could correctly predict very precise measurements not predicted by its predecessors unless there is "some truth" in it. This must not be interpreted to mean that it is improbable that the theory is not true (and hence probable that it is true). But it can be interpreted to mean that it is probable that the theory has both a high truth content and a high degree of verisimilitude; which means here only, "a higher degree of verisimilitude *than those of its competitors* which led to predictions that were less successful, and which are thus less well corroborated".

The argument is typically noninductive because in contradistinction to inductive arguments such as Carnap's the probability that the theory in question has a high degree of verisimilitude is (like degree of corroboration) inverse to the initial probability of the theory, prior to testing. Moreover, it only establishes a probability of verisimilitude relative to its competitors (and especially to its predecessors). In spite of this, there may be a "whiff" of inductivism here. It enters with the vague realist assumption that reality, though unknown, is in some respects similar to what science tells us or, in other words, with the assumption that science can progress towards greater verisimilitude.

166 In cases of crucial tests which, if accepted, would refute a cherished theory, agreement is often not easily reached. I alluded in section 8 of *L.d.F.* to the famous case of "the unexplained positive result of Michelson's experiment observed by Miller (1921-1926)". It has been suggested that the rejection of Miller's experiment by the scientific community was simply due to the dogmatic acceptance of special relativity. But Einstein said at once that if Miller's results were correct, he would abandon his theory. Yet the unreliability of Miller's results was commonly accepted by experimentalists, especially after a visit by Max Born to Miller's laboratory. Miller himself withdrew his first results; and the verdict of the scientific jury that his experiments were technically unreliable was based on findings such as those of Max Born, who found Miller's interferometer so badly put together that "a small movement of the hand, or a cough, made the interference fringes move, so that one could not determine their position". Here the test of the negative test was negative.

When writing those sections (8, 25-30) of *L.d.F.*, I had many such cases in mind. There were two in Vienna: Professor Felix Ehrenhaft, a brilliant experimentalist, had asserted for years that he had observed "sub-electrons", by the method later developed by Millikan in his famous determination of the electronic charge. The jury rejected Ehrenhaft's results and accepted Millikan's, and this verdict has been corroborated by many new methods since. I knew Ehrenhaft and I have seen his experiments, and I am satisfied that he was perfectly sincere in reporting his results. I am also satisfied that his results were wrong. I do not know the explanation, but it must lie in the *interpretation* of his observations. A case in which an explanation *was* found happened in the Vienna Radium Institute where some experiments of Rutherford's were repeated with quite different results. The explanation was that a substance used for sealing the apparatus emitted neutrons upon irradiation by α-particles; but since neutrons had not yet been discovered, this explanation had to wait for several years.

167 "The Aim of Science" [1957(i)]; a revised version has appeared as [1969(k)] and Chap. 5 of [1972(a)].

The footnote is numbered 5 in [1957(i)] (p. 27), and in [1972(a)] (p. 195), but is 3 in [1969(k)] (pp. 132 f.). It reads: "The term 'modified essentialism' was used as a description of my own 'third view' by a reviewer of my paper 'Three Views Concerning Human Knowledge' [in *The Times Literary Supplement*, **55** (1956), 527]. In order to avoid misunderstandings, I wish to say here that my acceptance of this term should not be construed as a concession to the doctrines of an 'ultimate reality', and even less as a concession to the doctrine of essentialist definitions. I fully adhere to the criticism of this doctrine which I have given in my *Open Society*, Vol. II, Chapter 11, section II (especially note 42), and in other places."

168 [1944(a)], [1957(g)], and later editions, section 19.

169 [1971(i)] and [1972(a)], Chap. 1, reprinted in part in sections 13 and 14 above.

170 See [1938(a)] (now in Appendix *ii of [1959(a)] and later editions), and esp. the new Appendices *iv and *v of [1959(a)]. Also devoted to this topic is [1963(g)] (see [1970(v)] for an important correction).

171 See my [1959(e)]; now also [1974(a)], Chap. 5.

172 I discovered Settle's omission to take full notice of [1959(e)] only when writing this reply, since when I previously read his paper I was without his footnotes. I had informed Settle that his Table 5 was clearly correct, and that I did not understand how he and Bunge could attribute to me anything like the instrumentalist or experimentalist position implied in his Tables 3 and 4. It

did not occur to me that he could have overlooked what I say on the point in my [1959(e)] which, after all, is my longest paper on the subject. My [1967(k)], with which Settle and Bunge worked, was a short outline, written especially for a joint conference of physicists and philosophers; this was the reason why I stressed the experimental aspects. (My unpublished *Postscript* is even more explicit than [1959(e)]; and so is section 4 of [1957(e)].)

173 The term "glossomorphic" seems to be due to Adolf Stöhr; see n. 154 above.

174 In my [1968(s)], where I spoke of the first, second, and third worlds. Their renaming as worlds 1, 2, and 3 is still more recent, and is thanks to the suggestion of Sir John Eccles in his *Facing Reality* (see n. 100 above).

175 Professor Alan Musgrave's contribution to this volume shows this very clearly, especially with respect to my *L.d.F.* For the presence of these ideas in my *O.S.* see esp. the *Addendum* I to Vol. II [1962(c)], which develops much older ideas from Vol. I, esp. pp. 64 ff. See also *C.&R.*, esp. the Introduction and Chaps. 1 and 10.

176 Cp. esp. my [1971(i)], now Chap. 1 of my [1972(a)].

177 For example, in section 79.

178 See the list of objectivist physicists on pp. 7 f. of my [1967(k)] ([1974(a)], Chap. 3). I should have mentioned Professor Margenau there, and I apologize for the omission. We can now also add Leslie E. Ballentine and Edward Nelson (see n. 138 in my *Autobiography*).

179 Leon Cohen, "Can Quantum Mechanics be Formulated as a Classical Probability Theory?", *Philosophy of Science,* 33 (1966), 317-22.

180 *International Encyclopedia of Unified Science* (Chicago: University of Chicago Press, 1939), Vol. I, No. 6.

181 Suppes just mentions my "Logic of Discovery" (*sic*), but there is nothing in his contribution to indicate that he remembers its content (or even its precise title). Nor does he ever refer to my [1957(e)] (now Chap. 4 of [1974(a)]) or to my [1963(g)].

182 See, for example, my recursive definition of n-termed independence or n-independence in [1969(h)], pp. 389 f.

183 See [1938(a)], reprinted in Appendix *ii of *L.Sc.D.*

184 We might call this "von Mises's principle", in recognition of the fact that it was von Mises who pointed out that we have at least to *interpret* "almost certainly" as "with frequency almost 1".

185 At present it seems that the class Ln is not empty; the velocity of light in a vacuum, the electronic charge, the masses and mass ratios of elementary particles, none seems to be subject to probabilistic scatter. The conservation laws appear slightly more suspect.

186 The paper [1957(l)] was an abridgement, made at my request, by Professor Agassi from Chap. II of my still unpublished *Postscript* which was then, and has been ever since 1957, in galley proofs. The following are significant corrections to be made in [1957(l)]: p. 355, second line after the second formula, insert *"the statements"* after "proximity of", and replace the last four words in the next line (before *"a"*) by "concerning the state of affairs described by the statement *a*". On p. 371, line 3, replace *"pi"* by *"p_i"* and on p. 371, line 6 from the bottom of the page, replace *"(ab)"* by *"(a,b)"*. On p. 367, the line before (3): replace "the logical theory" by "ordinary logic", and insert a new line after (3) as follows: "since both *a* and *b* are refuted by the evidence *c*." There are other corrections but they are less important.

187 Imre Fényes, "Eine wahrscheinlichkeitstheoretische Begründung und Interpretation der Quantenmechanik", *Zeitschrift für Physik,* 132 (1952), 81-106.

188 Edward Nelson, "Derivation of the Schrödinger Equation from Newtonian Mechanics", *Physical Review,* 150 (1966), 1079-85; and *Dynamical Theories of Brownian Motion* (Princeton: Princeton University Press, 1968).

189 In discussions of hidden variable theories it is often assumed that these theories must be of a deterministic character; but hidden variable theories may be indeterministic, as the example of Fényes and Nelson shows.

[190] John S. Bell, "On the Problem of Hidden Variables in Quantum Mechanics", *Reviews of Modern Physics*, **38** (1966), 447-52.

[191] Simon Kochen and E. P. Specker, "The Problem of Hidden Variables in Quantum Mechanics", *Journal of Mathematics and Mechanics*, **17** (1968), 59-87.

[192] David Bohm, "Classical and Non-Classical Concepts in the Quantum Theory", *British Journal for the Philosophy of Science*, **12** (1962), 265-80; and "A Proposed Topological Formulation of Quantum Theory", in *The Scientist Speculates*, ed. by I. J. Good (London: Heinemann, 1962), pp. 302-14.

[193] These are not, of course, the only promising attempts towards a new quantum mechanics; there is also the theory of Mendel Sachs; see Mendel Sachs and S. L. Schwebel, "A Self-Consistent Field Theory of Quantum Electrodynamics", *Nuovo Cimento*, supp. **21** (1961), 197-229. See also Mendel Sachs, "The Pauli Exclusion Principle from a Self-Consistent Field-Theory of Quantum Electrodynamics", *Nuovo Cimento*, **27** (1963), 1138-50, and the further development of this theory: *ibid.*, **31** (1964), 98-112; **34** (1964), 81-92; **37** (1965), 888-96 and 977-88; and **43** (1966), 1175-77.

[194] M. S. Bartlett, "Negative Probability", *Proceedings of the Cambridge Philosophical Society*, **41** (1945), 71-73; J. E. Moyal, "Quantum Mechanics as a Statistical Theory", *ibid.*, **45** (1949), 99-124; M. S. Bartlett and J. E. Moyal, "The Exact Transition Probabilities of Quantum-Mechanical Oscillators Calculated by the Phase-Space Method", *ibid.*, **45** (1949), 545-53.

[195] Leon Cohen, "Generalized Phase-Space Distribution Functions", *Journal of Mathematical Physics*, **7** (1966), 781-86; Henry Margenau and Leon Cohen, "Problems in Quantum Mechanics", in *Quantum Theory and Reality*, ed. by Mario Bunge (Berlin, Heidelberg and New York: Springer-Verlag, 1967), pp. 71-89; James L. Park and Henry Margenau, "Simultaneous Measurability in Quantum Theory", *International Journal of Theoretical Physics*, **1** (1968), 211-83. See also Leon Cohen, "Can Quantum Mechanics be Formulated as a Classical Probability Theory?", *Philosophy of Science*, **33** (1966), 317-22.

[196] For a discussion of the phrase "derive as an approximation" (which has to be taken as one term) see my [1957(i)] and [1969(k)]; [1972(a)], Chap. 5.

[197] "The Arrow of Time" [1956(b)], p. 538; now included in Chap. 10 of [1974(a)].

[198] E. L. Hill and A. Grünbaum, "Irreversible Processes in Physical Theory", *Nature*, **179**, 1296 f.

[199] "The Arrow of Time" [1956(b)].

[200] Erwin Schrödinger, *Mind and Matter* (Cambridge: Cambridge University Press, 1958), p. 86; in the combined reprint of *What is Life?* and *Mind and Matter* (Cambridge: Cambridge University Press, 1967), see p. 164.

[201] Kuhn mentions in section I two points in which (if I understand him rightly) he thinks we diverge: his "emphasis on the importance of...tradition" and his "discontent with the implications of the term 'falsification' ". I wonder whether he knows what I have written on the importance of tradition in *C.&.R.*, pp. 27 f., points 4 and 5, and Chap. 4.

[202] See [1970(w)] and also esp. J. W. N. Watkins, "Against Normal Science", in *Criticism and The Growth of Knowledge*, ed. by Lakatos and Musgrave (see n. 76 above), pp. 25-37: this is a brilliant defence of my views of science against Kuhn's criticism.

[203] See n. 202 above.

[204] Thomas S. Kuhn, *The Structure of Scientific Revolutions* (Chicago: University of Chicago Press, 1962; 2d enl. ed., 1970). The quotation is taken from a revised version of my [1963(h)], p. 961.

[205] Cp. Peter Havas, "Four-Dimensional Formulations of Newtonian Mechanics and their Relation to the Special and General Theory of Relativity", *Reviews of Modern Physics*, **36** (1964), 938-65; and Peter Havas, "Foundation Problems in General Relativity", in *Delaware Seminar in the Foundations of Physics*, ed. by Mario Bunge (Berlin, Heidelberg and New York: Springer-Verlag, 1967), pp. 124-49.

²⁰⁶ [1957(i)] and [1969(k)]; Chap. 5 of [1972(a)].

²⁰⁷ [1970(w)], pp. 56 f.

²⁰⁸ Thomas S. Kuhn, "Reflections on my Critics", in *Criticism and The Growth of Knowledge*, ed. by Lakatos and Musgrave (see n. 76 above), pp. 231-78; see esp. p. 232. (Italics mine.)

²⁰⁹ Compare with this my remarks about essentialism and the "essence of science" in *C.&R.*, p. 105, n. 17.

²¹⁰ See also my reply to Wild in the next section.

²¹¹ The two quotations are from *O.S.*, Vol. I, pp. 61 and 65. ("Improve" is newly italicized.)

²¹² *Ibid.*, pp. 64 f. (Italics are new.)

²¹³ *O.S.*, [1962(c)] and later editions, Vol. II, p. 375. Moral relativism, as I pointed out in the same *Addendum*, pp. 373 f., comes from the demand for *criteria*: it comes from *"criterion philosophy"*. I am greatly indebted to Professor F. Post (for a short time a student of mine) for drawing my attention in 1969 to an important point concerning this *Addendum*. It has to do with the first sentence of section 8 ([1962(c)] and later editions, p. 378), where I wrote of the "principle that *everything is open to criticism* (from which this principle itself is not exempt) . . .". This is an incautious way of writing because it is self-referring. Self-referring statements are by no means always dangerous (see Chap. 14 of *C.&R.*); but this particular statement *is a bad* self-referring statement because it occurs in a context in which truth and falsity play a role; and such self-referring statements are, as Tarski has shown, to be avoided if we wish to avoid the paradox of the liar. There are one or two other such passages in this *Addendum*, and they should be rewritten with some care; the one just referred to should read: "The metalinguistic principle that everything is open to criticism (a principle which, we can say in a metalanguage of higher order, should in its turn be open to criticism) . . . ." I do not think that any serious difficulty remains if the self-referring statements in the *Addendum* are rewritten, or interpreted, along these lines.

²¹⁴ [1962(c)], Vol. II, p. 386.

²¹⁵ Ronald B. Levinson, *In Defense of Plato* (Cambridge, Mass.: Harvard University Press, 1953).

²¹⁶ Unless I say otherwise, my references to *O.S.* will not be to the edition of 1950, to which Professor Wild refers (the first edition was 1945; the 1950 one-volume edition has not been available for many years), but to the fourth and later editions, which agree in pagination with the various paperback issues.

²¹⁶ᵃ Incidentally, my decision to adopt the word historicism, about which I was a little doubtful, was influenced by my finding the term "dialectical historicism" advocated in J. F. Hecker's *Moscow Dialogues* (London: Chapman and Hall, 1933), p. 76; see my *O.S.*, Vol. II, n. 4 to Chap. 15.

²¹⁷ See Samuel Butler, *Erewhon*, 1872 (New York and London: Everyman's Library, E. P. Dutton & Co. and J. M. Dent & Sons, 1932 and 1940), p. 135. The passage will also be found quoted in my *O.S.*, [1962(c)] and later editions, Vol. I, p. 136.

²¹⁸ See my *C.&R.*, pp. 27 f. (The italics are not in the original.)

²¹⁹ E. H. Gombrich, "Art and Self-Transcendence", in *The Place of Value in a World of Facts*, Nobel Symposium 14, ed. by Arne Tiselius and Sam Nilsson (Stockholm: Almqvist & Wiksell; New York, London and Sydney: John Wiley & Sons, 1970), pp. 125-33. The quoted passage (which refers to J. S. Bach) is on pp. 130 f.

²²⁰ *Ibid.* For the reference to world 3 see his p. 127 and the attached note (9) on p. 133. I may perhaps mention that the title of the last section of my *Autobiography*—"The Place of Values in a World of Facts"—was chosen quite independently of the title of this Nobel Symposium; both titles go back to Wolfgang Köhler. It was a remark of Professor Nabil Shehaby in the winter of 1968-69 about the first chapter of Köhler's book which led me to the choice of this title for the last section of my *Autobiography*.

221 See esp. E. H. Gombrich, *Art and Illusion* (New York: Pantheon Books, 1960); 2d ed. (London: Phaidon Press, 1962). This book contains examples of the emergence of new and objective artistic problems.

222 "Art and Self-Transcendence", pp. 127 f.

223 Quoted in n. 39 of [1966(f)], and also in my reply to Feigl and Meehl above; see text to n. 142.

224 "Art and Self-Transcendence", p. 132.

PART FOUR

BIBLIOGRAPHY OF THE WRITINGS OF KARL POPPER

(Compiled by Troels Eggers Hansen)

BIBLIOGRAPHY OF THE WRITINGS OF KARL POPPER

Edited and Revised by
TROELS EGGERS HANSEN
on the basis of lists of publications
partly compiled by other people

Key to Symbols Used

*	publication of original text
R	sheer republication or republication with minor corrections
Ṟ	republication with revisions and/or additions
T	sheer translation or translation with minor corrections
Ṯ	translation with revisions and/or additions
U	unpublished in the year under which it is entered.

PREFACE TO THE BIBLIOGRAPHY

I am greatly indebted to Sir Karl Popper, Arne Friemuth Petersen, Jeremy Shearmur, Margit Hurup Nielsen, and Gudrun Eggers Hansen for their assistance during the preparation of this bibliography.

The note to item 1935(a) and the bibliographical pieces of information to item 1944(c) contain quotations from *Bibliography of the Writings of Rudolf Carnap* (compiled by Arthur J. Benson), *The Library of Living Philosophers*, Vol. 11: *The Philosophy of Rudolf Carnap*. I wish to express my gratitude to *The Library of Living Philosophers, Inc.*, and to the Open Court Publishing Company, La Salle, Illinois, for the permission to make these quotations.

EGGERS HANSEN

DEPARTMENT OF PHILOSOPHY
UNIVERSITY OF COPENHAGEN

1925

* (a) Über die Stellung des Lehrers zu Schule und Schüler. Gesellschaftliche oder individualistische Erziehung?

    Schulreform (Vienna), 4. Jahrgang (1925), [Heft 4 (April, 1925)], pp. 204-208.

1927

* (a) Zur Philosophie des Heimatgedankens.

    Die Quelle (Vienna), 77. Jahr (1927), Heft (Folge) 10 ([Oktober], 1927), pp. 899-908.

    Einleitungsreferat zu einer Referatreihe über den *Heimatgedanken*, gehalten im Pädagogischen Seminar unter Leitung von Hofrat Dr. Eduard Burger am *Pädagogischen Institut der Stadt Wien*.

U (b) "GEWOHNHEIT" UND "GESETZERLEBNIS" IN DER ERZIEH-UNG. *Eine pädagogisch- strukturpsychologische Monographie.*

    Typed on foolscap typing paper, Vienna, 1927-1928 (approximate date). Pp. 135.

    A thesis presented (unfinished) to the *Pedagogic Institute* of the City of Vienna in 1927.

    Contents: *Vorbemerkung.* EINLEITUNG. *A. Pädagogische Problemstellung.* § 1. Pädagogische Voraussetzungen. § 2. Ein Problem der "Erziehung durch Gewöhnung". § 3. Ein Problem der Arbeitspädagogik. *B. Psychologische Problemstellung.* § 4. Einleitende Bemerkungen über das Verhältnis von dogmatischem und kritischem Denken. § 5. Allgemeine methodologische Voraussetzungen. § 6. Aufgabenstellung und Arbeitsplan. I. TEIL. PSYCHOLOGIE DES GESETZERLEBNIS-SES. *1. Abschnitt. Phänomenologie.* § 7. Typische Einstellungen gegenüber dem Unbekannten: 1. Die Angst vor dem "Fremden". Anhang zu 1: **Sicherung (Ablehnung des Neuen). 2. Angst und Setzungsbedürfnis: a)** Leichtgläubigkeit; b) Ordnungsbedürfnis. Anhang zu 2: c) Aberglauben. 3. Die "Neugierde" und die "Befangenheit". Anhang zu 3: Einstellungen mit direktem Hinweis auf die Setzung. § 8. Die Setzung des Sachverhalts: 1. Hinweis auf das "Material" der Setzung ("latente Sachverhalte"). 2. a) Die Setzung in ihren direkten Kundgebungen. 2. b) Selbstbeobachtungen. 3. a) Festhalten an irgend einer Bestimmung eines Gegenstandes: Begriffsbildung. 3. b) Auftauchen der Setzung in der Verteidigung derselben gegen eine Störung. Anhang zu § 8: 1. Festhalten eines Verfahrens. 2. Das Revisionserlebnis. § 9. Das Festhalten der Setzung: 1. Konservativismus. 2. Pedanterie. 3. Ritual. *Literaturverzeichnis.*

1928

U (a) ZUR METHODENFRAGE DER DENKPSYCHOLOGIE.

Dissertation, eingereicht zur Erlangung des Doktogrades der philosophischen Fakultät der Universität Wien.
Sommersemester 1928. Pp. v, 84, (Typewritten.)
Available at the University Library of Vienna.

Contents: Jnhaltsübersicht. *Einleitung:* Das Verhältnis der Methodologie zur praktischen Forschungsarbeit. ZUR METHODENFRAGE DER DENKPSYCHOLOGIE. § 1: *Der "Pluralismus der Aspekte".* § 2: *Kritik des Physikalismus.* 1. Der Standpunkt des Physikalismus. 2. Der Begriff der "vollständigen Erkenntnis" und die biologischen Wissenschaften. 3. Drei Thesen gegen den Physikalismus. 4. Kritik der parallelistischen Grundannahme. 5. Zusammenfassung und Ausblick. § 3: *Die Stellung der Aspekte in der Methode der Denkpsychologie.* 1. Die Fragestellung. 2. Der "Benehmensaspekt". 3. Der Aspekt der "objektiven geistigen Gebilde". 4. Der "Erlebnisaspekt". 5. Abschluss. *Verzeichnis der benützten Literatur.*

1929

U (a) AXIOME, DEFINITIONEN UND POSTULATE DER GEOMETRIE.

Typed on foolscap typing paper and bound in two volumes, Vienna, 1929. Pp. [xi], [156].

Contents: 1. HALBBAND. Jnhaltsuebersicht. Vorbemerkung. I. EINLEITUNGSTEIL: *Exposition der Grundprobleme.* § 1: Das "euklidische Programm" und die beiden Problemgruppen. § 2: Uebersicht über die mathematisch-logische Problemgruppe. § 3: Näheres zum Problem der Entbehrlichkeit. Teilsysteme. § 4: Anwendung: Teilabhängigkeiten. § 5: Uebersicht über die wissenschaftstheoretische Problemgruppe. § 6: Besprechung des Geltungsproblems. § 7: Bemerkungen zum historisch-genetischen Problem. § 8: Besprechung des Methodenproblems. II. HISTORISCHER TEIL: *Die Entwicklung der Probleme von EUKLID bis zur modernen Axiomatik.* § 9: Vorgeschichte. Aufbau des Systems bei EUKLID. § 10: Die euklidischen Definitionen, Postulate und Axiome vom Standpunkt der ersten Problemgruppe. § 11: Das Grundlagen-problem bei EUKLID. § 12: Die Entwicklung des Parallelenproblems und die Vorläufer der nichteuklidischen Geometrie. § 13: Philosophische Stellungnahmen. KANT. § 14: Die Begründer der nichteuklidischen Geometrie § 15: Zur nichteuklidischen Geometrie: Aeussere und innere Krümmung. § 16: Fortsetzung: Geodätische Linien. 2. HALBBAND. § 17. Fortsetzung: GAUSSsche Koordinaten. § 18: Das BELTRAMIsche Modell der nichteuklidischen Geometrien. § 19: Massetzung und Raum-art. § 20: Die Bedeutung der nichteuklidischen Geometrie für die erste Problemgruppe. § 21: Ansichten der Nichteuklidiker zur 2. Problem-gruppe. § 22: Die projektive Geometrie. § 23: Die Topologie ("Analysis situs"). Der projektive und der topologische Raum. § 24: Konventio-nalistische und empiristische Deutungen. § 25: Die Begründung der Axiomatik durch PASCH. *Beilage zum II. Teil:* Uebersicht über die Beantwortungen der Geltungsfrage. III. SYSTEMATISCHER TEIL: *Systematische Bearbeitung der beiden Problemgruppen.* § 26: Die Geltung und Anwendbarkeit der Arithmetik. § 27: Reine und ange-wandte Topologie. § 28: Die axiomatische Grundlegung der projektiven Geometrie und der metrischen Geometrien. § 29: Das Wesen der Impliziten Definition. § 30: Die ausgezeichnete Stellung der Geraden. § 31: Die Topologie und die implizite Definition der projektiven Geraden. § 32: "Erfüllungen" der impliziten Definition. Formale Geo-metrie und reine Geometrie. § 33: Die Tragweite der Axiome. § 34: Die Geltung der formalen und reinen Geometrie. § 35: Auflösung des HELMHOLTZschen Problems. Geometrie und Erfahrung. § 36: Physische und angewandte Geometrie. Der physische Raum. § 37: Der Sonderfall der angewandten Topologie. Der Koinzidenzbegriff. § 38: Zusammenfassung: Die Geltung der reinen und angewandten Geometrien. *Beilage zum III. Teil:* Uebersicht über die verschiedenen Geometrien nach der Art ihrer Geltung. *Literaturverzeichnis.*

1931

* (a) Die Gedächtnispflege unter dem Gesichtspunkt der Selbsttätigkeit.

Die Quelle (Vienna), 81. Jahr (1931), Heft (Folge) 6 ([Juni], 1931), pp. 607-619.

Thema der Wiener Bezirks-Volksschullehrerkonferenzen (10. Juni 1931).

1932

* (a) Pädagogische Zeitschriftenschau.

Die Quelle (Vienna), 82. Jahr (1932):

Heft (Folge)	3	([März], 1932), pp.	301–303;
—	—	7	([Juli], —), —	580–582;
—	—	8	([August], —), —	[6]46–647;
—	—	9 ([September], —), —	712–713;
—	—	10	([Oktober], —), —	778–781;
—	—	11 ([November], —), —	846–849;
—	—	12 ([Dezember], —), —	930–931.

U (b) DIE BEIDEN GRUNDPROBLEME DER ERKENNTNISTHEO-
RIE. [Band I: *Das Induktionsproblem.*]

Typed on foolscap typing paper, Vienna, 1932. Pp. [567].

Greatly abridged versions are contained in 1933(b) as ORIEN-
TIERUNG, [chapter I], and in 1934(b) as EINFÜHRUNG, chapter I.
Contents: Inhalt. 1. PROBLEMSTELLUNG. (1.) Induktionsproblem und Abgrenzungsproblem. 2. DEDUKTIVISMUS UND
INDUKTIVISMUS. (2.) Bemerkungen über den Lösungsweg und
vorläufige Angabe der Lösungen. (3.) Rationalismus und Empirismus
—Deduktivismus und Induktivismus. (4.) Die Möglichkeit einer deduk-
tistischen Erkenntnispsychologie. 3. DAS INDUKTIONSPROBLEM.
(5.) Der unendliche Regress ("HUMEs Argument"). (6.) Indukti-
vistische Positionen. *(Die Normalsatzpositionen.)* (7.) Die "Normalsatzpositionen": "Naiver Induktivismus", "strenger Positivismus" und
"Apriorismus". (8.) Kritik des "strengen Positivismus". Zweifache
"Transzendenz" der Naturgesetze. (9.) Die "transzendentale Methode".
—Darstellung des "Apriorismus". (10.) Kritik des "Apriorismus". (11.)
Zur Ergänzung der Kritik des Apriorismus. (Psychologismus und Trans-
zendentalismus bei KANT und bei FRIES.—Zur Frage der "empirischen Basis".) *(Die Wahrscheinlichkeitspositionen.)* (12.) Die Wahrscheinlichkeitspositionen.—Subjektiver Wahrscheinlichkeitsglaube. (13.)
Aussagen über die objektive Wahrscheinlichkeit von Ereignissen. (14.)
Wahrscheinlichkeit als objektiver Geltungswert allgemeiner Wirklichkeitsaussagen. (15.) Eine Möglichkeit, den Begriff der Wahrscheinlichkeit
einer Hypothese näher zu bestimmen. ("Primäre" und "sekundäre"
Hypothesenwahrscheinlichkeit.) Der Einfachheitsbegriff. (16). Der Begriff der "Bewährung" einer Hypothese.—Positivistische, pragmatisti-
sche und "wahrscheinlichkeitslogische" Deutung des Bewährungsbe-

griffes. (17.) Der unendliche Regress der Wahrscheinlichkeitsaussagen. *(Die Scheinsatzpositionen.)* (18.) Die "Scheinsatzpositionen": neue Fragestellung. (19.) Die Naturgesetze als "Anweisungen zur Bildung von Aussagen". (20.) "Wahr-falsch" oder "brauchbar-unbrauchbar"? Der "konsequente Pragmatismus". (21.) Schwierigkeiten des "konsequenten Pragmatismus". (22.) Werkzeug und Schema als rein pragmatische Gebilde. (23.) Die Naturgesetze als "Aussagefunktionen". (24.) Die "Scheinsatzpositionen" werden vorläufig verlassen: Der Konventionalismus. (25.) Die drei Interpretationen der axiomatischen Systeme. (Der Problemkreis des Konventionalismus.) (26.) Die konventionalistische "implizite" und die "explizite" Definition. Aussagefunktion und Aussagegleichung. (27.) Die konventionalistischen Aussagegleichungen als tautologische "generelle Implikationen". (28.) Können die axiomatisch-deduktiven Systeme auch als Folgerungssysteme von reinen Aussagefunktionen (von Scheinsätzen) aufgefasst werden? (29.) Die Zuordnungsdefinitionen des Empirismus: synthetische generelle Implikationen. (30.) Konventionalistische und empiristische Deutung, erläutert am Beispiel der angewandten Geometrie. (31.) Die "Implikation" und die "generelle Implikation". (32.) Die generelle Implikation und die Unterscheidung von "streng allgemeinen" und "besonderen" Sätzen. (33.) Allgemeinbegriff und Individualbegriff – Klasse und Element. (34.) Der "streng allgemeine" Satz – Induktionsproblem und Universalienproblem. (35.) Bemerkungen zum Universalienproblem. (36.) Rückkehr zur Diskussion der Scheinsatzpositionen. (37.) Symmetrie oder Asymmetrie in den Bewertungen der Naturgesetze? (38.) Die negative Wertung allgemeiner Sätze. Kritik der "streng symmetrischen" Interpretation der Scheinsätze. (39.) Ein unendlicher Regress von Scheinsätzen. (40.) Eine aprioristische Scheinsatzposition. (41.) Deutung der bisherigen Kritik; Bemerkungen über die Einheit von Theorie und Praxis. (42.) Ein letzter Ausweg für die Scheinsatzpositionen. (43.) Der Sinnbegriff des "logischen Positivismus". (44.) Sinnbegriff und Abgrenzungsproblem.—Die Grundthese des Induktivismus. (45.) Kritik des induktivistischen Sinndogmas. (46.) "Vollentscheidbare" und "teilentscheidbare" Wirklichkeitsaussagen. – Die Antinomie von der Erkennbarkeit der Welt. (Abschluss der Kritik der Scheinsatzpositionen.) (47.) Die "dialektische" und die "transzendentale" Bewährung der Lösung. (48.) Ist das Induktionsproblem gelöst? *Anhang:* Die Kritik des Induktionsproblems in schematischen Darstellungen.

U (c) DIE BEIDEN GRUNDPROBLEME DER ERKENNTNISTHEORIE. [Band II: *Das Abgrenzungsproblem.*]

Typed on foolscap typing paper, Vienna, 1932.

This item was never finished but replaced by 1933(b). The following sections (64 pp.) seem to be the only part of the manuscript which still exists: . . . *Entwurf einer Einführung: Gibt es eine philosophische Wissenschaft?* (Einführende Ueberlegungen zum "Abgrenzungsproblem".) . . . I. PROBLEMSTELLUNG. 1. Das Abgrenzungsproblem. 2. Tragweite des Abgrenzungsproblems. 3. Das Induktionsproblem. 4. Tragweite des Induktionsproblems. . . . *Zur Frage der Ausschaltung des subjektivistischen Psychologismus.* . . . UEBERGANG ZUR METHODENTHEORIE. 1. Ein Einwand gegen das Kriterium der Falsifizierbarkeit. 2. Kritik nicht-methodologischer Erkenntnistheorien. 3. Bemerkungen zur Frage: Konventionalismus oder Empirismus? 4. Der "empiristische Charakter" der Umgangssprache. – Die logische Auffassung als Voraussetzung der methodologischen. 5. Zur Kritik nicht-deduktiver und nicht-transzendentaler Erkenntnistheorien. 6. Gibt es eine Methodologie? 7. Universal- und Individualbegriff, – Klasse und Element. 8. Ueber den sprachkritischen Einwand gegen die Möglichkeit einer Methodologie. . . . *Die "Exhaustionsmethode".—"Sachverhalt" und "Tatsache".–Die "Allverschiedenheit".* . . . GRUNDRISS EINER THEORIE DER EMPIRISCH-WISSENSCHAFTLICHEN METHODEN (THEORIE DER ERFAHRUNG). *Grundsatz der Falsifizierbarkeit.* 1.) Kontinuitätsprinzip. 2.) These gegen den "strengen Positivismus". 3.) Erste These gegen den Konventionalismus: Satz von der Abgeschlossenheit des Systems. 4.) Zweite These gegen den Konventionalismus: Satz von der Beschränkung der singulären Hilfsannahmen (Ad-hoc-Hypothesen). . . .

1933

* (a) Ein Kriterium des empirischen Charakters theoretischer Systeme. (Vorläufige Mitteilung.)

Erkenntnis (Leipzig), Bd. 3 (Zugleich *Annalen der Philosophie,* Bd. 11) (1932/33), Heft 4/6 (5. September, 1933), pp. 426-427.

A letter to the editor.
English translation contained in 1959(a). The German text is reprinted in 1966(e).

LOGIK DER FORSCHUNG. [Original version.]

Typed on foolscap typing paper, Vienna, 1933.

An abbreviated version of this item was published as 1934(b). See notes to 1932(b) and to 1932(c).

Most of the manuscript seems to be lost.

Contents: INHALT. I. ORIENTIERUNG. GRUNDPROBLEME DER ERKENNTNISLOGIK. 1. Das Problem der Induktion. 2. Ausschaltung des Psychologismus. 3. Die deduktive Ueberprüfung der Theorien 4 Das Abgrenzungsproblem. 5. Erfahrung als Methode. 6. Falsifizierbarkeit als Abgrenzungskriterium. 7. Das Problem der Erfahrungsgrundlage. (Die "empirische Basis".) 8. Wissenschaftliche Objektivität und subjektive Ueberzeugung. ZUM PROBLEM DER METHODENLEHRE. 9. Die Unentbehrlichkeit methodologischer Festsetzungen. 10. Die "naturalistische" Auffassung der Methodenlehre. 11. Die methodologischen Regeln als Festsetzungen. II. BAUSTEINE ZU EINER THEORIE DER ERFAHRUNG. THEORIEN. 12. Kausalität, Erklärung, Prognosendeduktion. 13. Spezifische und numerische Allgemeinheit von Sätzen. 14. Universalien und Individualien. 15. Allsätze und universelle Es-gibt-Sätze. 16. Theoretische Systeme. 17. Deutungsmöglichkeiten eines axiomatischen Systems. 18. Allgemeinheitsstufen, der "modus tollens". FALSIFIZIERBARKEIT. 19. Die konventionalistischen Einwände. 20. Methodologische Regeln. 21. Logische Untersuchung der Falsifizierbarkeit. 22. Falsifizierbarkeit und Falsifikation. 23. "Ereignis" und "Vorgang". 24. Falsifizierbarkeit und Widerspruchslosigkeit. BASISPROBLEME. 25. Erlebnisse als Basis (Psychologismus). 26. Ueber die sogenannten "Protokollsätze". 27. Objektivität der Basis. 28. Die Basissätze. 29. Relativität der Basissätze. Auflösung des Trilemmas. 30. Theorie und Experiment. GRADE DER PRÜFBARKEIT. 31. Veranschaulichung und Programm. 32. Wie können Klassen von Falsifikationsmöglichkeiten verglichen werden. 33. Falsifizierbarkeitsvergleich mit Hilfe des Teilklassenverhältnisses. 34. Struktur der Teilklassenbeziehung. "Logische Wahrscheinlichkeit". 35. "Empirischer Gehalt", Implikationsbeziehung, Falsifizierbarkeitsgrad. 36. Allgemeinheit und Bestimmtheit. 37. Logische Spielräume,—Bemerkungen zur Messgenauigkeit. 38. Der Dimensionsvergleich. 39. Die Dimension einer Kurvenklasse. 40. Formale und materiale Einengung der Dimension einer Kurvenklasse. EINFACHHEIT. 41. Ausschaltung des aesthetisch-pragmatischen Einfachheitsbegriffes. 42. Das erkenntnistheoretische Einfachheitsproblem. 43. Einfachheit und Falsifizierbarkeitsgrad. 44. "Geometrische Form" und "Funktionsform". 45. Die Einfachheit der euklidischen Geometrie. 46. Der Einfachheitsbegriff des Konventionalismus. WAHRSCHEINLICHKEIT. 47. Das Interpretationsproblem. 48. Subjektive und objek-

tive Interpretationen. 49. Das Grundproblem der Zufallstheorie. 50. Die
v. MISESsche Häufigkeitstheorie. 51. Plan für einen Neuaufbau der
Wahrscheinlichkeitstheorie. 52. Relative Häufigkeit in endlichen Bezugsklassen. 53. Aussonderungen, Unabhängigkeit, Unempfindlichkeit, Belanglosigkeit. 54. Endliche Folgen. Stellenaussonderung und Umgebungsaussonderung. 55. n-Nachwirkungsfreiheit in endlichen Folgen. 56.
Abschnittsfolgen. Erste NEWTONsche Formel. 57. Unendliche Bezugsfolgen. Hypothetische Häufigkeitsansätze. 58. Diskussion des Regellosigkeitsaxioms. 59. Zufallsartige Folgen. Objektive Wahrscheinlichkeit.
60. Das BERNOULLIsche Problem. 61. Das Gesetz der grossen Zahlen
(Theorem von BERNOULLI). 62. BERNOULLIsches Theorem und
Interpretationsproblem. 63. BERNOULLIsches Theorem und Grenzwertsproblem. 64. Elimination des Grenzwertsaxioms. Auflösung des
Grundproblems. 65. Das Entscheidbarkeitsproblem. 66. Die logische
Form der Wahrscheinlichkeitsaussagen. 67. Wahrscheinlichkeitsmetaphysik. 68. Die Wahrscheinlichkeitsaussagen der Physik. 69. Gesetz und
Zufall. 70. Zur Deduzierbarkeit der Makrogesetze aus den Mikrogesetzen. 71. "Formalistische" Wahrscheinlichkeitsaussagen. 72. Zur Spielraumstheorie. BEMERKUNGEN ZUR QUANTENMECHANIK. 73.
Das HEISENBERGsche Programm und die Unbestimmtheitsrelationen.
74. Kurzer Bericht über die statistische Deutung der Quantenmechanik.
75. Statistische Umdeutung der Unbestimmtheitsrelationen. 76. Ausschaltung der Metaphysik durch Umkehrung des HEISENBERG-
Programms. Anwendungen. 77. Entscheidende Experimente. 78. Indeterministische Metaphysik. BEWÄHRUNG. 79. Die sogenannte
Verifikation von Hypothesen. 80. Kritik der Wahrscheinlichkeitslogik.
81. Induktionslogik und Wahrscheinlichkeitslogik. 82. Positive Theorie
der Bewährung. 83. Induktionslogik und Wahrscheinlichkeitslogik. 84.
Ueber den Gebrauch der Begriffe "wahr" und "bewährt". 85. Der Weg
der Wissenschaft. ANHANG. I. Definition der Dimension einer Theorie.
II. Zur allgemeinen Häufigkeitsrechnung in endlichen Klassen. III.
Ableitung der ersten NEWTONschen Formel (für endliche überdeckende
Abschnittsfolgen). IV. Konstruktionsangabe für Modelle von zufallsarti-
gen Folgen. V. Diskussion eines physikalischen Einwandes. VI. Ueber
ein "nichtprognostisches" Messverfahren. VII. Ergänzende Bemerkungen zu einem Gedankenexperiment. ANMERKUNGEN, *Zusätze und Litera-
turhinweise.* NAMENVERZEICHNIS.

1934

* (a) Zur Kritik der Ungenauigkeitsrelationen.

Die Naturwissenschaften (Berlin), 22. Jahrgang (1934), Heft 48 (30. November, 1934), pp. 807-808.

Dated: Vienna, 27. August, 1934.

* (b) LOGIK DER FORSCHUNG: *Zur Erkenntnistheorie der modernen Naturwissenschaft.*

Schriften zur wissenschaftlichen Weltauffassung, edited by Philipp Frank and Moritz Schlick, Band 9, Vienna: Verlag von Julius Springer, [1934] (with the imprint '1935'). Pp. vi, 248.

Abbreviated version of 1933(b). See notes to 1932(b) and to 1932(c).

Second German edition with new Appendices and other new material: 1966(e); third German edition, revised and enlarged: 1969(e); fourth German edition, revised: 1971(o). The text and the notes of the first edition are easily identified in the later, expanded editions.

English translation contained in 1959(a). For later editions and translations of 1959(a), see note to this item.

Japanese translation of EINFÜHRUNG: 1944(c).

Contents: Vorwort (Wien, im Herbst 1934). Inhaltsverzeichnis. EINFÜHRUNG. I. *Grundprobleme der Erkenntnislogik.* 1. Das Problem der Induktion. 2. Ausschaltung des Psychologismus. 3. Die deduktive Überprüfung der Theorien. 4. Das Abgrenzungsproblem. 5. Erfahrung als Methode. 6. Falsifizierbarkeit als Abgrenzungskriterium. 7. Das Problem der Erfahrungsgrundlage. (Die "empirische Basis".) 8. Wissenschaftliche Objektivität und subjektive Überzeugung. II. *Zum Problem der Methodenlehre.* 9. Die Unentbehrlichkeit methodologischer Festsetzungen. 10. Die "naturalistische" Auffassung der Methodenlehre. 11. Die methodologischen Regeln als Festsetzungen. BAUSTEINE ZU EINER THEORIE DER ERFAHRUNG. I. *Theorien.* 12. Kausalität, Erklärung, Prognosendeduktion. 13. Spezifische und numerische Allgemeinheit von Sätzen. 14. Universalien und Individualien. 15. Allsätze und universelle Es-gibt-Sätze. 16. Theoretische Systeme. 17. Deutungsmöglichkeiten eines axiomatischen Systems. 18. Allgemeinheitsstufen. Der "modus tollens". II. *Falsifizierbarkeit.* 19. Die konventionalistischen Einwände. 20. Methodologische Regeln. 21. Logische Untersuchung der Falsifizierbarkeit. 22. Falsifizierbarkeit und Falsifikation. 23. "Ereignis" und "Vorgang". 24. Falsifizierbarkeit und Widerspruchslosigkeit. III. *Basisprobleme.* 25. Erlebnisse als Basis (Psychologismus). 26. Über die sogenannten "Protokollsätze". 27. Objektivität der Basis. 28. Die Basissätze. 29.

Relativität der Basissätze. Auflösung des Trilemmas. 30. Theorie und Experiment. IV. *Grade der Prüfbarkeit.* 31. Veranschaulichung und Programm. 32. Wie können Klassen von Falsifikationsmöglichkeiten verglichen werden? 33. Falsifizierbarkeitsvergleich mit Hilfe des Teilklassenverhältnisses. 34. Die Struktur der Teilklassenbeziehung. "Logische Wahrscheinlichkeit". 35. "Empirischer Gehalt", Implikationsbeziehung, Falsifizierbarkeitsgrad. 36. Allgemeinheit und Bestimmtheit. 37. Logische Spielräume.—Bemerkungen zur Messgenauigkeit. 38. Der Dimensionsvergleich. 39. Die Dimension einer Kurvenklasse. 40. "Formale" und "materiale" Einengung der Dimension einer Kurvenklasse. V. *Einfachheit.* 41. Ausschaltung des ästhetisch-pragmatischen Einfachheitsbegriffes. 42. Das erkenntnistheoretische Einfachheitsproblem. 43. Einfachheit und Falsifizierbarkeitsgrad. 44. "Geometrische Form" und "Funktionsform". 45. Die Einfachheit der euklidischen Geometrie. 46. Der Einfachheitsbegriff des Konventionalismus. VI. *Wahrscheinlichkeit.* 47. Das Interpretationsproblem. 48. Subjektive und objektive Interpretationen. 49. Das Grundproblem der Zufallstheorie. 50. Die v. MISESsche Häufigkeitstheorie. 51. Plan für einen Neuaufbau der Wahrscheinlichkeitstheorie. 52. Relative Häufigkeit in endlichen Bezugsklassen. 53. Aussonderungen. Unabhängigkeit, Unempfindlichkeit, Belanglosigkeit. 54. Endliche Folgen. Stellenaussonderung und Umgebungsaussonderung. 55. n-Nachwirkungsfreiheit in endlichen Folgen. 56. Abschnittsfolgen. Erste NEWTONsche Formel. 57. Unendliche Bezugsfolgen. Hypothetische Häufigkeitsansätze. 58. Diskussion des Regellosigkeitsaxioms. 59. Zufallsartige Folgen. Objektive Wahrscheinlichkeit. 60. Das BERNOULLIsche Problem. 61. Das Gesetz der grossen Zahlen (Theorem von BERNOULLI). 62. BERNOULLIsches Theorem und Interpretationsproblem. 63. BERNOULLIsches Theorem und Grenzwertsproblem. 64. Elimination des Grenzwertsaxioms. Auflösung des Grundproblems. 65. Das Entscheidbarkeitsproblem. 66. Die logische Form der Wahrscheinlichkeitsaussagen. 67. Wahrscheinlichkeitsmetaphysik. 68. Die Wahrscheinlichkeitsaussagen der Physik. 69. Gesetz und Zufall. 70. Zur Deduzierbarkeit der Makrogesetze aus den Mikrogesetzen. 71. "Formalistische" Wahrscheinlichkeitsaussagen. 72. Zur Spielraumstheorie. VII. *Bemerkungen zur Quantenmechanik.* 73. Das HEISENBERGsche Programm und die Unbestimmtheitsrelationen. 74. Kurzer Bericht über die statistische Deutung der Quantenmechanik. 75. Statistische Umdeutung der Unbestimmtheitsrelationen. 76. Ausschaltung der Metaphysik durch Umkehrung des HEISENBERG-Programms. Anwendungen. 77. Entscheidende Experimente. 78. Indeterministische

Metaphysik. VIII. *Bewährung.* 79. Über die sogenannte Verifikation von Hypothesen. 80. "Hypothesenwahrscheinlichkeit" und "Ereignis-wahrscheinlichkeit"; Kritik der Wahrscheinlichkeitslogik. 81. Induktions-logik und Wahrscheinlichkeitslogik. 82. Positive Theorie der Bewährung. 83. Bewährbarkeit, Prüfbarkeit, logische Wahrscheinlichkeit. 84. Bemer-kungen über den Gebrauch der Begriffe "wahr" und "bewährt". 85. Der Weg der Wissenschaft ANHANG. I. Definition der Dimension einer Theo-rie. II. Zur allgemeinen Häufigkeitsrechnung in endlichen Klassen. III. Ableitung der ersten NEWTONschen Formel (für endliche überdeckende Abschnittsfolgen). IV. Konstruktionsangabe für Modelle von zufallsarti-gen Folgen. V. Diskussion eines physikalischen Einwandes. VI. Über ein "nichtprognostisches" Messverfahren. VII. Ergänzende Bemerkun-gen zu einem Gedankenexperiment. ANMERKUNGEN, *Zusätze und Litera-turhinweise.* NAMENVERZEICHNIS.

1935

* (a) "Induktionslogik" und "Hypothesenwahrscheinlichkeit".

Erkenntnis (Leipzig), Bd. 5 (Zugleich *Annalen der Philosophie*, Bd. 13) (1935), Heft 2/3 (18. Juni, 1935), pp. 170-172.

Presented at the Prague Preliminary Conference of the International Congresses for the Unity of Science, 31 Aug. to 2 Sept. 1934. (The Conference dates are incorrectly given as "30. August bis 1. September" on the *covers* of Heft 1 and 2/3.)

Heft 1 and 2/3 were issued also as a single "Sonderdruck aus *Erkenntnis*": *Einheit der Wissenschaft: Prager Vorkonferenz der internationalen Kongresse für Einheit der Wissenschaft, 1934.* Leipzig: Verlag von Felix Meiner, [1935]. Pp. [iv], 204.

This paper consists of some remarks made in a discussion of Hans Reichenbach's paper: Wahrscheinlichkeitslogik; *ibid.*, Heft 1 (31. März. 1935), pp. 37-43.

English translation contained in 1959(a). The German text is reprinted in 1966(e).

1938

* (a) A Set of Independent Axioms for Probability.

Mind (London), New Series, Vol. 47 (1938), No. 186 (April, 1938), pp. [275]-277.

Dated: Christchurch, N[ew] Z[ealand], November, 1937.

Errata: ibid., Vol. 47 (1938), No. 187 (July, 1938), p. 415; *ibid.*, Vol. 47 (1938), No. 188 (October, 1938), p. 552.

A Corrected version of this item is contained in 1959(a); the old system of axioms has been omitted and is replaced by the one on p. 53 in 1955(b).

* (b) Isaac Newton. A Notable Biography.

The Press (Christchurch, New Zealand), 15th October, 1938, p. 20, col. 6-8.

A review of *Isaac Newton 1642-1727*, by J. W. N. Sullivan, with a Memoir of the Author by Charles Singer, London: Macmillan & Co., New York: The Macmillan Company, 1938. Pp. xx, 275.

1940

* (a) What is Dialectic?

Mind (London), New Series, Vol. 49 (1940), No. 196 (October, 1940), pp. [403]-426.

A paper read to a philosophy seminar at *Canterbury University College*, Christchurch, New Zealand, in 1937.

Errata: To the Editor of "Mind". (4th February, 1941.) *Ibid.*, Vol. 50 (1941), No. 199 (July, 1941), pp. 311-312.

Also contained in 1963(a). German translation: 1965(b), 1965(n), 1966(n), and 1966(o).
See note to 1943(a).

* (b) Interpretation of Nebular Red-Shifts.

Nature (London), Vol. 145 (1940), No. 3663 (Jan. 13, 1940), pp. 69-70.

Errata: ibid., Vol. 145 (1940), No. 3679 (May 4, 1940), p. 701.

1943

* (a) Are Contradictions Embracing?

Mind (London), New Series, Vol. 52 (1943), No. 205 (January, 1943), pp. [47]-50.

A reply to Harold Jeffreys's note: Does a Contradiction Entail Every

Proposition?; *ibid.*, Vol. 51 (1942), No. 201 (January, 1942), pp. 90-91. In this note Jeffreys criticizes an argument in 1940(a).

1944

* (a) The Poverty of Historicism, I.

Economica (London; wartime address: Cambridge), New Series, Vol. 11 (1944), No. 42 (May, 1944), pp. 86-103.

Contents: [Parts I and II]; see note to 1957(g).

This item, 1944(b), and 1945(a) were translated into Italian and published in the form of articles: 1952(d) and 1953(e), and in book form: Italian: 1954(e), French: 1956(a) (reprint: 1969(o)).

Revised English book-edition: 1957(g).

2nd English edition (revised): 1960(c).

Revised 2nd English edition: 1961(b) (reprints: 1963(p), 1964(a), 1966(m), 1967(a), 1969(g), 1969(s), and 1972(b)).

Other translations: Arabic: 1959(b); Japanese: 1961(c), 1965(o), and 1966(l); Spanish: 1961(g); German: 1965(g), 1969(f), and 1971(p); Dutch: 1967(f); and Norwegian: 1971(d).

* (b) The Poverty of Historicism, II. A Criticism of Historicist Methods.

Economica (London; wartime address: Cambridge), New Series, Vol. 11 (1944), No. 43 (August, 1944), pp. 119-137.

Contents: [Part III]; see note to 1957(g).

For other editions and translations, see note to 1944(a).

T (c) Tankyû Ronrigaku Zyosetu.

In: *Kagaku Ronrigaku, Vīn Gakudan* [*The Logic of Science, by the Vienna Circle*], edited, with an introduction, by Katsumi Nakamura, [Tōkyō]: Nisshin Shoin, [1944]. (Pp. [xi], [401].) Pp. 311-349.

Japanese translation by Syûitirô Yosioka of the EINFÜHRUNG of 1934(b).

1945

* (a) The Poverty of Historicism, III.

Economica (London), New Series, Vol. 12 (1945), No. 46 (May, 1945), pp. 69-89.

Contents: [Part IV]; see note to 1957(g).

For other editions and translations, see note to 1944(a).

* (b) THE OPEN SOCIETY AND ITS ENEMIES. Volume I: *The Spell of Plato.*

London: George Routledge & Sons, Ltd., 1945. Pp. vii, 268.

Reprints: 1947(e) and 1949(c).
Revised and enlarged: 1950(a) (reprints: 1956(c) and 1956(d)).
2nd edition (further revised and enlarged): 1952(a).
3rd edition (further revised and enlarged): 1957(h).
4th edition (further revised and enlarged): 1962(c) (reprints: 1962(d), 1963(l), 1963(m), and 1963(n)).
5th edition (further revised and enlarged): 1966(a) (reprints: 1968(p), 1969(q), 1969(r), and 1971(b)).
Translations: Dutch: 1950(d); Spanish: 1957(c) and 1967(v); German: 1957(k) and 1958(i); Portuguese: 1959(c); Japanese: 1963(i) and 1973( ); Turkish: 1967(u) and 1968(l); and Italian: 197 ( ).
Contents: Preface ([1943]). Acknowledgements (Christchurch, [New Zealand], April 1944). Contents. Introduction. *Volume I: The Spell of Plato: The Myth of Origin and Destiny.* 1. Historicism and the Myth of Destiny. 2. Heraclitus. 3. Plato's Theory of Ideas. *Plato's Descriptive Sociology.* 4. Change and Rest. 5. Nature and Convention. *Plato's Political Programme.* 6. Totalitarian Justice. 7. The Principle of Leadership. 8. The Philosopher King. 9. Aestheticism, Radicalism, Utopianism. *Plato Attacks.* 10. The Open Society and its Enemies. *Notes* (pp. 178-268).

* (c) THE OPEN SOCIETY AND ITS ENEMIES. Volume II: *The High Tide of Prophecy: Hegel, Marx, and the Aftermath.*

London: George Routledge & Sons, Ltd., 1945. Pp. v, 352.

For later editions and translations, see note to 1945(b).
Contents: Contents. *The Rise of Oracular Philosophy.* 11. Aristotle. The Roots of Hegelianism. 12. Hegel and The New Tribalism. *Marx's Method.* 13. Sociological Determinism. 14. The Autonomy of Sociology. 15. Economic Historicism. 16. The Classes. 17. The Legal and The Social System. *Marx's Prophecy.* 18. The Coming of Socialism. 19. The Social Revolution. 20. Capitalism and Its Fate. 21. An Evaluation. *Marx's Ethics.* 22. The Moral Theory of Historicism. *The Aftermath.* 23. The Sociology of Knowledge. 24. Oracular Philosophy and the Revolt against Reason. 25. Conclusion. Has History any Meaning? *Notes* (pp. 268-346). *Index.*

* (d) [The Growth of German Historicism.]

    Economica (London), New Series, Vol. 12 (1945), No. 48 (November, 1945), pp. 259-261.

    A review of *The Growth of German Historicism* by F. Engel-Janosi, The Johns Hopkins University Studies in Historical and Political Science, Series LXII, No. 2, Baltimore· The Johns Hopkins Press, 1944. 101 pp.

* (e) Research and the University: A Statement by a Group of Teachers in the University of New Zealand.

    The Caxton Press (Christchurch, New Zealand), 10 July, 1945.

    Written in co-operation with R. S. Allan, J. C. Eccles, H. G. Forder, J. Packer, and H. N. Parton.
    Reprint: 1945(f); abridged version: 1945(g).

R (f) Place of Research in the University.

    Christchurch Press (Christchurch, New Zealand), 28 July, 1945.

    Reprint of 1945(e).

R (g) Research and the University.

    The Critic (Dunedin, New Zealand), Vol. 21 (1945), No. 11 (September 13, 1945), p. [1].

    Abridged version of 1945(e).

U (h) Principles of Scientific Method.

    In: *Principles of Scientific Method: Notes on Lectures by Dr. K. R. Popper given at the University of Otago from 22nd to 26th May, 1945*; available in Xerox at *Canterbury* and *Otago Universities* in New Zealand. (Pp. 26.) Pp. 1-20.

U (i) Principles of Indeterminacy.

    Ibid., pp. 21-22.

    Notes on an informal talk to a group of Physicists, May 19th, 1945.

U (j) Atomic Theory and Biology.

Ibid., pp. 23-26.

Notes on an informal talk to a group in the Medical School.

1946

* (a) "A Scientist Looks at History".

Time and Tide (London), Vol. 27 (1946), No. 5 (2 February, 1946), p. 107.

Letter to the Editor of *Time and Tide*. A reply to H. St. Lawrence's review of 1945(b) and 1945(c): The Scientist Looks at History; *ibid.*, Vol. 27 (1946), No. 2 (12 January, 1946), p. 38.

* (b) Why are the Calculuses of Logic and Arithmetic Applicable to Reality?

In: *Arisotelian Society, Supplementary Volume XX: Logic and Reality*, London: Harrison and Sons, Ltd., 1946. (Pp. [iii], 232.) Pp. [40]-60.

This was the third paper of a symposium: "Why are the Calculuses of Logic and Arithmetic Applicable to Reality?" held on July 6th, 1946, at the *Joint Session of the Aristotelian Society and the Mind Association* (Manchester, July 5-7, 1946). The two other symposiasts were G. Ryle and C. Lewy.
Also contained in 1963(a).

1947

* (a) New Foundations for Logic.

Mind (Edinburgh), New Series, Vol. 56 (1947), No. 223 (July, 1947), pp. [193]-235.

Errata: Corrections and Additions to "New Foundations for Logic"; *ibid.*, Vol. 57 (1948), No. 225 (January, 1948), pp. 69-70.

* (b) Logic Without Assumptions.

In: *Proceedings of the Aristotelian Society, New Series, Volume XLVII (1946-1947)*, London: Harrison & Sons, Ltd., 1947. (Pp. xx, 300.) Pp. [251]-292.

A paper read before the *Aristotelian Society* on May 5th, 1947.

* (c) Functional Logic without Axioms or Primitive Rules of Inference.

1. *Koninklijke Nederlandsche Akademie van Wetenschappen, Proceedings of the Section of Sciences* (Amsterdam), Vol. 50 (1947), No. 9 (1947), pp. [1214]-1224.

2. *Indagationes Mathematicae* ex actis quibus titulus (*Koninklijke Nederlandsche Akademie van Wetenschappen*, Amsterdam), Volumen 9 (1947), Fasciculus 5 (1947), pp. [561]-571.

>   Communicated by Prof. L. E. J. Brouwer at the meeting of October 25, 1947.

T (d) L'Utopie et la Violence.

>   *Les rencontres philosophiques des Bruxelles*, 1947.

>   An address delivered to the *Institut des Arts* in Brussels, in June 1947. French translation of 1948(a).

R (e) THE OPEN SOCIETY AND ITS ENEMIES.

>   London: George Routledge & Sons, Ltd., 1947.

>   Reprint of 1945(b) and 1945(c).

* (f) To the Editor of *Philosophy*.

>   *Philosophy* (London), Vol. 22 (1947), No. 82 (July, 1947), p. 191.

>   Dated: London, February 2nd, 1947.
>   A reply to Professor G. C. Field's review of 1945(b) and 1945(c); *ibid.*, Vol. 21 (1946), No. 80 (November, 1946), pp. 271-276.

1948

* (a) Utopia and Violence.

>   *The Hibbert Journal* (London), No. 181 = Vol. 46 (1947-1948), No. 2 (January, 1948), pp. 109-116.

>   Also contained in 1963(a). For abridged reprints, see 1971(f), 1971(y), and 1972(k).
>   Translations: French: 1947(d); Japanese: 1963(j); German: 1968(x).
>   See note to 1947(d).

* (b) On the Theory of Deduction, Part I. Derivation and its Generalizations.

1.   *Koninklijke Nederlandsche Akademie van Wetenschappen, Proceedings of the Section of Sciences* (Amsterdam), Vol. 51 (1948), No. 2 (1948), pp. [173]-183.

2.   *Indagationes Mathematicae* ex actis quibus titulus (*Koninklijke Nederlandsche Akademie van Wetenschappen*, Amsterdam), Volumen 10 (1948), Fasciculus 1 (1948), pp. [44]-54.

Communicated by Prof. L. E. J. Brouwer at the meeting of November 29, 1947.

* (c) On the Theory of Deduction, Part II. The Definitions of Classical and Intuitionist Negation.

1.   *Koninklijke Nederlandsche Akademie van Wetenschappen, Proceedings of the Section of Sciences* (Amsterdam), Vol. 51 (1948), No. 3 (1948), pp. [322]-331.

2.   *Indagationes Mathematicae* ex actis quibus titulus (*Koninklijke Nederlandsche Akademie van Wetenschappen*, Amsterdam), Volumen 10 (1948), Fasciculus 2 (1948), pp. [111]-120.

Communicated by Prof. L. E. J. Brouwer at the meeting of November 29, 1947.

* (d) Prediction and Prophecy and their Significance for Social Theory.

In: *Library of the Tenth International Congress of Philosophy*, Volume 1: *Proceedings of the Tenth International Congress of Philosophy* (Amsterdam, August 11-18, 1948), (*Bibliothèque du Xme Congrès International de Philosophie*, Volume 1: *Actes du Xme Congrès International de Philosophie*), edited by E. W. Beth, H. J. Pos and J. H. A. Hollak (assistant editor), Amsterdam: North-Holland Publishing Company, 1949. Fascicule 1 (pp. [x], 1-600), pp. 82-91.

An Address delivered to the Plenary Session.
Errata: ibid., Fascicule 2 (pp. [iv], [601]-1259), p. 1259.
Also contained in 1959(l) and 1963(a). German translation: 1965(m).

* (e) The Trivialization of Mathematical Logic.

Ibid., Fascicule 2 (pp. [iv], [601]-1259), pp. 722-727.

Errata: ibid., Fascicule 2, p. 1259.

* (f) What can Logic do for Philosophy?

In: *Aristotelian Society, Supplementary Volume XXII: Logical Positivism and Ethics*, London: Harrison and Sons, Ltd., 1948. (Pp. [iv], 215.) Pp. [141]-154.

This was the first paper of a symposium: "What can Logic do for Philosophy?" held on July 11th, 1948, at the *Joint Session of the Aristotelian Society and the Mind Association* (Durham, July 9-11, 1948). The two other symposiasts were W. C. Kneale and A. J. Ayer.

* (g) An Important Correction. To the Editor of the *Hibbert Journal*.

The Hibbert Journal (London), No. 182 = Vol. 46 (1947-1948), No. 3 (April, 1948), p. 275.

A correction of a statement made on p. 174 in S. H. Mellone: Survey of Recent Philosophical Theological Literature; *ibid*., No. 2 (January, 1948), pp. 174-177. The statement is a quotation from p. [317] in R. Rhees: "Social Engineering"; *Mind* (Edinburgh), New Series, Vol. 56 (1947), No. 224 (October, 1947), pp. [317]-331.

1949

* (a) A Note on Natural Laws and so-called "Contrary-to-Fact Conditionals".

Mind (Edinburgh), New Series, Vol. 58 (1949), No. 229 (January, 1949), pp. [62]-66.

* (b) Towards a Rational Theory of Tradition.

In: *The Rationalist Annual for the Year 1949*, edited by Frederick Watts, London: Watts & Co., [1949]. (Pp. 104.) Pp. 36-55.

This is a transcript of a lecture (corrected by the author) given at the *Third Annual Conference of the Rationalist Press Association* on July 26, 1948, at *Magdalen College*, Oxford.
Also contained in 1963(a).

R (c) THE OPEN SOCIETY AND ITS ENEMIES.

London: George Routledge & Sons, Ltd., 1949.

Reprint of 1945(b) and 1945(c).

* (d) Naturgesetze und theoretische Systeme.

In: *Gesetz und Wirklichkeit* (4. internationale Hochschulwochen des österreichischen College, Alpbach=Tirol, 21. August-9. September, 1948), edited by Simon Moser, Innsbruck, Vienna: Tyrolia Verlag, 1949. (Pp. [298].) Pp. 43-60.

2nd edition: 1964(e) and 1972(j). English translation contained in 1972(a).

1950

R (a) THE OPEN SOCIETY AND ITS ENEMIES.
*

Princeton, N. J.: Princeton University Press, 1950. Pp. xii, 732.

A revised and enlarged edition in one volume of 1945(b) and 1945(c) with a new preface: Preface to the Revised Edition (July 14, 1950).
Reprints: 1956(c) and 1956(d).

Indeterminism in Quantum Physics and in Classical Physics. Part I.

The British Journal for the Philosophy of Science (Edinburgh), Vol. 1 (1950-1951), No. 2 (August, 1950), pp. 117-133.

Expanded version of a paper read before the *Philosophy of Science Group* of the *British Society for the History of Science* (now the *British Society for the Philosophy of Science*), at their first Ordinary Meeting on November 15th, 1948.
Parts I and II also contained in 1974(a).

* (c) Indeterminism in Quantum Physics and in Classical Physics. Part II.

The British Journal for the Philosophy of Science (Edinburgh), Vol. 1 (1950-1951), No. 3 (November, 1950), pp. 173-195.

See note to 1950(b).

T (d) DE VRIJE SAMENLEVING EN HAAR VIJANDEN.
Deel I: De betovering door Plato.
Deel II: De Springvloed van Profetie: Hegel, Marx, en het Naspel.

Bussum, Holland: F. G. Kroonder, 1950. Deel I: pp. 306; Deel II; pp. 400.

Dutch translation of 1945(b) and 1945(c), by Justus Meijer.

1952

R (a) THE OPEN SOCIETY AND ITS ENEMIES. (Second English edition,
*   revised and enlarged.)

> London: Routledge and Kegan Paul, 1952. Vol I: pp. xi, 318; Vol. II: pp. v,
> 375.

> Further revised and enlarged edition of 1945(b) and 1945(c); see
> 1950(a).

* (b) Humanism and Reason.

> *The Philosophical Quarterly* (St. Andrews), Vol. 2 (1952), No. 7
> (April, 1952), pp. 166-171.

> An abridged review of: Ernesto Grassi und Thure von Uexküll
> *Von Ursprung und Grenzen der Geisteswissenschaften und Naturwis-*
> *senschaften, (Sammlung Überlieferung und Auftrag. Reihe Studia*
> *Humanitatis,* 1.), Bern: A. Franke AG, 1950. Pp. 252.
> The entire review is published in 1963(a).

* (c) The Nature of Philosophical Problems and their Roots in Science.

> *The British Journal for the Philosophy of Science* (Edinburgh), Vol. 3
> (1952-1953), No. 10 (August, 1952), pp. 124-156.

> The Chairman's address, delivered at the meeting of 28th April
> 1952, to the *Philosophy of Science Group* of the *British Society for*
> *the History of Science* (now the *British Society for the Philosophy of*
> *Science).*
> Also contained in 1963(a) and 1971(v).

T (d) La povertà dello storicismo.
*

> *L'industria* (Milano), 1952, No. 3 ([Summer], 1952), pp. 285-307.

> English summary: The Poverty of the Historical Method; *ibid.,*
> p. 454.
> Italian translation by Camilla Roatta of 1944(a), pp. 86-97. The English
> text has been revised by this translation.
> For book edition of this item and 1953(e), see 1954(e).

1953

* (a) Language and the Body-Mind Problem.

In: *Proceedings of the XIth International Congress of Philosophy* (Brussels, August 20-26, 1953), Vol. 7: *Philosophical Psychology*, (*Actes du XIème Congrès International de Philosophie* (Bruxelles, 20-26 Août, 1953), Vol. 7: *Psychologie philosophique*), Amsterdam: North-Holland Publishing Company, Louvain: Éditions E. Nauwelaerts, 1953. (Pp. 272.) Pp. 101-107.

Also contained in 1963(a).

* (b) The Principle of Individuation.

In: *Aristotelian Society, Supplementary Volume XXVII: Berkeley and Modern Problems*, London: Harrison and Sons, Ltd., 1953. (Pp. [iii], 230.) Pp. [97]-120.

This was the third paper of a symposium: "The Principle of Individuation" held on July 11th, 1953, at the *Joint Session of the Aristotelian Society and the Mind Association* (Dublin, July 10-12, 1953). The two other symposiasts were J. Lukasiewicz and G. E. Anscombe.

R (c) The Sociology of Knowledge: A Critique.

In: *Readings in Philosophy of Science: Introduction to the Foundations and Cultural Aspects of the Sciences*, arranged and edited by Philip P. Wiener, New York: Scribner, 1953. (Pp. ix, 645.) Pp. 357-366.

Reprinted from 1950(a), chapter 23, pp. 398-409, and notes, pp. 705-707.

* (d) A Note on Berkeley as Precursor of Mach.

The British Journal for the Philosophy of Science (Edinburgh), Vol. 4 (1953-1954), No. 13 (May, 1953), pp. 26-36.

This number of the *Journal* is devoted to commemorating the Bicentenary of George Berkeley (12th March 1685-14th January 1753).
Also contained in 1963(a), 1968(n), 1968(o), and 1970(g).

T (e) La povertà dello storicismo.
*

L'industria (Milano), 1953:

No. 1 ([January], 1953), pp. 69-93.
English summary: The Poverty of Historicism; *ibid.*, p. 177.
Italian translation of 1944(a), pp. 97-103; and 1944(b), pp. 119-124.

No. 2 ([March-May], 1953), pp. 283-307.
English summary: The Poverty of the Historical Method; *ibid.*, p. 374.
Italian translation of 1944(b), pp. 124-137.

No. 3 ([Summer], 1953), pp. 451-491.
English summary: The Poverty of the Historical Method; *ibid.*, p. 563.
Italian translation of 1945(a).

Translated by Camilla Roatta. The English text has been revised for this translation.
For book edition of 1952(d) and this item, see 1954(e).

1954

* (a) Philosopher of the Enlightenment. Karl R. Popper on Immanuel Kant.

The Listener (London), Vol. 51 (1954), No. 1303 (February 18, 1954), pp. 291-292, 303.

Broadcast under the title "Immanuel Kant: Philosopher of the Enlightenment" in the *BBC Third Programme* on the eve of the hundred and fiftieth anniversary of Kant's death, 12th February, 1954.
Also contained. in 1963(a).
German translation: 1954(b), 1957(k), and 1965(i).

T (b) Immanuel Kant. Zu seinem 150. Todestag am 12. Februar 1954.

Englische Rundschau (Köln), 4. Jahrgang (1954), Nr. 11 (19. März, 1954), pp. 166-167, 171.

German translation of 1954(a).
Also contained in 1957(k). An extract is contained in 1965(i).

* (c) Self-Reference and Meaning in Ordinary Language.

Mind (Edinburgh), New Series, Vol. 63 (1954), No. 250 (April, 1954), pp. 162-169.

Also contained in 1963(a).

* (d) Degree of Confirmation.

The British Journal for the Philosophy of Science (Edinburgh), Vol. 5 (1954-1955), No. 18 (August, 1954), pp. 143-149.

Errata: ibid., Vol. 5 (1954-1955), No. 20 (February, 1955), p. 334 and p. 359; 1959(a), p. 401, note *3.

Also contained in 1959(a).

R (e) MISERIA DELLO STORICISMO.
*

Collana di moderne opere economiche, diretta da Ferdinando di Fenizio, Milano: Editrice L'industria, 1954. Pp. 129.

Book edition with revised text of 1952(d) and 1953(e).

R (f) The Advocate of Democratic Criticism.

In: *The State versus Socrates: A Case Study in Civic Freedom*, edited and with an introduction by John D. Montgomery, Boston: The Beacon Press, 1954. (Pp. [xi], 247.) Pp. 160-166.

Reprint of 1950(a), pp. 184-189; part of chapter 10.

R (g) Has History Any Meaning?

In: *Contemporary Philosophy*, a book of readings edited by James Louis Jarrett and Sterling M. McMurrin, New York: Henry Holt and Company, 1954. (Pp. xvii, 524.) Pp. 433-440.

From chapter 25 of 1950(a).

1955

* (a) On a Proposed Solution of the Paradox of the Liar.

The Journal of Symbolic Logic (Groningen), Vol. 20 (1955), No. 1 (March, 1955), pp. 93-94.

Abstract of a paper contributed to the meeting of the *Association for Symbolic Logic* (Amsterdam, September 1, 1954).

* (b) Two Autonomous Axiom Systems for the Calculus of Probabilities.

The British Journal for the Philosophy of Science (Edinburgh), Vol. 6 (1955-1956), No. 21 (May, 1955), pp. 51-57.

Errata: ibid., Vol. 6 (1955-1956), No. 22 (August, 1955), p. 176.
Corrigendum: ibid., Vol. 6 (1955-1956), No. 24 (February, 1956), p. 351.

* (c) A Note on the Body-Mind Problem. Reply to Professor Wilfrid Sellars.

Analysis (Oxford), New Series No. 48 = Vol. 15 (1954-1955), No. 6 (June, 1955), pp. 131-135.

A reply to Wilfrid Sellars: A Note on Popper's Argument for Dualism; *ibid.*, New Series No. 43 = Vol. 15 (1954-1955), No. 1 (October, 1954), pp. 23-24.

Also contained in 1963(a).

* (d) A Note on Tarski's Definition of Truth.

Mind (Edinburgh), New Series, Vol. 64 (1955), No. 255 (July, 1955), pp. 388-391.

Also contained in 1972(a).

* (e) 'Content' and 'Degree of Confirmation': A Reply to Dr Bar-Hillel.

The British Journal for the Philosophy of Science (Edinburgh), Vol. 6 (1955-1956), No. 22 (August, 1955), pp. 157-163.

A reply to Yehoshua Bar-Hillel: Comments on 'Degree of Confirmation' by Professor K. R. Popper; *ibid.*, Vol. 6 (1955-1956), No. 22 (August, 1955), pp. 155-157.

T (f) Verso una teoria liberale dell'opinione pubblica.

Il Politico (Milano), Anno 20 (1955), No. 2 (1955), pp. 181-189.

Résumé, Summary, Zusammenfassung; *ibid.*, p. 333.
Italian translation by Silvia Boba of a paper read in English before the *Sixth Meeting of the Mont Pèlerin Society* at their Conference in Venice, September 1954.
See note to 1956(e).

U (g) THE DEMARCATION BETWEEN SCIENCE AND METAPHYSICS.

January, 1955. Distributed in a stencilled version since June, 1956. Pp. [i], 75.

A paper contributed in January, 1955, to *The Library of Living Philosophers*, Vol. 11: *The Philosophy of Rudolf Carnap*, edited by Paul Arthur Schilpp, La Salle, Illinois: The Open Court Publishing Company, 1963.
Contained in 1963(a) and 1964(b).

* (h) "The Illusion of the Epoch".

The Times Literary Supplement (London), 54th Year (1955), No. 2786 (July 22, 1955), p. 413.

A letter to the Editor containing an objection to a review of Harry Burrows Acton *The Illusion of the Epoch: Marxism-Leninism as a Philosophical Creed*, London: Cohen & West, 1955; *ibid.*, 54th Year (1955), No. 2783 (July 1, 1955), p. 359.

1956

T (a) MISÈRE DE L'HISTORICISME.
*

Paris: Librairie Plon, 1956. Pp. xvi, 196.

French translation by Hervé Rousseau of a revised and enlarged version of 1944(a), 1944(b), and 1945(a).
Préface à l'édition française (Penn, 12 décembre 1955); pp. [ix]-xi. Bibliographie des travaux de l'auteur jusqu'en 1956; pp. 175-179. Note sur la présente traduction; pp. 181-183.
Reprint: 1969(o).

* (b) The Arrow of Time.

Nature (London), Vol. 177 (1956), No. 4507 (March 17, 1956), p. 538.

Continued in 1956(g), 1957(d), 1957(f), 1958(b), 1965(f), 1967(b), and 1967(h).
Also contained in 1974(a).

R (c) THE OPEN SOCIETY AND ITS ENEMIES.

Princeton, N. J.: Princeton University Press, 1956.

Reprint of the one volume edition 1950(a).

R (d) THE OPEN SOCIETY AND ITS ENEMIES.

The Library of Science, New York: Basic Books, Inc., 1956.

Special book-club edition of 1950(a).

T (e) Die öffentliche Meinung im Lichte der Grundsätze des Liberalismus.
*

In: *Ordo: Jahrbuch für die Ordnung von Wirtschaft und Gesellschaft*, 8. Band, edited by Franz Böhm, Friedrich A. Lutz, and Fritz W. Meyer, Düsseldorf, Munich: Helmut Küpper vormals Georg Bondi, 1956. (Pp. xx, 412.) Pp. [7]-17.

German translation by Mira Koffka of a paper read in English before the *Sixth Meeting* of the *Mont Pèlerin Society* at their Conference in Venice, September 1954.
Spanish translation: 1963(f).
First published in English in 1963(a). For an Italian translation, see 1955(f).

* (f) Three Views Concerning Human Knowledge.

   In: *Contemporary British Philosophy: Personal Statements*, Third Series, edited by H. D. Lewis, (*The Muirhead Library of Philosophy*, edited by H. D. Lewis), London: George Allen & Unwin, New York: The Macmillan Company, 1956. (Pp. xiv, 501.) Pp. [355]-388.

   Also contained in 1963(a) and 1970(y).
   Translations: Italian: 1958(d), 1969(c), and 1969(d); Japanese: 1968(m).

* (g) Irreversibility and Mechanics.

   Nature (London), Vol. 178 (1956), No. 4529 (August 18, 1956), p. 382.

   A reply to Richard Schlegel: Irreversibility and Mechanics; *ibid.*, pp. 381-382.
   Continuation of 1956(b). Also contained in 1974(a).

* (h) Reply to Professor Carnap.

   The British Journal for the Philosophy of Science (Edinburgh), Vol. 7 (1956-1957), No. 27 (November, 1956), pp. 244-245.

   Reply to Rudolf Carnap: Remarks on Popper's Note on Content and Degree of Confirmation; *ibid.*, Vol. 7 (1956-1957), No. 27 (November, 1956), pp. 243-244.

* (i) Adequacy and Consistency: A Second Reply to Dr Bar-Hillel.

   The British Journal for the Philosophy of Science (Edinburgh), Vol. 7 (1956-1957), No. 27 (November, 1956), pp. 249-256.

   A reply to Yehoshua Bar-Hillel: Further Comments on Probability and Confirmation—A Rejoinder to Professor Popper; *ibid.*, Vol. 7 (1956-1957), No. 27 (November, 1956), pp. 245-248.

1957

* (a) Philosophy of Science: A Personal Report.

In: *British Philosophy in the Mid-Century: A Cambridge Symposium*, edited by C. A. Mace, London: George Allen and Unwin, 1957. (Pp. 396.) Pp. 155-191.

A lecture given at *Peterhouse*, Cambridge, in summer 1953, as part of a course on developments and trends in contemporary British philosophy, organized by the *British Council*.
Also contained in 1963(a) as: *Science: Conjectures and Refutations.* An extract is contained in 1965(a).
Italian translation: 1969(d).

* (b) A Second Note on Degree of Confirmation.

The British Journal for the Philosophy of Science (Edinburgh), Vol. 7 (1956-1957), No. 28 (February, 1957), pp. 350-353.

Addition and Correction: ibid., Vol. 8 (1957-1958), No. 32 (February, 1958), pp. 294-295, note 2. (Also in 1959(a), p. 406, note 1.)
Also contained in 1959(a).

T (c) LA SOCIEDAD ABIERTA Y SUS ENEMIGOS.

Biblioteca de Psicologia Social y Sociologia, Buenos Aires: Editorial Paidos, [1957]. Pp. 683.

Spanish translation of 1950(a), by Eduardo Loedel. Introduction by Norberto Rodríguez Bustamante.
For an *unauthorized* two-volume edition, see 1967(v).

* (d) Irreversible Processes in Physical Theory.

Nature (London), Vol. 179 (1957), No. 4573 (June 22, 1957), p. 1297.

A reply to E. L. Hill and A. Grünbaum: Irreversible Processes in Physical Theory; *ibid.*, pp. 1296-1297.
Continuation of 1956(b) and 1956(g).
Also contained in 1974(a).

* (e) The Propensity Interpretation of the Calculus of Probability, and the Quantum Theory.

In: *Observation and Interpretation; A Symposium of Philosophers and Physicists: Proceedings of the Ninth Symposium of the Colston Research Society held in the University of Bristol, April 1st-April 4th, 1957*, edited by S. Körner in collaboration with M. H. L. Pryce, (Volume 9 of the *Colston*

Papers), London: Butterworths Scientific Publications, 1957. (Pp. xiv, 218.) Pp. 65-70, 88-89.

This paper was read at the conference by P. K. Feyerabend. Pp. 88-89 contains the written reply to criticism.

Errata: The British Journal for the Philosophy of Science (Edinburgh), Vol. 8 (1957-1958), No. 32 (February, 1958), p. 301, note 1. These errata are also to be found in 1959(a), p. 414, note 7.

Reprint: 1962(o). Also contained in 1974(a).

* (f) Irreversibility; or Entropy since 1905.

The British Journal for the Philosophy of Science (Edinburgh), Vol. 8 (1957-1958), No. 30 (August, 1957), pp. 151-155.

Presented by the Chairman, Dr G. J. Whitrow, in the symposium on "The Status of Irreversible Processes in Physical Theory", September 23, 1956, at the *First Annual Conference of the Philosophy of Science Group of the British Society for the History of Science* (Manchester, September 21-23, 1956).

Erratum: ibid., Vol. 8 (1957-1958), No. 31 (November, 1957), p. 258.
Continuation of 1956(b), 1956(g), and 1957(d).
Also contained in 1974(a).

R (g) THE POVERTY OF HISTORICISM.
*

London: Routledge & Kegan Paul, Boston, Mass.: The Beacon Press, 1957. Pp. xiv, 166.

Revised English book-edition of 1944(a), 1944(b), and 1945(a). See 1944(a) for further editions and translations.

Contents: Historical Note. Preface (Penn, Buckinghamshire, July 1957). Contents. Introduction. *I. The Anti-Naturalistic Doctrines of Historicism.* 1. Generalization. 2. Experiment. 3. Novelty. 4. Complexity. 5. Inexactitude of Prediction. 6. Objectivity and Valuation. 7. Holism. 8. Intuitive Understanding. 9. Quantitative Methods. 10. Essentialism *versus* Nominalism. *II. The Pro-Naturalistic Doctrines of Historicism.* 11. Comparison with Astronomy. Long-Term Forecasts and Large-Scale Forecasts. 12. The Observational Basis. 13. Social Dynamics. 14. Historical Laws. 15. Historical Prophecy *versus* Social Engineering. 16. The Theory of Historical Development. 17. Interpreting *versus* Planning Social Change. 18. Conclusion of the Analysis. *III. Criticism of the Anti-Naturalistic Doctrines.* 19. Practical Aims of this

Criticism. 20. The Technological Approach to Sociology. 21. Piecemeal *versus* Utopian Engineering. 22. The Unholy Alliance with Utopianism. 23. Criticism of Holism. 24. The Holistic Theory of Social Experiments. 25. The Variability of Experimental Conditions. 26. Are Generalizations confined to Periods? *IV. Criticism of the Pro-Naturalistic Doctrines.* 27. Is there a Law of Evolution? Laws and Trends. 28. The Method of Reduction. Causal Explanation. Prediction and Prophecy. 29. The Unity of Method. 30. Theoretical and Historical Sciences. 31. Situational Logic in History. Historical Interpretation. 32. The Institutional Theory of Progress. 33. Conclusion. The Emotional Appeal of Historicism. *General Index.*

R (h) **THE OPEN SOCIETY AND ITS ENEMIES.** (Third English edition,
* revised and enlarged.)

London: Routledge and Kegan Paul, 1957. Vol. I: pp. xi, 322; Vol. II: pp. [vi], 391.

Further revised and enlarged edition of 1945(b) and 1945(c); see 1950(a) and 1952(a).

In the third edition Acknowledgements (Stanford, California, May 1957), an *Addendum:* Plato and Geometry, and an Index of Platonic Passages have been added to Vol. I. An Index of Subjects has been added to each volume.

* (i) The Aim of Science.

Ratio (Oxford), Vol. 1 (1957-1958), No. 1 (December, 1957), pp. 24-35.

Revised edition: 1969(k). Also contained in 1959(n) and 1972(a).
Translations: German: 1957(j), 1964(d), and 1972(i); Italian: 1962(j) and 1969(c).

T (j) Über die Zielsetzung der Erfahrungswissenschaft.

Ratio (Frankfurt a. M.), 1. Band (1957), Heft 1 = Jahrgang 1957/58, Heft 1 ([Dezember], 1957), pp. 21-31.

German translation of 1957(i). Revised reprints: 1964(d) and 1972(i). See note to 1957(i).

T (k) DER ZAUBER PLATONS. *Die offene Gesellschaft und ihre Feinde,* Band
* I.

Sammlung Dalp, Band 84, Bern: Francke Verlag, 1957. Pp. [436].

German translation by P. K. Feyerabend of 1952(a), Vol. I, with a new preface: Einführung zur deutschen Ausgabe (Penn, 31. Dezember 1955); and a reprint of 1954(b).

* (l) Probability Magic or Knowledge out of Ignorance.

Dialectica (Neuchâtel), Vol. 11 (1957), No. 3/4 (15.9.-15.12., 1957), pp. [354]-372.

Abstract, Résumé, Zusammenfassung; *ibid.*, pp. 372-374.
Part of the Abstract has been published in *The British Journal for the Philosophy of Science* (Edinburgh), Vol. 9 (1958-1959), No. 36 (February, 1959), p. 348.

1958

* (a) A Third Note on Degree of Corroboration or Confirmation.

The British Journal for the Philosophy of Science (Edinburgh), Vol. 8 (1957-1958), No. 32 (February, 1958), pp. 294-302.

Also contained in 1959(a).

* (b) Irreversible Processes in Physical Theory.

Nature (London), Vol. 181 (1958), No. 4606 (February 8, 1958), pp. 402-403.

A reply to R. C. L. Bosworth: Irreversible Processes in Physical Theory; *ibid.*, p. 402.
Continuation of 1956(b), 1956(g), 1957(d), and 1957(f).
Also contained in 1974(a).

T (c) Das Problem der Nichtwiderlegbarkeit von Philosophien.

Deutsche Universitätszeitung (Göttingen), 13. Jahrgang (1958), Nr. 1 (Januar, 1958), pp. 7-13.

German translation of Part II of 1958(f). See note to 1958(g).

T (d) TRE CONCEZIONI SULLA CONOSCENZA UMANA.

1. *L'industria* (Milano), 1958, No. 1 ([January-March], 1958), pp. 60-73; and No. 2, pp. 183-198.
    Appendice: Scritti di Karl R. Popper; *ibid.*, No. 2, pp. 198-201.

English summaries; *ibid.,* No. 1, pp. 138-139; and No. 2, p. 299.

2.   Milano: Editrice L'industria, [1958]. Pp. 32.

Italian translation of 1956(f) by Giulia Sanvisenti. For other Italian translations, see note to 1956(f).

* (e) Back to the Pre-Socratics.

In: *Proceedings of the Aristotelian Society, New Series,* Volume LIX (1958-1959), London: Harrison & Sons, Ltd., 1959. (Pp. [iv], 305.) Pp. [1]-24.

The *Presidential Address,* delivered before the meeting of the *Aristotelian Society* on 13th October, 1958.
Also contained in 1963(a), 1967(l), and 1970(t). An extract is contained in 1964(i).

* (f) On the Status of Science and of Metaphysics. Two Radio Talks:
I.   Kant and the Logic of Experience.
II. The Problem of the Irrefutability of Philosophical Theories.

Ratio (Oxford), Vol. 1 (1957-1958), No. 2 (December, 1958), pp. 97-115.

Two Radio Talks written for the *Free Radio-University*, Berlin.
Also contained in 1963(a). German translation: 1958(g).

T (g) Über die Möglichkeit der Erfahrungswissenschaft und der Metaphysik. Zwei Rundfunkvorträge:
I.   Kant und die Möglichkeit der Erfahrungswissenschaft.
II. Über die Nichtwiderlegbarkeit philosophischer Theorien.

Ratio (Frankfurt a. M.), Jahrgang 1957/58, Heft 2 ([Dezember, 1958]), pp. 1-16.

German translation of 1958(f).
Part II also contained in 1958(c), 1959(d), 1963(k), and 1969(t).

* (h) On Mr. Roy Harrod's New Argument for Induction.

The British Journal for the Philosophy of Science (Edinburgh), Vol. 9 (1958-1959), No. 35 (November, 1958), pp. 221-224.

T (i) FALSCHE PROPHETEN: HEGEL MARX UND DIE FOLGEN.
Die offene Gesellschaft und ihre Feinde, Band II.

Sammlung Dalp, Band 85, Bern: Francke Verlag, 1958, Pp. 483.

German translation by P. K. Feyerabend of 1952(a), Vol. II.

1959

T (a) THE LOGIC OF SCIENTIFIC DISCOVERY.
*

London: Hutchinson & Co., January 1959; New York: Basic Books, Inc.,
March 1959. Pp. [480].

Contains English translation of 1934(b), 1933(a), and 1935(a); also
1938(a), 1954(d), 1957(b), 1958(a), New Appendices, and other new material.
The translation was prepared by the author, with the assistance of Dr.
Julius Freed and Lan Freed.
Revised reprints: 1960(a), 1961(e), 1961(k), 1962(p), 1965(d), and 1965(e).
Second edition (revised and enlarged): 1968(a); third edition (revised and
enlarged): 1972(c).
Translations: Spanish 1962(r) and 1967(o); German: 1966(e), 1969(e), and
1971(o); Italian: 1970(e); Japanese: 1971(t) and 197 ( ); Serbo-Croat: 1973(c);
French: 1973(d).
Contents: Translators' note. Contents. Preface to the First Edition, 1934
(Vienna, Autumn 1934). Preface to the English Edition, 1958 (Penn,
Buckinghamshire, Spring 1958). PART I: INTRODUCTION
TO THE LOGIC OF SCIENCE. *Chapter I: A Survey of Some
Fundamental Problems.* 1. The Problem of Induction. 2. Elimination
of Psychologism. 3. Deductive Testing of Theories. 4. The Problem of
Demarcation. 5. Experience as a Method. 6. Falsifiability as a Criterion
of Demarcation. 7. The Problem of the 'Empirical Basis'. 8. Scientific
Objectivity and Subjective Conviction. *Chapter II: On the Problem of a
Theory of Scientific Method.* 9. Why Methodological Decisions are Indispen-
sable. 10. The Naturalistic Approach to the Theory of Method. 11.
Methodological Rules as Conventions. PART II: SOME STRUC-
TURAL COMPONENTS OF A THEORY OF EXPERIENCE. *Chapter
III: Theories.* 12. Causality, Explanation, and the Deduction of Predictions.
13. Strict and Numerical Universality. 14. Universal Concepts
and Individual Concepts. 15. Strictly Universal and Existential Statements.
16. Theoretical Systems. 17. Some Possibilities of Interpreting a System of
Axioms. 18. Levels of Universality. The Modus Tollens. *Chapter IV: Falsifiability.* 19. Some Conventionalist Objections. 20. Methodological Rules.
21. Logical Investigation of Falsifiability. 22. Falsifiability and Falsification. 23. Occurrences and Events. 24. Falsifiability and Consistency. *Chap-*

Metaphysical Elements by Inverting Heisenberg's Programme; with Applications. 77. Decisive Experiments. 78. Indeterminist Metaphysics. *Chapter X: Corroboration, or How a Theory Stands Up To Tests.* 79. Concerning the So-Called Verification of Hypotheses. 80. The Probability of a Hypothesis and the Probability of Events: Criticism of Probability Logic. 81. Inductive Logic and Probability Logic. 82. The Positive Theory of Corroboration: How a Hypothesis may 'Prove its Mettle'. 83. Corroborability, Testability, and Logical Probability. 84. Remarks Concerning the Use of the Concepts 'True' and 'Corroborated'. 85. The Path of Science. APPENDICES. i. Definition of the Dimension of a Theory. ii. The General Calculus of Frequency in Finite Classes. iii. Derivation of the First Form of the Binomial Formula. iv. A Method of Constructing Models of Random Sequences. v. Examination of an Objection. The Two-Slit Experiment. vi. Concerning a Non-Predictive Procedure of Measuring. vii. Remarks Concerning an Imaginary Experiment. NEW APPENDICES. *i. Two Notes on Induction and Demarcation, 1933-1934. [1933(a) and 1935(a).] *ii. A Note on Probability, 1938. [1938(a).] *iii. On the Heuristic Use of the Classical Definition of Probability, Especially for Deriving the General Multiplication Theorem. *iv. The Formal Theory of Probability. *v. Derivations in the Formal Theory of Probability. *vi. On Objective Disorder or Randomness. *vii. Zero Probability and the Fine-Structure of Probability and of Content. *viii. Content, Simplicity, and Dimension. *ix. Corroboration, the Weight of Evidence, and Statistical Tests. [1954(d), 1957(b), and 1958(a).] *x. Universals, Dispositions, and Natural or Physical Necessity. *xi. On the Use and Misuse of Imaginary Experiments, Especially in Quantum Theory. *xii. The Experiment of Einstein, Podolsky and Rosen. A Letter from Albert Einstein, 1935. INDICES, compiled by Dr. J. Agassi.

T (b) *'Uqm al-madhhab al-tārīkhī* (THE POVERTY OF HISTORICISM).

Alexandria: al-ma'ārif, 1959. Pp. 208.

Arabic translation by Abdulhamid Sabra of 1957(g).

T (c) A SOCIEDADE DEMOCRÁTICA E SEUS INIMIGOS.

Coleção espirito do nosso tempo, Vol. 1, Belo Horizonte, Brazil: Editôra Itatiaia Limitada, 1959, Pp. 737.

Portuguese translation by Milton Amado of 1957(h).

R (d) Über die Unwiderlegbarkeit philosophischer Theorien einschliesslich
*   jener, welche falsch sind.

Forum (Vienna), 6. Jahr (1959), Heft 61 (Januar, 1959), pp. 15-18.

A revised version of part II of 1958(g); see note to this item.
Also contained in 1963(k) and 1969(t).

* (e) The Propensity Interpretation of Probability.

  The British Journal for the Philosophy of Science (Edinburgh), Vol. 10
  (1959-1960), No. 37 (May, 1959), pp. 25-42.

  Errata: ibid., Vol. 10 (1959-1960), No. 38 (August, 1959), p. 171.
  Also contained in 1974(a).

* (f) Testability and 'Ad-Hocness' of the Contraction Hypothesis.

  The British Journal for the Philosophy of Science (Edinburgh), Vol. 10
  (1959-1960), No. 37 (May, 1959), p. 50.

  A reply to Adolf Grünbaum: The Falsifiability of the Lorentz-
  Fitzgerald Contraction Hypothesis: *ibid.,* Vol. 10 (1959-1960), No. 37
  (May, 1959), pp. 48-50.

* (g) Woran glaubt der Westen?

  In: *Erziehung zur Freiheit,* edited by Albert Hunold (*Sozialwis-
  senschaftliche Studien für das Schweizerische Institut für Auslandfor-
  schung,* edited by Albert Hunold, Band [7]), Erlenbach-Zürich, Stuttgart:
  Eugen Rentsch Verlag, 1959. (Pg. 387.) Pp. 237-262.

R (h) On the Sources of Our Knowledge.

  The Indian Journal of Philosophy (Bombay), Vol. 1 (1959-1960),
  No. 1 (August, 1959), pp. [3]-7.

  Forms part of 1960(d); see not to this item.

* (i) On Subjunctive Conditionals with Impossible Antecedents.

  Mind (Edinburgh), New Series, Vol. 68 (1959), No. 272 (October, 1959),
  pp. 518-520.

R (j) Has History Any Meaning?

  In: *The Philosophy of History in Our Time: An Anthology,* selected, and
  with an introduction and commentary by Hans Meyerhoff, (*A Doubleday*

Anchor Original A 164), Garden City, New York: Doubleday Anchor Books, Doubleday & Company Inc., 1959. (Pp. [ix], 350.) Pp. 301-311.

Extracts from chapter 25 of 1950(a).
Second [revised] edition: 1961(i).

R (k) Critical Rationalism.

In: *Philosophy for a Time of Crisis: An Interpretation with Key Writings by Fifteen Great Modern Thinkers,* edited by Adrienne Koch, New York: Dutton & Co., 1959. (Pp. 382.) Pp. 262-275.

Part of chapters 24 and 25 of 1950(a).
Arabic translation: 1964(c). See also 1962(l).

R (l) Prediction and Prophecy in the Social Sciences.
*

In: *Theories of History: Readings from Classical and Contemporary Sources,* edited with introductions and commentary by Patrick Gardiner, Glencoe, Illinois: The Free Press, 1959. (Pp. ix, 549.) Pp. 276-285.

A revised version of 1948(d). Also contained in 1963(a).
German translation: 1965(m).

* (m) "The Logic of Scientific Discovery".

The New Scientist (London), Vol. 5 (1959), No. 124 (2 April, 1959), p. 763.

A reply to Dr. Kurt Mendelssohn's review of 1959(a): Science and logic; *ibid.,* No. 121 (12 March, 1959), pp. 592-593.

U (n) THE LOGIC OF SCIENTIFIC DISCOVERY: POSTSCRIPT AFTER TWENTY YEARS.

London: Hutchinson Galley Proofs, 1958. [The proofs were received by Popper in March, 1957; the proofreading was stopped in 1959.]

Exists in partly corrected galley proofs and in the form of a typed manuscript (pp. [xx], 1068 (A4)) made from the corrected galley proofs.
Contents: [Mottoes]. INTRODUCTION: On the Non-Existence of Scientific Method (Stanford, California, November, 1956). POST-SCRIPT: AFTER TWENTY YEARS. *Preface to the Postscript:* The Theory of Knowledge and the Theory of Science. *Preface to the Postscript* (Penn, Buckinghamshire, Spring, 1958). *Author's Note* (Penn, Buckinghamshire, June, 1958). *Chapter I:* INDUCTION-

DEMARCATION-CORROBORATION. 1. A Puzzled Philosopher Abroad. 2. The Critical Approach. Solution of the Problem of Induction. 3. On So-Called Inductive Procedures, with Notes on Learning, and on the Inductive Style. 4. A Family of Four Problems of Induction. 5. Why the Fourth Stage of the Problem is Metaphysical. 6. Discussion of the Metaphysical Problem. 7. Metaphysical Realism. 8. Hume's Metaphysics. 'Neutral' Monism. 9. Why the Subjectivist Theory of Knowledge Fails. 10. A World without Riddles. 11. The Status of Theories and of Theoretical Concepts. 12. Criticism of Instrumentalism. Instrumentalism and the Problem of Induction. 13. Instrumentalism Against Science. 14. Science Against Instrumentalism. 15. The Aim of Science. [1957(i)]. 16. Difficulties of Metaphysical Realism. By a Metaphysical Realist. 17. The Significance of the Problem of Demarcation. 18. A Case of Verificationism. 19. Testability but not Meaning. 20. Non-Testable Statements. 21. The Problem of 'Eliminating' Metaphysics. 22. The Asymmetry between Falsification and Verification. 23. Why even Pseudo-Sciences may well be Meaningful. Metaphysical Programmes for Science. 24. Logical Remarks on Testability and Metaphysics. 25. Metaphysical Terms can be Defined by Empirical Terms. 26. The Changing Philosophy of Sense and Nonsense. 27. Corroboration: Certainty, Uncertainty, Probability. 28. 'Corroboration' or 'Probability'? 29. Corroboration or Confirmation? 30. The Problem of Degree of Corroboration. 31. Critical Remarks on Meaning-Analysis. 32. Corroboration. A Definition of Degree of Corroboration. 33. Humanism, Science, and the Inductive Prejudice. *Chapter II:* OBJECTIVE AND SUBJECTIVE PROBABILITY. 34. The Meanings of Probability. 35. Relative and Absolute Probabilities. 36. The Propensity Interpretation. Objective and Subjective Interpretations. 37. Experimental Tests and their Repetition: Independence. 38. The Logical Interpretation. 39. Comparing the Objective and Subjective Interpretations. 40. The Interpretation of 'b' in '$p(a,b)$'. 41. The Simple Inductive Rule. 42. How to Interpret the Simple Inductive Rule where it Works. 43. Summing up of the Status of 'b' in '$p(a,b)$'. 44. The Diminishing Returns of Learning by Induction. 45. The Paradox of Inductive Learning. 46. An Inductive Machine. 47. The Impossibility of an Inductive Logic. 48. Probability Logic *versus* Inductive Logic. 49. The Inductivist Interpretation of Probability. 50. The Redundancy of Theories. 51. No Point in Testing a Theory. 52. Summary of the Preceding Criticism. 53. The Case for Propensities. *Chapter III:* REMARKS ON THE OBJECTIVE THEORY OF PROBABILITY. 54. The Frequency Theory: Success and Failure. 55. Where the Frequency Theory Fails. 56. The Significance of the Failure. 57. The Neo-Classical and the

Frequency Theory Contrasted. 58. The Structure of the Neo-Classical Theory. 59. Singular Probability Statements. 60. Criticism of the Subjective and Logical Theories. 61. The Propensity Interpretation of the Probability of Single Events. *Chapter IV:* INDETERMINISM. 62. Determinism: Religious, 'Scientific', and Metaphysical. 63. Why-Questions. Causality and 'Scientific' Determinism. 64. The Principle of Accountability. 65. The Study of Behavior and the Principle of Accountability. 66. Critical Temperatures and the All-or-Nothing Principle. 67. Clocks and Clouds. 68. Arguments from Psychology. 69. The Determinist Picture of the World. 70. The Burden of Proof. 71. *Prima Facie* Determinism of Classical Physics. Laplace's Demon. 72. The Idea of 'Scientific' Determinism: Predictability from Within. 73. Two Definitions of 'Scientific' Determinism. 74. Does 'Scientific' Determinism follow from a *Prima Facie* Deterministic Theory? 75. A Result of Hadamard's. 76. Why I am an Indeterminist: Theories as Nets. 77. Comparison with Kant's View. 78. Is Classical Physics Accountable? 79. The Past and the Future. 80. The Verdict of Special Relativity. 81. Historical Prediction and the Growth of Knowledge. 82. Predicting the Growth of Theoretical Knowledge. 83. The Impossibility of Self-Prediction. 84. The Refutation of 'Scientific' Determinism. 85. An Argument of St. Augustine's, Descartes's, and Haldane's. 86. The Metaphysical Doctrines of Determinism and Indeterminism. 87. Why I Reject Metaphysical Determinism: A Conversation with Parmenides. 88. The Gain for Science: A Theory of Propensities. 89. *Prima Facie* Deterministic Theories and Probabilistic Theories. 90. Landé's Blade. 91. Landé's Blade and the Propensity Interpretation. 92. Conclusion. *Chapter V:* FURTHER OBSERVATIONS ON QUANTUM THEORY. 93. A Schism in Physics. 94. The Significance of Interpretations. 95. Subjective Probabilities, Statistical Probabilities, and Determinism. 96. The Objectivity of Statistical Mechanics. 97. The Subjectivist Interpretation of Statistical Mechanics. 98. Oscillations Between the Two Interpretations. 99. The Objectivity of Quantum Theory: The Boxes. 100. The Source of the Confusion: the 'Reduction of the Wave Packet'. 101. The Incompleteness of the Mathematical Formalism of Quantum Theory. 102. A Random Walk and the 'Transition from the Potential to the Actual'. 103. Particles, Waves, and the Propensity Interpretation. 104. Partial Anticipation of the Propensity Interpretation. 105. Are there Quantum Jumps? 106. Are there Particles? 107. Position Space. 108. Indeterminacy or Scatter? 109. The Experiment of Einstein, Podolsky, and Rosen. 110. The Two-Slit Experiment. 111. An Apology for having been Controversial. *Chapter VI:* A META-PHYSICAL EPILOGUE. 112. Metaphysical Ideas and Research Programmes, and the History of Physics. 113. Schisms, Programmes, and

Metaphysical Dreams. 114. Classical Determinism Modified by a Correspondence Argument. 115. Indeterminism and the So-Called 'Reduction of the Wave Packet'. 116. Replacing the Classical Films by Propensity Films. 117. A Rough Model of Quantum Theoretical Indeterminism. 118. Matter and Field. 119. Open Problems. 120. Conclusion.

1960

R (a) THE LOGIC OF SCIENTIFIC DISCOVERY.
*

London: Hutchinson & Co., January 1960.

Second impression (revised) of 1959(a) with *Acknowledgments*, 1960 (Summer 1959).

* (b) Probabilistic Independence and Corroboration by Empirical Tests.

The British Journal for the Philosophy of Science (Edinburgh), Vol. 10 (1959-1960), No. 40 (February, 1960), pp. 315-318.

Errata: ibid., Vol. 11 (1960-1961), No. 41 (May, 1960), p. 88; and No. 42 (August, 1960), p. 149.
A reply to Hugues Leblanc: On So-Called Degrees of Confirmation; *ibid.,* Vol. 10 (1959-1960), No. 40 (February, 1960), pp. 312-315.

R (c) THE POVERTY OF HISTORICISM. (Second revised edition.)
*

London: Routledge & Kegan Paul, 1960. Pp. xiv, 169.
A revised edition of 1957(g) with a new preface (Penn, Buckinghamshire, July 1959). See also 1944(a), 1944(b), and 1945(a).
Revised reprint: 1961(b).

* (d) On the Sources of Knowledge and of Ignorance.

Proceedings of The British Academy (London), Vol. 46 (1960), pp. [39]-71.

The *Henriette Hertz Trust Annual Philosophical Lecture* read before *The British Academy* on January 20th, 1960.
Published separately as 1961(f). Also contained in 1963(a) and 1966(k).
Abbreviated versions, see 1959(h) and 1962(n).
Translations: Spanish: 1962(q); Japanese: 1963(b); Italian: 1964(h) and 1969(c).

U (e) Philosophy and Physics.

A paper read before the *XIIth International Congress of Philosophy* (Venezia, September 12-18, 1958). For publication, see 1961(h).

1961

R (a) The Moral Theory of Historicism.

In: *Society, Law, and Morality: Readings in Social Philosophy,* edited with introductions by Frederick A. Olafson, Englewood Cliffs, N. J.: Prentice-Hall Inc., 1961. (Pp. ix, 518.) Pp. 286-297.

Reprint of part of chapter 22 of 1950(a).

R (b) THE POVERTY OF HISTORICISM. (Revised second edition.)

A Routledge Paperback, London: Routledge & Kegan Paul, 1961. Pp. x, 166.

A reprint, with some corrections, of 1960(c).
Reprints: 1963(p), 1964(a), 1966(m), 1967(a), 1969(g), 1969(s), and 1972(b).

T (c) *Rekishi-shugi no Hinkon* (THE POVERTY OF HISTORICISM).

Tokyo: Chuo-Koron Sha, Inc., 1961. Pp. [267].

Japanese translation by Saburo Ichii and Osamu Kuno.
First, second, and third printing 1961. Fourth printing: 1965(o); fifth printing: 1966(l).

* (d) Selbstbefreiung durch das Wissen.

In: *Der Sinn der Geschichte,* edited by Leonhard Reinisch, *(Beck'sche Schwarze Reihe,* Band 15), Munich: Verlag C. H. Beck, 1961. (Pp. 135.) Pp. [100]-116.

A broadcast on the *Bavarian Broadcasting Network* in February 1961, in a series of broadcasts *On the Meaning of History.*
Reprints: 1962(e), 1967(j), and 1970(u). English translation: 1968(t).

R (e) THE LOGIC OF SCIENTIFIC DISCOVERY.
*

New York: Science Editions, Inc., (paperback 598-S), 1961. Pp. [480].

Revised reprint of 1960(a).

R (f) ON THE SOURCES OF KNOWLEDGE AND OF IGNORANCE.
Annual Philosophical Lecture, Henriette Hertz Trust, British Academy,
1960.

London: Oxford University Press, [1961]. Pp. [39]-71.

Separate edition of 1960(d); see note to this item.

T (g) LA MISERIA DEL HISTORICISMO.

Madrid: Taurus Ediciones, 1961. Pp. 206.

Spanish translation by Pedro Schwartz of 1960(c).

* (h) Philosophy and Physics.

In: *Atti del XII Congresso Internazionale di Filosofia* (Venezia, 12-18
Settembre 1958), Volume Secondo: *Primo tema: l'uomo e la natura,*
(Proceedings of the XIIth International Congress of Philosophy, [Vol. 2]:
First Theme: Man and Nature), Firenze: G. C. Sansoni Editore, [1961]. (Pp.
vii, 511.) Pp. [367]-374.

While this work was published with the imprint 1960, it appears to have
been distributed in 1961.
Also contained in 1974(a).

R (i) Has History Any Meaning?

In: *The Philosophy of History in Our Time: An Anthology,* selected, and
with an introduction and commentary by Hans Meyerhoff, (*A Doubleday
Anchor Original* A 164), Garden City, New York: Doubleday Anchor Books,
Doubleday & Company Inc., 1961. (Pp. [ix], 350.) Pp. 300-311.

Second [revised] edition of 1959(j), containing expanded extracts from
chapter 25 of 1950(a).

U (j) EVOLUTION AND THE TREE OF KNOWLEDGE. *Herbert Spencer*
[*Memorial*] *Lecture.*

Mimeographed. October 30th, 1961. Pp. 21.

The lecture was delivered on October 30th, 1961, and the manuscript was
deposited on the same day in the *Bodleian Library,* Oxford.

Contained in 1972(a).

R (k) THE LOGIC OF SCIENTIFIC DISCOVERY.

New York: Basic Books, Inc., 1961. Pp. [480].

Reprint of 1960(a).

1962

* (a) On Carnap's Version of Laplace's Rule of Succession.

Mind (Edinburgh), New Series, Vol. 71 (1962), No. 281 (January, 1962), pp. 69-73.

Continued in 1967(c).

* (b) Historical Explanation [:An Interview].

Cambridge Opinion (Cambridge), No. 28 (1962), pp. [21]-25.

Replies to questions by Michael Tanner, John Dunn, and Alistair Young. Revised reprint: 1966(i).

R (c) THE OPEN SOCIETY AND ITS ENEMIES. (Fourth English edition,
* revised and enlarged.)

London: Routledge and Kegan Paul, 1962. Vol. I: pp. xi, 351; Vol. II: pp. [vi], 420.

Further revised and enlarged edition of 1945(b) and 1945(c); see 1950(a), 1952(a), and 1957(h).
In the fourth edition two new *Addenda* have been added to Vol. I: II. The Dating of the Theaetetus; III. Reply to a Critic. A new *Addendum* has been added to Vol. II: Facts, Standards, and Truth: A Further Criticism of Relativism.
Reprints: 1962(d), 1963(l), 1963(m), and 1963(n).

R (d) THE OPEN SOCIETY AND ITS ENEMIES.

Routledge Paperbacks No. 25 and 26, London: Routledge and Kegan Paul, 1962.

Paperback edition of 1962(c).

R (e) Selbstbefreiung durch das Wissen. (2. Auflage.)

In: *Der Sinn der Geschichte,* edited by Leonhard Reinisch, (*Beck'sche Schwarze Reihe,* Band 15), 2. Auflage, Munich: Verlag C. H. Beck, [1962]. (Pp. 135.) Pp. [100]-116.

Reprint of 1961(d).

* (f) Julius Kraft 1898-1960.

Ratio (Oxford), Vol. 4 (1962), No. 1 (June, 1962), pp. 2-12.

German translation: 1962(g).

T (g) Julius Kraft.

Ratio (Frankfurt a. M.), 4. Band (1962), Heft 1 ([Juni], 1962), pp. 2-10.

German translation of 1962(f).

* (h) Some Comments on Truth and the Growth of Knowledge.

In: *Logic, Methodology, and Philosophy of Science: Proceedings of the 1960 International Congress* (Stanford, California, August 24-September 2, 1960), edited by Ernest Nagel, Patrick Suppes, and Alfred Tarski, Stanford, California: Stanford University Press, 1962. (Pp. ix, 661.) Pp. 285-292.

A small part of chapter 10 of 1963(a). This part was presented at a Symposium on Theoretical and Empirical Aspects of Science, August 27, 1960.

* (i) Über Geschichtsschreibung und über den Sinn der Geschichte.

In: *Geist und Gesicht der Gegenwart: Gesehen durch das Spektrum Alpbach,* edited by Otto Molden, Zürich: Europa Verlag, 1962. (Pp. 223.) Pp. 111-142.

In part new, in part based on a revised version of chapter 25 of 1958(i).

T (j) Lo Scopo della Scienza.

La Scuola in Azione (Milano), 1961-1962, No. 13 (1962), pp. 5-22.

Italian translation of 1957(i). For another Italian translation, see 1969(c).

* (k) Die Logik der Sozialwissenschaften.

Kölner Zeitschrift für Soziologie und Sozialpsychologie (Köln), 14. Jahrgang (1962), Heft 2, pp. [233]-248.

An opening address to a discussion on "The Logic of the Social Sciences" at a congress of German sociologists in Tübingen, October 19th, 1961. Also contained in 1969(m), 1970(z₇), 1971(e), and 1972(l).

R (l) Critical Rationalism.

In: *Philosophy for a Time of Crisis* by Albert Einstein, E. M. Forster, Karl R. Popper, and Bertrand Russell, edited with notes by Kôzô Tada (*Modern English Series*), Tokyo: Kinseido Ltd., 1962. (Pp. [iii], 101.) Pp. [36]-53.

Reprint, with Japanese notes, of four of the essays contained in the book 1959(k).

* (m) A Comment on the New Prediction Paradox.

The British Journal for the Philosophy of Science (Edinburgh), Vol. 13 (1962-1963), No. 49 (May, 1962), p. 51.

A reply to Martin Gardner's note: A New Prediction Paradox; *ibid.*, p. 51.

R (n) On the Sources of Knowledge and of Ignorance.

Encounter (London), No. 108 = Vol. 19 (1962), No. 3 (September, 1962), pp. 42-57.

Abbreviated version of 1960(d); see note to this item.

R (o) The Propensity Interpretation of the Calculus of Probability, and the Quantum Theory.

In: *Observation and Interpretation in the Philosophy of Physics: With Special Reference to Quantum Mechanics,* edited by S. Körner in collaboration with M. H. L. Pryce, New York: Dover Publications (S 131), 1962. (Pp. xiv, 218.) Pp. 65-70, 88-89.

Paperback edition of 1957(e). *Errata,* see note to this item.

R (p) THE LOGIC OF SCIENTIFIC DISCOVERY.
*
London: Hutchinson & Co., June 1962.

Third impression (revised) of 1959(a).

T (q) Las Fuentes del Conocimiento y de la Ignorancia.

Cuadernos de Epistemologia (Buenos Aires), No. 50 (1962).

Spanish translation by Emilio O. Colombo of 1960(d).

T (r) LA LÓGICA DE LA INVESTIGACIÓN CIENTÍFICA.

Estructura y Funcion (edited by Enrique Tierno Galvan), No. 8, Madrid: Editorial Tecnos, S. A., 1962. Pp. 451.

Spanish translation, with some changes, of 1960(a) by Víctor Sánchez de Zavala.

Reprint: 1967(o).

1963

* (a) CONJECTURES AND REFUTATIONS: *The Growth of Scientific Knowledge.*

London: Routledge and Kegan Paul, New York: Basic Books, Inc., 1963. Pp. xiii, 412.

Dedicated to F. A. von Hayek.

2nd edition (revised and enlarged): 1965(c) (reprint: 1968(b)). 3rd edition (revised and enlarged): 1969(h) (reprint: 1969(i)). 4th edition (revised and enlarged): 1972(d).

Translations: Spanish: 1967(n); Italian: 1972(e); German: 197 ( ).

Contents: Preface (Berkeley, California, Spring 1962). Acknowledgements (Berkeley, California, Spring 1962). Contents. INTRODUCTION: On the Sources of Knowledge and of Ignorance. [1960(d)]. CONJECTURES: 1. Science: Conjectures and Refutations. *Appendix:* Some Problems in the Philosophy of Science. [1957(a)]. 2. The Nature of Philosophical Problems and their Roots in Science. [1952(c)]. 3. Three Views Concerning Human Knowledge. [1956(f)]. 4. Towards a Rational Theory of Tradition. [1949(b)]. 5. Back to the Presocratics. [1958(e)]. *Appendix:* Historical Conjectures and Heraclitus on Change. [1963(d)]. 6. A Note on Berkeley as Precursor of Mach and Einstein. [1953(d)]. 7. Kant's Critique and Cosmology. [1954(a)]. 8. On the Status of Science and of Metaphysics. [1958(f)]. 9. Why are the Calculi of Logic and Arithmetic Applicable to Reality? [1946(b)]. 10. Truth, Rationality, and the Growth of Scientific Knowledge. REFUTATIONS: 11. The Demarcation Between Science and Metaphysics. [1955(g)]. 12. Language and the Body-Mind Problem; a Restatement of Interactionism. [1953(a)]. 13. A Note on the Body-Mind Problem. [1955(c)]. 14. Self-Reference and Meaning in Ordinary Language. [1954(c)]. 15. What is Dialectic? [1940(a)]. 16. Prediction and Prophecy in the Social Sciences. [1948(d)]. 17. Public Opinion and Liberal Principles. [1955(f)], 18. Utopia and Violence. [1948(a)].

19. The History of Our Time: An Optimist's View. 20. Humanism and Reason. [1952(b)]. ADDENDA: *Some Technical Notes:* 1 Empirical Content; 2 Probability and the Severity of Tests; 3 Verisimilitude; 4 Numerical Examples; 5 Artificial vs. Formalized Languages. *Index of Names. Index of Subjects.*

T (h) Kindai Ninshikiron no Shinwa: Chishiki to Muchi no Gensen ni tsuite. (The Myth of Modern Epistemology: On the Sources of Knowledge and of Ignorance.)

Jiyu (Tokyo), Vol. 5 (1963), No. 1 (January, 1963).

Japanese translation by Tooru Yoshimura of 1960(d).

R (c) Plato as Enemy of the Open Society.

In: *Plato: Totalitarian or Democrat?,* essays selected and introduced by Thomas Landon Thorson, (*A Spectrum Book,* S - 68), Englewood Cliffs, N. J.: Prentice-Hall Inc., 1963. (Pp. [v], 184.) Pp. 41-102.

Part of 1950(a).

R (d) Kirk on Heraclitus, and on Fire as the Cause of Balance.

Mind (Edinburgh), New Series, Vol. 72 (1963), No. 287 (July, 1963), pp. 386-392.

An abridged version of "Appendix: Historical Conjectures and Heraclitus on Change" to chapter 5 of 1963(a).
A reply to G. S. Kirk: Popper on Science and the Presocratics; *ibid.,* Vol. 69 (1960), No. 275 (July, 1960), pp. 318-339.

* (e) The Erewhonians and the Open Society.

ETC.: A Review of General Semantics (San Francisco), Vol. 20 (1963), No. 1 (May, 1963), pp. 5-22.

This article was delivered as an address before the *Associated Students, San Francisco State College,* on March 14, 1962.

T (f) La Opinion Publica a la Luz de los Principios del Liberalismo.

In: *La Economia de Mercado,* Tomo 2, Madrid: Sociedad de Estudios y Publicaciones, 1963. (Pp. 273.) Pp. 137-152.

Spanish translation of 1956(e).

* (g) Creative and Non-Creative Definitions in the Calculus of Probability.

Synthese (Dordrecht-Holland), Vol. 15 (1963), No. 2 (June, 1963), pp. 167-186.

Reprinted in 1964(f); for corrections see 1970(v).

* (h) Science: Problems, Aims, Responsibilities.

Federation Proceedings (Baltimore), *Federation of American Societies for Experimental Biology*, Vol. 22 (1963), No. 4 (July-August, 1963): Part I, pp. 961-972.

Presented at the *47th Annual Meeting* of the *Federation of American Societies for Experimental Biology* (Atlantic City, New Jersey, April 16-20, 1963) at the *Federation Joint Session* in the evening, Wednesday, April 17, 1963.
Also contained in 1974(a). An abbreviated version is contained in 1971(h). Italian translations: 1966(h) and 1969(c).

T (i) *Jiyu Shakai No Tetsugaku to sono Ronteki* (THE PHILOSOPHY OF THE FREE SOCIETY AND ITS ENEMIES).

Osaka City: The Izumiya Co., Inc., 1963. Pp. [xiii], 138, 95.

Japanese translation by Hiromichi Takeda of chapters 11-17 in Vol. II of 1962(c). This translation is also provided with an English title: THE OPEN SOCIETY AND ITS ENEMIES, *Hegel & Marx* (1). (2) never appeared.

T (j) Yūtopia to Bōryoku (Utopia and Violence).

Shisō [Thought] (Tokyo: Iwanami Shoten), No. 469 (July, 1963), pp. 968-979 (pp. 66-77).

Japanese translation by Saburo Ichii of 1963(a), chapter 18 [1948(a)].

R (k) Über die Unwiderlegbarkeit philosophischer Theorien einschliesslich jener, welche falsch sind.

In: *Club Voltaire: Jahrbuch für kritische Aufklärung I*, edited by Gerhard Szczesny, Munich: Szczesny Verlag, 1963. (Pp. 419.) Pp. [271]-279.

Reprint of 1959(d). For reprint of *Club Voltaire I*, see 1969(t).

R (l) THE OPEN SOCIETY AND ITS ENEMIES.

Princeton, N. J.: Princeton University Press, 1963.

Reprint, in two volumes, of 1962(c); see note to this item.

R (m) THE OPEN SOCIETY AND ITS ENEMIES.

The Academy Library, New York and Evanston: Harper & Row, Publishers, (*Harper Torchbooks,* TB 1101 and 1102), 1963.

Paperback edition, in two volumes, of 1963(l).

R (n) THE OPEN SOCIETY AND ITS ENEMIES.

Routledge Paperbacks No. 25 and 26, London: Routledge and Kegan Paul, 1963.

Reprint of 1962(d).

* (o) Problems of Scientific Knowledge.

Bulletin of the International House of Japan (Tokyo), No. 12 (October, 1963), pp. [23]-28.

Japanese translation is contained in the Japanese Language Bulletin of the *International House of Japan: Kokusai Bunka Kaikan Kaiho* (Tokyo), No. 11.

R (p) THE POVERTY OF HISTORICISM.

London: Routledge & Kegan Paul, 1963.

A reprint of 1961(b).

U (q) Models, Instruments, and Truth.

A paper (so far unpublished except for the short extract 1967(d)) based on a lecture delivered in the *Department of Economics, Harvard University,* in February 1963.

1964

R (a) THE POVERTY OF HISTORICISM.

The Academy Library, New York and Evanston: Harper & Row, Publishers, (*Harper Torchbooks,* TB 1126), 1964. Pp. x, 166.

Paperback; reprint of 1961(b).

R (b) The Demarcation between Science and Metaphysics.

In: *The Library of Living Philosophers,* Vol. 11: *The Philosophy of Rudolf Carnap,* edited by Paul Arthur Schilpp, La Salle, Illinois: The Open Court Publishing Co., London: Cambridge University Press, [1964]. Copyright 1963. (Pp. xvi, 1088.) Pp. 183-226.

Contained in 1963(a). See also 1955(g).

T (c) Al-'Aql al-Naquid (The Critical Mind).

In: *Al-Falsafiyyah fi Azmat al-'Asr,* edited by Adrienne Koch, Cairo: Anglo, 1964.

Arabic translation by Mahmoud Mahmoud of 1959(k).

R (d) Die Zielsetzung der Erfahrungswissenschaft.
∗

In: *Theorie und Realität: Ausgewählte Aufsätze zur Wissenschaftslehre der Sozialwissenschaften,* edited by Hans Albert, (*Die Einheit der Gesellschaftswissenschaften,* Band 2), Tübingen: J. C. B. Mohr (Paul Siebeck), 1964. (Pp. [xi], 366.) Pp. [73]-86.

Revised reprint of 1957(j). Reprint: 1972(i).

R (e) Naturgesetze und theoretische Systeme.
∗

Ibid., pp. [87]-102.

New edition of 1949(d). Reprint: 1972(j). English translation contained in 1972(a).

R (f) Creative and Non-Creative Definitions in the Calculus of Probability.

In: *Form and Strategy in Science: Studies dedicated to Joseph Henry Woodger on the Occasion of his Seventieth Birthday,* edited by John R. Gregg and F. T. C. Harris, Dordrecht-Holland: D. Reidel Publishing Company, 1964. (Pp. vii, 476.) Pp. 171-190.

Reprint of 1963(g); for corrections see 1970(v).

R (g) [On Socrates.]

In: *The Socratic Enigma: A Collection of Testimonies Through Twenty-Four Centuries,* edited, with an introduction, by Herbert Spiegelberg in collaboration with Bayard Quincy Morgan, (*The Library of Liberal Arts*), Indianapolis, New York, Kansas City: The Bobbs-Merrill Company, Inc., (A Subsidiary of Howard W. Sams & Co., Inc., Publishers), 1964. (Pp. [xvi], 334.) Pp. 119-122.

Parts of chapters 7 and 10 of 1945(b).

T (h) SULLE FONTI DELLA CONOSCENZA E DELL'IGNORANZA.

1. *l'industria* (Milano), 1964, No. 2 (April-June, 1964), pp. 219-236; and No. 3 (July-September, 1964), pp. 337-354.
English summary; *ibid.,* No. 2, pp. 282-283, and No. 3, p. 459.

2. *Collana di moderne opere economiche,* edited by Ferdinando di Fenizio, Milano: Editrice L'industria, 1964. Pp. [39].

Italian translation by Giovanna Torre of 1960(d). For another Italian translation, see 1969(c).

R (i) Anaximander's Theory of the Earth.

The Christian Science Monitor (New England Edition: Boston, Mass.) 17 April, 1964, p. 8: *The Book Page.*

Extract from 1963(a), chapter 5 [1958(e)].

1965

R (a) Hume's Explanation of Inductive Inference.

In: *Human Understanding: Studies in the Philosophy of David Hume,* edited by Alexander Sesonske and Noel Fleming (*Wadsworth Studies in Philosophical Criticism*, edited by Alexander Sesonske and Noel Fleming, [Vol. 1]), Belmont, California: Wadsworth Publishing Company, 1965. (Pp. [ix], 116.) Pp. 69-74.

Extract from 1963 (a), chapter 1 [1957(a)].

R (b) Was ist Dialektik?

Student im Bild, edited by Karl Heinz Zenz, 10. Jahrgang (1965), Nr. 2 (Mai-Juni, 1965), pp. 42-45.

Abbreviated version of 1959(n), pp. [262]-274: 1, Erklärung der Dialektik. See note to this item.
Continued in 1966(n) and 1966(o).

R (c) CONJECTURES AND REFUTATIONS: *The Growth of Scientific Knowledge.* (Second edition, revised and enlarged.)

London: Routledge and Kegan Paul, New York: Basic Books, Inc., 1965. Pp. xiii, 417.

A revised and enlarged edition of 1963(a) with a new preface: Preface to the Second Edition (Penn, Buckinghamshire, January 1965), an addition to the end of chapter 5, a new *Addendum*: 6. A Historical Note on Verisimilitude (1964), a 'Supplementary Note', and new Indexes prepared by A. E. Musgrave.
Paperback edition: 1968(b). Spanish translation: 1967(n).

R (d) THE LOGIC OF SCIENTIFIC DISCOVERY.

London: Hutchinson & Co., 1965.

Fourth impression (revised) of 1959(a).

R (e) THE LOGIC OF SCIENTIFIC DISCOVERY.

The Science Library, New York: Harper & Row, Publishers, (*Harper Torchbooks*, TB 576), 1965. Pp. [480].

Revised paperback edition of 1965(d).

* (f) Time's Arrow and Entropy.

Nature (London), Vol. 207 (1965), No. 4994 (July 17, 1965), pp. 233-234.

Continuation of 1956(b), 1956(g), 1957(d), 1957(f), and 1958(b).
Also contained in 1974(a).

T (g) DAS ELEND DES HISTORIZISMUS.

Die Einheit der Gesellschaftswissenschaften, Band 3, Tübingen: J. C. B. Mohr (Paul Siebeck), 1965. Pp. xvi, 132.

Vorwort zur deutschen Ausgabe (Fallowfield, im November 1964), pp. [vii]-ix.

German translation by Dr. Leonhard Walentik of 1960(c) and 1964(a). Second impression: 1969(f); third impression: 1971(p).

R (h) Hat die Weltgeschichte einen Sinn?

In: *Versäumte Lektionen: Entwurf eines Lesebuchs*, edited by Peter Glotz and Wofgang R. Langenbucher, Gütersloh [Germany]: Sigbert Mohn Verlag, 1965; Stuttgart, Zürich, Salzburg: Europäischer Buchklub, Europäische Bildungsgemeinschaft, 1965. (Pp. [463].) Pp. 433-439.

Extract from chapter 25 of 1958(i).

R (i) Was ist Aufklärung?

Ibid., pp. 407-411.

Extract from 1954(b).

R (j) Unity of Method in the Natural and Social Sciences.

In: *Philosophical Problems of the Social Sciences*, edited by David Braybrooke, (*Sources in Philosophy, A Macmillan Series* edited by Lewis White Beck), New York; The Macmillan Company, London: Collier-Macmillan Limited, 1965. (Pp. v, 120.) Pp. 32-41.

Extract from 1960(c) and 1964(a).

R (k)   Social Science and Social Policy.

Ibid., pp. 99-107.

Extract from 1960(c) and 1964(a).

R (l) Historical and Generalizing Sciences.

In: *Philosophy of History*, edited by Alan Donagan and Barbara Donagan, (*Sources in Philosophy, A Macmillan Series* edited by Lewis White Beck), New York: The Macmillan Company, London: Collier-Macmillan Limited, 1965. (Pp. [vii], 115.) Pp. 86-89.

Extract from 1957(h).

T (m) Prognose und Prophetie in den Sozialwissenschaften.

In: *Logik der Sozialwissenschaften*, edited by Ernst Topitz, (*Neue Wissenschaftliche Bibliothek* 6: *Soziologie*, edited by Jürgen Habermas), Köln-Berlin: Kiepenheuer & Witsch, first and second editions 1965. (Pp. 568.) Pp. [113]-125.

German translation by Johanna and Gottfried Frenzel of 1959(l) [1948(d)].

T (n) Was ist Dialektik?

> *Ibid.*, pp. [262]-290.

German translation by Johanna and Gottfried Frenzel of 1965(c), chapter 15 [1940(a)].
For an abbreviated version of this translation, see 1965(b), 1966(n), and 1966(o).

R (o) *Rekishi-shugi no Hinkon* (THE POVERTY OF HISTORICISM).

> Tokyo: Chuo-Koron Sha, Inc., 1965.

> Fourth printing of 1961(c).

1966

R (a) THE OPEN SOCIETY AND ITS ENEMIES. (Fifth English edition, * revised and enlarged.)

> *Routledge Paperbacks* No. 25 and 26, London: Routledge & Kegan Paul, 1966. Vol. I: pp. xi, 361; Vol. II: pp. [vi], 420.

Further revised and enlarged edition of 1945(b) and 1945(c); see 1950(a), 1952(a), 1957(h), and 1962(c).
The fifth edition contains some new historical material (especially on page 312 of volume I and in the *Addenda*) and also a brief new *Addendum* in each volume.
Errata: p. 331, section (5), para. 2, line 4: *for* 'misrepresentation' *read* 'misinterpretation'; p. 337, footnote, lines 4, 5, 6, 7: *replace by* 'There are several other passages. See *Rep.*, 415d, and especially *Tim.*, 18e, proving that Plato finds his earlier advocacy of lying important enough to be included in a brief summary of the *Republic*. (See also *Laws*, 663d down to 664b.)'.
Reprints: 1968(p), 1969(q), 1969(r), and 1971(b).

* (b) Foreword.

> In: *Two Kinds of Values* by L. M. Loring, London: Routledge & Kegan Paul, 1966. (Pp. xii, [188].) Pp. [vii]-xii.

* (c) A Note on the Difference between the Lorentz-Fitzgerald Contraction and the Einstein Contraction.

The British Journal for the Philosophy of Science (Edinburgh), Vol. 16 (1965-1966), No. 64 (February, 1966), pp. 332-333.

* (d) A Comment on Miller's New Paradox of Information.

The British Journal for the Philosophy of Science (London), Vol. 17 (1966-1967), [No.] 1 (May, 1966), pp. 61-69.

Erratum: ibid., Vol. 17 (1966-1967), No. 3 (November, 1966), p. 264.
A comment on David Miller's note: A Paradox of Information; *ibid.,* Vol. 17 (1966-1967), [No.] 1 (May, 1966), pp. 59-61.
Continued in 1966(j).

R (e) LOGIK DER FORSCHUNG. (Zweite, erweiterte Auflage.)
*

Die Einheit der Gesellschaftswissenschaften, Band 4, Tübingen: J. C. B. Mohr (Paul Siebeck), 1966. Pp. xxvi, 441.
A revised and enlarged edition of 1934(b) containing a German translation by Dr. Leonhard Walentik of the *New Appendices* and the other new material in 1959(a). With new Indexes.
Redaktionelle Vorbemerkung, p. [v]. Vorwort zur zweiten deutschen Ausgabe (Penn, Buckinghamshire, im Frühjahr 1963), pp. [xxv]-xxvi.

* (f) OF CLOUDS AND CLOCKS: *An Approach to the Problem of Rationality and the Freedom of Man.*

St. Louis, Missouri: Washington University [Press], 1966. Pp. vii, 38.

The [Second] Arthur Holly Compton Memorial Lecture presented at *Washington University* (St. Louis, Missouri), April 21, 1965.
Introduction by Richard Rudner, Chairman, *Department of Philosophy,* May, 1966, pp. v-vii.
Erratum: p. 25 lines 6-9 to be inserted before the last line on p. 24.
Also contained in 1972(a). An excerpt is contained in 1969(u).
Italian translation: 1972(h).

* (g) A Theorem on Truth-Content.

In: *Mind, Matter, and Method: Essays in Philosophy and Science in Honor of Herbert Feigl,* edited by Paul K. Feyerabend and Grover Maxwell, Minneapolis, Minnesota: University of Minnesota Press, 1966. (Pp. [iv], 524.) Pp. 343-353.

T (h) PROBLEMI, FINALITÀ E RESPONSABILITÀ DELLA SCIENZA.

1. *l'industria* (Milano), 1966, No. 2, pp. 157-184.

English summary; *ibid.,* p. 321.

[Appendix]: 'Karl Popper's Life and Scientific Work (with a bibliographical note up to January 1966)'; *ibid.,* pp. 185-198. Italian summary; *ibid.,* pp. 321-322. This Appendix is also published separately, Milano: Editrice L'industria, [1966]. Pp. 15.

2. Milano: Editrice L'industria, [1966]. Pp. 30.

Italian translation of 1963(h) by Giulia Sanvisenti. For another Italian translation, see note to 1963(h).

R (i) Historical Explanation: An Interview with Sir Karl Popper.
*

University of Denver Magazine (Denver, Colorado), Vol. 3 (1965-1966), No. 4 (June, 1966), pp. 4-7.

A revised reprint of 1962(b).

* (j) A Paradox of Zero Information.

The British Journal for the Philosophy of Science (London), Vol. 17 (1966-1967), No. 2 (August, 1966), pp. 141-143.

Continuation of 1966(d).

R (k) On the Sources of Knowledge and of Ignorance.
*

In: *Studies in Philosophy: British Academy Lectures,* selected and introduced by J. N. Findlay, (*Oxford Paperbacks* No. 112), London: Oxford University Press, 1966. (Pp. [v], 266.) Pp. 169-212.

A revised and enlarged reprint of 1960(d) and of the Introduction to 1965(c).
Italian translation contained in 1969(c).

R (l) *Rekishi-shugi no Hinkon* (THE POVERTY OF HISTORICISM).

Tokyo: Chuo-Koron Sha, Inc., 1966.

Fifth printing of 1961(c).

R (m) THE POVERTY OF HISTORICISM.

London: Routledge & Kegan Paul, 1966.

A reprint of 1961(b).

R (n) Was ist Dialektik?

Student im Bild, edited by Karl Heinz Zenz, 11. Jahrgang (1966), Nr. 1.

Abbreviated version of 1965(n), pp. 274-283: 2. Die Hegelsche Dialektik.
See note to this item.
Continuation of 1965(b).

R (o) Was ist Dialektik?

Student im Bild, edited by Karl Heinz Zenz, 11. Jahrgang (1966), Nr. 2
(Mai, 1966), pp. 42-44.

Abbreviated version of 1965(n), pp. 283-288: 3. Die Dialektik nach Hegel.
See note to this item.
Continuation of 1965(b) and 1966(n).

1967

R (a) THE POVERTY OF HISTORICISM.

New York: Basic Books, Inc., 1967.

A reprint of 1961(b).

* (b) Time's Arrow and Feeding on Negentropy.

Nature (London), Vol. 213 (1967), No. 5073 (January 21, 1967), p. 320.

A reply to W. Büchel: Entropy and Information in the Universe; *ibid.,* pp.
319-320.
Continuation of 1956(b), 1956(g), 1957(d), 1957(f), 1958(b), and 1965(f).
Also contained in 1974(a).

* (c) The Mysteries of Udolpho: A Reply to Professors Jeffrey and Bar-Hillel.

Mind (Oxford), New Series, Vol. 76 (1967), No. 301 (January, 1967), pp.
103-110.

Erratum: ibid., No. 303 (July, 1967), p. 462.
A continuation of 1962(a) and a reply to Richard C. Jeffrey: Popper on the
Rule of Succession; *ibid.,* Vol. 73 (1964), No. 289 (January, 1964), p. 129;
and to Y. Bar-Hillel: On an Alleged Contradiction in Carnap's Theory of Inductive Logic; *ibid.,* Vol. 73 (1964), No. 290 (April, 1964), pp. 265-267.

* (d) La rationalité et le statut du principe de rationalité.

In: *Les Fondements Philosophiques des Systemes Economiques: Tex-
tes de Jaques Rueff et essais rédigés en son honneur 23 août 1966,* edited by

Emil M. Claassen, (*Biblioteque Economique et Politique*), Paris: Payot, 1967. (Pp. 523.) Pp. [142]-150.

French translation of 'Rationality and the Status of the Rationality Principle' (mimeographed, pp. 13); see note to 1963(q).
Spanish translation: 1968(v).

* (e) Zum Thema Freiheit.

In: *Die Philosophie und die Wissenschaften: Simon Moser zum 65. Geburtstag,* edited by Ernst Oldemeyer, Meisenheim am Glan [Germany]: Anton Hain, 1967. (Pp. xii, 412.) Pp. 1-12.

T (f) DE ARMOEDE VAN HET HISTORICISME.
*

Floret-Boeken Nr. 12, Amsterdam: N. V. De Arbeiderspers, 1967. Pp. 174.

Dutch translation of 1960(c).
Voorwoord bij de Nederlandse Uitgave (Fallowfield, november 1964), pp. 5-8.

T (g) Die Wissenschaft als Institution des Fortschritts.

In: *Sozialer Wandel Zivilisation und Fortschritt als Kategorien der soziologischen Theorie,* edited, with an introduction, by Hans Peter Dreitzel, (*Soziologische Texte* 41), Neuwied und Berlin: Hermann Luchterhand Verlag, 1967. (Pp. 514.) Pp. 305-312.

German translation of part of section 32 of 1963(p) by Professor Dr. Otto Kimminich, Bochum.

* (h) Structural Information and the Arrow of Time.

Nature (London), Vol. 214 (1967), No. 5085 (April 15, 1967), p. 322.

A reply to Harold W. Woolhouse: Negentropy, Information and the Feeding of Organisms; *ibid.*, Vol. 213 (1967), No. 5079 (March 4, 1967), p. 952.
Continuation of 1956(b), 1956(g), 1957(d), 1957(f), 1958(b), 1965(f), and 1967(b).
Also contained in 1974(a).

* (i) The Cosmological Origins of Euclidean Geometry.

In: *Proceedings of the International Colloquium in the Philosophy of Science* (London, July 11-17, 1965), Vol. 1: *Problems in the Philosophy of*

Mathematics, edited by Imre Lakatos, (*Studies in Logic and the Foundations of Mathematics,* edited by A. Heyting, A. Robinson, and P. Suppes), Amsterdam: North-Holland Publishing Company, 1967. (Pp. xv, 241.) Pp. 18-20.

R (j) Selbstbefreiung durch das Wissen. (3. Auflage.)

In. *Der Slnn der Geschlchte,* edited by Leonhard Relnisch, (*Beck'sche Schwarze Reihe,* Band 15), 3. Auflage, Munich: Verlag C. H. Beck, 1967. (Pp. 135.) Pp. [100]-116.

Reprint of 1961(d). English translation: 1968(t).

* (k) Quantum Mechanics without "The Observer".

Chapter 1 in: *Quantum Theory and Reality,* edited by Mario Bunge, (*Studies in the Foundations, Methodology, and Philosophy of Science,* edited by Mario Bunge et al., Volume 2), Berlin, Heidelberg, New York: Springer-Verlag, 1967. (Pp. [v], 117.) Pp. [7]-44.

This volume consists of papers prepared for the *International Symposium on the Foundations of Physics,* held at Oberwolfach in July 1966 by the *Académie Internationale de Philosophie des Sciences.*
Also contained in 1974(a).

R (l) The Pre-Socratics and the Rationalist Tradition.

ETC.: A Review of General Semantics (San Francisco), Vol. 24 (1967), No. 2 (June, 1967), pp. 149-172.

Reprint of 1963(a), chapter 5 [1958(e)].

R (m) Plato as a Totalitarian Ideologist.

In: *Totalitarianism: Temporary Madness or Permanent Danger?,* edited with an introduction by Paul T. Mason, published in the series: *Problems in European Civilization,* edited by Ralph W. Greenlaw and Dwight E. Lee, Boston: D. C. Heath and Company, 1967. (Pp. xvii, 121.) Pp. 17-21.

A selection from chapters 6, 7, 8, and 9 of 1963 (l).

T (n) EL DESARROLO DEL CONOCIMIENTO CIENTIFICO: CONJETURAS Y REFUTACIONES.

Biblioteca de Filosofia, edited by Gregorio Klimovsky and Saad Chedid, *Serie Mayor* 2, Buenos Aires: Editorial Paidos, 1967. Pp. 463.

Spanish translation of 1965(c) by Nestor Miguez.

R (o) LA LOGICA DE LA INVESTIGACIÓN CIENTIFÍCA.

Estructura y Funcion (edited by Enrique Tierno Galvan), No. 8, Madrid: Editorial Tecnos, S. A., 1967. Pp. 451.

Second impression of 1962(r).

T (p) Wieczny Ideał Społeczeństwa Otwartego.

In: *Demokracja a ideał społeczny: wybór pism,* edited by Jan Ostaszewski, London: Ośrodek Wydawniczy Szkoła Nauk Politycznych i Społecznych w Londynie, 1967. (Pp. xxxvi, 400.) Pp. 373-400.

Polish translation of chapter 10 'The Open Society and Its Enemies' of 1957(h).

* (q) Epistemology and Scientific Knowledge.

In: *Abstracts of Papers, 3rd ICLMPS, Amsterdam 1967,* edited by B. van Rootselaar, Amsterdam: *Third International Congress for Logic, Methodology and Philosophy of Science* (Amsterdam, August 25-September 2, 1967), 1967. (Pp. viii, 167.) P. 72.

See note to 1968(s).

R (r) Reply to a Critic (1961).
*

In: *Plato, Popper and Politics: Some Contributions to a Modern Controversy,* edited by Renford Bambrough, (*Views and Controversies about Classical Antiquity,* edited by M. I, Finley), Cambridge: W. Heffer & Sons, New York: Barnes & Noble, 1967. (Pp. viii, 219.) Pp. 199-219.

Reprint, with errata, of *Addenda* III and IV to 1966(a), volume I.

* (s) Homage to Norwood Russell Hanson.

In: *Boston Studies in the Philosophy of Science,* Vol. III: *In Memory of Norwood Russell Hanson,* (*Proceedings of the Boston Colloquium for the Philosophy of Science 1964/1966*), edited by Robert S. Cohen and Marx W. Wartofsky, (*Synthese Library*), Dordrecht-Holland: D. Reidel Publishing Company, 1967. (Pp. xlix, 489.) Pp. xxxiii-xxxiv.

* (t) [Einstein's Influence on My View of Science: an Interview.]

In: *Einstein: the Man and his Achievement,* a series of broadcast talks under the general editorship of G. J. Whitrow, London: British Broadcasting Corporation, 1967. (Pp. xv, 94.) Pp. 23-28.

Interview by G. J. Whitrow.
Reprint: 1970(z_1). Spanish translation: 1969(w). See also 1969(v).

T (u) AÇIK TOPLUM VE DÜŞMANLARI. Cilt I: *Platon' un Büyüsii.*

Türk Siyasî İlîmler Derneği Yayınları [Publications of the Turkish Society for Political Sciences, USIS, Ankara]: *Siyasî İlîmler Serisi* 13, Ankara: Sevinç Matbaasi, 1967. Pp. [xv], [408].

Turkish translation of Vol. I of 1963(l). Translated and introduced by Mete Tunçay.

R (v) LA SOCIEDAD ABIERTA Y SUS ENEMIGOS.

Biblioteca del hombre contemporáneo Vol. 182, Buenos Aires: Editorial Paidos, 1967. Tomo I: pp. 353; Tomo II: pp. 401.

An *unauthorized* two-volume edition of 1957(c) without Footnotes, Preface, etc.

1968

R (a) THE LOGIC OF SCIENTIFIC DISCOVERY. (Second English edition,
* revised and enlarged.)

London: Hutchinson & Co., 1968. SBN 09 086630 4 (cased). SBN 09 086631 2 (paperback: *A Radius Book*). Pp. [480].

A revised and enlarged edition of 1959(a) with four new *Addenda* and *Acknowledgments,* 1968 (November 1967). The title of the preface to the first English edition has been changed to: Preface to the First English Edition, 1959.

R (b) CONJECTURES AND REFUTATIONS: *The Growth of Scientific Knowledge.*

New York and Evanston: Harper & Row, Publishers, (*Harper Torchbooks,* TB 1376), 1968. Pp. xiii, 417.

Paperback edition of 1965(c).

* (c) Remarks on the Problems of Demarcation and of Rationality.

In: *Proceedings of the International Colloquium in the Philosophy of Science* (London, July 11-17, 1965), Vol. 3: *Problems in the Philosophy of Science*, edited by Imre Lakatos and Alan Musgrave, (*Studies in Logic and the Foundations of Mathematics*, edited by A. Heyting, A. Robinson, P. Suppes, and A. Mostowski), Amsterdam: North-Holland Publishing Company, 1968. (Pp. ix, 448.) Pp. 88-102.

* (d) Non-Apparent Depth, Depth, and Pseudo-Depth.

Ibid., pp. 139-140.

* (e) Is there an Epistemological Problem of Perception?

Ibid., pp. 163-164.

* (f) On so-called Paradoxes in Physics.

Ibid., pp. 202-204.

* (g) Mathematics, Observation and Physical Thought.

Ibid., pp. 242-244.

* (h) On Rules of Detachment and so-called Inductive Logic.

In: *Proceedings of the International Colloquium in the Philosophy of Science* (London, July 11-17, 1965), Vol. 2: *The Problem of Inductive Logic*, edited by Imre Lakatos, (*Studies in Logic and the Foundations of Mathematics*, edited by A. Heyting, A. Robinson, P. Suppes, and A. Mostowski), Amsterdam: North-Holland Publishing Company, 1968. (Pp. viii, 417.) Pp. 130-139.

* (i) Theories, Experience, and Probabilistic Intuitions.

Ibid., pp. 285-303.

* (j) A Revised Definition of Natural Necessity.

The British Journal for the Philosophy of Science (London), Vol. 18 (1967-1968), No. 4 (February, 1968), pp. 316-321.

A reply to G. C. Nerlich and W. A. Suchting: Popper on Law and Natural Necessity; *ibid.*, Vol. 18 (1967-1968), No. 3 (November, 1967), pp. 233-235.

* (k) Plato.

In: *International Encyclopedia of the Social Sciences*, edited by Alvin Johnson, David L. Sills, and W. Allen Wallis, Vol. 12, New York: The Macmillan Company & The Free Press, London: Collier-Macmillan, Ltd., 1968. (Pp. 638.) Pp. 159-164.

T (l) AÇIK TOPLUM VE DÜŞMANLARI. Cilt II: *Hegel ve Marx*.

Türk Siyasî İlîmler Derneği Yayınları [Publications of the Turkish Society for Political Sciences, USIS, Ankara]: *Siyasî İlîmler Serisi* 14, Ankara: Sevinç Matbaasi, 1968. Pp. [viii], 448.

Turkish translation of Vol. II of 1963(m) by Harun Rizatepe.

T (m) Chishiki ni taisuru Mittsu no Mikata.

In: *Kagaku no Tetsugaku* (Philosophy of Science), edited, with an Introduction, by Saburo Ichii, Tokyo: Heibun-sha, 1968. (Pp. [407].) Pp. 271-308.

Japanese translation by Saburo Ichii of 1963(a), chapter 3 [1956(f)].

R (n) A Note on Berkeley as Precursor of Mach and Einstein.

In: *Berkeley's PRINCIPLES OF HUMAN KNOWLEDGE: Critical Studies*, edited by Gale W. Engle and Gabriele Taylor, (*Wadsworth Studies in Philosophical Criticism*, edited by Alexander Sesonske, [Vol. 7]), Belmont, California: Wadsworth Publishing Company, 1968. (Pp. viii, 173.) Pp. 90-100.

Reprint of 1965(c), chapter 6 [1953(d)].

R (o) A Note on Berkeley as Precursor of Mach and Einstein.

In: *Locke and Berkeley: A Collection of Critical Essays*, edited by C. B. Martin and D. M. Armstrong, (*Modern Studies in Philosophy*, edited by Amelie Rorty), Garden City, New York: Anchor Books, Doubleday & Company Inc., (*A Doubleday Anchor Original*, AP 6); London, Melbourne: Macmillan and Co. Ltd., (SBN 333 10069 7 (hard cover), SBN 331 10073 5 (*Papermacs*)), 1968. (Pp. [xi], 463.) Pp. [436]-449.

Reprint of 1965(c), chapter 6 [1953(d)].

R (p) THE OPEN SOCIETY AND ITS ENEMIES. Volume I: *The Spell of Plato*.

London: Routledge and Kegan Paul, [1968] (with the imprint '1966').

Fifth edition, revised and enlarged, of 1945(b). Hardback edition reprinted from the paperback 1966(a).

* (q) Birkhoff and von Neumann's Interpretation of Quantum Mechanics.

Nature (London), Vol. 219 (1968), No. 5155 (August 17, 1968), pp. 682-685.

Also contained in 1974(a).

* (r) On the Theory of the Objective Mind.

In: *Akten des XIV. Internationalen Kongresses für Philosophie (Proceedings of the XIVth International Congress of Philosophy)* (Vienna, September 2-9, 1968), Band I, [edited by Leo Gabriel], Vienna: University of Vienna, Verlag Herder, 1968. (Pp. xx, 656.) Pp. [25]-53.

Expanded version of an address delivered in German to the Plenary Session on September 3rd, 1968.
Also contained in 1972(a). Spanish translation: 1970(j).
See also 1970(h).

* (s) Epistemology Without a Knowing Subject.

In: *Proceedings of the Third International Congress for Logic, Methodology and Philosophy of Science* (Amsterdam, August 25-September 2, 1967): *Logic, Methodology and Philosophy of Science III,* edited by B. van Rootselaar and J. F. Staal, (*Studies in Logic and the Foundations of Mathematics,* edited by A. Heyting, A. Mostowski, A. Robinson, and P. Suppes), Amsterdam: North-Holland Publishing Company, 1968. (Pp. [xiv], [554].) Pp. [333]-373.

Most of this paper was read to the Congress as an *Invited Hour Address,* August 25, 1967.
Also contained in 1969(n) and in 1972(a). See also 1967(q).
Italian translation: 1972(h).

T
* (t) Emancipation through Knowledge.

In: *The Humanist Outlook,* edited by A. J. Ayer, London: Pemberton Publishing Company in association with Barrie & Rockliff, 1968. SBN 301 66764 0. (Pp. [vi], 296.) Pp. 281-296.

English version by K. R. Popper of 1967(j). See note to 1961(d).

R (u) Has History Any Meaning?

In: *Science, Faith, and Man: European Thought Since 1914*, edited by W. Warren Wagar, (*Documentary History of Western Civilization*, edited by Eugene C. Black and Leonard W. Levy), New York: Harper & Row (*Harper Torchbooks*, TB 1362), 1968; New York: Walker and Company (clothbound edition), 1968. (Pp. vi, 337.) Pp. 247-262.

Reprint of chapter 25 of 1963(l).

T (v) La explicación en las ciencias sociales (La racionalidad y el *status* del principio de racionalidad).

Revista de Occidente (Madrid), Año 6 (1968), No. 65 (Agosto, 1968), pp. [133]-146.

Spanish translation of 1967(d).

R (w) The Autonomy of Sociology.

In: *Mill: A Collection of Critical Essays*, edited by J. B. Schneewind, New York: Doubleday & Company, Anchor Books Edition, (paperback), 1968. (Pp. [xxiii], 455.) Pp. [426]-442.

Reprint of chapter 14 of 1966(a). See also 1969(p).

T (x) Utopie und Gewalt.

In: *Utopie: Begriff und Phänomen des Utopischen*, edited, with an introduction, by Arnhelm Neusüss, (*Soziologische Texte* 44), Neuwied und Berlin: Hermann Luchterhand Verlag, 1968. (Pp. 525.) Pp. 313-326.

German translation of 1963(a), chapter 18 [1948(a)].

* (y) Quantum Theory, Quantum Logic and the Calculus of Probability.

In: *Akten des XIV. Internationalen Kongresses für Philosophie* (*Proceedings of the XIVth International Congress of Philosophy*) (Vienna, September 2-9, 1968), Band III, edited by Leo Gabriel, Vienna: University of Vienna, Verlag Herder, 1969. (Pp. xvi, 694.) Pp. [307]-313.

Also contained in 1974(a).

* (z) Summary [of Paul Weingartner's three talks on "Modal Logics with two

Kinds of Necessity and Possibility" at the University of London, February 1967].

Notre Dame Journal of Formal Logic (Notre Dame, Indiana), Vol. 9 (1968), No. 2 (April, 1968), pp. 152-153.

This summary was given in a letter to Paul Weingartner from April 1967 who published it, with acknowledgements, in his paper "Modal Logics with two Kinds of Necessity and Possibility"; *ibid.*, pp. 97-159.

1969

* (a) The Moral Responsibility of the Scientist.

Encounter (London), Vol. 32 (1969), No. 3 (March, 1969), pp. 52-54, 56-57.

Also contained in 1970(z_3), 1971(q), 1971(s), and 1974(a). German translation: 1970(z).
See note to 1970(z_3).

* (b) Popper's "Moral Responsibility".

Encounter (London), Vol. 33 (1969), No. 1 (July, 1969), pp. 95-96.

A reply to Professor Henry D. Aiken's criticism of 1969(a): Popper's "Moral Responsibility"; *ibid.*, p. 95.

T (c) SCIENZA E FILOSOFIA: *Problemi e scopi della scienza. Cinque saggi.*

Nuovo Politecnico 29, Torino: Giulio Einaudi editore, 1969. Pp. 218.

Contents: Tre punti di vista a proposito della conoscenza umana. [1965(c), chapter 3 [1956(f)]]. Lo scopo della scienza. [1957(i), revised 1967]. Le fonti della conoscenza e dell'ignoranza. [1966(k), revised 1966]. Problemi, scopi e responsabilità della scienza. [1963(h)]. Verità, razionalità e accrescimento della conoscenza scientifica. [1965(c)], chapter 10].
Italian translation by Mario Trinchero.

T (d) [1]. Tre orientamenti epistemologici. [2]. Il criterio della rilevanza scientifica. [3]. La tematica induttiva: congetture e confutazioni. [4]. Enunciati probabilistici, teorie, spiegazione.

In: *Il Neoempirismo,* edited by Alberto Pasquinelli, (*Classici della*

Filosofia, edited by Nicola Abbagnano, No. 4), Torino: Unione Tipografico-Editrice Torinese, 1969. (Pp. 975.) Pp. [659]-751.

[1], pp. [659]-696: Italian translation of 1965(c), chapter 3 [1956(f)]; [2]-[4], pp. 697-751: Italian translation of 1965(c), chapter 1 [1957(a)].

R (e) LOGIK DER FORSCHUNG. (Dritte, vermehrte Auflage.)

Die Einheit der Gesellschaftswissenschaften, Band 4, Tübingen: J. C. B. Mohr (Paul Siebeck), 1969. Pp. xxvi, 441.

A revised and enlarged edition of 1966(e) [1934(b)] with eight new *Addenda* and a new Preface: Vorwort zur dritten deutschen Auflage (Penn, Buckinghamshire, im Herbst 1968), pp. [xxv]-xxvi.

R (f) DAS ELEND DES HISTORIZISMUS. (Zweite, unveränderte Auflage.)

Die Einheit der Gesellschaftswissenschaften, Band 3, Tübingen: J. C. B. Mohr (Paul Siebeck), 1969. Pp. xvi, 132.

Second impression of 1965(g).

R (g) THE POVERTY OF HISTORICISM.

London: Routledge & Kegan Paul, 1969. SBN 7100 1965 3 (hardback).

A reprint of 1961(b).

R (h) CONJECTURES AND REFUTATIONS: *The Growth of Scientific Knowledge.* (Third edition, revised and enlarged.)

London: Routledge and Kegan Paul, 1969. SBN 7100 6507 8. Pp. xiii, 431.

A revised and enlarged edition of 1965(c) [1963(a)] with a new preface: Preface to the Third Edition (Penn, Buckinghamshire, April 1968); two new *Addenda*: 7. Some Further Hints on Verisimilitude (1968), 8. Further Remarks on the Presocratics, especially on Parmenides (1968); and an Index of Mottoes.
The *Addendum* '9. The Presocratics: Unity or Novelty?' is identical with the 'Supplementary Note' in 1965(c).
Paperback edition: 1969(i).

R (i) CONJECTURES AND REFUTATIONS: *The Growth of Scientific Knowledge.*

London: Routledge and Kegan Paul, 1969. SBN 7100 6508 6. Pp. ix, 431.

Paperback edition of 1969(h).

* (j) A Pluralist Approach to the Philosophy of History.

In: *Roads to Freedom: Essays in Honour of Friedrich A. von Hayek,* edited by Erich Streissler (managing editor), Gottfried Haberler, Friedrich A. Lutz and Fritz Machlup, London: Routledge & Kegan Paul, 1969. ISBN 0 7100 6616 3. (Pp. xix, 315.) Pp. 181-200.

Based on a lecture delivered in Oxford on November 3, 1967. Reprint: 1970(z_8).

R (k) The Aim of Science.
*

In: *Contemporary Philosophy: A Survey,* edited by Raymond Klibansky, III: *Metaphysics, Phenomenology, Language and Structure, (La Philosophie Contemporaine: Chroniques,* III: *Métaphysique, Phénoménologie, Langage et Structure),* Firenze: La Nuova Italia Editrice, 1969. (Pp. xii, 410.) Pp. [129]-142.

A revised version of 1957(i). Also contained in 1972(a).

R (l) The Hypothetical-Deductive Method and the Unity of Social and Natural Science.

In: *The Nature and Scope of Social Science: A Critical Anthology,* edited by Leonard I. Krimerman, New York: Appleton-Century-Crofts, Educational Division, Meredith Corporation, 1969. (Pp. xi, 796.) Pp. 47-53.

Reprint of section 29 of 1961(b).

R (m) Die Logik der Sozialwissenschaften.

In: *Der Positivismusstreit in der deutschen Soziologie,* edited by Heinz Maus and Friedrich Fürstenberg, *(Soziologische Texte* 58), Neuwied und Berlin: Hermann Luchterhand Verlag, 1969. (Pp. [348].) Pp. 103-123.

Reprint of 1962(k). For reprints of this volume, see 1970(z_7), 1971(e), and 1972(l).

R (n) Epistemology Without a Knowing Subject.
*

Chapter 11 in: *philosophy today,* No. 2, edited by Jerry H. Gill, New York: The Macmillan Company, London and Toronto: Collier-Macmillan Ltd., 1969. (Pp. vii, 310.) Pp. [225]-277.

A revised reprint of 1968(s); see note to this item.

R (o). MISÈRE DE L'HISTORICISME.

> *Recherches en sciences humaines (Série grise)* 8, Paris: Librairie Plon, [1969]. Pp. xvi, 196.

> Reprint of 1956(a).

R (p) The Autonomy of Sociology.

> In: *Mill: A Collection of Critical Essays,* edited by J. B. Schneewind, Notre Dame, Indiana: University of Notre Dame Press, (hardbound); (*Modern Studies in Philosophy,* edited by Amelie Rorty), London, Melbourne: Macmillan and Co. Ltd., (SBN 333 10524 9 (hardbound), SBN 333 10526 5 *(Papermacs)*), 1969. (Pp. [xxiii], 455.) Pp. [426]-442.

> Reprint of chapter 14 of 1966(a). See also 1968(w).

R (q) THE OPEN SOCIETY AND ITS ENEMIES.

> London: Routledge and Kegan Paul, 1969. SBN 7100 1967 X (hardback).

> Fifth edition of 1945(b) and 1945(c); reprint of 1966(a).

R (r) THE OPEN SOCIETY AND ITS ENEMIES.

> *Routledge Paperbacks* No. 25 and 26, London: Routledge & Kegan Paul, 1969. SBN 7100 4625 1.

> Reprint of 1966(a).

R (s) THE POVERTY OF HISTORICISM.

> *A Routledge Paperback,* London: Routledge & Kegan Paul, 1969. SBN 7100 4616 2 (paperback).

> A reprint of 1961(b).

R (t) Über die Unwiderlegbarkeit philosophischer Theorien einschliesslich jener, welche falsch sind.

> In: *Club Voltaire: Jahrbuch für kritische Aufklärung I,* edited by Gerhard Szczesny, (*Rowohlt Paperback,* R73), Reinbek bei Hamburg: Rowohlt Taschenbuch Verlag, 1969. (Pp. 419.) Pp. [271]-279.

Reprint of 1963(k) [1959(d)].

R (u) Of Clouds and Clocks.

Architectural Design (London), Vol. 39 (1969), No. 9 (September, 1969), pp. 491-492.

An excerpt from 1966(f) made by the editor of the journal.

R (v) [Einstein's Influence on My View of Science: an Interview.]

In: *Einstein: the Man and his Achievement,* edited by G. J. Whitrow; edited with notes by Hirokazu Nakayama and Toshio Fuse, [Tokyo]: Asahi Press, 1969. (Pp. [vii], 83.) Pp. 20-22.

Abridged version of 1967(t).

T (w) [Einstein's Influence on My View of Science: an Interview.]

In: *Einstein el hombre y su obra,* edited by G. J. Whitrow, (*Colección Minima* 23), México: Siglo XXI Editores, S. A., 1969. (Pp. [136].) Pp. 46-53.

Spanish translation by Julieta Campos of 1967(t).

1970

* (a) Dialectical Methodology.

The Times Literary Supplement (London), 69th Year (1970), No. 3552 (March 26, 1970), pp. 338-339.

A letter to the Editor occasioned by a review of 1969(m); *ibid.,* No. 3550 (March 12, 1970), pp. [269]-272.
An expanded version of this letter is contained in 1970(z₄).

R (b) Has History Any Meaning?

In: *The Nature of Historical Enquiry,* edited by Leonard M. Marsak, New York: Holt, Rinehart & Winston, 1970. (Pp. viii, 181.) Pp. 155-157.

Reprint from chapter 25 (pp. 278-280) of 1963(l) and 1966(a).

R (c) The Open Society and Its Enemies (Chapter 22): The Moral Theory of Historicism.

In: *Philosophical Perspectives for Education,* edited by Carlton H.

Bowyer, Glenview, Illinois: Scott, Foresman and Company, 1970. (Pp. [xiii], 402.) Pp. 261-270.

Reprint from chapter 22 of 1966(a).

* (d) Plato, *Timaeus* 54E-55A.

The *Classical Review* (Oxford), New Series, Vol. XX (1970), No. 1 (March, 1970), pp. 4-5.

T (e) LOGICA DELLA SCOPERTA SCIENTIFICA: *Il carattere autocorrettivo*
* *della scienza.*

Einaudi Paperbacks 14, Torino: Giulio Einaudi editore, 1970. Pp. [xxxi], 549.

Italian translation by Mario Trinchero of 1968(a).
Prefazione all'edizione italiana, 1970 (Penn, Buckinghamshire, marzo 1970.), pp. [xiii]-xv.

T (f) Adevăr, raţionalitate şi progresul cunoaşterii ştiinţifice.

In: *Logica Ştiinţei,* edited by Gh. Enescu & Cornel Popa, Bucuresti: Editura Politică, 1970. (Pp. 599.) Pp. [99]-155.

Roumanian translation of chapter 10 of 1963(a).

R (g) A Note on Berkeley as Precursor of Mach and Einstein.

In: *George Berkeley: A Treatise Concerning the Principles of Human Knowledge—with Critical Essays,* edited by Colin Murrey Turbayne (*The Bobbs-Merrill Text and Commentary Series,* edited by Harold Weisberg, TC 2), Indianapolis, New York: The Bobbs-Merrill Company, 1970. (Pp. [xxvii], 338.) Pp. 129-144.

Reprint of 1965(c), chapter 6 [1953(d)].

* (h) Eine objektive Theorie des historischen Verstehens.

Schweizer Monatshefte (Zürich), 50. Jahr (1970-1971), Heft 3 (Juni, 1970), pp. 207-215.

Based on an address delivered to the Plenary Session of the *XIVth International Congress of Philosophy* (Vienna, September 2-9, 1968) on September 3rd, 1968. See also 1968(r).

Material from this paper (in English) is incorporated in 1972(a), chapter 4.

* (i) Palabras de apertura del simposio.

In: *Simposio de Burgos: Ensayos de Filosofia de la Ciencia—En torno a la obra de Sir Karl R. Popper* (Burgos, September 23-25, 1968), edited by Miguel Boyer, Víctor Sánchez de Zavala, and Pedro Schwartz, *(Serie de Filosofia y Ensayo de Editorial Tecnos),* Madrid: Editorial Tecnos, 1970. (Pp. 241.) Pp. [13]-14.

T (j) Sobre la teoria de la inteligencia objetiva.

Ibid., pp. [202]-237.

Spanish translation of 1968(r) by Víctor Sánchez de Zavala.

* (j₁) [Remarks on Norman Barraclough's paper "El principio de simetria como origen de una realidad matematicamente estructurada" *(ibid.,* pp. [27]-36).]

Ibid., pp. [37]-38.

* (j₂) [Remarks on Víctor Sánchez de Zavala's paper "Sobre las ciencias de 'complexos' " *(ibid.,* pp. [39]-63).]

Ibid., pp. [64]-69.

* (j₃) [Remarks on Luis Angel Rojo's paper "El metodo empirico y el conocimiento economico" *(ibid.,* pp. [92]-108).]

Ibid., pp. 110-116.

* (j₄) [Remarks on Pedro Schwartz's paper "El individualismo metodologico y los historiadores" *(ibid.,* pp. [117]-140).]

Ibid., pp. 150-152.

R (k) The Sociology of Knowledge.

In: *The Sociology of Knowledge: A Reader,* edited by James E. Curtis and John W. Petras, New York, Washington: Praeger Publishers, 1970. (Pp. vii, 724.) Pp. 649-660.

A reprint of chapter 23 of 1966(a).

* (l) A Realist View of Logic, Physics, and History.

In: *Physics, Logic, and History,* edited by Wolfgang Yourgrau and Allen D. Breck, New York and London: Plenum Press, 1970. SBN 306 30360 4. (Pp. xiv. 336.) Pp. 1-30, 35-37.

Discussion, pp. 30-37; reply, pp. 35-37.
This book is based on the *First International Colloquium* held at the *University of Denver* (Denver, Colorado), May 16-20, 1966.
Also contained in 1972(a).

* (m) [Remarks on André Mercier's paper "Knowledge and Physical Reality" (*ibid.,* pp. 39-50).]

Ibid., pp. 56-57.

* (n) [Remarks on Willard V. O. Quine's paper "Existence" (*ibid.,* pp. 89-98).]

Ibid., p. 98 and p. 103.

* (o) [Remarks on Jaakko Hintikka's paper "On Semantic Information" (*ibid.,* pp. 147-168).]

Ibid., pp. 169-170.

* (p) [Remarks on Czesław Lejewski's paper "Quantification and Ontological Commitment" (*ibid.,* pp. 173-181).]

Ibid., p. 189.

* (q) [Remarks on Jean-Pierre Vigier's paper "Possible Internal Subquantum Motions of Elementary Particles" (*ibid.,* pp. 191-197).]

Ibid., pp. 199-200.

* (r) [Remarks on Alfred Landé's paper "Non-Quantal Foundations of Quantum Mechanics" (*ibid.,* pp. 297-306).]

Ibid., p. 308.

* (s) [Remarks on György Ránki's paper "Some Problems of the Connection

between Technical Development and Economic History" (*ibid.*, pp. 311-315).]

> *Ibid.*, pp. 316-317.

R (t) Back to the Presocratics.

> In: *Studies in Presocratic Philosophy,* Vol. I: *The Beginnings of Philosophy,* edited by David J. Furley and R. E. Allen, (*International Library of Philosophy and Scientific Method,* edited by Ted Honderich), London: Routledge & Kegan Paul, New York: The Humanities Press, 1970. ISBN 0 7100 6759 3. (Pp. x, 429.) Pp. 130-153.

> Reprint of chapter 5 [1958(e)] of 1963(a), or later editions.

R (u) Selbstbefreiung durch das Wissen. (4. Auflage.)

> In: *Der Sinn der Geschichte,* edited by Leonhard Reinisch, (*Beck'sche Schwarze Reihe,* Band 15), 4. Auflage, Munich: Verlag C. H. Beck, 1970. ISBN 3 406 02415 7. (Pp. 135.) Pp. [100]-116.

> Reprint of 1961(d).

* (v) Correction.

> *Synthese* (Dordrecht-Holland), Vol. 21 (1970), No. 1 (March, 1970), p. [107].

> A correction to 1963(g) and 1964(f).

* (w) Normal Science and Its Dangers.

> In: *Proceedings of the International Colloquium in the Philosophy of Science* (London, July 11-17, 1965), Vol. 4: *Criticism and the Growth of Knowledge,* edited by Imre Lakatos and Alan Musgrave, London: Cambridge University Press, 1970. SBN 521 07826 1. (Pp. viii, 282.) Pp. 51-58.

> Paperback edition: 1970(x). Also contained in 1974(a).

R (x) Normal Science and Its Dangers.

> Paperback edition of 1970(w). SBN 521 09623 5.

R (y) Three Views Concerning Human Knowledge.

> In: *The Foundations of Knowledge,* edited by Charles Landesman, (*Cen-*

tral Issues in Philosophy Series), Englewood Cliffs, New Jersey: Prentice-Hall, Inc., 1970. (Pp. viii, 184.) Pp. 93-123.

A reprint of 1965(c), chapter 3 [1956(f)].

T (z) Die moralische Verantwortlichkeit des Wissenschaftlers.
*

Schweizer Monatshefte (Zürich), 50 Jahr (1970-1971), Heft 7 (Oktober, 1970), pp. 561-570.

A revised translation of 1969(a). See note to 1970(z_3).

R (z_1) Einstein: Early Years.

In: *Physics and Man,* edited by Robert Karplus, New York: W. A. Benjamin, Inc., 1970. (Pp. xxii, 343.) Pp. 47-52.

Reprint of 1967(t).

* (z_2) [Contributions to a discussion of a paper by A. Grünbaum.]

In: *Induction, Physics, and Ethics: Proceedings and Discussions of the 1968 Salzburg Colloquium in the Philosophy of Science* (Salzburg, August 28-31, 1968), edited by Paul Weingartner and Gerhard Zecha, *(Synthese Library)*, Dordrecht-Holland: D. Reidel Publishing Company, 1970. SBN 90 277 0158 X. (Pp. x, 382.) Pp. [167]-168.

Remarks on Adolf Grünbaum: Simultaneity by Slow Clock Transport in the Special Theory of Relativity; *ibid.,* pp. [140]-166.

R (z_3) The Moral Responsibility of the Scientist.

Ibid., pp. [329]-336.

A paper read to a session *Science and Ethics: The Moral Responsibility of the Scientist.* The papers in this section of the Colloquium were all read at the *University of Vienna* on September 3, 1968, in connection with the *14th International Congress of Philosophy* (Vienna, September 2-9, 1968).
A reprint of 1969(a).

* (z_4) Reason or Revolution?

Archives européennes de sociologie (Paris), Tome XI (1970), No. 2 (November, 1970), pp. 252-262.

A much expanded version of 1970(a).

* (z₅) On the Philosophy of Bertrand Russell: Karl Popper, Peter Strawson and Geoffrey Warnock Take Part in a Discussion Chaired by Bryan Magee.

The Listener (London), Vol. 83 (1970), No. 2146 (May 14th, 1970), pp. [633]-636, 638; and No. 2147 (May 21st, 1970), pp. 685-686.

A Radio Discussion broadcast in the *BBC Third Programme.* Reprinted in 1971(m).

* (z₆) Russell, Popper, and Oxford.

The Listener (London), Vol. 83 (1970), No. 2149 (June 4th, 1970), p. 753.

A reply to Ray Bloomfield's letter; *ibid., p. 753.*

R (z₇) Die Logik der Sozialwissenschaften.

In: *Der Positivismusstreit in der deutschen Soziologie,* edited by Heinz Maus and Friedrich Fürstenberg, (*Soziologische Texte* 58), second edition, Neuwied und Berlin: Hermann Luchterhand Verlag, 1970. (Pp. [348].) Pp. 103-123.

Reprint of 1969(m) [1962(k)].

R (z₈) A Pluralist Approach to the Philosophy of History.

In: *Roads to Freedom: Essays in. Honour of Friedrich A. von Hayek,* edited by Erich Streissler (managing editor), Gottfried Haberler, Friedrich A. Lutz and Fritz Machlup, London: Routledge & Kegan Paul, 1970. ISBN 0 7100 6616 3. (Pp. xix, 315.) Pp. 181-200.

Reprint of 1969(j).

1971

* (a) Conversations with Philosophers—Sir Karl Popper talks about some of his basic ideas with Bryan Magee.

The Listener (London), Vol. 85 (1971), No. 2180 (January 7th, 1971), pp. 8-12.

The fifth in a series of 13 *Conversations with Philosophers* broadcast in the *BBC Third Programme.*
Slightly expanded in 1971(l). Danish translation: 1972(n).

R (b) THE OPEN SOCIETY AND ITS ENEMIES. Vols. I and II.

Princeton Paperbacks 219 and 220, Princeton, New Jersey: Princeton University Press, 1971. ISBN 0 691 01968 1 and 0 691 01972 X.

Reprint of 1966(a).

R (c) Nachrevolutionäres Risiko—oder freie, offene Gesellschaft? Gegensätzliche politische Entwürfe von Herbert Marcuse und Karl Popper zum Thema "Revolution oder Reform".

Süddeutsche Zeitung, No. 14 (16./17. Januar 1971), *SZ am Wochenende: Feuilleton-Beilage der Süddeutschen Zeitung*, pp. [1]-[2].

Abridged version of 1971(g).

T (d) SAMFUNNSVITENSKAP OG PROFETI.

Praktisk filosofi, No. 6 *(Studiefakkel)*, Oslo: Gyldendal Norsk Forlag, 1971. Pp. xiii, 133.

Norwegian translation, with an introduction, by Bernt Vestre of 1961(b).

R (e) Die Logik der Sozialwissenschaften.

In: *Der Positivismusstreit in der deutschen Soziologie*, edited by Heinz Maus and Friedrich Fürstenberg, (*Soziologische Texte* 58), third edition, Neuwied und Berlin: Hermann Luchterhand Verlag, 1971. (Pp. [348].) Pp. 103-123.

Hardback and paperback editions of 1969(m) [1962(k)].

R (f) Utopia and Violence.

In: *The Good Society,* a book of readings edited by Anthony Arblaster and Steven Lukes, London: Methuen & Co., 1971. SBN 416 08350 1 (hardbound). SBN 416 08430 3 (*A University Paperback Original* UP 400). (Pp. xi, 436.) Pp. 380-386.

An abridged reprint of 1969(h), chapter 18 [1948(a)]. See also 1971(y) and 1972(k).

* (g) [Revolution oder Reform?]

In: *Revolution oder Reform? Herbert Marcuse und Karl Popper—Eine Konfrontation,* edited by Franz Stark, Munich: Kösel-Verlag, 1971. (Pp. 48.) Pp. [3], [9]-10, [22]-29, [34]-39, and [41].

An enlarged version of a TV-interview broadcast on the *Bavarian Broadcasting Network* on January 5th, 1971.
Reprints: 1971(z) and 1972(g). An abridged version is contained in 1971(c).
Translations: Dutch: 1971(w); English: 1972(f) and 1972(m).

R (h) Science: Problems, Aims, Responsibilities.

In: *Science and Public Policy,* edited by Louise B. Young and William J. Trainor, New York: Oceana Publications, 1971. (Pp. xiv, 626.) Pp. 20-35.

A partial reprint of 1963(h).

* (i) Conjectural Knowledge: My Solution of the Problem of Induction.

Revue Internationale de Philosophie (Brussels), No. 95-96 ([Thème]: *Hypothèse et Confirmation*) = 25^e année (1971), fasc. 1-2, pp. [167]-197.

Also contained in 1972(a).

* (j) Einstein's Greatness.

The Sunday Telegraph (London), May 23rd, 1971, p. 11.

A letter to the Editor by P. B. Medawar and K. R. Popper occasioned by Nigel Dennis's review of *The Born-Einstein Letters* (Macmillan); *ibid.,* May 9th, 1971, p. 11.

* (k) Einstein's Error.

The Listener (London), Vol. 86 (1971), No. 2208 (July 22nd, 1971), p. 115.

A reply to Dr. G. Burniston Brown's letter; *ibid.,* No. 2206 (July 8th, 1971), p. 52.

R (l) Conversation with Karl Popper.

In: *Modern British Philosophy* by Bryan Magee, London: Secker & Warburg, New York: St. Martin's Press, 1971. SBN 436 27103 6 (hard cover). SBN 436 27104 4 (paperback). (Pp. xi, 234.) Pp. [66]-82.

A slightly expanded reprint of 1971(a), see note to this item. Danish translation: 1972(n).

R (m) Discussion among Karl Popper, Peter Strawson and Geoffrey Warnock: *The Philosophy of Russell: II.*

Ibid., pp. [131]-149.

A reprint of 1970(z_5), see note to this item.

* (n) Particle Annihilation and the Argument of Einstein, Podolsky, and Rosen.

In: *Perspectives in Quantum Theory: Essays in Honor of Alfred Landé,* edited by Wolfgang Yourgrau and Alwyn van der Merwe, Cambridge, Massachusetts, and London: M. I. T. Press, 1971. ISBN 0 262 24014 9 (hard cover). (Pp. xxxvii, 283.) Pp. [182]-198.

Also contained in 1974(a).

R (o) LOGIK DER FORSCHUNG. (Vierte, verbesserte Auflage.)
*

Die Einheit der Gesellschaftswissenschaften, Band 4, Tübingen: J. C. B. Mohr (Paul Siebeck), 1971. Pp. xxvi, 441.

A revised and slightly enlarged edition of 1969(e) [1966(e), 1934(b)] with a small *Addendum* on p. 96: *Zusatz (1971).*

R (p) DAS ELEND DES HISTORIZISMUS. (Dritte, verbesserte Auflage.)

Die Einheit der Gesellschaftswissenschaften, Band 3, Tübingen: J. C. B. Mohr (Paul Siebeck), 1971. Pp. xvi, 132.

Third impression, with a few corrections, of 1965(g).

R (q) The Moral Responsibility of the Scientist.

Bulletin of Peace Proposals (Oslo), Vol. 2 (1971), No. 3 (1971), pp. 279-283.

A revised version of 1969(a). See note to 1970(z_3).
Erratum: p. 283, first column: the last and second to last lines have been printed in the wrong order, i.e. it should read: ". . . everybody has a special responsibility in the field in which he has either special power or special knowledge. Thus, in the main, only scientists can . . .".

R (r) Wider die grossen Worte: Ein Plädoyer für intellektuelle Redlichkeit.

Die Zeit (Hamburg), 26. Jahrgang (1971), Nr. 39 (24. September, 1971), p. 8.

An excerpt from 1971(u).

R (s) The Moral Responsibility of the Scientist.

In: *Akten des XIV. Internationalen Kongresses für Philosophie (Proceedings of the XIVth International Congress of Philosophy)* (Vienna, September 2-9, 1968), Band VI, edited by Leo Gabriel, Vienna: University of Vienna, Verlag Herder, 1971. (Pp. xii, 609.) Pp. [489]-496.

See note to 1970(z_3).

T (t) *Kagakuteki Hakken no Ronri* (THE LOGIC OF SCIENTIFIC DIS-COVERY). Vol. I.

Tokyo: Koseisha-Koseikaku, 1971. Pp. 268, 23.

Japanese translation by I. T. Mori and G. Ouchi of 1959(a): Translators' Note; Preface to the First Edition, 1934; Preface to the English Edition, 1958; and chapters I-VIII. This volume also contains a translation of 1966(e): Vorwort zur zweiten deutschen Auflage; and a translation of the first three of the eight new *Addenda* in 1969(e). A *Translators' Postscript* (Sendai, 1st February, 1971) has been added on the last 23 pages.

In this translation the copyright has, incorrectly, been ascribed to Basic Books Inc.—it resides with Karl R. Popper.

* (u) Philosophische Selbstinterpretation und Polemik gegen die Dialektiker.

In: *Verfall der Philosophie: Politik deutscher Philosophen* by Claus Grossner, *(Die Zeit Bücher)*, Reinbek bei Hamburg: Christian Wegner Verlag, 1971. ISBN 3 8032 0041 5. (Pp. 348.) Pp. [278]-289.

For an excerpt, see 1971(r).

R (v) The Nature of Philosophical Problems and their Roots in Science.

In: *Plato's Meno: Text and Essays*, edited by Malcolm Brown, Indianapolis, New York: The Bobbs-Merrill Company, Inc., 1971. (Pp. xxxiv, 314.) Pp. 128-179.

Reprint of 1969(h), chapter 2 [1952(c)].

T (w) [Sociale Revolutie of Sociale Hervorming?]

In: *Herbert Marcuse/Karl Popper: Sociale Revolutie of Sociale Hervorming—Een Confrontatie*, edited by Franz Stark, Baarn: Het Wereldvenster, 1971. (Pp. 47.) Pp. 5, 9-11, 22-29, 34-38, and 40.

Dutch translation by A. Kreykamp of 1971(g).

R (x) Kritik des Sozialutopismus.

In: *Wort und Sinn: Lesebuch für den Deutschunterricht* (edited by Karl-Ernst Jeismann and Gustav Muthmann), Oberstufenband 2, edited by Konrad Gründer, Paderborn: Ferdinand Schöningh (*Schöningh-Buch* 28580), 1971. ISBN 3 506 28580 7. (Pp. 422.) Pp. 221-231.

Reprint of 1957(k), chapter 9.

R (y) Utopia and Violence.

In: *The Good Society*, a book of readings edited by Anthony Arblaster and Steven Lukes, New York: Harper & Row, Publishers, (*Torch Library*), 1971. ISBN 0 06 136054 6. (Pp. xi, 436.) Pp. 380-386.

An abridged reprint of 1969(g), chapter 18 [1948(a)]. See also 1971(f) and 1972(k).

R (z) [Revolution oder Reform?]

In: *Revolution oder Reform? Herbert Marcuse und Karl Popper—Eine Konfrontation*, edited by Franz Stark, second edition, Munich: Kösel-Verlag, 1971. ISBN 3 466 42022 9. (Pp. 48.) Pp. [3], [9]-10, [22]-29, [34]-39, and [41].

Reprint of 1971(g).

1972

* (a) OBJECTIVE KNOWLEDGE: *An Evolutionary Approach.*

Oxford: at the Clarendon Press, 1972. ISBN 0 19 824370 7 (hard cover). ISBN 0 19 875024 2 (paperback). Pp. x, 380.

Dedicated to Alfred Tarski.
Contents: Preface (Penn, Buckinghamshire 24th July 1971). Acknowledgements. Contents. 1. Conjectural Knowledge: My Solution of the Problem of Induction [1971(i)]. 2. Two Faces of Common Sense: An Argument for Commonsense Realism and Against the Commonsense Theory of Knowledge. 3. Epistemology Without a Knowing Subject. [1968(s)]. 4. On the Theory of the Objective Mind. [1968(r) and 1970(h)]. 5. The Aim of Science. [1957(i), 1969(k)]. 6. Of Clouds and Clocks. [1966(f)]. 7. Evolution and the Tree of Knowledge. [1961(j)]. *Addendum.* The Hopeful Behavioural Monster. 8. A Realist View of Logic, Physics, and History. [1970(1)]. 9. Philosophical Comments of Tarski's Theory of Truth. [197 ( )]. *Addendum.* A Note on Tarski's Definition of Truth. [1955(d)]. APPENDIX.

The Bucket and the Searchlight: Two Theories of Knowledge. [1949(d), 1964(e)]. *Index of Names. Index of Subjects.*

R (b) THE POVERTY OF HISTORICISM.

London: Routledge & Kegan Paul, 1972. ISBN 0 7100 1965 3 (hardback). ISBN 0 7100 4616 2 (paperback: *A Routledge Paperback*). Pp. x, 166.

A reprint of 1961(b).

R (c) THE LOGIC OF SCIENTIFIC DISCOVERY. (Third English edition, * revised and enlarged.)

London: Hutchinson & Co., 1972. ISBN 0 09 111720 8 (cased). ISBN 0 09 111721 6 (paperback: *A Radius Book*). Pp. [480].

A revised and enlarged edition of 1968(a) [1959(a)].

R (d) CONJECTURES AND REFUTATIONS: *The Growth of Scientific* * *Knowledge.* (Fourth edition, revised and enlarged.)

London: Routledge and Kegan Paul, 1972. ISBN 0 7100 6507 8 (cased). ISBN 0 7100 6508 6 (paperback), Pp. xiii, 431.

A revised and enlarged edition of 1969(h) [1963(a)].

T (e) CONGETTURE E CONFUTAZIONI: *Lo sviluppo della conoscenza scientifica.*

Collezione di testi e di studi: Filosofia, Bologna: Società editrice il Mulino, 1972. Pp. lxvii, 726.

Italian translation by Giuliano Pancaldi of 1969(h) [1963(a)]. Introduction by Giorgio Sandri, pp. [vii]-lxvii.

T (f) On Reason & the Open Society: A Conversation. *

Encounter (London), Vol. 38 (1972), No. 5 (May, 1972), pp. 13-18.

English translation by Maxwell Brownjohn of 1971(g). The text, and the translation, has been revised and added to by Professor Popper. Reprint: 1972(m).

R (g) [Revolution oder Reform?]

In: *Revolution oder Reform? Herbert Marcuse und Karl Popper—Eine Konfrontation*, edited by Franz Stark, third edition, Munich: Kösel-Verlag,

1972. ISBN 3 466 42022 9. (Pp. 48.) Pp. [3], [9]-10, [22]-29, [34]-39, and [41].

Reprint of 1971(g).

T (h) EPISTEMOLOGIA, RAZIONALITÀ E LIBERTÀ.

Filosofia o problemi d'oggi, 13, Roma: Armando Armando Editore, 1972. Pp. 135.

Contents: Epistemologia senza soggetto conoscente. [1968(s)]. Nuvole ed orologi: saggio sul problema della razionalità e della libertà dell'uomo. [1966(f)].
Italian translation by Dario Antiseri.

R (i) Die Zielsetzung der Erfahrungswissenschaft.

In: *Theorie und Realität: Ausgewählte Aufsätze zur Wissenschafts-lehre der Sozialwissenschaften*, edited by Hans Albert, (*Die Einheit der Gesellschaftswissenschaften*, Band 2), 2nd revised edition, Tübingen: J. C. B. Mohr (Paul Siebeck), 1972. ISBN 3 16 503851 1. (Pp. xii, 431.) Pp. [29]-41.

Reprint of 1964(d) [1957(j)].

R (j) Naturgesetze und theoretische Systeme.

Ibid., pp. [43]-58.

Reprint of 1964(e) [1949(d)].

R (k) Utopia and Violence.

In: *The Good Society*, a book of readings edited by Anthony Arblaster and Steven Lukes, New York: Harper & Row, Publishers, (*Harper Torchbooks*, TB 1641), 1972. ISBN 0 06 131641 5. (Pp. xi, 436.) Pp. 380-386.

An abridged reprint of 1969(h), chapter 18 [1948(a)]. See also 1971(f) and 1971(y).

R (l) Die Logik der Sozialwissenschaften.

In: *Der Positivismusstreit in der deutschen Soziologie*, edited by Heinz Maus and Friedrich Fürstenberg, (*Soziologische Texte* 58), fourth edition, (*Sonderausgabe der Sammlung Luchterhand*), Neuwied und Berlin: Hermann Luchterhand Verlag, 1972. (Pp. [348].) Pp. 103-123.

Paperback edition of 1969(m) [1962(k)].

R   (m) On Reason and the Open Society — A Conversation.

Congressional Record (Washington), Vol. 118 (1972), No. 83 (May 23, 1972), pp. E 5625-E 5627.

Reprint of 1972(f).
Erratum: p. E 5626, first column: lines 26-27 should read: ". . . Dictatorships are more stable, and so are utopias, . . .".

T   (n) Den kritiske metode til eliminering af fejltagelser: En dialog om sandheden.

Berlingske Aftenavis: Weekendavisen (Copenhagen), 224. årgang (1972), nr. 21 (2. juni, 1972), pp. 14-15.

Danish translation by Niels Chr. Stefansen and Knud Haakonssen of 1971(l) [1971(a)].

R   (o) Basisprobleme.

In: *Ideologiekritik in der Erziehungswissenschaft,* edited by Heinrich Kanz, (*Erziehungswissenschaftliche Reihe,* Band 13), Frankfurt am Main: Akademische Verlagsgesellschaft, 1972. ISBN 3 400 00167 8. (Pp. vi, 177.) Pp. [37]-49, 158-160.

Reprint of 1969(e), chapter 5, pp. 60-76.

R   (p) The Open Society and Its Enemies: [Utopian Engineering].

In: *Experimentation with Human Beings: The Authority of the Investigator, Subject, Professions, and State in the Human Experimentation Process*, edited by Jay Katz with the assistance of Alexander Morgan Capron and Eleanor Swift Glass, New York: Russell Sage Foundation, 1972. ISBN 87154 438 5. (Pp. xlix, 1159.) Pp. 266-268.

An abridged reprint of 1966(a), chapter 9, pp. 157-163.

1973

*   (a) Indeterminism is Not Enough. A Philosophical Essay.

Encounter (London), Vol. 40 (1973), No. 4 (April, 1973), pp. 20-26.

R   (b) From *The Poverty of Historicism.*

In: *Modes of Individualism and Collectivism,* edited by John O'Neill, London: Heinemann Educational Books, Ltd., 1973. ISBN 0 435 82664 6 (cased). ISBN 0 435 82665 4 (paperback: *An H.E.B. Paperback*). (Pp. x, 358.) Pp. 68-87.

A reprint of 1961(b), sections 29 to 32.

T (c) LOGIKA NAUČNOG OTKRIĆA.

Biblioteka savremene SYMPOSION strani autori, Beograd: Nolit, 1973. Pp. 496.

Serbo-Croat translation of 1968(a) [1959(a)] and the new *Addenda* in 1969(e) and 1971(o) by Dr. Staniša Novaković. Appendices *IV and *V have been translated from 1971(o).

Introductory essay by the translator: *Metodološka i filosofska gledišta Karla Popera* [Methodological and Philosophical Views of Karl Popper], pp. [11]-39; *Napomena prevodioca* [Translators Note], pp. [495]-496.

T (d) LA LOGIQUE DE LA DÉCOUVERTE SCIENTIFIQUE.

Bibliothèque Scientifique, Paris: Payot, 1973. ISBN 2 228 11390 5. Pp. [vii], 480.

Translation into French by Nicole Thyssen-Rutten and Philippe Devaux, based on 1968(a) [1959(a)], 1970(e), and 1971(o).

With a *Préface* (August 1972) by Jacques Monod, Prix Nobel, pp. [1]-6; *Note des traducteurs,* p. [7]; and an acknowledgement by Karl R. Popper, p. [9].

1974

* (a) PHILOSOPHY AND PHYSICS: *Essays in Defence of the Objectivity of Physical Science.*

Oxford: at the Clarendon Press, 1974.

Contents: Preface (Penn, Buckinghamshire, England Christmas 1971). 1. Philosophy and Physics. [1961(h)]. 2. Science: Problems, Aims, Responsibilities. [1963(h)]. 3. Quantum Mechanics without 'The Observer'. [1967(k)]. 4. The Propensity Interpretation of the Calculus of Probability, and the Quantum Theory. [1957(e)]. 5. The Propensity Interpretation of Probability. [1959(e)]. 6. Particle Annihilation and the Argument of Einstein, Podolsky, and Rosen. [1971(n)]. 7. Quantum Theory, Quantum Logic and the Calculus of Probability. [1968(y)]. 8. Birkhoff and von Neumann's Interpretation of Quantum Mechanics. [1968(q)]. 9. Indeterminism in Quantum Physics and in Classical Physics. [1950(b) and (c)]. 10. On the Objectivity of the Arrow of Time and the Current Theory of Entropy. [1956(b), 1956(g), 1957(d), 1958(b), 1957(f), 1965(f), 1967(b), 1967(h), and: Further Arguments against the Subjectivist Theory of Entropy]. 11. Time, Probability and Indeterminism. 12. Normal Science and its Dangers. [1970(w)]. 13. The Moral Responsibility of the Scientist.[1969(a)].

This table of contents is provisional.

* (b) Intellectual Autobiography.

In: *The Philosophy of Karl Popper*, edited by Paul Arthur Schilpp, (*The Library of Living Philosophers*, edited by Paul Arthur Schilpp, Vol. 14), La Salle, Illinois: The Open Court Publishing Company, 1974. Book I. ISBN 0 87548 141 8. Pp. [3]-181.

Written for the present volume.
Acknowledgements contained in Book I.

* (c) Replies to My Critics.

Ibid., Book II. ISBN 0 87548 142 6. Pp. [961]-1197.

Written for the present volume.

* (d) The Myth of the Framework.

In: The Abdication of Philosophy: Philosophy and the Public Good (The Schilpp Festschrift), edited by Eugene Freeman, LaSalle, Illinois: Open Court Publishing Company, 1974, forthcoming.

INDEX
(by Pappu S. S. Rama Rao)

verisimilitude of a, 305
Hyppolite, Jean, 887 n
hypothetico-deductive method, 280 ff, 302

Ichii, Saburo, 1242, 1249, 1264
icon(s), 472, 475, 477
id, 532
idealism 60 64 f 108 f 120 128 185 198
609, 1093, 1140 ff, 1188 n; Berkeleyan, 99,
165 n; epistemological, 64, 198; Gödel's,
103; Hume's, 1017 f; Machian, 99; subjective, 114
ideas, 14, 371, 393, 398, 565; and impressions,
406; association of, 209; bold, 977 ff; growth
of, 721 f; guide to actions, 222, 238; history
of, 846; innate, 442, 499, 501, 502, 1071 f;
metaphysical, 91; objective, 399, 974; origin
of, 238, 499; Platonic, 146, 148, 469, 586;
simple, 60; testing of, 239; true, 996
identity thesis, 557
ideographic characters, 358
ideology, 33, 907
Iggers, G. G., 906, 923 n
illusion, Hiroshima as, 128; Müller-Lyer, 110
images, 60, 1017
imagination, 274 f; and hypothesis, 1026 ff;
poverty of, 920
imitation, 431 ff; learning by, 39
immateriality, 528
"immunizing stratagems," 982, 1004 f, 1007,
1186 n f
imperative, hypothetical, 1036
implication, 635, 638; strict, 678
importance, meaning of, 1165 f
impressions, 1017, 1065
impressionism, 936
"imprinting," 34, 39, 1024
improbability, 83, 236
indeterminism, 74, 102 f, 120, 123, 371 ff, 392,
407, 479 ff, 513, 522, 531, 728, 730, 976,
1053, 1051 f, 1067; metaphysical, 373 f,
387; not conclusive, 522; not enough, 1074 f;
not normative, 400; objective, 388; sustained by ignorance, 387; tychistic, 481;
physical, 405, 1074; Popper's case for,
385 ff; quantum, 529; relation to interactionism, 394 f; scientific, 374, 387
indeterminacy, Heisenberg's, 73, 76, 86,
168 n; micro-, 385 f; Newton's, 375; princi-

ple of, 730; propensity interpretation of,
385; psychobiological, 405
index, 475, 477
indifference, principle of, 722
individual, a priori in, 443
individualism, 1169; institutionalistic, 693;
methodological, 895, 926; psychological,
495
individuality, 885
induction, 34, 62, 69, 98, 120, 190, 219, 223,
252, 256, 262, 265 n, 270 n, 288, 292, 300 f,
400, 418, 428, 438, 486, 510, 514, 694,
697 ff, 722, 742 n f, 750, 806, 962, 964, 968,
975, 976, 994, 1014, 1031, 1037, 1040, 1046,
1117, 1121; and knowledge, 613; and scientific method, 277 f; as guessing, 190; as synthetic a priori, 222; Baconian, 278; by
repetition, 41, 116, 1018, 1032; circularity
of, 239, 996; deductivist approach to, 268 n;
dissolving the problem of, 326; guarantee-
ing, 704; Goodman's puzzles on, 330;
Hume's problem of, 68, 87, 1013 ff;
iterative, 276; justification of, 190, 260,
322 f, 1043; learning without, 34 ff; logical
problem of, 1018, 1020 ff, 1042 ff; meaning
of, 220 f, 276; metaphysical, 261; method
of, 63; myth of, 63, 68, 112, 118, 274 ff,
1032 f; nature of, 208; passive, 416;
Popper's solution of, 221 f, 322 ff, 1013 ff;
pragmatic problem of, 1025 ff; probabilistic
theory of, 262, 697, 1032; problems of, 66,
68, 175 n, 242 ff, 315, 322, 703; psychological problem of, 1018 ff; relation to
demarcation, 242, 253, 255; stages in, 286;
three principles of, 323; validity of, 116 ff,
400, 1027
inductivism(ist), 134, 185, 201, 223, 253, 256,
346, 527, 576, 584 f, 685, 693 f, 703 ff, 1060,
1193 n; and determinism, 406; critique of,
190 f, 258 ff; truth in, 228 f
inference, 164 n; inductive, 428, 1014 f; inductive and deductive, 112 ff; logic of, 415;
rules of, 115, 649; scientific, 826; theory of
deductive, 632 f, 639 f, 644, 645, 647 f
infinity, potential and actual, 10, 98; problem
of, 10
informative content, 18 ff, 31, 33, 130, 147,
158 n, 982, 1022, 1051, 1102
Infeld, Leopold, 169 n

INDEX

1310

Oldemeyer, Ernst, 1259
Olmütz, Archbishop Kohn of, 84
omniscience, basic, 1107
ontology, 395; foundations of, 642; Leśniewski's, 642, 654 n; Plato's, 862; physicalistic, 544; realistic, 481 f
open systems, irreversibility of, 782
operationalism(ist), 70 ff, 104, 345, 516 n, 608, 1120; definitional, 448 f; Heisenberg's, 77
opinion, and knowledge, 563
Oppenheim, Paul, 93, 102
optics, 802
ordinary language, 78, 210, 414, 649, 1097 f; philosophy of, 99
Ordinary of Francis Joseph, 5
organism(s), 10, 34, 41, 82, 102 f, 109, 135, 373, 419, 423, 532, 1108; and environment, 421; and machines, 525 ff; as problem-solving, 142; dualism in, 389 f; evolution of, 389 ff; not passive, 401; Popper's view of, 388 ff; problems of, 143, 391 f; sequences of, 600; states of, 535; three suppositions concerning, 389
originality, a gift of gods, 49
orthogenetic trends, 138, 141
Osborn, H. F., 426, 453 n
Ostaszewski, Jan, 1261
Ostwald, Wilhelm, 7, 11
Otago, University of, 1049
Ouchi, G., 1281
Oxford, 73, 86, 99, 349

pacifism(ist), 8, 24
Packer, J., 1216
painting, 943; abstract, 954; contemporary, 939
Palace of Versailles, 700
Paleolithic Age, 354 f
panpsychism, 173 n, 180 n
Pan-Slavic Movement, 9
Pap, Arthur, 160 n, 482
paradigm, 339, 490 ff, 811 f, 817 n, 1150 f; acceptance of, 236; and conjectures, 1069; and empirical content, 833; change in, 236 f, 830 ff; explained, 810; exploitation of, 827, 832, 839; falsification of, 229; Kuhn's concept of, 832 ff; meaning of, 490; nature of a, 229; replacement of, 234; natural selection of, 437; shifts in, 436; supplanting of, 230

paradox(es), 671 ff; Hempel's, 218 f; logical, 93; Rosen, 758 (see also Liar's Paradox)
parallelism, 150, 1056; linguistic, 393
Pareto, Vilfredo, 1172
Paris, 100, 186, 936
Park, James L., 167 n, 759 n, 1195 n
Parliament, Austrian, 5; English, 5
Parmenides, 16, 102 f, 158 n, 729, 980
Parsegian, V. L., 759 n
particles, 73, 785; fundamental, 122; gas, 779; interference, 76; picture, 74
particulars, 754
Parton, Hugh, 90, 171 n, 1216
Passmore, John, 69 ff, 166 n, 517 n
Pasteur, L., 835
pathempiricism, 164 n
patriotism, 8
Pauli, Wolfgang, 122, 607, 986
Pavlov, 61, 538
peace, 24
Pearl Harbor, 91
Pearson, Egon S., 616, 630 n
Pearson, Karl, 278 f, 281, 290 n
Pedagogic Institute (Vienna), 57 f, 66
Peierls, R. E., 167 n
Peirce, C. S., 75, 167 n, 259, 276, 278, 283, 286, 290 n, 417, 436, 438 ff, 456 n, 464, 467 ff, 508 ff, 516 n, 698, 722, 724 ff, 737 ff, 742 n, 747 n, 1032, 1065 f, 1072, 1101, 1119; critique of, 513 f
Pelles, Geraldine, 956 n
Pennett, W., 168 n
Penrose, 781, 788, 796 n f
Pepper, S. C., 434, 445, 451 n, 459 n, 462 n
perception, 40, 198, 399, 402, 413, 473 ff, 970 f; as a knowledge process: Kant's categories of, 441 ff; sense, 327, 754; subjective, 111
perceptual assurance, 562 f, 568, 588 n
perceptual experience, 563, 568, 590 n
perceptual judgment, 473 f
percepts, 465
Percival, 781, 788, 796 n f
Pericles, 812 f, 852 f
Perrin, Burton, 413 n
Perry, R. B., 747 n
person, concept of a, 399; identity of, 533
Petersen, Arne, x, 172 n, 1057, 1199
Petras, John W., 1273